NELSON'S

ILLUSTRATED GUIDE TO RELIGIONS

WITHDRAWN

NELSON'S
ILLUSTRATED
GUIDE TO
RELIGIONS

JAMES A. BEVERLEY

THOMAS NELSON
Since 1798

NASHVILLE   DALLAS   MEXICO CITY   RIO DE JANEIRO   BEIJING

Published in Nashville, Tennessee, by Thomas Nelson. Thomas Nelson is a registered trademark of Thomas Nelson, Inc.

Page design and production by Robin Crosslin, Crosslin Creative, Spring Hill, TN.

Thomas Nelson, Inc., titles may be purchased in bulk for educational, business, fund-raising, or sales promotional use. For information, please e-mail SpecialMarkets@ThomasNelson.com.

Library of Congress Cataloging-in-Publication Data available upon request

ISBN-13: 9780785244912
ISBN-10: 0785244913

Printed in the United States of America

09 10 11 12 13 RRD 6 5 4 3 2 1

DEDICATION

This book is dedicated to
my wife, Gloria;
our adult children,
Andrea and Derek;
our son-in-law, Julien;
and our granddaughter,
Dorothée—

with all my love.

TABLE OF CONTENTS

PREFACE

In a general sense this work is a product of over thirty years of study and teaching in the worlds of religion and philosophy. More to the point, I began specific work on this project during a sabbatical in 1999–2000. Two earlier books (*Understanding Islam* and *Religions A to Z*) resulted from the research for this larger work, but I have kept returning to this book as one of my major academic and spiritual tasks of the last decade.

Though the introduction provides an outline of my perspective on religion, let me make more personal observations up front. This book illustrates my dual citizenship as a member of the academic world and an evangelical Christian. While these two worlds sometimes collide, I feel at home in both. I realize that my Christian perspective will create tensions at certain points with followers of other religions or with academics of no religious persuasion. My criticisms of various groups and leaders are offered with a deep recognition of my own fallibility. Consequently, I welcome input on what I have written though I also ask for civility in dialogue.

Like any author, I also hope that readers will grant me benefit of the doubt as regards motives and basic decency. When I offer negative verdicts on various theories or individuals it is not done in malice or in any sense of hate. As I state in the introduction, whatever critique is offered is done because I believe that it is both true and necessary. It is not my intention to minimize the good in almost every religion. Likewise, critique is not meant to support those who crush religious liberties in various parts of the globe.

I owe much to a circle of friends, both past and current, who provided encouragement as the research and writing continued on this project. So, thanks to John and Trish Wilkinson, Marta Durski, Annie McKeown Bain, Gary and Peg LeBlanc, Kevin and Sandy Quast, Rodney and Adonica Howard-Browne, John Axler, Larry and Beverly Matthews, Carol Greig, Rick and Darlene George, Frank Beckwith, Stephen and Dawn Stultz, Siddiqi Ray, Doug and Pat Markle, Larry Willard, Ken and Miriam MacLeod, Ralston and Cheryl Nickerson, John and Teresa Reddy, Tom Dikens, Randy and Cindy McCooeye, Sam Mikolaski, Bob and Mary Gunn, Norm Keith, Kevin and Jill Rische, Dave Collison, Rick and Charis Tobias, Clark Pinnock, Rick Love, Gladys Chan, Gary Habermas, Bruxy and Nina Cavey, Mike Homer, Bob and Ann Young, Daveed Gartenstein-

Ross, Terrance and Berry Trites, Pat Minichello, Reg and Linda Horsman, Phil Sherwood, Randy and Susan Campbell, Jim Penton, Cheryl Geissler, Bryan and Jeannie Taylor, Wade Wry, Jerry and Karen Reddy, Sharon Geldart, and Bill and Mary-Lynne Rout.

I also want to acknowledge the influence of several academics in my life. Eileen Barker, Massimo Introvigne, Todd Johnson, Don Wiebe, and Gordon Melton are valued friends and constant sources of learning about the world of religion, even when we disagree. Since 2003 I have worked with Gordon as Associate Director of his Institute for the Study of American Religion. In 2007 I became friends with Martin Gardner, the famous author, and his interest in my work has been wonderful. I am also grateful for continuing encouragement from Hans Küng, my former professor during Ph.D. work at the Toronto School of Theology. His breadth of learning and courage in theological life is a source of inspiration.

Tyndale Seminary has been my academic home since 1988. I am grateful to Tyndale administration for their support: Brian Stiller, Janet Clark, Winston Ling, and Randy Henderson. Thanks also to two former deans, Ian Rennie and Brian Cunnington, for their enthusiasm and interest in this work. All of my faculty colleagues over the years have been supportive but a special nod to John Kessler, David Sherbino, Victor Shepherd, and Kaarina Hsieh. Thanks also to Andrew Smith and Toby Goodman of the I.T. department at Tyndale. I owe a lot to current and former administrative assistants, including Tina Kim, Dahlia Fraser, Cathy Nguyen, and Lynda Marshall.

I am very grateful to several friends who have provided academic assistance and help in research: Agnes Choi, Rachel Collins, Darren Hewer, Chad Hillier, and Rebekka Ries. I also am in debt to key personnel at Thomas Nelson who have assisted me during the past decade. It was great to work with Robin Crosslin, a magnificent designer and typesetter, and with The Bates Corporation, whose team provided excellent editorial suggestions and proofreading skills.

Some of the material in this book first saw light in magazine format. Thanks to *Christianity Today* editors David Neff and Mark Galli for their support and the same thanks to Gail Reid and Bill Fledderus, editors at *Faith Today* magazine. Lee Grady at *Charisma* magazine has been very supportive of my writing on charismatic Christianity. I am also so grateful to scholars around the world who helped me in their particular areas of expertise. Thanks also to those scholars and others who sent photos for use in the book.

I am surrounded by a great circle of relatives, including Bill and Margaret Bulman, Reta Lutes, Norman and Phyllis Gillcash, my step-mother Mary Beverley, David and Darlene Keirstead, Gerry and Judy Gillcash, Cindy Beverley, James A. Beverley (my namesake) and Mary Jo Beverley, Lorne and Linda Gillcash, Billy and Nancy Bulman, Jack and Grace Stultz, and Keith and Mary Beverley. My twin brother Bob Beverley is a constant source of love and enthusiasm. As ever, and most important, I am so grateful to my immediate family to whom this book is dedicated: my wife Gloria, our adult children, Derek and Andrea, and Julien, our son-in-law. And, during the last year of research and writing, our grand-daughter Dorothée arrived and she is a wonderful gift from God.

James A. Beverley
Professor of Christian Thought and Ethics
Tyndale Seminary, Toronto, Canada
Associate Director
Institute for the Study of American Religion
Santa Barbara, USA
February 2009
jamesbeverley@sympatico.ca
www.jimbeverley.com

INTRODUCTION

How can one navigate the complex maze of religious groups and sort out the various claims made by both world and new religions? This book attempts to introduce readers to all of the major religions of the world and hundreds of new ones, profiling many religious leaders, doctrines, beliefs, and practices. In so doing, it aims to serve as a guide to understanding some of the most controversial religious groups and issues.

Readers have a right to know the perspective that I bring to this study. *The Nelson's Illustrated Guide to Religions* offers more than simply bare facts about the various groups and leaders covered. Rather, it provides opinion and commentary both about many controversial issues related to the study of religion in general and specific religious groups. While every entry contains basic material that is beyond dispute, I also provide what I believe are necessary criticisms on relevant and important points.

TEN LEADING HISTORIANS OF RELIGION

- Friedrich Max Müller (1823–1900)
- Cornelis Petrus Tiele (1832–1902)
- Chantepie de la Saussaye (1818–74)
- Wilhelm Brede Kristensen (1867–1953)
- Rudolf Otto (1869–1937)
- Gerardus van der Leeuw (1890–1950)
- Joachim Wach (1898–1955)
- Mircea Eliade (1907–86)
- Wilfred Cantwell Smith (1916–2000)
- Ninian Smart (1927–2001)

Several important issues must be addressed in terms of proper method in the study of religion. Significant choices arise immediately in introducing and responding to the various religions of the world, whether major or minor, old or new, popular or controversial. We can consider these choices in terms of the following questions.

1. Do we adopt a postmodern outlook on religions?

We live increasingly in a postmodern context where pluralism and relativism are at the core of the dominant ideological outlook. Christian notions of exclusivity are automatically suspect because the prevailing notions of postmodernism are so powerful. People are pluralists because it is the mood of the day. Most people do not believe all religions are paths to the Ultimate because they have studied these religions. Rather, the postmodern spirit of the age leads to an automatic and implicit acceptance of all religions and of every sincere and authentic path to the divine.

2. Do we accept a religious understanding of religion?

It has been accurately pointed out that one does not have to be a horse to understand horses, but many scholars believe only a religious person can understand religion. Obviously, the religions of the world adopt a religious understanding of religion. Thus, Muslims interpret the religions of the world through what they believe the Qur'an teaches about reality, while Jews accept the teaching of the Torah about religion. Most academic study of religion is built upon a religious understanding as well. The American Academy of Religion, for example, does not adopt an atheistic or agnostic attitude about religions and religious beliefs.

Some academics believe that the only proper way to understand religion is by adopting a non-religious perspective. One such scholar, Donald Wiebe, believes that a truly scientific and rational approach to religion demands abandoning all religious interpretation of religion, whether Christian, Muslim, New Age, Buddhist, or the implicit pro-religious views of the American Academy of Religion and similar academic bodies.

DONALD WIEBE AND THE IRONY OF THEOLOGY

Prolific and controversial scholar of religion Donald Wiebe was raised a Mennonite in Canada and was an evangelical Christian philosopher for many years. Pursuing Ph.D. studies under the famous scholar Ninian Smart, Wiebe gradually abandoned traditional Christian views, coming to believe the improbability of reconciling science and religion. Wiebe has been a professor at Trinity College in Toronto for nearly thirty years.

Wiebe believes that the theological enterprise and the academic study of religion represent two radically different modes of thought. He argues in his most well-known work, *The Irony of Theology*, that theologians undermine their own faith by seeking to give it credibility of a scientific kind. He further maintains that true academic study of religion demands abandoning the religious understanding of religion. To be part of the modern research university involves, according to Wiebe, adopting a scientific, objective and neutral approach to the study of religion.

Many scholars, including Francis Schüssler Fiorenza, have criticized Wiebe's views as positivistic and naïve. These scholars have been particularly upset by his argument that the history of religion shows a failure of nerve in avoiding a truly scientific approach. Wiebe believes that liberal scholars have exercised bad faith in introducing a crypto-theological agenda in religious studies, especially in Europe and North America.

3. Do we accept a pluralistic understanding of religion?

If we believe that a religious understanding of religion is proper, we then must decide if we believe in a pluralistic outlook on religion. This is the view accepted by postmodernists, but one does not have to be a postmodernist to adopt pluralism. The Dalai Lama, the famous Buddhist teacher, believes that humans are designed to follow different religious paths, even though these religions do not always agree. Some liberal Christians no longer teach that Jesus is the only Savior.

4. If we do not accept a pluralist model, what specific religion or theology guides us in the study of religion?

If one has already chosen a specific religious group as the path of truth, then he or she is likely to measure all religions by that specific group. Scientologists, for example, view the world through the teachings of L. Ron Hubbard. Followers of the Hare Krishna movement are guided by the teachings of their guru A. C. Bhaktivedanta Swami Prabhupada. Disciples of Sun Myung Moon believe that he offers the ultimate truth about salvation, while theosophists follow the teachings of Madame Blavatsky.

5. **If one follows Christian tradition, which theological perspective influences the study of religion?**

Since the Christian tradition is ancient and diverse, the options here are also considerable. Roman Catholicism offers a particular perspective on religion, as does the Orthodox tradition. In both the Catholic and Orthodox world there are further choices to be made about the extent of commitment to tradition. For example, if one is a Roman Catholic, does one adopt the theology of the pope or that of the more liberal Catholic thinker Hans Küng?

HANS KÜNG

Hans Küng (b. 1928) is probably the most influential Catholic scholar of modern times. Trained in Rome and Paris, the Swiss-born priest became well known for his book on *Justification* (1957) and for his writing on Vatican II and the Roman Catholic Church. His critique of the 1968 papal ban on the birth control pill and his 1970 book against papal infallibility created considerable controversy in Rome. In 1979 the Vatican removed Küng as an approved Catholic scholar though this only increased his popularity worldwide and as a professor at the University of Tübingen.

In the latter part of his career Küng turned his attention to world religions and ethics, producing *Judaism, Christianity and the World Religions, Christianity and Chinese Religions, A Global Ethic,* and *Global Responsibility.* The English edition of his massive work *Islam: Past, Present and Future* was published in 2007. He is the president of the Global Ethic Foundation.

Küng has resisted requests from pluralists to abandon a Christ-centered theology and has stated that Christianity is for him "the only true religion." He believes that Christians should make a distinction between "domestic policy" in addressing internal issues in theology and "foreign policy" in regard to judgment about other religions. Küng holds respect for those of other faiths but does not hesitate to raise critical questions about specific issues in these faiths. He has also passionately urged world leaders to realize that peace on Earth will come only if peace exists among the religions of the world. Küng is not advocating utopia on Earth since he is realistic about human folly, but he asks for followers of all faiths to follow the core human and ethical values common to all religions.

Author with Hans Küng in Germany

Photo: Courtesy of Jim Beverley

If one is a Protestant, then choices must be made about a particular denominational outlook (Lutheran, Baptist, Pentecostal, etc.). In the Protestant world, one can be influenced by fundamentalist views and by the contours of evangelical theology, or by the stances of a more liberal ideology. Do we, for example, adopt the views of Bob Jones or Norman Geisler, or of C. S. Lewis, Clark Pinnock, or John Cobb?

6. Do we believe that religion is basically good?

Most religious traditions have a positive view of religion per se even if an exclusivist or non-relativist position is adopted. Many Muslims have a high view of Christians and Jews as followers in the same tradition that led to Muhammad. Hindus often teach that all religions lead to God. Even conservative Christians can be optimistic about non-Christian religions as paths that God will use to bring people to the greater truth in Jesus.

Over against this dominant view stands the theology of Karl Barth, the famous Reformed theologian, who resisted Hitler and Nazism during World War II. Barth, by his own admission, did not know world religions in detail. However, he believed that a thorough grasp of Christian revelation in Jesus leads automatically to a radical suspicion of religion. Barth believed that the gospel of Jesus Christ was a word of radical judgment against all religions, including Christianity.

7. Do we accept that some religions should be viewed as cults?

For the last three decades it has become popular to make a distinction between religions and cults. According to this distinction, some groups are so strange or dangerous or heretical as to deserve a special term or category to distinguish them from real religion. Thus, the word *cult* has been used of hundreds of different groups, most often describing new religions that have arrived in the West since the mid-1960s.

8. Do we believe that liberty should be granted to all religions?

Even if we have a very low view of particular religious groups we may, at the same time, believe that the liberty of all religions should be a fundamental reality of human life on planet Earth. There are many religious people who do not share this view. Often those who target the so-called cults believe that these groups should be restricted in terms of freedom, or even that their members should be kidnapped and deprogrammed out of the group.

9. Do we accept scientific and academic analysis of religion?

Many religious groups and theologies remain deeply suspect about the scientific understanding of religion. In the Christian tradition there has been a long history of mistrust about universities, going back to battles over the academy in the high Middle Ages. Is psychological assessment of religion important? Can sociologists of religion help us understand religion? Can the study of one religion aid us in the understanding of another?

10. Is it safe to study religion?

Some religious people believe strongly that it is very dangerous to explore beliefs outside of one's particular fellowship. For example, Jehovah's Witnesses are forbidden to read any literature that is critical of its Watchtower Bible & Tract Society. Some conservative Christians argue that visiting non-Christian groups and reading non-Christian religious texts opens a person to the false (and perhaps even demonic) spirits behind these religions.

A Proper Response to Religions

The various religious traditions in this work are studied from my perspective as an evangelical Christian scholar. I realize that many readers will not share this paradigm or worldview; however, I ask those following other philosophies to grant some epistemic patience for the faith tradition that I bring to this study, one that I believe to be the truth. I recognize that this book would be different if written from a Buddhist, Muslim, esoteric, or other tradition. It would also be a different book if it adopted the standpoint of relativism or postmodernism, or the perspective of the so-called objective academic.

Stained glass, St. Boniface Church, Bunbury, UK

Photo: TD

I have also written this book with a deep recognition of my own fallibility. Criticisms are offered only when I believe that they are truly necessary. Even then, negative statements are not meant to ignore or downplay the ways in which virtually every religion offers love, identity, and meaning to its followers. I am also aware that evangelical Christians have at times been careless in their response to other religions. Further, even after years of study of particular groups, it is possible to make mistakes of fact and interpretation. Consequently, I welcome input and correction on what I have written, though I also ask for civility in critique.

Over time I have presented in various books a list of ten essentials that form a proper Christian response to religions. These ten principles construct the framework I have used in responding to the hundreds of groups and leaders covered in this book. While these core points offer a multifaceted and balanced Christian paradigm for assessing religions, they also are built on an appreciation for everything true and valid that can be learned from those in other religions, or from non-Christian academics who provide serious research on new and world religions. Collectively, they offer what I believe to be a proper Christian response to religions.

1. **All religions and philosophies are to be measured by the final revelation of God in Jesus Christ.** The Christian must interpret all religious claims and spiritual views in light of the ultimate truth embodied in Jesus Christ. The binding Christian confession of Jesus as the only Son of God and as God's final and ultimate Word is the foundation for all assessment of religions. Contrary to relativism, the Bible does not teach that all roads lead to God. Rather, the orthodox Christian tradition has always taught the uniqueness and supremacy of Jesus. Karl Barth, the great Protestant theologian, has stated that Jesus is the one distinction between truth and error.

2. **Commitment to Jesus demands that the study of religion be carried out in love.** Bigotry and ignorance are incompatible with the command of Jesus to love. Christian response to other religions has often been marked by hatred, not only in words but in wars. Further, the evangelical study of religions has frequently been superficial and careless. Though this work includes critique of various groups, these concerns are raised with the aim of providing truthful and important analysis.

3. **Christian response to religions involves a commitment to truth.** A commitment to truth means not only dedication to Christ as the Truth but also a devotion to accuracy in the world of theology and religion. The commandment not to bear false witness against one's neighbor includes avoiding lies, half-truths, and distortions about the religion of others. Sadly, some of the most inaccurate books on various religious groups have been written by evangelicals.

4. **Christians must recognize the contradictions and ultimate disunity that exist among the religions of the world.** Contrary to popular opinion, the religions of the world often disagree—even on basic points. For example, Buddhists do not believe in God. Jews and Muslims do not accept the Trinity. Mormon males believe they will progress to Godhood in eternity. Unificationists believe that Sun Myung Moon is the Messiah. Jehovah's Witnesses trust the Watchtower Society alone for spiritual guidance. Santeria followers kill animals for religious worship. What should be obvious in the study of religions is their lack of similarity rather than their alleged unity.

5. **Disciples of Jesus must recognize every significant point of agreement with people of other religions and even with those of no faith.** No harm exists in seeing God's common grace at work in the religions and peoples of the world. Thus, atheists can love their children. Hindus can understand the value of love. Muslims can detest the evils of global terrorism. Non-Christians can serve as moral examples to the Christian community. The reality of goodness and truth in non-Christian paths needs emphasis by evangelicals because we can be prone to negativity when it comes to other faiths.

   Evangelicals must resist paranoia about those in other religions. We too readily ascribe demonic elements where none exist or we question motives where motives are pure. Satan's influence is invoked as a causal explanation too quickly at times and we fail to interpret a group, its leaders or its followers, with any level of sensitivity.

6. **Those who trust the gospel of Jesus must recognize the power of the dominant liberal perspective on religion and religious study.** For over a century the West has seen an increasing emphasis on relativism. Since the 1893 World's Parliament of Religions, the acceptance of all religions as paths to God has grown. Mainline denominations have

often downplayed the missionary enterprise, and liberal theologians have argued that Jesus is not the only Savior. Further, postmodernism has eroded confidence in the Christian gospel.

7. **The Christian church must affirm that the mercy and love of God shown in Jesus are sufficient to answer all concerns about God's fairness in a world of religions.** The Christian must resist attempts to downplay the supremacy of Jesus or to overstate the unity of religions as a means of making Christian faith more acceptable in a climate of relativism. The wideness of God's mercy is shown best by the grace given at Calvary. If there is to be any optimism about God's grace toward non-Christian paths, it must be rooted in optimism about the grace of God in Jesus Christ.

Slave plantation, South Carolina–Complicity in slavery is just one example of how Christians have sometimes carried out evil under God's alleged blessing.

Photo: Jim Beverley

8. **Those who trust in the Christian gospel must not forget the wrath of God that stands against the wickedness of a fallen world.** The message of God's justice is a necessary balance to overstatements of God's mercy and grace. This applies to both secular and religious domains since the Lord's name is taken in vain in both. People often carry out

evil under God's alleged blessing. The good news in Jesus is a word of judgment about the folly and sin of a lost humanity. Paradoxically, trust in God's judgment can be an anchor of hope for those who have experienced evil and injustice.

9. **Christians must repent in sorrow for the ways in which we have not allowed the gospel to critique the church through the ages.** Karl Barth has pointed prophetically to the ways in which the message of Christ must be heard by all religions, even Christianity. Barth was correct to recognize that religion can be unbelief, even among those who claim to follow Christ. The story of Christianity stands under the judgment of the gospel just as much and sometimes more than the non-Christian paths.

KARL BARTH ON RELIGION

Karl Barth (1886–1968) is considered by many scholars to be the most influential theologian of modern times. Trained under liberal Christian scholarship in Europe, Barth abandoned many of liberal Christianity's central precepts during his early preaching days when he was dramatically impacted by the theology of Paul's epistle to the Romans.

Barth held a very negative view of natural religion and placed his emphasis instead on God's revelation in Jesus Christ. He wrote in a famous section of his *Church Dogmatics* that "religion is unbelief." For Barth, Christian tolerance is not about accepting the validity of religions but about receiving humanity in the patience of Christ. The gospel of Jesus Christ is the final revelation of God and the standard under which all religions, including the Christian religion, are to be judged.

Even though Barth said a decisive "Nein" to natural religion, he is often accused of being a universalist. This emphasis did not come from a high view of humanity's goodness or religious identity but because of God's election of humanity in Jesus. For Barth, the "one distinction between truth and error" is Jesus Christ. Barth allowed his belief in the gospel to guide him in resisting the German churches that embraced Nazism.

Evangelicals have often been too critical of Barth based on serious misreading of him by critics like Cornelius Van Til. Barth did more than any other theologian to combat the liberal theology of nineteenth-century Germany.

10. **A Christian response to religion must include respect for human liberty.** Christians must defend the right of all humans to exercise their free choice on religious matters. A decision for the gospel is real only if made in freedom. Likewise, the Christian respects the freedom of humans to reject any religion, including the Christian gospel, believing that coercion is antithetical to the manner in which Jesus himself treated others.

Cross near Orthodox Church in Mtskheta-Mtianeti region, Georgia

Photo: Steffen Schuelein, Georgia Tourism Association

BASICS OF THE CHRISTIAN FAITH

- There is only one God, the omnipotent Creator, who is a Spirit Being who is all-powerful and all-loving (Gen. 1:1; Deut. 6:4; Is. 43:10; John 17:3).

- This one God exists eternally in three Persons: Father, Son and Holy Spirit (Matt. 28:19–20; John 1:1; Eph. 4:4–6).

- The Bible is the Word of God and is the ultimate authority for God's people (2 Tim. 3:14–17).

- Jesus Christ is human and divine. He was born of the Virgin Mary and is both Son of God and Lord. He is the only Savior (Luke 1:34–35; John 14:6; Acts 4:12; Phil. 2:5–9).

- The life, teaching, and miracles of Jesus serve as a model of truth and goodness for Christians and all of humanity (Matt. 7:24, 28; Luke 8:24–25).

- Humans are made in the image of God and are also fallen because of disobedience and sin (Gen. 1—3; Rom. 1—3).

- Jesus died for the sins of a fallen humanity (John 3:16; Rom. 3:21–26; 5:1–21).

- Jesus rose bodily from the grave (Matt. 28:8–9; Luke 24:36–43; John 20:24–29).

- Jesus Christ will return visibly to the earth again (Matt. 24:23–31; 1 Thess. 4:13–18).

- The church is the body of Christ. There is only one body of Christ (Matt. 16:18). Union with Christ and the church is shown in baptism and the celebration of the Lord's Supper.

- Heaven and hell are realities beyond death (John 14:1–6; Matt. 25:46; Rev. 21—22).

- Salvation is by grace, not works (Eph. 2:8–9; Gal. 2:14—4:31); works follow true faith (Gal. 5:13–26; 1 John 2:3–6).

- The Christian is under grace, not law (Gal. 3:1–5).

- The Christian is justified by faith in Christ and is to live a life of faith in Christ (Rom. 5—8).

- The Christian is to be holy (2 Pet. 1:3–11) and is to live a sanctified life, full of the Holy Spirit and the fruits of the Spirit (1 Cor. 12; Eph. 5:16–26).

- The church is to live in love and by love (1 Cor. 13; 1 John 4:7–8).

- Christians are called to prayer and spiritual discipline (Luke 11:1–4).

- Christians are to care for the poor and the oppressed (Luke 4:18).

- God created the world as good. This world is real, though temporal (2 Cor. 4:16–18).

- Christians are to follow Jesus as "the Truth" and are to be people of the truth (John 8:32; 1 John 4:1).

Altar to ancestors, Hanoi

Photo: Eileen Barker

In or Out, True or False?

Christians may refer to themselves (or be referred to as) exclusivists, inclusivists, or pluralists. The exclusivist view or tradition asserts that only by explicit faith in Jesus Christ can any hope of salvation be found. In previous centuries this strict doctrine would have been applied to both unbaptized infants and all those who have not heard the gospel. Most exclusivists today, however, would be more open on the question of the fate of infants and the mentally challenged who die before being able to accept Jesus Christ as their Savior.

Inclusivists embrace the more recent view in Christian thought that God's message in Jesus Christ includes the hope of redemption for those in other faiths who have lived up to the light available to them. The inclusivist position is adopted by the Second Vatican Council and by some evangelical authors like Clark Pinnock and John Sanders.

CLARK PINNOCK

Q: Does Clark Pinnock no longer believe that Jesus is the only Savior?

A: Clark Pinnock's position in his controversial book *A Wideness in God's Mercy* has often been misunderstood. His approach is based on the belief that God's grace in Christ Jesus is so deep that it will reach those in other religions who live up to the light they have. Pinnock believes that Jesus is the only Savior and that his mercy is wider than most evangelicals have believed.

While I believe Pinnock is overly optimistic regarding the world's non-Christian religions as paths that God uses to bring people to Christ, I admire his concern for humans who have simply never heard the gospel or who have only a dim understanding of it. Further, his emphasis on God's mercy provides a necessary balance to the ways in which conservative theology can be judgmental and mean-spirited.

Pluralists view all religions as paths to the Ultimate and assert that no one religion has a full grasp of truth. John Hick and Paul Knitter are two persuasive advocates of the pluralistic view. Pluralism is the dominant ideology in university religious studies departments and in liberal Christian seminaries. Under this paradigm, there is no need for persons to be converted to Christ alone to be saved. Rather, salvation or enlightenment comes through following the paths of Buddhism, Hinduism, Islam, Taoism, Judaism, Christianity, or other religions. Scholars like Hick and Knitter are not ignorant about the differences between religions. Both have studied world religions in detail; however, they believe that the Ultimate Spirit (or God) affirms all religious paths that offer goodness and beauty. (They also assert that religion can be evil and that some religions can be basically wicked.)

Shrines for the departed, Hong Kong

Photo: Eileen Barker

Ten Tests for Truth in Religion

Whether inclusivists, exclusivists or pluralists, Christians should apply the following multifaceted tests in approaching their own faith tradition and that of any religious group:

- **The God Test**—Does the group in question recognize the one God of the Bible as the true God, the God who is the almighty Creator of heaven and earth? Does the group believe in the God and Father of our Lord Jesus Christ? Does the religion believe that God is Father, Son, and Holy Spirit?

- **The Christological Test**—Does the group in question exalt Jesus Christ as the only eternal Savior, as the only eternal Son of God? Does the particular religion look to Jesus as the final revelation of God? Does it consider Jesus to be God incarnate?

- **The Biblical Test**—Does the group really follow the Bible? Are the clear and dominant teachings of Scripture believed? Are the many and varied commands of the Bible obeyed? Does the particular religion or denomination add to, take away from, or ignore God's Word?

- **The Love Test**—Does the group in question follow the high moral standard of the Old and New Testaments? Is love central in the group, and is it really practiced by the leaders and members? Does the particular religion illustrate that love is seen as the chief goal by loving both God and their neighbors?

- **The Spirit Test**—Does the group show a desire for following the Holy Spirit? Does a desire for purity and authentic spirituality exist? Do signs of legalism or shallow ritualism pervade the ethos of the particular movement?

- **The Freedom Test**—Does the group offer real freedom to individuals? Do the religious leaders offer psychological wholeness? Does the religious group advocate a sexuality that honors biblical teaching about sex? Is your money safe in this group?

- **The Psychological Test**—Is the specific religious group mentally healthy? Are the leaders arrogant and proud? Does the group allow self-criticism? Do the leaders show signs of grandiosity and paranoia?

- **The Social/Political Test**—Does the group care for the social well-being of individuals? Does it care about the political needs of humanity? Are its leaders doing anything practical to address poverty, disease, and injustice?

- **The Prophetic Test**—Have the leaders of the group claimed prophetic status and made false prophecies?

- **The Rational Test**—Are the specific teachings of the religion true? Does the group respect wisdom and reason, or do the leaders teach wild and erroneous ideas? Does a given idea seem reasonable, in keeping with the path of wisdom and truth? Is the specific claim of a religious leader, in fact, true?

The Cult Distinction

In spite of the popularity of the term *cult* in the language of religion, the word remains problematic and debate continues on whether its use should be eliminated altogether. Some Christian scholars like J. Gordon Melton have argued that the word is used so carelessly and has such a nasty impact that it should be abandoned. Many other Christian scholars believe that the vast majority of groups labeled cultic actually deserve the title.

Gordon Melton at the Melton collection
University of California at Santa Barbara

Photo: Jim Beverley

It is difficult to overstate the power of the word *cult*. Once a religious group is labeled as a cult it becomes very difficult to break down the strong barriers of suspicion created by that single four-letter word. Groups that appear on the lists of some cult-monitoring organizations can labor for years at clearing their reputation. In the West the term *cult* has become a synonym for wacky and brainwashed. The word may even conjure up images of fanatics intent on self-destruction or the harm of others.

Additionally, the word *cult* is applied inconsistently. Usually world religions are treated separately from so-called cult groups, but the Hare Krishna movement was labeled a cult when it began to attract a following in the 1970s in London, New York, and Los Angeles. (The Hare Krishna movement is not a new religion, but a branch of ancient Hinduism.) Often minority groups are labeled cultic in the media after only brief and shallow research into their origins and beliefs.

Speaker's Corner, Hyde Park, London, England

Photo: Jim Beverley

Over the last one hundred years the word *cult* has been used in three different ways.

First, *cult* has been used as a sociological term to describe religious groups that are isolated from mainstream society. By this understanding *cult* is used in contrast to words like *church* or *denomination* or even *sect*. Ernst Troeltsch made famous the distinctions *church*, *sect*, and *cult*, and this typology has continued in the discussions by sociologists of religion.

Second, the word *cult* is also used in the anti-cult movement to indicate those religious groups that allegedly brainwash people and use deceptive means to recruit and maintain membership. In this understanding *cult* is a very pejorative term that stigmatizes the group to which it refers. It has been used of religious groups that are viewed as extreme either in beliefs or practices, such as Jim Jones and his suicidal followers in Guyana, or David Koresh and his Branch Davidian followers in Waco, Texas.

Finally, the word *cult* is used as a theological term to describe groups that do not measure up to a standard of orthodoxy. Evangelical Christians make distinctions between groups that follow the Bible and groups that are cultic because they do not follow the basic claims of Scripture. Thus, according to evangelicals, Mormonism is cultic because of its doctrinal deviations from classical Christian theology.

The power of the word *cult* illustrates the importance of paying attention to the ordinary and popular use of words. Although the term continues to be used in a non-judgmental and technical way by scholars of religion, the vast majority of people take the word *cult* to mean a dangerous or crazy religion. In other words, the scholarly use of the term *cult* has very little sway in ordinary discourse.

CULTS Q&A:

1. What leads to situations like the Guyana tragedy (1978) or the apocalyptic ending to the Branch Davidian group in Waco, Texas?

   In both cases highly authoritarian and unstable leaders (Jim Jones and David Koresh) kept their membership in seclusion and tensions heightened in the face of outside pressure. In the case of Jonestown, the followers were convinced the U.S. army was preparing to attack them. In the Branch Davidian situation, the raid by law enforcement officers led to wounding and death. The subsequent standoff with the FBI created tensions on both sides that spurred further acts of violence.

2. Are the famous cult groups wealthy?

   Some groups do extremely well financially while others exist on the verge of financial ruin. Remember, the mere fact that a group has large financial holdings does not prove anything negative. The key distinction revolves around a group's demonstrated integrity in raising and handling money.

3. Are so-called cult leaders sincere in their beliefs?

   The study of the new religions should lead almost anyone to see that most leaders are sincere in belief in their own message. In my opinion, these leaders do not go to bed at night saying: "I fooled them again." Though some may be con artists, most show their sincerity by duplicating what we see in any committed followers of a religion: hard work, a willingness to face adversity or to die for the cause, and a commending of one's faith to family and friends.

4. What if a friend or family member joins a group regarded as cultic or dangerous?

First, you should try to obtain accurate and balanced information about the group. You should find experts on the group who know what the group believes, how they live, how they handle criticism, etc. Then process a critique of the group with your loved one (in a relaxed setting, if possible) and communicate your unconditional love and interest.

5. How popular are the so-called cult groups?

In spite of all the attention cults receive, most new religious groups are quite small in size. University of Chicago professor Martin Marty has said: "It puts things in perspective when you realize there are more Baptists in one Baptist Church in Dallas, Texas, than there are Moonies in all of North America." While this is true of many religious groups, a few like the Mormons and Jehovah's Witnesses have worldwide memberships in the millions.

6. What websites offer the best help in understanding controversial religions?

From among the academic sites, I find the Religious Movements homepage (created by sociologist Jeff Hadden, now deceased) and the CESNUR site (www.cesnur.org) most helpful. Of the evangelical groups, I would turn first to the Spiritual Counterfeits Project (www.scp-inc.org) and Watchman Fellowship (www.watchman.org), especially since they provide lots of data. From the secular cult awareness sites, the International Cultic Studies Association, formerly the American Family Foundation (www.icsahome.com), offers very comprehensive data.

7. What about the allegation that some scholars are "cult apologists"?

Cult apologist is applied most often to J. Gordon Melton, Massimo Introvigne, and Eileen Barker and is used to question their scholarship and their basic integrity. This attack is unfair for several reasons. First, all three have provided some of the best research ever done on new religions. Second, their defense of so-called cult groups is largely concerned with defending their religious liberties and freedoms. Third, each of these scholars can be quite critical of the beliefs and practices of given groups.

Eileen Barker at conference in Lithuania

Photo: Jim Beverley

Conclusion

Readers of this book will quickly discover that it is impossible to harmonize the contradictory teachings of all religions. Religions vary in size, beliefs, style, impact, structure, history, and leadership. Scientology has a very high degree of structure in contrast with a group like Theosophy. The New Age movement has made a major impact on our society while the Arica Institute remains largely unknown. Buddhists do not believe in God while most other religions do. Catholics believe in papal infallibility and Baptists do not. Many Muslims do not believe that the Holocaust ever happened. Fundamentalist Mormons believe in polygamy while mainline

Mormons do not. These differences are wide and cannot simply be dismissed or overlooked.

What should the Christian's response be with regard to the critique of other religions? Should Jesus' teaching "Do not judge, or you too will be judged" (Matt. 7:1) be applied in light of these many differences? I believe that the Christian's first and most important response is to resist the temptation to downplay the importance of this command of Jesus. Fundamentalist and evangelical Christians in particular need to monitor the judgmental spirit that permeates their writings about many topics— and especially about other religions.

"Do not judge" is a very important first principle in responding to other religions. But beyond this, the words of Jesus do not forbid all judgment. Jesus states that criticism of others must be (a) preceded by self-criticism and repentance and (b) rooted in the desire to help others. Jesus himself warns against false prophets. Further, Christians are told to defend "the faith that was once for all entrusted to the saints" (Jude 3). Balance, love, and a respect for biblical truth should rule our actions in this regard; and it should be every Christian's desire to help anyone to a full and deep knowledge of the gospel of Jesus Christ.

HENDRIK KRAEMER ON CHRISTIANS AND MISSIONARIES

"A Christian and a missionary should live by the ardent desire that all men will surrender to Christ as the Lord of their lives. Whosoever does not stress that, does not sufficiently consider the passionately prophetic and apostolic spirit of the Gospel. The core of the Christian revelation is that Jesus Christ is the sole legitimate Lord of all human lives and that the failure to recognize this is the deepest religious error of mankind."

BAHA'I

Baha'i Gardens in Haifa

Photo: Hillel Cohen

The Baha'i faith, now considered a distinct world religion, cannot be understood apart from its connections to a sect of Shi'ite Islam known as the Babi movement. Shi'a Islam has a core doctrinal position that the world awaits the return of a *madhi*, or Messiah figure, at the end of time. In 1844 a Muslim by the name of Sayyid 'Ali Muhammad (1819–50), building on this apocalyptic notion, proclaimed that he was the "Bab" or gate to God.

After the Bab's execution in 1850, orthodox Shi'a leaders continued to persecute his followers. In 1852 many Babis were arrested, including Mirza Husayn 'Ali Nuri. Husayn 'Ali, born in Persia in 1817, founded the Baha'i faith. He is now known in history as Baha'u'llah, which means "the glory of God." He was exiled to Baghdad in 1853. Ten years later he proclaimed himself to be the *madhi* promised by the Bab and by all religions. In 1868 he was exiled to Acre on the coast of Syria. He died there in 1892.

After the founder's death, leadership of the movement passed to Abdul-Bahá, the son of Baha'u'llah. Under Abdul-Bahá (b. 1844) the Baha'i faith became a world movement. He helped formulate official teaching on many theological and ethical topics and also successfully warded off attacks from his stepbrother through a decade of conflict between competing heirs. When Adbul-Bahá died in 1921, his grandson, Shoghi Effendi, led the movement until his death in 1957.

Shoghi Effendi's death created a crisis in the movement, since no heir remained to follow as the One Guardian. Leadership eventually passed to those known as the Hands of the Cause of God and then to the members of the Universal House of Justice, in Haifa, Israel. In 1960 Charles Remey proclaimed himself the Guardian of the Baha'i faith, but very few chose to follow him. In the early '60s Remey taught that an impending catastrophe would lead to the death of two-thirds of the world's population. He died in Italy in 1974.

2008 Baha'i Convention

Photo: © Baha'i International Community

NINE LEADERS OF HOUSE OF JUSTICE

Elected at Tenth International Baha'i Convention, May 2008:

- Farzam Arbab
- Kiser Barnes
- Peter Khan
- Hooper Dunbar
- Firaydoun Javaheri
- Paul Lample
- Payman Mohajer
- Shahriar Razavi
- Gustavo Correa

Baha'i Leaders of the Universal House of Justice

Photo: © Baha'i International Community

Baha'i and Christianity

Despite its complex Islamic past, the central beliefs of the Baha'i religion are quite straightforward. Among the most important: (1) all religions are one, (2) religion must conform to science and reason, (3) all humans are one, (4) Baha'u'llah is the manifestation of God for the present age, (5) women and men are equal, and (6) there should be one universal language. Followers also believe in previous manifestations of God, including Moses, Zoroaster, Krishna, Buddha, Muhammad, Jesus, and the Bab.

Christian critique of the Baha'i faith involves two major issues.

First, no amount of rhetoric or argumentation can rationally support the view that all religions are the same. While most world religions agree on some general moral principles, they emphatically disagree on other moral issues and on essential doctrinal matters. The Baha'i emphasis on the unity of religions seems more of a tactical and ideological move designed to lead people to join the Baha'i faith.

Second, the Baha'i faith has a faulty assessment of Jesus Christ. Baha'u'llah did not believe in the historical reality of the miracles of Jesus. While he taught that Jesus died on the cross (a departure from his Islamic roots), he denied the physical resurrection. He also misunderstood both the divinity of Jesus and the New Testament doctrine of his second coming, that Jesus will return as *Jesus* and not as Baha'u'llah. In fact, Baha'u'llah fulfills the prediction of Jesus that *false* teachers will proclaim themselves to be the returning Messiah.

PRINCIPLES OF THE BAHA'I FAITH

Baha'i:

- Recognizes the unity of God and his prophets

- Upholds the principle of an unfettered search after truth

- Condemns all forms of superstition and prejudice

- Teaches that the fundamental purpose of religion is to promote concord and harmony

- States that religion must go hand-in-hand with science and that it constitutes the sole and ultimate basis of a peaceful, ordered and progressive society

- Inculcates the principle of equal opportunity, rights, and privileges of both sexes

- Advocates compulsory education

- Abolishes extremes of poverty and wealth

- Recommends the adoption of an auxiliary international language

- Provides the necessary agencies for the establishment and safeguarding of a permanent and universal peace

—Shoghi Effendi, First Guardian of the Baha'i Faith

Baha'is and Religious Liberty

Contrary to popular image, the mainstream Baha'i movement has often exercised intolerance toward more liberal Baha'is. Frederick Glaysher, one prominent dissident, started the Reform Baha'i Faith (based in Haifa, Israel) as an alternative to mainstream Baha'i. Glaysher published ninety-five theses as a means of reformation. The first thesis states that Reform Baha'is will resolve:

"To witness the truth of the deviation of the organized, incorporated Baha'i Faith from the Path, and its imposition of manifest corruptions and innovations, over many lamentable decades, that have wrought ever-increasing alienation, fear, censorship, coercion, misrepresentation, distortion, and damage, all the stratagems of despots and dictators, political and religious, upon individual Baha'is, their families, and the community of believers."

Shrine of the Bab, Haifa, Israel

Photo: © Baha'i International Community

Juan Cole, a great Baha'i scholar, was excommunicated from the movement in 1996. Initially he reacted by renouncing his faith in Baha'u'llah. "At the time," he said, "the entire thing seemed to me clearly contrary to every principle I had ever believed about the Baha'i faith, from the importance of the rule of law to the right of every Baha'i to declare his conscience and express his views (guaranteed by Shoghi Effendi himself) as long as those views were advertised as non-authoritative (which I always did). I have to admit, with some shame, that my faith in Baha'u'llah was shattered by this episode."

In 1999 Cole wrote, "For better or worse, I'm introverted, an intellectual, a mystic, and an individual. As a professional academic historian, my life is dedicated to free inquiry and I cannot allow an outside body to dictate how I write history. There could not have been a worse fit between a personality and a religion than that between me and the Baha'i World Faith." He also had concluded, however, that he still believed the essence of Baha'u'llah's message: "I therefore feel the obligation publicly to say that I feel myself a believer in and a follower of Baha'u'llah. (That feels so right to say!) And that I formally disavow my earlier disavowal of Him."

Prison where Baha'u'llah was held in Palestine

Photo: © Baha'i International Community

The International House of Justice excommunicated Canadian Michael McKenny in 1997. McKenny had become open to paganism. He wrote of his stance: "I cannot conceive how I could demonstrate the harmony of humanity by claiming to be a Baha'i heretic, when my understanding is that the Founders of the Baha'i Faith intended that heresy not exist. I am, indeed, pagan, and enjoying the thrill of flexing my paganism openly. I took a break in the writing of this to go out at dawn to stand inside a tree-ring communing with the spirits of that place."

In January 2008 Judge Amy J. St. Eve of the U.S. District Court of Northern Illinois tried a civil case involving the National Spiritual Assembly (NSA) of Wilmette, Illinois, against three minority Baha'i groups. The NSA argued that the smaller groups should be held in contempt for violation of a 1996 ruling about proper use of Baha'i symbols. The court ruled against the NSA and the case is under appeal.

BAHA'I TIMELINE

1817—Birth of Mirza Husayn 'Ali Nuri (later known as Baha'u'llah) on November 12

1835—Baha'u'llah marries Nawab (first of three wives)

1844—Sayyid 'Ali Muhammad discloses his role as the Bab ("Gate" in Arabic) on May 23

1850—The Bab is executed on July 9

1852—Baha'u'llah imprisoned and then exiled to Baghdad

1863—Baha'u'llah sent to Istanbul

1866—Baha'u'llah announces status as "He whom God shall make manifest"

1868—Baha'i leader sent to Acre

1892—Baha'u'llah dies on May 29

1892—Abdul-Bahá, son of Baha'u'llah, becomes leader

1921—Shoghi Effendi becomes head of movement after death of Abdul-Bahá

1953—House of Worship dedicated in Wilmette, Illinois

1957—Death of Shoghi Effendi

1963—Baha'i World Congress in London

1983—Universal House of Justice takes permanent seat in Israel

1992—Second Congress (New York City)

2001—Opening of the Terraces on Mount Carmel

MASON REMEY PROCLAMATION

"The Baha'i people the world around know that The Beloved Guardian singled me, Mason Remey, out from amongst all of the Believers upon earth to occupy the position of President of the Baha'i International Council. This is the only position suggestive of authority that Shoghi Effendi ever bestowed upon anyone, the only special and specific appointment of authority to any man ever made by him.

"I, standing single and alone against the entire Baha'i world, but confirmed and steadfast in my assurance of ultimately saving the cause from this calamity. My assurance is based upon the authority that The Beloved Guardian gave me as President of the Council, the authority enabling me to act and assume command of the Baha'is that came to me at His death."

—Mason Remey, prominent American Baha'i, 1960

◼ Leland Jensen and Prophecy

Eschatology has always preoccupied the Baha'i faith. Various figures not only predicted the emergence of the Messiah (*mahdi*) in Shi'a Islam, but also the second coming of Christ. Factions within the Baha'i world adopt specific prophetic strategies in order to defend their distinct identity.

The followers of Leland Jensen (Baha'is Under the Provisions of the Covenant), for example, argue that the details of Jensen's life conform to Bible prophecy—including the notion that the Old Montana Territorial Prison in Deer Lodge, Montana, matches the dimensions of Ezekiel's temple. Jensen's followers teach that he was made aware of his messianic status while falsely imprisoned there.

Jensen states: "I started right in on that date prophesied by Daniel, defending the Faith. I was opposed by Satan on April 21, 1963—on that day my ministry started. I wasn't elected to that Assembly because I was in opposition to Satan. I was defending the Faith against Satan, Rex King. Today, I'm not liked by the Christians because I'm in opposition to Satan, as the pope wears the fish hat of Satan. He has the crosier of Satan. He has the keys of Satan—of Janus and Cybele. And he has the red robe of Satan, the red devil. And the pope is defending what? Of all things, a pagan triune god!"

Jensen even argues that he fulfills prophetic details given in the Great Pyramid of Egypt: "The same thing happened here, and the day was April 29, 1971, 108 years after Baha'u'llah's proclamation on April 21, 1863. In the floor of the King's Chamber are 108 red granite blocks. You add 108 to April 21, 1863, and you get April 21, 1971. But I made my proclamation on April 29. Baha'u'llah had already made it a holy day; it's one of the nine holy days of the Baha'i year, and it so happens that there are nine granite beams in the ceiling of the King's Chamber. April 21 is the first day of Ridvan and April 29 is the ninth day of Ridvan, and that gives us April 29, 1971, when I told Harry Stroup, 'Yes, I am the Joshua or the Jesus to come to establish my Father's kingdom—Baha'u'llah's. I'm a Knight, and I'm revealing the things that the people need to know so that everybody can become Baha'i.'"

BAHA'I	
Founder	Baha'u'llah (1817–92)
Main Group Website	www.bahai.org
Other Groups	Reform Baha'i movement (Frederick Glaysher): www.reformbahai.org Orthodox Baha'i group (Joel Marangella): http://www.rt66.com/~obfusa/council.htm Fourth Guardian Group (Jacques Soghomonian): www.guardianshipofthebahaifaith.org Tarbiyat Baha'i group (Rex King): www.tarbiyatcenter.org Baha'is Under the Provisions of the Covenant (Leland Jensen): http://bupc.montana.com Baha'is Under the Provisions of the Covenant (Neal Chase): www.bupc.org
Other Sites	www.bahai.com http://bahai-library.com www-personal.umich.edu/~jrcole/bahai.htm (Juan Cole) www.h-net.org/~bahai
Ex-Baha'i Website	Eric Stetson (Christian Universalist): www.bahai-faith.com
Recommended Reading	Francis J. Beckwith, "The Baha'i World Faith," in Ronald Enroth, ed. *A Guide to New Religious Movements* (Downers Grove: InterVarsity, 2005) Peter Smith, *A Concise Encyclopedia of the Baha'i Faith* (Oxford: Oneworld, 2000) William McElwee Miller, *What Is the Baha'i Faith?* (Grand Rapids: Eerdmans, 1977) Margit Warburg, *Baha'i* (Salt Lake City: Signature, 2001)

Universal House of Justice, Haifa, Israel

Photo: © Baha'i International Community

BAHA'IS TOP TEN	
Country	**Followers**
India	1,823,631
USA	593,075
Iran	409,869
Vietnam	376,328
Kenya	368,093
Congo-Zaire	318,876
South Africa	252,159
Philippines	247,499
Zambia	224,488
Bolivia	206,029

Source: World Christian Database 2008

2

THE BRANCH DAVIDIANS

(DAVID KORESH)

Tank used to ram church structure

Photo: FBI

The Branch Davidian movement forever will be identified with the leadership of David Koresh and the fire that consumed him and many of his followers at their Waco compound on April 19, 1993. Yet the Branch Davidians trace their origin to the work of Victor Houteff, a native of Bulgaria, who joined the Seventh-day Adventists in 1919.

Houteff focused his Bible interpretation on a phrase in Micah 6:9: "Hear ye the rod." Houteff believed that God chose him to reveal the secrets of the scroll protected by seven seals, as described in Revelation 5. Like Jehovah's Witnesses, Houteff took the 144,000 figure of Revelation

7 literally. He believed he would gather this faithful remnant to Palestine where they would set up the Kingdom of David.

He founded the Mount Carmel Center near Waco in 1935 and spread his version of Adventist doctrine around the world. His death in 1955 created a crisis in the movement, but his wife, Florence, assumed leadership. The movement did well until she predicted the world would end on April 22, 1959. That false prophecy caused an exodus of members, internal fragmentation, and financial collapse. Several groups subsequently emerged that continued to espouse the views of Victor Houteff, collectively known as Davidian Seventh-day Adventists (as distinguished from the Branch Davidians connected to Ben Roden).

Roden took control of the Mount Carmel property when he bought it from other Davidians and soon declared himself the fifth angel of Revelation 9:1. (Victor Houteff had claimed to be the fourth angel of Revelation 8:12.) When Roden died in 1978, his wife, Lois, assumed leadership of the group and claimed to be the sixth angel of Revelation 9:16. A year before her husband's death, she announced a revelation that the Holy Spirit is female.

In 1981 Vernon Howell joined the group. He gathered his own followers, but in 1984 George Roden, Lois's son, forced him out of Mount Carmel. Howell took control of Mount Carmel in 1988 when Roden was jailed for contempt of court. The previous year Howell and Roden had engaged in a gun battle after Roden had dug up the corpse of Anna Hughes and challenged Howell to a "resurrection contest." Howell declined and asked the Waco sheriff's department to charge Roden with abuse of a corpse. A gun battle ensued when Howell and his men returned to the property to get a picture of the corpse.

CHRONOLOGY RELATED TO BRANCH DAVIDIANS

1782—Birth of William Miller

1827—Ellen G. White born in Gorham, Maine

1831—William Miller predicted that the world would end in 1843

1843—Millerites changed end of world date to October 22, 1844

1844—Millerites experienced "the Great Disappointment" over failed prophecy

1863—Birth of Seventh-day Adventist movement in Battle Creek, Michigan

1885—Victor Houteff born in Bulgaria

1915—Death of Ellen G. White

1919—Houteff joins Seventh-day Adventist movement

1930—Houteff publishes *The Shepherd's Rod* Part One

1932—*The Shepherd's Rod* Part Two published

1934—Dismissal from Seventh-day Adventist organization

1935—Houteff starts new headquarters in Waco, Texas, at Mount Carmel. Group is known as The Shepherd's Rod Seventh-day Adventists

1943—Houteff renames group Davidian Seventh-day Adventist Association

1955—Houteff dies and his widow, Florence, takes over after dispute with Ben Roden

1955—Roden founds the Branch Davidian Seventh-day Adventists (BDSDA)

1959—Florence Houteff predicts end of world on April 22

1959—Vernon Howell born on August 17

1962—Roden and his followers take over Mount Carmel

1977—Lois Roden claims that Holy Spirit is feminine

1978—Ben Roden dies and wife Lois assumes leadership

1979—Vernon Howell joins Seventh-day Adventist Church in Tyler, Texas

1981—Vernon Howell becomes handyman at Mount Carmel

1983—Howell is alleged to have cohabited with Lois Roden

1984—George Roden removes Howell from Mount Carmel. Howell sets up headquarters in Palestine, Texas

1984—Howell marries Rachel Jones (age 14)

1985—Howell claims revelation that he is Cyrus

1985—Howell visits General Conference of Seventh-day Adventists in New Orleans

1986—Karen Doyle, age 14, is claimed as second "wife"

1986—Howell said to have slept with Michele Jones, 12, sister of Rachel Jones

1986—Marc Breault joins Howell's group

1986—Lois Roden dies on November 10

1986—Howell makes first trip to Australia

1986—Howell teaches that he can engage in polygamy

1987—Allegations that Robyn Bunds sleeps with Howell

1987—Howell allegedly takes Sherri Jewell as "wife"

1987—Gunfight between Howell and George Roden on November 3

1988—George Roden jailed and Howell regains control of Mount Carmel

1988—One of Howell's "wives," Dana Okimoto, has child on September 10

1988—Robyn Bunds gives birth to Shaun in November

1989—In April Howell makes controversial tape that mentions a dream where he sleeps with an underage girl

1989—Breault marries Elizabeth Baranyai on April 28

1989—Breault leaves Howell's group in September

1989—Turmoil among Howell followers in Australia and New Zealand

1990—Howell changes name to David Koresh

1990—Robyn Bunds leaves group

1990—Raid by La Verne police on local Koresh site

1991—David Jewell gains custody of daughter Kiri

1992—*Waco Tribune Herald* investigates Koresh

1992—BATF begins criminal investigation of Koresh in May-June

1993—BATF raid on Mount Carmel on February 28

1993—Fire kills seventy-four members, including Koresh, on April 19

Howell changed his name to David Koresh in 1990. He believed himself to be the Lamb of Revelation 5 and claimed that he would open the seven seals described in that chapter, thereby ushering in the second coming of Jesus. Koresh began the practice of taking "spiritual wives" in 1984, claiming to be the male figure to create a new line of God's children. He predicted apocalypse in America and out of this teaching adopted a survivalist mentality, stockpiling weapons and food. His teachings created both a loyal following and fierce criticism from ex-members.

Agents from the Bureau of Alcohol, Tobacco, and Firearms (BATF) raided the Branch Davidian compound on February 28, 1993, after a search warrant was issued on February 23. Reports of child abuse filed by ex-members, most notably Marc Breault, influenced the BATF investigation and raid.

Six Davidians and four BATF agents died in the raid. A subsequent FBI siege of the compound lasted fifty-one days. Koresh was allowed to broadcast a sermon on March 2, but reneged on his word to surrender. He then announced on April 14 that he would give up after he finished his commentary on the seven seals. The FBI attacked the compound on April 19, however, and the building erupted in flames. Seventy-four members died in the blaze, including twenty-one children. Thirty-five members fled during the siege (fourteen adults and twenty-one children), nine members survived the fire, and another six members were away from Mount Carmel at the time of the raid.

Seven Koresh followers received prison sentences for their involvement in the attack on BATF officers: Livingstone Fagan, Paul Fatta, Graeme Craddock, Renos Avraam, Jaime Castillo, Brad Branch, and Kevin Whitecliff. Some observers view Fagan as Koresh's successor, since he was tasked with releasing some of Koresh's last prophetic material to the world. Both Fagan and Renos Avraam have written religious material since 1993. Some surviving Koresh followers have expressed displeasure with Avraam for what they perceive as departures from Koresh's teachings.

Livingstone Fagan in London, England

Photo: Jim Beverley

A few of Koresh's followers continue to visit Mount Carmel and worship in the new sanctuary. Clive Doyle supervised the building of a modest structure and is often viewed as the group spokesperson. He declared himself a follower of Ben and Lois Roden and later accepted Koresh as leader. His youngest daughter died in the compound fire.

A KORESH APOLOGIST

During the final siege of the Waco compound, Livingstone Fagan was sent out to deliver Koresh's message to the public. Fagan was convicted and sentenced in 1994 for his participation in the attack on BATF officers. He was released from prison in 2007 and now lives in England. He has been very open, both in his lectures and in private conversations, about his continued commitment to David Koresh. He continues to claim that God led Koresh to have sexual relations with many females, including some underage girls.

Fagan told Judge Walter J. Smith the following just before his sentencing at the 1994 trial:

> Two thousand years ago when Christ was on the cross, we know that he was innocent. But he didn't have an appeal, did he? The system killed him. Is that appeal going to bring back [my wife] Evette, David, the children and all of the rest? No, it's not. Appeal doesn't mean nothing to me. But we also serve a God who sits on a throne, like you, a judge. He's got a book in his hand, sealed with seven seals. Men don't know his judgment. Consequently, Mount Carmel happened the way that it did. As you have judged, so, too, you will be judged. This is only an opportunity, from our perspective, for you, not for ourselves.

Waco: Q&A

1. Why did the BATF raid fail?

The February 28, 1993, raid failed largely because Koresh's brother-in-law, David Jones, tipped off Koresh about the attack. Two reporters who planned to cover the BATF raid, asked Jones, who was away from the compound at the time, how to get to Mount Carmel.

2. Why did the bureau launch such a raid?

The bureau considered the raid justified since it suspected illegal weapons had been stockpiled at Mount Carmel. Any such discovery would have given agents the authority to arrest Koresh.

3. Did the BATF know the raid was compromised?

Yes, but the issue is a bit complicated because of contradictory testimony by BATF agents. The BATF had an informant in the Koresh group named Robert Rodriguez, who was known in the group as Robert Garcia. When Rodriguez found out that Koresh knew about the attack, he left the compound. He claims that he clearly told BATF agent Chuck Sarabyn that the raid had been compromised. Sarabyn testified that he thought Rodriguez's warning was too vague to abandon the plan. Rodriguez stated in his testimony: "These two men know what I told them. They knew exactly what I meant. They lied to the public, and in doing so they just about destroyed a great agency." Sarabyn was dismissed and then reinstated to a desk job.

4. Did Koresh have illegal weapons on the compound?

Mark Swett, a leading expert on Waco, reports that he did, but other Waco researchers disagree. Koresh's attorney, Dick Deguerin, testified during a congressional investigation that Koresh told him that he had illegal weapons at the Mount Carmel site, some of which the Texas Rangers later retrieved. Finally, the BATF affidavit outlining its evidence of illegal weapons appears quite persuasive.

5. Was Koresh hit in the BATF raid?

He was shot in an index finger and in the pelvis area. He thought he was dying. He left a phone message with his mother, Bonnie Haldeman, in which he said, "Hello, Mama, it's your boy. They shot me and I'm dying, all right? But I'll be back real soon, OK? I'm sorry that you didn't learn the seals, but I'll be merciful, OK? I'll see y'all in the skies."

6. Were any children killed in the original raid?

No. Though Koresh originally claimed that children died in the raid, he later retracted that statement. One Waco researcher altered evidence to prove that a Davidian child had been killed.

7. Who was in charge when the FBI took over?

Jeff Jamar, from the FBI office in San Antonio, was the lead agent. Byron Sage, supervisor of the Waco office, also provided major leadership. William Sessions headed the FBI at the time, while Janet Reno served as U.S. Attorney General.

8. Did Koresh threaten the safety of those inside the compound?

At one point he suggested that children would be killed if the FBI did not allow the group to have outside contact with the world: "You guys are telling the public of this country that you don't want any blood. All right, now, I made a deal with you. You tell these boys they better get our lines back operable, OK? Or they're going to go to bed every night with the knowledge that they're the ones that killed these little children."

9. How did Koresh's emphasis on the "seven seals" impact the standoff?

Koresh interpreted the raid in light of his prophetic understanding of the seven seals of the Book of Revelation. In the final days of the standoff, the FBI largely ignored his desire to complete his commentary on the seven seals.

10. Did Koresh break a promise to leave the compound?

Yes. The FBI agreed to let Koresh broadcast on the radio on the condition that he and his followers vacate the buildings after airing of the broadcast. Koresh's rambling message, delivered under considerable physical pain, was played on both Texas radio and stations across the U.S. The broadcast also ran on CNN. FBI negotiators persuaded the Davidian leader to say, "I, David Koresh, agree upon the broadcasting of this tape, to come out peacefully with all the people immediately." He did not keep his word but claimed that God told him, in an audible voice: "Wait."

11. What kept the Branch Davidians from peaceful surrender?

On the one hand, the FBI made some strategic errors that made it difficult for Koresh and his followers to trust the Bureau. But more important, the members' devotion to Koresh and his message kept them from walking away from the building. Mark Swett stated, "Although no one was forced at gunpoint to stay inside Mt. Carmel, we can say that the Branch Davidians were spiritual hostages to the seven seals message."

12. Was there ever any hope of a peaceful solution?

An opportunity for peace seemed very real when Koresh said he would surrender after finishing his work on the seven seals. He felt impressed by the serious consideration given to his work by scholars James Tabor (University of North Carolina at Charlotte) and Phillip Arnold (Reunion Institute). Nevertheless, the FBI did not believe that Koresh would keep his promise to surrender after he finished his writing.

INTERVIEW WITH WACO SURVIVOR

In 1999 Michael W. Lynch interviewed David Thibodeau, a Waco survivor, for *Reason* magazine. Here is an exchange on Koresh and sex with underage girls:

Lynch: In your book, you complain that the media demonized Koresh. But don't you think much of the material in your book— especially his attraction to young girls—vindicates some of the harsher portraits of Koresh?

Thibodeau: That's no reason to go in and kill the people. But as for the allegations that Koresh slept with minors, in some of the cases it's true and some of the cases are not. Most of the women were of age. There were only a couple that weren't. I can't deny [that some of the girls were underage]. I wish I could. But I can't.

13. Was Janet Reno fully informed about the situation in Mount Carmel?

No. The evidence indicates that when she gave the order to gas the compound, she did not even know about Koresh's alleged plans to surrender after writing his commentary on the seven seals. Also, she had been misinformed about allegations of child abuse at the compound during the standoff.

14. Was Koresh sincere in his offer to surrender?

This is one of the most disputed issues regarding the standoff with the FBI. Despite Koresh's promise to surrender, there exists some clear evidence that leaders inside the compound had a mass suicide in mind. Steve Schneider, a top Koresh lieutenant, stated on April 18, just a day before the end: "At least we're going up. I'd rather go up in a puff of smoke than out the door and in a Bradley." The same day he told another member, "You always wanted to be a charcoal briquette."

15. How did Koresh portray himself as he negotiated with the FBI?

His declaration of March 7 speaks for itself: "I'm trying to tell you that I love this world more than you could ever imagine. But I'm trying to tell you that someone greater than I is telling me to wait. I'm just a poor cult leader out here in the middle of Waco, Texas. Ya know what I mean? And I ain't hurting nobody. I never have hurt anybody. They don't believe I'm Christ, do they? They will when they make me into a carcass, though, won't they? I have to bear sins of others, don't I? Christ can be born more than once, you know."

16. Who set the fires that consumed the compound?

Contrary to popular perception, Koresh followers themselves set the fires of April 19. Bugs the FBI had planted picked up many comments of key members stating that they had spread available fuel. There is no evidence that they were making weapons to resist the FBI. Furthermore, the group refused to surrender when the FBI began to pour tear gas into the compound at 6 A.M. A little after 11:30 that morning a voice was recorded, saying, "He said to light it." The voice came from one of David Koresh's followers inside the compound.

17. Did the FBI make its wishes clear on the final day?

FBI agent Byron Sage told the group, "We are going to place a significant increase in gas unless you put out a white flag right now. Give the signal and we will advise the people in the armored vehicles to stand back and allow a peaceful and orderly exit, but your opportunity is at hand right now. David. You have the capability right now—right now, of calling an end to it. Do not subject yourself or your children to any more discomfort. You have some precious kids in there. We do not—we do not intend to, nor do we want to inflict any injury on those kids. The same applies to you and your followers. Please. David. It is time to bring this to an end."

18. How did Koresh die?

An autopsy revealed that he died from a gunshot wound to the forehead. Both FBI agent Robert Ricks and U.S. Army colonel Robert Rawlings suggested that Steve Schneider shot Koresh when he tried to flee. No released FBI tapes confirm this theory. Ricks later recanted his claim.

19. Did the FBI engage in a cover-up?

The most significant lack of disclosure involved the federal agency not informing the public that agents fired pyrotechnic ferret rounds into the building on April 19 to force members out. That revelation came six years after the tragedy.

20. What is the debate about FLIR tapes?

On the last day of the siege the FBI used a forward-looking infrared (FLIR) video camera from a plane to take images of the compound. Some experts believe that the FLIR tapes show the Davidians under fire from the outside. Other experts believe that the images of light on the film merely reflect sunlight.

21. Were any law enforcement officials fired because of Waco?

BATF supervisors Chuck Sarabyn and Phillip Chojinacki were fired but were later brought back to the bureau at a lower rank. No FBI officials were disciplined. Both Janet Reno and William Sessions received enormous criticism for their roles and decisions.

22. How should we think about conspiracy theories regarding Waco?

The wildest conspiracy theories involve claims that Koresh himself was a government agent or that the survivors were part of a government plot. Some claim that officials at the highest levels of the U.S. government fully planned the deaths of the Davidians. These ideas deserve little respect in light of all of the evidence that points both to Koresh's utter commitment to his beliefs and to government agents bungling the case.

23. What are some of the biggest mistakes made at Waco?

Most people forget that six hours elapsed between the beginning of the FBI assault on the compound and the start of the fire that engulfed the compound. This gave Koresh and his followers plenty of time to surrender. They chose not to do so. It is possible that they feared that the FBI would kill them if they walked out. It is far more likely, however, that they chose to remain inside simply because that is what Koresh wanted them to do.

24. What is considered the most tragic part of FBI planning during the standoff?

It is tragic that the FBI did not take Koresh's theology seriously. They did not have to believe it or think him rational, but things might have turned out very differently if agents had tried harder to understand his worldview. They failed to give enough attention to the way the bureau's aggressive actions fit into his theories about government and "end times."

25. Who provides good information on Waco?

Mark Swett is a great analyst of Waco and has provided help to most major scholars who have written about Koresh. Swett's vast collection on Waco is available at Baylor University. The best book on the topic is James Tabor and Eugene V. Gallagher's *Why Waco?* (University of California, 1997).

Internet Sources

Davidian Massacre homepage: http://carolmoore.net/waco/

PBS Front Line "Waco: The Inside Story": www.pbs.org/wgbh/pages/frontline/waco

Waco: the Rules of Engagement: www.waco93.com/

BATF affidavit on illegal weapons: www.thesmokinggun.com/fall/waco1.html

Rick Ross on Waco: www.rickross.com/groups/waco.html

Reason magazine interview with David Thibodeau: http://reason.com/bi/int-thib.shtml

John Mann website: http://www.fountain.btinternet.co.uk/koresh/index.html

Texas Rangers September 1999 Waco report: www.txdps.state.tx.us/director_staff/public_information/branch_davidian

3

BUDDHISM

Buddhist temple grounds, Richmond, Virginia

Photo: Derek Beverley

Buddhism probably enjoys the best public image of any world religion, in general because of Buddhist emphasis on peace, serenity, and compassion. More specifically, Buddhism has become a religion of choice because of the singular impact of His Holiness the Dalai Lama, the spiritual leader of Tibet, a monk renowned for his great character, humility, and humor.

Buddhism originated nearly 2,500 years ago with an Indian reformer named Gautama who is now known to us as the Buddha. If one accepts traditional Buddhist accounts of Gautama's life, he was raised as a prince in complete isolation from the reality of ordinary life. One day he was startled to discover that sickness and death are real, and he set out on a spiritual journey to discover how humanity can be delivered from malady. He abandoned some traditional Hindu teachings of his time and achieved enlightenment through intense study and reflection. He chose then to stay on Earth to help liberate others.

At first glance Buddhism appears to be a very simple religion that relies on universal moral principles about following paths of peace. However, this exterior gives way to extensive guidelines about life as a monk, complex philosophical views, and very strange esoteric rituals. Further, as one learns about Buddhist history, it becomes clear that Buddhism is understood very differently over time, and that radical differences exist between the various types of Buddhism.

Buddhist nuns, Plum Village, France

Photo: Jim Beverley

This chapter provides an introduction to basic Buddhist perspectives and major Buddhist leaders and organizations, and offers extensive material on the life, views, and impact of His Holiness the Dalai Lama. I had the opportunity to interview the Dalai Lama in 2000 for *Christianity Today* magazine, and a record of that interview is included as well. This chapter also provides a Christian response to Buddhism.

According to a 2008 survey of religion in the United States, less than one percent of Americans identify themselves as Buddhists. However, Buddhism has a high profile in the country not only because of the Dalai Lama but also because of Chinese persecution of Tibetan Buddhists and the high profile that Buddhism has in certain Hollywood circles. Globally, there are about 400 million Buddhists, comprising about 6 percent of the world's population.

BUDDHISM 101

- There is no God or Supreme Creator.

- The current universe has evolved through natural law.

- Truth has been given through countless ages by various Buddhas, or enlightened beings.

- Gautama Buddha, who lived twenty-five hundred years ago, is the teacher for our time period.

- While salvation depends on individual effort, the Buddhist is to take refuge in the Buddha, his teaching (dharma), and the Buddhist community (sangha).

- The Buddha taught Four Noble Truths: (1) suffering is real; (2) suffering is caused by selfish desire; (3) suffering will cease when selfish desire is eliminated; and (4) selfish desire will cease through following the Noble Eightfold Path.

- The Noble Eightfold Path that leads to Nirvana involves having the (1) right view, (2) right resolve, (3) right speech, (4) right action, (5) right livelihood, (6) right effort, (7) right mindfulness, and (8) right concentration.

- All living things are subject to the law of karma, the principle of cause and effect, which controls the cycle of reincarnation.

- The Buddhist is to abstain from:
  —killing   —stealing
  —forbidden sex   —lying
  —use of illicit drugs and liquor

- Buddhism is not irrational.

- Buddhism is not pessimistic.

- Buddhism is not nihilistic.

THE PALI CANON

The Buddhist Pali Canon serves as scripture or sacred text for Theravada Buddhists. Some parts of the Pali Canon are also recognized by Mahayana and Vajrayana Buddhists. The Pali Canon is usually referred to as the Tipitaka or Three Baskets because of the division into three sections.

There is great divergence among scholars over to what extent the Pali texts represent the actual words or stories of Gautama. Some parts claim to be from disciples of the Buddha.

First Basket: Vinaya Pitaka (rules of conduct)

1. Suttavibhanga
2. Mahavagga
3. Cullavagga
4. Parivara

Second Basket: Sutta Pitaka (contains more than 10,000 discourses)

1. Digha Nikaya
2. Majjhima Nikaya
3. Samyutta Nikaya
4. Anguttara Nikaya
5. Khuddaka Nikaya

Third Basket: Abhidhamma Pitaka

1. Dhammasangani
2. Vibhanga
3. Dhatukatha
4. Puggalapaññatti
5. Kathavatthu
6. Yamaka
7. Patthana

▥ Buddha: A Life in Twelve Acts

The different traditions in Buddhism do not agree on the details about Gautama, the historical Buddha. However, his life is often captured in twelve crucial Acts, the first having to do with his pre-incarnate state:

1. Waits in *Tushita* (the eternal realm)
2. Grows in the womb of Queen Mayadevi, his mother
3. Is birthed out of his mother's side
4. Attains intellectual and physical skills
5. Marries Yashodhara and fathers a son (Rahula)
6. Renounces royal life and departs from palace
7. Chooses ascetic path of extreme denial
8. Seeks enlightenment at the Bodhi Tree
9. Defeats Mara (the Lord of Samsara)
10. Attains enlightenment
11. Teaches Buddhist dharma
12. Enters Nirvana

Alleged supernatural elements exist in parts of Buddha's life story. When he was in his mother's womb, his father is said to have seen him sitting in a meditation posture inside a wonderful box. After Gautama was born he allegedly took seven steps and proclaimed: "I alone in the world am the Honored One." When Gautama's mother died, she purportedly became a goddess whose womb is preserved in the heavens. Gautama escaped from the royal palace on his horse, Kanthaka. The horse is said to have died of a broken heart when Gautama had to leave him, but Kanthaka subsequently became a god. When Gautama defeated Mara, he is believed to have done so, in part, by turning demons to flowers.

CHRONOLOGY OF BUDDHISM

566–486/490–410 B.C.—Siddhartha Gautama, the historical Buddha

486 B.C.?—First Buddhist Council at Rajagrha

386 B.C.—Second Council at Vaisali

367 B.C.—Non-Canonical Council at Pataliputra

272–231 B.C.—King Asoka converts to Buddhism

c. 250 B.C.—Asoka's son Mahinda goes as missionary to Sri Lanka

250 B.C.—Third Council at Pataliputra

250 B.C.—Pali Canon finished

200 B.C.—Beginnings of Mahayana Buddhism

Second century B.C.—Nagasena's famous dialogue with King Milinda

25 B.C.—Pali Canon written in Sri Lanka

First century A.D.—Fourth Buddhist Council at Kagmir

First century—Lotus Sutra composed

First century—Buddhism spreads to Central Asia

Second century?—Asvaghosa composes *Buddha-Carita*

Second century—Nargarjuna forms Madhyamika school

Third century—Buddhism spreads to Southeast Asia

310–90—Life of Asanga, founder of Yogacara school

Fourth century—Vajrayana Buddhism starts in India

372—Buddhism spreads to Korea

334–416—Life of Hui-yuan (translator of Chinese texts)

344–413—Life of Kumarajiva, founder of Madhyamika in China

405—Fa-hsien, Chinese monk, arrives in India

420–500—Life of Vasubandhu, author of Vijnaptiimatra Sutra

Fifth century—Nalanda monastery founded in India

Fifth century—Buddhaghosa composes *Visuddhimagga* (Path of Purity)

Fifth century—Amitabha (Amida) Pure Land school
starts in China

520—Bodhidharma goes to China

538—Buddhism reaches Japan

602–64—Life of Hsan-tsang (Chinese translator
and pilgrim)

638–713—Life of Huineng, sixth Patriarch of
Ch'an Buddhism

Eighth century—Hosso, Jojitsu, Kegon, Kusha, Ritsu and
Sanron schools

Eighth century—Padmasambhava travels to Tibet to help
spread Buddhism

Eighth century—Nyingma-pa sect in Tibet begins

767–822—Life of Saicho (founder of Tendai
school)

774–835—Life of Kukai (founder of Shingon
school)

845—Buddhism under attack in China

Ninth century—Diamond Sutra written in China

983—Szechuan Canon printed

1008–64—Life of Buston, great Tibetan textual
scholar

1012–96?—Life of Marpa, founder of Kargyupa sect

1040–1123—Life of Milarepa, disciple of Marpa

c. 1040—Atisha (982–1054) starts Kahdampa
school in Tibet

c. 1050—Sakyapa Tibetan school begins

1133–1212—Life of Honen, founder of Jodo Shinshu
(Shin Buddhism)

1141–1215—Life of Eisai, founder of Rinzai Zen
Japanese sect

1173–1263—Life of Shinran, founder of True Pure
Land Japanese sect

1200—Nalanda University destroyed

1200–53—Life of Dogen, founder of Soto Zen
Japanese sect

1222–1282—Life of Nichiren

Thirteenth century—Vajrayana spreads to Mongols

Fourteenth century—Bu-ston edits Tibetan Buddhist Canon

1360—Theravada becomes state religion in Thailand

1355–1417—Life of Tsongkhapa, founder of Gelugpa Tibetan sect

Fifteenth century—Dalai Lama lineage in Tibet begins

1587—Altan Khan gives Gelugpa leader title of Dalai Lama

1686–1769—Life of Hakuin, famous Rinzai teacher of koans

1862—Sri Lankan monks get reordained in Burma

1862—Western translation of Dhammapada

1870—Birth of D. T. Suzuki, Japanese Zen teacher

1871—Fifth Buddhist Council at Mandalay, Burma

1891—Anagarika Dharmapala (1865–1933) starts Maha Bodhi

1893—Buddhist monks at World's Parliament of Religions in Chicago

1904—Birth of Ven. U. Sobhana (Vispassana reformer)

1907—Birth of Ven. Walpola Rahula, Sri Lankan reformer

1926—Founding of Buddhist Society by Christmas Humphreys

1926—Birth of Thich Nhat Hanh, famous Vietnamese Buddhist

1928–9—T'ai-Hsu, b. 1889, Chinese monk, travels in Europe

1932—Buddhadasa establishes Suan Mokkhabalarama in Chaiya

1935—Birth of Dalai Lama

1950—Communist persecution of Tibet

1954–6—Sixth Buddhist Council at Rangoon, Myanmar

1956—Ambedkar (1891–1956) espouses Buddhism

1959—Dalai Lama flees Tibet

1960—Soka Gakkai president Daisaku Ikeda visits America and forms first chapter of Soka Gakkai

1962—San Francisco Zen Center founded by Shunryu Suzuki-roshi

1965— *Three Pillars of Zen* (author: Philip Kapleau)

1966—D. T. Suzuki dies

1967—Zen Center of Los Angeles founded by Taizan Maezumi

1971—Shunryu Suzuki-roshi dies

1972—Lama Ole Nydahl starts Vajrayana Center in Copenhagen

1974—Naropa Institute founded by Chogyam Trungpa

1975—Vietnamese Buddhists emigrate in larger numbers to U.S.

1982—Thich Nhat Hanh starts Plum Village near Bordeaux, France

1983—Conflict over Richard Baker's leadership at Zen Center

1987—Death of Chogyam Trungpa in Halifax, Nova Scotia

1988—Controversy over sexual mores of Osel Tendzin (Thomas F. Rich) of Shambhala group

1989—Dalai Lama receives Nobel Peace Prize

1995—Death by drowning of Zen leader Taizan Maezumi

1995—Dorje Shugden debate

1997—Hollywood focus on Buddhism

1998—Tamil Tigers attack Temple of the Tooth in Sri Lanka

2001—Taliban destroy two Buddhist statues

2004—Death of Kapleau

2007—Dalai Lama receives Congressional Medal and visits President George W. Bush

2008—Tibetan monks rebel against Chinese authority

■ The Dalai Lama: A Special Report

His official titles are "Jetsun Jamphel Ngawang Lobsang Yeshe Tenzin Gyatso," meaning "Holy Lord, Gentle Glory, Eloquent, Compassionate, Learned Defender of the Faith, Ocean of Wisdom." After Pope John Paul II and Billy Graham, he is probably the most recognized religious figure on our planet. His is the voice of Buddhism to the nations and he is often called the "god-king" of Tibet. He was awarded the Nobel Peace Prize in 1989, and his best-selling *Ethics for a New Millennium* has made him a spiritual guide for many non-Buddhists. He is treated with immense respect by secular media and draws crowds up to 300,000 at his public talks.

These titles and accolades belong to Buddhism's leading apostle, the Dalai Lama. Born as Lhamo Thondup in 1935 in northeast Tibet, he was chosen as the fourteenth Dalai Lama (Tibet's highest religious figure) at age 2. He was enthroned in 1940 and became political leader of Tibet at age 15, just after Mao's armies began their takeover of Tibet. In exile since 1959, the Dalai Lama has become a world leader in ethics, politics, and religion.

He has also become the de facto leader of millions of spiritual seekers in the West. Christians who want to evangelize our culture do well to understand the extent of the Dalai Lama's influence, especially in pop culture, as well as the exact nature of his beliefs. To this end, in the summer of 2000, *Christianity Today* magazine sent me to the Dalai Lama's home-in-exile in Dharamsala, India, to ask him about the popularity of Buddhism, his faith's relation to other faiths, and, most of all, what he thinks about Jesus.

Hollywood's Guru

The Dalai Lama's influence and the allure of Tibet in Hollywood and pop culture are explored in Orville Schell's *Virtual Tibet*. Schell notes that by the mid-1990s, Hollywood's "unparalleled engine of invention had alighted on Tibet as one of its chosen subjects." The Dalai Lama became the unseen star of two large-budget films, Jean-Jacques Annaud's *Seven Years in Tibet* and Martin Scorsese's *Kundun*.

Scorsese told one interviewer about his meeting with the Dalai Lama: "Something happened. I became totally aware of existing in the moment. It was like you could feel your heartbeat; and as I left, he looked at me. I don't know, but there was something about the look, something sweet. . . . I just knew I had to make the movie."

Hollywood actor Richard Gere is probably his most famous devotee. After an initial foray into Zen, Gere was drawn to the Dalai Lama, telling *Shambhala Sun* magazine, "It completely changed my life the first time I was in the presence of His Holiness. No question about it." Gere introduced the Dalai Lama to New Yorkers in 1999 when the Buddhist leader spoke in Central Park. The actor also led a protest rally for a free Tibet when the Dalai Lama visited Washington in 2000.

Prayer wheels, Dharamsala, India

Photo: Jim Beverley

The Dalai Lama is also a major spiritual influence on actress Sharon Stone, composer Philip Glass, Adam Yauch of the Beastie Boys, and muscle actor Steven Seagal. "The Dalai Lama's been a great friend to me, and I don't want to use that for anything but my personal spiritual sustenance," Seagal told Schell. "He is the great mother of everything nurturing and loving. He accepts all who come without judgment. He has a very serious impact on the degenerate times in which we live and on bringing us back to a more pure realm."

The Dalai Lama's international image, in fact, is virtually shatterproof. There was a minor ripple about his credibility when Heinrich Harrer's Nazi past was exposed just before the movie *Seven Years in Tibet* was released. On that subject, the Dalai Lama does not claim omniscience, and says Harrer simply kept the truth from him. Likewise, the Dalai Lama had endorsed Shoko Asahara, the guru of the Aum Shinrikyo movement in Japan, but withdrew his support after that movement's poison-gas attacks on Tokyo subways. Again, his sympathetic comment about Saddam Hussein in a *New York Times* interview drew only passing criticism. Geshe Kelsang Gyatso, a famous Tibetan guru who now lives in England, led a brief international campaign against the Dalai Lama, accusing him of dictatorship and hypocrisy, to no result.

One consequence of Hollywood's attention to the Dalai Lama is that Buddhism, especially the Tibetan strain, has entered mainstream America. Madison Avenue uses Buddhist lingo to sell goods, and Buddhist terminology crops up on *The Simpsons* and other high-profile television shows. Ads for Tibetan root beer proffer a "gently invigorating cardamom and coriander in a Tibetan adaptation of Ayurvedic herbs." Washington's Smithsonian Institution featured Tibetan culture in its folk life festival in the summer of 2000. At the National Mall visitors could hear Buddhists monks chanting, watch a sand mandala being created, buy Tibetan medicines, and even join in prayer before an image of Avalokitesvara, the protector deity of Tibet.

Westerners can even be chosen as incarnations of high lamas, as has been claimed of Jewish-born Catharine Burroughs, Vancouver native Elijah Ary, and Steven Seagal himself. Penor Rinpoche, head of the Nyingma lineage in Tibetan Buddhism, declared that Seagal was the current manifestation of Chungdrag Dorge, a renowned seventeenth-century teacher. Ary, born in 1972, now goes by Tenzin Sherab and is said to be the incarnation of Geshe Jatse, a sage who died in a Tibetan cave more then thirty years ago. Burroughs, titled as Jetsunma Ahkon Lhamo, heads a large Tibetan monastery in Poolesville, Maryland. Her story is told in Martha Sherill's *The Buddha from Brooklyn*.

TWO MAIN BRANCHES OF BUDDHISM

	Theravada	Mahayana
Main geographical location	Sri Lanka, Myanmar, Thailand, Laos, Cambodia, Vietnam	China, Tibet, Japan, Korea, Taiwan, Nepal, Mongolia
View of Buddhas	Emphasis on Gautama and previous Buddhas plus belief in Maitreya (the Buddha to come)	Emphasis on Gautama plus the Buddhas for our time (Amitabha and others) and Maitreya
Concept of salvation	Focus on self-liberation through monastic life	Self-liberation plus focus on bodhisattva ideal of liberating others
Scripture	Pali Canon	Pali material plus Mahayana sutras
Schools	No major divisions	Chan (Zen), Pure Land, Tibetan and others
Ritual	Simple worship, austere	Elaborate and complex involving mudras, mantras, tantric formulas, mandalas, trance states, dances

Special Note: For the sake of simplicity Tibetan Buddhism is included under Mahayana. It is often treated as a separate form known as Vajrayana.

■ The Romance of Tibet

The influence of the Dalai Lama comes in part because of the allure of Tibet on the Western imagination for the last two centuries. Tibet has captured the hearts of figures as diverse as famous psychoanalyst Carl Jung, Theosophy founder Madame Blavatsky, and Alexandra David-Neel, an explorer extraordinaire. At age 55, David-Neel reached Lhasa, Tibet's capital, after a 2,000-mile trek from India. James Hilton's famous 1933 novel *Lost Horizon* located paradise in northern Tibet in a hidden valley he called Shangri-La.

Hilton may have been borrowing on the Tibetan Buddhist belief that there is a pure kingdom known as Shambhala. Richard Gere told a *Frontline* documentary that Tibet promises "Release. Light. Happiness. I would say that the West is very young; it's very corrupt. We're not very wise. And I think we're hopeful that there is a place that is ancient and wise and open and filled with light." That Tibet has been pillaged by Communist China has only added to Western longings for the paradise that has been lost.

The most extreme claims about Tibet as a kingdom of magic come from the writings of T. Lobsang Rampa. Claiming to be a Tibetan priest with supernatural powers, he recounted his phenomenal life story in his best seller *The Third Eye* (1956), followed by *Doctor from Lhasa* (1959) and *The Rampa Story* (1960). The first volume was greeted with ridicule by Tibetan specialists, and their skepticism was confirmed when a private investigator revealed that Rampa was really Cyril Henry Hoskin, a native of Devonshire, England, who had never been to Asia. Despite the debunking, Rampa's first volume remains in print and is one of the most popular guides to Tibetan religion.

Myths about a Tibetan paradise extend to the sexual dimension as well. Western devotees and students of Asian thought have long been fascinated with aspects of Hindu and Buddhist tantra, which sometimes add sexual practice to divine rituals. A few American religious groups trace their sexual libertarianism to what they call the sex magic of Tibet. Jeffrey Hopkins, a leading scholar of Buddhism, has even argued that Tibetan Buddhism is a great vehicle for gay liberation.

The Dalai Lama himself is one source to counter many of the utopian visions of Tibet. He routinely dismisses stories about flying monks and levitating lamas. He told his Central Park audience that he does not know how to do miracles and has never seen one. He suggested to one interviewer that the only way a Buddhist monk could fly is by jumping off a cliff, spreading his robes, and hoping for a soft landing. The Dalai Lama has also acknowledged that pre-Communist Tibet had the weaknesses—corruption, illiteracy, and violence, for example—one would expect from a semi-feudal and premodern society.

Tenzin Taklha, one of the Dalai Lama's top aides who used to manage his security in Dharamsala and in his world travels, told me in my interview for *Christianity Today* that he holds the Dalai Lama in high esteem as a wonderful boss and a fabulous person—but that people who believe he has magical powers are simply mistaken. He was equally direct about claims regarding tantra. He denied any idea that tantric sex is a common practice among Tibetan Buddhists.

Statue in Choijing Lama Temple, Mongolia

Photo: Massimo Introvigne

Various scholars echo his view, saying that the tantric doctrine became at most a convenient way for a few Tibetan masters to break their celibate vows in the West. These experts also said that homosexual abuse by senior monks would be a more likely reality in Tibetan monasteries. Missionaries to the Tibetan Buddhist world told me of isolated cases in which monks used their status to seduce young women in local villages in Nepal, Bhutan, and Tibet, equivalent to cases of Christian pastors using their spiritual status for sexual abuse.

The mythology about Tibet has been explored in depth by Donald Lopez Jr.'s masterful work *Prisoners of Shangri-La*. Lopez makes a persuasive case that "the continued idealization of Tibet—its history and religion—may ultimately harm the cause of Tibetan independence." Whatever the case, there is no doubt that naïve understandings of Tibet, both past and present, shape public response to the Dalai Lama, just as he, by virtue of his connection with Tibet, seems larger than life to the thousands who flock to his teachings and buy his many books.

Internet Sources

www.savetibet.org

http://www.savetibet.org/campaigns/pl/history.php

THE MISSING PANCHEN LAMA

The Panchen Lama is the second highest religious authority in Tibet. There has been a decade-long ideological battle over the true Panchen Lama and an international outcry against the abduction of the eleventh Lama chosen by His Holiness the Dalai Lama. This tragic story is told in Isabel Hilton's, *The Search for the Panchen Lama* (Norton, 2000).

Timeline:

1989—Death in January of the tenth Panchen Lama: Lobsang Trinley Lhundrup Choekyi Gyaltsen

1989—April 29: Birth of Gendun Choekyi Nyima

1995—January: Recognition of Gendun Choekyi Nyima as the eleventh Panchen Lama by the Dalai Lama

1995—May: Public announcement of the eleventh Panchen Lama by the Dalai Lama

1995—May 17: Chinese government abducts eleventh Panchen Lama and takes him into hiding

1995—Arrest of Chadrel Rinpoche (Senior Tibetan Abbot) who led the search team for the eleventh Panchen Lama

1995—Chinese select own Panchen Lama: Gyaincain Norbu

1996—Chinese government admits to holding Gendun Choekyi Nyima

2004—Gyaincain Norbu praises Chinese rule in Tibet in first public interview

■ A Conversation with the Dalai Lama

I interviewed the Dalai Lama in Dharamsala, India, the site of the Tibet Government in Exile and the home of the Dalai Lama since 1960. Situated in the state of Himachal Pradesh, Dharamsala is nestled on the side of one of the mountains that form part of the Outer Himalayas. The Dalai Lama himself lives in a modest setting in Upper Dharamsala or McLeod Gang, 1,800 meters above the fertile plains of the Kangra Valley.

Author with Dalai Lama, August 2000, Dharamsala, India

Photo: Office of the Dalai Lama

Dharamsala is not a high-class tourist haven. The best hotels are mediocre by Western standards. Tourist guides warn about the lack of sanitary conditions in many of the restaurants. Cows wander the narrow, unpaved streets at will, in competition with an amazing number of taxis. Goods are sold in small booths along both sides of the streets. Most prices are set, though you can barter with Kashmir merchants selling carpets, Buddhist icons, and precious gems. There are several pleasant second-hand bookstores and a lot of travel agencies. Buddhist prayer flags dominate the buildings, as do pictures of the Dalai Lama.

Pilgrims usually get to Dharamsala by bus, train, or taxi from New Delhi, an arduous twelve-hour journey. A two-hour flight to Amritsar or Jammu will cut the journey to a five-hour cab ride.

Despite the difficulty of the journey, visitors from all over the world flock to what is called "little Lhasa." The Dalai Lama holds frequent public audiences and gives public teachings at least once a year in the Buddhist temple opposite his residence. Private sessions with the Dalai Lama are arranged through Taklha, his deputy secretary, who receives 50 to 100 interview requests daily. Soldiers of the Indian army guard the Dalai Lama. Visitors who enter the residence area have to walk through metal detectors and are searched by a member of the Dalai Lama's security team.

Two days before my interview, I was briefed by the Dalai Lama's personal secretary, who, along with the Dalai Lama's personal translator, was present for the interview. I was given no rules on protocol, and when the Dalai Lama was ushered into the interview room, he was introduced without any fanfare. After an exchange of greetings, the Dalai Lama expressed concern about the health of Billy Graham.

We ranged back and forth over a variety of topics in the interview, as the following summary of our conversation reveals.

Sinless Nonsense

Nicholas Vreeland, director of the Tibet Center in Manhattan, told me at the Central Park event that he regards the Dalai Lama as sinless, a view shared by many practitioners of Tibetan Buddhism. When the Dalai Lama arrived at the Parliament of the World's Religions in Chicago in 1993 under heavy police guard, his Buddhist devotees greeted him with tears, shouts of joy, and an adulation that bordered on worship. The Dalai Lama's charisma is legendary.

When I reviewed such incidents, as well as some people's claims that he is a god-king, sinless and perfect, the Dalai Lama answered with one word: "Nonsense." Then he laughed.

He does believe that he is a reincarnation of a previous Dalai Lama, but he is not sure of the details. "According to some of my dreams, I have some very close connection with the 13th Dalai Lama as well as the 5th Dalai Lama." He said that he must not focus on his fame. "It does not matter whether people regard me as a very high being, almost like Buddha, or a counterrevolutionary. What matters is whether I remain a genuine Buddhist monk and accordingly make some contribution for the betterment of other sentient beings."

The Dalai Lama is remarkably candid about his personal failings. His struggles to control his temper are recounted in *Freedom in Exile,* his second autobiographical work. Taklha said he has seen his boss lose his temper on more than one occasion, though only once did he feel he was out of control. In several interviews the Dalai Lama has admitted that he struggles with lust. He told *Tricycle,* a leading Buddhist magazine, that when he thinks about beautiful women, he has to remember classical Buddhist teaching that the human body will one day be a rotting corpse.

Avalokiteshvara Buddha of Compassion

Photo: Derek Beverley

His aides in Dharamsala tell the Dalai Lama that he works too hard, but he joked in the interview about his laziness when it comes to things he hates to do. He did admit that the demands of being a teacher and politician have forced him to give up hobbies like gardening and repairing watches. He follows a regular routine of early-morning prayers and meditation and midmorning administrative work and then gives his afternoons to interviews and public forums. Though his schedule is tight, he is flexible. At one point in the interview, when his attention was drawn to the time, he said, "This is not New York or Washington. Let's keep talking."

Buddhism and Other Religions

The Dalai Lama said he is generally not discouraged about the type of Buddhism he sees when he visits the West. He believes that people from different areas should keep their own faith. "Changing religion is not easy," he said. "Sometimes it creates more confusion." If someone in the West finds Buddhism more suitable, "it is their individual right, but it is extremely important to keep their respect towards their own traditional religion."

He expressed appreciation for Richard Gere's efforts as a celebrity to spread Buddhist *dharma* (or teaching). He did not seem concerned about the depth or style of Buddhist devotion in America, except to make a point against what he called New Age Buddhists who take concepts from every religion. "If they do that and make clear this is something new, that is all right. If they claim that such a mixture is traditional Tibetan Buddhism, then this is not right."

The Dalai Lama is no advocate of one world religion, as some New Age Buddhists seem to believe. He has consistently spoken against this in his public speeches. "So if one is always trying to look at things in terms of similarities and parallels, there is a danger of rolling everything up into one big entity," he writes in *The Good Heart,* his book about the teachings of Jesus. "I do not personally advocate seeking a universal religion; I don't think it advisable to do so. And if we proceed too far in drawing these parallels and ignoring the differences, we might end up doing exactly that!"

But if not a universal religion, what about a universal following of Buddha? Why does he not simply urge people to follow the path of Buddha as the only truth?

He replied by citing India's pluralistic past and said that contradictions in Buddha's own philosophical teaching have forced Buddhists to realize that "one teaching or one view will not satisfy."

"To some people Christianity is much more effective, in some other case, Islam, Judaism, Hinduism, or Zoroastrianism," he said. "Even if I say that Buddhism is the best, that everybody should follow Buddhism, everybody is not going to become a Buddhist."

He laughed.

"But you do believe Buddhism is the best, don't you?"

"Yes," he replied, "I can say that for me personally, Buddhism is best because the Buddhist approach is most effective to me."

"This does not mean Buddhism is best for everyone. No," he said when pushed further. "Now, for my Christian brother or sister, Christianity is best for him or for her." But Christianity, he said, is not the best for him.

"Here, the concept of one religion, one truth, is very relevant for the individual," he said, qualifying his other statements about one religion. "But for the community it must be several truths, several religions."

He believes this solves the contradiction between religions, though he said that there is a unity of all major religions on "the message of compassion, forgiveness, tolerance, contentment, simplicity, and self-discipline."

In terms of his own faith, the Dalai Lama drew a parallel between emotional love for Buddha and Christian love for Jesus. He said that his reflection on Buddha's teaching and sacrifice has led him to tears at times.

Does he thank Buddha for the good things in his life?

"Frankly speaking, my own happiness is mainly due to my own good karma," he said. "It is a fundamental Buddhist belief that my own suffering is due to my mistakes. If some good things happen, that is mainly due to my own good actions, not something related to a direct connection with Buddha."

The Integrity of Jesus

In our interview, we devoted considerable time to the identity and integrity of Jesus. The Dalai Lama seemed at ease with the questioning, even while admitting that this was possibly the toughest area for exploration between evangelical Christians and Buddhists.

I reminded him of his belief that Jesus is "a fully enlightened being," and asked, "If Jesus is fully enlightened, wouldn't he be teaching the truth about himself? Therefore, if he is teaching the truth, then he is the Son of God, and there is a God, and Jesus is the Savior. If he is fully enlightened, he should teach the truth. If he is not teaching the truth, he is not that enlightened."

As the Dalai Lama felt the momentum of the question, he laughed more than at any other time in the interview. He obviously understood the argument, borrowed from *Mere Christianity* by C. S. Lewis.

"This is a very good question," he said. "This is very, very important, very important." Even in Buddha's case, he said, a distinction must always be made between teachings that "always remain valid" and others that "we have the liberty to reject."

He argued that the Buddha knew people were not always ready for the higher truth because it "wouldn't suit, wouldn't help." Therefore, lesser truths are sometimes taught because of the person's ignorance or condition. This is known in Buddhist *dharma* as the doctrine of *uppayah*, or skillful means. The Dalai Lama then applied this to the question about Jesus.

"Jesus Christ also lived previous lives," he said. "So, you see, he reached a high state, either as a *Bodhisattva,* or an enlightened person, through Buddhist practice or something like that. Then, at a certain period, certain era, he appeared as a new master, and then because of circumstances, he taught certain views different from Buddhism, but he also taught the same religious values as I mentioned earlier: Be patient, tolerant, and compassionate. This is, you see, the real message in order to become a better human being." He said that there was absolutely no lying involved since Jesus' motivation was to help people.

The True Light

I came away from the interview perplexed about many matters, but mostly regarding the Dalai Lama's views of Jesus. Here is the core of what separates Buddhists and Christians and thus must become a key element in conversations with Buddhists.

While the Dalai Lama's claim that Jesus is a fully enlightened being offers some common ground with Christian faith, he does not seem to grasp the difficulties inherent in his position.

In the four Gospels the integrity of Jesus' moral teaching is intimately linked with the accuracy of his self-identity, not only by the opponents and disciples of Jesus, but also by Jesus himself. It is virtually impossible to picture an enlightened Jesus once a Buddhist perspective is used to evaluate his truth claims. For example, Jesus praised Peter for his belief that Jesus is the Messiah, the Son of the living God. Jesus said God revealed this to the disciple. From a Buddhist perspective, there is no God to reveal anything. If there is no God, then Jesus is not the Son of God, and Peter's confession is false. What does this suggest about the integrity of Jesus as a teacher?

Furthermore, why is it that humans in Jesus' day could not be given the same Buddhist message delivered by Gautama just a few centuries earlier in India? The Dalai Lama rightly recognizes that good teaching modifies itself to the audience to some degree. Was the karma so bad in Palestine to require withholding the Buddha's teachings on reincarnation, the Four Noble Truths, the Eightfold Path, and the nature of enlightenment?

Finally, claims that Jesus is really a Buddha in disguise is no compliment to Jesus or to Buddha. How would Buddhists feel if Christians claimed that Gautama was really a Christian figure ahead of his time?

Still, it is no small matter that the most famous Buddhist on earth has a high regard for Jesus Christ. When he was asked to compare himself with Jesus in an interview with *The New York Times* in 1993, the Dalai Lama refused to do so. However limited his grasp of the identity of Jesus, his recognition of the greatness of Jesus provides a hope for further engagement with what it really means that Jesus is a great master and a fully enlightened being. "Perhaps," one might suggest on another occasion, "Jesus is so enlightened that he is truly the light of the world."

NECHUNG ORACLE

The Nechung Oracle refers to the spirit who provides guidance and protection to His Holiness the Dalai Lama and Tibet. The Oracle is believed by Tibetan Buddhists to indwell a select individual who is used as a spirit medium. The current holder is Venerable Thupten Ngodup, who was born in Tibet on July 13, 1958.

Ngodup moved to Dharamsala in 1969, three years after he and his family escaped to Bhutan. He did his spiritual training at the Gadong and Nechung monasteries. He was chosen as the medium in 1987, three years after the death of the previous medium, Lobsang Jigme.

Ngodup goes into a trance during the ritual. He describes it this way: "Normally, when I am seated on the throne with my costumes on, I do my meditations while reciting the mantras of Hayagriva. Slowly, I get possessed through a deeper state of absorption, and then gradually feel distant from my own identity and surroundings. It is like having a dream and not remembering it the next morning. The same is the case with me before and after I come out of trance."

The trance takes place during the first month of the Tibetan calendar. Ngodup wears an elaborate costume known as the Gye-Che. Tibetans believe that the Oracle was led to protect Tibet under the orders of the famous Buddhist teacher Padmasambhava, who is a second Buddha figure to Tibetans.

COMPETING HEIRS FOR TIBETAN BUDDHIST GROUP

The Kagyu tradition makes up one of the four major schools of Tibetan Buddhism. The spiritual head of the Kagyu is known as the Karmapa. After the death of the sixteenth Karmapa in 1981 there was a controversy about who was the proper claimant to the throne. One group of Buddhists has chosen Urgyen Trinley Dorge (b. 1985) while the other believes that Trinley Thaye Dorje (b. 1983) is the rightful leader. Urgyen Trinley Dorge made world headlines when he escaped from Tibet into India in late 1999. He has been accepted by the Dalai Lama as Karmapa, though the Dalai Lama is not from the Kagyu tradition.

Opposing Heirs to the Kagyu Throne	
Trinley Thaye Dorje (Approved by H. H. Kunzig Shamar Rinpoche) Born 1983	**Urgyen Trinley Dorge** (Approved by Dalai Lama) Born 1985
http://www.karmapa.org	http://www.kagyu.org

Blood and Tears in Tibet

The uprisings in Tibet in 2008 have once again brought world attention to the issue of Communist oppression of Tibetan culture and religion. "It is essential that the world at large be made aware of what has taken place in Tibet." So writes the Dalai Lama in the foreword to Mary Craig's *Tears of Blood: A Cry for Tibet.* Craig's book provides chilling reports of the physical and psychological assault on Tibetans, from the invasion of Mao's armies in 1950 through to 1991.

In one account three monks are thrown into a deep pit. "The public were made to urinate on them while the Chinese urged the monks to fly out of the pit." In another report, "A monk who begged the Chinese not to use the Buddhist scriptures as toilet paper had his arm cut off and was told to ask God to give him another one."

The Tibetan Government in Exile reports that 6,000 monasteries were destroyed by the Chinese armies in the first decade of their rule in Tibet. More than a million deaths have been attributed to Chinese oppression. Tibetans have been subject to mass reeducation programs, and resistance has meant abuse, rape, torture, and imprisonment.

One nun gave this testimony of her beating by Chinese guards: "They told me to take off my clothes. They made me take off everything. They told me to lie with my face down, and started beating me with sticks. I died with shame as so many people were watching. Later the beating was so unbearable that I forgot about my shame."

As of 1998 there were over 1,000 Tibetans in prison for their political, religious, and ethical views. That number has increased with the public crackdown in 2008. The Beijing government has outlawed pictures of the Dalai Lama and forced Tibetan monks to denounce him. Tibetan women are often forced to be sterilized, to use contraception, and if conception occurs, to abort their children. Some reports estimate that almost one-fourth of China's nuclear missile force is now located in Tibet. Chinese immigrants now outnumber Tibetans in their own land. Tibetans have been systematically robbed of their language, culture, and religion.

Buddha Ba Na Mountain, Vietnam

Photo: TD

Gautama image, Penang, Malaysia

Photo: Gordon Melton

The International Commission of Jurists (ICJ), based in Geneva, has documented the case against Beijing since the late 1950s. The ICJ writes in its report *Tibet: Human Rights and the Rule of Law* (1997): "Tibetans are a people under alien subjugation entitled to the right of self-determination. The Tibetan people have not yet exercised this right which requires a free and genuine expression of their will. The ICJ therefore calls for a referendum in Tibet under United Nations supervision to ascertain the wishes of the Tibetan people."

In his interview with *Christianity Today* the Dalai Lama said he deeply appreciates the help of Christians in addressing the Communist oppression of Tibet. "I urge Christian brothers and sisters as spiritual brothers and sisters to study more about the situation in Tibet, especially in regard to religious freedom." He also said it would help if Christians wrote the United States government on Tibetan matters. When asked about donations of money, he said that that many Christians have provided immense help to the Tibetan people, and "We will always be grateful."

Empathy for the Dalai Lama's role in leading the Tibetan Government in Exile does not demand an uncritical endorsement of his every political move, past or present. Melvyn Goldstein, one of the leading scholars of Sino-Tibetan relations, makes this point in *The Snow Lion and the Dragon*. Goldstein writes, "The Dalai Lama knows intellectually that he needs more friends and supporters in Beijing, not Washington or New York City, but he finds it emotionally difficult to take appropriate actions to achieve that end."

Given the brutalization of Tibet since the Communist invasion in 1950, both Christian and Buddhist belief systems are now under threat. Christian presence in Tibet has been minimal through the centuries. This was due largely to Tibet's geographical isolation but also to hostility to a missionary presence, especially when Tibetans became followers of Christ. There have been occasional acts of violence against the small Christian communities.

If the Dalai Lama were able to exercise leadership again in Tibet, would he allow freedom of religion?

"Certainly!" he said. He talked about the Muslim presence in Tibet during the last four centuries and claimed there had been no government discrimination against Christians when the Dalai Lamas ruled Tibet. He said that he values religious witness as long as it is not coercive.

"And if a Christian wants to tell you that you should accept Jesus, it's a free world, they can say it?"

"Oh yes," he said. "Oh yes."

Buddhist Leaders and Organizations

Ajahn Maha Boowa

Ajahn Maha Boowa is one of the most famous teachers in the Theravada Buddhist tradition. Born in Thailand in 1913, Maha Boowa was a student of the Venerable Ajahn Mun (1870–1949). Maha Boowa follows the Forest Monk tradition, also known as Kammatthana. He is the founder of the Help Thai Nation Project and abbot of Wat Pa Bahn Tahd. Maha Boowa teaches at the Forest retreat with Ajahn Pannavaddho, one of the senior Western monks in Thailand.

In a talk in London in 1974, Maha Boowa commented on Buddhism and other religions: "Please understand that Buddhism does not teach people to draw away from each other. Buddhism and Christianity both teach people to be good so that they will be happy and go to heaven. If we compare the city of London to heaven, we could tell people that there are many ways to enter the city. When they have chosen a way and made use of it, all of them will reach London. Whatever religion one has, one should practice it accordingly. They will meet in heaven."

Internet Source

www.luangta.com/english

Aum Shinrikyo

On March 20, 1995, twelve Japanese died as a result of sarin gas poison released during the morning rush hour in Tokyo. The killings were found to be the work of Aum Shinrikyo, one of the most notorious religious groups of modern time. Aum Shinrikyo founder Asahara Shoko was formerly known as Matsumoto Chizuo. He was born in 1955 in Kyushu, a southern island of Japan, and claimed to have received enlightenment while alone in the Himalayas in 1986.

The violence in the Aum Shinrikyo movement can be traced back to 1989 when the group was targeted in the media and the political movement suffered total loss in elections. Aum became the object of public ridicule. In November a prominent opponent of the group, lawyer Sakamoto Tsutsumi, disappeared along with his infant son and wife. Their bodies were discovered almost six years later. Sakamoto had disproven Aum Shinrikyo founder Asahara's claim that his blood contained unique DNA.

Two hundred members of the Aum Shinrikyo group were arrested after the March 20, 1995 poisoning, including Asahara. Some of the accused received death sentences while others were given long jail terms. Asahara was sentenced to death in February 2004. The judge's verdict read in part: "This was an evil and serious series of crimes brought about by the extremely malevolent and fantastic lies of Chizuo Matsumoto, who fed the illusion that his existence was absolute and on par with that of a god and who planned to build the group's forces and rule Japan under the guise of being a savior."

Laughing Buddha

Photo: Derek Beverley

Aum Shinrikyo combined yoga, Tibetan ritual, and apocalypticism. Asahara was obsessed with Nostradamus and the Book of Revelation. At one time he received the endorsement of His Holiness the Dalai Lama, but this was withdrawn after the group began to engage in criminal activity.

Asahara was adored by his followers both before and after the 1995 poisonings. In 2000 one pro-Asahara website stated: "With divine powers developed through the practice of meditation and with enlightened wisdom, Master Asahara shows his genius not only in the spiritual domain, but in various fields such as science, medicine, music, writing, translation, education, etc. In this age of crisis, his unique leadership with altruism and devotion has a great significance to world peace and the survival of human beings." Since 2000, however, his popularity diminished radically among members with increasing evidence of his involvement in the planning of the gas attacks.

Former members of the Aum group started Aleph in 2000, a new movement built on the nonviolent aspects of Asahara's teachings. Aleph has apologized for the criminal actions of Aum and its founder. The new group has also provided financial remuneration for victims. In spite of this attempt at a fresh start, Aleph members are stigmatized because of their connection with Aum. Since the 1995 poisoning, various government leaders, police officials, and newspapers in Japan have called for specific laws against religions that are "cultic."

AUM SHINRIKYO	
Typology	Buddhist Sectarian
Founder	Asahara Shoko
Special Note	Aum's founder and top leaders were involved in the 1995 gas poisoning in the Tokyo subway system. The group later dissolved and some former members founded Aleph.
Recommended Reading	Robert Jay Lifton, *Destroying the World to Save It* (New York: Metropolitan, 1999). Ian Reader, *Religious Violence in Contemporary Japan* (University of Hawaii Press, 2000)
Website	http://english.aleph.to

Bhikkhu Bodhi

Bhikkhu Bodhi is a native of New York. Born in 1944, he earned a Ph.D. from Claremont in 1972. He left his Jewish heritage after developing a deep interest in Buddhism. He was ordained by Venerable Balangoda Ananda Maitreya Mahanayaka in Sri Lanka. He is known most for his work with the Buddhist Publication Society of Sri Lanka. His publications include *The Connected Discourses of the Buddha*. His essays can be read at www.accesstoinsight.org.

Chen Tao

Hon-Ming Chen, leader of Chen Tao ("True Way," aka God's Salvation Church), was born and educated in Taiwan. In the early 1990s he became a member of a Taiwanese religious group known as the Association for Research on Soul Light, rising to become the leader of the group a few years later. Based on alleged divine guidance, Chen moved to the United States, locating first in California and then in Garland, Texas.

In 1997, a vision led him and his followers to search for a Christ-figure in Vancouver, Canada, a mission that did not succeed. The group achieved international fame with Chen's prediction that God would appear on television on March 25, 1998, and in person to everybody in the world on March 31. Reporters followed the group closely in the days leading up to the two failed prophecies. Chen subsequently lost most of his followers although about thirty members moved with him later in 1998 from Texas to Lockport, New York.

In the year 2000 Chen wrote the American people, President Clinton, and pharmaceutical companies to inform them of the possibility of major cures for cancer and AIDS. He claimed that God wanted Central Park to become the "medical base of God's super high-tech salvation." Chen claims to be the reincarnation of Joseph, father of Jesus Christ.

Chen is the author of *God's Descending in Clouds (Flying Saucers) on Earth to Save People* and *The Practical Evidence and Study of the World of God and Buddha.*

Chin Kung

Born Hsu Yae-hong in China in 1927, Chin Kung is an influential teacher of Pure Land Buddhism. In 1949 he moved to Taiwan and began study of Buddhism. He was ordained as a monk in 1959 and since that time has established over fifty Pure Land Centers throughout the world. In 1977 he began to travel and teach outside of Taiwan, immigrating to the United States in 1985. Chin Kung later moved to Singapore and then Australia, and he has played a major role in inter-faith dialogue.

Internet Source

www.amtb.org.tw/e-bud/e-bud.htm

Buddha images in stone near Shanghai

Photo: TD

D. T. Suzuki

Daisetz Teitaro Suzuki is one of the most famous Buddhist scholars of the last two centuries. He was born in Japan in 1870 and studied Zen in his student days at Tokyo University. Suzuki moved to America in 1897 and worked with Paul Carus at Open Court Publishing. In 1909 he moved back to Japan and over the next four decades he taught in Japan, starting the Eastern Buddhist Society in 1921 and becoming a professor at Otani University in Kyoto. He wrote extensively on Zen and Japanese religion and was also a frequent visiting professor at Columbia University. Suzuki died in 1966.

According to Suzuki, "The basic idea of Zen is to come in touch with the inner workings of our being, and to do so in the most direct way possible, without resorting to anything external or superadded. Therefore, anything that has the semblance of an external authority is rejected by Zen. Absolute faith is placed in a man's own inner being. For whatever authority there is in Zen, all comes from within."

Frederick P. Lenz III

One of the more controversial gurus of the twentieth century, Frederick P. Lenz III was known as "Zen Master Rama" and author of the best sellers *Surfing the Himalayas* and *Snowboarding to Nirvana*. Lenz committed suicide in April 1998 at his Long Island mansion. He was born in San Diego in 1950 and grew up in Connecticut. Lenz married in May 1971 but was divorced within a year. Lenz obtained a Ph.D. in English literature from Stony Brook and was once a follower of Sri Chimnoy, the Hindu guru based in Queens. After a falling out with Chimnoy in 1981 Lenz began his own group in California, turning quickly to Zen as his professed tradition. He demanded both intense emotional and financial commitment from his followers, and he was accused of sexual abuse by former members.

After his death a legal battle for his estate ensued between the Audubon Society (one of Lenz's favorite charities) and a foundation started by Lenz associate Norman Marcus. Most of the estate went to Marcus, who helped found the Frederick P. Lenz Foundation for American Buddhism. Lenz's father, a former mayor of Stamford, Connecticut, sits on the board. Followers of Lenz continue to maintain a web presence in honor of their guru. One member recalls a moment of enlightenment in his presence:

"As the meditation began, I could feel myself filling up with light. How can you feel light? I don't know, but felt it I did. It actually started down by my legs and rose up my body, just like filling a container with fluid. As the light continued to climb in my chest, I felt myself dissolving. By the time it had risen to my head, there weren't many thoughts of 'me' left. Shortly before the light reached the top of my head, 'I' was gone, like so many meditations before."

Lenz claimed to know the importance of sincerity and humility. "As inspirational writers, we have to practice what we preach. And if we can't laugh at ourselves, each other and the world around us, I think we have missed not only our own message but the essence of the teachings of our own teachers—which is to lose self-importance and to care more for the welfare of others and the magical world around us, than we do for ourselves and our own self-images."

Internet Sources

Pro-Lenz websites:

www.himalaya.com

www.fredericklenz.com

www.ramalila.com

Critic sites:

www.ex-cult.org

www.trancenet.org

Lama Michel

Lama Michel is the Buddhist title for Michel Lenz Cesar Calmanowitz, a young boy from São Paulo, Brazil, said to be the reincarnation of a high Tibetan master. The boy's family follow Tibetan Lama Gangchen (b. 1941) who started a Dharma center ("Shi De Choe Tsog") in São Paulo in 1988. Gangchen went to Brazil after developing a friendship with Monica Benvenuti, who met the Lama when he lived in Italy. Benvenuti introduced the Lama to Isabel Villares Lenz Cesar, the mother of Michel (b. July 1981) and a younger sister Fernanda. Gangchen first met Michel in 1987, and his status as a Western *tulku* was approved by several Tibetan masters. In 1994 Michel moved to a Tibetan monastic community in southern India. Gangchen claims that the young man is the reincarnation of a fifteenth-century High Lama named Drubtchok Gualwa Samdrup.

Frank Usarski of the Pontifical Catholic University of São Paulo, Brazil, has done extensive study on Lama Michel.

Internet Source

Gangchen Peace website: www.lgpt.net

Lama Ole Nydahl

Ole Nydahl is a Western teacher in the Karmapa tradition of Tibetan Buddhism. Ole and his wife Hannah committed to Buddhism while on their honeymoon in Nepal in 1968. They had met Rangjung Rigpe Dorje (1924–81), the sixteenth Gyalwa Karmapa, a leading Tibetan master, and spent three years studying with him in the Himalayas. Lama Ole is based in Copenhagen and heads about 400 Diamond Way Buddhist centers worldwide. He is the West's ambassador for Trinley Thaye Dorje, one of the two Tibetan claimants to the title of the seventeenth Karmapa.

Internet Sources

www.lama-ole-nydahl.org

www.karmapa.org

www.diamondway-buddhism.org

Pema Chödrön

Pema Chödrön is one of the most well-known female Tibetan masters. A native of New York City, she was born Diedre Blomfield-Brown in 1936. She became a nun in 1974, ordained by His Holiness the Sixteenth Karmapa in London. She studied with Chögyam Trungpa Rinpoche from 1974 until his death in 1987. In 1984 Chödrön became the Director of Gampo Abbey in Cape Breton, Nova Scotia. She has written several books, including *The Wisdom of No Escape.*

Internet Source

www.gampoabbey.org

KARMAPA LINEAGE IN TIBETAN BUDDHISM

Karmapa Leader	Dates
Dusum Chenpa (Khyenpa)	1110–93
Karma Pakshi	1204–83
Rangjung Dorje	1284–1339
Rolpe Dorje	1340–83
Deshin (Dezhin) Shegpa	1384–1415
Tongwa (Thongwa) Donden	1416–53
Chodrag Gyamtso (Gyatsho)	1454–1506
Mikyo Dorje	1507–54
Wangchug (Wangchuk) Dorje	1556–1603
Choying Dorje	1604–74
Yeshe Dorje	1676–1702
Changchub Dorje	1703–32
Dudul Dorje	1733–97
Thegchog Dorje	1798–1868
Khakhyab Dorje	1871–1922
Rangjung Rigpe Dorje	1924–81
Trinley Thaye Dorje . . . or Urgyen Trinley Dorge	1983– 1985–

Philip Kapleau

Philip Kapleau is one of the most influential Western teachers of Zen Buddhism. Born in 1912, Kapleau authored *The Three Pillars of Zen*, an excellent guide to Zen Buddhism. He was raised in New Haven, Connecticut, and became a court reporter; then he was eventually chosen to work at the Nuremberg Trials and the War Crimes Trials in Tokyo, Japan. While in Japan he met D. T. Suzuki. Kapleau returned to the United States in 1950 and studied with Suzuki at Columbia University. In 1953 he returned to Japan and spent thirteen years in Zen training. He was ordained by Hakuun Yasutani-roshi in 1965. That same year *The Three Pillars of Zen* was published, and he founded the Rochester Zen Center. Kapleau died in May 2004.

Internet Source

www.rzc.org

SCANDAL AT THE SAN FRANCISCO ZEN CENTER AND RICHARD BAKER

"One of the things that had set Zen Center apart from earlier Japanese and Japanese-American temples—and Baker himself had strongly urged this innovation—was its encouragement of women to study and progress on equal terms with men. But the opportunity cut both ways. Even before Baker became abbot in 1971, the deference of female students to his priestly authority gave him easy sexual pickings in the northern California world of Zen. Thereafter, as some women confided to Downing, they had been tapped for bed service in much the same spirit as they might have been called upon to act as one of Baker's personal secretaries or, for that matter, to scrub pots or weed a garden. And understandably, their *zazen* practice had become hollow or simply impossible once they were made the concubines of their allegedly enlightened master."

—Source: From Frederick C. Crews, "Zen and the Art of Success," *New York Review of Books* (March 28, 2002). Review of Michael Downing, *Shoes Outside the Door* (Berkeley: Counterpoint, 2001)

Shambhala

Shambhala is the Buddhist tradition connected with Chögyam Trungpa Rinpoche (1939–87), one of the most important Tibetan Buddhist masters of modern times. He was considered a *tulku*—a reincarnated master—of the Kagyu lineage, one of the major schools in Tibetan religion. Trungpa was also trained in the Nyingma tradition. He fled Tibet in 1959 and taught for four years in Dalhousie, India, and then at Oxford University from 1963 through 1966. The next year he founded a Tibetan center in Scotland. In 1969, having abandoned his monastic vows, he married Diana Pybus and immigrated to America.

Once in America, Trungpa founded the Tail of the Tiger (now known as Karme-Choling) meditation center in Vermont. During the 1970s he traveled widely and began his unique program of Shambhala Training. He also started Naropa University and founded the Gampo Buddhist monastery in Cape Breton, Nova Scotia, Canada. He died in April 1987.

Sakyong Mipham Rinpoche (b. 1962), Trungpa's eldest son, now leads Shambhala. He was born Ösel Rangdröl Mukpo but was later viewed as Sakyong (earth protector and dharma-king) and as the reincarnation of Mipham the Great (1846–1912), a revered Tibetan lama.

The Shambhala movement has faced serious criticism regarding the immoral behavior of Rinpoche and also of Osel Tendzin. Tendzin (Thomas F. Rich) was appointed as Trungpa's Vajra Regent or Dharma heir in 1976. He created an enormous scandal in 1988 when it was revealed that he contracted AIDS in 1985 and did not inform his sexual partners about it. John Dart reported on the crisis created by Tendzin in *The Los Angeles Times* on March 3, 1989. Tendzin remained in leadership in the movement until his death in 1990.

Royal Palace in Ulanbaatar, Mongolia

Photo: Massimo Introvigne

Rinpoche was known for his wild excesses, particularly involving liquor and sex. Pema Chödrön (born Diedre Blomfield-Brown), one of his most famous disciples, admitted in an interview with *Tricycle* magazine that Rinpoche "did not keep ethical norms," and yet she claims that her "devotion to him is unshakable." Chödrön, who heads the Gampo Abbey, responded about his sexual indiscretions in this way: "I don't know what he was doing. I know he changed my life. I know I love him. But I don't know who he was. And maybe he wasn't doing things to help everyone, but he sure helped me. I learned something from him. But who was that masked man?" She also stated: "I can actually hold my devotion purely and fully in my heart and still say, maybe he was a madman."

Stupa

Photo: Jim Beverley

Sakyong Mipham Rinpoche became engaged to Semo Tseyang Palmo, the daughter of a famous Tibetan teacher, in May 2005. The Shambhala leader also took part in the Boston marathon the previous month. He is author of *Turning the Mind into an Ally,* which was released in 2004. Like his father, the Sakyong places emphasis on the Buddhist teaching of no-self. "To know the truth is to see the transitory nature of who we are—the selflessness of ourselves and others. It's to see the suffering that comes from imagining we are solid and permanent entities."

SHAMBHALA

Typology	Tibetan Buddhist
Founder	Chögyam Trungpa Rinpoche (1939–87)
Leader	Sakyong Mipham Rinpoche (1962–)
Homepages	www.shambhala.org www.mipham.com

Stephen Batchelor

Born in Scotland in 1953, Stephen Batchelor is now known most famously for his defense of an agnostic version of Buddhism. He traveled to India in 1972 and studied with Tibetan masters in Dharamsala, then moved to Switzerland in 1975 and received ordination in 1978. Batchelor studied Zen in Korea from 1981 through 1984, then in 1985 gave up his monastic vows and married Martine Fages. He and his wife then settled in England for fifteen years; in August 2000 they relocated to France.

Batchelor has argued that it is not necessary to believe in karma and reincarnation in order to be faithful to Buddhism. He expressed this in his 1998 work *Buddhism Without Beliefs*. He claims that there is symmetry between humanistic, agnostic Western culture and Buddhism. In arguing this he points to a famous statement by the Buddha from the Pali Canon.

"Suppose, Malyunkyaputta, a man were wounded by an arrow thickly smeared with poison, and his friends and companions brought a surgeon to treat him. The man would say, 'I will not let the surgeon pull out the arrow until I know the name and the clan of the man who wounded me, whether the bow that wounded me was a longbow or a crossbow, whether the arrow that wounded me was hoof-tipped or curved or barbed.' And all this would still not be known to that man and meanwhile he would die. So too, Malyunkyaputta, if anyone should say, 'I will not lead the noble life under the Buddha until the Buddha declares to me whether the world is eternal or not eternal, finite or infinite, whether the soul is the same as or different from the body, whether or not an awakened one continues or ceases to exist after death.' That would still remain undeclared by the Buddha and meanwhile that person would die."

Prayer wheels, rural France

Photo: Gordon Melton

In an essay on "Deep Agnosticism" Batchelor writes: "This kind of agnosticism is not based on disinterest. It's not based on saying, 'I just don't really care about the great matter of birth and death.' It's recognizing that, *I do not know* in a very passionate way, in a passionate sense, where, perhaps we find our deepest integrity as human beings. So it's not just something that one would periodically reflect upon, but really something that one brings to heart, that I do not really know where I did come from. I do not really know where I am going. I do not really know what will happen after death. The only honest stance I can take toward the doctrine of rebirth is to say I just do not know."

Internet Source

www.stephenbatchelor.org

Nichiren Shoshu temple, Washington, DC

Photo: Gordon Melton

Thich Nhat Hanh

Next to the Dalai Lama, Thich Nhat Hanh is probably the most famous living Buddhist teacher. He was born in Vietnam in 1926, but now lives in exile in France. He became a Buddhist monk when he was 16 and was forced to leave Vietnam in 1966. He practices "Engaged Buddhism," which combines core Buddhist values with a search for justice and peace. Hanh runs a retreat center known as Plum Village and is a founder of the Unified Buddhist Church.

Hanh said, "I would like to publish the book with the title: *Buddha and Jesus as Brothers*. In fact, they could have taken each other's hands and practiced walking meditation, so why not the two of you, one as a Buddhist and one as a Christian? You are the continuation of the Buddha, and you are the continuation of Jesus Christ. That is only beautiful, if you can share your wisdom, your insights, and you can learn from each other and enrich yourselves. That is what I envision for the future, that we remove the barriers between different spiritual traditions."

According to Hanh, "The Zen master Ling Chi said that the miracle is not to walk on burning charcoal or in the thin air or on the water; the miracle is just to walk on earth. You breathe in. You become aware of the fact that you are alive. You are still alive and you are walking on this beautiful planet. That is already performing a miracle. The greatest of all miracles is to be alive. We have to awaken ourselves to the truth that we are here, alive. We are here making steps on this beautiful planet. This is already performing a miracle."

Internet Source

www.plumvillage.org

"WHAT IS THIS?" A KOREAN ZEN KOAN

In Korean Zen students learn from a famous Zen master named Huineng (A.D. 638–713) who taught his disciples to reach enlightenment through asking: "What is this?"

Martine Batchelor has this to say of the question. "The practice is very simple. Whether you are walking, standing, sitting, or lying down, you ask repeatedly, *What is this? What is this?* You have to be careful not to slip into intellectual inquiry, for you are not looking for an intellectual answer. . . . We are not speculating with our mind. We are trying to become one with the question. The most important part of the question is not the meaning of the words themselves but the question mark. We are asking unconditionally, *What is this?* without looking for an answer, without expecting an answer. We are questioning for questioning's own sake. . . . As we throw out the question *What is this?* we are opening ourselves to the moment. There is no place we can rest. We are letting go of our need for knowledge and security, and our body and mind themselves become a question."

—Source: *Tricycle,* Fall 2008

Thich Nhat Hanh's Plum Village, France

Photo: Jim Beverley

■ Responding to Buddhism

The Dalai Lama has said that he has "no doubt" at all about the main principles of Buddhism but that he has become very skeptical about aspects of Buddhist astrology and cosmology. He noted that he often urges his Tibetan followers to avoid superstition.

The Dalai Lama states in his book *The Opening of the Wisdom-Eye* that Tibetan Buddhist teachings and rituals "were taught by Lord Buddha in person." This claim has two serious weaknesses.

First, there are the crucial differences in belief and ritual between the late Buddhism of Tibet and the earlier Buddhisms of India and Sri Lanka, in addition to the forms of Buddhism provided in China and Japan. For example, Tibetan Buddhist *tantric* ritual, including visualization of wrathful deities in explicit sexual poses, lacks harmony with earlier forms of Buddhist meditation.

Beyond differences between various Buddhisms, there is the more serious historical integrity of the earliest documents about Buddha. These texts, in Pali and Sanskrit, were written between four and five centuries after the death of Gautama. In *A Short History of Buddhism*, Edward Conze, the devout Buddhist scholar, dismisses any "confident assertions" about what the Buddha really said as "mere guesswork." Conze wrote in the introduction to *Buddhist Scriptures*: "Buddhists possess nothing that corresponds to the New Testament."

Many elements of Buddhist belief and practice defy rational belief, quite apart from historical issues. In spite of repeated Buddhist claims to rationality and skepticism, aspects of Buddhism should give pause at the intellectual level. The Tibetan emphasis on consultation with spirit mediums is a case in point. The Dalai Lama himself regularly consults with the Nechung Oracle, said to be a spirit deity who takes over the body of a chosen Tibetan Buddhist. It is hard to given credence to this practice, given the poor divination granted to the Dalai Lama in the torturous years of his interaction with Chairman Mao. Further, the fear that grips many Buddhists about the spirit world reflects a superstitious core to elements of Buddhism. Many rituals, likewise, reflect a magical view of reality, as if the number of prostrations and turns of a prayer wheel is all it takes to impact the ever-pervasive karmic forces.

The notions of karma and reincarnation have an explanatory function in dealing with life's events, but they, too, come at a price. The Dalai Lama writes in one of his books that a person killed by a lightning bolt has earned that fate by some misdeed in a previous life. That example, though grim, does not address the deeper implications of the Buddhist view. What of the many Buddhist nuns raped by Communist soldiers during the purge of Tibet? Was this their karmic debt? The doctrine of karma also has serious implications for Christian belief about the death of Jesus. Did Jesus deserve to die? Was this his karmic death for his sin in previous lives? How could trust in the atoning work of Christ be compatible with any Buddhist view that suggested that Christ's death was his necessary karma for his failings in previous lives? It seems impossible to reconcile Christ with karma.

These are questions that Western students of Buddhism may want to ponder as Eastern views of karma and reincarnation gain popularity.

While the Dalai Lama's assertion that Jesus was an enlightened being is consistent with Buddhist philosophy, this belief strains rationality. First, the Dalai Lama has no warrant to ignore the gospel's claims about the identity of Jesus while elevating the ethic of Jesus. Second, the level of duplicity in the teaching of Jesus becomes staggering as soon as one starts to work through the Gospels to dismiss all the non-Buddhist elements. Third, it is hard to imagine any reason why humans in the time of Jesus could not be given the same Buddhist message delivered by Gautama just a few centuries earlier in India. Lastly, claims that Jesus is really a Buddha in disguise is no compliment to Jesus or Buddha. How would Buddhists feel if Christians claimed that Gautama was really a Christ in disguise, and that for reasons known only to God, he was not able to give the full truth of the gospel before the birth of Jesus?

Buddha reaches Enlightenment

Photo: Jim Beverley

■ Buddhism Glossary

Agamas: a collection of beliefs/practices or laws

Alaya: the term for consciousness in any and all sentient beings

Amitabha (Amida, Amita, Amitayus): the most popular name for Buddha in the Mahayana schools; can also refer to the true and enlightened Mind

Arhat: Buddhist saint who is liberated from the cycle of death and birth

Asura: major demons

Attachment: the craving of self that is the fundamental cause of suffering

Avalokitesvara: name for the Bodhisattva of compassion (known as Guan Yin/Kuan Yin in China and Kannon in Japan)

Avatamsaka (Flower Ornament) Sutra: one of the most famous teachings in the Buddhist Canon, said to be given immediately after Shakyamuni attained enlightenment

Bardo: the intermediate state between death and reincarnation

Bhiksu: male Buddhist monk

Bhiksuni: female Buddhist monk

Bhaisajyaguru: the Buddha of health

Bodhi: Sanskrit for enlightenment

Bodhisattva: enlightened being who aspires to save others

Brahma Net Sutra (aka Brahmajala Sutra): major document in Mahayana Buddhism

Buddha Nature: term in Mahayana Buddhism for the true nature that is possible for all beings to attain

Caitya: location where Buddha relics are stored

Ch'an-Ting: Chinese term for meditation

Citta: Asian term for mind and heart

Dana: being generous and charitable

Delusion (Ignorance): the error of believing that appearances are reality

Devakanya: the goddess of the sun and moon

Devas: gods

Dharini: a lengthy mantra used in esoteric Buddhism

Dharma: term for the teachings of the Buddhas, and for Buddhist law and duty

Dharmakara: the Bodhisattva, famous for his forty-eight vows, who later became Amitabha Buddha

Dhyana: a term for concentration or meditation

Heresy: sixty-two different views were held to be incompatible with the teaching of the Buddha

Hinayana: "the lesser vehicle," a derogatory designation for Theravadan Buddhism by Mahayanists

Icchantika: a very depraved and immoral person

Kalpa: period of time or age

Karma: used both as a reference to individual will and volition and also to the result of one's choices in life or previous lives

Kasaya: the robe of a monk

Ksanti: term for patience (one of six Paramitas)

Laksana: term for any of the thirty-two signs to distinguish a Buddha

Lotus Grades: refers to the nine degrees of rebirth possible in the Pure Land

Maha-Bodhisattva (aka Mahasattva): advanced Bodhisattva

Mahakaruna: wonderful compassion

Maitreya: the next Buddha who will come to our world

Mantra: sacred word, syllable or verse that aids in enlightenment when repeated

Middle Vehicle (aka Madhyarnika): one of the main schools in Mahayana Buddhism

Nirvana: popular Buddhist term for the ultimate state of enlightenment

Ocean-Wide Lotus Assembly: the assembly of Amitabha, Bodhisattvas, and all the saints in the land of ultimate Bliss

Paramitas: the six moral practices that lead to Nirvana

Parinirvana: the final Nirvana of the Buddha

Pratyeka Buddha: term for any Buddha who does not teach others the path to enlightenment nor has any wish to do so

Priyavacana: caring and loving speech that leads others to the truth

Samadhi: focus of the mind in peace

Samantabhadra: a leading Bodhisattva famous for moral practice

Samatha: calmness, peace of mind

Samsara: cycle of birth and death

Sangha: Buddhist community

Sariputra: leading disciple of Buddha

Sastra: term for commentary in scriptures

Sila: moral principles

Skandhas: parts of the human that are always in flux like feelings and impulses

Tao: Way/path (aka Marga in Sanskrit)

Theravada: means the school of the elders; the tradition in Buddhism that places emphasis on the Pali Canon and the notion that enlightenment is basically for the few who can follow its difficult path

Three bodies of the Buddha (Skt. trikaya): 1. Dharmakaya: the transcendental and inconceivable realities; 2. Sambhogakaya: the celestial body that dwells in the Pure Land; 3. Nirmanakaya: the visible body of the Buddha when incarnation takes place to help others achieve enlightenment

Tripitaka: term that means three baskets and refers to the three divisions of the earliest Buddhist Canon: sutras, rules of Discipline (Vinaya), and commentaries (sastras)

Upasaka/Upasika: lay disciple (man/woman)

Upaya: Skillful means

Vairocana: key Buddha in the Avatamsaka Sutra

Vipaka: the fruit of one's karma

Vipasyana: wisdom, accurate perception

Yana: path of spirituality

BUDDHISM	
Web sites	BuddhaNet www.buddhanet.net DharmaNet www.dharmanet.org Buddhist Studies Virtual Library www.ciolek.com/WWWVL-Buddhism.html Government of Tibet in Exile (Dalai Lama) www.tibet.com
Recommended Reading	Rick Fields, *How the Swans Came to the Lake* (Boston: Shambhala, 1992) Donald S. Lopez, Jr., *The Story of Buddhism* (San Francisco: HarperSanFrancisco, 2001) J.Isamu Yamamoto, *Beyond Buddhism* (Downers Grove: InterVarsity, 1982)
Special Note	Harold Netland and Keith Yandell, two leading Christian philosophers of religion, provide one of the best critiques of Buddhism in a forthcoming volume by Paternoster in London and InterVarsity in the USA. The Paternoster title will be *Spirituality Without God? Buddhist Enlightenment and Christian Salvation.*

4

CHRISTIAN SCIENCE

Mother Church, Boston, Massachusetts

Photo: Mark Shane

Christian Science is the popular designation for the Church of Christ, Scientist, the controversial movement founded by Mary Baker Eddy in Lynn, Massachusetts, in 1879. Eddy was born in Bow, New Hampshire, on July 16, 1821, and published *Science and Health with Key to the Scriptures,* the central defining text of the religion, in 1875.

She claims that the turning point of her spiritual life came in February 1866 after life-threatening injuries from a fall on the sidewalk were reversed when she discovered the healing methods of Jesus. Critics not only dispute her account of the healing but also the underlying ideology of her view of sickness and health.

Eddy began publicly teaching her method of healing in 1870, founded her church in 1879, and chartered the Massachusetts Metaphysical College in 1881. The Christian Science movement grew rapidly in the final two decades of the century in spite of widespread criticism in the media and from religious leaders like A. J. Gordon. The Mother Church in Boston was dedicated in January of 1895 and the movement published the first issue of *The Christian Science Monitor* in 1908.

Mary Baker Eddy, 1903

Photo: Courtesy Mary Baker Eddy Library, Boston, Massachusetts

MARY BAKER EDDY: A CHRONOLOGY

July 16, 1821—Mary Morse Baker is born in Bow, New Hampshire, the youngest of six children

1829—First claim of hearing an unseen voice

1838—Joins the Congregational Church (Sanbornton Bridge, New Hampshire)

December 10, 1843—Marries George Washington Glover

June 27, 1844—Glover dies

September 12, 1844—A son, George Washington Glover II, is born

1849—Mary's mother dies

May 1851—Son George goes to live with the Cheney family

June 21, 1853—Marries Daniel Patterson (a dentist)

April 1856—Son George moves to Minnesota (Does not see mother again until 1879)

1862—Mary seeks healing from Phineas Parkhurst Quimby

June 1864—Mary moves to Lynn, Massachusetts

1865—Mary's father dies

January 16, 1866—Phineas Quimby dies

February 1, 1866—Mary falls on icy sidewalk in Lynn, Massachusetts

February 4, 1866—She claims divine healing

August 1870—Mary begins teaching Christian Science

1873—Mary is divorced from Patterson (who deserted her in 1866)

October 1875—Publishes first edition of *Science and Health*

July 1876—Organizes Christian Scientist Association

January 1877—Marries Asa Gilbert Eddy (her former student)

April 1879—Forms Church of Christ, Scientist

January 1881—Charters Massachusetts Metaphysical College

November 1881—Mrs. Eddy ordained pastor

June 1882—Asa Gilbert Eddy dies (Mrs. Eddy blames animal magnetism for his death)

Fall 1882—Calvin Frye becomes Eddy's secretary

April 1883—Publishes first issue of *The Christian Science Journal*

1885—Eddy defends herself at Boston's Tremont Temple

1887—Opening of First Church in New York under Augusta Stetson

1888—Eddy adopts Ebenezer J. Foster

June 1889—Moves to Concord, New Hampshire

1889—Founding of Unity by Myrtle Fillmore (ex-Scientist)

1890—Founding of *New Thought Journal*

1890—Josephine Woodbury, famous Christian Science teacher, has illegitimate child

1891—Fiftieth edition of *Science and Health* published

1891—Publishes *Retrospection and Introspection* (autobiographical work)

September 1892—Reorganizes her church

1893—Eddy's controversial *Christ and Christmas* published

1894—Ordains the Bible and *Science and Health* pastor of church

1894—Mother Church building finished

1895—Publication of *Church Manual*

1896—Josephine Woodbury excommunicated

1897—Eddy severs ties with adopted son

1897—Publishes *Miscellaneous Writings*

1898—Establishes Committee on Publication

1899—Woodbury attacks Eddy in *Arena* magazine; sues over Eddy's June Communion message

1903—Eddy takes morphine to relieve pain

1906—Extension finished on Mother Church

1907—*McClure's* magazine begins critical series; Mark Twain publishes *Christian Science*

1907—Eddy wins "Next Friends" suit about her mental fitness

November 1908—*The Christian Science Monitor* published

1909—Former pastor and leader Augusta Stetson forced to resign for insubordination and false teaching

1909—Publication of Willa Cather and Georgine Milmine's *Life of Mary Baker Eddy and the History of Christian Science*

December 3, 1910—Mary Baker Eddy dies at home

Mrs. Eddy died on December 3, 1910, at age 89, in her home in Chestnut Hill. During her life, in her dying days, and since her death, she has been the subject of much debate. Her followers often write about her with complete adulation while her critics question her ethics, theology, medical theories, and even her sanity. Controversy has also surrounded the movement she founded from its beginning.

Christian Science represents Mrs. Eddy's metaphysical understanding of Christian faith. Though the movement uses the standard terms of Christian orthodoxy, they are invested with the ideology of the Mind Science tradition popular in America in the 1800s, most notably through the work of Phineas Parkhurst Quimby (1802–66), a pioneer in the field of mesmerism in the United States. Eddy turned to Quimby in 1862 for medical assistance but later minimized his influence on her theories of divine healing.

The Christian Science movement has faced crisis in the last few decades. Several ex-members have launched massive campaigns against Christian Science for its neglect of the health needs of children. Doug and Rita Swan, for example, blamed church ideology and practice for the death of their son Matthew from spinal meningitis. They formed an organization named C.H.I.L.D. (Children's Healthcare Is a Legal Duty) to monitor Christian Science and other groups accused of putting children at risk.

Caroline Fraser, a prominent ex-member, created considerable controversy when she chronicled the death of Christian Science children in an article in *The Atlantic Monthly* in 1995. Fraser's later work *God's Perfect Child*, published in 1999, created further turmoil for Christian Science. Her work highlighted the case of Robyn Twitchell, a two-year-old who died in 1986 of a medically treatable bowel obstruction. Robyn's parents,

David and Ginger Twitchell, claimed that their reliance on prayer alone was allowed under a religious exemption clause added to the state of Massachusetts' law on child neglect in 1971. The Twitchells were convicted in 1990 of involuntary manslaughter.

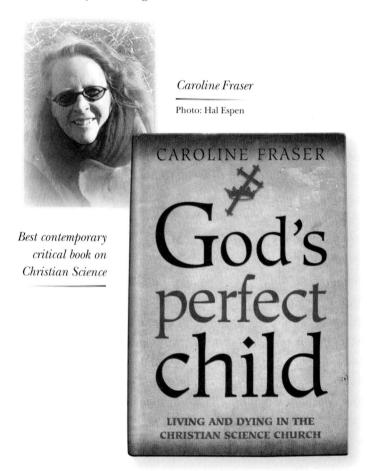

Caroline Fraser

Photo: Hal Espen

Best contemporary critical book on Christian Science

CAROLINE FRASER

God's perfect child

LIVING AND DYING IN THE
CHRISTIAN SCIENCE CHURCH

Critics of Christian Science have also accused church leaders of hypocrisy for their decision to publish a book entitled *The Destiny of the Mother Church* by Bliss Knapp. Knapp was born in 1877 to prominent Christian Scientists Ira and Flavia Knapp. He published his book privately in 1947 but the Christian Science Publishing Society rejected it, considering it faulty for its apocalyptic flavor and its undue exaltation of Mrs. Eddy.

Before Knapp's death in 1958 he made a provision in his will to leave his inheritance to the church on the condition that the church would publish his book by 1993. His inheritance stood at over $90 million by that date. The church published the book but denied any wrongdoing, precipitating a worldwide outcry from many members. Senior editors of church publications resigned in protest of the leadership's decision.

The Bliss Knapp case surfaced at a time when the church was undergoing severe internal strain over declining membership, loss of revenue at the *Christian Science Monitor* and financial losses in a failed media venture. Those at the top of the Mother Church have been accused of hiding the truth about finances and being closed to legitimate criticism and dissent. Stephen Gottschalk, the leading scholar within Christian Science, went public on these matters after church officials ignored his opinion and attempted to pressure him into silence.

In recent years Christian Science has sought to appeal to those attracted to the New Age movement and to modern notions of spirituality. Virginia Harris, the current head of the Mother Church, has campaigned aggressively to present a fresh image of the movement. She has appeared on *Larry King Live* and on PBS, and has been interviewed by *The New York Times*, *Forbes Magazine*, and *The Los Angeles Times*. Mrs. Harris is also on the Board of the Mary Baker Eddy Library for the Betterment of Humanity, which opened in September 2002.

■ The Fall in Lynn: Facts and Statements

Mary Baker Eddy dates the origins of modern Christian Science to her healing after a fall that occurred in February 1866. At the time she was married to Daniel Patterson, so accounts of that day refer to her as Mrs. Patterson:

Thursday evening, February 1, 1866

- Mary trips on an icy sidewalk in Lynn, Massachusetts, and is taken to the nearest home

- Dr. Alvin Cushing treats her and returns later for a second examination

Friday, February 2, 1866

- At her request Mary is moved to her own home by sleigh after receiving morphine

- George Newhall, a milkman, travels to tell Rev. Jonas B. Clark of Mary's injuries

- Dr. Cushing visits her twice

Saturday, February 3, 1866

- Mary rests at home

- Dr. Cushing visits her

- Newspaper account appears in *Lynn Reporter:*

  "Mrs. Mary M. Patterson fell upon the ice on Thursday evening and was severely injured. She was taken up in an insensible condition and carried to the residence of S. M. Bubier, Esq., nearby, where she was kindly cared for during the night. Dr. Cushing, who was called, found her injuries to be internal, and of a very serious nature, including spasms and intense suffering. She was removed to her home yesterday afternoon though in a very critical condition."

Sunday, February 4, 1866

- Rev. Clark visits Mary at her bedside

- Mary tells her friend Ira Brown that she will be walking by her friend's next visit

- Mary claims healing in afternoon as she reads about Jesus in the Bible

- Rev. Clark is said to be astonished at her recovery when he visits in evening

Monday, February 5, 1866

- Dr. Cushing visits Mary

February 15, 1866

- Mary writes letter to Julius Dresser (fellow-student of Phineas Parkhurst Quimby):

  "I am constantly wishing that you would step forward into the place he [Quimby] has vacated. I believe you would do a vast amount of good, and are more capable of occupying his place than any other I know of. Two weeks ago I fell on the sidewalk, and struck my back on the ice, and was taken up for dead, came to consciousness amid a storm of vapors from cologne, chloroform, ether, camphor, etc., but to find myself the helpless cripple I was before I saw Dr. Quimby. The physician attending said I had taken the last step I ever should, but in two days I got out of bed alone and will walk; but yet I confess I am frightened. . . . Now can you help me? I believe you can."

August 10, 1866

- Dr. Cushing treats Mary for bad cough

1891

- Mary Baker Eddy writes in *Retrospection and Inspection:*

"It was in Massachusetts, in February 1866, and after the death of the magnetic doctor, Mr. P. P. Quimby, whom spiritualists would associate therewith, but who was in no wise connected with this event, that I discovered the Science of divine metaphysical healing which I afterwards named Christian Science.

"My immediate recovery from the effects of an injury caused by an accident, an injury that neither medicine nor surgery could reach, was the falling apple that led me to the discovery how to be well myself, and how to make others so. Even to the homoeopathic physician who attended me, and rejoiced in my recovery, I could not then explain the *modus* of my relief. I could only assure him that the divine Spirit had wrought the miracle—a miracle which later I found to be in perfect scientific accord with divine law."

August 13, 1904

- Dr. Cushing writes in an affidavit:

> "I did not at any time declare, or believe, that there was no hope of Mrs. Patterson's recovery, or that she was in a critical condition, and did not at any time say, or believe that she had but three or any other limited number of days to live; and Mrs. Patterson did not suggest, or say, or pretend, or in any way whatever intimate, that on the third day or any other day, of her said illness, she had miraculously recovered or been healed, or that discovering or perceiving the truth or the power employed by Christ to heal the sick, she had, by it, been restored to health."

Mrs. Eddy's Most Tragic Error

Christian Science is one of the few religions in the world that contains a core teaching that is often deadly when put into practice. Mrs. Eddy repeatedly taught that matter is not real and that sin, disease, and death are only illusions. This notion is captured in one of the most famous lines from *Science and Health*: "There is no life, truth, intelligence, nor substance in matter. All is infinite Mind and its infinite manifestation, for God is All-in-all" (p. 468).

Later, she writes that "Man is not matter, he is not made up of brain, blood, bones, and other material elements" and that "Man is incapable of sin, sickness, and death" (*Science and Health*, p. 475). In further reflection on the nature of humanity she states: "To the five corporeal senses, man appears to be matter and mind united; but Christian Science reveals man as the idea of God, and declares the corporeal senses to be mortal and erring illusions" (p. 477).

In a famous passage on the origin and nature of evil, *Science and Health* claims: "God, or good, never made man capable of sin. It is the opposite of good—that is, evil—which seems to make men capable of wrong-doing. Hence, evil is but an illusion, and it has no real basis. Evil is a false belief. God is not its author" (p. 480). Eddy then argues: "Sin, sickness, and death will seem real (even as the experiences of the sleeping dream seem real) until the Science of man's eternal harmony breaks their illusion with the unbroken reality of scientific being" (p. 494).

It is tragic that such intellectual and theological nonsense passes for brilliance in the Christian Science world. The utter falsity of Mrs. Eddy's ideology is proven by the simple fact that no Christian Scientist can live consistently with the belief that matter is unreal. Christian Scientists are forced to trust their material senses almost all the time. Mrs. Eddy cared enough about the material world to be known for her beautiful clothing. Her followers have to obey traffic lights, wear seat belts, avoid jumping off tall buildings, and they are known to wear glasses, get bones fixed and go to the dentist.

THE ASHLEY KING CASE

Ashley King, age 12, was kept out of school in late 1987 through early 1988 so that her bone cancer could be dealt with by the healing methods of Christian Science. Authorities intervened on May 5, 1988, when Child Protective Services obtained a court order so that the child could be examined at a hospital. Here is author Caroline Fraser's description of the case:

"Judging by photographs taken a year or so before her death, Ashley King was a beautiful girl, with long, straight dark-brown hair and high cheekbones. When she was taken to Phoenix Children's Hospital, she had a tumor on her right leg that was forty-one inches in circumference.

"Her hemoglobin count, according to Paul Baranko, the physician who examined her, was 'almost incompatible with life.' Her heart was enlarged from the burden of pumping blood to the tumor, her pulse was twice normal, the cancer had spread to her lungs, and she was in immediate danger of dying from congestive heart failure. Immobilized by the tumor, she had been lying in the same position for months. Her buttocks and genitals were covered with bedsores."

Ashley King died on June 5, 1988. A year later her parents were found guilty of reckless endangerment.

—Caroline Fraser, "Suffering Children and the Christian Science Church," *Atlantic Monthly* (April 1995).

Alas, good Christian Scientists do not go to doctors and hospitals or take medicine. When so-called illness or disease comes their way the true Christian Scientist prays for healing. This is a perfect example of a false and deadly piety that can kill its practitioners. What must never be forgotten here is that the prayer is not directed against real sickness but against the false belief that disease is present. The testimonies of Christian Science healing sound credible to outsiders only because they assume that there is a real physical malady being cured.

Caroline Fraser's book, *God's Perfect Child,* offers a heart-breaking description of the death of Michael Schram. Fraser knew Schram when they attended Christian Science Sunday School together as children. In September 1979 Michael Schram, at age 12, began experiencing stomach pains. He missed school all week and by Thursday was showing signs of serious illness. Schram died that evening from a ruptured appendix. His mother and another Christian Scientist prayed until Sunday for his resurrection. Then they called the funeral home.

Michael's father, Jack, had never really embraced Christian Science ideology. He was estranged from his wife at the time of his son's death and was not informed of his sickness. Had he heard, he would have realized his son's peril given Christian Science's belief that evil is unreal, sickness is unreal, and therefore, that a ruptured appendix is unreal. Fraser tells of Jack coming home one night and reporting to his family about seeing a flaming car crash on the highway. His wife told him: "You're listening to error. You didn't see any car on fire."

■ Christian Science Q&A

1. Was Mrs. Eddy sincere in her beliefs?

Yes. While fame and fortune are part of her story, there is no reason at all to interpret her as a con artist or as a fraud.

2. Is Christian Science orthodox in its teaching and practice?

No. Mrs. Eddy and her followers deny by misinterpretation many of the classical doctrines of Christianity. The doctrine of the Trinity is not upheld by Christian Scientists and *Science and Health* explicitly states that Jesus is not God. Mrs. Eddy spiritualizes the virgin birth of Jesus and does the same in her writings on the miracles of Jesus, his atonement, and his resurrection. Christian Science errors about doctrine involve radical misunderstanding of the Bible rather than overt denial of some of its teachings.

3. Did Mrs. Eddy follow only the Bible in the formation of Christian Science?

Though she claims that the Bible was her "only textbook" it is obvious that Mrs. Eddy's theories rose directly from her early contact with Phineas Parkhurst Quimby and his views on divine healing. Over time Mrs. Eddy radically downplayed the influence of Quimby on her own life and theories. In her first lessons as a Christian Science teacher, however, she actually distributed copies of material that she received from her former guide.

4. Is *Science and Health* plagiarized from Quimby?

No direct plagiarism exists, but deep parallels are evident between the two with regard to many terms and ideas. Eddy was guilty of overt plagiarism involving other authors later in her life. For example, two articles in her *Miscellaneous Writings* were taken from the writings of others. The Christian Science Church continues to publish this volume without acknowledgement of the plagiarism.

5. What is animal magnetism?

Animal magnetism is the term used in Christian Science for the belief that humans can damage the emotional and physical health of others through mental thought, even while being at considerable geographical distance. Mrs. Eddy blamed the death of her third husband on animal magnetism in spite of evidence that he died of heart problems. She was also paranoid about animal magnetism in her final years as a recluse in her own home.

6. Is it true that Mrs. Eddy did not care about the existence of Jesus?

Yes. In a conversation with scholar James Wiggin, Eddy stated: "I do not find my authority for Christian Science in history, but in revelation. If there had never existed such a person as the Galilean Prophet, it would make no difference to me. I should still know that God's spiritual ideal is the only real man in His image and likeness" (*The First Church of Christ, Scientist and Miscellany*, p. 319). No doubt Christian Scientists would be upset with anyone who said: "If there had never existed such a person as Mrs. Eddy, it would make no difference to me."

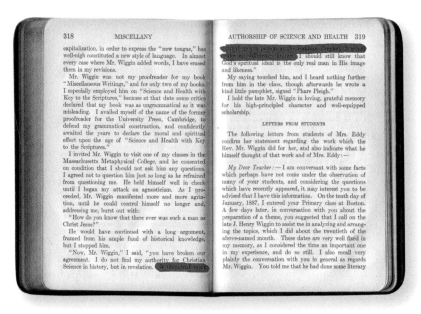

Eddy denies importance of historicity of Jesus

7. Was Mrs. Eddy as wonderful in character as many Christian Scientists believe?

Their famous leader conducted herself well in public and was often very generous and kind to her followers, especially to those who worked for her. However, these positive realities do not obscure abundant evidence of a darker side to Mrs. Eddy. Here are the words of a sympathetic biographer: "Even the most devoted of Mrs. Eddy's staff admitted freely and emotionally that what made their service to her hardest was her anger, the fury of her rebukes, the storm of criticism and reproach and invective that might fall upon their heads at any time. . . . She could be bad tempered, irrational, capricious, inconsiderate, domineering, sanctimonious, unkind" (Gillian Gill, *Mary Baker Eddy*, pp. 401, 405).

8. Are Christian Scientists allowed to go to regular doctors for treatment of illness?

Technically, yes. There is no official announcement from the Mother Church that absolutely forbids going to the hospital or a regular doctor. However, the movement radically frowns on traditional medical procedures and exerts tremendous pressure on individual Scientists to stay away from doctors, except for the treatment of broken bones, dental issues, and the use of eyeglasses.

9. What is wrong with Christian Science reliance on prayer for healing?

The Christian Science method of healing is marred by adherence to Mrs. Eddy's wild belief that sickness is not real. Prayer for healing in her view is not about prayer for the healing of real disease but the healing of false belief that disease is real. In orthodox Christianity one prays for the healing of cancer. In Christian Science one prays for the healing of thinking that cancer is real.

▪ Christian Science Splinter Groups

The Work of Ann Beals

Ann Beals was a member of the Mother Church until 1974 when her publication of material on animal magnetism led to fallout with church leaders. Beals helped Reginald Kerry send his controversial Kerry letters attacking the Mother Church for corruption and immorality. In 1980 Beals started The Bookmark to make early Christian Science works available, as well as her own writings.

Internet Source

Website: www.thebookmark.com

Mary Baker Eddy Institute (Helen Wright site)

Helen Wright started the Mary Baker Eddy Institute, based in Captiva, Florida, in 1988. The Institute makes available online the works of Eddy and also publishes Wright's many works, including *America: Cradle for the Second Coming of Christ.* This work attempts to document how divine providence led to the creation of America, the land that birthed Christian Science.

Internet Source

Website: www.mbeinstitute.org

Christian Science Endtime Center

This group believes that they represent the true "Boston school" of Christian Science that was taught by Eddy and then preserved by Stanley C. Larkin in study courses in the 1960s. The CSEC and The Church of Transfiguration carry on Larkin's work.

They differ from mainline Christian Science in teaching that Mrs. Eddy is the fulfillment of the prophecy of a God-crowned woman in Revelation 12. The group also believes that Stanley C. Larkin is the fulfillment of a prophecy from Mrs. Eddy: "I calculate that about one half century more will bring to the front the man that God has equipped to lift aloft His standard of Christian Science."

The CSEC also draws support from the writings of Bliss Knapp, author of the controversial work *The Destiny of the Mother Church.*

Internet Source

Website: www.endtime.org

Joel Goldsmith and The Infinite Way

Born in 1892, Joel Goldsmith developed an interest in Christian Science after his father experienced healing in 1915. Goldsmith was involved in Christian Science until 1945 when he resigned. In 1947 he published *The Infinite Way,* which describes his mystical understanding of Christian Science. After Goldsmith's death in 1964, his wife Emma carried on a tape ministry, continued later by Thelma G. (Geri) McDonald, Emma's daughter from a previous marriage. Emma died in 1986.

The Infinite Way has no churches but seeks simply to spread Joel's teaching tapes to the world. "Joel's work came from divine inspiration. Joel often mentioned that many times in his lecture work that revelations would come through in a Class and they would be the first time he heard it as well."

Internet Source

Website: www.joelgoldsmith.com

INTERNET SOURCES

Sites Supporting Christian Science

Church of Christ, Scientist website: www.tfccs.com

The Mary Baker Eddy Library: www.marybakereddylibrary.org

Christian Science Community Board: www.lii.net/tcscb

The Longyear Museum: www.longyear.org

Spirituality.com: www.spirituality.com

Christian Science E-News: www.csenews.com

Emergence International (pro-gay Christian Scientists): http://www.emergence-international.org

Sites Critical of Christian Science

God's Perfect Child (Caroline Fraser): www.godsperfectchild.com

Caroline Fraser on "Suffering Children": http://www.theatlantic.com/unbound/flashbks/xsci/suffer.htm

Children's Health Care Is a Legal Duty (CHILD, Inc.): www.childrenshealthcare.org

Christian Way: www.christianway.org

Ex-Christian Scientists

Quackwatch (Stephen Barrett, M.D.): www.quackwatch.org

■ A Christian Science Bibliographical Guide

The controversies surrounding the life and teachings of Mary Baker Eddy are so significant that a word must be said about some of the most important works and authors. Among Christian Scientists, Robert Peel remains the master scholar of Eddy's life. His three-volume biography is a tremendous source of information, though it is heavily biased in favor of Eddy. Stephen Gottschalk, a leading Christian Science scholar, is the author of *The Emergence of Christian Science in American Religious Life* (California, 1973). Adam Dickey's *Memoirs of Mary Baker Eddy* (1929) is also important since Dickey served as her longtime assistant.

Among recent authors who are not believers in Christian Science, Gillian Gill's *Mary Baker Eddy* (Perseus, 1998) demonstrates an incredible grasp of detail, although Gill could be far more critical of Mrs. Eddy. Robert Davis Thomas's *With Bleeding Footsteps* (Knopf 1994) is also noteworthy. Caroline Fraser's *God's Perfect Child* (Henry Holt, 1999) is the best work in terms of offering extensive and powerful critique of Mrs. Eddy and Christian Science. Martin Gardner's *The Healing Revelations of Mary Baker Eddy* (Prometheus, 1993) should be consulted as well.

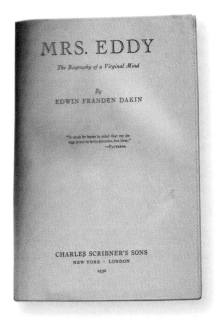

Title page subtitle shows
Dakin's view of Mrs. Eddy

Of the older critiques of Christian Science, the work by Ernest S. Bates and John V. Dittemore (Mary Baker Eddy: *The Truth and the Tradition*, 1932) is by far the most important though Edwin Dakin's biography *Mrs. Eddy* (1929) is also significant. Dakin's subtitle, "The Biography of a Virginal Mind," captures the spirit of his book. The polemic works by Willa Cather and Georgine Milmine (*The Life of Mary Baker G. Eddy and the History of Christian Science*, 1909) and Mark Twain (*Christian Science*, 1907) are crucial to note because of their impact during Eddy's lifetime.

5

CHRISTIAN SECTARIAN GROUPS

Three historic figures important to Rastafarians:
Marcus Garvey, Haile Selassie, and Bob Marley

Painting and photo: Derek Beverley

Seen globally and from the span of more than twenty centuries, the vast majority of the Christian story involves the narratives of Roman Catholic, Orthodox, and Protestant Christians. However, these three Christian traditions do not capture the complete story of those groups through history that claim to be Christian. For want of a better term, there are also sectarian Christian groups that are distinct from the Catholic, Orthodox, and Protestant options. The best known include the Church of Jesus Christ of Latter-day Saints (Mormons), Jehovah's Witnesses, Unification Church, The Family International, Peoples Temple, Branch Davidians, and various non-traditional Church of Christ movements (like the Iglesia ni Cristo in the Philippines).

The above groups retain a Protestant ethos about them even as they depart in various ways from classical Christian doctrine. There are also sectarian Christian groups shaped by Catholic, Orthodox, or a Western esoteric paradigm. The best-known Catholic sects are the Army of Mary (a Quebec-based group centered on Marie-Paule Giguere), the Apostles of Infinite Love (Pope Jean Gregory XVII), and the Vatican in Exile (Pope Michael I).

The most significant sectarian groups rooted in Western esotericism are Christian Science, Unity, New Thought, and the various Swedenborgian churches. These metaphysical movements achieved even greater distance from classical Christian understandings of God, Jesus, divine revelation, and humanity, though often expressed in obtuse language.

What do these sectarian groups have in common?

First, apart from the few Catholic bodies, they usually adopt a non-Trinitarian perspective to a greater or lesser degree. For example, Jehovah's Witnesses deny the deity of Christ but remain monotheistic. Mormons affirm the deity of Christ but in a context of affirming the possibility of human exaltation to a similar divine status. Sun Myung Moon teaches that Jesus is the Son of God but also that Jesus is really subordinate to Moon. Esoteric Christian groups tend to emphasize the divinity in each human so that Christ becomes an example more than a divine Savior.

Second, each group retains the language of Christian faith even if the substance is not retained on particular matters. In Christian Science the second coming of Christ is the emergence of the work of Mary Baker Eddy. Members of The Family International view holiness through the perspective of a radical sexual libertarianism. Salvation in Mormonism involves obedience to temple rituals that were borrowed in part from Joseph Smith's experiences in the Masonic Lodge.

Last, and most important, each group has been shaped by an authoritarian and often narcissistic leadership, particularly at inception. This may explain to some degree how new and even radical templates are created in the ongoing Christian narrative. It is as if the Roman Catholic obedience to the pope or the Protestant submission to Scripture is duplicated in allegiance to a new leader, be it Joseph Smith, Mary Baker Eddy, Sun Myung Moon, or Pope Michael I. The darkest extremes of authoritarianism found expression in the violent deaths associated with Jim Jones

(Peoples Temple) and David Koresh (Branch Davidians) or in the sexual abuse of followers, as in the case of David Berg.

Of course, the story of these marginal Christian groups is expressed best by discontinuities rather than common themes. The groups are so distinct that they each amount to a new understanding of Christian faith, as seen from the older and larger Christian traditions. Of course, each marginal group views itself as faithful to the original Christian gospel and central to the ongoing work of God's kingdom, so much so that most sectarian groups view it as wrong to form ecumenical associations with anyone else. Given this, each marginal group has to be understood through its own unique narrative.

African Hebrew Israelites of Jerusalem (AHI)

The AHI is a group of "Black Hebrews" living in Dimona, Israel. The vegetarian and polygamous group migrated from Chicago to Israel in 1969 under their leader Ben Ammi Ben Israel, who was born as Ben Carter in 1939. Ben Ammi claims he received a vision from the angel Gabriel in 1966 telling him that his African heirs were part of the ten lost tribes of Israel.

About two thousand AHI members now live in Israel. The famous pop star Whitney Houston visited the movement's headquarters in May 2003. The AHI have centers in various American cities, including Chicago, Washington, and Houston. The group operates a catering and restaurant business under the banner of Soul Vegetarian.

Ben Ammi and his followers deny any connection to Yahweh ben Yahweh, the convicted leader of a radical Black Hebrew group based in Miami.

Internet Source

AHI website: www.africanhebrewisraelitesofjerusalem.com

Aggressive Christianity Missions Training Corps

"General" Jim Green and his wife, Lila, started the Aggressive Christianity Missions Training Corps in 1982 in Sacramento, California. They view themselves as a spiritual army sent to battle the forces of darkness. They have also been identified as Free Love Ministries. Christian cult watchers expressed concerns about their military style and elitism as early as 1984. One Sacramento radio station refused to carry their broadcasts.

"The Corps" lost its California property as a result of court action brought against the group in 1988. That year Maura Schmierer sued the group for holding her captive and for emotional abuse. She told *The Sacramento Bee* that the Greens "told me I was a witch, that I was a whore." She claims that she was forbidden to bathe or have hot water for six months and that she was pressured into getting a divorce and giving her husband custody of their three children. She was kicked out of the group in July 1987. One report claims that Lila Green received a prophecy from God in late 1988 that Maura's lawyer Bob Blasier would be run over by a truck. The group lost the court case and was ordered to pay the ex-member $1.2 million.

The Corps settled for a while in Klamath Falls, Oregon, but is now based in Fence Lake, New Mexico. Lila now goes by Deborah L. Green. The movement places great emphasis on battling demonic forces and giving direct prophecies from God. On September 12, 2001, The Corps released the first of a long series of messages from God about the meaning of the attacks on the World Trade Center and the Pentagon. In a radio program released in June 2003, the group claims that God told them: "Therefore, I say do not fret thyselves over enemies of my purpose. But know that I the Living God am well-able to execute my vengeance upon them. I say when men will put on a pretentious show, claiming that they are mine, I say that I vindicate myself upon their wantonness."

Internet Source

ACMTC homepage: http://www.aggressivechristianity.net

■ Alamo Christian Ministries

Alamo Christian Ministries represents the work of Tony Alamo. His name is often linked with that of his first wife, Susan, who died on April 8, 1982. The Alamos had a significant street ministry in Hollywood during the hippie revolution of the 1960s. Disillusioned hippies were attracted to their message of the gospel and their call to a new type of communal living. The Alamos carried on their ministry under the name Music Square Church and also the Tony and Susan Alamo Christian Foundation.

Tony was born in Joplin, Missouri, on September 20, 1934, as Bernie Lazar Hoffman. Susan was born Edith Opal Horn and, like Tony, was from a Jewish family. Tony and Susan met in California and adopted Alamo as their last name. After they started their church work in California, they branched out to Arkansas and other southern states in the 1970s.

The Alamos' ministry became the target of both anti-cult groups, particularly the Cult Awareness Network, and law enforcement agencies. In 1976 the U.S. Labor Department charged that church members who work for the church should be subject to the Fair Labor Standards Act and viewed as employees and not volunteers—a position the U.S. Supreme Court upheld in 1985.

Tony Alamo has had other brushes with the law. After Susan died, she was buried in a mausoleum on church property in Georgia Ridge, Arkansas. In 1991 Alamo removed Susan's body after the government confiscated the property. Christhiaon Coie, Susan's estranged daughter, charged Tony with stealing her body, and her stepfather had the body relocated under court order. In the 1980s and 1990s the IRS targeted Alamo, the church, and its businesses for income tax evasion. Alamo was convicted on four tax-related charges in 1994 and was sentenced to six years in prison. He was released in 1998 but arrested again in September 2008.

The movement follows a fundamentalist ideology and views the King James Version as the only valid translation of the Bible. Tony Alamo adopts conspiracy theories about the Roman Catholic Church and taught that the Cult Awareness Network was a branch of the Vatican. He calls the Catholic Church "the Queen of Whores" and cited John Paul II for his criminal past. Alamo claimed that the Gulf War was a Vatican plot to distract attention from U.S. judicial persecution against him. In 1999 he announced that UFOs are real and are a part of God's end-time prophecy.

The extent of Alamo's conspiracy mind-set can be seen in this description of former president Clinton. "Check it out for yourself. Clinton, as a child, attended Catholic parochial school, graduated from Catholic Georgetown University, and received a Catholic Rhodes scholarship to Catholic Oxford University in Oxford, England. For political reasons, Clinton temporarily became a Baptist; now as President, he is unashamedly and zealously showing his true Catholic colors. By the way Clinton is obediently performing for Rome, he can, with assurance, predict future bloody Christian massacres. If he continues being faithful to the Pope's evil leadership, why maybe he could even plan on being the next Führer."

ALAMO CHRISTIAN MINISTRIES

Typology	Christian Protestant Fundamentalist Sectarian
Homepage	Alamo Ministries: www.alamoministries.com

Apostles of Infinite Love

This is one of various groups that claim to be the true version of Roman Catholicism. Michael Collin, a former priest, founded the Apostles of Infinite Love. The movement is based in Saint-Jovite, Quebec, and is currently led by Gregory Tremblay (b. 1928), whom the group views as Pope Jean Gregory XVII. The group also goes by the title "The Catholic Church of the Apostles of the Latter Times." Their Quebec site is home to The Order of the Magnificat of the Mother of God.

The movement claims its origins lie in what are known as the La Salette prophecies, or revelations Mary gave to Mélanie Calvat and Maximin Giraud, two children, on September 19, 1846, in La Salette, France. The Vatican accepts the La Salette apparition but has condemned groups who have used the revelations in ways contrary to Rome. Rome condemned Michael Collin, who died in 1974, three times—in 1951, 1956, and 1961—for his disobedience to Vatican policies.

The first verdict against Collin reads: "By a decree dated January 17, 1951, the Supreme Sacred Congregation of the Holy Office has reduced to the status of a layman the priest Michael Collin of the Order of the Sacred Heart, already dismissed from the said Order, traveling through several dioceses, frequently and in various ways violating rules of the Sacred Canon."

The Order, founded in 1962, has this to say about its alleged divine roots: "In Her loving mercy, the Virgin of La Salette has transported Her great light to Quebec soil, where the Order of the Magnificat of the Mother of God, the Order of the Apostles of the Latter Times, has been formed under Her direction and protection. In a turn of events whose initiative the Virgin took upon Herself, the Order has been developing in Quebec and in many countries all over the world for the past thirty-five years."

In April 1999 an arrest warrant was issued in Quebec against Mr. Tremblay and three other members of the group, including two nuns. Police raided the group at the time and took children into custody for examination. The charges involved allegations of sexual abuse and assault. Tremblay surrendered to authorities two weeks after charges were laid, but the Quebec courts dropped the case in 2001 because of insufficient evidence to proceed to trial.

The Order claims that it has been the constant victim of persecution. "Time has not altered the rage of the enemy of God and his henchmen— quite the contrary. Those who have followed our progress through court trials, newspaper articles, etc., know that our path has been sown with a thousand snares. The Order of the Mother of God is now founded, but it has been established and is holding its own through opposition and persecution."

APOSTLES OF INFINITE LOVE

Typology	Christian Roman Catholic Sectarian
Leader	Gregory Tremblay, aka Pope Jean Gregory XVII
Homepage	www.magnificat.ca

Army of Mary

The Army of Mary is a Quebec-based Marian work founded by Marie-Paule Giguere. She was born on September 14, 1921, and married George Cliche on July 1, 1944. The couple had five children, but Marie-Paule left her husband in 1957. She claims that Jesus and the Virgin Mary have appeared to her since she was a teenager.

She states that God told her of her Marian work in 1954. She also claimed that Jesus told her in 1958 that the church would persecute her: "It will be those of my priesthood who will crucify you. Like me, you are innocent, but on all sides, voices will cry out that you are hateful, that you are the most infamous of creatures. All those of my priesthood who are sinning through pride, egoism, through sensuality in all its forms, will cast stones at you."

The Army of Mary was officially founded on August 28, 1971, and received endorsement as a Pious Association by Cardinal Maurice Roy, the Archbishop of Quebec, on March 10, 1975. Marie-Paule's work also received the blessing of Ida Peerdeman (1905–1996), a Marian mystic based in the Netherlands. The movement came under scrutiny from the Vatican and from the Canadian Catholic authorities in the 1980s. Suspicion was due in part to the fact that Belgian member Marc Bosquart wrote two books contending that Mary was mystically indwelling Marie-Paule. On May 4, 1987, Cardinal Louis-Albert Vachon, then Archbishop of Quebec, revoked the status of the Army of Mary as a Pious Association.

On March 31, 2000, the Vatican formally objected to Marie-Paule's *Life of Love,* a fifteen-volume autobiography. In 2001 the Canadian Conference of Catholic Bishops spoke decisively against the movement, and the Vatican ratified their verdict. The Canadian Conference stated: "The Army of Mary's on-going activities and teachings pose dangers for the Catholic Church in Canada and to the faith of its members. In view of this and the continuing threat to the integrity and unity of the Catholic faith, the Bishops of Canada declare, and hereby inform all the Catholic faithful, that the Army of Mary, regardless of its claims to the contrary, is not a Catholic association. Some of the teaching it propagates about redemption, the Virgin Mary and reincarnation are profoundly at variance with the teaching and profession of the faith of the Catholic Church."

The Canadian bishops were particularly disturbed by the claims of the Army of Mary that Marie-Paule is a reincarnation of the Virgin Mary. They also objected to the insubordination of Army leaders to the direct wishes of Catholic authorities: "The Catholic Bishops of Canada regret the way the leaders of the Army of Mary continue to defy ecclesial authority and refuse to heed the legitimate pastoral admonitions and injunctions of the Archbishop of Quebec."

On April 4, 2005, Marc Cardinal Ouellet, the Archbishop of Quebec and Primate of Canada, issued a further warning against the Army. He cited these words of Marc Bosquart, given in 2001, as an example of the Army's faulty understanding of its leader:

"So, let's believe it, let's say it, let's proclaim it: in the Kingdom of the Spirit, in that Kingdom which is coming, in that Kingdom which has already begun, everywhere, side by side, there will be Jesus Christ and Marie-Paule, the Redeemer and the Co-Redeemer of all humankind."

The Army of Mary is based in Lac-Etchemin, sixty miles south of Quebec City.

ARMY OF MARY

Typology	Christian Roman Catholic Sectarian
Leader	Marie-Paule Giguere (1921–)
Homepage	www.communaute-dame.qc.ca

■ Aryan Nations

The Aryan Nations is one of the major racist religious groups in America. The movement teaches a version of "Christian identity," that is, the belief that only Anglo-Saxons are children of God, that non-whites are "mud people," and that the "Canaanite Jew . . . a child of Satan" is "the natural enemy of our Aryan (White) Race." Richard Butler (1918–2004) founded the Aryan Nations in the mid-1970s, with roots in the Church of Jesus Christ Christian, started by Wesley Swift. Butler worked with Swift from 1961 until the latter's death a decade later. He then moved to Hayden, Idaho, and formed the Aryan Nations.

Nations members believe that Adam is the father of the white race only and that whites represent the twelve tribes of Israel. They claim the swastika as their symbol, believing early Christians used it to point to Christ as a cornerstone. Butler taught that his ideology is rooted in a love for the white race that leads him to war with "the anti-Christ Jews, mongrel hordes and liberal White race-mixers." Butler was a great admirer of Adolf Hitler.

Butler's group suffered a major financial blow in 2000 when the Southern Poverty Law Center won a $6.3 million civil suit against the group. Membership in the Aryan Nations costs thirty-five dollars. The member declares: "I am of the White Aryan Race. I concur that Aryan Nations is only Aryans of Anglo-Saxon, Germanic, Nordic, Basque, Lombard, Celtic and Slavic origin. I agree with Aryan Nations' biblical exclusion of Jews, Negroes, Mexicans, Orientals, and Mongrels." The movement experienced schism after Butler's death.

Charles John Juba claimed leadership for several years but there is now an alternative Aryan Nations group (www.aryannations.org) based in Coeur d'Alene, Idaho. Juba argued that Butler passed the national director's position on to Ray Redfeairn in September 2001 and that the latter resigned that position the next March. Juba then assumed the position and then claimed that Redfeairn was a traitor to the cause. "Redfeairn is riding Pastor Butler's coattails for power, and trying to bully and intimidate anyone in his way for his grasp for power. In doing so, he has those around him do his bidding like the work of Jews, by trying to rule by dividing and conquering."

Juba announced an alternative to WWJD? (What Would Jesus Do?) in his WWHD? (What Would Hitler Do?), calling for an aggressive campaign against the impact of Jews in American society. Juba also stated: "We are *not* a non-violent organization, we believe that our Race is on the verge of extinction, and will do anything in our powers to secure a white safe future for our children and our children's children." Juba left the movement in early 2005 shortly after moving the headquarters to Kansas City. August B. Kreis now heads the group, which is based in South Carolina. Its website stated: "We have encapsulated the quintessence of this work in two words: Aryan Jihad." Now the site refers to Aryan War and no longer uses the word *Jihad.*

ARYAN NATIONS

Typology	Christian Identity
Founder	Richard Butler
Headquarters	Lincoln, Alabama
Homepage	www.aryannations.org (Coeur d'Alene, Idaho)
Critic Site	Southern Poverty Law Center www.splcenter.org
Recommended Reading	Michael Barkun, *Religion and the Racist Right* (Chapel Hill: University Of North Carolina Press, 1997) Mattias Gardell, *Gods of the Blood* (Durham: Duke, 2003) Jeffrey Kaplan, ed, *Encyclopedia of White Power* (Lanham: Creek: AltaMira, 2000)

■ Carol Balizet

Carol Balizet is the founder of Home in Zion Ministries, based in Tampa, Florida. Born in 1933 in Georgia, Balizet is known for her radical views on childbirth and separation from society. She teaches that proper birthing of children is to take place in the home and not in the hospital since hospitals are demonic sites. She condemns the use of drugs in childbirth and home visits by doctors. She teaches that Christians are to avoid medicine and exercise faith in response to health emergencies. Surgery is wrong because it represents a spirit of mutilation.

Balizet's views on childbirth are given in her book *Born in Zion*, which contrasts so-called spiritual "Zion births" from those of "Egypt" (man-made medical systems). Balizet also believes that birth by Caesarean section is particularly wicked since women who have Caesareans have "the spirit of Caesar" in them.

■ British-Israelism

The term *British-Israelism* refers to the idea that the ten lost tribes of Israel settled in Great Britain and that there is a direct link between the ancient Israelites and the Anglo-Saxon people. British-Israelites even claim that the Stone of Scone used in British royalty ceremonies is the same one used in the coronation of King David in Israel.

Theories about a connection between Britain and ancient Jews circulated in some form among Puritans and a few writers of the eighteenth century. Richard Brothers was one of these early British-Israelites. Brothers was born in Canada in 1757, and by the turn of the century he was claiming that he was descended from King David and was the proper heir to the British throne. He was committed to an asylum and died in 1824.

Most scholars trace British-Israelism to John Wilson, a native of Ireland who authored *Lectures on Our Israelitish Origin* in 1840. After Wilson's death in 1871, Edward Hine spread his ideas throughout England and the United States. British-Israelism also had some impact on the theories of William Miller and early Adventists. A conscious anti-Semitic element emerged in British-Israelism through the views of Howard Rand of the Anglo-Saxon Federation of America in 1928.

The most popular exponent of British-Israelism in the twentieth century was Herbert W. Armstrong, founder of the Worldwide Church of God. In 1967 Armstrong authored *The United States and British Commonwealth in Prophecy*, a work that owed much to the views expressed in J. H. Allen's *Judah's Sceptre and Joseph's Birthright*, first published in 1902. After Armstrong's death, the Worldwide Church of God abandoned British-Israelism, though many splinter groups retain the ideology.

British-Israelism is advanced today through several organizations, most notably the British-Israel World Federation, organized in 1919. The BIWF has branches in Australia, New Zealand, and Canada. The federation contends that "the Royal House of Britain is descended from King David" and that "the British Monarchs are anointed in the same way as

Zadok the Priest anointed the Kings of Israel." The organization also maintains that God's promise that Israel will not be defeated is proved by British victories in World Wars I and II and "in many other great battles such as the Spanish Armada, Trafalgar and Waterloo." The federation argues in its booklet "As Birds Flying Over Jerusalem" that the Royal Flying Corps fulfilled a 2,600-year-old Bible prophecy.

British-Israelism is based on superficial Bible study and careless historical judgments. Its claims are refuted in detail in Joseph Hopkins's *The Armstrong Empire* and in Walter Martin's classic work, *The Kingdom of the Cults.* The subtle racism in British-Israelism turns far more sinister in the radical white supremacist movements that have embraced its emphasis on Anglo-Saxons as the people of God.

BRITISH ISRAELISM	
Typology	Christian Protestant Sectarian
Homepage	British-Israel World Federation: http://www.britishisrael. co.uk
Critical Websites	Worldwide Church of God critique: www.wcg.org/lit/ prophecy/anglo/usbrit1.htm British-Israelism and the WCG: www.wcg.org/lit/prophecy/anglo/howanglo.htm Robert Roberts 1879 reply to Edward Hine: http://mm91007.tripod.com/book/anglo.htm

■ Christadelphians

Christadelphians trace their modern roots to the work of John Thomas, a native of England. Thomas was born in 1805 and immigrated to the United States in 1832. He was associated for some time with Restorationist movements (the Campbellites and the Millerites) but kept refining his own theological positions. He gained a following both in England and the United States and in 1864 adopted the name "Christadelphian" (meaning "brothers in Christ") for his group. Though some of his date-setting and apocalyptic warnings about England created unrest, his followers remained united until his death in 1871. Robert Roberts led the English branch of the movement after the founder's death while Thomas Williams led the American group.

Christadelphians affirm the inerrancy of Scripture but hold some views distinct from classical Christian orthodoxy. They deny the Trinity and the personal nature of the Holy Spirit. They believe Jesus to be the Son of God but do not believe that He is one in essence with the Father and Spirit. Christadelphians state: "Jesus is a Man, not God!" They also deny that Jesus had a sinless nature. They do believe in the virgin birth of Jesus, accept the Gospel accounts of his miracles, and believe that Jesus will come again to Earth.

Christadelphians deny the immortality of the soul, eternal punishment, and the existence of Satan. They affirm the notion of soul sleep and believer's baptism, even contending that baptism is necessary for salvation. They reject the typical Protestant understanding of "grace alone" for salvation, arguing "we reject the doctrine that the Gospel alone will save, without obedience to Christ's commandments." The group also condemns Christian involvement in the military and politics.

The Christadelphians have endured major internal tensions throughout their history over what constitutes true doctrine. There have been divisions over the understanding of Christ's nature, the issue of biblical inerrancy, and the proper place of leadership within the body. The most significant division occurred in the 1890s over whether the dead who once followed Christ would be raised to judgment. The bitter controversy over a rather arcane point led to amendment of the Statement of Faith. Some Christadelphians follow the Birmingham Unamended Statement of Faith (or BUSF). The majority follow the Birmingham Amended Statement of Faith (or BASF). Frequent attempts to bridge the schism have failed, though there is less tension on the issue in recent decades.

Christadelphians have no central ecclesiastical authority, though they are bound by their common heritage from Thomas and by the many doctrines common to both Statements of Faith. There are more then three hundred local congregations in Britain and more than four hundred in the United States.

The Christadelphian serves as the main magazine for Amended fellowships while *The Christadelphian Advocate* reaches those who follow the Unamended Statement of Faith.

CHRISTADELPHIANS

Typology	Christian Protestant
Founder	John Thomas (1805–1871)
Websites	www.christadelphia.org www.thechristadelphians.org
Recommended Reading	Charles H. Lippy, *The Christadelphians in North America* (Lewiston, New York: Edwin Mellen,1989)

■ Christian Educational Services (CES)

CES, headquartered in Indianapolis, Indiana, is a split-off movement from The Way International, the controversial sect founded by Victor P. Wierwille. In October 1986 prominent Way researcher John Schoenheit was fired for writing a paper on "Adultery and Fornication" in which he defended traditional Christian teaching. Schoenheit's conclusions were at variance with the views and practices of Way leaders who tried to justify adultery.

Schoenheit's firing led to an internal crisis in The Way, and the leadership threatened dismissal for simply reading his paper. In March 1987 a few brave members, including John and Pat Lynn, called for reformation in the movement. John was fired on April 1, and that fall he teamed up with Schoenheit, Mark Graeser, and others to form "American Fellowship Services." That was the precursor to CES, which was officially incorporated in September 1988.

CES has become a spiritual home for many ex-Way members. CES retains some unorthodox views from its Way roots, including denial of the Trinity and of the preexistence of Jesus with the Father. Like The Way, CES also teaches a distinction between "the Holy Spirit" (used as another name for God the Father) and "holy spirit" (the spirit planted in Christians when they are born again).

Internet Sources

CES homepage: http://stfonline.org

Ex-CES website: http://ex-ces.faithweb.com

■ The Church of Bible Understanding (COBU)

Stewart Traill started this controversial group in 1971 in Allentown, Pennsylvania. Traill was born in Quebec, Canada, in 1936. In 1959 he married Shirley Rudy and they had five children. Traill said later that having children led him back to God. He was kicked out of an independent pentecostal church in Allentown in 1970 and started his own movement, one that had similarities to the Jesus People. Traill's followers were originally known as the Forever Family.

Traill divorced in 1976 and married his secretary, Gayle Gillespie, who was 20 at the time. The divorce and remarriage created internal dissent, and many left the movement. According to *Philadelphia Magazine* COBU bought a $435,000 home in Princeton, New Jersey, which served at the time as home base for Traill and his wife. Female church members helped clean the home.

Traill has been frequently criticized for authoritarianism and emotional abuse of members. In the early 1980s four of Traill's followers were convicted for beating his son Donald. The four said that the boy's father ordered them to punish the 12-year-old for alleged shoplifting. He went to Children's Hospital in Philadelphia in serious condition. Further church turmoil was created in a famous March 4, 1989, meeting at which Traill admitted that he had been guilty of adultery with a young female follower. His request for grace struck many members as hypocritical given his harsh treatment of others.

At the repentance meeting Traill stated: "In some sense or other, I have a framework somehow, that I can keep going—does that make any sense?—that you don't have. I wasn't seeing grace, nevertheless I could include enough of it in some sort of pseudo-framework to, ah, keep going, enough to, ah, seem right. Got it? You know the whole while, I never tried to take Jesus' place. No way and I was always speaking against it. And yet that's what the devil arranged. God purposely made me blind to it. . . . And who is the emptiest of all? Me. I was devoid, I was unconscious of grace. I really wonder if some of you were more aware of grace than I. I really think so, because it's zero with me."

The church does mission and relief work in Haiti. Church members work together in the antique business, carpet cleaning, and the repair of photographic equipment. Though The Church of Bible Understanding follows much of the doctrinal paradigm of Scripture, the focus on

Traill as the supreme interpreter of Scripture leaves much to be desired. As well, the reports by ex-members of emotional abuse in the group are often heartbreaking.

Jim Greiner, a former leader in the group, issued a public apology in 1999 for his abuse of members. "I am very sorry for all the anger and hurt I have caused you. I am very sorry for the abuse and hateful things I said. I had no right at all to treat any of you the way I did. There is no excuse for the way I treated any of you. I am sorry for all the negative effects I have had in your lives. I also know that no words can take away all the pain I have caused you. Please forgive me for my sin against you."

THE CHURCH OF BIBLE UNDERSTANDING

Typology	Christian Protestant Fundamentalist Sectarian
Critic Websites	X-COBU website: www.angelfire.com/nm/cobu
Recommended Reading	Sabrina Rubin Erdely, "I'll Be Damned," *The Philadelphia Magazine* (June 1999) Christopher J. Kelly, "On the Traill: Difficult to Peg Reclusive Leader," *Scranton Times Tribune* (February 9, 2003)

Concerned Christians

Monte Kim Miller, the leader of Concerned Christians, was born April 20, 1954. A native of Colorado, he was converted under the ministry of Bill Bright. Miller was originally connected with the evangelical counter-cult movement, but in the late 1980s he adopted an isolationist ideology that made him the target of cult watchers.

Miller uses files from his former radio program, *Our Foundation*, to spread his views. In 1996 he claimed to have a message from God for the radio stations that used to run his program: "You are to begin airing the program for free on the air. Do not laugh. He is serious. We will not be sending you any more funds. It is time for you to serve the Lord with all your heart, soul, and mind." He filed for bankruptcy the next year.

Miller denies the allegation that he predicted that Denver would be destroyed on October 10, 1998. Miller left the Denver area in September of that year. He is also said to have prophesied that he would be gunned down in Israel in 1999 and rise again. Some of Miller's followers were arrested in Israel in late 1998. They were sent back to the United States out of fear that, as the end of the millennium approached, they would commit violence in order to bring about their vision of Armageddon.

Miller claims that he is "the Prophet" of God speaking God's message to the last days. The tone of his message is expressed in this announcement to the world: "Fear God, for it is he who gathered athletes from precisely 77 nations on the 770th day of the millennium, February 8, 2002, the Opening of the Winter Olympic Games. It is he who ordained, on the very same day, the completion of his 777th tape and CD of detailed explanations of his coordination of world history, this all being 7 days before the 777th day of the millennium, February 15, 2002, his day that The Seventh Angel Sounds."

The United States is the target of much of Miller's prophetic wrath: "It is God *or* country, not God *and* country. If a Christian does not denounce in his heart the *Declaration of Independence* principles that America was founded upon, that is, 'life, liberty, and the pursuit of happiness,' that Christian will be considered by God to have a heart of treason against the Kingdom of Heaven. A man who is willing to die for America is a man who will not enter the kingdom of God."

Miller claims to offer precise details of biblical prophecy. He states that the space shuttle *Challenger*'s destruction was foretold in Scripture. Also, the Manhattan Project was directed out of rooms 5120 and 5121 in the War Department Building in Washington in order to fulfill Jeremiah 51:20 and 51:21. Furthermore, God ordained that a recent bomb in the American arsenal be named MOAB (Massive Ordnance Air Burst) since Moab was the son of Lot's daughter. This connection with Sodom proves, according to Miller, that America is the modern kingdom of Babylon.

Early in the new millennium Miller dropped out of sight. His current whereabouts are unknown.

CONCERNED CHRISTIANS

Typology	Christian Protestant Sectarian
Founder	Monte Kim Miller (1954–)
Website	www.kimmillerconcernedchristians.com

▨ Darwin Fish and "A Local Church"

Darwin Fish leads what he calls "A Local Church" in Southern California. Fish was born on May 5, 1961, and raised in the United Methodist tradition. After taking some interest in Mormonism, he joined John MacArthur's Grace Community Church in Panorama City. He was connected with MacArthur for about thirteen years and left in 1992–1993. He attacked MacArthur as a false teacher in 1994. Later Fish resigned from his work as a probation officer and now pastors a small group originally called "God's Word Fellowship" but now known as "A Local Church."

As to whether Fish's church is the only true church, its website states: "We do not know. There was a church in Murfreesboro, TN, but that has since dissolved. Other than that, we have not yet, as of this date (1–11–03), found another church that is in the truth (1 John 4:6), and we have been to many." The question, "Can you name any other true believers/teachers since the early church (A.D. 100) until now?" gets the answer: "No."

Fish condemns as "false teachers" some of the famous leaders in evangelical Christianity, including MacArthur, Charles Stanley, Jack Hayford, Greg Laurie, James Dobson, and Billy Graham. He also condemns all of the early church fathers and accuses Charles Spurgeon of being an "ecumenical false teacher."

Phillip R. Johnson, the elder who led Fish's excommunication from Grace Community Church, provides ongoing critique of Fish's current ministry. A Local Church is not connected in any way with The Local Church of Witness Lee.

Internet Sources

Johnson's Fish Critique: www.atruecult.info/dfishfaq.htm

A Local Church: www.atruechurch.info

▨ Davidian Adventism

Most people connect Davidian Adventism with David Koresh's Branch Davidian movement and the fiery apocalypse that engulfed Koresh and most of his followers on April 19, 1993. However, the Koresh group must be distinguished from others who are part of the larger Davidian tradition.

In 1955 Ben and Lois Roden started the Branch Davidians after the death of Victor Houteff, founder of the Davidian Seventh-day Adventist Association. Houteff's wife, Florence, won a leadership battle against Ben Roden after her husband's demise. But she lost control of her own followers in the early 1960s, and Ben Roden purchased Mount Carmel after its financial collapse.

Some of Victor Houteff's followers set up a continuation of his work in Riverside, California, in 1961, under the leadership of M. J. Bingham. They moved to Exeter, Missouri, and are known as the Bashan Davidians. Bingham (b. February 22, 1905) died on August 1, 1988. His wife, Jemmy (b. December 3, 1928), now leads the movement. She met Bingham when he preached the message of the shepherd's rod in her native Guyana, and they were married in 1955. The group owns twelve hundred acres at Bashan Hill in Exeter.

M. T. Jordan split from Bingham's group and started the Gilead Davidians in Canada. Don Adair moved from California to be with a Davidian group in Salem, South Carolina, and he is now the group's leader. Wanda Blum (formerly Adair's wife) and others split from the Salem group and eventually settled in northern California. Tony Hibbert, a Jamaican living in New York, also led a group of Davidians who split from the Adair movement, and they have their headquarters in Mountain Dale, New York. Some of the Mountain Dale members moved to Waco in 1991 and started a separate Davidian group.

The South Carolina movement is based in the town of Tamassee. They use the title General Association of Davidian Seventh-day Adventists. Adair goes by the title vice president because Victor Houteff is viewed as the last and final president. They have reprinted all forty of Houteff's books and pamphlets.

The New York Davidians are based in Mountain Dale, New York. They use the title General Association of Davidian Seventh-day Adventists and make explicit reference to the works of Victor Houteff as well. The group in Waco refers to itself as Davidian Seventh-day Adventists. They bought the original Mount Carmel site, which Lois Roden had sold to Presbyterians.

All Davidian Adventist groups share many of the doctrines and practices of their Seventh-day Adventist heritage. Where they gain their unique identity, whether as a collective or as individual groups, is the ways in which they have reshaped these doctrines to adopt a different understanding of the church, eschatology, law, and Christian life. Their central unique claim has to do with the prophetic claims made about Victor Houteff. In the case of David Koresh, the apocalyptic element in Davidian Adventism was taken to an extreme. This became a factor in the events that led up to the standoff with government authorities in Waco in 1993.

DAVIDIAN ADVENTISM	
Typology	Christian Protestant Adventist Sectarian
Founder	Victor Houteff (1885-1955)
Websites	General Association of Davidian Seventh-day Adventists Don Adair group (South Carolina): www.davidian.org The Shepherd's Rod (Mountain Dale, NY): www.shepherds-rod-message.org The Shepherd's Rod (Hendersonville, NC) www.shepherds-rod.org

■ Doukhobors

The term *Doukhobor* means "spirit wrestlers," which is a pejorative a Russian Orthodox archbishop used against a sectarian group that resisted the Orthodox religious path. The Doukhobors believed that there was no need for priests or churches and that God can be found through direct spiritual contact. The group suffered intense persecution after its members resisted military inscription. As a signal of their belief in peace, they destroyed their own firearms on June 29, 1895.

Russian authorities allowed more than seven thousand Doukhobors to move to Canada in 1899. The famous Russian novelist Leo Tolstoy aided them in their emigration. They arrived in Halifax, on Canada's east coast, on January 20 and then moved to Saskatchewan where they settled in sixty-one villages. Peter Vasilievich Verigin, their leader, joined them in 1902. The commune lost their land over a legal dispute with the Canadian government in 1907, and many moved to southern British Columbia the next year. Verigin died in a train explosion in 1924. Assassination was suspected, but the case was not solved.

In 1938 those Doukhobors who wanted to maintain communal life organized into the Union of Spiritual Communities of Christ under the leadership of Peter P. Verigin. Most Canadian Doukhobors live in the area of Grand Forks, British Columbia, and in parts of Saskatchewan. The

Doukhobors are now celebrated as part of the Canadian mosaic, though the government of Canada has frequently victimized them.

The Doukhobors have often been identified with the actions of a radical minority group known as The Sons of Freedom. This group, which was centered in Krestova, British Columbia, engaged in acts of terror in response to government persecution in the 1930s. They also were infamous for their nude marches in protest of government policies against them. In 1950 S. S. Sorokin became their leader, and they changed their name to the Christian Community and Brotherhood of Reformed Doukhobors.

Doukhobors are usually pacifists and vegetarian, and they adopt a mystical approach to faith. They reject typical outward symbols of faith, including baptism, though they usually have bread, salt, and water at meetings as symbols of the basic elements of life. The Bible gives way to emphasis on the oral tradition of the movement, especially expressed in hymns. Doukhobors place great stress on living in obedience to the teachings of Jesus.

Doukhobor life retains a deep connection to its Russian roots, in spite of decades of persecution. One Doukhobor hymn reflects a bittersweet reflection on their Canadian base:

Many years we have sojourned, Dear Brethren,

In a land that is foreign and cold,

And your people still have no conception,

Of the truth that we strive to uphold.

Our life here is not for excesses,

But for bringing of life from above;

Let Humanity be as one family,

On the basis of freedom and love.

DOUKHOBORS	
Typology	Christian Orthodox Sectarian
Websites	Voice of the Doukhobors: www.iskra.ca Koozma J. Tarasoff site: www.spirit-wrestlers.com Doukhobors Genealogy: www.doukhobor.org
Recommended Reading	Koozma J. Tarasoff, *Spirit Wrestlers: Doukhobor Pioneers' Strategies for Living* (Ottawa: Legas Publishing)

Efraim

H. J. A. van Geene leads a group known as Efraim, which is based south of Amsterdam. Van Geene claims to be Elijah the prophet, chosen to prepare the bride of Christ for the Second Coming. The group has about one hundred members. It maintains a website that offers elaborate prophetic and biblical speculations about 9/11, the Holy Land, and the end of the world.

The site makes it clear that Efraim followers believe they represent the one church of Jesus. One message reads: "There exists only one bride of Christ, even if they say otherwise a hundred times. Only with us can you really join His bride and only with us will you receive the real special food that God the Father has now only for the bride of His Son. It cannot be that in your country there is now also a bride of Jesus Christ without us knowing it. Neither can there be a leader of the bride of Jesus Christ without us knowing it."

Internet Source

Efraim Website: www.prophetelijah.org

Faith Tabernacle (Philadelphia)

Founded by Charles Reinert, the Faith Tabernacle in Philadelphia has gained notoriety because of the death of members who refuse medical attention. In the summer of 2002 Joyce Reinert died of natural causes a week after she had a miscarriage. She did not seek a doctor as her health worsened. At the end of the year her son Benjamin, age 9, died of a treatable form of leukemia. In 1991 several children from the group died in an outbreak of measles.

The Family International (David Berg)

The Family International is the current name of the group formerly known as the Children of God, the Family of Love, and The Family. This controversial movement started by David Berg in 1968 has been the target of frequent police action, litigation, and media scrutiny worldwide. Berg is known affectionately in the movement as Dad, Father David, and Moses David.

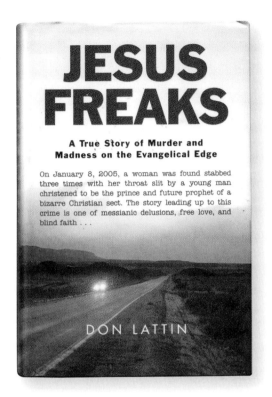

JESUS FREAKS

A True Story of Murder and Madness on the Evangelical Edge

On January 8, 2005, a woman was found stabbed three times with her throat slit by a young man christened to be the prince and future prophet of a bizarre Christian sect. The story leading up to this crime is one of messianic delusions, free love, and blind faith . . .

DON LATTIN

Journalist explores murder/suicide
tragedy in The Family International

David Brandt Berg was born in 1919 to an evangelist mother. Berg married Jane Miller in 1944 and four years later became a minister himself in a Christian and Missionary Alliance church in Arizona. He was forced out in 1951. In 1968 Berg moved with his wife and four children to Huntington Beach, California. Reaching out to the hippies of Southern California, he soon had a small group of followers.

In 1969 Berg led his group out of California, traveling in the United States, settling for a while in Quebec, Canada, and then moving to Jordan's Soul Clinic in Texas in February 1970. By 1972 the group was under pressure from critics, and Berg issued a warning about judgment against America. He and his members soon dispersed to different nations. Berg and his family moved to London, England. He was joined there by his mistress Maria (birth name Karen Zerby), who was twenty-seven years his junior.

Berg communicated with his followers through what were known as "MO letters" or MLs. One of these communications, ML 273, was issued in January 1974 and encouraged the membership to engage in sexual activity with strangers in order to win them to Jesus. This practice was known as "flirty fishing" and constituted one of the most notorious aspects of Berg's ideology. He elaborated on this teaching in 1976 in a string of MO letters known as "King Arthur's Nights."

The group observed liberal sexual policies internally. Sexual activity was encouraged between adults and also between adults and children. Female members made soft-core videos for Father David. Some members-only Family material contained very graphic language and illustrations related to Berg's sexual instructions. The open model of sexuality was curtailed somewhat with MO letter 1434 "Ban the Bomb" (March 1983), which restricted sex to adults in one's own house group. However, flirty fishing continued until 1987.

DAVID BERG AND GROUP TIMELINE

1919—David Brandt Berg is born in Oakland, California (February 18)

1924–33—Virginia Berg (mother) builds and pastors Miami Gospel Tabernacle

1937—Berg moves to California

1941–42—Berg is drafted into US Army and discharged due to poor health

1944—Berg marries Jane Miller (Mother Eve)

1947—Berg studies at Southern California Bible College

1948—Berg becomes a full-time pastor at the Christian and Missionary Alliance Church in Valley Farms, Arizona

1949—Hosea is born; Berg builds church in Valley Farms

1950—Church dismisses Berg as pastor

1951—Berg attends University of Arizona, Tempe

1952—Berg teaches Christian elementary school, California

1953—Berg attends Fred Jordan's Soul Clinic in Los Angeles and Thurber, Texas

Receives the prophetic "Call of David" message

1954—Berg teaches Christian elementary school

1955—Berg starts Miami Soul Clinic in order to train missionaries

1956—Berg starts working for Fred Jordan, booking his TV show nationwide

1959—Berg starts a new Soul Clinic in Miami

1963—Berg and family leave Miami

1963–67—Berg and family live at Texas Soul Clinic (Thurber, Texas)

1968—Berg starts "Teens for Christ" at the Light Club in Huntington Beach

Virginia Berg dies

1969—Berg takes Karen Zerby (aka Maria, present-day leader) as his mistress

Berg and Teens for Christ leave California

1970—A "spirit helper," Abrahim, is revealed to and speaks through Berg

Berg and Zerby leave for Europe and Israel

Berg starts writing MO Letters

1971—Rock star Jeremy Spencer of Fleetwood Mac joins

Fred Jordan evicts COG members from his properties

Berg writes "All Things Revolution" setting the stage for sexual promiscuity in the group

1972—Berg writes that he will die in 1989 and Jesus will return in 1993

2,300 members in forty countries

1973—Berg's oldest son Aaron dies on a mountain near Geneva

Berg publishes *Women in Love (292)*, condoning homosexual relationships between women

Berg and Zerby begin "flirty fishing" (or FF: refers to COG women members using sexual favors to convert and influence prominent men)

1974—Berg publishes the first "FF" MO Letter *The Flirty Little Fishy (293)*

Berg and Zerby move to Tenerife, Canary Islands

Berg writes *The Law of Love* promoting libertarian sexuality

1975—Maria's son, Davidito, born in Tenerife (not announced until 1977)

1976—Group adopts name Family of Love

Berg writes that Jesus had sexually transmitted diseases

1977—Berg and Zerby flee Tenerife

1978—Berg announces that Flirty Fishing should involve payment

Daughter Deborah leaves group

Berg becomes seriously ill due to acute alcoholism

Maria and Davidito proclaimed to be future Two Witnesses of Revelation 11

Davidito Letters begin on upbringing of Davidito (including sexual details)

1979—Defection of two top leaders (Rachel and Timothy)

Peter Amsterdam becomes Berg's right-hand man

1980—Group adopts The Family as name

Berg predicts imminent nuclear war

1981—Prominent member Justus Ashtree leaves

1982—Berg, Zerby, and staff move to Philippines where they stay until 1987

Berg teaches that he has spiritual sex with the Holy Spirit

1983—MO letter bans sex outside of one's Family group home

1984—Halley's Comet in 1986 will herald beginning of the seven-year Great Tribulation

The Children of God: The Inside Story, a book by Deborah, Berg's eldest daughter, is published

1985—*Teen Sex* encourages sex between children before the kids are capable of reproduction

1986—Maria directs Family adults to cease their sexual contact with children and teens

1987—Threat of AIDS curtails sex with outsiders

Flirty Fishing abandoned

1988—U.S. network films abduction of four group children from the group's home in Thailand

1989—Berg and Zerby live in British Columbia

1992—*Summit Jewels* published

Police raid on Family homes in Sydney, Australia

London trial involving Family and child custody case begins

1993—Youth revolt

1994—David Berg (Father David) dies in Portugal (October 15)

1995—Justice Ward delivers verdict in London child custody case

Love Charter promotes less authoritarianism in group

Love Jesus teaching begins promoting sexual intimacy with Jesus

1998—Top World Services staff member James Penn leaves group

2000—Penn writes "No Regrets"

2000–01—Davidito leaves mother and group

2001—MovingOn.org founded for ex-members

2004—Group changes name to Family International

2005—Davidito (aka Ricky Rodriguez) kills Angela Smith and himself

Xfamily.org started

2007—Noah Thomson's film *Children of God: Lost and Found* premieres at Sundance

Not Without My Sister (Kristina Jones, Celeste Jones, Juliana Buhring) published

Jesus Freaks (Don Lattin) published

The Family International faced its most intense scrutiny from the media and the courts from 1988 through 1996. ABC covered the abduction of children from a Family home in Thailand on its *20/20* program in 1988. Two years later the police raided a group home in Barcelona. The Australian Family was raided in 1992, and the British court system targeted The Family in 1992 in a trial that was to last three years. The Argentine Family was raided in 1993. In all these situations concerns were raised about child abuse, particularly allegations of incest, though more attention should have been given to the trauma created on group children by the police raids. Berg died in 1994. Maria then married Peter Amsterdam, and they serve as leaders of the group. Maria and Peter instigated major policy changes in Family practice, including warnings against physical, emotional, and sexual mistreatment of children. They also adopted a more relaxed model of church leadership, expressed in The Family's "Love Charter" that was released in 1995. These changes led the British court to adopt a more open attitude to The Family in its rulings about child custody.

Berg held many of the beliefs central to classical Christianity, though his understandings of salvation, the Trinity, biblical authority, and the nature of the church were warped. His prophetic announcements were reckless, and he held racist views about blacks and Jews. As is obvious to virtually everyone, Berg was a deviant in relation to sex. His views and practices led to enormous sexual and emotional harm to children in his group.

Family leaders distanced themselves from Berg's worst sexual teachings after his death. Leaders have issued the strictest warnings against sex with children, for example. The Family retains the belief that it is morally right to have sex with other adults in one's house group who are of the opposite sex. They also teach that both males and females should think of Jesus as a love partner while engaging in masturbation and think of Jesus as lover during sexual intercourse.

On January 8, 2005, Ricky Rodriguez, Maria's son, killed long-time Family member Angela Smith and then shot himself. Rodriguez (known in the group as Davidito) taped a video before his death and blamed The Family for the rage that led to the murder-suicide. He was once championed as the future leader of the movement but left it in 2001. Family leaders blame the media and the anti-cult movement for fueling Rodriguez's anger and violence. The 2005 rampage led to renewed media focus and greater determination by many ex-members to expose the dark side of The Family.

The Family website offers a sanitized version of Family history and beliefs. The ex-member sites are much more important for gaining details about David Berg and past Family history and literature. These sites provide primary material in abundance. The inside, members-only data is very disturbing and very graphic. It provides abundant proof that Berg was a false prophet and a deceiver.

CONCLUSIONS OF JUSTICE WARD

From February 1992 to November 1995, Sir Alan Ward, a judge in the Court of Appeal of England and Wales and Her Majesty's Most Honourable Privy Council, presided over a prominent court case involving The Family International. He concluded with regard to The Family:

1. I am totally satisfied that there was widespread sexual abuse of young children and teenagers by adult members of The Family, and that this abuse occurred to a significantly greater extent within The Family than occurred in society outside it.

2. Berg was well aware when he propounded his Law of Love that there was a high risk that many who followed it were not mature enough wisely and responsibly to use the freedom (that "dangerous toy") conferred on them in a way which did not cause harm. Harm to children was readily foreseeable as soon as he had schooled The Family to accept that even young children were sexual beings. By endowing children with the same sexual responses as were enjoyed by adults, he made them objects of sex. He placed them within the scope of the Law of Love. That law depends upon full free and informed consent being given to the contemplated activity. Children's consent to sexual activity can never be the product of a free will both because they do not have the maturity to understand the emotional consequences of any sexual engagement, but also because, due to the imbalance of power between adult and child, any decision of the

child is made under influence and pressure. Apparent consent is thereby vitiated.

3. It is, therefore, quite unacceptable for The Family to cast the blame upon the immature or weak members and not to face up to what is a harsh truth unpalatable to them that Berg bears responsibility for propagating the doctrine which so grievously misled his flock and injured the children within it.

With regard to David Berg:

I am completely satisfied that he was obsessed with sex and that he became a perverted man who recklessly corrupted his flock and did many of them serious damage which he made no attempt to redress and for which he never admitted any personal responsibility. Hypocritically he did not practice what he preached, that confession and repentance are good for the soul. Now he is dead. May the Lord have mercy on his soul. There will be many who will not mourn his passing.

With regard to accusations of sexually inappropriate conduct:

By the Law of Love and the belief that to the pure, all things are pure, Berg freed his flock from the restraints which in society control licentious behavior. He knew that he was giving his people "a dangerous toy," the danger being that lust would be mistaken for love. Having encouraged the sexuality of children, they became, as he must have been aware, objects of the Law of Love when he must have appreciated that by reason of their want of age and understanding they were unable to give full and free consent especially under the pressure of advances made upon them by adults. He also must have realized that harm would be caused to them.

THE FAMILY INTERNATIONAL

Typology	Christian Protestant Sectarian
Founder	David Berg (1919–94)
Family Websites	Main Homepage: www.thefamily.org Family Care Foundation: www.familycare.org Aurora Productions: www.auroraproductions.com
Critic Sites	XFamily: www.xfamily.org/ ExFamily.org: www.exfamily.org/ New Day News: www.newdaynews.com Data on Family Care Foundation: www.angelfire.com/ clone/charityalert Family Art Corner: www.geocities.com/familyartcorner
Recommended Reading	William Bainbridge, *The Endtime Family* (Albany: State University of New York Press, 2002) James D. Chancellor, *Life in the Family* (Syracuse University Press, 2000) Deborah Davis, *The Children of God* (Grand Rapids: Zondervan, 1984) Kristina Jones, Celeste Jones, Juliana Buhring, *Not Without My Sister* (London: HarperCollins, 2007) Don Lattin, *Jesus Freaks* (San Francisco: HarperOne, 2007) James R. Lewis & J. Gordon Melton, editors, *Sex, Slander, and Salvation* (Stanford: Center for Academic Publication, 1994) J. Gordon Melton, *The Children of God* (Salt Lake: Signature, 2004) David Van Zandt, *Living in the Children of God* (Princeton: Princeton University Press, 1991) Miriam Williams, *Heaven's Harlots* (New York: William Morrow, 1988)

▓ Father Divine

Father Divine was one of the most flamboyant religious leaders of the twentieth century. He founded the International Peace Mission, based in Philadelphia, but achieved infamy through his claim to be God on Earth. Father Divine was born George Baker, but there is debate about his year of birth. Some accounts suggest 1877 and others 1883. He died in 1965.

Though he was often maligned for his claims of divinity and for his wealthy lifestyle, Father Divine orchestrated massive campaigns for social justice in the bleak years of the Great Depression. He attracted a wide following among blacks in Harlem in the 1930s. The antagonism of mainline religion and the justice system against Father Divine only served to unite his followers. Father Divine was sentenced to a year in jail in 1932 for being a menace to society. The judge died three years after sentencing; and, according to one account, when Father Divine was told of the judge's sudden demise, he responded: "I hated to do it."

Though Father Divine taught chastity to his followers, he was married twice. His first wife was a woman named Pinninnah. They were recognized as husband and wife by 1919. She died in 1937, but Father Divine claimed that his second wife was her reincarnation. Father Divine's followers believed this testimony in spite of the physical differences between the two physical forms. Pinninnah was a large black woman while his next wife was white and slender. The second Mother Divine was Edna Rose Ritchings, a native of Canada. They married on April 29, 1946, a day declared to be the fulfillment of the Marriage Supper of the Lamb described in the Book of Revelation.

Internet Source

International Peace Mission: http://fdipmm.libertynet.org

■ Followers of Christ Church (Walter White)

Based in Oregon, the Followers of Christ Church was founded by Walter White. The church has not had a pastor since White's death in 1969. The movement has been attacked for its faith healing practices. One newspaper report claimed that twenty-one children in the church have died as a result of failure to receive proper medical attention. In 2000 Steven and Ruth Shippy, a couple from Alberta, Canada, received three-year suspended sentences arising from the death of their 14-year-old son, Calahan Shippy, who died on December 30, 1998, from complications related to diabetes. His parents are connected with the Oregon church.

■ The Geftakys Assemblies

In 1971 George Geftakys began a house-church movement in Fullerton, California, based largely on a Plymouth Brethren model of Christianity. Over the next three decades Geftakys, along with his wife, Betty, became leaders to more than fifty different assemblies in the United States. There are also several assemblies in Canada, England, Mexico, and Africa.

The Assembly fell into turmoil in late 2002 and early 2003 when it was revealed that George Geftakys and other leaders did not exercise proper discipline toward George's son David, who was accused of repeated physical assault on his wife and daughter. On January 17, 2003, elders in the Fullerton congregation issued a letter of excommunication against Geftakys.

Internet Sources

Assembly Reflection: www.geftakysassembly.com

Bulletin Board (Brian Tucker): www.briantucker.net/bb

▨ The Global Church of God

Former members of the Worldwide Church of God, the famous group radio preacher Herbert W. Armstrong started in 1934, established the Global Church of God in 1993. Armstrong's successor, Joseph W. Tkach, instituted significant changes in the WCG that led to the formation of many splinter groups, including the Global Church of God. Roderick C. Meredith, one of Armstrong's famous evangelists, originally led GCG. However, Global's Board removed Meredith in 1998 in a dispute over his claim to primacy. Almost 80 percent of the membership went with Meredith, who started the Living Church of God. The Global Church folded under financial pressure, though the remnant in that group formed "The Church of God, a Christian Fellowship." This church merged with the United Church of God in 2001.

Internet Source

Dr. Brian M. Hoselton homepage: www.gcg1.net

▨ Greater Grace World Outreach (Carl H. Stevens)

Carl H. Stevens, the founder of a church movement known as The Bible Speaks, leads this Baltimore-based ministry. Stevens, a one-time baker, began his ministerial work in Maine in 1964. He moved to a new location in South Lennox, Massachusetts, in 1976. While there he was targeted as a cult leader. In the mid-1980s the church went through bankruptcy because a former member, Elizabeth Dovydenas, sued to retrieve

$6 million she had given to the church from 1983 to 1985. The court forced the church to sells its property. Stevens then moved to Baltimore.

Greater Grace World Outreach adopts a standard evangelical doctrinal framework, though cult-watching groups have been critical of Stevens for allegedly inflating his importance to God's kingdom. The church runs the Maryland Bible College and Seminary and has done mission work in 180 countries. Stevens can be heard regularly on his radio program *The Grace Hour*. There are fifty-two churches affiliated with GGWO in the United States.

Internet Source

Greater Grace World Outreach: www.ggwo.org

■ House of Yahweh (Abilene)

Yisrayl Hawkins founded the Sacred Name Assembly in 1980. Hawkins uses elaborate and eccentric points from Hebrew words to argue that Scripture actually prophesies the location and name of his group. He claims that he and his older brother Jacob (founder of the House of Yahweh in Odessa, Texas) are the "two witnesses" of the Book of Revelation.

Yisrayl Hawkins was born in Oklahoma. He and his brother had a radio program in the 1950s that dealt with biblical prophecy and Mosaic Law. Jacob started a House of Yahweh in 1973 in Nazareth, Israel, after he learned that this was the inscription on a newly discovered sanctuary from the time of Jesus. He then built a church with the same title in Odessa, Texas, in 1975. He and Yisrayl parted ways over the use of *Elohim* as a word for God (Jacob was in favor), and Yisrayl started a new House of Yahweh in 1980. Jacob died on March 22, 1991.

Critics have alleged that Yisrayl's group is under his authoritarian spell and that they engage in reckless prophetic speculation. On the latter, Hawkins announced that a nuclear holocaust would occur on September 12, 2006. When no explosion took place, Hawkins announced that the nuclear baby would take nine months to deliver (June 12, 2007). He then argued that God had delayed the nuclear holocaust.

In 2008 Hawkins was arrested on charges of bigamy. He claims that he is a victim of persecution.

Internet Sources

House of Yahweh: www.yahweh.com

Yisrayl Hawkins: www.yisraylhawkins.com

International Churches of Christ

The International Churches of Christ (ICOC) is a controversial movement founded by Kip McKean. The ICOC has roots in the older Church of Christ tradition, also known as the Stone-Campbell Restoration Movement. In the early nineteenth century several Christian leaders, upset at diverse Protestant movements, attempted to return to the original Church of Christ described in the New Testament.

The ICOC emerged from the stricter churches in the Stone-Campbell Movement.

McKean was baptized in the Crossroads Church of Christ in Gainesville, Florida, in 1972. While leading the Lexington Church of Christ near Boston in 1979, he led thirty people to a more radical commitment to Christian life and evangelism. Out of this emerged what became known as the Boston Church of Christ, also known as the Boston Movement. McKean pulled away from the larger Church of Christ tradition in 1987. The title International Churches of Christ was chosen in 1993.

The ICOC has always been criticized for its exclusivist ideology, given its long-standing internal belief that it is *the* body of Christ in the world. As well, critics argue that the movement adopts a legalistic understanding of baptism, especially given the urgency with which members want outsiders to be baptized in order for their sins to be forgiven. The ICOC has also been sharply condemned for its authoritarian style, a possible reflection of Kip McKean's military background.

On November 11, 2001, it was announced that Kip and his wife Elena would take a sabbatical from their leadership roles. Earlier in the year their daughter Olivia had left the church. These two happenings brought discomfort to ICOC members, but there was more shock when Kip McKean announced on November 6, 2002, that he was resigning his position as World Missions Evangelist and top World Sector leader.

McKean stated in his resignation letter: "This hour is personally a time of tears. God through His Word, through circumstances and through true brothers has made it clear that my leadership in recent years has damaged both the Kingdom and my family. My most significant sin is arrogance—thinking I am always right, not listening to the counsel of my brothers, and not seeking discipling for my life, ministry and family. I have not followed Jesus' example of humility in leadership."

The ICOC went through incredible worldwide turmoil in the wake of McKean's departure. Several prominent churches left the movement. In February 2003 Henry Kriete, a leader in the London Church of Christ, wrote a stinging open letter about the systemic evil in the movement. Major ICOC leaders were forced to apologize for their duplication of the leadership style of McKean. The once-united grouping of churches fragmented as different theologies and styles of church life were adopted.

On July 13, 2003, McKean wrote a fifty-page circular letter to all ICOC churches under the title "From Babylon to Zion." He described his spiritual downfall in detail and argued for the movement to return to its original vision. He announced that he had become the leader of the church in Portland, Oregon, and that he and his wife had found a new zeal for Christian work: "Rest assured, at this time Elena and I are totally committed to brotherhood and to evangelizing the world through the fellowship of the ICOC. 'Our highest joy' is Zion. (Psalm 137:6) Therefore, we solicit your prayers that the Spirit will guide us to begin to rebuild the wall, alongside each of you."

INTERNATIONAL CHURCHES OF CHRIST CHRONOLOGY

April 11, 1972—Kip McKean baptized at Crossroads Church of Christ (Gainesville, Florida)

1976—Kip McKean works as campus minister at Heritage Chapel Church of Christ; marriage to Elena

June 1979—Kip McKean leads Lexington Church of Christ (Massachusetts); McKean calls thirty disciples to total commitment

1982—Boston World Missions Seminar; start of Chicago and London churches

1983—NYC Church founded

1985—Toronto Church started

1986—Church plants in South Africa, India, and Europe

1987—*Christian Chronicle* (mainline Church of Christ paper) critiques BCC; McKean pulls away from mainline group; founding of HOPE *worldwide*

1988—World Sector Leaders chosen

1990—Kip and Elena McKean move to Los Angeles

1991—Rick Bauer leaves movement after fourteen years; Ayman Akshar leaves London Church of Christ; Church has 50,000 in attendance; Moscow Church becomes one hundredth church plant

1993—Discipleship Publications International (DPI) started; name "International Churches of Christ" adopted; most of ICOC Mission team in Milan leaves movement

1994—*Evangelization Proclamation* (February 4); Ed Powers leads Indianapolis Church out of movement; ICOC has 146 churches in 53 nations with attendance at 75,000; Kingdom News Network (KNN) started

1995—Los Angeles Church reaches 10,000 in Sunday worship

1996—Michelle Campbell and Catherine Hampton start REVEAL for ex-members; ICOC disciples sent to Jerusalem

1997—ICOC plants three-hundredth church, in Armenia

1998—Kingdom Kids program launched

1999—Movement reaches almost 200,000 members in 372 churches in 158 countries; first International Youth Ministries Conference, "Revolution X," held in Los Angeles

2000—ICOC reaches six-year goal in evangelism

2001—HOPE *worldwide* reaches over half a million in poverty; Olivia McKean, Kip and Elena's daughter, leaves group; announcement that Kip and Elena would take sabbatical (November 11)

2002—Death of Ayman Akshar, prominent ex-member, on March 5; resignation letter from Kip McKean (Wednesday, November 6); unity meeting in Los Angeles (week of November 11)

2003—Evangelist Henry Kriete writes Open Letter to ICOC (February); Los Angeles elders release apology; *Boston Globe* gets interview from McKean for May 17 article; McKean writes fifty-page letter "From Babylon to Zion"

2005—84 ICOC leaders reject McKean

2007—McKean starts separate Sold-Out movement

INTERNATIONAL CHURCHES OF CHRIST

Typology	Christian Stone-Campbell Restoration Sectarian
Founder	Kip McKean
Headquarters	Los Angeles
Critic Sites	www.reveal.org www.rightcyberup.org http://icoc.blogspot.com www.tolc.org

■ Israelite House of David

This group centers on the work of Benjamin Purnell (1861–1927), who believed himself to be the Seventh Messenger of Revelation 10:7. The earlier messengers were Joanna Southcott (d. 1814), Richard Brothers, George Turner, William Shaw, John Wroe, and James Jershom Jezreel (d. 1885). Purnell and his wife, Mary, were members of the Michael Mills commune in Detroit from 1891 to 1895. Mills was a controversial evangelist of the New and Latter House of Israel, the name of the followers of Jezreel who were based in Gillingham, England.

After leaving the Mills group in 1895, Benjamin and Mary engaged in an itinerant ministry for seven years and then settled in Fostoria, Ohio, in 1902—the same year that they published their 780-page work *The Star of Bethlehem*. They moved to Benton Harbor, Michigan, in 1903, claiming divine revelation for the new location. Followers of Wroe's group in Australia linked with Brother Benjamin in 1904. Brother Benjamin taught that he was the spiritual Shiloh predicted by Joanna Southcott, though her prophecies seemed to imply that she was to give literal birth to a physical child.

After Benjamin Purnell's death in 1927 many members followed H. T. Dewhirst as leader. Others chose to follow Mary Purnell, who created the Israelite House of David as Reorganized in 1930. Her group follows the same ideology as the original with the exception of giving Mary an increased status in divine history. Mary's group claims that she opted for an out-of-court settlement with Dewhirst to spare her community from further bitterness and strife.

Both groups have emphasized celibacy, though there were frequent allegations that Benjamin Purnell engaged in sexual relations with some of his female followers. The Israelites in both groups stressed vegetarianism and pacifism. Many members also took the Nazirite vow to not cut their hair.

The original group attracted attention for their House of David baseball team, which traveled the country. When the House split in 1930, Mary's group also sponsored a team.

Internet Sources

Israelite House of David: www.israelitehouseofdavid.org

Mary Purnell's Israelite group: www.maryscityofdavid.org

Christian Israelite Church (Australia): www.cichurch.asn.au

▪ Jesus Christians (Dave McKay)

Dave McKay was born in Rochester, New York, and moved to Australia in 1968. He was involved with the Children of God (now known as The Family International) for a brief time and then broke away from them to form his own group. McKay has a small following, but his followers have received worldwide attention because of charges that they kidnapped a

British boy into their group. They have also received significant attention because members have adopted a policy of donating kidneys to those in need of a transplant.

The Lord Our Righteousness Church

The Lord Our Righteousness Church is a small but controversial movement started in Idaho in 1987 by Wayne Bent. Bent (b. 1941) is a former Seventh-day Adventist pastor. He and his congregation moved to Strong City, New Mexico, in 1987–88. Bent views himself as a messiah figure and contends that he has a role in fulfilling Bible prophecy. He took the name Michael Travesser (Travesser is a creek near Strong City) and identified two females in the church as the "Two Witnesses" of Revelation 11. The Strong City group believed that 2007 was the end of the 70 weeks prophesied in Daniel 9:24.

Image of Wayne Bent, convicted leader
of Strong City group, New Mexico

Photo: The Lord Our Righteousness Church

In 2008 Bent was convicted on charges of sexual misconduct with two minors who were part of a group of seven virgins chosen to "sleep with the Lord." Bent denied having intercourse with the two minors and argued that the touching that took place was spiritual in nature. The group was the object of police investigations in 2002 and 2004 over allegations of a possible mass suicide.

Bent wrote about his sentencing: "As I sat at the desk at 8:20 a.m., waiting for the jurors to come into court before the beginning of deliberation for the second day, the Father revealed to me what the verdict was going to be. What came to me was, 'guilty on all counts.' I wrote 8:20 a.m. and GOAC on a piece of tissue paper, the only paper available to me at the moment. He also showed me why the world had to convict me. It was because they were now going to be convicted by the heavenly court and found guilty for all of their hidden offenses before heaven. They convicted the Son of man and now they were going to be convicted."

There are about 50 members left in the group. The church is profiled in a BBC documentary called *The End of the World Cult*, directed by Ben Anthony.

THE LORD OUR RIGHTEOUSNESS CHURCH

Founder	Wayne Bent (aka Michael Travesser)
Websites	http://strongcity.info/
Critic Sites	Prudence Welch (ex-member) http://www.travesser.info/ Mark Horner http://beyond90seconds.com/

◾ Metropolitian Community Churches

The association of Metropolitan Community Churches dates back to October 6, 1968, when Troy Perry started a church based on a positive attitude toward homosexuality. The first meeting took place with twelve people in Perry's home in Huntington Park, California. Perry writes: "There wasn't a dry eye in the place. A hush fell over the place and everybody in that small living room was weeping silently. We all felt that we were a part of something great. God was preparing to move. We were to see God's handiwork, and that would be unbelievable." The MCC now has more than three hundred congregations spread across twenty-two countries.

Since the formation of the MCC, other denominations have adopted a pro-gay view, including the United Church of Christ, the Episcopal Church, and the United Church of Canada. The Anglican movement worldwide has experienced enormous friction because of the Episcopal Church's 2003 decision to ordain Gene Robinson, an openly gay pastor, as Bishop of New Hampshire.

Virtually all mainline denominations have a lobby in favor of acceptance of gays, lesbians, bisexuals, and transgender persons. There are pro-gay groups for a range of religious groups and movements: Evangelicals Concerned is pro-gay while Dignity USA reaches Catholics and "A Common Bond" reaches Jehovah's Witnesses.

The MCC is quite conservative in its overall theology. Its Statement of Faith affirms the Trinity and adopts a high view of Scripture. This contrasts with some pro-gay churches that are quite radical in their Christology and that explicitly repudiate the authority of Scripture. The MCC website states: "Lesbians and gay men face discrimination because of societal attitudes. Unfortunately, these attitudes are often taught by the church. Sadly, the Bible is often used as a weapon to 'bash' gays and lesbians. It is important to remember that such hurtful things are not a reflection of Christ, or the way God wants the church to be, or even what the Bible really says."

How should evangelical Christians respond to pro-gay churches like the MCC?

First, response must be rooted in love, especially since gays endure so much hate in both church and society. Evangelicals should find disturbing anti-gay rhetoric that amounts to hate speech, as illustrated by Fred Phelps's infamous work at Westboro Baptist Church in Topeka, Kansas. Phelps warns against "the maudlin, kissy-pooh, feel-good, touchy-feely preachers of today's society."

Second, the position that homosexuality is wrong is based on the clear teaching of Scripture and is the dominant tradition in the history of Christian faith. Robert Gagnon has defended the traditional interpretation about Scriptural teaching in his exhaustive work *The Bible and Homosexual Practice*. Bruce Metzger, the famous Princeton New Testament scholar, wrote a stinging rebuke of his own denomination's task force on homosexuality because of its neglect of the plain reading of the Bible. Resistance to pro-gay theology is rooted in the Creation mandate of heterosexual marriage, in the prohibitions against same-sex acts in both Old and New Testament, and in the teachings of the church fathers and leaders of the Reformation.

METROPOLITAN COMMUNITY CHURCHES

Typology	Christian Protestant Pro-Gay
Founder	Troy Perry
Website	www.mcchurch.org
Other Pro-Gay Sites	Religious Archives Network: www.lgbtran.org Whosoever Magazine (Online): www.whosoever.org Evangelicals Concerned: www.ecwr.org
Sites Critical of Pro-Gay Theology	Exodus Global Alliance (Pat Lawrence): http://exodusglobalalliance.org Exodus International: http://exodus.to Sy Rogers: www.syrogers.com Genesis Counseling (Joe Dallas): www.genesiscounseling.org National Association for Research and Therapy of Homosexuality: www.narth.com, www.robgagnon.net P.A.T.H.: www.pathinfo.org
Recommended Reading	Joe Dallas, *A Gay Gospel?* (Eugene: Harvest House, 2007) Robert Gagnon, *The Bible and Homosexual Practice* (Nashville: Abingdon, 2001) David Greenberg, *The Construction of Homosexuality* (Chicago: University of Chicago Press, 1988) Stanton Jones and Mark Yarhouse, *Homosexuality: The Use of Scientific Research in the Church's Moral Debate* (Downers Grove: InterVarsity, 2000) Elizabeth Moberly, *Homosexuality: A New Christian View* (Cambridge: James Clark, 1983)

■ Peoples Temple

The Peoples Temple will forever be associated with the mass suicide and murders of more than nine hundred of its members on November 18, 1978, in the jungles of Guyana. The deaths and killings in Jonestown immediately framed popular discourse about so-called cult groups; and Peoples Temple founder, the Reverend Jim Jones, has become the archetype of a cult leader.

James Warren Jones was born in 1931. His group, known originally as Wings of Deliverance, started in Indianapolis in 1955. In 1959 the group became part of the Disciples of Christ. Jones and a small cadre spent a few years in Brazil in the early 1960s and then moved to northern California in 1965. The group had a significant outreach to the poor in both San Francisco and Los Angeles. Jones was a dynamic preacher, but he was also increasingly paranoid and controlling. His early Christian vision gave way to a Marxist and anarchistic utopianism.

Jim Jones (right rear) with followers

Photo: Jonestown Institute

In 1976 the Peoples Temple leased almost four thousand acres from the government of Guyana. Jones and the majority of his followers moved there the next year. By then Jones had attracted a vocal opposition in California, particularly from a group known as the Concerned Relatives. They charged Jones and the top leadership of Peoples Temple with financial mismanagement and fake healings and even with conducting suicide drills. The Concerned Relatives also engaged in a custody battle over John Victor Stoen, a boy in the group.

In June 1978, six months before the massacre, Jonestown escapee Deborah Layton, in an affidavit to the United States government, warned of a potential massacre and also complained about suicide drills. This and other allegations led Congressman Leo Ryan on a fact-finding mission to Jonestown in November. While Ryan and others were waiting at an airstrip to fly back home, several young men from the compound opened fire on them. Ryan and four others (three members of the media and one defector) were killed. Others were wounded. Shortly after the assault, Jones led his followers in a mass suicide ritual known as the White Night. A total of 913 persons died at the compound. Larry Layton, Deborah's brother, was imprisoned for his role in the shootings at the airport, though he did not kill anyone.

Several factors make the tragedy of Jonestown more complex than discourse about cultic religion usually involves. First, Jones was an ordained minister in the Disciples of Christ, a mainstream Protestant denomination. Second, he was widely supported in the political and civic worlds of California. He was recognized as a passionate supporter of social justice— a fact often ignored in later discussions about him. Third, the group did experience intense opposition, fueling Jones's paranoia and leading his hard-core followers to adopt his apocalyptic response to criticism.

None of these caveats absolve Jones and his top leaders of their responsibility for the murders and suicides. Apart from a few conspiracy theorists, most writers on the Peoples Temple recognize that Jones's pathology was the ultimate explanation for the events of November 18, 1978. The vast majority of new religions survive the death of the founder. This is not so with the religion Jim Jones built. The Peoples Temple no longer exists and the Jonestown site is not maintained.

PEOPLES TEMPLE

Founder	Jim Jones (1931–78)
Websites	Alternative Considerations of Jonestown & Peoples Temple (Rebecca Moore and Fielding M. McGehee III): http://jonestown.sdsu.edu Deborah Layton: www.peoplestemple.com
Recommended Reading	David Chidester, *Salvation and Suicide* (Bloomington: Indiana University, 1988, 2003) John Hall, *Gone from the Promised Land* (New Brunswick: Transaction Books, 1987, 2004) Deborah Layton, *Seductive Poison* (New York: Doubleday, 1998) Rebecca Moore, *A Sympathetic History of Jonestown* (Lewiston, N.Y.: Edwin Mellen Press, 1985) Tim Reiterman and John Jacobs, *Raven* (New York: Dutton, 1982)

◾ Rastafarian

Rastafarian is a religious and political movement that emerged in Jamaica in the third decade of the twentieth century. Early Rastafarian leaders like Leonard Howell and Joseph Nathaniel Hibbert found their original inspiration from the radical teachings of Black Nationalist prophet Marcus Garvey (1887–1940). Most people know Rastafarian through reggae or the dreadlock hairstyle of its followers. Bob Marley and Burning Spear have been the movement's most famous vocal ambassadors. The religion is also known for its ritual use of marijuana or *ganja*.

Burning Spear in concert

Photo: Derek Beverley

The term *Rastafarian* comes from Ras Tafari, who became Emperor Haile Selassie I of Ethiopia in 1930. Early Rastafarians looked to him as a messianic figure who would lead blacks out of oppression. Rastas placed great import on the titles given to Haile Selassie. He was called "King of Kings, Lord of Lords, Conquering Lion of the Tribe of Judah, Defender of the Faith and Light of the World." Haile Selassie was also claimed to be 225th descendant from Solomon, the son of King David.

These factors led early Rastafarians to proclaim that the emperor was divine, even though he had formal ties with the Ethiopian Orthodox Church. The emperor was disconcerted by Rastafarian worship of him when he visited Jamaica in 1966. While the emperor was alive, Rastafarians believed that he would bring Africans back to their homeland. With his death in 1975, that affirmation is taken in a less literal sense. Rastafarians often identify Haile Selassie as Jesus Christ.

There is little rigidity in Rastafarian doctrine and lifestyle, particularly in the last several decades. Most followers believe that blacks, the true descendants of the Hebrews, were sent into slavery and exile because of disobedience to Jah or Jehovah. Rastafarians claim that whites have kept them in Babylon. Some Rastas use Bible references to defend the use of ganja. Other Rastas protest the use of the Christian Bible as a tool of the white race. Many Rastas use a version of the Bible known as the Holy Piby, compiled by Robert Athlyi Rogers of Anguilla from 1913 through 1917. Generally, Rastafarian culture is patriarchal, though women have increasing leadership roles outside of the home. This is documented in Barry Chevannes's significant ethnographic fieldwork in Jamaica.

There is no one organization or person that speaks for all Rastafarians. The better known groups are The Twelve Tribes of Israel, the House of Bobo, and the Nyahbinghi Order. The Order states in its anthem: "To advance, to advance with truths and rights, To advance, to advance with love and light. With righteousness leading. I n I Hail to Rastafari I n I King, Imanity is pleading, One Jah for I n I." ("I n I" is a common Rastafarian phrase that reflects unity with Jah.) Some Rastas have argued that the popularization of Rasta music and culture has led to an accommodation with the larger white culture once so widely vilified.

RASTAFARIAN	
Websites	Nyahbinghi Order: www.nyahbinghi.org House of Bobo: http://houseofbobo.com Ras Adam Simeon site: http://web.syr.edu/~affellem Rasta Times: www.rastafaritimes.com Rastafari Speaks: www.rastafarispeaks.com
Recommended Reading	Leonard Barrett, *The Rastafarians* (Boston: Beacon Press, 1997) Barry Chevannes, *Rastafari* (Syracuse University Press, 1994) William David Spencer, *Dread Jesus* (London: SPCK, 1999) Nathaniel Murrell, William David Spencer, and Adrian McFarlane, eds. *Chanting Down Babylon* (Philadelphia: Temple, 1998)

The Roberts Group

In 1971 Jim Roberts founded a nomadic group of followers most famously known as the Garbage Eaters. They are also known as the Brotherhood and The Brethren. Composed of about one hundred members, they travel within North America in small groups. Roberts has taught them to embrace suffering and poverty in order to gain salvation. They earned the name Garbage Eaters because of their practice of searching dumpsters for discarded food. The Roberts Parents Group calls this "Dumpster Diving." The group's members dress very simply, travel by bicycle, and take Hebrew names. Followers separate completely from their natural family.

New members often send a letter home saying that they are well but will never write again. The parents' group posts letters on their website addressed to their children and even to their leader. One of the letters to Roberts implores: "I am asking you to ask your followers to email their parents (we can't find out their whereabouts through email) and let them know they are OK that they are not perishing in the woods in the freezing snow. Teach them a lesson in compassion and love. They love their parents. They are making great sacrifice to follow you and your spoken and unspoken wishes."

Jim Guerra tells of his ten years in the group in his book *From Dean's List to Dumpsters* (Pittsburgh: Dorrance Publishing). Guerra also wrote an open letter to his former colleagues in which he accuses Roberts of being anti-biblical in his control over the group, in his discouragement of marriage, and in his resistance to criticism. He writes: "What has happened to the church since it started out in 1971 as just a traveling Christian ministry? How has it gotten to its current state, where members are distrustful of one another, secretive, deceitful, self-righteous, hateful toward their families, unwilling to be corrected? Very simply. Your leader is not accountable to anyone."

Gene Scott

Gene Scott, a former denominational executive, was the controversial and enigmatic pastor of the Los Angles University Cathedral. Dubbed the "largest Protestant cathedral," the church, which Scott described as "the most unique ministry in the 2,000 years of the church," claims fifteen thousand members. He began a nightly television show in 1975 called "The University Network," which broadcasts twenty-four hours a day in most of the world.

Scott earned a Ph.D. in Philosophies of Education from Stanford in 1957. His television show made him infamous, given his unusual broadcasting style, which included on-air cursing, cigar smoking, focus on his equestrian team, and insulting comments to his studio and television audience. A major report in *The Los Angeles Times* pictured him this way on his show: "Piercing blue eyes stare through half-framed reading specs and gold-rimmed shades, worn one on top of the other. A mouthful of perfectly aligned, pearl-white teeth sneers behind a wispy beard. Shocking white hair stands out each night from under assorted head wear—a Stetson, a Stanford cap, a crown, even a sombrero."

Scott was born on August 14, 1929, in Buhl, Idaho. His family moved to northern California in the 1930s. He married Betty Ann Frazer in the early 1950s but divorced her after twenty-three years. Scott called her "the Devil's sister" and said on his show, "I hate her. If I go to heaven and she's there, I'm going to another planet." He remarried, divorced a second time, and married a third time before his death in February 2005.

In earlier years Gene Scott helped Oral Roberts establish his university in Tulsa, Oklahoma. Scott also worked for years in the Assemblies of God, resigning in 1970. In 1975 he became pastor of the Glendale, California Faith Center Church, which moved later to its current downtown location. The University Cathedral can be reached at P.O. Box 1, Los Angeles. Visitors need to get a ticket (at no cost) in order to attend Sunday worship. The Cathedral has an incredible collection of artwork. Scott's widow, Melissa, now leads the University Cathedral.

Sources

Official Dr. Gene Scott website: www.drgenescott.org

Melissa Scott: www.pastormelissascott.com

Glenn F. Bunting, "The Shock Jock of Televangelism," *Los Angeles Times* (7/10/94)

▪ Sold-Out Discipling Movement Churches

Kip McKean, the controversial founder of the International Churches of Christ (ICOC), founded the Sold-Out Discipling Movement Churches in 2006. The ICOC, a split-off of the older Church of Christ movement, was known originally as the Boston Church of Christ.

McKean led the ICOC until his resignation as World Leader in 2002. He had hoped to regain leadership in 2003 but was rejected by the major leaders in the movement. In 2005 eighty-four of these leaders withdrew their fellowship from Kip. McKean had become a leader in Portland, Oregon, and many of the ICOC members followed McKean as part of the Sold-Out group. McKean started a Los Angeles group in 2007 known as the City of Angels International Christian Church. McKean is now world evangelist for the new movement.

The split between ICOC and the Sold-Out churches is largely over allegiance to McKean as leader. Doctrinally, both groups adopt a conservative, evangelical Protestant theology with the Church of Christ emphasis on believer's baptism. The ICOC is now the more open of the two churches. The ICOC no longer places as much emphasis on worldwide church government and uniformity.

As of mid-2008, the Sold-Out movement has fourteen congregations in the U.S. and sixteen international congregations.

Internet Sources

City of Angels International Christian Church: http://www.upsidedown21.org

City of Angels International Christian Church homepage: www.caicc.net

Kip McKean biography: www.kipmckean.org

▪ Twelve Tribes

Twelve Tribes is the latest designation for a Christian commune Elbert Eugene ("Bert") Spriggs leads. The group was known for years as the Northeast Kingdom Community Church, based in Island Pond, Vermont. Spriggs and his followers moved to Vermont in 1978, after six years of ministry based in Chattanooga, Tennessee. Spriggs is known as Yoneq in the group.

Twelve Tribes Community, California

Photo: Eileen Barker

In the 1980s the group came under intense scrutiny from cult-watching groups and from Vermont law enforcement. There were concerns about child abuse involving excessive discipline of children, and ex-members also accused the leadership of authoritarianism, hypocrisy, and illegal activities (involving failure to comply with birth registries and burial permits). Tensions heightened in 1983 over claims that Spriggs and his wife, Marsha, took away a young girl named Lydia Mattatall without the consent of her father, Juan (who had legal custody of Lydia). Furthermore, Eddie Wiseman, the number-two leader in the group, was blamed for beating a young girl named Darlynn Church in May 1983. (The criminal case against him was eventually dropped.)

These issues and others led Vermont state officials to authorize a police raid on the homes of church members. The raid took place in the predawn hours of June 22, 1984, and involved ninety Vermont police officers. One hundred twelve children were taken from their homes in order to be examined by social workers. However, the legality of the raid was questioned immediately, and the children were allowed to return home. A Vermont judge ruled that the raid was unconstitutional. In the last two decades the communal group has continued to face child custody issues, though not in the fashion of the 1984 raid.

On a personal note, I was involved in public debates about this group in the 1980s. At the time, after careful investigation, I concluded that Eddie Wiseman was too harsh in his discipline of Darlynn Church. I base my view on interviews with her and her family and also from a medical report on Darlynn. The Mattatall case should be viewed in favor of the Twelve Tribes. Lydia's father, Juan, was a pedophile, and the group was right in their arguments in court that the mother should have retained custody of Lydia and the other children. Juan lied to me and others about himself and the group. Juan's own mother murdered him in 1990, just before she committed suicide.

The Twelve Tribes have homes in the United States, Canada, the United Kingdom, Australia, Argentina, Brazil, France, Germany, and Spain. Group members view themselves as the body of Christ, dismissing both the Catholic and the Protestant traditions. The Twelve Tribes refer to Jesus as "Yahshua" and believe that communal living is necessary for salvation. They do not send their children to public schools, colleges, or universities. They do not allow the use of television but maintain an attractive website.

Evangelical Christian scholars argue that the Twelve Tribes is sectarian in its ideology. The movement is prone to legalism and works-righteousness. Leaders put too much emphasis on issues such as dress codes and hairstyles. They would do well to foster more independence among members and abandon their simplistic dualism that creates unnecessary conflicts with ex-members, courts, and the world outside their group. Insiders have been taught that blacks are a slave class and that Martin Luther King's murder was a good thing.

Yoneq fosters dependence upon his rule through false comparisons with New Testament apostles, developing an antirational mind-set in the group and equating his word with the direction of the Lord. His teachings are rarely self-critical, and he is obsessed with the Twelve Tribes as the only work of God on the earth.

Several websites provide careful critique of the Twelve Tribes, including Bob Pardon's reports at his New England Institute of Religious Research. James Howell and Michael Painter, two prominent ex-members, have also provided extensive analysis of the movement. Howell was a former top aide to Yoneq.

TWELVE TRIBES

Typology	Christian Protestant Sectarian
Homepage	Twelve Tribes: www.twelvetribes.com
Critical Websites	NEIRR research (Bob Pardon): http://neirr.org/mcconclu.html Twelve Tribes-Ex: www.twelvetribes-ex.org Jacob Eberhardt site: http://www.twelvetribesteachings.com Yoneq and the Twelve Tribes: http://yattt.blogspot.com/

▪ The Two-by-Two's

"Two-by-Two's" is one of several terms outsiders have given to several groups that can be traced to the ministry of a Scotsman named William Irvine (1863–1947). Irvine was associated for several years with Faith Mission, which George Govan (1861–1927) founded in 1886. Irvine departed from the Mission in 1901, and Edward Cooney and others joined him. Irvine created a split in the movement because of his claims about 1914 being the end of the age of grace. Irvine also taught that he was one of the two witnesses mentioned in Revelation 11. Irvine excommunicated Cooney (b. 1867) in 1928. Cooney moved to Australia and died there in 1960. Irvine maintained a small following until his death in Jerusalem.

The Two-by-Two's are often called Irvineites and Cooneyites in spite of the schisms. They are also called Black Stockings, a reference to the stockings preachers of the movement allegedly wore in its earliest years. Members refer to themselves simply as Christians and as followers of "The Truth." They often register with governments as "Christian Conventions" and "Assemblies of Christians." They gather in house churches and believe that church buildings are contrary to New Testament teaching. Their focus has been on the support of ministers who go two-by-two, according to their interpretation of Matthew 10:7. A slogan in the movement picks up these emphases: "the ministers without a home, and the church in the home."

Critics of this house-church movement, in its various forms, accuse it of legalism, authoritarianism, denial of the Trinity, and works-righteousness. Followers believe that they are the one church of Jesus and that other churches are false. David Stone argues in *The Church Without a Name* that the movement is emotionally damaging to both members and those who leave the fellowship.

Internet Sources

Anti-Two-by-Two's

Research and Information Services: www.workersect.org

The Lying Truth: www.thelyingtruth.info

Pro-Two-by-Two's

Friends of Truth: www.friendsoftruth.net

Topics in Bible: www.homestead.com/prosites-hobarker/topicsinbible.html

The Way International

Victor Paul Wierwille founded The Way International (TWI), based in New Knoxville, Ohio. Born on December 31, 1916, Wierwille was ordained in 1941 in the Evangelical and Reformed Church; and in 1942 he started a radio ministry known as Vesper Chimes. He pastored St. Peter's Church (Van Wert, Ohio) until 1957. He claims that he received the baptism of the Holy Spirit through speaking in tongues in 1951. Two years later he produced the first version of his Power for Abundant Living course. He resigned from his denomination in 1958.

TWI became the target of the counter-cult movement in the 1970s. The most notorious charge had to do with allegations of weapons training for TWI membership. The Way leadership said that these charges were a result of misunderstanding The Way's participation in a state program on hunting safety. TWI also underwent an internal crisis in 1986 and 1987 over evidence of sexual libertarian practices by Wierwille and other Way leaders. John Juedes has provided extensive evidence that Wierwille plagiarized from various sources and that he was careless about major claims in his spiritual journey.

Religious positions of the TWI founder raise concerns. Wierwille believed that the Bible was originally written in Aramaic (it was actually written mostly in Hebrew and Greek). Wierwille taught that Christians are not subject to the Gospels and the Book of Acts; he placed emphasis instead on Paul's later epistles. The Way leader also denied the Trinity in his work *Jesus Christ Is Not God.*

CRAIG MARTINDALE ON EX-MEMBER

"Oh, I love the one comment the former moron, ex-follower, that they quote so often, guy hasn't got two brains to rub together, I tell you what, two brain cells to rub together, the spirits have chewed him up so bad. He says I got more control over you than the Pope does over the Roman Catholics. How do you like that, Bible fans? How do you like that? Well at least I don't wear a big stupid hat!"

—Sunday Night Service Video #1876; May 4, 1997

Similar problematic positions appear in TWI's theology. The group rejects water baptism and communion. Members believe that it is necessary to speak in tongues to be a Christian. And while they affirm the atonement of Jesus and his resurrection from the dead, they believe that Jesus died on a Wednesday and rose on Saturday.

Craig Martindale became the second president of The Way International in 1982, three years before its founder's death in 1985. Martindale and his wife, Donna, adopted an aggressive policy against members who were not totally devoted to Way leadership. Donna stated that a female follower died in a plane crash because the girl's father was not obedient to the group's leadership. The Way's most serious internal crisis took place in 1987 when ex-members provided evidence of sexual indiscretions by Wierwille, Craig Martindale, and other top leaders.

In early 2000 Paul and Frances Allen sued for fraud, sexual assault, and breach of contract against TWI. Frances claimed in the suit that she was coerced into sex with Craig Martindale. Martindale resigned as president shortly after the Allen suit was launched. He denied the assault charge but admitted to having an affair. The Allen couple accepted a settlement from the group in late 2000. Their case created a crisis in the movement. After Martindale's multiple sexual affairs were revealed to The Way's board, it moved to suspend him from office, investigated the charges, and eventually removed him from any leadership role in the organization.

The TWI homepage makes no mention of Wierwille or Martindale. Rosalie F. Rivenbark is the current president.

Several splinter groups formed because of objections to either Wierwille or Martindale. The largest group is Christian Educational Services, based in Indianapolis and led by John Schoenheit, John Lynn, and Mark Graeser. A lot of members left The Way after reading Chris Geer's account of Wierwille's last days in "The Passing of a Patriarch." Christian Family Fellowship formed in 1996 and is based in Tipp City, Ohio.

THE WAY INTERNATIONAL

Typology	Christian Protestant Sectarian
Founder	Victor Paul Wierwille (1916–86)
Homepage	www.theway.com
Critic Sites	The Path of Christ Ministry (Patrick Roberge): www.waychrist.com The Cult that Snapped (Karl Kahler site): www.ex-way.com Grease Spot Café: www.greasespotcafe.com
Splinter Groups	Christian Family Fellowship: www.cffm.org Christian Educational Services (CES): http://stfonline.org Ex-CES site: http://ex-ces.faithweb.com

6

HINDUISM

Hindu temple, Calabasa

Photo: Gordon Melton

The word *Hinduism* is now used in a way that implies that there is a unified view of India's majority religious tradition. However, the narrative of the Hindu tradition is actually a story of many traditions, both complex and contradictory. For example, Hindus have not had a consistent or constant understanding of God throughout history. The earliest Hindu scriptures express belief in a host of gods and goddesses. Thus, the first Vedic (earliest Hindu strand) material mentions the worship of Agni, Soma, Varuna, Indra, and other deities. Gradually this polytheism became replaced by a focus on the famous trinity of Hinduism: Brahma, Vishnu, and Shiva.

In Hinduism, Vishnu and Shiva have been the dominant gods in the last two millennia, though Krishna also emerges as a powerful deity. Hindus have continued to worship the feminine aspect of the divine in goddesses like Durga or the divine consorts of Vishnu, Shiva, and Krishna. There is also a longstanding adoration of Ganesh, the elephant-headed god, and Hanuman, the famous monkey god, and many other deities peculiar to particular regions of India or specific traditions in Hinduism.

HINDUISM 101

- Hindus believe the one supreme God manifests in various forms.

- Hindus have often venerated a triad of deities: Brahma, Vishnu, and Shiva.

- There are thousands of gods and goddesses in Hinduism.

- Hinduism is pantheistic, and humans share in the divine reality.

- Some Hindus believe that God is impersonal; others hold that God is personal.

- Hindus believe that the deities dwell in images that the devotee is to adore.

- Hinduism has a vast corpus of scripture, including the Vedas and the Upanishads.

- The Bhagavad-Gita is the most loved of Hindu scriptures.

- Humans are caught in the cycle of *samsara* (karma and reincarnation).

- Salvation is known as *moksha* and means release from *samsara*.

- This world is one of *maya* or illusion.

- Realization that the soul (*atman*) is divine (*Brahman*) is the key to salvation.

- Some Hindus believe that individuality will be merged with divinity.

- Other Hindus believe that individuals will be in union with God but retain identity.

- Orthodox Hindus believe God created the caste system.

- Hindus believe that gods come to earth (*avatars*) to help humanity.

- Krishna is the favorite avatar in the Hindu religion.

- Salvation is both by the grace of the gods and the work of human beings.

- Most Hindus believe that the stories of their deities are historically true.

- Proper living involves faith in God, good works, and proper worship.

- Hinduism places great stress on having a guru to guide one's spiritual path.

- Hinduism puts much emphasis on mystical experience.

- Hindus believe the world was created 311,040 billion years ago.

- All life is sacred, and non-injury (*ahimsa*) is to be adopted toward all living things.

- Hinduism places focus on annual pilgrimages to holy sites throughout India.

Western scholars have often overstated Hindu commitment to God as ultimately impersonal, a position known as *advaitism*. They commonly argue that all Hindus believe in a pantheistic or monistic understanding of God. Of course, many Hindu gurus and philosophers defend this view as essential to Hinduism. However, there are still millions of Hindus who believe that God is ultimately personal. The Hare Krishna movement, for example, has made the personalist position widely known worldwide.

TEN AVATARS OF VISHNU

1. Matsya	5. Vaman	8. Balaram or Buddha
2. Kurma	6. Parasuram	9. Krishna
3. Varaha	7. Rama	10. Kalki
4. Narasingh		

Hindu Scripture

Hindu scholars distinguish between sacred writings believed to be direct revelations from God and writings that serve as lesser vehicles of religious truth. The former category is known as *sruti* (Sanskrit for "what is heard"). This highest category of revelation is applied to the Vedas and the Upanishads. There are four famous Vedic collections: the Rigveda, the Samaveda, the Yajurveda, and the Atharveda. The Vedas comprise the earliest scriptures for Hindus, while the Upanishads comprise a second phase of divine revelation.

Hindus give enormous weight to a second level of religious texts. The Bhagavad-Gita has gained particular honor and is often called the "Bible" of Hinduism, even though it is part of a long epic poem. R. C. Zaehner, the famous scholar of Hinduism, stated that the Gita is "the most important, the most influential, and the most luminous of all the Hindu scriptures" (*Hinduism*, p. 10). The traditions of the gods and goddesses are recorded in the Puranas. Most famous here are the stories about the pastimes of Lord Krishna. The Laws of Manu provide details on ritual and moral guidance.

Transcendental Meditation Golden Dome at Maharishi University

Photo: Lucy Lowe

NINE ESSENTIALS OF HINDUISM

1. Hindus believe in the divinity of the Vedas, the world's most ancient scripture, and venerate the Agamas as equally revealed. These primordial hymns are God's word and the bedrock of Sanatana Dharma, the eternal religion that has neither beginning nor end.

2. Hindus believe in a one, all-pervasive Supreme Being who is both immanent and transcendent, both Creator and Unmanifest Reality.

3. Hindus believe that the universe undergoes endless cycles of creation, preservation, and dissolution.

4. Hindus believe in karma, the law of cause and effect by which each individual creates his own destiny by his thoughts, words, and deeds.

5. Hindus believe that the soul reincarnates, evolving through many births until all karmas have been resolved, and moksha, spiritual knowledge and liberation from the cycle of rebirth, is attained. Not a single soul will be eternally deprived of this destiny.

6. Hindus believe that divine beings exist in unseen worlds and that temple worship, rituals, sacraments, as well as personal devotionals create a communion with these devas and Gods.

7. Hindus believe that a spiritually awakened master, or satguru, is essential to know the Transcendent Absolute, as are personal discipline, good conduct, purification, pilgrimage, self-inquiry and meditation.

8. Hindus believe that all life is sacred, to be loved and revered, and therefore practice ahimsa, "noninjury."

9. Hindus believe that no particular religion teaches the only way to salvation above all others, but that all genuine religious paths are facets of God's Pure Love and Light, deserving tolerance and understanding.

—From the Himalayan Academy, founded by Gurudeva

■ Hinduism and Salvation

Hindus believe humans are caught in *samsara*, the cycle of birth, death, and afterlife. In this age of bondage (*kali-yuga*), Hindus hope for *moksha* (the term for liberation or salvation) by getting beyond the impact of negative karma. Hindus believe in reincarnation and hope that by obedience to God that they will achieve better status in the next life and eventually move beyond the cycles of transmigration.

Salvation in Hinduism is largely a matter of works, though Hindus do speak of the grace and mercy of God. Karmic doctrine explains evil and suffering and has been used to justify the caste system. One's success or pain in this life is caused by what one has done in previous lives. Thus, according to some orthodox Hindu gurus, the outcaste deserves his low status because of bad karma. Even though Hindus believe that this is a world of *maya* or illusion, humans are responsible for their actions and beliefs.

For many Hindus, enlightenment is achieved through realization that the self (*atman*) is God (*Brahman*). Hence the famous line: atman is Brahman. Other Hindus would speak of oneness with God without advocating the loss of individual self-identity. For all Hindus, salvation involves following the moral duties that apply to all humans and to the particular responsibilities connected with individual stages in life.

The vast majority of Hindus forbid eating of meat, drunkenness, and illicit sexuality. Some Hindus adopt a radical path of achieving enlightenment through sensual pleasure. This path is known as tantrism. Both Hinduism and Buddhism have a tantric aspect, though critics of both religions have often overemphasized this. Nevertheless, it is true that some gurus and devotees have broken normal boundaries in the pursuit of meat, drink, and sex.

The Hindu Trinity	
	Consort
Brahma (Creator)	Saraswati (the goddess of knowledge)
Vishnu (preserver)	Lakshmi (the goddess of love)
Shiva (destroyer)	Kali (the goddess of power and destruction)

Hindu Leaders and Groups

Adidam

Adidam is the contemporary spiritual movement devoted to the famous and controversial teacher Adi Da. Since his emergence as a guru in 1972, he has taken several names, including Bubba Free John and Da Free John. His original community was known, among several other titles, as the Dawn Horse Communion, then the Crazy Wisdom Fellowship.

Adi Da was born Franklin Albert Jones on November 3, 1939, in Jamaica, New York. He was raised in Long Island and studied at Columbia and Stanford universities. He has four daughters, one of whom—Shawnee Free Jones—is a Hollywood actress.

Adi Da claims to be God incarnate and says that he was born in a fully enlightened state. He pursued Eastern religions and studied with the famous Hindu guru Swami Rudrananda (aka Rudi). Adi Da also claimed spiritual lineage with the famous teachers Muktananda, Bhagavan Nityananda, Rang Avadhoot, and also with the cosmic goddess Ma. Adi Da broke away from Muktananda in 1973. Adi Da teaches his devotees at the group's main centers in California, Hawaii, and the Fiji Islands.

Adi Da's followers believe that he dwells in a state known as "Bright." Chris Tong, a scholar in the movement, states that Adi Da is "the only complete Incarnation of the Divine." Adi Da has taught that two female devotees—Ruchira Adidama Sukha Dham Naitauba and Ruchira Adidama Jangama Hriddaya Naitauba—have reached profound levels of spiritual realization.

Adi Da has been the subject of intense debate for more than three decades. Ex-members and critics of Adidam accuse the guru of narcissism, drunkenness, sexual abuse, and living a life of splendor, especially with his inner circle. Alice, one of his former "wives," states in one Web forum: "Da is a user. He is abusive and manipulative. In summary, he cares for his own pleasure and amusement and is full of humiliation and inconsideration." One devotee dismissed this as "superficial." Followers claim that Adi Da can operate above traditional values, as in the "crazy wisdom" teachings in Buddhism that allow an enlightened master to rise above the normal rules of karma.

Adi Da's devotees adore their guru. They sometimes raise funds through auctioning Adi Da's possessions among his followers. In one auction, the starting price for a Q-tip Adi Da used was $108. His disciples express their commitment to him in very emotive language. Members are often in rapture when he grants them the opportunity to be in his presence (*darshan*) and experience what they regard as his transcendent love.

The Adidam website states this of his darshan in the summer of 2005: "Darshan is Avatar Adi Da's greatest Gift. When receiving His Darshan, when sitting in His all-Embracing, all-Blessing Divine Company, when receiving His Love-Blissful Divine Regard, you are magnetized to His Divine Attractiveness. The Way of Adidam is the Way of the relationship to Avatar Adi Da Samraj—a relationship of attraction to His Divine Human Body and obedience to His Divine Heart-Word of Instruction, for the sake of Divine Self-Realization."

When Adi Da was sick in 2000, Carolyn Lee, one of the movement's leaders, wrote of her anguish and love: "Please let this Leela [account] of Beloved's Anguish break and convert your heart. Our love for our Beloved Guru is beyond any other love, and yet, we tend to abstract Him, even especially in the moments of His most extreme vulnerability and Distress. Beloved is not only seriously ill, He is in danger of not being able to go on in the Body at all, unless He is relieved of the sense that His Work is failing, and that He is truly protected and Set Apart and Given everything He needs in human terms to Bless and transform the world." Adi Da died unexpectedly of a heart attack on Thursday, November 27, 2008, at his Fiji island site.

He spoke of his passing in a 1976 address: "Grief is good—it is a way of being attentive. But you must allow yourself to be transformed, by My apparent absence, into a community of devotees most fully far beyond any realization of your common life that existed during the Lifetime of This Appearance. That is What I am Telling you. And I expect you to remember this when This One finally Goes."

ADI DA	
Typology	Hindu Sectarian
Pro Adi Da Websites	www.adidam.org www.aboutadidam.org www.beezone.com
Critical Website	http://lightmind.com/daism

Advaita Fellowship (Ram Tzu)

Wayne Liquorman, a follower of the Indian guru Ramesh S. Balsekar, leads the Advaita Fellowship, which is based in Redondo Beach, California. Liquorman uses a pen name of Ram Tzu for some of his publications, including *No Way for the Spiritually Advanced.* Liquorman teaches a form of non-dualist Hinduism, though with an obvious Western style. In one of his poems, Ram Tzu states: "You can only be lost If you are trying to get somewhere." Liquorman/Ram Tzu is quite critical of New Age spirituality: "Your New Age is neither new nor will it last an age."

Internet Source

Advaita website: http://advaita.org

AMOOKOS

AMOOKOS stands for the "Arcane Magical Order of the Knights of Shambhala." It is an esoteric group that claims its roots lie in the ancient Nath tantric traditions of Hindu India. The Magical Order dates officially to 1982 through the work of His Holiness Shri Gurudev Mahendranath, more popularly known as Dadaji. It is claimed that Dadaji is the twenty-third chief guru in the Adinatha lineage, going back to the famous tantric master Matsyendranath (c. A.D. 900) and his disciple Gorakhnath.

Dadaji was born in London in April 1911. He claimed that he received pagan initiation at age 11 from an English aunt. In his twenties he is supposed to have had contact with the famous British occultist Aleister Crowley. It is also suggested that Dadaji went to India in 1949 and spent three decades following the mystic's path. His followers believe that he was ordained into the Nath tradition in 1953 through Shri Lokanatha the Digambar-Avadhoot. It is also alleged that he was trained in Tibetan Buddhism, Zen, and Taoism. Dadaji died in 1992.

Dadaji issues this invitation to the Nath tradition: "If you are interested in solving the problems of life and gathering know-how for a future existence on any plane, then the Nath-Yogi-Magician way of life could be the best for you. What we have we treasure, but we will share it with others if they are ready and willing. If you can shed inhibitions, false modesty, dirty thinking, shyness, superstitions about sex and certain parts of the body, you need no longer be ashamed of yourself, ashamed of others or anything. A Nath can do no wrong. This is our spiritual way of life. What a Nath sees fit to do, they do, in private or in public. The only restraint is not to hurt the feelings of lesser-developed people."

Internet Source

Michael Magee website: www.shivashakti.com

Deities at ISKCON temple, Toronto, Canada

Photo: Jim Beverley

Ananda Church of Self-Realization (Swami Kriyananda)

In 1968 Swami Kriyananda founded the spiritual community Ananda. The swami is also known as J. Donald Walters and claims to be a direct disciple of Paramhansa Yogananda (1893–1952), author of the influential *Autobiography of a Yogi*. Yogananda's work is chiefly identified with the Self-Realization Fellowship (SRF).

Kriyananda was involved in the SRF from 1948 until its board of directors expelled him in 1962. Kriyananda has constantly argued that his dismissal was unjust. The main site for Kriyananda's community is the Ananda Village, located on 840 acres near Nevada City, California.

Ex-members have accused Kriyananda and other Ananda leaders of emotional and sexual abuse. The most significant case involved Anne-Marie Murphy (formerly Anne-Marie Bertolucci). In 1994 she launched legal action and was eventually awarded $1.8 million. Swami Kriyananda denied wrongdoing in the case. In 2004 police raided the Italian Ananda community, and nine leaders were charged with fraud and labor law violations.

Kriyananda teaches in the non-dualist Hindu tradition. In his essay on "The Divine Mother," he writes: "In essence, we are a part of the Infinite, and it's God who's playing our particular role in life. God is uniquely present in each one of us, and has His own song to sing through everyone. The whole purpose of this great drama is—to realize that you are God. But we must be careful. We can't correctly say, 'This body is God. This personality is God.' No. But God is you—this is correct. In the end, Self-realization means to know that the whole universe is a part of our own reality, and that in our basic nature, we are infinite."

Internet Sources

Kriyananda site: www.ananda.org

Critical sites

Ananda Awareness Network: www.anandainfo.com

Ananda Uncovered: www.anandauncovered.com

Ananda Marga (Prabhat Rainjan Sarkar)

In 1955, Prabhat Rainjan Sarkar—who was born in Jamalpur, India, on May 21, 1921—founded Ananda Marga (Path of Bliss). Ananda Marga followers believe that Sarkar was able to translate ancient Tantric Yoga into a scientific philosophy for modern times. His devotees believe he is a miracle worker and God incarnate, with power to know if an individual follower is correctly observing the ten principles of morality, known as *yama* and *hiyama*.

The Society first ordained monks in 1962 and nuns in 1966. Ananda Marga arrived in the United States in 1969. By the mid-'70s Sarkar's followers numbered about three thousand. Today Ananda Marga reports societies in more than 160 countries, with almost one million members. In addition to its spiritual theories, the organization has focused on worldwide social and humanitarian relief, including environmental awareness and disaster relief. Their political activism has sparked much controversy.

YOGA

Yoga is a widely used term, not only in Hinduism and Buddhism, but also in the New Age and other forms of modern spirituality. Yoga is also viewed as simply physical exercise for the body. Hindus refer to this type of yoga as *hatha yoga*. Among the other common yogas are *bhakti yoga* (devotional meditation), *karma yoga* (performing good deeds), and *jnana yoga* (proper use of the mind). Hindus believe that these forms of yoga are meant to culminate in spiritual growth and union with the divine. *Tantric yoga* is the most controversial of yogic practices since it can involve engaging in illicit sex and drunkenness as a path to spiritual liberation.

Most Hindus have been taught that there are seven power points in the body known as *chakras*. These energy centers run from the genitalia to the top of the head. Yogic practice is designed to align these *chakras* to release divine energy. Some forms of yoga give considerable attention to release and control of the energy at the base of the spine. This is known as *kundalini*, and this spiritual force is often pictured as a serpent ready to release its power.

Hatha yoga can include just physical exercise in toned-down style for Western consumption. It usually involves an eightfold path: (1) body purification, (2) postures, (3) mudras (postures that produce spiritual energy), (4) breath control, (5) stilling the mind, (6) concentration, (7) meditation, and (8) union with God.

Christian concern about yoga must revolve around the issue of whether a particular yoga teaching involves non-Christian meditation and spiritual exercises. If a class in yoga only involves physical exercise, participation would be a matter of personal conscience.

Ananda Marga emphasizes the practice of yoga and follows P. R. Sarkar's Sixteen Points, a system of spiritual practices to maximize personal growth. Ananda Marga espouses a theory known as PROUT, or "Progressive Utilization Theory," which calls for a new social order based on just distribution of the world's resources

In apparent response to his condemnation of corrupt Indian officials, Sarkar was arrested in 1971 but was cleared of all charges after seven years in prison. He also composed more than five thousand songs from

1982 until his death on October 21, 1990. Sarkar's spiritual name was Shrii Shrii Anandamurti.

Internet Sources

Ananda Marga website: www.anandamarga.org

Proutist Universal website: www.prout.org

South Asian Institute for Advanced Christian Studies, Bangalore, Karnataka

Photo: Jim Beverley

Babaji's Kriya Yoga (Marshall Govindan)

In Quebec, Canada, a group of Hindus, led by Marshall Govindan, foster the Kriya yoga of an alleged immortal master named Babaji. According to Govindan, Babaji was born in A.D. 203 in Tamil Nadu, India. He achieved total enlightenment while meditating in a cave in the Himalayas. Over the centuries, he has guided Hindu masters, including Shankara and Kabir. Babaji also appeared to Sri Yukteswar about 1860 and then to Yukteswar's disciple Paramahansa Yogananda, author of *Autobiography of a Yogi* and founder of the Self-Realization Fellowship.

Govindan argues that the SRF has neglected Babaji and actually altered Yogananda's book in order to hide the need for following Babaji. According to Govindan, Babaji worked in the early 1940s with two Indians: S. A. A. Ramaiah and V. T. Neelakantan, a student of Annie Besant, the famous theosophical leader. Ramaiah and Neelakantan founded the Kriya Babaji Sangah in 1952, enduring opposition from the SRF. Babaji taught his 144 techniques of Kriya yoga to Ramaiah, who initiated Govindan in 1970–71. Babaji, who has the appearance of a 16-year-old, revealed himself to Govindan in 1988.

Babaji describes himself: "I am Existence-Knowledge-Bliss absolute. I am the One in all and the All in one. I am the impersonal Personality of the whole universe. What can make me afraid? I care not for nature's laws. Death is a joke to me and I am the death of death. I beat in every breast, see in every eye, throb in every pulse, smile in every flower, shine in the lightning and roar in the thunder. I flutter in the leaves. I hiss in the winds and I roll in the surging seas. . . . I am the immutable and indescribable Atman, the dynamic principle of Existence and the infinite ocean of everlasting Glee. In my presence all hells and heavens are effaced into shadowy nothingness and the whole universe is a mere bubble ever ready to burst."

Internet Source

Group site: www.babaji.ca

Brahma Kumaris (Dada Lekhraj)

Dada Lekhraj is the founder of the Brahma Kumaris movement. He was born in India in 1876 and became a prominent businessman, but in 1936 he experienced a series of visions that led him to pursue the path of a Hindu mystic. In 1937 he chose eight women to form a Trust to spread his message of Raja Yoga. His members call him Brahma Baba. He died in 1969.

The Brahma Kumaris operate more than three thousand meditation centers in seventy countries. Dadi Prakashmani, one of the original eight Trust members, served as the movement's administrative head from 1969 to her death in 2007. The movement is now led by Dadi Janki.

Internet Source

Brahma Kumaris official website: www.bkwsu.com

Chinmayananda

Swami Chinmayananda, born on May 8, 1916, in Kerala, India, is the founder of the Chinmaya mission. His birth name was Balakrishna Menon. He was raised in a devout Hindu home and recalls early fascination with pictures of the Hindu gods, particularly Lord Shiva. Chinmayananda was involved in the Indian independence movement in the 1940s and was jailed briefly. He studied law and English literature in university and became a journalist with *The National Herald* in New Delhi in 1945.

In 1947 Chinmayananda visited the ashram of the famous Hindu guru Swami Sivananda (1887–1963), who initiated him on February 25, 1949. Chinmayananda spent eight years in the Himalayas studying Hindu scriptures with Sri Swami Tapovan. He then spent time wandering India as a beggar before Swami Sivananda sent him on a mission to teach Hinduism to India and the world.

Chinmayananda died in 1993 in San Diego, and the movement is now led by Swami Tejomayananda, who was born in 1950.

Internet Source

Chinmayananda website: www.chinmaya.org

Gandhi

Mohandas Karamchand Gandhi is probably the most famous Hindu of modern times. He was born on October 2, 1869, in Porbander, Gujarat, India. He studied law in England in his early twenties and returned to India in 1891. He moved to South Africa in 1893 and moved back to India in 1915. For the remainder of his life he worked for Indian independence, the rights of the Untouchables (people deemed unclean because they are outside even the lowest caste), and peaceful Muslim-Hindu relations.

He advocated non-violence and was arrested seven times between 1917 and 1942. He also fasted as a way of protest. In 1942 he implored Britain to "Quit India." His wife died in 1944. His defense of the outcaste was presented without equivocation. "To say that a single human being, because of his birth, becomes an untouchable, unapproachable or invisible, is to deny God." An orthodox Hindu assassinated Gandhi in New Delhi on January 30, 1948.

Gandhi was raised in a devout Hindu home. He was influenced by Jainism and was attracted to the monotheism of Islam. He also found ethical inspiration in the Sermon on the Mount. He always resisted the idea of conversion, believing in the unity of religions. He was a strong advocate of vegetarianism and was most famous for his strength of moral character. In 1918 British scholar Gilbert Murray wrote this about Gandhi: "Persons in power should be very careful how they deal with a man who cares nothing for sensual pleasure, nothing for riches, nothing for comfort or praise, or promotion, but is simply determined to do what he believes to be right. He is a dangerous and uncomfortable enemy, because his body which you can always conquer gives you so little purchase upon his soul."

Hare Krishna temple, Los Angeles, California

Photo: Gordon Melton

Hare Krishna (ISKCON)

The Hare Krishna movement is officially known as the International Society for Krishna Consciousness, or ISKCON. It is both a new religious movement and part of ancient Hinduism. Western awareness of the movement goes back five decades, to a time when Srila A. C. Bhaktivedanta Swami Prabhupada, the movement's founder and guru, brought the Hare Krishna faith to the United States. The movement is recognized most famously by its dancing in the streets, chanting of the

Hare Krishna mantra, and by the saffron robes and shaved heads of male Krishna devotees.

Prabhupada was born on September 1, 1896, in Calcutta. He studied at Scottish Churches' College and was married in 1918, then spent most of his life as a pharmacist and business manager. He was initiated as a disciple of Srila Bhaktisiddhanta Sarasvati Thakur in 1932. On August 13, 1965, after years of preparation, Prabhupada set sail for the United States in order to bring the message of Krishna consciousness to the West. He attracted a significant number of followers in Manhattan, and the movement spread quickly to other parts of the world. Prabhupada died November 14, 1977, in India.

ISKCON is modeled after the larger Vaisnava (or Vaishnava) tradition in Hinduism. It places emphasis on bhakti yoga, the ecstatic love of God. Hare Krishna devotees object strongly to the Advaitist position that the Divine is impersonal. In ISKCON the believer does not become one with God in an ontological sense. ISKCON members view Krishna as the Supreme Personality of the Godhead and believe that liberation is attained through hearing and chanting about Krishna. Most ISKCON devotees still look to Prabhupada as their main guru and spiritual guide.

Prabhupada was known for his strict adherence to Hindu morals. Unlike many Eastern gurus who came to the West, he did not use his status to seduce his followers sexually. He never entertained doubts about his belief system. He even denied that Neil Armstrong had landed on the moon, since the Hindu scriptures teach that the moon is farther away than the sun and is inhabited.

Prabhupada took the Hindu scriptures literally, including the claim that earlier beings engaged in space travel. Based on this belief, Prabhupada wrote a booklet called *Easy Journey to Other Planets*. His commentaries take the stories of Hindu gods and goddesses as literal historic narratives. The guru believed that his understanding of Hinduism represented its purest form.

When Prabhupada died, eleven of his disciples assumed the mantle of leadership. These gurus were (1) Harikesa Swami, (2) Jayatirtha dasa Adhikari, (3) Hamsaduta Swami, (4) Hrdayananda Gosvami, (5) Ramesvara Swami, (6) Bhagavan dasa Adhikari, (7) Kirtanananda Swami, (8) Tamala Krsna Goswami, (9) Satsvarupa dasa Goswami, (10) Bhavananda Goswami, and (11) Jayapataka Swami. The movement has undergone enormous turmoil since Prabhupada died, particularly in relation to Kirtanananda.

The ISKCON Governing Body (GBC) expelled Kirtanananda, and a West Virginia judge sentenced him to thirty years in prison for using murder, kidnapping, and fraud to protect an illegal, multimillion-dollar enterprise. He entered prison in 1991 and was released on June 16, 2004. This crime story is covered in the books *Monkey on a Stick* and *Betrayal of the Spirit.*

In 2000 former members who were raised as children in ISKCON brought a lawsuit against the group because of neglect and abuse (emotional, physical, and sexual) in the movement's schools. In 2005 ISKCON reached an agreement with the U.S. bankruptcy court system to create a multimillion-dollar fund for the victims. The internal chaos in ISKCON since its founder's death has led to the exodus of most of the original disciples, including Stephen J. Gelberg, one of the major academics in the movement.

ISKCON devotees doing kirtan, London, England

Photo: Gordon Melton

HARE KRISHNA (ISKCON)

Founder	A . C. Bhaktivedanta Swami Prabhupada (1896–1977)
Official ISKCON Websites	www.iskcon.com www.prabhupada.com www.krishna.com
Other Websites	Surrealist.org (Nori J. Muster): http://surrealist.org/links/ harekrishna.html ISKCON Revival Movement: www.iskconirm.com Chakra: www.chakra.org
Recommended Reading	Edwin Bryant and Maria Ekstrand, eds. *The Hare Krishna Movement: The Postcharismatic Fate of a Religious Transplant* (New York: Columbia University Press, 2004) John Hubner and Lindsey Grueson, *Monkey on a Stick: Murder, Madness, and the Hare Krishnas* (New York: Harcourt, Brace, Jovanovich, 1988) Nori Muster, *Betrayal of the Spirit* (Champaign, IL, University of Illinois Press, 1997). Federico Squarcini and Eugenio Fizzotti, *Hare Krishna* (Salt Lake City: Signature, 2004)

Integral Yoga (Aurobindo and the Mother)

Sri Aurobindo Ghose is one of the most influential gurus of modern times. He was born on August 15, 1872. Sent to England by Mira Richards at age 7, Aurobindo returned to India in 1893, having had a thorough training in a Western classical education. He was involved in business for several years and then became a prominent and controversial political activist. He moved to Pondicherry, India, in 1910 and turned to the spiritual path.

He spent four decades in contemplation, writing, teaching, and building a spiritual community.

Aurobindo's devotees believe that on November 24, 1926, Krishna descended to the physical plane so that a new age for humanity became possible in the attainment of Ananda (bliss) and what Aurobindo called "the Overmind." This is known as the Day of the Siddha.

Aurobindo's name is always associated with Mira Richards (b. 1878), who became known as The Mother. She stated in one of her writings: "As soon as I saw Sri Aurobindo I recognized in him the well-known being whom I used to call Krishna." She claimed at one time "Sri Aurobindo and myself are one and the same consciousness, one and the same person." Mother's devotees speak of her in supernatural terms. "Even today there is a continuous flow of a rare divine energy from the reclining chair she was using. The same flow will also be there in all the articles received through her lotus hands."

After 1926 Aurobindo communicated with his followers through Mother. He died on December 5, 1950. Mother died in 1973, just five years short of her hundredth birthday. She suggested when she was in her forties that following Aurobindo's yoga techniques caused her to look only 18 at the time.

Internet Source

Integral Yoga website: www.miraura.org

Kriya Yoga Institute (Swami Paramahamsa Hariharananda)

The Kriya Yoga Institute claims to be continuing the yogic tradition of the famed Hindu teacher Paramahamsa Yogananda (1893–1952), author of *Autobiography of a Yogi*. Paramahamsa Hariharananda, born May 27, 1907, near Calcutta, led the Institute for decades but died on December 3, 2002, in Miami. He was initiated by the famous yogi Swami Shriyukteshwar in 1932 and by Yogananda in 1935. Hariharananda's followers believe that the eternal Yogi Babaji appeared to him in 1949 to bless his mission to bring Kriya yoga to the world. The swami made his first trip to the West in 1974.

When asked one time, "What is God?" Hariharananda replied: "God is all-pervading, omniscient, omnipotent. He is in every human being. Having made the whole universe, created man and woman, He entered into His creation. He is hiding in the whole body of all beings, and in the whole universe. Everything is God. All human beings are born for God-realization, because they are rational beings. Animals cannot realize God."

Paramahamsa Prajanananda now leads the Kriya Yoga Institute. The U.S. headquarters is in Homestead, Florida.

Internet Source

Kriya Yoga International homepage: www.kriya.org

Hindu deity, India

Photo: Jim Beverley

Ma Jaya Sati Bhagavati

Ma Jaya Sati Bhagavati, known as Guru Ma, is a Hindu teacher famous for her work among AIDS victims. Guru Ma was born Joyce Green and raised in poverty in a Jewish home in Brooklyn, New York. She turned to Eastern religion in 1972. Her first teacher was Hilda Charlton, a well-known New York teacher. Ma also claims direct guidance from Jesus and the famous Hindu master Neem Karoli Baba. In 1974 Ram Dass became a devotee of Guru Ma, but he split from her in 1975 and wrote a negative article about her in the *Yoga Journal* the next year. Ma is head of the Kashi Ashram in Sebastian, Florida.

Ma is also a Trustee of the Parliament of the World's Religions and co-founder, with Tenzin Choegyal (brother of the Dalai Lama), of World Tibet Day. Ma is legendary for her sense of humor. When one reporter asked her about how she handled criticism, she replied: "Honey, I was taught to walk on like an elephant and let the puppies fight at my feet."

Ma's most famous devotee is folk singer Arlo Guthrie. Guru Ma blessed his Guthrie Center, based in the former Trinity Church (the church mentioned in the song "Alice's Restaurant") in Great Barrington, Massachusetts. She wrote these words on the door: "One God—Many Forms, One River—Many Streams, One People—Many Faces, One Mother—Many Children."

Statues of Krishna and Radha

Photo: Gordon Melton

Guru Ma has been targeted as a cult leader. Her most prominent critic is Richard Rosenkranz, who was one of her followers from 1976 through 2000. Once the group's media person, his high-profile divorce proceedings in 2001 involved allegations against the Kashi Ashram. In 2002 Rosenkranz wrote in a Florida newspaper: "Sure, we were naïve, overly trusting and made mistakes. But we were victims in my opinion of fraud, deceit, manipulation and abuse. No amount of smoke and mirrors excuses that."

Ex-members Dr. Harry Brodie and his wife, Roseanne, also criticize the Florida-based guru. In 1981 the couple gave their firstborn child, Tess, to Guru Ma; but after they left the group they used law enforcement officers to regain custody of their daughter in 1989.

Ma's worship of the Hindu goddess Kali is captured in these words: "The All Good and All Powerful One, Kali is without beginning or end. Where her consort creates, she preserves and withdraws the world of extended matter. May She, the Black One of the Dead Night's Glory, forgive those who live in the silence and have never—due to lack of meditation—felt her Hand on their breast. I am Ma, and I beg you to go deeper into the place of the terrifying horror of the dying ego. I shall be there with you."

Internet Sources

Kashi website: www.kashi.org

Critic website: www.kashiashram.com

Mother Meera

Followers of Mother Meera believe her to be the incarnation of the Divine Mother. She was born in southern India in 1960, and her birth name was Kamala Reedy. As a teenager she received guidance from the famous Hindu teacher Sri Aurobindo. Reedy traveled to Europe in 1979 and formed the first Mother Meera Society in Canada in the early 1980s. Mother Meera now resides in Germany but also owns property in Madanapalle, India. She was married in 1982.

Devotees travel from all parts of the world to hear from Mother Meera in an audience (*darshan*) of silence. Cliff Bostock writes: "Four evenings a week, a couple hundred devotees who have made reservations weeks in advance come to sit in plastic chairs or on the floor in her basement in total silence. They take turns kneeling before her in complete silence. She takes the head of the devotee in her hands for a few moments. Then, the devotee sits back and she looks into the eyes. This brief experience, so reminiscent of a mother's gazing into an infant's eyes, is life changing for many." Source: Bostock, "Revisiting Mother Meera," *Soul Work* (www. soulworks.net)

Mother Meera became famous through Andrew Harvey's *Hidden Journey* (1991), a work that explores his devotion to the young Hindu guru. That love relationship was lost when Mother Meera refused to endorse Harvey's homosexual relationship. Harvey attacked Mother's credibility in a second work, *The Return of the Mother*, published in 1995, and then in *Sun at Midnight*. Mother Meera has also been studied in Martin Goodman's *In Search of the Divine Mother*.

Mark Matousek, author of the famous work *Sex Death Enlightenment*, credits Mother Meera for her initial impact on his spiritual transformation. Matousek, a native of Brooklyn, had a tormented childhood and found false solace in the hedonistic world of New York pop culture. Finding himself lost in drugs and sex, he decided to travel to India to escape his inner demons. He stopped in Germany to visit Mother Meera and claimed a feeling of resurgence as he rested his head on the pillow at her feet.

Mother Meera stated, "I have come to say that all paths are as good as each other and all lead to the Divine, and that therefore the various believers should respect each other's ways. For example, Muslims, Christians, Hindus, Buddhists and other religious people can believe and follow their own faith, but should not hate or fight others' faith. People who follow any path can come to me—I help them to remember the Divine, and give them peace and happiness when they are in trouble."

Ganges River, Benares, India

Photo: Jim Beverley

Osho (aka Bhagwan Shree Rajneesh)

Osho was one of the most famous and controversial Hindu gurus of the twentieth century, known especially for owning more than ninety Rolls-Royces while living in America in the early 1980s.

Osho was born Rajneesh Chandra Mohan in 1931 in central India and claimed enlightenment on March 21, 1953, when he was a philosophy student. He received an M.A. degree in 1956 and was a professor from 1957 through 1966 at the University of Jabalpur.

In 1966 he began to focus on public communication of his spiritual message. He moved to Mumbai (formerly Bombay) in 1970 and started to invite people into discipleship under him. During this time he was known as Bhagwan Shree Rajneesh and became one of the most popular gurus for Westerners flocking to India in search of enlightenment. From 1974 to 1981 Osho led his own ashram in Pune, India, and moved to the United States in 1981.

Osho's followers purchased a 64,000-acre ranch in Oregon, which became known as Rajneeshpuram. Osho resided there until 1985 when the spiritual commune broke up in disarray after several leaders (including Ma Anand Sheela, Osho's personal secretary) were found guilty of criminal acts involving food poisoning, arson, and wiretapping. Ma was sentenced to prison for her involvement.

On October 28, 1985, Osho was arrested at gunpoint in Charlotte, North Carolina, and spent twelve days in jail. Some of his followers claim that he was poisoned while in custody in Oklahoma, on his return to Oregon. His critics contend that he was addicted to Valium and nitrous oxide, and some of his close followers acknowledge his frequent use of nitrous oxide (more commonly known as laughing gas). Osho was deported from the United States in November after pleading guilty to immigration fraud and paying a fine of $400,000.

Osho's 1986 world tour was marred by frequent denial of entry into various countries or by expulsion soon after his arrival. He returned to his ashram in India in January 1987. He adopted the name of "Osho" in 1989. His longtime girlfriend, Vivek, committed suicide shortly before Osho died in January 1990. Following Hindu custom, his body was cremated.

Many of Osho's devotees still view him as the perfect embodiment of enlightenment. Other disciples, notably Christopher Calder, claim that he was both enlightened and corrupt. Many devotees left Rajneesh/Osho after the debacle in Oregon and suffered incredible agony and disillusionment. Since his death he has become the guru for a whole new generation of followers. The Osho Commune International maintains the spiritual community in Pune, India.

On his tombstone is engraved:

OSHO

Never Born – Never Died

Only Visited this Planet Earth between

December 11, 1931–January 19, 1990

OSHO

Typology	Hindu
Headquarters	Pune, India
Recommended Reading	Judith M. Fox, *Osho Rajneesh* (Salt Lake: Signature, 2000) Satya Bharti Franklin, *The Promise of Paradise* (New York: Station Hill Press, 1992) Tim Guest, *My Life in Orange* (London: Granta, 2004)
Main Websites	www.osho.com www.oshoworld.com Friends of Osho: www.sannyas.net Sannyasworld: www.sannyasworld.com

Ramakrishna (1836–86)

Ramakrishna is one of the most influential of modern Hindu gurus. He was born in 1836 in Bengal, India. Sarada Devi (1853–1920) was pledged to marry him at a young age. She joined him in Calcutta in her teen years, but the relationship was a spiritual one. After her master's death in 1886, she continued his work. Ramakrishna's mission is carried on through the Ramakrishna Order in India and through the Vedanta Society in other parts of the world.

Ramakrishna was particularly devoted to Kali, one of Hinduism's most popular female manifestations of God. Some of Ramakrishna's followers came to believe that he himself was an incarnation of the divine. He is known most through the work of his most famous devotee, Swami Vivekananda (1863–1902). Ramakrishna was inspirational in Vivekananda's decision to represent Hinduism at the first World's Parliament of Religions (Chicago, 1893).

Ramakrishna believed that Ultimate Reality, or Brahman, embraces all faiths. Ramakrishna wrote: "Different people call on [God] by different names: some as Allah, some as God, and others as Krishna, Siva, and Brahman. It is like the water in a lake. Some drink it at one place and call it 'jal,' others at another place and call it 'pani,' and still others at a third place and call it 'water.' The Hindus call it 'jal,' the Christians 'water,' and the Moslems 'pani.' But it is one and the same thing."

Jeffrey Kripal created enormous controversy with his 1995 work *Kali's Child* (University of Chicago Press). Kripal, a student of the famous Indologist Wendy Doniger, analyzed alleged homoerotic elements in Ramakrishna's life. His book was condemned in India and in Hindu communities throughout the world. Both Swami Tyagananda (the Hindu chaplain at Harvard) and Rajiv Malhotra (Infinity Foundation) questioned his facility in the original Bengali documents and familiarity with Indian culture. Kripal, now a professor at Rice University, acknowledged some mistakes in translation but has repeatedly defended the fundamental perspective of his book.

Internet Sources

Vedanta Society: www.vedanta.org

Jeffrey Kirpal and *Kali's Child:* www.ruf.rice.edu/~kalischi

Infinity Foundation: www.infinityfoundation.com

Hindu priest

Photo: Jim Beverley

Sathya Sai Baba

Sathya Sai Baba is the most influential and controversial Hindu guru in the world today. According to most accounts, he was born on November 23, 1926, in Puttaparthi, southeastern India, and named Sathyanarayana Raju. Sathya Sai Baba claims to be the reincarnation of Shirdi Sai Baba, a Hindu guru of an earlier generation. Sathya Sai Baba's followers believe that supernatural signs marked his birth and that he miraculously survived a scorpion sting in 1940, the year when he proclaimed his divine essence. He held his first world conference in 1968 in Bombay.

Since the 1950s Sai Baba has devoted funds to the building of hospitals and educational institutions in India. He has also been involved in the creation of a major waterworks project that brings clean water to hundreds of villages near his main residence. In 1995 the president of India inaugurated its third phase. In 2001 Sai Baba opened a major specialty hospital in Bangalore. The guru visited eastern Africa in 1968, his only travel outside India.

Benares University

Photo: Jim Beverley

Miracle stories circulate widely about him, but prominent ex-members and investigators view them as trickery and sleight-of-hand. The "anti-guru" Besava Premanand has written critiques of Sai Baba's miracles in *The Indian Skeptic.* He has also accused Indian police and government officials of sloppy investigation into murders at Sai Baba's residence in 1993. Further, ex-members have charged Sai Baba with the sexual abuse of young men in his group. One of the earliest to raise this issue was Tal Brooke, one of the leaders in the Spiritual Counterfeits Project. Brooke wrote about his sojourn with Sai Baba in *Avatar of the Night*, published in 1976 and released in an expanded edition in 2008.

In 1999 former followers David and Faye Bailey issued *The Findings*, a report on their own disillusionment with Sai Baba, which they based on extensive interviews with boys and young men the guru allegedly had abused. BBC2 raised the sexual abuse question in a 2004 documentary *Secret Swami*. Followers usually respond by questioning the integrity of the accusers or by claiming that Sai Baba sometimes touches his devotees in order to raise their *kundalini*, or spiritual energy. Many members, due to their complete trust in their guru, simply ignore the accusations.

Indulal Shah, a top international leader in the movement, advised devotees, "We know how Bhagavan does not spare Himself in the service to Humanity. We all know that Bhagavan's Life is His Message. We also know that when we have our own experience to rely upon, we have no time or space to pay any heed to the malicious allegations that are innately false and devious."

Sai Baba claims that he lives above both criticism and adulation. He once wrote to his brother, "Have you not heard of dogs that howl at the stars? How long can they go on? Authenticity will soon win. I will not give up My Mission, or My determination. I know I will carry them out; I treat the honor and dishonor, the fame and blame that may be the consequence, with equal equanimity. Internally, I am unconcerned. I act but in the outer world; I talk and move about for the sake of the outer world and for announcing My coming to the people; else, I have no concern even with these."

There are more than twelve hundred Sai Baba centers worldwide. Michael Goldstein, who leads the American branch of the Sai Baba movement, gave this assessment of his guru: "We believe that Sri Sathya Sai Baba is Jesus Christ. Sri Sathya Sai Baba is Buddha. Sri Sathya Sai Baba is the founder of all of the world's religions. Sri Sathya Sai Baba has always been God."

The Hindu guru also predicted that he would die around 2022 and that his third incarnation will take place in the person of Prema Sai Baba.

Brian Steel conducted the most rigorous study of Sathya Sai Baba. Steel is a former devotee who gave up spiritual commitment to Baba as a result of both his own study of Sai Baba's discourses and the evidence provided in *The Findings*. He also wrote a stinging critique of Bill Aitken's book *Sri Sathya Sai Baba: A Life*.

SATHYA SAI BABA

Typology	Hindu
Sathya Sai Baba Websites	www.sathyasai.org www.srisathyasai.org.in www.saibabalinks.org
Critic Websites	www.saiguru.net www.exbaba.com http://bdsteel.tripod.com http://www.saibaba-x.org.uk/ www.saibabaexpose.com
Recommended Reading	Bill Aitken, *Sri Sathya Sai Baba. A Life* (New Delhi: Penguin Books India, 2004) Tal Brooke, *Avatar of the Night* (End Run Publishing, 1999) R. Padmanaban, R. *et al, Love Is My Form. Vol. 1 The Advent (1926–1950)*. Prasanthi Nilayam, Sai Towers, 2000
Special Note	Brian Steel, an ex-Sai follower, has an extensive bibliography on Sai Baba on his site noted above.

Self-Realization Fellowship

The Self-Realization Fellowship fosters the memory and work of the famous Hindu guru Paramahansa Yogananda. Yogananda was born Mukunda Lal Ghosh in 1893 in Gorakhpur, India. He arrived in the United States in 1920 and became one of the most influential exponents of Hinduism in the West. He is best known for his *Autobiography of a Yogi*, published in 1946. He died on March 7, 1952.

SRF has groups in fifty-four countries and across the United States. Sri Daya Mata, one of Yogananda's earliest devotees, has been a major leader in the movement. She worked closely with her guru for twenty years. She told SRF members that Yogananda told her just before he died: "When I am gone, only love can take my place. Be so drunk with the love of God night and day that you won't know anything but God; and give that love to all."

SRF won litigation against the Ananda Church of Self-Realization (led by Swami Kriyananda, aka J. Donald Waters) over copyright issues related to Yogananda's books.

Internet Source

Self-realization Fellowship: www.yogananda-srf.org

Shree Maa

Shree Maa is one of the famous women gurus of India. She was raised in wealth but left home to follow the mystical path inspired by her hero Ramakrishna, the nineteenth-century holy man of Bengal. Maa spent considerable time in the foothills of the Himalayan Mountains, where she practiced meditation, spoke little, and took part in extreme fasting. (Her followers claim that at one point she weighed just over sixty pounds.) She roamed India, and in 1980 met Swami Satyananda Saraswati, an American-born guru. Satyananda viewed Maa as the embodiment of the goddess Durga.

Maa and Satyananda moved to America in 1984. Their temple grounds are located in Napa, California.

Internet Source

Shree Maa website: www.shreemaa.org

Street scene, Bangalore, Karnataka

Photo: Jim Beverley

FIVE OBLIGATIONS OF A HINDU

1. Worship, upasana: Young Hindus are taught daily worship in the family shrine room—rituals, disciplines, chants, yogas and religious study. They learn to be secure through devotion in home and temple, wearing traditional dress, bringing forth love of the Divine and preparing the mind for serene meditation.

2. Holy days, utsava: Young Hindus are taught to participate in Hindu festivals and holy days in the home and temple. They learn to be happy through sweet communion with God at such auspicious celebrations. Utsava includes fasting and attending the temple on Monday or Friday and other holy days.

3. Virtuous living, dharma: Young Hindus are taught to live a life of duty and good conduct. They learn to be selfless by thinking of others first, being respectful of parents, elders and swamis, following divine law, especially ahimsa, mental, emotional and physical noninjury to all beings. Thus they resolve karmas.

4. Pilgrimage, tirthayatra: Young Hindus are taught the value of pilgrimage and are taken at least once a year for darnana of holy persons, temples and places, near or far. They learn to be detached by setting aside worldly affairs and making God, Gods and gurus life's singular focus during these journeys.

5. Rites of passage, samskara: Young Hindus are taught to observe the many sacraments which mark and sanctify their passages through life. They learn to be traditional by celebrating the rites of birth, name-giving, head-shaving, first feeding, ear-piercing, first learning, coming of age, marriage and death.

—From the Himalayan Academy, founded by Gurudeva

Sidda Yoga

Sidda Yoga is the creation of Swami Muktananda, one of the most famous Hindu gurus of the twentieth century. The Sidda Yoga Dham of America (SYDA) now maintains the movement. Muktananda, born in 1908, was a disciple of Bhagawan Nityananda (d. 1961). Muktananda brought his teaching to the West in 1970 and started more than six hundred meditation centers in North America and around the world. SYDA is based in South Fallsburg in upstate New York.

Before his death in 1982, Muktananda appointed Malti Shetty (Swami Chidvilasananda) and her brother Subhash (Swami Nityananda) as his successors. In October 1985 Nityananda (b. 1962) was removed as a guru after a confrontation with his sister at the group's headquarters in India. This disruption was chronicled in a major investigative report by Lis Harris in *The New Yorker* (November 14, 1994). Her followers know Chidvilasananda (b. 1954) affectionately as "Gurumayi." Nityananda now leads his own group (based in Walden, New York), but he and his sister have never reconciled.

Near the end of his life, prominent ex-members accused Muktananda of sexually abusing several female devotees. Harris and William Rodarmor reported these allegations in "The Secret Life of Swami Muktananda" in *The Co-Evolution Quarterly* (Winter 1983).

Former member Stan Trout (now Swami Abhayananda) wrote an Open Letter to Muktananda in 1981 about emotional and sexual abuse. Trout stated to fellow devotees: "I sincerely regret that I must be the bearer of this news, and wish like you that it could all be proven false. I have learned, and I think you will too, that although they are hard, these sad tidings are the key to a future of freedom. And though it's a frightening and lonely vista at first, the initial anger at having been deceived for so long will subside."

Muktananda responded to Trout's accusations by arguing: "Still, this is nothing new. It is a part of the lineage that I belong to. Mansur Mastana was hanged, Jesus was crucified, and all of Tukaram's books were thrown into the river. You should be happy that I am still alive and healthy and that they haven't tried to hang me."

SYDA's critics continue to focus on Muktananda's sexual abuse. Sarah Caldwell, a Hindu scholar, has sought to defend the sexual practices of the guru through his professed adoption of Tantric sexual rites, an esoteric tradition in both Hinduism and Buddhism. Caldwell was once a disciple of Muktananda. She provides evidence of Muktananda's interest in Tantric teachers and practices. Her viewpoint is based in part on firsthand interviews with devotees who had sexual interaction with the famous guru.

Remnants of ancient Hindu site, Vietnam

Photo: TD

SYDA'S TRAUMATIC ABUSE

"I had slowly and painfully begun to acknowledge to myself and others that there were aspects of SYDA and its leaders that I found unethical and disturbing. In particular, I had witnessed and personally experienced Gurumayi verbally and emotionally abusing her followers, publicly shaming and humiliating those with whom she was displeased in cruel and harsh ways. I had heard her tell lies and witnessed her deliberately deceiving others.

I witnessed her condoning and encouraging illegal and unethical business and labor practices, such as smuggling gold and U.S. dollars in and out of India, and exploiting workers without providing adequate housing, food, health care, or social security.

I was aware that for many years, Gurumayi, and her predecessor, Swami Muktananda, had been using spies, hidden cameras, and microphones to gather information about followers in the ashram. I had heard whispers that Muktananda, contrary to his claims of celibacy and renunciation, had extensive sexual relations with female followers, which he then lied about and attempted to cover up with threats of violence to those who sought to expose him. Later, after I exited Siddha Yoga in 1994, I came to recognize in Muktananda's and Gurumayi's behavior toward their followers the hallmarks of abuse: the use of power to seduce, coerce, belittle, humiliate, and intimidate others for the ultimate purpose of psychological enslavement and parasitic exploitation."

—From Daniel Shaw, "Traumatic Abuse in Cults: A Psychoanalytic Perspective" (full article posted at www.danielshawlcsw.com/traumatic_abuse.htm)

Sidda Yoga follows the typical themes of the advaitist or impersonalist tradition in Hinduism. The essence of liberation involves realization that the Self is divine. This is ultimately experienced through relationship with a guru who can channel divine energy to the devotee. Sidda Yoga refers to spiritual awakening as *shaktipat*, which is achieved by connection with the guru.

William Mahoney, a professor of religion and a follower of Gurumayi, states: "The living master, the outer Guru, is a human being who has become totally at one with the Guru tattva, the Guru principle. Totally at one with that power of divine grace, she is identical with divine grace itself. There is no difference between the two. She is the Guru."

SIDDA YOGA (MUKTANANDA)	
Typology	Hindu
Current Leader	Swami Chidvilasananda (Gurumayi)
Sidda Yoga Website	www.siddhayoga.org
Other Websites	www.leavingsiddhayoga.net eXSY Yahoo group: http://groups.yahoo.com/group/eXSY/ Swami Nityananda site (Gurumayi's estranged brother): www.shantimandir.com

Sri Chimnoy

Sri Chimnoy was born in East Bengal in 1931. After his parents' deaths in 1944, he went to the Aurobindo Ashram. He moved to New York City in 1964. He is known for his music and athletics, including the spiritual/weight lifting program called "Lifting Up the World with a One-Ness Heart." The guru regularly invited famous people to a site in Queens, where he would power lift them over his head. Sri Chimnoy often led meditations at the United Nations. Carlos Santana, the famous musician, was a devotee of Chimnoy from 1972 until 1981. Sri Chimnoy died on October 11, 2007.

Former followers disputed some of his weight-lifting claims and accused him of emotional and sexual abuse.

Internet Source

Official Sri Chinmoy website: www.srichinmoy.org

Subramuniyaswami

Satguru Sivaya Subramuniyaswami, born in 1927, was recognized worldwide as a leader of Hinduism. Jnanaguru Yogaswami, a famous Hindu guru, initiated him into the life of a monk in 1949. Subramuniyaswami's followers knew him as "Gurudeva." He had a major impact through his

Saiva Siddhanta Church, his temple building, his Himalayan Academy, and his famous magazine *Hinduism Today*. He was a major Hindu presence at the 1993 Parliament of the World's Religions in Chicago.

Gurudeva, a native of California, moved his headquarters to Hawaii in 1970. He died in December 2001. Satguru Bodhinatha Veylanswami now leads the movement. On October 21, just weeks before death, Gurudeva called his closest monks to his bedside. He passed his pendant, bracelet, and one of his rings to Bodhinatha, and then stated: "You are the guru now."

Internet Sources

Kauai's Hindu Monastery website: http://www.himalayanacademy.com

Hinduism Today website: www.HinduismToday.com

TEN FAMOUS GURUS

Guru	Dates	Group/Organization
Ramakrishna	1836–86	Ramakrishna Order
Swami Vivekananda	1863–1902	Ramakrishna Order
Sri Aurobindo	1872–1950	Integral Yoga
Paramahansa Yogananda	1893–1952	Self-Realization Fellowship
Swami Prabhupada	1896–1977	Hare Krishna
Swami Muktananda	1908–82	Siddha Yoga
Prabhat Rainjan Sarkar	1921–90	Ananda Marga
Subramuniyaswami (Gurudeva)	1927–2001	Hinduism Today
Osho (aka Rajneesh)	1931–90	Osho Commune International
Sathya Sai Baba	1926–	Sathya Sai

Transcendental Meditation

TM is one of the most recognized modern movements in the study of religion. The meditative program, which guru Maharishi Mahesh Yogi made famous, has been the subject of controversy concerning its purported status as a science. Followers claim that it combines the best of Western science with Vedic Science (or SCI: Science of Creative Intelligence) and should not be dismissed as a religion. Critics argue that the techniques of TM involve explicit religious practices, including the recitation of Hindu mantras. They also point to a groundbreaking court case in 1978 in New Jersey, when TM was banned from public schools because of its religious nature.

Maharishi was born Mahesh Prasad Varma in Uttar Pradesh, India. His birthday is typically given as January 12, 1917. He became a follower of Swami Brahmananda Saraswati (1871–1953) in the 1940s and worked as his assistant until the latter's death in 1953. Maharishi and TM devotees refer to Saraswati as "Guru Dev" and invoke his blessing in the TM initiation *puja* (ceremony). Maharishi went public with his meditation technique in 1958 and first visited the United States in 1959.

TM grew dramatically after the Beatles met with Maharishi in London on August 24, 1967. They heard him speak at the Park Lane Hilton and received initiation the next week. Their enchantment lasted only about a year but created a fascination with the guru within their circles. John Lennon targeted Maharishi in the song "Sexy Sadie." The Beatles had grown concerned about financial pressure on them from Maharishi, plus they had heard of allegations that Maharishi had sexually assaulted some of his female followers.

TM has been viewed as a helpful, non-religious meditation exercise. Maharishi has aimed for every person on earth to engage in TM. A World Plan Executive Council is in charge of implementing the wide-ranging vision. The claims proponents of TM make are astounding. They argue that if 1 percent of the world meditated then all war would come to an end and that if 1 percent of any city's population meditated then that city would see a drop in crime. They claim TM improves every area of personal life, including one's intelligence, health, and job performance. The movement claims that more than five hundred scientific studies have proven that TM works. Some scientists have disputed these studies and argue that TM can actually be harmful to some people.

Maharishi's vision is expressed through his Open University, the Corporate Development Program, and the TM organization. The Natural Law Party was created on the basis of TM, but its work is now carried on by the U.S. Peace Government, which John Hagelin, a major leader in TM, heads. The U.S. Peace Government is part of TM's Global Country of World Peace.

Maharishi has offered products from Vedic Medicine over the years, but he gained most scrutiny for offering advanced courses in yogic-flying. Ex-members have said that the flying simply amounts to learning to bounce from a sitting position on a mattress one or two feet in the air with a forward motion of three or four feet. Early advertisements for TM promised levitation, invisibility, and supernormal hearing and sight.

The claim that TM is not religious is difficult to sustain in the face of Maharishi's Hindu roots, the explicit use of Hindu mantras, his overall ideology, and his own clear statements made over the years in private publications and conversations. The initiation ceremony of TM contained this invocation: "To Lord Narayana, to lotus-born Brahma the Creator, to Vashishta, to Shakti, and to his son, Parashar, to Vyasa, to Shukadava, to the great Gaudapada, to Govinda, ruler among yogis, to his disciple, Shri Trotika and Varttika-Kara, to others, to the tradition of our masters I bow down. To the abode of the wisdom of the Shrutis, Smritis and Puranas, to the abode of kindness, to the personified glory of the Lord, to Shankara, emancipator of the Lord, I bow down. To Sharkaracharya, the redeemer, hailed as Krishna and Badarayana, to the commentator of the Brahma Sutras, I bow down again and again."

Two of the U.S. court cases that affirmed the religious nature in TM are: MALNAK v. YOGI, APPEAL FROM THE UNITED STATES DISTRICT COURT FOR THE DISTRICT OF NEW JERSEY, (D.C. Civil Action No. 76-0341) and MALNAK v. YOGI, Nos. 78-1568, 78-1882, UNITED STATES COURT OF APPEALS, THIRD CIRCUIT, 592 F.2d 197, December 11, 1978, Argued, February 2, 1979.

When a student reporter at UCLA interviewed Maharishi, he gave this answer to a question on the meaning of enlightenment: "Enlightenment means lack of darkness, absence of darkness. And absence of darkness means no mistake, no weakness, no shortcoming—success everywhere, fulfillment of desire everywhere. That is enlightenment. One is living in full accord with Natural Law. Spontaneously Nature is supporting us: then we are not in the dark about anything."

Maharishi lived out his later years in the Netherlands. He died on February 5, 2008.

TRANSCENDENTAL MEDITATION

Typology	Hindu
Founder	Maharishi Mahesh Yogi
Websites	www.tm.org www.alltm.org www.natural-law.org

Critic Sites	Falling Down the TM Rabbit Hole (Joe Kellett):
	    www.suggestibility.org
	Meditation Information Network (Mike Doughney):
	    http://minet.org
	TM-Free Blog (John Knapp): http://tmfree.blogspot.com/

Recommended Reading	Paul Mason, *The Maharishi* (Lyndhurst: Evolution, 2008)

Special Note	The original TranceNet site (www.trancenet.org) was
	    devoted to critical material on TM. That site was
	    discontinued in 2005 but the domain now points to an
	    Italian organization that offers meditation techniques that
	    are less expensive than TM.

Virato

Swami Nostradamus Virato is a guru in the tradition of the famous and controversial Hindu teacher Rajneesh/Osho. Virato, a native of Brooklyn, was born on December 14, 1938. He claims that Jesus appeared to him when he was 9 years old. In 1972 he left his wife and three children to pursue spiritual enlightenment. He became a *sannyasin* (disciple) of Rajneesh on January 10, 1980, and he directed the group's center in Philadelphia from 1982 to 1984.

Swami Virato claims that both Osho and Nostradamus appeared to him in holographic form out of a large plant in his office on January 19, 1990—at the same moment Osho died. The Swami is married to Dhiraga, a native of Russia who works with him in Theatre Tantra.

Like Osho, Virato is known for a radical style and rhetoric. In one message he stated: "During my discourses in America and Russia I always tell listeners not to believe me. . . . Beliefs, including being an 'enlightenment junky,' will keep you from your destination, be it Nirvana, Heaven, God, or whatever you choose to call it. Religions and spiritual paths do just this by 'dogmafying' the way."

Internet Source

Virato website: www.newfrontier.com

Swami Vivekananda

Swami Vivekananda, born in Calcutta in 1863, is one of the most celebrated of Hindu gurus. He is most famous for his exposition of Hinduism at the 1893 World's Parliament of Religions, held at the World's Fair in Chicago. Vivekananda was a disciple of Sri Ramakrishna, a celebrated Vendanta guru who died in 1886. Vivekananda founded the Ramakrishna Order after his master's death. In the West, Vivekananda's name is usually connected with the Vedanta Society. His *Complete Works* are available in nine volumes.

In one of Vivekananda's Parliament speeches, he dealt with the question of idol worship: "The Hindus have discovered that the absolute can only be realized, or thought of, or stated, through the relative, and the images, crosses, and crescents are simply so many symbols—so many pegs to hang the spiritual ideas on. One thing I must tell you. Idolatry in India does not mean anything horrible. It is not the mother of harlots. On the other hand, it is the attempt of undeveloped minds to grasp high spiritual truths. The Hindus have their faults, they sometimes have their exceptions; but mark this, they are always for punishing their own bodies, and never for cutting the throats of their neighbors."

Vivekananda also addressed the unity of religions. "To the Hindus, then, the whole world of religions is only a traveling, a coming up, of different men and women, through various conditions and circumstances, to the same goal. Every religion is only evolving a God out of the material person, and the same God is the inspirer of all of them. Why, then, are there so many contradictions? They are only apparent, say the Hindus. The contradictions come from the same truth adapting itself to the varying circumstances of different natures. It is the same light coming through glasses of different colors. And these little variations are necessary for purposes of adaptation. But in the heart of everything the same truth reigns."

Internet Source

Swami Vivekananda website: www.vivekananda.org

HINDUISM TIMELINE

c. 272 B.C.—King Asoka rules India

c. 200 B.C.—Composition of Gita

c. A.D. 200—The Laws of Manu finished

   c. 500—*Kama Sutra*

   c. 800—Sankara (788–820) expounds Advaitist position

   c. 1100—Ramanuja (1017?–1137) defends Vaisnava theism

   1206—Mughal rule in India

   1518—Death of Kabir, famous devotional poet

   1542—Francis Xavier begins mission in India

   1556—Accession of the emperor Akbar

   1583—Caitanya, Bengali Vaisnava bhakti leader

   1757—British rule established in Calcutta

   1828—Ram Mohan Roy starts Brahmo Samaj

   1829—Banning of Sati (widow burning)

   1875—Dayananda Sarasvati founds Arya Samaj

   1893—Vivekananda at World's Parliament of Religions in Chicago

   1914—Aurobindo founds ashram in Pondicherry

   1947—Independence of India

   1948—Assassination of Gandhi

   1984—Sikh Golden Temple assaulted by Army

   1984—Indira Gandhi assassinated

   1985—Downing of Air India 182 (Sunday, June 3)

   1991—Rajiv Gandhi assassinated

   1992—Muslim-Hindu clashes

   1996—Victory of BJP party

   1999—Graham Staines and two sons burned alive

   2001—Suicide attacks on Indian Parliament

   2002—Muslim-Hindu clashes

   2004—Congress party wins election

■ The Christian Response to Hinduism

The following items represent the chief concerns Christians must raise about the major elements of Hinduism:

1. The legends and stories about the gods and goddesses of Hinduism do not have the ring of historicity to them. Granted, the vast majority of Hindus really believe the stories about Krishna, Hanuman, Shiva, and other deities. However, there is no historical evidence to support these legends. During my Ph.D. course work, I interviewed A. L. Basham, one of the world's greatest scholars on India and its religions. He told me that there was no proof at all of the historical reality of Krishna. His answer was not based on any stance of faith but came out of his immense historical erudition. The mythical nature of the Hindu deities is in total contrast to the historical evidence for God's incarnation in Jesus Christ.

2. The polytheistic nature of Hinduism is contradictory to the Bible's message of one God. Of course, Christians must note that Hindus usually believe that the thousands of deities in the Hindu world are manifestations of one ultimate God. Nevertheless, biblical faith mandates worship only of the God and Father of the Lord Jesus Christ. The Bible also explicitly and repeatedly condemns the worship of idols.

3. The law of karma is fatalistic in nature and undermines the biblical teaching on grace and mercy. Likewise, the theory of reincarnation is not taught in the Bible. Hinduism teaches that karma is absolute, while Christian faith teaches that God's mercy can override the wages of sin.

THE POWER OF CASTE

Although caste is *the* defining feature of most of Indian society, I knew nothing of its power until one afternoon of 1952, at the University of Allahabad. As a student in Jorhat (1946–49) I had swept floors, cleaned toilets, and happily worked in the gardens to pay for my room and board. My parents and Christian mentors had taught me that all work was honorable, better than begging.

So I never imagined that a sweeper was different from me or my fellow students . . . that is not until about 4 o'clock that fateful day. A classmate of mine and I were walking home to our hostel. Our hostel sweeper was walking a little ahead of us. The winter evening sun cast his long shadow on us. I didn't even notice it but my friend did. He suddenly flew into a rage. "You *Bhangi*!" he screamed at the sweeper, "You scum of the earth! Are you blind? Your shadow fell on me. You have polluted me!"

—Rochunga Pudaite (Bibles for the World)

4. The caste system denies the dignity and equality of all humans. The ancient Hindu scriptures clearly advocate the caste system. In spite of India's laws about equality, the country remains divided along caste lines. Indian society still teaches that some people are Untouchable. These individuals are known as Dalits. Sixty percent of Indian Christians are from a Dalit background. It is estimated that Dalits number over 250 million in India.

5. Hindu leaders in India often protest that Christians try to convert Hindus to Jesus. However, Hindu gurus have consistently attempted to convert a Western audience to Hinduism. Religious freedom should include the right to change one's religious convictions. Tragically, Hindu extremists have resorted to violence against Christians in the last decade.

6. It is evident that many famous Hindu gurus who have come to the West have used their alleged spiritual status to engage in sexual and financial exploitation of disciples. While this does not prove that Hin-

duism is false, this pattern of abuse illustrates the dangers of gullible and naïve faith in so-called spiritual masters.

7. The Hindu appreciation for Jesus Christ is not matched by a recognition and acceptance of the Gospels' teaching that Jesus is the only Son of God, the One who died for our sins and rose to heavenly glory.

First Hindu temple in U.S., Flushing, New York

Photo: Gordon Melton

Glossary of Hindu Terms

Agni: god of fire
ahimsa: the principle of non-violence
atman: the self or soul
avatar: manifestation or incarnation of god or goddess on earth
avidya: ignorance about morals and delusion about reality
bhakti: practice of devotion and worship
Brahman: the force and power behind all things; Ultimate Reality
Brahmin: highest of the four castes (Varnas)
deva/devi: god/goddess
dharma: (a) duties and obligations, often related to caste, (b) virtue
gopi: daughter or wife of farmer/milkmaid
guru: spiritual teacher

hatha yoga: type of yoga devoted to bodily exercise

Ishvara: means "Lord of the Universe"

jati: sub-caste

jiva: soul of person

jnana: knowledge

kama: pleasure (aesthetic, sexual, and otherwise)

karma: one's just reward for good and evil

kshatriya: warrior or leader; second of four castes

lila: play, festival, drama, sport

linga/m: oblong stone that symbolizes Shiva

mantra: sacred words and sounds used in meditation

maya: the world of appearance and illusion

moksha: salvation from cycle of death and rebirth

om: most well-known mantra or sacred sound

puja: offering of food, flowers and love to the divine

puranas: stories of the gods/goddesses

Ramayana: major epic about the love of Rama for Sita

sadhu: one who renounces normal life for ascetic path

shakti: term for power, especially related to goddesses

samadhi: final stage of meditation when one grasps the Ultimate

samsara: cycle of death and rebirth

sannyasin: another term for sadhu; also can mean disciple

Shaivism: the worship of Shiva, one of the most famous Hindu gods

shudra: lowest Hindu caste

student: first of four life stages

outcaste: the Untouchables, those below the lowest class

vaishya: trade and merchant caste, including farmers

Vaishnavism: worship of Vishnu (and Rama and Krishna, Vishnu's avatars)

varna: caste

vidya: learning, knowledge, spiritual enlightenment

yogi: a practioner of yoga

Bibliography

Wesley Ariarajah, *Hindus and Christians* (Grand Rapids: Eerdmans, 1991)

Jonah Blank, *Arrow of the Blue-Skinned God* (New York: Doubleday, 1992)

Elisabeth Bumiller, *May You Be the Mother of a Hundred Sons* (New York: Random, 1990)

David Burnett, *The Spirit of Hinduism* (Tunbridge Wells: Monarch, 1992)

Frederick Copleston, *Religion and the One* (London: Search Press, 1982)

Harold Coward, ed. *Hindu-Christian Dialogue* (Maryknoll, NY: Orbis Books, 1989)

Diana Eck, *Encountering God* (Boston: Beacon Press, 1993)

Franklin Edgerton, trans. *The Bhagavad Gita* (New York: Harper & Row, 1944)

Gavin Flood, *An Introduction to Hinduism* (Cambridge University Press, 1996)

Klaus Klostermaier, *A Concise Encyclopedia of Hinduism* (Oxford: Oneworld, 1998)

Julius Lipner, *Hindus* (London: Routledge, 1998)

Geoffrey Parrinder, *Avatar and Incarnation* (New York: Oxford University Press, 1970)

Sarvepalli Radhakrishnan, *Selected Writings* (New York: Dutton, 1970)

R. C. Zaehner, *Hinduism* (Oxford University Press, 1966)

7

ISLAM

Mosque, Kuala Lumpur, Malaysia

Photo: Gordon Melton

Like all religions, Islam has a core, an essence, a sort of DNA that has defined the religion from the beginning. The best way to capture this basic and fundamental identity is to grasp four absolutely key realities in the faith of all Muslims. Even if you knew everything there was to know about Islam, these keys to understanding the Muslim faith would be essential.

1. What is absolutely primary in Islam is a total belief in Allah (the Arabic term for God). Muslims inherited from Jewish and Christian tradition the conviction that there is one Supreme Creator, an infinite, eternal Power who can do all things and knows all things.

   According to Muslims, Allah is the perfect, wise, merciful and just Guide who holds all humans accountable for their deeds, both good and bad. All of this is captured in the first verses of the Qur'an, the Muslim scripture. "In the name of Allah, Most Gracious, Most Merciful. Praise be to Allah, the Cherisher and Sustainer of the worlds." It continues: "Master of the Day of Judgment. You do we worship, and Your aid we seek. Show us the straight way."

ISLAM'S NINETY-NINE NAMES OF GOD

Allah—The God	Al Rahman—The Compassionate
Al Rahim—The Merciful	Al Malik—The King
Al Quddus—The Holy	As Salam—The Peace
Al Mu'min—The One with Faith	Al Muhaymin—The Protector
Al 'Aziz—The Mighty	Al Jabbar—The Repairer
Al Mutakabbir—The Imperious	Al Khaliq—The Creator
Al Bari'—The Maker	Al Musawwir—The Fashioner
Al Ghaffar—The Forgiver	Al Qahhar—The Dominant
Al Wahhab—The Bestower	Al Razzaq—The Provider
Al Fattah—The Opener	Al 'Alim—The Knower
Al Qaibid—The Contractor	Al Basit—The Expander
Al Khafid—The Humbler	Al Rafi'—The Exalter
Al Mu'izz—The Honorer	Al Mudhill—The Abaser
As Sami'—The Hearer	Al Basir—The Seer
Al Hakam—The Judge	Al 'Adl—The Just
Al Latif—The Subtle	Al Khabir—The Aware
Al Halim—The Gentle	Al 'Azim—The Mighty
Al Ghafur—The Forgiving	Ash Shakur—The Grateful
Al 'Ali—The Lofty	Al Kabir—The Great
Al Hafiz—The Guardian	Al Muqit—The Nourisher
Al Hasib—The Reckoner	Al Jalil—The Majestic
Al Karim—The Generous	Ar Raqib—The Watcher
Al Mujib—The Responder	Al Wasi'—The Englober
Al Hakim—The Wise	Al Wadud—The Loving
Al Majid—The Glorious	Al Ba'ith—The Resurrector
Ash Shahid—The Witness	Al Haqq—The Truth
Al Wakil—The Trustee	Al Qawi—The Strong
Al Matin—The Firm	Al Wali—The Friend
Al Hamid—The Praiseworthy	Al Muhsi—The Counter
Al Mubdi'—The Originator	Al Mu'id—The Restorer
Al Muhyi—The Life-Giver	Al Mumit—The Death-Giver
Al Hayy—The Living	Al Qayyum—The Self-Subsistent

Al Wajid—The Finder	Al Majid—The Noble
Al Ahad—The One	As Samad—The Eternal-Absolute
Al Qadir—The Able	Al Muqtadir—The Powerful
Al Muqaddim—The Expediter	Al Mu'akhkhir—The Deferrer
Al Awwal—The First	Al Akhir—The Last
Az Zahir—The Manifest	Al Batin—The Hidden
Al Wali—The Governor	Al Muta'ali—The Exalted
Al Barr—The Benefactor	At Tawwab—The Acceptor of
Al Muntaqim—The Avenger	Repentance
Ar Ra'uf—The Pardoner	Al 'Afuw—The Pardoner
Dhu 'l-Jalal wa 'l-Ikram—Lord of	Malik al-Mulk—The Ruler of the
Majesty and Generosity	Kingdom
Al Jami'—The Gatherer	Al Muqsit—The Equitable
Al Mughni—The Enricher	Al Ghani—The Self-Sufficient
Ad Darr—The Distresser	Al Mani—The Preventer
An Nur—The Light	An Nafi'—The Benefactor
Al Badi—The Incomparable	Al Hadi—The Guide
Al Warith—The Inheritor	Al Baqi—The Enduring
As Sabur—The Patient	Ar Rashid—The Rightly Guided

2. Muslims also believe that Allah has spoken to the world through Muhammad, the final, ultimate and greatest prophet. The vast majority of Muslims believe that Muhammad (who died in A.D. 632) was sinless. Every area of Islamic life is patterned after what Muhammad taught, what he did, how he dressed, how he responded to threats, and what he said had been revealed to him by Allah.

   The reverence and adulation of Muhammad is hard to overestimate, though Muslims do not believe he was divine. However, those who cast aspersions on the Prophet are in extreme danger, as Salman Rushdie, the Indian-born Muslim, discovered when he wrote *The Satanic Verses*. The Iranian Ayatollah Khomeini issued a death threat on the author because he thought Rushdie had slandered Muhammad.

3. Further, the Qur'an is absolutely pivotal to all Muslims. This is *the* Holy Book of Islam. Muslims believe the Qur'an (Koran is the old English term) was revealed to Muhammad and is the literal, actual

Word of Allah. It should be recited in Arabic, the original language, and memorized, studied, but never questioned.

Islamic views on everything are determined by what the Qur'an says or by what can be deduced from its general teachings. Thus, polygamy is acceptable because the Qur'an says so. Muslim veiling of women is derived from one passage that demands modesty. The hand of a thief is amputated simply because the Qur'an says this is to be the punishment. Muslims have certain views about Jesus because the Muslim holy book teaches them.

4. Islam is also a religion of law. While every religion has general principles, some religions, like orthodox Judaism and Roman Catholicism, have elaborate rules and regulations. This is even more so in Islam, since Islamic law extends to every area of life, including how Muslim nations are to obey God's will. *Shariah* is the Arabic term for way or path, and Muslims believe that Islamic law is God's law or way.

AMERICAN MUSLIMS AND ISLAMIC LEGAL RULINGS

In 1986 experts in Islamic law from the United States and Canada formed the Fiqh Council of North America to provide legal opinion on all aspects of Muslim life. The Council website (www.fiqhcouncil. org) provides answers to hundreds of questions, ranging from "Can Muslims attend non-Muslim funerals?" (Yes) to "Should Muslim men wear beards?" (It is a good practice but not absolutely necessary).

The history of Islamic jurisprudence is very long and complicated, especially after Islam experienced a serious division following the death of Muhammad. Basically, however, Islamic law is derived first from the Qur'an, and then from the example (*sunnah*) of Muhammad. When neither the Qur'an nor the Prophet's life and teachings speaks directly on an issue, most Muslim legal authorities depend on reason and consensus to formulate new laws or judgments based on the massive codes of law given in the three centuries after Muhammad's death.

The scope of *shariah* law is amazing to most non-Muslims. Take, for example, some of the matters addressed in *Islamic Laws*, written by

Ayatullah al Uzama Sye Ali-al-Husaini Seestani, a famous judge in Iran. He provides rulings (known as *fatwas*) on thousands of topics, including: (a) what direction should be faced when using the bathroom? (b) when does swallowing thick dust make fasting void? (c) how much is owed Allah in alms-giving if a Muslim owns sixty-one camels?

Grave of al-Bukhari, hadith collector

Photo: Massimo Introvigne

ISLAM 101

The Five Pillars of Islam

- *Shahadah: Confession of Faith:* "There is no God but Allah, and Muhammad is His messenger."

- *Salat: Prayer:* All Muslims are to pray five times per day, facing Mecca, the holiest city.

- *Zakat: Tithing:* Muslims must give financially to the poor and the needy. This involves giving at least 2.5 percent of their total wealth.

- *Sawm: Fasting:* During the holy month of Ramadan, Muslims are to refrain from food, water, and sex from sunrise to sunset.

- *Hajj:* As far as possible, at least once in a lifetime, Muslims are to travel to Mecca to engage in rituals of prayer and worship at the central shrine in Islam's holiest city.

The Prophet

- Most Muslims believe that Muhammad was sinless.

- Muhammad is not viewed as divine.

- Most Muslims believe that the Prophet was illiterate.

- The prophetic status of Muhammad is not to be questioned.

- Muhammad provides the greatest example for all aspects of life.

- The traditions about the Prophet are known as *hadith.*

- The Prophet was given permission by Allah to have twelve wives.

The Qur'an

- Muslims believe the Qur'an is the perfect Word of Allah.

- The Qur'an contains 114 chapters or *surahs.*

- Muslims believe that the Qur'an was revealed to Muhammad by the archangel Gabriel.

- The Qur'anic material was composed from 610 through Muhammad's death in 632.

- The final compilation of the Qur'an was completed about A.D. 650.

- The Qur'an is basically ordered by chapter length. The shorter chapters appear later but are usually from the earlier part of Muhammad's ministry.

The Five Pillars of Islam

Just as the Ten Commandments shape Judaism, the five pillars of Islam constitute core patterns of faith for most Muslims. The primary pillar is a confession of faith known as the *shahadah*, which reads: "There is no God but Allah, and Muhammad is His messenger." Once a person makes this confession with sincerity he or she has become a Muslim. By reference to Allah, Muslims are speaking about the God of Islamic faith and not simply affirming belief in one God.

The second pillar involves the discipline of prayer (*salat*) and the call to all Muslims to pray at five specific times every day, facing Mecca, the holiest city. The five prayers are (a) *Salat-Ul-Fajr*: the Morning Prayer, which is to take place between dawn and just before sunrise, (b) *Salat-Ul-Zuhr*: the Noon Prayer, to be said sometime between when the sun reaches its zenith and mid-afternoon, (c) *Salat-Ul-Asr*: the Afternoon Prayer, to occur between mid-afternoon and just before sunset, (d) *Salat-Ul-Maghrib*: the Evening Prayer, to be offered just after sunset or up to an hour and a half later, and (e) *Salat-Ul-Isha*: the Night Prayer, which can be said anywhere from an hour and a half after sunset through till the next day's dawn.

Muslims are supposed to give at least 2.5 percent of their total wealth as a means of addressing the imbalances between rich and poor. This third pillar is known as *zakat*, from an Arabic root word that means purification and growth. Zakat is not to be understood as charity but rather as the way in which Allah wants the world to be a place of greater justice. This third pillar represents a matter of obligation; giving beyond 2.5 percent constitutes charity. In both kinds of giving it is normally expected that the identity of the giver will be kept a secret unless it will be helpful for the greater good for the identification to be made public.

As is well known, Muslims are to intensify their spiritual focus through another pillar, that of fasting during the month of Ramadan. This fourth pillar is known as *sawm* and involves refraining from smoking, eating, drinking, and sexual intercourse during the daylight hours of the month. Muslims are only excused from fasting for serious medical conditions. At the end of Ramadan Muslims celebrate a feast known as *Eid al-Fitr*.

FOOD AND ISLAM

Many Muslims obey food laws in much the same way that orthodox Jews follow kosher dietary laws in the Jewish faith. The Arabic term *halal* refers to food that Muslims are allowed to eat, while the term *haram* applies to forbidden food. Muslims cannot eat pork products and are not supposed to drink alcohol.

The last pillar, known as the *hajj*, is the command for all able-bodied Muslims to make a pilgrimage to Mecca at least once in their lifetime. The *hajj* takes place just over two months after the end of Ramadan, and about two million Muslims annually make their way to Mecca for this major spiritual exercise. During the week-long pilgrimage Muslims engage in a five-part ritual designed to reenact major events in the sacred history of Islam and draw closer to God and fellow Muslims. The *hajj* ends with the feast known as *Eid al-Adha* (Festival of Sacrifice).

MONTHS OF THE ISLAMIC CALENDAR

1. Muharram	7. Rajab
2. Safar	8. Sha'ban
3. Rabi' al-awwal (Rabi' I)	9. Ramadan
4. Rabi' al-thani (Rabi' II)	10. Shawwal
5. Jumada al-awwal (Jumada I)	11. Dhu al-Qi'dah
6. Jumada al-thani (Jumada II)	12. Dhu al-Hijjah

■ Other Major Items in Islam

Just as all faithful Muslims believe that Allah is the one true God, they also want to emulate Muhammad, obey the Qur'an, pray, give financially, fast, take the pilgrim's journey to Mecca, and obey the law of God in all things. Beyond these overriding and paramount aspects of Islam, there are seven other fundamental beliefs that further enhance an accurate picture.

1. Contrary to popular opinion, Muslims do **not** believe that their religion began with Muhammad. They assert that Islam started at creation when God created Adam and Eve, and that Islam was the religion of faithful Jews and Christians. Thus, Jews in the time of Moses were Muslims, and Christians in the time of Jesus were Muslims! Younis Shaikh, who taught at a medical college in Pakistan, was arrested in October, 2000, for allegedly saying that Muhammad's parents were not Muslims and that Muhammad did not become a Muslim until he was 40.

2. Though Muslim views derive in part from Christian tradition, Muslims do **not** believe in original sin. (This is the concept that all human beings are born with a sinful nature.) Muslims do believe that Adam rebelled against God's law in the Garden of Eden as is taught by most Christian groups, but there was no fall of the human race. Humans are frail and weak, prone to temptation, obviously, but not predisposed toward sin.

3. Islam's emphasis on the majesty and total sovereignty of God cannot be overstressed. In parts of Afghanistan goals in soccer games are celebrated by shouting "Allahu Akbar" or "God is great." When visiting Kenya in 1994, I saw a vivid display of Islamic trust in God in a poor Muslim area. There, on top of the most pitiful little "house" imaginable, the "home owner" had a sign, almost bigger than his house, proclaiming his faith in the great Allah.

   Muslim theologians developed a very rigid doctrine of predestination out of the emphasis on Allah's total supremacy. If God is all-knowing and all-powerful, is he not, in some sense, responsible for everything? If nothing really deviates from his will, then, since He knows the future, everything must be predestined, or so it has been argued. Some analysts of Muslim culture believe that a sense of fatalism has emerged as a result of this Islamic preoccupation with predestination.

4. Islam also teaches that our universe is home to angels, devils, and another kind of spirit beings known as *jinns*. Islam shares with Christian tradition a belief in Satan or the supreme devil, an angel who chose to rebel against Allah. Muslims also believe in angels, disembodied spirits who obey God. The English term *genie* derives from Muslim stories about the *jinn*, supernatural entities who can do both good and evil.

5. Islam has very definite views about the Day of Judgment. At a time known only to Allah, the world will end. All humans will be judged by their deeds. Humans await either eternal punishment in hellfire or eternal bliss in heaven. Islam has no notion of purgatory and virtually no openness to any idea that all humans will eventually reach paradise.

   The explicitness of Islam on the severity of hellfire makes tough reading, as can be said of much of the traditional Christian images of hell, as evidenced in Dante's famous *Inferno*. One noted verse in the fourth *surah* (chapter) of the Qur'an states: "Those who reject our Signs, We shall soon cast into the Fire: as often as their skins are roasted through, We shall change them for fresh skins, that they may taste the penalty: for God is Exalted in Power, Wise" (v. 56).

6. Islam views heaven as the eternal abode of those chosen by Allah. Heaven is a paradise of bliss and perfection, where sin, evil, pain, sorrow, and death are no more. This parallels the Christian understanding of heaven, obviously. Both males and females will be in heaven, and there is a significant emphasis in Islamic history on the promise that faithful Muslim males will enjoy sexual pleasure in heaven with their own harem of virgins.

   This teaching has been the focus of recent study because of promises made to Palestinian suicide bombers that their death will lead them to a paradise where virgins await their arrival. As well, Judith Miller, a reporter for *The New York Times*, writes in her book *God Has Ninety-Nine Names* about radical Egyptian clerics who also encourage terrorist acts by promising their young male followers that they will have eternal sex on the other side of a suicide mission.

Surah 37:43–48 of the Qur'an reads like this: "In Gardens of Felicity,

"Facing each other on Thrones (of Dignity): Round will be passed to them a Cup from a clear-flowing fountain, crystal-white, of a taste delicious to those who drink (thereof),

"Free from headiness; nor will they suffer intoxication therefrom. And beside them will be chaste women, restraining their glances, with big eyes (of wonder and beauty)."

7. Muslims claim that Jesus is a prophet of Islam. Given the bitter hostilities between Islamic and Christian empires in history, it is often assumed that Muslims have no interest in Jesus. While Muhammad is the chief prophet, Muslims also look to Jesus as a spiritual guide. Often when Muslims speak of Jesus, they will add the phrase "Peace Be Upon Him"—just as they do when Muhammad's name is mentioned either vocally or in print. For short, in writing you will often see "Muhammad (PBOH)" or "Jesus (PBOH)."

There are significant differences between Muslim and Christian understandings of Jesus. This is most easily seen by a list of Muslim negative assertions about Christian views. For Islam, Jesus is *not* the Son of God and *not* an incarnation of God. Jesus is *not* divine. He did *not* die on the cross at Calvary. His death is *not* a sacrifice for sin. He was *not* put in a tomb outside Jerusalem. The Christian story of Easter is *not* true, though Muslims do believe that Jesus went to heaven when he died, years after attempts to have him crucified failed.

Muslims do agree with Christianity on the following points: Jesus was born of the Virgin Mary, was a prophet of God, lived a holy life, taught with wisdom and love, and performed many miracles. Muslims also unite with Christian tradition in teaching that Jesus was persecuted for his faith, was opposed to idol worship (as most Jews would be), and is now in heaven.

■ The Branches of Islam

Like all religions, Islam has not retained its original unity. In fact, within a generation of the Prophet's death, Muslims were at war with each other over political leadership and the proper interpretation of Islamic spirituality. Muslims can be grouped under three major branches or types.

The three are: (a) Sunni, (b) Shi'a, also known as Shi'ite, and (c) Sufi.

Sunni Islam represents the largest grouping in Islam. Of the world's 1.2 billion Muslims, over one billion are Sunni, which represents over 90 percent of all Muslims. Sunni Muslims trace themselves back to the Prophet but separate from Shi'a Muslims over the question of proper authority in Islam, the shape of Islamic law, and the nature of salvation.

There are 170 million Shi'a Muslims globally. Though they represent a minority among the three main Islamic groups, the Shi'a version of Islam became the most well known in the West after the Islamic revolution in Iran in 1979. The Shah of Iran was deposed and the Ayatollah Khomeni, the well-known Shi'a Muslim leader, returned from exile in France to run the country.

Grave of Sufi leader Baha-ud-Din Naqshband Bukhari (1318–89)

Photo: Massimo Introvigne

In Sunni Islam the *imam* is the person who leads prayer in the mosque. The same word in Shi'a Islam stands for leaders like the Ayatollah and, most importantly, for the succession of singular figures said to be chosen by Allah to guide Islam in its earliest and most important years. One Shi'a group believes there were seven imams, while another extends the number to twelve. Each group believes the last imam to be alive, but that Allah has placed him in a state of supernatural hiddenness until the end of time.

Shi'a Muslims give enormous significance to the martyrdom of Husayn, whose father, Ali, was the son-in-law of the Prophet. Sunni Muslims killed Husayn and his comrades at Karbala, Iraq, on the tenth day of the Muslim month of Muharran in A.D. 680. Every year Shi'a Muslims engage in elaborate rituals to honor Husayn's memory. His shrine in Karbala is one of the holiest Shi'a pilgrimage sites.

The Sufis represent the mystical side of Islam. Today, they number more than 240 million throughout the world. Sufism emerged in the twilight years of the earliest Muslim dynasties. Al-Ghazali, the great Islamic devotional writer, turned to Sufism as an alternative to the speculative and uncertain paths of philosophy and reason. The Sufi path is best known through the Whirling Dervish, a type of dance used to resist outside stimuli and focus on the mind of Allah.

▩ Muhammad: the Prophet of Islam

Some secular historians, who have no desire to follow Muhammad, believe that he is the most significant person in human history. Though Christianity claims more adherents, Muhammad is viewed by these historians as having a greater impact on history, given the breadth of Islamic political power, the depth and range of Islamic spirituality, and the pervasive way in which Islam brings its ideology to bear on every facet of life.

Whatever the merit of this judgment, anyone who knows the history of the world since the seventh century can see the absolutely profound impact Muhammad made in his lifetime and ever since. Muslims believe, of course, that the most important fact to grasp is that Muhammad is *the* Prophet, the final Messenger of Allah. For this claim alone, if not for the others, our understanding of Islam is intrinsically linked with our knowledge and assessment of its Prophet.

The Contours of a Prophet's Life

Scholars of Islam are divided over how much is historically certain about Muhammad. For this outline of his life we will use the perspective adopted by most Muslims and by some non-Islamic scholars. Muslims believe that Muhammad was born about A.D. 570. According to Islamic tradition, his father died before Muhammad was born and his mother died shortly after his birth. Muslims believe that this is the context for the rhetorical question in Surah 93:6 "Did He not find thee an orphan and give thee shelter (and care)?" Again, tradition states that Muhammad was raised by his grandfather and then by an uncle (Abu Talib) who watched over him until Muhammad reached his teen years.

The standard Muslim biographies report that Muhammad visited Syria on trading missions with his uncle. These reports provided an apologetic motif for evidence of Muhammad's acumen in business and for early witness to his future spiritual leadership.

A woman merchant named Khadijah came into Muhammad's life and they were married in 595, when Muhammad was about 25. Though she was considerably older than he, she bore him at least six children (two boys died early), and by all indications they had a loving marriage. Muhammad did not have other wives until after Khadijah's death in 619.

Muhammad's life changed forever in the year 610, on the seventeenth night of the Arabic month of Ramadan. Muhammad claimed that the angel Gabriel visited him on Mount Hira, near Mecca, in a powerful, terrifying, and transforming encounter. According to the earliest Muslim accounts, Muhammad returned home, shaken by this encounter, and turned to his wife for confirmation of his prophetic call.

Three years later Muhammad began to preach to his Meccan neighbors. His message of one God met fierce resistance. Arabs were polytheistic and Mecca's main shrine, the Kaba, said to be built by Abraham, was home to many gods. Muhammad gained some converts immediately, one of the most famous being his friend Abu Bakr. The earliest Muslims came mainly from the poor clans of Mecca, drawn to Muhammad's message of social reform.

Muslims believe that in 620, one year after the death of Muhammad's first wife, the angel Gabriel brought Muhammad by night to Jerusalem on the back of a heavenly horse named Buruq. In the holy city the prophet conversed with Jesus, Moses, and Abraham. Then, according to the Qur'an,

Muhammad and his angel companion were taken by ladder (called a *miraj*) to the seventh heaven. Muslims believe that the Dome of the Rock in Jerusalem is built on the spot from where Muhammad ascended.

Two years later in 622, in year one of the Muslim calendar, Muhammad was forced to flee to Medina, about 250 miles north of Mecca. Then, for eight long and bitter years, the Prophet engaged in repeated military battles with his Meccan enemies. There were significant victories (most notably on March 15, 624, at Badr) and major setbacks (one being at Uhud just a year later).

By January 630, however, Muhammad triumphed, took control of Mecca, and destroyed the idols in the Kaba. Medina continued to be his home base. He led military campaigns in northern Arabia and returned to Mecca for a final pilgrimage in early 632. He was in poor health at the time, traveled back to Medina, and died on June 8, 632, in the embrace of Aisha, one of his wives.

Alfred North Whitehead once said, "Philosophy is one long footnote to Plato." Likewise, Islamic history is one long footnote to Muhammad. Thus, Muhammad's journey—in all of its detail, from the mode of his prayer life, to his treatment of Jews and Christians, to what he did in battle—becomes the paradigm for all Muslims.

Muhammad's life must not be compartmentalized, as if his spiritual life is distinct from his family life, or military career, or political strategies, or economic views. For Muhammad and for Muslims, they are part of a seamless whole. Islam continued this pattern by absolutely refusing to think that the religious and the secular should be divorced. Thus, Muhammad would have no respect for the American model of the separation of "church and state."

Historical Accuracy and Muhammad

As we will see in the next section, there is a wide range of opinion about Muhammad. Part of that difference arises out of varied estimates about how certain we can be historically about his life. There are two major sources for historical analysis: the Qur'an and, secondly, what is called the *hadith* or the non-Qur'anic traditions about Muhammad that were gathered by Muslims after his death.

The study of the *hadith* represents one of the most fascinating aspects of Islam. Muslim scholars had to sort through the hundreds of thousands of traditions about Muhammad in order to decide what reports were accurate. The most famous collection of what Muslims regard as authentic *hadith* was done by al-Bukhari (d. 870).

Through his lifetime al-Bukhari examined over 200,000 separate traditions about Muhammad, discarded those he felt were bogus, and then published seven thousand that he believed were genuine. Almost all Sunni Muslims accept his collection but also augment al-Bukhari's work with other collections. Shi'a Muslims have their own separate collection of traditions, but there is large agreement about the basics of Muhammad's life.

Western scholars have been divided over the value of the *hadith* in terms of what we can know about Muhammad. The traditions obviously tell us what Muslims and others were saying about the Prophet, and that has an interest for its own sake. Though a few have expressed total skepticism about their integrity, most non-Muslim scholars suggest that the *hadith* have some value in getting us to the real Muhammad.

F. E. Peters writes in his *Muhammad and the Origins of Islam* that "it is inconceivable that the community should have entirely forgotten what Muhammad did or said at Mecca and Medina." This valid point does not solve the issue of what memories of the community are accurate or what parts of the standard biographies (like Ibn Ishaq's *Life of the Apostle of God*) are faithful to history.

Further, an immense gap remains between Muslim scholars who accept everything from the Qur'an and the *hadith* and those non-Muslim historians who retain the right to judge both in terms of historical integrity, moral authenticity, spiritual depth, and intellectual power. Thus, a Western academic may accept a particular saying or deed of Muhammad as historical but use that teaching or action as proof that Muhammad is not the Prophet of God.

Three Views of Muhammad

That there is an extreme range of opinion about Muhammad should come as no surprise, given the radical divergence about him in his lifetime and given the incredible things said for him and against him through the centuries. Many wars have been fought over his ideology, even among Muslims. In the Iran-Iraq conflict in the early 1980s, where hundreds of thousands died, both countries claimed to have Muhammad on their side, much like both Irish Catholics and Protestants asserted that

Jesus was with them when they fought each other during their various civil wars.

Three distinct views cover the range of interpretation about the Prophet. Of first significance is the orthodox Muslim understanding of Muhammad. While orthodox Muslims do not worship Muhammad, they view him as the sinless Prophet and as an infallible guide. The Muslim ethic and social life is rooted in the example of the Prophet. For example, al-Ghazali, one of Islam's greatest philosophers, cut his toenails based on Muhammad's pattern. Al-Ghazali (1058–1111) even states that levity on such matters will lead to a closing of the door of happiness. The modern Muslim intellectual Tariq Ramadan uses Muhammad as exemplar in his work *In the Footsteps of the Prophet.*

Out of this immense adulation of Muhammad comes an equal anger against any who are said to ridicule the Prophet. This was shown in the furor in 2005 and 2006 over the Danish cartoons of Muhammad. Salman Rushdie (1947–) received death threats because of his perceived attacks on the prophet in his novel *The Satanic Verses.* Ahmed Deedat, one of the most popular defenders of Islam, circulated a pamphlet called *How Rushdie Fooled the West.* His conclusion speaks for itself: "Mired in misery, may all his filthy lucre choke in his throat, and may he die a coward's death, a hundred times a day, and eventually when death catches up with him, many he simmer in hell for all eternity!"

A second assessment of Muhammad is one step removed from Islamic orthodoxy, though a major step. We move to those who have a high opinion of Muhammad but do not accept, for various reasons, that he is *the* prophet of God, or that Islam is the one true religion. Karen Armstrong, a former Catholic nun, has defended this view in her popular, though overly optimistic book *Muhammad: A Biography of the Prophet.* Here is a high view of Muhammad from Alphonse de LaMartaine, writing in 1854 in his *History of the Turks*:

> If greatness of purpose, smallness of means, and astonishing results are the three criteria of a human genius, who could dare compare any great man in history with Muhammad? The most famous men created arms, laws, and empires only. They founded, if anything at all, no more than material powers which often crumbled away before their eyes. This man moved not only armies, legislations, empires, peoples, dynasties, but millions of men in one-third of the then inhabited world; and more

than that, he moved the altars, the gods, the religions, the ideas, the beliefs and the souls.

There is also a developing trend in Christian thought to advance a high view of Muhammad, though shy of the Muslim view. This change has been championed by some great Christian scholars of Islam, including W. Montgomery Watt, Kenneth Cragg, Wilfred Cantwell Smith, and Hans Küng.

Küng first took up the question of Muhammad's status in his book *Christianity and the World Religions*. He presents seven parallels between Muhammad and the prophets of Israel, outlines the immense contribution of Muhammad, and concludes by citing Vatican II where one of the documents states that the Catholic Church "also looks upon the Muslims with great respect: They worship the one true God who has spoken to man."

Küng, who does not believe that Muhammad was sinless or that Islam is the one true religion, then offers this assessment: "In my opinion, that Church—and all the Christian Churches—must also 'look with great respect' upon the man whose name is omitted from the declaration out of embarrassment, although he alone led the Muslims to the worship of the one God, who spoke *through* him: Muhammad the Prophet."

The third view moves to a whole other realm, one in which Muhammad becomes the embodiment of evil. This tradition of contempt began in the early Middle Ages as Christian and Muslim armies fought for land control from North Africa, across the Middle East, and into Europe. The wars were viewed by many Christians as the necessary struggle against the Antichrist himself—Muhammad.

Dante's *Inferno* puts the Islamic leader in the lower realms of hell. William E. Phipps, author of *Muhammad and Jesus*, describes Dante's vision of Muhammad's fate. "There he receives everlastingly some of the worst punishment that hell has to offer. A gash from throat to anus causes his intestines to hang between his legs. Many of the damned are so horrified by the mutilated Muhammad spectacle that they forget momentarily their own torment."

Such diatribes against Muhammad continue from Dante through the Reformation period, culminating in Luther's invective, quoted by Phipps: "Should you be called a prophet, who were such an uncouth blockhead and ass? When the spirit of lies had taken possession of Muhammad, and the devil had murdered men's souls with his Qur'an and had destroyed the faith of Christians, he had to go on and take the sword and set about to murder their bodies."

Tunisian mosque

Photo: Eileen Barker

Secular writers have dismissed Muhammad with less bile, but their views often follow the same pattern: Muhammad was ignorant, barbaric, and immoral. He was either a hypocrite or delusional, perhaps the victim of epileptic seizures, whose success with converts had more to do with promises of sexual reward, material gain, and the proverbial Islamic sword.

In the aftermath of September 11, some editorials in the secular press hint at Muhammad's dark side, with subtle accusations that the terror that reigned down on New York and Washington had its roots in the life and teaching of the Muslim prophet. They cite Muhammad's all-or-nothing mentality, his expansionist vision, his dictatorship, and, of course, his love for *jihad*.

One interesting factor here is that human beings arrive at radically different views while dealing with the same person, the same documents, and the same history. One right-wing Christian author calls Muhammad racist, lustful, a murderer, and a pedophile. This person contends that his views are based on careful reading of the *hadith* material about Muhammad. Muslims read the same traditions and regard them as proof that Muhammad is sinless and the greatest person who has ever lived.

If we look at a particular issue in *hadith* interpretation, we will discover that the debate is not usually over what this or that tradition states. Muslim scholars know very well what particular *hadith* is being used to justify each specific attack on Muhammad. The difference of opinion has to do with larger philosophical, religious, and psychological realities that are brought to the given issue.

Take for instance the incredible accusation that Muhammad was a pedophile. It is hard to imagine a more explosive thing to say about a religious leader, or anyone for that matter. Some Muslim scholars may want the accuser to die, but they know that he is referring to a time in the Prophet's life when he took Aisha to be his wife when she was very young, perhaps as young as 6.

How could any Muslim scholar defend this today? First, some would simply refuse to entertain any possibility that Muhammad could sin. "He is the Prophet (Peace Be Upon Him), he is sinless. I cannot question God's Apostle (Peace Be Upon Him)." A second tactic would be to explain the event by reference to different cultural norms in Muhammad's day. "Who are we to judge another culture and their norms in marriage and family life?"

Finally, other Muslim scholars might say that the Prophet is exempt from the moral standards that apply to normal humans. "Allah, the Sovereign Lord, alone decides what is right. His ways are beyond our understanding. We must trust him no matter what. Allah, in his infinite wisdom, gave the young bride to Muhammad (Peace Be Upon Him). Allah knows what is best."

A more likely process is for Muslims to resist all accusations against Muhammad by a reflex action that turns to refuge in the sacred and eternal truths that have been given by Allah through His Prophet. The thought that these truths can be shaken is simply beyond the imagination of most Muslims. Where else can the Muslim turn but to the promises of Allah given to Muhammad?

MUHAMMAD'S LIFE AT A GLANCE

A.D. 570— Birth in Mecca.

575— After death of mother, Muhammad is raised by grandfather and uncle.

595— Marries Khadijah, a travel merchant.

610— Claims to have divine revelations through mystical experience. These revelations form the basis of the Qur'an.

613— Begins to preach monotheistic message and endures persecution.

613— Muhammad adds then deletes "Satanic verses" out of Qur'an because of false revelation that said worship of three idols was acceptable.

619— After the death of Khadijah, Muhammad marries Sawdah, first of many other wives.

620— Muhammad is taken by the angel Gabriel to Jerusalem and ascends to seventh heaven on a ladder (called the *miraj*).

622— Escapes to Medina to avoid persecution in Mecca.

624— Muhammad defeats Meccan enemies at the Battle of Badr.

627— Marries Zaynab, his cousin, who was previously married to the Prophet's adopted son Zayd.

627— Raids the Jewish clan of Qurayzah and orders death of hundreds of Jewish men.

628— Signs treaty with Meccan leaders at Hudaybiyyah.

630— Muhammad conquers his enemies at Mecca and removes idols from city.

632— Muhammad dies on June 8 after a period of ill health.

MIRACLE STORIES ABOUT MUHAMMAD

1. The Qur'an as perfect book proves Allah as author.

2. Taken on supernatural trip to Jerusalem and heaven.

3. Prophet splits the moon in two to prove Islam.

4. Angel opens Prophet's chest and washes his heart.

5. Prophet multiplies food to feed hungry disciples.

6. Water supply flows through Prophet's fingers.

7. Wolf praises Muhammad's ministry.

8. Muhammad heals crying palm tree.

9. Three thousand angels help Muhammad in battle.

10. Two trees move to provide privacy for Prophet.

WRITERS ON MUHAMMAD

Tor Andrae, *Mohammed: The Man and His Faith.* Translated by
   T. Menzel (New York: Harper & Brothers, 1960)
Karen Armstrong, *Muhammad* (San Francisco: Harper, 1992)
James A. Beverley, "Muhammad," *Encyclopedia of the Qur'an*
   (London: Routledge, 2005)
Clinton Bennett, *In Search of Muhammad* (London: Continuum,
   1998)
F. Buhl and Alford T. Welch, "Muhammad," *Encyclopedia of
   Islam,* Vol. 7 (Leiden: E. J. Brill, 1993)
Michael Cook, *Muhammad* (New York: Oxford University Press,
   1983)
Kenneth Cragg, (2004) "Hadith," *Encyclopaedia Britannica*
   Online
Patricia Crone and Michael Cook, *Hagarism* (Cambridge:
   Cambridge Press, 1977)

A. Guillaume, *The Life of Muhammad.* Translation of Ibn Ishaq's
   Sirat Rasul Allah (London: Oxford University Press, 1955)

Asma Hasan, *Why I Am a Muslim* (Element Books, 2004)

Martin Lings, *Muhammad* (Rochester: Inner Traditions, 1983)

Fatima Mernissi, *The Veil and the Male Elite.* Translated by Mary
   Jo Lakeland (New York: Perseus, 1991)

Harald Motzki, ed. *The Biography of Muhammad* (Leiden: Brill,
   2000)

F. E. Peters, *Muhammad and the Origins of Islam* (Albany: SUNY
   Press, 1994)

Tariq Ramadan, *In the Footsteps of the Prophet* (New York: Oxford
   University Press, 2007)

Maxime Rodinson, *Muhammad.* Translated by Anne Carter
   (Middlesex: Penguin, 1976)

Abdulaziz Sachedina, *The Islamic Roots of Democratic Pluralism*
   (Oxford: Oxford University Press, 2001)

Annemarie Schimmel, *And Muhammad Is His Messenger* (Chapel
   Hill: University of North Carolina Press, 1985)

Wilfred Cantwell Smith, *Islam in Modern History* (Princeton:
   Princeton University Press, 1977)

Robert Spencer, *The Truth about Muhammad* (Washington:
   Regnery Gateway, 2006)

John Wansbrough, *Quranic Studies* (Oxford: Oxford University
   Press, 1977)

Ibn Warraq, ed. *The Quest for the Historical Muhammad* (Buffalo:
   Prometheus, 2000)

W. Montgomery Watt, *Muhammad: Prophet and Statesman*
   (London: Oxford University Press, 1964)

▨ The Qur'an: The Muslim Holy Book

Yusaf Ali's English translation of the Qur'an runs to 597 pages in a
paperback edition, one indication of the space taken up by the Qur'an's
six thousand or so verses. What is amazing about the Qur'an is not its
size—it is that many Muslims, including young boys and girls, have memorized the entire Qur'an, cover to cover, in Arabic.

This remarkable feat is an indication of the incredible stature of the Qur'an to the Muslim world. It is a sin for a Muslim to place any book or object on top of the Qur'an. Every debate in Muslim law is settled by what the Qur'an teaches. Muslim scholars who have condemned the September 11, 2001, terrorist attacks have done so on the basis of their belief that the Qur'an condemns such evil.

The Origin of the Qur'an

Most Muslims believe that the origin of the Qur'an lies in the eternal mind of Allah. Then, when the time was right, according to the will of Allah, the angel Gabriel dictated the revelations to Muhammad. The Prophet recited the words to his wife and then to the small group that became his first followers. The earliest members not only memorized the unfolding contents but also began to write them down. After Muhammad died a number of Muslim scholars formed the final edition of the Qur'an.

Most Muslims pay no attention to skeptical attacks on the Qur'an. They absolutely reject theories about its alleged human origins. Islam states quite plainly that the Qur'an has one author: Allah. It is not Muhammad's book. It is not, they say, a human book. It is divine. To question the Qur'an is to risk eternal punishment. To obey it is to gain eternal life.

Muslims believe that the Qur'an is perfect and contains no errors. The Prophet faithfully passed on what Allah revealed to him, with one startling exception, according to Islamic tradition. Early on in his work as a prophet, Muhammad was fooled by Satan into thinking that true followers of Allah could worship three Arab deities. For a very brief period one of the chapters of the Qur'an contained approval of such pagan worship.

As soon as Allah told Muhammad of the deception by Satan, the Prophet quickly removed the offending passage. Ever since, these verses have been called "the Satanic verses." This episode in the life of the Prophet is mentioned in the Qur'an, in the *hadith* or traditions about the Prophet, and in countless books. It is from this incident that Salman Rushdie titled his controversial novel.

The Structure of the Qur'an

The Qur'an contains 114 *surahs* or chapters and over six thousand verses. The surahs are arranged by size, with the shorter chapters near the end. It is generally believed that the chapters nearer the end of the Qur'an were actually written first, most during the time when the Prophet was in Medina (A.D. 622–30). The longer chapters were written last and were revealed after the Prophet conquered Mecca in A.D. 630.

The titles of the various chapters are based on some word or idea that appears in the chapter, though the titles do not usually suggest the main theme of the chapter, if one exists. Some Muslim scholars have attempted to show that there are hidden scientific truths and mathematical wonders in the Qur'an. For example, one writer argues that the divine inspiration of the Qur'an is proven by the fact that the Arabic word for "Most Merciful" is used 114 times, which matches exactly the number of surahs of the Qur'an.

The Major Themes of the Qur'an

Many first-time readers of the Qur'an find it confusing. It does not seem orderly, as most Muslims will readily acknowledge. The text does not follow a narrative, and it is not written in a systematic fashion. The surahs are not arranged by content, and there is no single theme in most chapters. The best way to understand the Qur'an is to first grasp the major themes that it addresses on its pages.

1. **Allah**. The Qur'an is absolutely dominated by references to God. Verse after verse, page after page, beginning to end, Allah is everything to the Qur'an. The term *Allah* appears more than 2,500 times. Anyone who says that the Qur'an is mainly about something else has never read the Qur'an. It is a book saturated with references to God. Here are ten major things, in alphabetical order, that the Qur'an says about Allah.

   - He is the Creator. Surah 6:101–102 states: "He created all things, and He hath full knowledge of all things. That is God, your Lord! There is no god but He, the Creator of all things." Another passage expresses a similar assertion: "He is God, the Creator, the Evolver, the Bestower of Forms (or Colours). To Him belong the Most Beautiful Names: whatever is in the heavens and on earth, doth declare His Praises and Glory: and He is the Exalted in Might, the Wise" (59:24).

- He is Eternal. "God! There is no god but He, the Living, the Self-subsisting, Eternal. No slumber can seize Him, nor sleep" (2:225). Verse 2 of Surah 3 states: "God! There is no god but He, the Living, the Self-Subsisting, Eternal." The 112th Surah simply says: "God, the Eternal, Absolute" (v. 2).

- He is the Guardian. In Surah 89:14, near the end of the Qur'an, we read: "For thy Lord is (as a Guardian) on a watch-tower." An earlier Surah reads: "O mankind! reverence your Guardian-Lord, who created you from a single person, created, of like nature, His mate, and from them twain scattered (like seeds) countless men and women; reverence God, through whom ye demand your mutual (rights), and (reverence) the wombs (that bore you): for God ever watches over you" (4:1).

- He is Holy: "Whatever is in the heavens and on earth, doth declare the Praises and Glory of God, the Sovereign, the Holy One, the Exalted in Might, the Wise" (62:1). God's holiness is also expressed in his goodness, as in 3:26: "In Thy hand is all good." Later, in the same Surah, we read: "God loves those who do good" (v. 134).

- He is the Lord of All: "And do ye join equals with Him? He is the Lord of (all) the Worlds" (41:9). This theme is also expressed in terms of God's sovereignty, as in these powerful words from Surah 59:23: "God is He, than Whom there is no other god; the Sovereign, the Holy One, the Source of Peace (and Perfection), the Guardian of Faith, the Preserver of Safety, the Exalted in Might, the Irresistible, the Supreme: Glory to God!"

- He is the All-knowing: Surah 35:38 speaks of the scope of God's knowledge. "Verily God knows (all) the hidden things of the heavens and the earth: verily He has full knowledge of all that is in (men's) hearts." An earlier Surah also reads: "He knows all that goes into the earth, and all that comes out thereof; all that comes down from the sky and all that ascends thereto."

- He is Merciful: "He is the Most Merciful of those who show mercy!" (12:64). The phrase "Oft-forgiving, Most Merciful" is used over and over again in the Qur'an, six times in Surah 9 alone. Another powerful expression of God's mercy is given in an earlier Surah: "Those who believed and those who suffered exile and fought (and strove and struggled) in the path of God, they have the hope of the Mercy of God: And God is Oft-forgiving, Most Merciful."

- He is the Revealer: The Qur'an longs for people to trust in God's revelation and expresses astonishment that humans ignore what Allah has shown them. "If only they had stood fast by the Law, the Gospel, and all the revelation that was sent to them from their Lord, they would have enjoyed happiness from every side" (5:56). In Surah 3 we find a celebration of Jews and Christians who follow Allah's revelation: "And there are, certainly, among the People of the Book, those who believe in God, in the revelation to you, and in the revelation to them, bowing in humility to God: They will not sell the Signs of God for a miserable gain! For them is a reward with their Lord" (v. 199).

- He is the Sustainer: One of the more beautiful passages is Surah 7:54, which reads: "Your Guardian-Lord is God, Who created the heavens and the earth in six days, and is firmly established on the throne (of authority): He draweth the night as a veil o'er the day, each seeking the other in rapid succession: He created the sun, the moon, and the stars, (all) governed by laws under His command. Is it not His to create and to govern? Blessed be God, the Cherisher and Sustainer of the worlds!"

- He is worthy of Worship: This is expressed by stating repeatedly that God is worthy of praise. God himself commands worship, as in 20:14: "Verily, I am God: There is no god but I: So serve thou Me (only), and establish regular prayer for celebrating My praise."

2. **Muhammad.** The Prophet himself is at the center of the Qur'an, though often as a figure behind every chapter. His name is mentioned only four times, but he is the subject of many passages. Muslims do not believe that Muhammad is writing about himself, however. Islam

teaches that Gabriel dictated to Muhammad material that was to be put in the Qur'an about Muhammad. Further, when the Qur'an quotes words from Muhammad, Muslims believe that these are words that Allah tells Muhammad to say.

Muhammad has, according to the Qur'an, an incredible status because Allah called him as a prophet. In fact, he is "the Seal of the Prophets," a phrase from the famous passage in Surah 33 that is used by Muslims to argue that Muhammad is the final prophet. In addition, Muhammad is a judge to his followers (4:65) and is to be respected by them (2:104; 4:46).

Allah himself is a witness to Muhammad's mission (13:43; 46:8). Further, the Qur'an teaches that Muhammad's prophetic work was predicted by both Moses (46:10) and by Jesus, of whom the Qur'an says: "And remember, Jesus, the son of Mary, said: 'O Children of Israel! I am the apostle of God (sent) to you, confirming the Law (which came) before me, and giving Glad Tidings of an Apostle to come after me, whose name shall be Ahmad.'" (Ahmad is a shortened form of Muhammad.)

Muhammad is the universal messenger from God (34:28), the symbol of Allah's mercy to the world (9:61; 28:46–47; 76:24–26), and inspired by Allah. Surah 53:10–12 says: "So did (God) convey the inspiration to His Servant—(conveyed) what He (meant) to convey. The (Prophet's) (mind and) heart in no way falsified that which he saw. Will ye then dispute with him concerning what he saw?"

The Qur'an describes Muhammad as gentle (3:159), very concerned about his followers (9:128), and in deep distress for unbelievers (12:97; 25:30). It says he was a man of prayer (74:3) and had an "exalted standard of character" (68:4). He was often mocked by his enemies in Mecca, and he was accused of being mad (7:184) and under the power of demons (81:22).

Muhammad is told to adore Allah (96:19), faithfully stick to the message that he is given from God (46:9), follow Allah's duty for him (30:30), and work hard (66:9). In Surah 33 Muhammad is told by Allah that he can take women as wives as long as he pays their dowry or they are "prisoners of war." He can also marry his cousins and any woman he wants "who dedicates her soul to the prophet."

Muhammad's followers are told to visit the Prophet's home only when they have permission. They are to arrive right at mealtime (not before), leave quickly after the meal, and avoid "familiar talk" with the Prophet. It is said that "such (behavior) annoys the Prophet: he is ashamed to dismiss you, but God is not ashamed (to tell you) the truth."

3. **Qur'an.** The Qur'an also takes up itself as a subject. Satan, we are told, is not the author of the Qur'an. Muhammad could not be the author either, since, the Qur'an argues, he was completely illiterate. Only Allah could have produced such a book. The Qur'an says of itself that it is clear, understandable, written in pure Arabic, free from error, and that it contains the universal message, one that will guide its hearers into health and into eternal salvation.

Men's ritual cleansing area in mosque

Photo: Derek Beverley

4. **Biblical Material.** The Qur'an gives considerable attention to various Old and New Testament figures. As said earlier, Muslims claim that Islam began with creation and that Allah revealed himself to Jews and Christians, though both groups altered their Scriptures. Muslims use this to explain why Old and New Testament accounts of people and events often differ radically from those reported in the Qur'an.

Of biblical figures, Moses gets the most mention, with more than five hundred verses or almost 10 percent of the text dealing with him. The Qur'an also gives information about Noah, Abraham, Moses, Joshua, David, Jesus, Mary, and others. Muslims find it easy to draw comparisons between Muhammad and Moses the law-giver, and also with King David, the warrior for God.

5. **Jesus.** The Qur'an treats Jesus with great respect, as a prophet, a teacher, and a sign from God. It also states that Jesus was born of the Virgin Mary, performed miracles, and that his followers were called Muslims. The Qur'an points out that it is a serious error to think that Jesus is the Son of God or that God is a trinity of three Persons, as in Christian tradition. For the Qur'an, Jesus is an apostle, but no more than that.

As said earlier, Muslims do not believe that Jesus died on the cross. Surah 4:157, one of the famous verses of the Qur'an, speaks about enemies of Allah who insulted the Virgin Mary and who brag: "We killed Christ Jesus the son of Mary, the Apostle of God." The text then reads: "but they killed him not, nor crucified him, but so it was made to appear to them, and those who differ therein are full of doubts, with no (certain) knowledge, but only conjecture to follow, for of a surety they killed him not."

6. **True Believers.** Hundreds of verses in the Qur'an are devoted to a portrait of the true believer. The vast majority of these passages deal with behavior, both the path that is right, and the path that is wrong. This is in keeping with the common assertion that Islam is a religion about the right path, much more than it is a religion about right ideas.

Even though Islam is a religion of law, the Qur'an is focused more on the larger principles behind the law. These have to do, first of all, with positive things that are expected of all Muslims. The Muslim is a follower of Allah, fears him, and has turned from all false gods. The believer patterns his life after the model of the prophet Muhammad.

The Muslim is also a person of prayer and contemplation. He or she is peaceful, faithful, humble, and forgiving. True believers strive to do good works and protect one another. Muslims are to be charitable, according to the Qur'an, and are to be united in their faith. The disciple of Allah engages in fasting and follows Allah's will on proper marriages and proper inheritance laws. Believers are to remember the rewards of heaven and the pains of hell.

Resistance to evil and sin also identify the true believer. The Qur'an teaches that Muslims are to avoid gambling and drinking. Usury is a sin. Certain foods are forbidden, as in Orthodox Judaism. Muslim males cannot have more than four wives. Allah's followers should avoid contact with skeptics and should avoid being too inquisitive about their faith. Sexual lust is wrong and therefore female believers are to dress modestly.

The Qur'an also teaches that excess in eating is sinful and warns about the dangers of excess in religion. (Muhammad said one time that there was going to be no monkery in Islam, referring to a celibate priesthood.) This idea of excess also involves avoiding certain ideas. Thus, Surah 4:171 states: "O People of the Book! Commit no excesses in your religion: Nor say of God aught but the truth. Christ Jesus the son of Mary was (no more than) an apostle of God. Say not 'Trinity': desist: it will be better for you: for God is one God: Glory be to Him: (far exalted is He) above having a son."

7. **Unbelievers.** The whole human setting of the Qur'an involves the storm created by Muhammad's prophetic call to decision. His message creates two options: belief or unbelief. There is considerable discussion of those that the Qur'an calls hypocrites and unbelievers.

Those who reject Allah's message are deaf, blind, and full of disease. They are arrogant, foolish, hate the truth, live in delusion, and their prayers are in vain. The unbeliever is a liar, a coward, vain, and a deceiver. Muslims should avoid unbelievers given their perversity. They will be sent into the depths of hell unless they repent.

8. **Heaven, Hell, and Judgment Day.** The Qur'an gives enormous weight to life after death. There are hundreds of verses about paradise, the pains of hell, and the reality of a final judgment by God. Though Muslim scholars debate to what extent certain verses about heaven and hell are to be taken literally, the overall message is clear. Heaven is pictured as a garden paradise with mansions, fountains, food and drink, and sexual pleasure, where believers are full of happiness, peace, and joy in the presence of God.

The Qur'an depicts hell as a place of blazing, eternal fire. The unbelievers will taste the boiling fluids of hell, with their faces covered in flame. They will wear garments of fire, will live in eternal regret at the folly of their rebellion against Allah, and will beg for destruction. The Day of Judgment is an absolute certainty, according to the Qur'an, though the righteous have no reason to fear. Justice will be done and human deeds will be weighed in the balance, when the last trumpet sounds.

Women in Islam

The immense literature on the subject of women in Islam reveals an absolute and total division in opinion. In fact, the difference is so extreme that one wonders if the same subject is being debated. On the one hand, orthodox Muslims believe that women gain true freedom in Islam, that the Prophet liberated females, that there is essential equality between males and females, and that non-Muslims have misunderstood the whole topic.

On the opposite extreme, critics of Islam argue that women are in bondage in Islam, that the Prophet was a chauvinist, and that the Qur'an contains very offensive material about women. It is also commonly held that Islamic law and tradition treat women as second-class citizens and that women are subject to abuse in most Muslim countries of the world.

Orthodox Islamic Ideals

In understanding the place of women in Islam, we can start with a listing of very positive ideals that are taught in Orthodox Islam. These principles may not always be followed, but they present the orthodox Islamic teaching in its best light. Here are fifteen key points gathered from various Muslim authors, including Hammudah Abdalati and Jamal A. Badawi, two well-known Muslim writers:

1. The Qur'an teaches against the view that women are inferior to men.

2. Islam stopped the practice of female infanticide in the Arab world.

3. Women are equal to men but have different roles.

4. Women are allowed to receive education just as men.

5. Women are to be given freedom of expression.

6. Marriage and family life are very sacred.

7. Motherhood is given incredible honor in Islam.

8. Husbands are to love their wives and treat them kindly.

9. Husbands are to make sure wives are satisfied sexually.

10. The separation of females in worship is done for reasons of purity.

11. Divorce is to be allowed only when absolutely necessary.

12. Women receive just inheritance in Islamic family law.

13. Veiling of Muslim women is done for protection and purity.

14. The seclusion of women is practiced for reasons of social purity.

15. Polygamy is allowed only if all wives can be supported and loved.

In one of Badawi's essays on the status of women he quotes Surah 4:1 from the Qur'an: "O mankind! Reverence your Guardian-Lord, who created you from a single person, created, of like nature, His mate, and from them twain scattered (like seeds) countless men and women."

Of this passage, Badawi writes: "In the midst of the darkness that engulfed the world, the divine revelation echoed in the wide desert of Arabia with a fresh, noble, and universal message to humanity." Badawi then cites an unnamed scholar on the same text: "It is believed that there is no text, old or new, that deals with the humanity of the woman from all aspects with such amazing brevity, eloquence, depth, and originality as this divine decree."

The Qur'an on Women

Some of these lofty principles find solid support in the Qur'an. Such instances of support should be noted before addressing more controversial issues. The Qur'an affirms the unity of males and females in the original creation by Allah. At least fifteen passages in the Qur'an make this point, including Surah 7:189, which reads: "It is He Who created you from a single person, and made his mate of like nature, in order that he might dwell with her (in love)."

Further, the Qur'an teaches that Allah will reward women, as well as men, for their labor. "For Muslim men and women, for believing men and women, for devout men and women, for true men and women, for men and women who are patient and constant, for men and women who humble themselves, for men and women who give in Charity, for men and women who fast (and deny themselves), for men and women who guard their chastity, and for men and women who engage much in God's praise, for them has God prepared forgiveness and great reward" (33:35).

Grand Mosque, Paris, France

Photo: Gordon Melton

The Qur'an also describes husbands and wives as friends (4:36) and says that there is to be "tranquility, love and mercy" between them (30:21). In heaven, there will be delight, love, and joy between spouses (36:55–57; 55:51–53). If divorce occurs in this life, women are to be treated with grace (2:237) and with justice (2:231; 65:2), and there should be arbitration in conflict (4:35).

Critics of Islam point to other passages, however, to complain about the status and treatment of women in the Qur'an. The dominant charges are: (1) the Qur'an teaches that the testimony of women is worth only half that of males, (2) the Qur'an grants more power to husbands in the divorce process than is given to wives, (3) the Qur'an often grants greater inheritance rights to males than females, (4) the Qur'an grants men access to female slaves for sexual purposes, (5) the Qur'an allows polygamy for males, and (6) the Qur'an actually teaches that husbands are superior to wives and can beat them.

Muslim apologists admit to the factual reality of these points but seek to blunt criticism by arguing that (a) the Qur'an's teaching improved the status of women in contrast to pre-Islamic Arabic life, (b) social conditions explain the need for polygamy, and for the differences about legal testimony and inheritance rights, (c) military realities of Muhammad's day warranted the use of female slaves, and (d) Allah's Word is to be trusted and not treated with suspicion and doubt.

The idea that a husband can beat his wife is rooted in Surah 4:34, which reads: "Men are the protectors and maintainers of women, because God has given the one more (strength) than the other, and because they support them from their means." The verse continues: "As to those women on whose part ye fear disloyalty and ill-conduct, admonish them (first), (Next), refuse to share their beds, (And last) beat them (lightly)."

Many ancient and modern Muslim authorities have accepted the plain meaning of the text. For example, Abdul-latif Mushtahiri, a contemporary scholar, writes: "If admonishing and sexual desertion fail to bring forth results and the woman is of a cold and stubborn type, the Qur'an bestows on man the right to straighten her out by way of punishment and beating provided he does not break her bones nor shed blood. Many a wife belongs to this querulous type and requires this sort of punishment to bring her to her senses!"

Muhammad and Women

The teaching of the Prophet on women and the example he set with women is crucial in understanding the Islamic heritage about women. Obviously, Muhammad would affirm all of the ideal principles noted earlier. Muslims love to cite stories from the *hadith* about his care for girls, his concern about women who were being mistreated, and about his tender relations with Khadijah, his first wife.

Critics of Islam target Muhammad for some of the same things noted about material from the Qur'an. Thus, Muhammad is viewed as a male chauvinist because of his views on inheritance rights, the legal value of a woman's testimony, male dominance in divorce proceedings, and the inferiority of women. Critics also question Muhammad's moral character in terms of his engagement in polygamy, the sexual use of female slaves, and his defense of the Qur'an when it teaches that wives can be beaten.

Muslim apologists use the same arguments to defend the Prophet as they do for defending the Qur'an. However, they also must address other things in the course of Muhammad's life, including complaints that the Prophet (a) taught that there are more women in hell than men, (b) believed brief contractual marriages are sometimes right given the sexual needs of males, (c) married one of his wives when she was just six years old, (d) married his own stepson's wife, (e) taught that women are mentally inferior to men, and (f) believed that the prayer of a man is invalid if a donkey, dog, or woman walks in front of him while he is praying.

Contrary to what non-Muslims might think, these allegations were not invented by enemies of Muhammad. Islamic scholars grant that most of these allegations arise out of genuine traditions about the Prophet. In other words, there is often no dispute over the basic facts. Differences arise in how to interpret the specific controversial claims and actions of the Prophet and also on the fundamental trust granted to Muhammad as the sinless Prophet of Allah.

For the orthodox Muslim it is absolutely unthinkable that the Prophet might be wrong in his views or in his deeds. So, if the Prophet taught, for example, that women outnumber men in hell, then that is a truth that is to be accepted. If he taught that women are mentally inferior, that is the case. If he advocated brief contractual marriages, then he was right to do so. If he said that prayers of a man are invalid if a woman walks in front of him, then so be it. Who is anyone to question the word of the Prophet?

The controversy surrounding Muhammad's marriage to Aisha when she was allegedly 6 years old illustrates how one's fundamental worldview determines perspective and judgment. According to some accounts in the *hadith*, Muhammad did in fact marry her when she was 6, though they did not consummate their marriage until she was 9. Muslim scholars have gone to great lengths to defend the Prophet.

Some argue that Aisha was much older, in her mid-teens, when the Prophet first slept with her and that the *hadith* that suggest she was only 6 are mistaken. Another author stated that Allah wanted Aisha to marry at 6 so that she might be given a longer time to know the great Prophet. One Muslim writer actually dismisses the whole controversy about Aisha by arguing that the average age of Muhammad's wives when they marry him is quite high.

Other Muslims simply declare that Allah gave Aisha at age 6 to the Prophet in marriage and that there is absolutely nothing wrong with him sleeping with her when she was 9. This was the will of Allah, the perfect Creator, for his sinless Prophet. One writer contends: "Only in Islam can one with good conscience accept 'the whole package' without ignorantly or hypocritically denying things that they don't like. This is how true internal peace and balance are achieved."

Women in Modern Islam

As complex as the debate is over the ideals of Islamic orthodoxy, it is obviously much more difficult to write with accuracy about the actual realities of life for Muslim women in a global perspective. Given the number of Muslim women in the world, given the diversity of Muslim states, given the power of feminism, the only thing that can be written with certainty is that no one picture can capture what it is like to be a Muslim woman in our day. Here are some snapshots that capture the diverse realities, gathered from newspaper reports and website material.

- In Britain and other Western countries secular women are turning to Islam as an alternative to a materialistic culture that treats women as objects for sexual gratification.

- In Jordan rape victims find themselves cut off from their families and even killed because of the shame brought to the home because of the loss of virginity.

- Many American female college students are converting to Islam, according to the Council for American-Islamic Relations. One source says that four out of five converts to Islam are women.

- In one Middle Eastern country a woman had acid thrown on her face because she had allowed a wisp of hair to appear from beneath her head covering.

- Zeenah Ibraheem and Fatima Yunus, two Muslim women from Nigeria, convinced Mary Walker, the production coordinator for the BBC2 series on *Living Islam* that the veil can actually be a source of liberation and not a signal of repression.

- Fareena Alam, a Bengali woman living in London, started the website "Islam—The Modern Religion" at age 18, stating that "Islam's attitude toward woman is a dream come true for anyone who is interested in equal rights and feminism."

- In Saudi Arabia rich princesses obey Muslim law while at home and then adopt a Western mind-set as soon as their private jets take them to weekend parties in Paris and London.

- One Muslim woman condones certain kinds of sports for women, but adds that no Muslim woman should use deodorants with a fragrance. "What must be kept in mind is the Prophet's warning: The woman who perfumes herself and passes through a gathering is an adulteress."

- A Canadian woman converts to Islam from a liberal Protestant church. She loses her two children in a custody suit with her non-Muslim husband. At her mother's funeral she is told by her uncle, a Christian pastor: "When we bury her, we bury you."

- A young woman from Australia recalls the experience of converting to Islam: "I finally dropped the mental wall that had been stopping me. I was to repeat in Arabic after the sister. With her first word I cried. It is a feeling that I can't explain. I felt so much power around me."

- A Muslim woman from the Middle East decides to become a Christian. She is tortured for her decision and her face shows marks of the brutality. She flees to Canada to escape threats of death.

- The average Muslim woman in Yemen lives in a home with a total family income under $1,500 per year.

- Karamah, an organization of Muslim female lawyers, monitors human rights abuses from its base in Fairfax, Virginia, protesting abuses of women by Muslim leaders around the world.

- "Revolutionary Women of Afghanistan" rally against the Taliban's abuse of power and provide shocking proof of the torture, rape, and killing of Muslim women. One video clip from their website shows the execution of a woman, totally shrouded in blue, by military officials

- Muslim women in Saudi Arabia are forbidden to drive. A 1991 protest by Saudi women over their lack of freedom was met by fierce resistance from Muslim clerics and the state.

- Sister Power! operates a website to bring skilled Muslim women together to increase job opportunites and business success.

Muslim women in Bangladesh

Photo: Christopher R. Wigginton

ISLAM AND FEMALE CIRCUMCISION

In recent years the world community has been alarmed by the practice of female circumcision, also known as female genital mutilation (FGM), a ritual performed in more than thirty countries of the world. Female circumcision involves a range of medical procedures from the removal of the clitoris to the cutting away of all outer genital tissue. Scholars suggest that two million girls endure this rite every year and about 15 percent die as a result.

Muslims leaders throughout history have defended female circumcision on the basis of various alleged sayings of Muhammad. Even in recent years these sayings of Muhammad and some material in the Qur'an have been used to defend both male and female circumcision. Nearly a decade ago, some Egyptian clerics wanted a *fatwa* (ruling) calling for the death penalty for any Muslim judge who did not favor male circumcision. An Egyptian court has ruled that female circumcision could not be outlawed because of certain sayings of the Prophet that seemed to favor it.

Some Muslim leaders seek to defend female circumcision by arguing that it protects young girls from sexual temptation and affords less likelihood of female masturbation or other sexual activities. One writer has argued that the experience of going through the rite is actually beneficial in other ways, too, since the young girl receives presents and is surrounded by a loving community—support that gives her a better sense of self.

Female circumcision is practiced, to varying degrees, in the following Muslim countries: Sudan, Egypt, Somalia, Yemen, the United Arab Emirates, Bahrain, Qatar, Oman, and some areas of Saudi Arabia, Mauritania, Indonesia, Malaysia, Pakistan, and India. The practice continues, although the vast majority of Muslims abhor FGM and the world's most influential Muslim jurists and clerics have ruled against it.

THE MUSLIM FEMINIST COWGIRL

Asma Gull Hasan calls herself as "the Muslim feminist cowgirl." She grew up in Chicago but now lives in Colorado and has played a prominent role in shaping public opinion about Islam. Hasan is a frequent guest on radio and television talk shows, has written significant newspaper editorials about Islam, and is the author of *Why I Am a Muslim*.

Hasan combines her love for the United States with a love for her Islamic faith, but much of traditional Islam may not be open to her. In her book *American Muslims: The Next Generation* she states: "I'm tired of Muslim women having to make concessions, like sitting somewhere else besides the position of honor [which is in the front of the mosque] or wearing *hijab* [a special headcovering for women] because men can't control themselves."

Hasan is a powerful example of a free-spirited Muslim woman. She is willing to confront the hardened traditions in Islam but says that she does so because of her deep trust in Allah and Muhammad. Some reviewers have suggested, however, that her book illustrates a naïve and far too optimistic view of Muhammad as a liberator of women.

Internet Source

www.asmahasan.com

■ Jihad and September 11

September 11 has forever altered the significance of the word *jihad* to the modern world. While many Muslims assert that the word simply means spiritual struggle, militant Islam has a far more sinister understanding: "Holy War." Rick Bragg reported in *The New York Times* about Muslim boys running through their school compound on September 11, "celebrating, stabbing the fingers on one hand into the palm of the other, to simulate a plane stabbing into a building.

In February 1998, three and a half years before September 11, Osama bin Laden made his own views clear. Along with other extremists from Egypt, Pakistan, and Bangladesh, he issued a *fatwa* or ruling that called on Muslims "to kill the Americans and their allies—civilian and military." He called this "an individual duty for every Muslim who can do it in any country in which it is possible to do it. In the winter of 2001 Osama bin Laden told ABC News producer Rahimullah Yousafsai that he would kill his own children if necessary in order to hit American targets.

In contrast, the vast majority of Muslim states have opposed Osama bin Laden since September 11. Here is one news report of enormous significance for world peace: "Iran has vehemently condemned the suicidal terrorist attacks in the United States and has expressed its deep sorrow and sympathy with the American nation" (*Iran Today*, September 24, 2001, front page report). The governments of Bahrain, Egypt, Lebanon, Oman, Pakistan, Palestine, Qatar, Saudi Arabia, Turkey, United Arab Emirates, and Yemen also expressed their condemnation of the terrorist attacks.

American Muslim groups condemned the terrorist attack immediately. One prominent group issued this press release on September 12: "The Islamic Supreme Council of America (ISCA) categorically condemns yesterday's airline hijackings and attacks against the World Trade Center, the Pentagon, and all other targets. From coast to coast, we join our neighbors, coworkers and friends across ethnic, cultural and religious lines in mourning the devastating loss of precious life, which Islam holds as sacred. We pray for the thousands of innocent victims, for their families, for law enforcement and emergency workers, for stranded travelers, and for all whose confidence and security have been shaken. We pray that God's Infinite Mercy reaches us all."

The tragedies of September 11 have brought to the surface a long and bitter struggle between between Muslims over the meaning of *jihad* and the nature of true Islam. These contemporary conflicts about Islam's real identity are rooted in ancient debates about the teaching of the Qur'an, the example of the Prophet, the legitimacy of non-Muslim governments, and the place of war in Islamic ideology.

GEORGE BUSH ON ISLAM

"I also want to speak tonight directly to Muslims throughout the world. We respect your faith. It's practiced freely by many millions of Americans, and by millions more in countries that America counts as friends. Its teachings are good and peaceful, and those who commit evil in the name of Allah blaspheme the name of Allah. The terrorists are traitors to their own faith, trying, in effect, to hijack Islam itself. The enemy of America is not our many Muslim friends; it is not our many Arab friends. Our enemy is a radical network of terrorists, and every government that supports them."

—President George W. Bush, September 20, 2001

AMERICAN ISLAM ON ATTACKS ON CHRISTIANS

Contrary to popular impression, American Muslims are not simply concerned about the situation in their own country. When Christians in Pakistan were killed during Sunday worship in October 2001, the American Muslim Alliance expressed its outrage at the murders. An AMA Press release said: "AMA chairman Dr. Agha Saeed said that the killing of the innocent Christians was a heinous crime. He urged Pakistan's president, General Pervez Musharraf, to bring the perpetrators to justice and provide safety and security to all the citizens and particularly to the minorities."

◼ Background to the Two Islams

The current debates between Muslims about *jihad* are better understood in the context of several crucial facts. Anyone who studies even briefly the history and nature of Islam will discover these items to be beyond dispute, though what these facts mean is a source of considerable debate. Here are some key facts that shape the world of Islam today:

- The Qur'an uses the term *jihad* in terms of spiritual struggle.

- The Qur'an also uses *jihad* about "holy war" or just war.

- The Prophet engaged in battles of war.

- The Prophet taught that Islam must be spread to the whole world.

- Islamic law justifies self-defense and certain acts of war.

- Muslims conquered non-Arab lands and peoples through war.

- Muslims divide the world into two: Islam and non-Islam.

- Many Muslims believe that all countries should follow Islamic law.

- Many Muslim countries are non-democratic and crush dissent.

Out of the vortex of these realities two basically different perspectives have emerged among modern Muslims. The vast majority of Muslims believe that none of the above points justifies terrorism. They believe that the Qur'anic defense of war does not apply to the attacks of September 11. They believe that the Prophet would condemn Osama bin Laden, that this extreme terrorist has broken Islamic law, that he has disgraced Islam and is therefore doomed to eternal punishment.

Muslim extremists believe the opposite. They view their actions as a true *jihad* or "holy war" against infidels and the enemies of Islam. They believe it is right to target America as "the great Satan." Osama bin Laden himself clearly believes that the Qur'an supports his campaign, that the Prophet would bless his cause, that Islamic law justifies his actions, and that Allah is on his side. In the end, we are left then with a world of two Islams.

▓ Major Islamic Terrorist Groups

There are about seventy major terrorist groups operating in the world. Of these, more than thirty are Islamic in orientation. Of the rest, only a few are well known, like the Irish Republican Army or the Aum group that spread poison gas in the Tokyo subway system. Among the Islamic groups, the most famous are:

- Abu Nidal Organization (aka Black September)

- Islamic Group or IG (aka Al-Gama'a al-Islamiyya)

- Armed Islamic Group (GIA)

- Hamas

- Hizballah (Party of God, aka Islamic Jihad)

- al-Jihad (aka Islamic Jihad)

- al-Qaida (of Osama bin Laden)

Before September 11, Americans for the most part did not worry about such groups. Europeans had a far greater sensitivity to terrorism because of the militant groups operating in Ireland and Spain. Israel has had firsthand experience with several militant Islamic groups, but America seemed safe, even with the attacks on American embassies in Kenya and Tanzania, and on the USS *Cole* in South Yemen.

It had been stated in lectures on terrorism that an American was more likely to die from a fall in the bathtub than from a terrorist attack. As absurd as it sounds, that point had merit prior to September's attack. The U.S. State Department lists a total of seventy-seven American casualties in terrorist attacks from 1995 through 2000, and then on one infamous day thousands perished at the World Trade Center alone.

The Islamic terrorist groups have several aims: (a) use violence to bring their version of Islam to particular Muslim countries, (b) establish a Palestinian state, (c) destroy the State of Israel, (d) crush dissent against their views, and (e) attack the United States of America. These goals are expressed in the language of religious hate. On Sunday, October 9, 2001, al-Jazeera satellite TV released a statement from Osama bin Laden that captures his style and ideology. Here are excerpts:

"America is filled with fear. America has been filled with horror from north to south and east to west, and thanks be to God what America is tasting now is only a copy of what we have tasted. God has blessed a group of vanguard Muslims to destroy America and may God bless them and allot them a supreme place in heaven.

"I swear to God that America will never dream of security or see it before we live it and see it in Palestine, and not before the infidels' armies leave the land of Muhammad, peace be upon him."

Of course, behind these words lie deeds of terror. Judith Miller reported from the militant Middle East for *The New York Times* for years and recorded her observations in her book *God Has Ninety-Nine Names*. Her powerful, evocative prose captures the depth of tragedy and evil in militant Islam, whether in the Sudanese slave trade, or the execution of moderates in Egypt, the slaughter of Kurdish Muslims in Iraq, the gang-rape of devout Muslim women in Algeria by Muslim extremists, or the killings of journalists in the same country, eighteen in 1994 alone, some by decapitation.

In the year prior to September 11, Israel was repeatedly the target of terrorism. Here are ten examples from a much longer list:

- January 17, 2000—In the West Bank, Ofir Rahum, a Jewish high school student, is killed after being shot more than fifteen times.

- February 14, 2000—Eight persons are killed when a Palestinian bus driver plows into a crowd near Tel-Aviv.

- April 1, 2000—Dina Guetta, 42, of Haifa, is killed as part of an initiation rite into a terrorist cell.

- May 9, 2000—Two 14-year-old Jewish boys are stoned to death at a cave near their small town of Tekoa in the West Bank.

- June 1, 2000—A Palestinian suicide bomber associated with Hamas denotates an explosives belt that injures one hundred twenty and kills twenty at a nightclub in Tel-Aviv.

- August 9, 2000—A bombing at a pizza place in Jerusalem kills fifteen, including six children, and injures eighty. Hamas is blamed.

- August 12, 2000—A suicide bombing at a cafe in Kiryat Motzkin, Israel, wounds twenty-one.

- August 25, 2000—The Democratic Front for the Liberation of Palestine takes responsibility for two Palestinians who killed three Israeli soldiers in the Gaza Strip.

- October 30, 2000—A bomb blast at pizza joint in Jerusalem kills fifteen and injures one hundred thirty.

- November 22, 2000—Two Israelis are killed near Hadera, Israel, when a car bomb explodes near a bus, wounding thirty others.

THE ROOTS OF ISLAMIC MILITANCY

Many writers often refer to the Middle Ages when they attempt to explain Islamic militancy. However, the militant side of Islam owes more to events in the last three centuries. The extreme form of Islam that dominates Saudi Arabia goes back to the writings of Muhammad al-Wahhab (1703–92), the ideological founder of the Wahhabi movement. Al-Wahhab influenced other Islamic radicals, including Jamaluddin al-Afghani (1838–97) and his student Muhammad 'Abduh (1849–1905).

Islamic militancy is not simply a revolt against the West (as expressed in Ali Shariati's influential work *Westoxication* in 1962) but is also an attack against Arab governments that are viewed as un-Islamic and corrupt. Islamic militants have struck against governments in Egypt, Algeria, Kuwait, and Syria, for example; and Iran became the home of Shi'ite radicalism after the demise of the Shah's regime in 1979.

The Muslim Brotherhood was an early radical movement formed by the youthful Hasan al-Banna (1906–49) in 1928. Sayyid Abul A'la Mawdudi (1903–79) championed Muslim ideals in both India and Pakistan through his Jamaat-e-Islami movement. Hasan al-Banna was assassinated in 1949 for his push for radical reform in Egypt. Sayyid Qutb (1906–66), unimpressed by his student days in America, pushed for a more radical Islam in Egypt and was executed by the Egyptian government.

Understanding Islamic Terrorism

"How could they do it?" A year or so of planning, waiting in Florida, New Jersey, or Maine, enjoying life in America, and then, the unimaginable: two planes flown into the World Trade Center, one flown into the Pentagon, and another brought down in a field in Pennsylvania. Our first response was a failure of imagination. This simply could not be happening. How can we understand it?

Six dominant interpretations have been offered of the events of September 11. They are:

1. The paradigm of *mental illness*. In this view, the terrorists are crazy, mad, insane. Nothing can explain what they did because their actions fall outside any ordinary discourse of reason and sense. Their deeds are irrational, beyond the understanding of any decent human being. Terrorists such as these are monsters of insanity, proof that humans can abandon all rationality.

2. The paradigm of *evil*. The terrorists are the embodiment of wickedness. Their behavior can only be explained on the grounds of hellish hate. These are people without conscience, possessing no moral compass. They are fanatics whose hearts are darkened by their alliance with evil.

   This interpretation, valid or not, must take serious note of the fact that the evil is done under the guise of good, in the name of Allah. This brings to mind the thesis of Phillip Hallie's book *The Paradox of Cruelty*: most evil is done with "good" intentions. Hallie argues the need for a profound recognition of the power of delusion in the human mind.

3. The paradigm of the *terrorist ideology*. To Osama bin Laden and his colleagues, there is no mystery to understanding why September 11 happened. The United States deserved what it got. It is an enemy of Allah, opposed to Islam, and worthy of destruction. Islamic terrorists believe what they are doing is right. Thousands of young Muslim boys are being instructed daily in this ideology. It will constitute their only schooling, and they are not allowed to ask questions.

4. The paradigm of *Islam-bashing*. The killings on September 11 prove once and for all that Islam is the religion of the sword. In this view, all Muslims are terrorists and Islam is the chief cause of the wickedness. From this paradigm, some Americans have attacked Muslims at will. One member of the Sikh faith, a religion very distinct from Islam, was killed on a street in Arizona simply because his turban looked like that of the Taliban leaders.

5. The paradigm of *America-blaming*. From this angle, while the events of September 11 are wrong, America has created its own karma through its abuse of power, its arrogance as the only reigning superpower, and its military attacks on Muslim peoples. Further, American complicity

in the abuse of Palestinians by Israel has created legitimate anger toward the United States.

Two professors, Edward Said of Columbia University, and Noam Chomsky, the linguistics expert from MIT, have famously articulated this approach. Chomsky argues that Western intellectuals turn a blind eye to American atrocities and the American people remain largely ignorant. For example, Chomsky stated in one interview:

"The U.S. has already demanded that Pakistan terminate the food and other supplies that are keeping at least some of the starving and suffering people of Afghanistan alive. If that demand is implemented, unknown numbers of people who have not the remotest connection to terrorism will die, possibly millions. Let me repeat: the U.S. has demanded that Pakistan kill possibly millions of people who are themselves victims of the Taliban. This has nothing to do even with revenge. It is at a far lower moral level even than that."

Referring to September 11, Chomsky writes: "It is correct to say that this is a novel event in world history, not because of the scale of the atrocity—regrettably—but because of the target. How the West chooses to react is a matter of supreme importance. If the rich and powerful choose to keep to their traditions of hundreds of years and resort to extreme violence, they will contribute to the escalation of a cycle of violence, in a familiar dynamic, with long-term consequences that could be awesome. Of course, that is by no means inevitable. An aroused public within the more free and democratic societies can direct policies towards a much more humane and honorable course."

The events of 9/11 and its aftermath have led some non-Muslim activists to reconsider their rhetoric against both Israel and the United States. Of most significance, Australian activist, Helen Darville, author of *The Hand That Signed the Paper* writes: "I have watched, since that day, the cozy leftist pieties of my youth disintegrate. Those pieties will be familiar to many of you. Chief among them is the old saw that to understand horrors, one must be willing to contextualize them. And if that mitigates them, so be it."

6. The paradigm of *failure in the Muslim world*. The attack on America is, according to this view, a result of a Muslim ignorance that lacks the will or freedom to be self-critical. The Muslim hatred of America is

fueled by jealousy of that country's wealth and freedom in contrast to the poverty and dictatorship in the Muslim world. Thus, America is blamed for calamity, oppression, and evil that is actually rooted in the corruption, sloth, and inadequacies in Muslim nations.

This point has been articulated well by Kanan Makiya, author of the famous works *Republic of Fear* (on Saddam's Iraq) and *Cruelty and Silence*, a powerful protest against the silence of Arab intellectuals about the dark side of the militant Islamic Middle East. In a London *Observer* article on "Fighting Islam's Ku Klux Klan," Makiya writes of the incredible price that Muslims will pay if they continue to wallow in a victim mentality to the point of losing "the essentially universal idea of human dignity and worth that is the only true measure of civility."

Makiya continues: "Arabs and Muslims need today to face up to the fact that their resentment at America has long since become unmoored from any rational underpinnings it might once have had; like the anti-Semitism of the interwar years, it is today steeped in deeply embedded conspiratorial patterns of thought rooted in profound ignorance of how a society and a polity like the United States, much less Israel, functions." His article ends with these words:

"Muslims and Arabs have to be on the front lines of a new kind of war, one that is worth waging for their own salvation and in their own souls. And that, as good out-of-fashion Muslim scholars will tell you, is the true meaning of jihad, a meaning that has been hijacked by terrorists and suicide bombers and all those who applaud or find excuses for them. To exorcise what they have done in our name is the civilisational challenge of the twenty-first century for every Arab and Muslim in the world today."

Islam: A Religion of Peace?

President George W. Bush has stated publicly on several occasions: "Islam is a religion of peace." He was making reference to the Islam that condemns terrorism, to the millions of Muslims who deplore Osama bin Laden, and to the significant Islamic traditions that support peace between religions and between all peoples. By the "Islam of peace" the president was referring to the ways in which Islam has brought meaning and stability to the lives of millions of its followers.

September 11 proves that there is another Islam, that of Muslims who readily kill in the name of Allah. The terrorists who hijacked one of the planes at Logan Airport in Boston left behind their instructions on what to do if a passenger interfered in their plot: "If God grants any one of you a slaughter, you should perform it as an offering on behalf of your father and mother, for they are owed by you. Do not disagree among yourselves, but listen and obey. If you slaughter, you should plunder those you slaughter, for that is a sanctioned custom of the Prophet's." When the president spoke of a peaceful Islam, Muslims of another stripe burned the American flag and dreamed of more attacks on America.

There is an Islam of peace. It is in the millions of Muslims who live every day in love and gentleness. It is in the Muslim who prays five times each day for no more days like September 11. It is in those mosques where clerics preach that Islam is not a religion of the sword. It is in those Afghan Muslims who know that Osama bin Laden has betrayed their country. It is in those Muslims everywhere who know that such a hateful Islam could not possibly be from Allah, the One All-merciful Creator.

Jay Smith, Brethren in Christ missionary to Islam,
Speakers Corner, London, England

Photo: Jim Beverley

AL-YAZEED SAYS JIHAD WILL CONTINUE

"So, the killing of these heroic chiefs doesn't—and won't—end the march of jihad (holy war) or extinguish its torch or put out its light as the enemies imagine. Rather, their killing, in fact, pushes the march forward and strengthens, stabilizes, sharpens and stimulates it."

—Mustafa Abu al-Yazeed, Al-Qaida's Afghanistan leader on revenge for the death of Abu Laith al-Libi and other militants

■ A Christian Response to Islam

A proper evangelical response to Islam must be multifaceted in light of the breadth of Islamic history, the vast spread of Islam globally, the variety within Islam, and the tangled sociopolitical realities of the Middle East and other parts of the Muslim world. In other words, analysis of Islam must not be simplistic, as in the popular desire to say that Islam is or is not a religion of peace, with no qualifications.

Since September 11, 2001, it bears repeating that Christian witness to Islam should focus more on the positive news of the gospel and less on the weaknesses in Islam. Though the following remarks contain some negative assessments of Islam in general and Muhammad in particular, the most important thing a Christian can do with a Muslim is bear witness to the full message given in Jesus Christ.

With this in mind, some general judgments must be made when thinking about Islam in its totality. I believe that the following points represent the central elements in a Christian critique of Islam and must be kept in mind as the Christian church tries to pursue a redemptive and loving witness to the Muslim world, a necessary corrective to a rising vitriolic attack on Islam in some Christian circles.

1. Islam fails in its core denial that Jesus is the Son of God. This error about the identity of Jesus strikes at the very integrity of Islam as a revelation from God. Muhammad's failure to capture the very essence of the New Testament teaching on Jesus shows how little he knew of the Gospel accounts. This error alone constitutes sufficient reason for abandoning any notion that Muhammad was a prophet of God.

How could a prophet living after the time of Jesus be so misinformed about the identity of God's Messiah?

2. The Muslim denial that Jesus died on the cross is further illustration that Muhammad had no real sense of what constitutes the heart of Christianity. The Islamic notion that Jesus was replaced on the cross shows complete disregard for the Gospel records and for ancient historical testimony about his death. Muslims are forced to deny the crucifixion on the basis of a few verses in a book written six hundred years after the death of Jesus, while denying hundreds of verses that attest to his death in books written at the time of Jesus.

Cross at Ground Zero, New York City, New York

Photo: Kaarina Hsieh

3. On a broader level, Christians must remain extremely skeptical about the Qur'an, given its abundant distortion of biblical stories and teachings, not simply in relation to Jesus, but to the whole range of scriptural data. Muhammad's knowledge of the Bible derived from his minimal contacts with Jews and Christians of his day and their

reliance on extrabiblical traditions about the Jewish and Christian Scriptures.

Though the Qur'an contains many teachings in harmony with Christian faith and with Old Testament tradition, it is difficult to believe that it is a product of divine revelation, given its lack of order, its redundancy, and its increasing mean-spiritedness. It proves itself to be largely a product of Muhammad's thirst for prophetic status and unquestioned authority, especially in light of his growing use of the sword as a defense for his divine calling.

Old Dir aiyah in Riyadh, Saudi Arabia
Ancestral home of al-Saud family

Photo: Massimo Introvigne

4. Christians must also express serious reservations about the prophet Muhammad, especially in contrast to the Person of Jesus Christ. This does not demand treating Muhammad as if he were the embodiment of evil. However, Muhammad's life reads more like that of Moses or David, as if we were taken back to the wars of the Old Testament, proof that Islam was not properly exposed to the grace and mercy revealed in the New Testament.

To be more specific, the Christian tradition has always had enormous difficulty with the following aspects of Muhammad's life: (a) episodes of extreme brutality both in war and in dealing with some of his enemies, (b) his lack of tolerance toward critics and those who chose not to follow Islam, (c) his adoption of polygamy and arrogance toward his wives, especially by use of his prophetic status to crush dissent, (d) the consummation of his marriage to Aisha when she was only nine, (e) his marriage to Zaynab, his stepson's wife, while the stepson was still alive.

MUSLIMS AND THE GOSPEL OF BARNABAS

Muslims frequently refer to the Gospel of Barnabas as a reliable guide to the person and work of Jesus. Muslims are attracted to this gospel because it contains ideas in agreement with Islam, including the teaching that Jesus did not die on the cross. Some Muslim apologists even argue that this gospel is more accurate than the four Gospels of the New Testament.

Muslims are particularly attracted to the explicit mention of Muhammad as the final prophet of God. In section 163 of the Gospel of Barnabas, Jesus is said to have predicted another who will fully reveal God's will. The disciples asked Jesus: "O Master, who shall that man be of whom you speak, who shall come into the world?" Jesus answered with joy of heart: 'He is Muhammad, Messenger of God.'"

The Gospel of Barnabas teaches that Jesus was taken to heaven by angels and that Judas was mistakenly identified as Jesus and died on the cross. It asserts that Jesus was then sent from heaven to confirm to his mother and other disciples that He did not perish on the cross. However, Barnabas is then told by Jesus: "God, in order that I be not mocked of the demons on the day of judgment, has willed that I be mocked of men in this world by the death of Judas; making all men to believe that I died upon the cross. And this mocking shall continue until the advent of Muhammad, the Messenger of God, who, when he shall come, shall reveal this deception to those who believe in God's Law" (Section 220).

The Gospel of Barnabas is actually a fabrication written sometime during the Middle Ages, possibly by a Muslim convert. No known copy of the gospel exists before the fifteenth century, and no Christian Father or theologian quotes it during the first fifteen centuries of church history. Muslim scholars also do not refer to the Gospel of Barnabas prior to the sixteenth century. The gospel also contains historical anachronisms, including use of the Latin Vulgate and a quotation from Dante's *Inferno.*

5. Christians must also reject central elements in the Islamic understanding of salvation. Islam has little concept of the New Testament doctrines of salvation by faith alone and grace alone, apart from the works of the law. Islam's emphasis on law and obedience leads to uncertainty about assurance of salvation. As well, the Qur'an puts such an emphasis on the sovereignty of Allah's will in salvation that the ordinary Muslim cannot be certain of eternal destiny.

6. The Islamic treatment of women must remain a matter of concern for Christians. Though Christian tradition has often abused women, this is no ground for ignoring the plight of women in many Muslim countries. Generally, Muslim women in non-Western countries have little access to the freedoms taken for granted by Muslim females in the West.

7. The lack of human rights and freedom under Islam must also continue to be the object of Christian critique. The repression of non-Muslims, in one form or another, has been a constant reality in Muslim history. This is not saying that Muslim leaders forced Jews or Christians to become Muslims. Rather, Jews and Christians were generally treated as second-class citizens under Islamic caliphs.

Muslims have a distorted memory when it comes to the issue of the Crusades. They have every right to object to the wicked aspects of the Crusades carried about by the church against Islam. However, the early Islamic empires were built on a Crusade model, as Islamic armies overthrew Christian and Jewish peoples across North Africa, Palestine, and southern Europe.

Let us assume that Islam granted total freedom to other religions, that its record on women's rights was exceptional, and that Muhammad was the epitome of gentleness, humility, and love. Even making these assumptions, Islam must be found wanting because of its cardinal errors about the Person of Jesus, his death and resurrection, and the path of salvation. For these reasons alone, it is the Christian's duty to witness in love to the Muslim world.

HUMAN RIGHTS IN ISLAM

Is Islam fundamentally opposed to human rights by its inherently theocratic thrust? Why do Muslim countries have such deplorable records on human rights? Data made available by Freedom House, an organization that monitors political and civil rights in every country of the world, supports this assertion. Of the forty-one countries whose population is at least 70 percent Muslim, twenty-six are considered not free and thirteen are partly free. Only two are considered free—meaning they protect political and civil rights as defined by the United Nations Declaration of Human Rights.

The abuse of human rights in Muslim countries can be demonstrated in other ways. The government of Saudi Arabia welcomed Allied Forces to free Kuwait, but forbids entry of non-Muslims to its country. Western governments allow Muslims to talk freely about their faith, but Christians cannot do the same in many Muslim countries. Muslims rightfully express concern about the denial of liberties to Palestinians, but the rights of Jews are not protected in Iran, and Hindus are not free in Pakistan.

Human beings are being traded as slaves in Sudan, a fact documented in Paul Marshall's *Their Blood Cries Out,* yet the government in Khartoum has hardly been flooded with protests from every corner of the Muslim world. Likewise, no one can deny the lack of women's rights under Islam, regardless of Muslim polemic to the contrary. The widespread practice of female genital mutilation in Muslim countries alone signals the reality of female oppression. Women are forbidden even to drive cars in Saudi Arabia.

Until they were freed suddenly in mid-November 2001, eight expatriate Christians stood trial in Afghanistan on charges of Christian evangelism. They denied the charge, but not their faith. Followers of Jesus in many Muslim countries today can be put to death for sharing what they believe. It would be wonderful to know that the Muslim leaders who joined President Bush in public to express solidarity against Osama bin Laden were already on record condemning the persecution of these Christians in Afghanistan.

Muslims who abandon their faith and embrace Christianity have received death threats—not in Sudan, or Libya, or Iraq, but in the

United States. Are American Muslim leaders disturbed that members of their own communities threaten former Muslims with death on the basis of Shari'ah law, which mandates that Muslims who abandon their faith be put to death?

Avicenna (Ibn Sina 980–1037), portrait from museum in birthplace in Uzbekistan

Photo: Massimo Introvigne

ISLAM TIMELINE [632-2007]

632—Death of the prophet Muhammad

634—Death of Abu Bakr, the first *caliph* or successor to Muhammad

637—Capture of Jerusalem by Muslim leaders

661—Assassination of Ali, the fourth *caliph* to Muhammad

680—Murder of Husayn, grandson of the Prophet

690—Construction of the Dome of the Rock in Jerusalem

628—Death of Hasan al-Basri, early Sufi leader

732—Muslims defeated at Battle of Tours

750—Rise of the Abbasid Dynasty, based in Baghdad

765—Split among Shi'ite Muslims over new leader

850—Death of al-Bukhari, specialist on Islamic *hadith*

940—Twelfth Shi'a Imam becomes the "hidden imam"

950—Death of Al-Farabi, the Muslim Aristotle

975—Founding of Al-Azhar university in Cairo

1037—Death of Ibn Sina (aka Avicenna), a great Islamic philosopher

1099—Crusaders capture Jerusalem

1111—Death of al-Ghazali

1187—Saladin recaptures Jerusalem

1198—Death of Averroës

1258—Mongols sack Baghdad

1273—Death of Rumi (b. 1207)

1300—Rise of Ottoman Empire

1315—Death of Raymond Lull, Christian missionary to Muslims

1389—Ottomans defeat Balkan allies at Battle of Kosovo

1453—Ottomans capture Constantinople and rename it Istanbul

1492—End of Muslim rule in Spain

1517—Salim I conquers Egypt

1520—Rise of Suleiman the Magnificent, the Ottoman emperor

1526—Muslim armies under Babur enter India

1563—Akbar gains power in India

1566—Death of Suleiman

1683—Ottoman forces defeated at Battle of Vienna

1798—Napoleon in Egypt

1803—Wahhabi movement gains control in Saudi Arabia

1830—France occupies Algeria

1881—British take control of Egypt

1893—Alexander Russell Webb at World's Parliament of Religions (Chicago)

1897—First Zionist Congress (Basle)

1902—Qasim Amin pioneers feminism in Egypt

1910—Oil prospects in Persia

1914—Start of World War I (August 4)

1915—British and French forces defeated at Gallipoli (April)

1915—Beginning of Armenian genocide

1916—Arab revolt led by Sharif Hussein against Ottoman rule

1916—Sykes-Picot agreement between Britain and France

1917—Balfour Declaration (November)

1920—Lebanon separated from Syria by French

1920—Arab revolts in Jerusalem (April)

1920—Formation of the Haganah (Jewish underground militia)

1923—Turkey becomes republic under Mustafa Kemal Atatürk

1925—Abdul Aziz ibn Saud captures Mecca from Sharif Hussein

1928—Muslim Brotherhood founded by Hassan al-Banna

1929—Jews killed by Arabs at Hebron (August)

1931—Formation of the Irgun

1932—Political independence in Iraq

1936—Arab revolt in Palestine led by Haj Amin Al-Husseini

1936—Peel Commission on Palestine mandate (report: 1937)

1939—Start of World War II (September 3)

1941—Mohammad Reza Pahlavi becomes Shah of Iran

1946—Syria gains independence from France

1946—Irgun bombing of King David Hotel (July 22)

1947—Creation of Pakistan

1948—Jewish attack on Deir Yassan (April 9)

1948—Founding of the State of Israel (May 14)

1949—Hassan al-Banna assassinated

1952—Nasser leads coup in Egypt

1953—CIA aids coup against Iranian leader Mohammad Mosaddeq

1954—Algerian war of independence begins

1955—Sudan gains independence from British-French rule

1956—Suez Canal crisis

1962—Algeria gains independence

1964—Formation of the Palestinian Liberation Organization

1965—Assassination of Malcolm X in New York City

1966—Sayyid Qutb executed in Egypt (August 29)

1967—Six-Day War between Israel and Egypt (June 5–10)

1969—Qaddafi stages coup in Libya

1970—Death of Egypt president Nasser (September 28)

1972—"Black September" attack on Israeli Olympic athletes (September 5)

1973—October War between Israel and Arabs

1974—Peace treaty between Jordan and Israel

1975—Start of civil war in Lebanon

1977—Anwar Sadat makes historic peace trip to Jerusalem (November 19)

1978—Saddam Hussein controls Baath party in Iraq

1979—Islamic revolution in Iran under Khomeini (February)

1979—USSR invades Afghanistan

1979—Iranian hostage crisis (November 4)

1980—Iran-Iraq War (September 22, 1980–August 20, 1988)

1981—Israel destroys nuclear reactor in Iraq (June 7)

1981—Assassination of Anwar Sadat (October 6)

1981—Release of U.S. hostages in Iran (January 20)

1982—Syrian army massacres Muslim Brothers in Hama (February)

1982—Israeli invasion of Lebanon (June 6)

1982—Massacre at Sabra and Shatila camps in Beirut (September 16–19)

1983—Attack on U.S. and French soldiers in Beirut (October 23)

1985—Palestinian terrorists hijack *Achille Lauro* (October 7)

1987—Intifada begins in Palestine

1988—Pan Am flight 103 blown up over Lockerbie, Scotland

1989—Iranian *fatwa* against Salman Rushdie for *The Satanic Verses*

1991—Gulf War to liberate Kuwait

1991—Military conflicts begin in former Yugoslavia

1992—Seige of Sarajevo begins (April 1992–February 1996)

1993—Bombing of the World Trade Center (February 26)

1993—Oslo Accords (Washington signing September 13)

1994—Jordan recognizes State of Israel

1995—Massacre in Srebrenica (July)

1995—Assassination of Yitzhak Rabin (November 4)

1996—Osama bin Laden announces Jihad against the U.S.

1996—Taliban take control of Kabul

1997—Collapse of Albania

1998—World Islamic Front issues Declaration against the U.S. (February 23)

1998—U.S. embassies in Kenya and Tanzania bombed (August 7)

1999—War in Kosovo

2000—USS *Cole* attacked in Yemen (October 12)

2000—Breakdown of President Clinton's Israel-Palestine peace talks

2001—September 11 terrorist attack on America

2001—Defeat of Taliban in Afghanistan

2002—Heightened suicide bombings in Israel

2002—Israel government approves security wall

2002—Terrorist bombing in Bali kills 202 (October 12)

2003—U.S. attacks Iraq (March)

2004—Crisis in Darfur escalates

2004—Madrid train bombings (March 11)

2004—Killing of Dutch filmmaker Theo van Gogh (November 2)

2004—Death of Arafat (November 11)

2005—Mahmoud Abbas elected Palestinian leader

2005—Rafik Hariri killed in Beirut (February 14)

2005—London bombings (July 7)

2005—Israeli forces leave Gaza and West Bank (August)

2005—Danish cartoon controversy erupts (September–December)

2006—Hamas defeats Fatah in general election (January)

2006—Arrest of suspected terrorists in Toronto (June 3)

2006—Israeli-Lebanese war (July 12–August 14)

2006—Pope Benedict XVI controversy (September)

2007—Fighting between Hamas and Fatah in Gaza

2007—Muslim and Christian leaders start new dialogue

2008—Gaza under Israeli attack (December 27–January 19, 2009)

ISLAM

General Reading	James A. Beverley, *Understanding Islam* (Thomas Nelson, 2001) _____ *Islamic Faith in America* (Facts on File, 2002) Robert Fisk, *The Great War for Civilization* (Knopf, 2005) Samuel Huntington, *The Clash of Civilizations* (Simon & Schuster, 1996) Martin Kramer, *Ivory Towers in the Sand* (Washington Inst for Near East Policy, 2001) Bernard Lewis, *Islam and the West* (Oxford, 1993) Paul Marshall, ed., *Religious Freedom in the World* (Broadman & Holman, 2000) V. S. Naipaul, *Among the Believers* (Penguin, 1982) Seyyed Nasr, ed., *Islamic Spirituality: Manifestations* (SCM, 1991) Vali Nasr, *The Shia Revival* (Norton, 2006) Fazlur Rahman, *Islam* (University of Chicago Press, 1979) Andrew Rippin, *Muslims* (Routledge, 2000) Reinhard Schulze, *A Modern History of the Islamic World* (NY University Press, 2000) Mark Sedgwick, *Islam and Muslims* (Intercultural Press, 2006) _____ *Sufism: The Essentials* (AUC Press, 2003) Ibn Warraq, *Why I Am Not a Muslim* (Prometheus, 1995)
Christian Response	James A. Beverley, *Christ and Islam* (College Press, 2001, second edition) George W. Braswell Jr., *Islam* (Broadman & Holman, 1996) Kenneth Cragg, *The Call of the Minaret* (Orbis, 1985) Norman Geisler and Abdul Saleed, *Answering Islam* (Baker, 1993) Rick Love, *Muslims, Magic and the Kingdom of God* (William Carey, 2001) Hans Küng, *Islam* (Oneworld, 2007)
Jihad, Militant Islam, and Terrorism	Peter L. Bergen, *Holy War Inc.* (Free Press, 2001) Michael Bonner, *Jihad in Islamic History* (Princeton University Press, 2006) Ian Buruma, *Murder in Amsterdam* (Penguin, 2006) Steve Coll, *Ghost Wars* (New York: Penguin, 2004) _____ *The Bin Ladens* (Penguin, 2008) Paul Fregosi, *Jihad in the West* (Prometheus, 1998) Daveed Gartenstein-Ross, *My Year Inside Radical Islam* (Tarcher, 2007) Roland Jacquard, *In the Name of Osama bin Laden* (Duke, 2002) Kanan Makiya, *Cruelty and Silence* (W. W. Norton, 1993) Monte and Princess Palmer, *At the Heart of Terror* (Rowman & Littlefield, 2004) Daniel Pipes, *Militant Islam Reaches America* (Norton, 2003) Ahmed Rashid, *Taliban* (Yale, 2001) _____ *Descent into Chaos* (Viking, 2008) Thomas Ricks, *Fiasco* (Penguin, 2006) Michael Scheuer, *Marching toward Hell* (Free Press, 2008) Stephen Schwartz, *The Two Faces of Islam* (Anchor, 2003) Bob Woodward, *State of Denial* (Simon & Schuster, 2006) Lawrence Wright, *The Looming Tower* (Knopf, 2006)

Christian Websites on Islam	Answering Islam http://www.answering-islam.org Muslim-Christian Debate Web site (features work of Jay Smith): www.debate.org.uk
Academic Sites	Carl W. Ernst (University of North Carolina) www.unc.edu/~cernst/index.html Alan Godlas (University of Georgia) www.uga.edu/islam Martin Kramer (Olin Institute, Harvard) www.martinkramer.org Daniel Pipes www.danielpipes.org
Muslim Sites	Al-Muhaddith (download site for Qur'an, hadith, Islamic legal material): www.muhaddith.org Mamalist of Islamic Links www.jannah.org/mamalist Islamic Gateway (an Islamic site with great graphics and links): www.ummah.org.uk IslamiCity (a popular Muslim site that emphasizes evangelism): www.islam.org Musalman: the Islamic portal (Islamic site with good news coverage): www.musalman.com
Ex-Muslim Sites	www.faithfreedom.org www.apostatesofislam.com
Terrorism Analysis Sites	Counterterrorism Blog http://counterterrorismblog.org Foundation for Defense of Democracies http://defenddemocracy.org ICT - Terrorism & Counter-Terrorism www.ict.org.il Jihad Watch www.jihadwatch.org
CD Christian Resource	*The World of Islam* (GMI, 2001) www.gmi.org Features major work by Dudley Woodberry, Fuller seminary scholar

8

JEHOVAH'S WITNESSES

Convention in Moscow

Photo: Eileen Barker

Nearly everyone has at some point had Jehovah's Witnesses come knocking at their door. In 2002 the dedicated members of the Watchtower Society spent 1.2 billion hours in what they call "public Bible educational work." In 2002 alone the Jehovah's Witnesses baptized 265,469 new members, an increase of 2.8 percent from the previous year, a growth probably linked to the events of 9/11. In 2004 they performed 262,416 more baptisms. As of the beginning of 2005 there were almost 97,000 Jehovah's Witnesses congregations worldwide.

WATCHTOWER 101

- Jehovah's Witnesses alone are true Christians. If you are not a Jehovah's Witness, you are not a Christian.

- God is not a triune being; the doctrine of the Trinity is satanic.

- Jesus is to be called "a god" and not God. Thus, Jehovah's Witnesses translate John 1:1 this way: "In the beginning the Word was, and the Word was with God, and the Word was a god."

- While Jesus is worthy of honor, he is not to be worshiped.

- Jesus is a created being. He is not eternal in his preexistence but rather was created by Jehovah as Michael the Archangel.

- Jesus died on a stake and not on a cross. The cross is a pagan symbol.

- Jesus did not rise physically from the grave. Rather, Jehovah raised his spirit from death and then provided another body for his appearances to his disciples.

- The second coming of Jesus took place in 1914, when Jesus returned invisibly to Earth.

- The Holy Spirit is not the third Person of the Trinity but rather an impersonal force.

- The Governing Body of Jehovah's Witnesses constitutes "the faithful and discreet slave" mentioned in Matthew 24:45–47 and serves as the only body on Earth who can properly interpret the Bible.

- Only 144,000 saints will be in heaven.

- Witnesses who are not part of the 144,000 will be raised from death to live forever on paradise Earth.

- Blood transfusing is forbidden; it is sin deserving destruction.

- Celebrating Christmas, Easter, and birthdays is immoral.

- True Christians must not be involved in politics or in saluting the flag of any nation.

- Jehovah's Witnesses cannot take part in military service.

- All Jehovah's Witnesses must go door-to-door in announcing the message of Jehovah's Kingdom.

- Witnesses must obey the teachings of the Watchtower Society and be in total unity with God's organization.

- The Witness must not read any material critical of the Society. This literature is viewed as "spiritual pornography."

- Witnesses must shun anyone who has left or been excommunicated from the Society.

Loyalty to the Organization

To understand the Jehovah's Witnesses' religion, it is essential to understand how much they rely on the Watchtower leadership for everything and also to understand the total commitment required of the membership to the Watchtower Society. Witnesses believe loyalty to the organization is equivalent to loyalty to the Divine. They hold that one's obedience to God can be measured by one's submission to the Governing Body of Jehovah's Witnesses and that to dissent from the "faithful and discreet slave" is to reject God's counsel.

Ironically, however, this unrelenting emphasis on obedience to the organization is in direct opposition to the explicit teaching of Charles Russell, the founder of the movement. Russell feared large organizations and warned against religious organization where "the church creed is the role" and where one finds "the exultation of the teachings of the organization above the word of God" (Russell, quoted in *The Finished Mystery*, p. 209).

JEHOVAH'S WITNESSES TIMELINE

1852—Birth of Charles Taze Russell in Old Allegheny, Pennsylvania

1879—Publication of *Zion's Watchtower and Herald of Christ Presence*

1886—*The Plan of the Ages* published as first volume of *Studies in the Scriptures*

1897—First separation of Russell and his wife

1906—Court case results in divorce

1913—Grand jury trial between Russell and J. J. Ross of Hamilton

1916—Russell dies on October 31

1917—Judge Rutherford elected president on January 6

1920—*Millions Now Living Will Never Die* published

1931—Name "Jehovah's Witnesses" adopted

1939—Bitter leadership rivalry leads to Olin Moyle's dismissal from Society

1942—Rutherford dies. Nathan Knorr becomes president

1945—Blood transfusions forbidden

1960—*New World Translation* is completed

1968—Focus on 1975 as end of the world begins

1971—Formation of Governing Body

1977—Knorr dies. Frederick Franz becomes president

1980—Apology from Governing Body about 1975. Purge of so-called apostates from Brooklyn

1981—Raymond Franz, former Governing Body member, excommunicated

1984—International protest by ex-members at Brooklyn

1992—Frederick Franz dies. Milton Henschel becomes leader

2000—Reorganization of Watchtower Society leadership

2001—Watchtower Society gives up NGO status at United Nations

2002—Media attention over child abuse cover-up allegations

2003—Witnesses persecuted in former Soviet countries

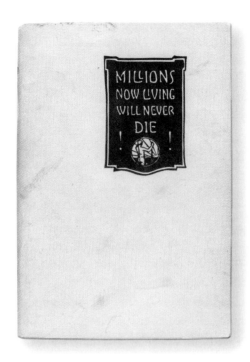

A 1908 *Watchtower* article stated: "Fallen human nature is considerably the same at all times and in all places; and so we find that amongst those who have named the name of the Lord during this Gospel Age, there have been similar tendencies [to the Israelites' wanting a king] to overlook the Lord as this great Head of the church, a great protector of its interest, a great governor of its affairs. Two centuries of the Gospel Age had not passed when the worldly spirit called them for more organization in the Lord and established through Jesus and the apostles."

The required allegiance to the Watchtower Society explains two trends among Jehovah's Witnesses. First, Witness dedication to the Governing Body keeps Jehovah's Witnesses from carefully checking into biblical doctrine or allegations concerning false prophecy, faulty scholarship, and injustice. Alan Rogerson has noted in his work *Millions Now Living Will Never Die* that "for the most part the Witness remains in a state of certainty that only inward doubts can remove. Such dogmatism is not restricted to Jehovah's Witnesses—it is typical of other systems. It is characterized by complete absence of tolerance and the presence of a rigid opinion that the possessor refuses to alter even in the face of contrary facts—it is the facts that are altered or ignored where they do not fit in."

This allegiance to the Watchtower Society also explains why Witnesses defend the harsh treatment of those who question the Society. Those who leave or who are expelled from the organization are sentenced to a religious Siberia—at enormous emotional cost, both for the one excommunicated and for those who are forced, against their deepest wishes, to have nothing to do with that person.

THE GOVERNING BODY OF JEHOVAH'S WITNESSES

Jehovah's Witnesses are constantly taught that the Governing Body of the Society is the "faithful and discreet slave" of Matthew 24:45–47. This body makes the major decisions for all Jehovah's Witnesses, interprets the Bible for them, and counsels that Witnesses must use Watchtower material. The Governing Body also believes that there is to be unity at all costs.

In the entire history of people claiming to be Christians, it is likely that only Witnesses have interpreted Matthew 24:45–47 to refer to a group of men from Brooklyn, New York. Actually, Witnesses used to believe that Charles Russell alone was the wise and faithful servant ("faithful and discreet slave"). Ultimately, the Governing Body has not proven to be "discreet" or "faithful" to the Scripture.

The Bible says Christians are to follow God's Word even if it goes against human counsel (Acts 5:29) and that we are to test the spirits (1 John 4:1) and prove all things (1 Thess. 5:21). Witnesses ignore these scriptural teachings and give incredible power to their leaders, following all their dictates, no matter how debatable or harmful.

In the 1970s the Governing Body subjected Witnesses all over the world to rules concerning what constituted adultery and what married couples were allowed to do in the privacy of their own bedroom. The Governing Body taught for several years that homosexual acts or sex with animals did not constitute adultery. Witnesses who divorced spouses over such acts were kicked out of the Society.

Jehovah's Witnesses and 1914

Since the founding of the Watchtower movement, Jehovah's Witnesses have been absorbed with Bible prophecy. For almost a century the Society has given prominence to their teaching that 1914 marks the invisible return of Jesus to Earth and the beginning of the end-times. Though the details surrounding the 1914 doctrine involve some complex issues, one can quite readily grasp the basic rationale for the Witness view by understanding the following:

1. Witnesses believe they can calculate the timing of Jesus' return to Earth by referring to "the time of the Gentiles" mentioned in Luke 21:24. They believe that the Second Coming took place in 1914 because, they argue, that was the year Gentile domination of Jerusalem ended.

2. The Society teaches that Gentile control of Jerusalem began in 607 B.C., the year the Witnesses claim the Babylonians conquered Jerusalem and removed the Jewish leaders from their rule over the Holy City. Witnesses are taught that historical evidence proves that 607 B.C. is the start of "the time of the Gentiles."

3. Witnesses then argue that Gentile control of Jerusalem is predicted in Daniel 4:23 to last "seven times." But what does "seven times" mean? According to the Witnesses, this "seven times" is prophetic language used in the Bible for 2,520 days. They base this on their interpretation of Revelation 12:6 that 1,260 days equals three and one-half times. If three and a half equals 1,260, they claim, then seven times equals twice that amount, which adds up to 2,520 days.

4. Witnesses then state that the Bible teaches that one day in prophecy actually equals one year. They base this on the "a day for a year" principle given in Ezekiel 4:6 where the prophet Ezekiel is told that every day of his symbolic action of God's wrath stands for one year of judgment against Israel. This means that 2,520 days equals 2,520 years. Therefore, the Gentile control of Jerusalem will last 2,520 years.

5. Finally, since the Gentile times began in 607 B.C., according to Witnesses, then one can simply add 2,520 years to that date to calculate that the Gentile times will end in A.D. 1914, the year that the

Society teaches that Jesus returned invisibly to guide the Jehovah's Witnesses.

Errors in the 1914 Doctrine

Though the Society claims that its teaching on 1914 and the return of Jesus is based on plain Bible teaching, these theories are actually based on the theories of Charles Russell and subsequent movement leaders. Here are some reasons to question their understanding of the return of Jesus:

- Charles Russell taught for most of his life that 1874, not 1914, would mark the invisible return of Jesus. Judge Rutherford, the Society's second leader, also taught this until 1934.

- Jehovah's Witnesses use the wrong date for the fall of Jerusalem. The Babylonians invaded the city in 587/586 B.C., not 607 B.C.

- Jehovah's Witnesses' interpretions of chapter 4 of Daniel are highly idiosyncratic. Most Christians believe that this chapter is about the length of God's punishment of Babylonian King Nebuchadnezzar.

- There was no end of the world in 1914, as Russell predicted. Also, 1914 did not bring an end to the Gentile domination of Jerusalem. The Jewish people did not regain control of Israel until 1948, and control of the whole city of Jerusalem came in 1967.

- Jehovah's Witnesses claim that Jesus returned secretly. According to the Bible, his return will be visible and obvious (see Matt. 24; Mark 13; Luke 21).

- Jehovah's Witnesses taught for decades that 1914 plus one generation equals the end of the world.

- The Watchtower Society excommunicates critics, rather than answering them.

- Jesus warned his followers about those who say he has already returned.

PROPHECY AND THE GREAT PYRAMID

Watchtower founder Charles Russell borrowed the view that the Great Pyramid of Egypt was a reliable guide to Bible prophecy. He described it as a "great witness of stone eloquently proclaiming the wisdom in power and grace of our God" (*Thy Kingdom Come*, p. 376). The 1891 edition of *Studies in the Scriptures* (volume 3) uses the length of one passage in the pyramid to prove that 1870 marks the beginning of the "time of trouble." The 1912 edition attempts to prove that 1914 is the beginning of the same event—by simply declaring that the measurement of the pyramid's passage is 3,457 inches, the number necessary to make the formula work out to 1914.

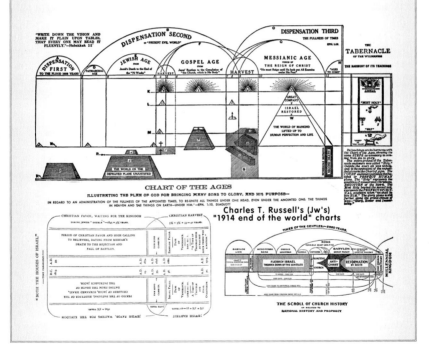

Charles T. Russell's (Jw's)
"1914 end of the world" charts

Jehovah's Witnesses and False Prophecy

The Society's teaching about 1914 fits into a larger story of Witness leaders' false prophecies. Jehovah's Witnesses have confidently asserted that they make up a "prophet-class." The Society has passed judgment on others who falsely predicted the end of the world, saying that such false prophecy shows clearly that God's Spirit is not with them.

Witnesses still believe that Charles Russell, Judge Rutherford, Nathan Knorr, Frederick Franz, and the current Society leadership are accurate in their understanding of prophecy. Some evidence even shows that the increase in membership in the organization is directly proportional to the zeal with which dates are set for apocalyptic events. Only a handful of Witnesses realize the extent of Watchtower errors in prophecy. Yet no evidence indicates that the Society will abandon its obsession with prophecy or its reluctance to face up to past prophetic blunders.

Charles Russell duplicated the prophetic focus that swept many Christian bodies in the nineteenth century. The elaborate system of prophecy Russell constructed failed on nearly every point. Modern Society publications make brief reference to Russell's predictions about 1914 and suggest that he prophesied the outbreak of World War I. But modern Witnesses are not told of Russell's overall prophetic framework. Actually, the Jehovah's Witnesses founder predicted that the world would end in 1914.

THE UNITED NATIONS COVER-UP

The Watchtower Society has often argued in their literature that the United Nations fits the description of the "evil beast" described in the Book of Revelation. The Society teaches that the "Whore of Babylon" that rides the "evil beast" is the term for the false religions of the world, including all Protestant denominations. One Society publication states: "Yes, the League of Nations, along with its successor, the United Nations, truly became an idol, a 'disgusting thing' in the sight of God and of his people."

On October 8, 2001, a story by Stephen Gates in *The Guardian* newspaper reported that the Watchtower Bible and Tract Society actually had Non-Governmental Organization (NGO) status with the United Nations since 1992. Two days after the story appeared, in the midst of worldwide interest in Gates's report, the Society withdrew its membership. The Society tried to excuse the NGO identification by saying it was the only way to have access to library material at the UN. This was a false claim, as was the Society's argument that the leaders in Brooklyn did not know about the membership.

Russell taught throughout his life that the years A.D. 539, 1799, 1828, 1846, and 1873 were all significant in Bible prophecy, a view that no modern Witness would recognize. As well, Russell taught that 1874 was the beginning of Christ's invisible presence on the Earth. He also predicted that 1878 would mark the coming of Christ in power and the beginning of the heavenly resurrection, an idea reworked when the world did not end in that year.

Russell's whole prophetic outlook was not original; he adapted most of these ideas from the works of Nelson Barbour, George Storrs, John Aquila Brown, William Miller, Joseph Seiss, and Benjamin Wilson. The Watchtower leader also copied the idea that the Great Pyramid in Egypt was a reliable guide to Bible prophecy. Russell showed hesitation about his prophecies only as the dates approached in which supernatural events were to occur. Other than that, his confidence was staggering.

In *The Time Is at Hand*, Russell judged his speculations a matter of "unquestionable certainty." In the conclusion to *The Plan of the Ages*, he wrote: "And be it known that no other system of theology even claims, or has ever attempted, to harmonize in itself every statement of the Bible; yet nothing short of this can we claim for these views. This harmony not only with the Bible, but with the divine character and with sanctified common sense, must have arrested the attention of the conscientious reader already, and filled him with awe, as well as with hope and confidence."

New Leadership—More Failed Prophecies

Though Judge Joseph Rutherford, Russell's successor, changed most of Russell's eschatological framework, he admitted to being careless in regard to his predictions about 1925. That year was to "mark the return of Abraham, Isaac, Jacob and the faithful prophets of old to the condition of human perfection." Even after that prophecy failed, Witnesses remained confident enough in these men's imminent return to purchase a beautiful home in San Diego for them. The mansion was known as Beth-Sarim, Hebrew for "House of the Princes." In the late 1930s and nearly 1940s the Society's prophetic zeal increased again. Society literature spoke of the impropriety of marriage and having children, since Armageddon was just months away.

After Nathan Knorr became the Society's third president in 1942, the Society demonstrated more restraint about predicting the future. This continued until the 1966 publication *Life Everlasting in Freedom of the Sons of God* focused on 1975 as the end of the world. Though most of the statements in Society literature were nuanced, Frederick Franz, Knorr's successor, became known for his more bombastic claims about that year. In the May 1974 issue of *Kingdom Ministry*, the Society's Brooklyn headquarters had this to say: "Reports are heard of brothers selling their homes and property and planning to finish out the rest of their days in this old system in the pioneer service [full-time evangelism]. Certainly this is a fine way to spend the short time remaining before the wicked world's end."

The 1975 prediction had such a negative impact on worldwide membership that the Society leadership issued an apology in the March 15, 1980 edition of *The Watchtower.* However, the Society's candor about 1975 has never really extended to its century-long prophetic errors. Uninformed Witnesses think that the Society has made only a few mistakes and that past failures were largely results of an overzealous response to the leadership's veiled prophetic statements.

Explaining Away the Errors

When I wrote my first book, *Crisis of Allegiance,* I interviewed Walter Graham, at the time the public relations director for the Watchtower Society's Canadian branch. We spent some time discussing whether the Society had made mistakes in the area of prophecy. Here is part of that conversation:

Beverley: "What is your view or the Society's view of failures in past prophetic outlook?"

Graham: "Well, we don't feel that they were failures as such or wrong prophecy."

Beverley: "Would you admit that some of the statements in the Society's literature have been, on any interpretation, just simply wrong?"

Graham: "Well, we don't feel them wrong in the context of their being maliciously put there or with the wrong motive, but indeed, we had indeed modified our belief in many of these things, and that we feel is normal."

Beverley: "But do you mind saying that these were clear-cut mistakes?"

Graham: "Yes, because that statement can be taken out of context. And so of course we mind saying that such statements were wrong or mistakes, because we don't believe they were."

Graham later admitted to me that based on an ordinary understanding of the word *mistake*, some of the Society's past prophetic statements were mistaken. But he added that since Jehovah allowed the mistakes, he did not want to say that God made errors. He admitted that Witnesses have been overly enthusiastic and sometimes expected "the wrong thing at the right time." That is exactly the language Charles Russell used to excuse William Miller, the famous Adventist preacher, when he predicted the end of the world in 1844.

■ Jehovah's Witnesses and Intellectual Honesty

In describing Watchtower ideology, James Beckford, a leading sociologist of religion, argues that the movement's rationalistic appearance accounts in part for the extreme commitment of its membership. Since the beginning of Russell's ministry, the Society has placed much stress on rationality, and consequently Witnesses believe that genuine scholarship supports their views.

In earlier years, the Bible Students (the original title for Russell's followers) viewed Russell as "the faithful and discreet slave" of Matthew 24, a title the pastor accepted in private conversation. But the extent to which people admired Russell can only be understood when one widely reads Society literature following his death. *The Finished Mystery*, a 1917 Watchtower publication, described him in this way:

> The amount of work that Pastor Russell performed is incredible, and it is doubtful whether it was ever equaled by any other human being. For 50 years he suffered constantly with sick headaches, due to a fall in his youth, and for 25 years had such distressing hemorrhoids that it was impossible for him to rest in the easiest chair; yet in the past 40 years he traveled one million miles, delivered 30,000 sermons and table talks— many of them two and a half hours long—wrote over 50,000 pages of advanced biblical exposition, often dictated 1,000 letters per month, managed every department of a worldwide evangelistic campaign employing 700 speakers, personally compiled the most wonderful Biblical drama ever shown; and with all that, he has been seen, unobserved by himself, to stand by his mantle all night in prayer, in one position.

According to the Witnesses of Russell's day, God had chosen him as the messenger to deliver the final warnings to apostate Christendom. It is surely quite ironic that Jehovah's Witnesses today pay virtually no attention to their founder. The early Bible Students said that he was "the beautiful voice of the Lord: strong, humble, wise, loving, gentle, and just, merciful, faithful, self-sacrificing; one of the noblest, grandest characters of all history."

THE FINISHED MYSTERY

The Finished Mystery should be consulted as an example of how dogmatic Witnesses can be. The book argues that the Book of Job predicts the invention of the steam engine and that Nahum describes a railway train in motion. Further, a distance mentioned in Revelation 14:20 is said to refer to the distance between Scranton, Pennsylvania (where *The Finished Mystery* was written), and Brooklyn, New York (where it was printed). The Watchtower Society endured a major schism over the book's contents, and few Witnesses today know anything about the book that was once viewed as a fulfillment of Bible prophecy.

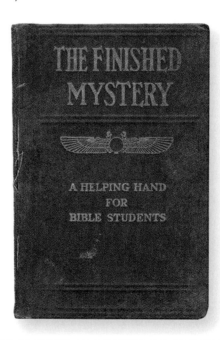

Academics and experts on religion seldom cite Watchtower material as a source of insight, careful exegesis, or profound theological reflection. Further, while Witness publications cite various authorities, there are often clear misrepresentations of their views of the scholars who are quoted. For example, Edwin Thiele, William Barclay, Julius Mantey, Edward Campbell, and David Noel Freedman (all scholars of religion) have each complained about distorted use of their work.

One cannot turn to Society literature even for a reliable outline of the Society's own history. Discussion of Russell's status as "the faithful and discreet slave" is often misleading, as is the treatment of his marital problems. Watchtower reporting on the 1917 schism that occurred when Rutherford took over the Society is inaccurate. Likewise, Witnesses have never been told that their own organization attempted to ingratiate itself with Adolf Hitler and the Nazi regime.

A Naïve Worldview

The Watchtower Society has regularly approached and handled politics and society simplistically. Even worse, the leaders apparently make decisions with no regard for the impact they will have on the lives of ordinary Witnesses.

In his book *Crisis of Conscience*, former Jehovah's Witness Raymond Franz documented an example of these kinds of decisions. Franz cited the inconsistency of Watchtower leadership in giving directions for how Witnesses should respond to government policies in Mexico that were different from those for Witnesses in Malawi, an East African country. In Mexico, Jehovah's Witnesses were allowed to bribe authorities and lie about military service. But in Malawi, Witnesses suffered loss of property, torture, rape, and death because they followed the Society's instruction not to pay for the ruling party's political membership card.

RAYMOND FRANZ

One of the most influential people in the Watchtower Society is actually an ex-Witness named Raymond Franz. He is a former member of the Governing Body and was the main person behind the Society's *Aid to Bible Understanding*. Franz became a Witness in 1939, but he was pushed out of the Society in 1981 following turmoil at the Bethel headquarters in 1979 and 1980. Ray's uncle Frederick Franz was president at the time, but he did nothing as "Jehovah's organization" turned against his nephew.

After Raymond Franz left the Society in 1981, he wrote *Crisis of Conscience*, the most important modern book—now in its fourth edition—about the Witnesses. Its significance lies not only in its detailed report of life at the top of the Watchtower but in its powerful critique of dominant themes in Witness ideology. He documents the Society's leadership cover-ups, duplicity in the formulation of doctrine, and hypocrisy in the application of Society rules. His account of the way Society leadership treated him illustrates the abuse of power by religious authorities.

As a prominent member of the Governing Body, Franz had enormous influence in the Society. Since his ousting, he has shown many ex-Witnesses that there is life beyond the Watchtower.

(*Crisis of Conscience* is available from Commentary Press, Box 43532, Atlanta, GA 30336-0532 and at www.commentarypress.com.)

■ Jehovah's Witnesses and Ideological Stability

Witness history is replete with doctrinal changes, medical quackery, and revised prophecies. How do Witnesses respond to these realities? Usually they refer to the idea of "progressive revelation," which they believe is described in Proverbs 4:18: "but the path of the righteous ones is like the bright light that is getting lighter and lighter till today is firmly established." The *Watchtower* even made reference to the navigational maneuver of "tacking into the wind" to justify, by analogy, the Society's confusing doctrinal changes over the years. Also, the Society constantly tells Witnesses to "avoid running ahead of Jehovah" by trying to correct error in his organization.

The idea of "progressive revelation" is not accompanied with humility about official teachings. Society leaders advance their teachings in the most dogmatic manner, are ready to exercise discipline on those who disagree, and are unwilling to recognize that their "truth" of today might be tomorrow's error.

Judge Rutherford was not even considerate of the heritage he received from Charles Russell. Timothy White states in his work *A People for His Name*:

> An examination of the Watchtower through the 1920s will convince any logical mind that in no case did Rutherford point out in an honest manner faults in Russell's teachings. Usually he merely stated his change without any acknowledgment that it contradicted a long-established and well-reasoned view. Where he did mention a view he said was Russell's it was either a thorough distortion or oversimplification of it, or, at times, a view Russell simply did not have and even expressly denied.

Finally, progressive revelation is no excuse for extreme doctrinal ambivalence. Paul warns that "we will no longer be infants, tossed back and forth by the waves, and blown here and there by every wind of teaching and by the cunning and craftiness of men" (Eph. 4:14). The difference between early Watchtower teaching and current doctrine is so extreme that Charles Russell, if he were alive today, would be excommunicated if he held to the views that built the Society in his day.

The Watchtower leaders have also changed their minds twice on the same issue. For example, Russell taught that the phrase "higher authorities" as it is used in Romans 13 refers to human government. Rutherford then applied this text to Jehovah and Jesus, but later the Society adopted Russell's view. Russell gave considerable liberty to elders and deacons, but Rutherford, in moves to consolidate his personal power, abolished these biblical offices in 1932. The Society reinstated these offices in the early 1970s, largely as a result of the evidence Raymond Franz gathered for the Society's *Aid to Bible Understanding*.

Two further items are of importance in relation to the ambivalence of the Governing Body on doctrine and policy. First, the Governing Body is actually a recent creation in Society history—a fact most Witnesses do not know. The organization's first three presidents ruled like monarchs, as Franz documents in chapter 3 of *Crisis of Conscience*. Second, the mere listing of doctrinal vacillations cannot convey the heartache brought to

Jehovah's Witnesses who sacrificed career, marriage, children, and health on the altar of changing Watchtower positions.

■ Jehovah's Witnesses and Child Abuse

In 2000 William Bowen of Calvert City, Kentucky, discovered that one of his fellow elders in the local Kingdom Hall had molested a child many times over. The Watchtower Society told Bowen that the person would be removed as an elder but that Bowen was not to report the incident to the police. Bowen disobeyed the Society, resigned as an elder, and went public with his observation that the Society's policies often protect pedophiles. He started www.silentlambs.org to provide a setting where victims of abuse could protest Witness cover-ups and to serve as "a place for the lambs to roar." Bowen was kicked out of the Society in the summer of 2002.

Barbara Anderson, who for a time worked at Watchtower headquarters, went public with her charges that the Society has mishandled child-abuse cases in its midst. Anderson was responsible at "Bethel" (the spiritual term for headquarters) for drafting and shaping policies for the worldwide Witness community, and her job gave her access to details concerning Watchtower handling of child-abuse cases. She said she decided to speak out because she could not have lived with herself if she did not do something to protect little children. She was excommunicated for her actions, even though she told Watchtower officials that she simply wanted to protect children in the Society.

What do Bowen and Anderson believe is wrong with Society policies? (1) Kingdom Hall elders do not have the necessary training to deal with child abusers or child-abuse victims, (2) elders often do not report cases of child abuse to the police unless local law demands it, (3) the Society teaches that nothing can be done about reports of child abuse unless they are substantiated by two witnesses, (4) the Society has not always followed its own rules, and (5) the Society has dealt more harshly with critics of its child-abuse policies than it has with actual child molesters in its midst.

Heartbreaking stories of abuse cover-up by the Society have been reported on NBC *Dateline*, BBC *Panorama*, CNN *Connie Chung Tonight*, the Canadian Broadcasting Corportation's program *The Fifth Estate*, Australian *Channel 9*, and *The New York Times*, among others.

The Watchtower Society has responded to criticism with a strong public relations campaign. Society personnel like J. R. Brown have argued that the organization does not condone child abuse and that the Society has cooperated with police fully in relevant cases. They have also contended that it is important for the Society to maintain confidentiality with parishioners.

However, Anderson and Bowen both maintain that the Society's policies still do not do enough to expose the pedophilia inside the Society. Anderson's 100-page commentary, which is part of her CD *Secrets of Pedophilia in an American Religion*, is available for free on the Internet.

■ Jehovah's Witnesses and Blood Transfusions

In Acts 15:20, 29 and 21:25 Gentile Christians are advised to abstain "from blood." Most Christians interpret this to mean to abstain from the *eating* of blood. The Watchtower Society has taught since 1945 that this means that true Christians are to avoid blood transfusions. The Society leadership equated receiving a blood transfusion with eating blood, and many Jehovah's Witnesses have chosen death instead of accepting a life-saving blood transfusion. (The May 22, 1994 edition of *Awake!* magazine featured pictures of twenty-six Witness children who died in cases involving the refusal of blood transfusion.)

Early Society literature on the subject relied on outdated ideas about blood to substantiate its position that the blood in a transfusion actually nourishes the body. The Associated Jehovah's Witnesses for Reform on Blood (AJWRB, Box 190089, Boise, Idaho 83719-0089, www.ajwrb.org), which provides help for Witnesses who have doubts about the Society's policies about transfusions, makes this point: "blood, in and of itself, is not a nutrient, and because of this a blood transfusion does not nourish the body, does not have as its design the nourishing of the body, and is not given because the patient needs nourishment."

In 1980 the Society reversed its ban against organ transplants and thus weakened its position on blood transfusion. In recent years Watchtower leaders have often spoken of God's ban "on taking in blood to sustain life." It should be obvious that this wording is a deceptive way of equating transfusion with eating blood since "taking in blood" can be used to describe both eating of blood and blood transfusion.

A MOTHER'S ANGUISH

"He was 15 years old and in the 9th grade when he and another young Witness were in a terrible auto accident. The other boy was driving my son home from the Sunday meeting when he raced the car, lost control and flipped. I was a faithful Witness for 29 years, and my husband and I trained our son to refuse blood transfusions. He told the ambulance drivers, 'No blood!' and he said it again at the first hospital before he became unconscious. When he was airlifted to the trauma center, he was immediately transfused because he was unconscious and a minor.

"Secretly, I had hoped the doctors would give him blood despite our wishes—if a transfusion could save his life. The doctor said they restarted his heart twice, and that gave us a glimmer of hope. But twenty minutes later, with tears in his eyes, the doctor said they couldn't restart his heart a third time—he had died.

"My husband and my two other sons and I cried and cried and cried. I have never known such anguish and physical pain! I wanted to die. The pain was unbearable. I kept thinking, 'Would he have lived if he got blood at the first hospital?' A spiral of profound change began in my life.

"My heart is completely broken—my child is dead. I beg of you who read my story, don't let this happen to you. Educate yourself now before you are faced with a similar tragedy. If any child can be saved by their parents thinking now rather than after they lose their child, perhaps my son's death will not have been for nothing."

—Mary, from Associated Jehovah's Witnesses for Reform on Blood

The current Watchtower ban on transfusions is tragic for three reasons.

First, over the last few decades the Society has relaxed its rules against the use of blood components. This has led to the bizarre situation where Witnesses are allowed to use most of the parts that make up blood but cannot take blood itself. For example, the Society allows hemoglobin transplants, even though hemoglobin makes up 97 percent of the dry weight in red blood cells.

The second tragedy has to do with the irony behind the Witness ban on blood transfusion. The biblical ban against eating blood is rooted in respect for blood as a symbol of life. In the case of blood transfusion, however, the Witness policy actually leads to death. One rule celebrates God's gift of life, while the other rule terminates God's gift of life in the Witnesses who follow the Society's policy.

In the spring of 2000 the Society changed its treatment of Witnesses who break Watchtower policy concerning blood transfusion. Previously anyone who voluntarily received a transfusion would be subject to a Judicial Committee hearing and would be excommunicated. Now those who receive transfusions are said to have, by their own actions, automatically removed themselves from the Society. The Jehovah's Witnesses call this "disassociation." The end result is the same: Society members are to shun the ex-Witness unless there is repentance for not refusing the transfusion and request for reinstatement.

◼ Only 144,000 in Heaven?

Jehovah's Witnesses have long taught that there are two classes of Christians.

First, there are the "anointed ones" who will be among the 144,000 who go to heaven. The Watchtower Society takes this number from the Book of Revelation—chapters 7 and 14, where the apostle John wrote of a crowd of 144,000—and accepts it literally. However, if these texts are to be taken literally, John was referring to 12,000 Jewish virgin males from each of the twelve tribes of Israel. The Watchtower Society takes everything symbolically except the total numerical figure.

The Society teaches Jehovah's Witnesses that there is a second group of believers who will live forever, not in heaven but on Earth. This crowd will be composed of all the Old Testament saints and any Jehovah's Witnesses who are not part of the 144,000. Modern-day Witnesses who are not part of the "anointed class" are not to take part in the Lord's Supper. Further, Witnesses who *are* part of the 144,000 but who leave the Society lose their place in the heavenly crowd and are replaced by other Witnesses who are still alive. Jehovah selects the replacement, and that particular Witness has an inner testimony from the Holy Spirit that he or she is now part of the heavenly crowd.

The famous Witness teaching on the 144,000 is paradoxical because the same section of Scripture that uses this number also pictures another scene. Revelation 7:9 states: "After this I looked and there before me was a great multitude that no one could count, from every nation, tribe, people and language, standing before the throne and in front of the Lamb. They were wearing white robes and were holding palm branches in their hands." The plain wording of the verse, especially in its context, implies that there will be many more than 144,000 believers in heaven.

Christians should have no major objection to the teaching that God will create a paradise on Earth as part of the redemption of the cosmos. However, the Witness teaching that only 144,000 believers go to heaven contradicts the plain teaching of Revelation 7:9. Likewise, this teaching denies Jesus' promise to his disciples that he was going to prepare a place in his Father's house for them. Likewise, the Witness teaching that there will be no Old Testament saints in heaven contradicts the obvious message in Matthew 8:11, which reads: "I say to you that many will come from the east and the west, and will take their places at the feast with Abraham, Isaac and Jacob in the kingdom of heaven."

■ Did Jesus Die on a Cross . . . or on a Torture Stake?

For the first half-century after its founding in 1879, the Watchtower Society taught that Jesus died on the cross. In 1928 Judge Rutherford, the Society's second president, started to distance himself from the traditional Christian emphasis on the cross, arguing instead that the cross was actually a pagan symbol. Witnesses are now taught that Jesus actually died on what they call a "torture stake," which they believe was a single pole with no cross-beam.

To defend their position, Witness authors have misrepresented archaeological and historical evidence and distorted the work of scholars. There is no reason to believe that the English word *cross* is a mistranslation of the relevant Greek words New Testament writers used. Likewise, there is plenty of evidence that Romans used a cross with a side-beam for executions, although they also used "crosses" with no side-beam. The horizontal bar Romans used in a complex cross was known as the *patibulum*. This was probably what Jesus carried on his way to Golgotha.

IS JESUS MICHAEL THE ARCHANGEL?

Jehovah's Witnesses believe that, before his incarnation, Jesus was actually Michael the archangel and that he assumed the same name after his resurrection. Witnesses base this on the argument that the work of Michael the archangel in Daniel 12 and Revelation 12 is the same as the work of Jesus, and therefore, the two are the same person. Further, they argue that Jesus is now an archangel in heaven because 1 Thessalonians 4:16 states that when he returns it will be "with the voice of the archangel." Witnesses believe that Jesus is also the glorified Son of God in heaven.

The Witness position loses all credibility in light of the following: (a) hundreds of Bible verses point to the identity of Jesus as the Son of God and not as Michael the Archangel, (b) the Book of Hebrews makes it explicit that Jesus is greater than angels, and (c) the author of Hebrews even argues that angels are commanded to worship Jesus as Lord. The reference in 1 Thessalonians is better interpreted as a reference to the angelic company that returns with Jesus at his second coming.

■ Light from the Past?

When Charles Russell started the Witness movement in 1879 he did not teach that his Bible Students were the only faithful Christians in the world. However, he became increasingly arrogant about his unique understandings of Scripture, particularly related to Bible prophecy. During the leadership of Judge Rutherford, Witnesses came to believe that they were the one true church of Jesus.

When one looks at past Watchtower teaching, it becomes clear that Society views and practices have changed considerably and that Jehovah's Witnesses have been dogmatic on a wide range of issues.

The Danger of Aluminum: "As a result of the publication of wholesome truth on the subject, there are fewer people now purchasing aluminum cooking utensils than heretofore. There is also a pronounced drop in the cancer death rate. Much aluminum used: many cancers. Less aluminum used: fewer cancers" (Source: *The Golden Age,* 1930, p. 650).

Anti-Semitism: "The greatest and the most oppressive empire on earth is the Anglo-Saxon Empire. By that is meant the British Empire, of which the United States of America forms a part. It has been the commercial Jews of the British-American Empire that have built up and carried on Big Business as a means of exploiting and oppressing the peoples of many nations. This fact particularly applies to the cities of London and New York, the stronghold of Big Business. This fact is so manifest in America that there is a proverb concerning the city of New York which says: The Jews own it, the Irish Catholics rule it, and the Americans pay the bills" (Source: Yearbook, 1934, p. 134).

No Children Since the End Is Near: "Would it be Scripturally proper for them to now marry and begin to rear children? No, is the answer, which is supported by the Scriptures. . . . Those Jonadabs who now contemplate marriage, it would seem, would do better if they wait a few years, until the fiery storm of Armageddon is gone . . ." (Source: *Face the Facts*, 1938, pp. 46, 49–50).

No Need for Career: "If you are a young person, you also need to face the fact that you will never grow old in this present system of things. Why not? Because all the evidence in fulfillment of Bible prophecy indicates that this corrupt system is due to end in a few years. Of the generation that observed the beginning of the 'last days' in 1914, Jesus foretold: 'This generation will by no means pass away until all these things occur.' Therefore, as a young person, you will never fulfill any career that this system offers" (Source: *Awake!* May 22, 1969, p. 15).

Salvation Only in Jehovah's Organization: "Do not conclude that there are different roads, or ways, that you can follow to gain life in God's new system. There is only one. There was just one ark that survived the Flood, not a number of boats. And there will be only one organization— God's visible organization—that will survive the fast-approaching "great tribulation." It is simply not true that all religions lead to the same goal. . . . You must be a part of Jehovah's organization, doing God's will, in order to receive his blessing of everlasting life . . ." (Source: *You Can Live Forever*, 1982, p. 255).

The Bible Cannot Be Understood Apart from Watchtower: "Thus the Bible is an organizational book and belongs to the Christian congregation as an organization, not to individuals, regardless of how sincerely they may believe that they can interpret the Bible. For this reason the Bible cannot be properly understood without Jehovah's visible organization in mind" (Source: *Watchtower*, October 1, 1967, p. 587).

Vaccination Dangerous: "Vaccination summed up is the most unnatural, unhygienic, barbaric, filthy, abhorrent, and most dangerous system of infection known. Its vile poison taints, corrupts, and pollutes the blood of the healthy, resulting in ulcers, syphilis, scrofula, erysipelas, tuberculosis, cancer, tetanus, insanity, and death" (Source: *The Golden Age*, January 3, 1923, p. 214).

Pyramid Corridor Proves Bible Prophecy about 1874: "This calculation shows A.D. 1874 as marking the beginning of the period of trouble; for 1542 years B.C. plus 1874 years A.D. equals 3,416 years. Thus the Pyramid witnesses that the close of 1874 was the chronological beginning of the time of trouble such as was not since there was a nation—no, nor ever shall be afterward. And thus it will be noted that this 'Witness' fully corroborates the Bible testimony on this subject . . ." (Source: *Thy Kingdom Come*, 1904 edition, p. 342).

Same Pyramid Corridor Later Used to Prove Bible Prophecy about 1914: "This calculation shows A.D 1915 as marking the beginning of the period of trouble; for 1542 years B.C. plus 1915 years A.D. equals 3,457 years. Thus the Pyramid witnesses that the close of 1914 will be the beginning of the time of trouble such as was not since there was a nation—no, nor ever shall be afterward. And thus it will be noted that this 'Witness' fully corroborates the Bible testimony on this subject . . ." (Source: *Thy Kingdom Come*, 1910 edition, p. 342).

God Lives on the Pleiades Constellation: "The constellation of the Pleiades is a small one compared with others which scientific instruments disclose to the wondering eyes of man. But the greatness in size of other stars or planets is small when compared to the Pleiades in importance, because the Pleiades is the place of the eternal throne of God" (Source: J. F. Rutherford, *Reconciliation*, 1928, p. 14).

JEHOVAH'S WITNESSES

Typology	Christian Protestant Adventist Sectarian
Founder	Charles Taze Russell (1852–1916)
Headquarters	Brooklyn, New York
Homepage	www.watchtower.org
Critic Sites	Watchers of the Watch Tower World—Randall Watters site: www.freeminds.org/ Watchtower Documents LLC (Barbara Anderson): www.watchtowerdocuments.com Comments from the Friends—David Reed: www.cftf.com/ Watchtower Information: www.watchtowerinformationservice.org Giving Voice to a Voiceless Community: www.disfellowshipped.org Child Abuse and the Watchtower (Bill Bowen): www.silentlambs.org Dissenting JWs on Blood Transfusion: www.ajwrb.org Reasoning with Jehovah's Witnesses (Kevin Quick): www.kevinquick.com
Recommended Reading	Raymond Franz, *Crisis of Conscience* (Atlanta: Commentary Press, 1983) M. James Penton, *Apocalypse Delayed* (Toronto: University of Toronto Press, 1985) David A. Reed, *Answering Jehovah's Witnesses* (Grand Rapids: Baker, 1996) Ron Rhodes, *Reasoning from the Scriptures with Jehovah's Witnesses* (Eugene: Harvest House, 1993)

9

JUDAISM

Synagogue in Bukhara, Uzbekistan

Photo: Massimo Introvigne

As of 2008, there are about 15 million Jews in the world, with about 5 million in Israel and 6 million in the United States. While these are not large figures on the scale of major world religions, the numbers are amazing when one considers that Jewish people exercised no independent political rule in Palestine from 63 B.C. until 1948. The survival of the Jewish people becomes even more remarkable in light of the Holocaust and the persecution of Jews through the centuries.

Judaism forms the matrix for the emergence of both Christianity and Islam, even though both movements move beyond Jewish orthodoxy. Sadly, both traditions neglected to appreciate their origins in Judaism and the rulers in Christendom and in Islamic states often persecuted Jewish people. Anti-Semitism has marred the face of both church and Islamic history. It is no wonder that many Jewish people have a deep resentment toward both church and mosque.

Contrary to popular impression, most Jews are secular and not religious. However, Judaism remains the meta-narrative for many secular Jews, particularly in relation to annual holy days, rites of passage, kosher food, and any sense of spiritual longing. Many secular Jews follow certain religious practices even though there is no explicit belief in God.

The split between religious and secular Jew carries more importance in Israel than in the United States. This is due to the political power of Orthodox Jews in Israel and the strong disagreements that Israeli Jews have over the influence that religion should have in Jewish politics. What makes these issues even more complex is that there are serious divisions among both secular and religious Jews about Zionism, the Israel-Palestinian conflict, and the proper response to Orthodox political power.

JEWS AND THE SEVEN LAWS OF NOAH

Contrary to popular perception, the vast majority of Orthodox Jews do not believe that Gentiles must obey Jewish laws. Rather, Gentiles are obligated to obey the seven laws given in God's covenant with Noah:

1. Establish justice and the rule of law.

2. Do not engage in idolatry.

3. Do not blaspheme God's name.

4. Do not engage in sexual misconduct.

5. Do not take the life of another human.

6. Do not steal.

7. Do not tear a limb from a living animal.

▉ Main Branches of Judaism

Judaism, like all world religions, has its divisions. As noted at the start of the chapter, most Jews are secular. In terms of religious Jews, most fall into the following three categories: orthodox, conservative, and reform. Generally speaking, there is less distance between Conservative and Reform Jews than between Orthodox and other religious Jews.

Orthodox Judaism is the most complex of the three divisions since the Orthodox can be further divided into a whole number of sub-groups, especially in Israel and areas of the U.S. where there is a large Orthodox presence.

1. Orthodox Judaism

Orthodox Judaism usually includes the Hasidic movements. Hasidic Jews share much in common with the larger Orthodox world and usually resent being called Ultra-Orthodox. Orthodox Jews, including Hasidim, place great emphasis on the Torah (the first five books of the Bible) since it provides the written Law God gave Moses on Mount Sinai. They also believe that Moses received the Oral Law from God. This Oral Law is contained in the Mishnah and the Talmud. Orthodox Jews believe that the Torah contains 613 *mitzvots* or commandments. Orthodox rabbis are often trained at Yeshiva University.

Internet Source

Main website: www.ou.org

ORTHODOX JUDAISM 101

- Orthodox Jews believe in the One God who has revealed himself to Israel.

- Orthodox Jews follow the 613 Commands or *mitzvot* given in the Torah.

- Orthodox Jews follow an Oral Law they believe God gave Moses.

- Orthodox Jews obey the laws presented in the Mishnah.

- Orthodox Jews receive guidance from the Talmud.

- Orthodox Jews follow *gezerot*: rabbinic laws that provide "a fence around the Torah" to ensure that Jews do not accidentally break a mitzvah.

- Orthodox Jews obey the laws connected to Israel's holy days.

- Orthodox Jews rest on the Sabbath day.

- The Talmud forbids thirty-nine categories of work on the Sabbath.

- Orthodox Jews obey the *Kashrut* or Jewish dietary laws.

- Orthodox Jews have three formal prayer times every day.

- Women and men have separate seating in synagogue services.

- Orthodox Judaism forbids marriage to non-Jews.

- Orthodox Jews discourage but do not forbid Gentile conversion.

- Orthodox Jews are not to consider themselves better than non-Jews.

- The Jewish boy becomes a Bar Mitzvah (son of the law) at age thirteen, and celebrations are usually held.

- Sabbath laws can be broken in order to save a life.

- Husband and wife are to obey the law of *niddah*: separation during the wife's menstrual period.

- Certain forms of birth control (like the pill) are allowed under certain circumstances.

- Jewish law forbids homosexual acts.

- The Talmud allows Jewish men to divorce for any reason or no reason.

- The wife receives a *get* or document of release from the marriage.

- Jews are to base their lives on the teaching of God as given in Scripture, Mishnah, Talmud, and Kabbalah.

- Abortion is commanded if a mother's life is at stake.

- Jewish law forbids cremation.

- The body of a dead person is to be cleaned and not left alone until burial.

- Open caskets are not permitted under Jewish law.

Synagogue in Lithuania

Photo: Jim Beverley

2. Conservative Judaism

Dr. Solomon Schechter was the leader behind the formation in America in 1913 of the United Synagogue of Conservative Judaism. However, the broader movement began in Germany in the mid-1800s, centering in the work of Zecharias Frankel (1801–75), who founded the Jewish Theological Seminary of Breslau in 1854. Conservative Judaism provides a middle ground between Orthodoxy and Reform. The Jewish Theological Seminary in America was started in 1886. There are about eight hundred Conservative synagogues in the United States.

Internet Source

Main website: www.uscj.org

MONTHS AND HOLY DAYS IN THE JEWISH CALENDAR

	Month	Length	Holy Days in Month	Gregorian Calendar
1	Nissan	30 days	Passover	March–April
2	Iyar	29 days		April–May
3	Sivan	30 days	Shavu'ot	May–June
4	Tammuz	29 days		June–July
5	Av	30 days		July–August
6	Elul	29 days		August–September
7	Tishri	30 days	Rosh Hashanah Yom Kippur Sukkot	September–October
8	Cheshvan	29 or 30 days		October–November
9	Kislev	30 or 29 days	Chanukkah	November–December
10	Tevet	29 days		December–January
11	Shevat	30 days		January–February
12	Adar	29 or 30 days	Purim	February–March
13	Adar II	29 days		March–April

3. Reform Judaism

Reform Judaism grew out of the work of Rabbi Isaac Mayer Wise (1819–1900), who trained in Europe but came to America in 1846 and sought to unify American Jews under a more liberal understanding of

Jewish tradition. Reform Jews do not believe that the Torah or the Talmud are the explicit revelation of God, and they believe they have the right and duty to decide which laws apply to today's world. The principles of Reform Judaism were announced in the Pittsburgh Platform (1885), in the Columbus Platform (1937), in the Centenary Perspective (1976), and in the recent Statement of Principles for Reform Judaism (1999).

Considerable controversy arose among Reform Jews as the leadership moved to adopting the 1999 Statement of Principles. Rabbi Robert Seltzer stated in *Reformed Judaism* magazine, "We must guard against turning Reform Judaism into Conservative Judaism Lite." Seltzer was responding specifically to "Ten Principles for Reform Judaism," which Rabbi Richard Levy drafted in anticipation of the 1999 annual meeting in Pittsburgh.

There are more than nine hundred Reform synagogues in the United States, and they are joined under The Union of American Hebrew Congregations. Wise founded the Hebrew Union College (HUC) in 1875 in Cincinnati. The HUC merged with the Jewish Institute of Religion (JIR) in 1959. The resulting HUC-JIR is the primary place for rabbinical training among Reform Jews, with training centers in Cincinnati, New York, Los Angeles, and Jerusalem.

Internet Sources

Main websites: www.uahc.org and www.rj.org

Rabbi Michael Skobac of Jews for Judaism

Photo: Jim Beverley

JEWISH STATEMENT OF FAITH

- G-d exists.

- G-d is one and unique.

- G-d is incorporeal.

- G-d is eternal.

- Prayer is to be directed to G-d alone and to no other.

- The words of the prophets are true.

- Moses' prophecies are true, and Moses was the greatest of the prophets.

- The Written Torah (first five books of the Bible) and Oral Torah (teachings now contained in the Talmud and other writings) were given to Moses.

- There will be no other Torah.

- G-d knows the thoughts and deeds of men.

- G-d will reward the good and punish the wicked.

- The Messiah will come.

- The dead will be resurrected.

4. Hasidic Judaism

Hasidic Jews can be regarded as the charismatics and mystics of Judaism. Their origin lies in the work of Rabbi Israel ben Eliezer, who is known famously as the *Ba'al Shem Tov* or Master of the Good Name. The Rabbi was born about 1700 in the Ukraine and was known early as a meditative type and a student of the Kabbalah. He is said to have revealed his mission at the age of thirty-six. He became legendary for his simple stories and parables. Miracle stories about him abound in Hasidic legends.

MAIN HASIDIC GROUPS

Amshinov	Ger (Gur)	Radziner
Alecsander	Karlin-Stoliner	Satmar
Belzer	Kloisenberger	Skvirer
Bobover	Lubavitcher	Slonimer
Bostoner	(Chabad)	Tauscher
Boyaner	Modzitzer	Vizhnitzer
Breslov	Muncatz	

The Ba'al Shem Tov encouraged emphasis on emotion in Jewish life, study, and worship—a characteristic not considered in relation to traditional Talmudic study. The Rabbi helped restore confidence in their teachers among many European Jews. This was in contrast to the cynicism that prevailed in prior decades because of hypocrisy and opulence among many rabbis. The Ba'al Shem Tov taught the immanence of God in the world, a fact that suggests that Jews should express their joy in dancing in worship, in drinking, in storytelling, and in song.

HASIDIC SOCIAL AND RELIGIOUS PRACTICE

- Most men wear hats, often a distinctive type related to specific group tradition.

- Most women wear head coverings, including wigs.

- Hasidic men often wear the *yarmulke* or skullcap to bed.

- Men do not usually wear shorts or go without a shirt.

- Many men have long hair curls and do not trim their beards.

- Men often wear a small shawl with fringes attached to its four corners.

- Hasidic couples do not use a sheet with a hole in the middle during sex.

- Hasidic men often wear black or dark clothes.

- Hasidic men often rock back and forth in prayer and worship.

After the Hasidic founder's death, other rabbis and their descendants spread his teachings. Some of the earliest and most influential leaders were Rabbi Dov Baer (Meseritz), Rabbi Jacob Joseph (Polnoye), Rabbi Shneiur Zalman (Ladi), Rabbi Nachman (Breslov), Rabbi Levi Isaac (Berditshev), and Rabbi Menahem Mendel (Kotzk). Rabbi Zalman founded the Chabad school in Lithuania, now known as the Chabad-Lubavitch movement.

Lubavitch

The Lubavitch movement, now based in Brooklyn, New York, is one of the most famous groups in world Judaism. The group traces its roots to eighteenth-century Europe but became famous through the work of Rabbi Menachem Mendel Schneerson, the seventh and last Lubavitcher *rebbe*. Rabbi Schneerson was born in 1902, chosen as the rebbe in 1950, and died in 1994. His fame as a teacher, mystic, and leader inspired a worldwide following.

Lubavitch are famous for their aggressive evangelism, not to Gentiles but to secular Jews. In 1972 Rabbi Schneerson announced the creation of *mitzvah tanks* to spread the message of Chabad on the streets of New York. Lubavitchers would appeal to non-observant Jewish men to come into their van (the group now uses refurbished mobile homes) and put on *tefillin* and say a short prayer. They also offered Jewish women guides to the lighting of candles before the start of the Sabbath.

Schneerson married Rebbetzin Chaya Mushka, the daughter of the sixth Lubavitcher Rebbe, in December 1928 in Warsaw. Schneerson's wife remained out of public attention through their fifty-nine years of marriage. She died on February 10, 1988, and fifteen thousand people, under police escort, joined in the procession to her burial.

Rabbi Schneerson remained active as leader until he suffered a stroke on Monday afternoon, March 2, 1992. He lost the ability to speak and was paralyzed on his right side. He died on June 12, 1994, and his body was put to rest at the *Ohel Chabad Lubavitch* at 226-20 Francis Lewis Blvd., Cambria Heights, New York 11411, next to the burial spot of his father-in-law, Rabbi Joseph Isaac Schneersohn, the sixth Rebbe.

Lubavitch come from all over the world to visit Schneerson's *Ohel* (*Ohel* is the term for a tent that is placed over the burial site of a holy person). The website www.ohelchabad.org provides details about visiting or sending a letter to the Rebbe. Visitors are encouraged not to wear leather shoes; men are to wear a hat and women are to wear a head covering. Usual practices are to write a letter to the Rebbe before entering the *Ohel* and to leave by walking backward as a sign of respect.

HOLY DOLLAR BILLS

In 1986 the famous Lubavitcher Rabbi Schneerson started a visitor's line at the Lubavitch headquarters in Brooklyn. He would greet people, pass on brief advice, and give them a one-dollar bill. A web biography states: "The Rebbe wished to elevate each of the thousands of encounters of the day to something more than a meeting of two individuals; he wanted that each should involve the performance of a 'mitzvah' (good deed), particularly a mitzvah that also benefits another individual." In spite of his age (he was born in 1902), the Rebbe would often stand in line for nine hours passing out one-dollar bills.

In Rabbi Schneerson's later years, even just before his death, his followers held considerable hope that he was the Messiah. Some Lubavitchers even refused to believe he had died, while others maintained that he would be resurrected. After his death, the movement decided not to choose another rebbe. Rabbi Yehuda Krinsky, Schneerson's top assistant, has held top administrative power since 1994. In 1995 Rabbi Shmuel Butman published a lengthy work, *Countdown to Mochiach*, which argued that Schneerson is the Messiah. However, Butman has since abandoned that view. There have even been a few Lubavitch in Israel who claimed that the famous rabbi is God.

A FALSE MESSIAH

Shabbetai Zvi is one of the most famous figures in Jewish history. A native of Smyrna, he was born in 1626 and became known for his knowledge of both the Kabbalah and the Talmud. He was also known as a mystic and ecstatic and drew both praise and scorn from the Jewish community. Zvi was declared to be the Messiah when he was in Jerusalem and he accepted the title. He attracted a group of followers, and by 1665 reports of his messianic role were creating excitement in Jewish groups across Europe.

Some Jews proclaimed him the king of Israel. However, on September 15, 1666, the so-called Messiah denied the Jewish faith when the Islamic Sultan forced him to choose between death and conversion to Islam.

In 1996 the Rabbinical Council of America indirectly censored the view that Schneerson could be the Messiah: "In light of disturbing developments which have recently arisen in the Jewish community, the Rabbinical Council of America in convention assembled declares that there is not and has never been a place in Judaism for the belief that Mashiach ben David [Messiah son of David] will begin his Messianic Mission only to experience death, burial and resurrection before completing it."

The Chabad-Lubavitch movement has an impressive web presence, due largely to its first Internet leader, Rabbi Yosef Yitzchak Kazen, a native of Cleveland, Ohio. The Lubavitch world headquarters is located at 770 Eastern Parkway, Brooklyn, New York 11213. Most Lubavitch know the address simply as "770."

LUBAVITCH

Typology	Judaism Orthodox Hasidic
Famous Leader	Menachem Mendel Schneerson (1902–94)
Headquarters	770 Eastern Parkway, Brooklyn, New York 11213
Websites	www.lubavitch.com www.therebbe.org www.chabad.org
Critic Site	http://failedmessiah.typepad.com/

Breslov Hasidim

The Breslov movement started with the work of Rebbe Nachman, who was born in 1772 in Medzeboz, Ukraine. He became known as a Jewish saint or *tzaddik*, following in the tradition of his great-grandfather Rabbi Israel, the Ba'al Shem Tov, the founder of Hasidic Jewry. Rebbe Nachman lived for eight years in the Ukrainian city of Breslov, from which the movement gets its name. He died in 1810 after moving to Uman.

Following the Rebbe's death, his immediate followers could find no one to take his place. To this day the Breslov movement still looks to him as their Rebbe. Rebbe Nachman's followers run the Breslov Research Institute, which publishes his works and supports scholarly study of his life. Most information about the Breslov Rebbe comes from Reb Noson (1780–1844), who became the Rebbe's chief disciple soon after the two men first met in 1802.

Internet Source

Breslov website: www.breslov.org

■ Karaite Judaism

Karaite Jews claim to represent the authentic Judaism of the Old Testament. Claiming historic ties to the first Jewish leaders, modern Karaites distinguish themselves by their allegiance solely to the written Law. They oppose all forms of Judaism that make use of the Oral Law. Thus, they do not use the Mishnah or the Talmud, since both are based on an acceptance of the Oral Law God allegedly gave Moses on Mount Sinai.

The word *Karaite* comes from a Hebrew term meaning "Followers of Scriptures." It is difficult to trace the history of the Karaites, though the movement's modern roots go back to the work of the Jewish leader Anan ben David, who lived in the eighth century under Muslim rule. He persuaded Muslim authorities to protect Jews who did not follow the Talmud from persecution by Orthodox Jews.

The Karaites claim to follow the Jewish calendar and the holidays mentioned in the Old Testament and argue that Orthodox Jews depart from the strict teachings of Scripture on both holy days and the calendar year in general. The Karaites also claim that they follow the proper Torah rules for the wearing of fringes (or *Tzitzit*) on the edge of their clothing. The Karaite *Tzitzit* have blue in them, unlike those of Orthodox Judaism.

The Karaites also depart from Orthodox Judaism in that they do not wear *tefillin*, black leather boxes containing Scripture passages, on their forehead and left arm. That is because they believe that Torah passages that refer to wearing the law "like a sign on your hand and a reminder on your forehead" (Ex. 13:9) are to be understood metaphorically. Strict Karaites will sit in the dark on the Sabbath, however, in deference to the command against lighting a fire on that day.

Since there is no longer a Temple, the Karaites do not obey the Temple sacrifice laws. However, they look for Jews who can prove their lineage to the priests mentioned in Ezra 2:61 in order to resume sacrifices not connected with the Temple. They also do not believe in offering ritual sacrifices until obtaining the ashes of the Red Heifer in order to purify themselves. Unlike Samaritan Jews, the Karaites do not sacrifice a Paschal lamb at Passover.

Contemporary Karaism owes much to the work of Mordecai Avraham Alfandari. Born of Jewish parents in New York in 1929, Alfandari discovered some Karaite literature and came to the belief that all humans, not just Jews, should follow the religion of the Old Testament. He moved to Israel in 1950, met with some leading Karaites, and over time became a significant figure in Jerusalem's Karaite community. He helped rebuild the Karaite Synagogue after the Six-Day War in 1967.

In his writings, Alfandari was blunt against the beliefs of both Talmudic Jews and Christians. In his "Light of Israel" he wrote: "There *is* an alternative to the horror-story theology of Christianity with its crucified god-man who was murdered because his 'father' loved the world! THE ALTERNATIVE IS YHVH! There *is* an alternative to modern Rabbinic Judaism with its mumbled prayers and its de-personalized God. THE ALTERNATIVE IS YHVH!"

Internet Source

Karaite website: www.karaite-korner.org

▓ Kabbalah

Question: Do the signs of the zodiac influence human fate? Answer: Yes. Question: How can we hasten the Messiah's return? Answer: By performing good deeds. Question: How do I resist the powers of the Evil Eye? Answer: By wearing a Red String. Question: What is the proper positioning for my bed? Answer: Along an east-west axis. Question: Is reincarnation true? Answer: Yes. Question: What magical ceremony can I use to curse an enemy? Answer: The Beating by Fire. Question: Where does all this come from? Answer: Kabbalah.

If you think you have heard that term before, you can probably thank Madonna. The former "Material Girl" is now the most famous advocate of this ancient Jewish mystical path. She became interested in Kabbalah about 1997. Around 2004 she adopted the Hebrew name Esther, and since then, she has flashed Hebrew words on projection screens at her concerts. Madonna is linked to The Kabbalah Centre and the work of its leader, Rabbi Philip Berg. It has been reported that she has given millions to the Centre's work in the United States and in the United Kingdom.

THE RED STRING

Why do Madonna and other contemporary Kabbalists wear the Red String around their left wrist? According to the Kabbalah Centre, ancient concerns about the Evil Eye are not rooted in superstition but in real danger. Kabbalists believe the Red String works like a modern vaccine in providing resistance to evil glances that represent envy and hatred. Red is the color of danger, and the Red String has been previously taken to Israel and wound around Rachel's tomb. Rachel is the matriarch of the Bible, and her spiritual force of protection is infused into the Red String.

Kabbalists wear the string on the left wrist because they believe energy enters the body on the left side. The string has seven knots tied in it, each corresponding to one of seven important spiritual realities. A loved one is to tie the string to the left wrist, and then to pray for spiritual power to do good deeds and ward off evil. The Kabbalah Centre sells the Red String in quantities of seven for $26.

The History of Kabbalah

The Kabbalah's history is difficult to trace. The answer to the question of where the Kabbalah began depends on whom you ask. Some Jewish mystics trace the Kabbalah's roots back to the *Sefer Yetzirah*, said to have been written by the patriarch Abraham. However, most scholars argue that this brief but very obscure document dates from the early Christian era, when mysticism was becoming a major reality in Jewish life. These scholars, including Gershom Scholem, also argue that the most famous texts of Kabbalah date from the medieval period and not from the time of Christ or earlier.

The core books of Kabbalah are the *Sefir-ha-Bahir* (The Book of Brightness) and, most importantly, *The Zohar* (The Book of Splendor). Many Kabbalists insist that Rabbi Shimon bar Yochai wrote *The Zohar* around

A.D. 150, but the linguistic and textual evidence shows that it originated from an early fourteenth-century Spanish Kabbalist named Moses ben Shem Tov de Leon.

The Kabbalah grew in importance in Judaism through the Renaissance and Reformation eras. Seminal rabbinical figures like Moses Cordovero (1522–70) and Isaac Luria (1534–72), nicknamed "The Lion," spread the tradition. Luria's followers claimed that he had supernatural powers and that he had frequent interviews with the Old Testament prophet Elijah. To this day, Lurianic Kabbalism is one of the more dominant Kabbalah schools. Luria's tomb in Israel is a sacred site for Jewish pilgrims.

Kabbalism received a major setback in 1666 when a so-called Jewish messiah named Shabbetai Zvi abandoned Judaism and converted to Islam—under the coercion of a Turkish sultan. Prominent Jewish leaders had sanctioned Zvi, and a wave of messianic fever had swept across Europe, only to be dashed when Zvi renounced his faith. Kabbalism revived in the next century under the enormous impact of Israel ben Eliezer (1698–1760), better known as the Ba'al Shem Tov, who founded the Hasidic movement, which became the dominant keeper of the Kabbalah in Orthodox Jewry.

Like all Orthodox Jews, the Hasidim base their life on the Torah and the Talmud (said to be the Oral Law given to Moses and written down in the first four or five centuries after Christ). The Hasidim also place great emphasis on striving for unity with God, which is expressed in ecstatic worship and in following the teachings of their particular Rebbe. The most popular Hasidic movement in modern times is the Lubavitch. Their current understanding of the Kabbalah comes from the teaching of Menachem Mendel Schneerson (1902–94), their seventh and last rabbi.

THE KABBALAH CENTRE

The Kabbalah Centre, based in Los Angeles, is the most controversial organization in modern Kabbalism. Its leaders are Rabbi Philip Berg, his second wife, Karen, and their two sons, Michael and Yehuda. Philip Berg was born Fevil Gruberger in 1930. He worked in the insurance industry before emerging as a teacher of Kabbalah in the early 1970s. His first wife was the niece of Rabbi Yehuda Tzvi Brandwein, a famous Kabbalist who taught in Israel. Berg left his first wife and their eight children to marry Karen, his former secretary. Karen recently told a British reporter that she and Berg knew one another in a previous life during the Spanish revolution.

Since the mid-'90s the Kabbalah Centre has often been targeted as a cult, with the typical allegations of money-grabbing, deceptive marketing, hero worship, and abuse of members. Various Jewish leaders and organizations also accuse Berg and his organization of abandoning authentic Judaism and offering "Kabbalah Lite." The Centre argues that the Kabbalah "was never meant for a specific sect. Rather, it was intended to be used by all humanity to unify the world." Berg has stated that his critics are simply jealous of his success. The organization has centres in ten cities of the United States and in fourteen other countries. It also claims to have four million students throughout the world.

It is hard not to notice hype in Centre promotions and publications. An e-mail advertisement for a recent book states: "*The Prayer of the Kabbalist: The 42-Letter Name of God* by Yehuda Berg is truly groundbreaking, as it teaches everyone for the first time how to use the powerful prayer known as the *Ana Bekho'ah* to make miracles happen every day. Find out why '42' is the answer to everything." On a more serious note, in one of his other books, Yehuda tries to argue that *The Zohar*, the most important Kabbalistic text, prophesied the events of 9/11 and the actual name *bin Laden*.

The Basics of Kabbalah

Most people who have studied the famous texts of Kabbalah find them strange and difficult to decipher. Arthur Goldwag, a sympathetic Kabbalah observer, wrote that "many kabbalistic texts are virtually impossible to understand." Other Jews, both religious and secular, dismiss the Kabbalah as nonsense and superstition. One tradition in Orthodox Judaism holds that the study of Kabbalah's most important texts is dangerous, both physically and spiritually.

KABBALAH FOR CHILDREN

One ancient guideline in Kabbalah is that its learning is for Jewish males over the age of 40 only. Today, however, females and children of both genders study the Kabbalah. In fact, Madonna has written several books for children built around Kabbalistic stories and ideas, including *Lotsa de Casha*, which tells the story of a rich person who learns the true meaning of happiness. Also, Karen Berg of The Kabbalah Centre has developed a whole program called "Spirituality for Kids."

What is at the heart of Kabbalah? The answer, once again, depends on whom you ask. Philip and Karen Berg have worked overtime to argue that Kabbalah is not necessarily tied to Judaism. For them, the Kabbalah is the most ancient mystical path that can illuminate every religion. Thus, they believe, Christians, Buddhists, Muslims, Hindus, and secularists can follow the Kabbalah without adopting Jewish beliefs and rituals. It is quite fashionable in Kabbalah Centre circles to argue that Kabbalah is not really about religion but about spirituality.

Traditional Jews, however, must read the Kabbalah in its obvious Jewish light. It is a Jewish path designed for Jews who want to know God and obey Jewish law. Australian Rabbi Aron Moss puts it this way: "Taking Kabbalah out of its Jewish context is like picking a flower from a garden. It looks beautiful and smells nice for a while, but soon it starts to wither, rot, and stink. Kabbalah is a living, breathing spirituality that is nourished by the rich soil of Jewish wisdom and practice."

When one reads Kabbalah material in detail, it appears that Moss is correct. Kabbalistic stories are about *Jewish* rabbis taking trips to heaven to meet ancient *Jewish* sages. *The Zohar* focuses heavily on the deeper truths about *Jewish* understandings of God, humanity, angels, demons, holiness, past lives, and the return of the Messiah. It is the twenty-two letters of the *Hebrew* alphabet that influence the created order. The Kabbalistic emphasis on the spiritual significance of numbers (known as "Gematria") has to do with numbering of passages in the *Jewish* Bible.

One way to see what is at the heart of Kabbalah—and to see how Jewish it truly is—is to reflect on what Jewish Kabbalists have written on two issues: the nature of God and the return of the Messiah. According to all

Kabbalistic texts, God is ultimately unknowable, but we can see glimpses of Him since creation through emanations known as the *sefirot*. According to most Kabbalists, there are ten *sefirot*: *keter* (crown), *chochma* (wisdom), *bina* (understanding), *chesed* (kindness), *gevura* (might), *tiferet* (beauty), *netzach* (endurance), *hod* (splendor), *yesod* (foundation), and *shekinah* (presence). All of these English words have their roots in Hebrew terms derived from the Hebrew Bible and Jewish writing.

The Kabbalastic understanding of the coming of the Messiah (Hebrew: *Mashiach* or "anointed one") is likewise thoroughly Jewish. The world is fallen, as noted in Genesis 3, and the light of God's original creation has been shattered. The restoration of the original creation will happen when the Messiah comes. His arrival will be hastened as Jews obey the 613 laws of Moses and the Talmudic laws derived from them. The good works of Jews (and righteous Gentiles) rise like sparks to heaven, restoring the primal light and hastening the coming of the Jewish Messiah. He will be a Jewish king, a descendant of David who will bring peace to Earth. Some teachers say that the Kabbalah confirms the Orthodox Jewish teaching that the Messiah will return before the Hebrew year 6000 (or 2240 in the Gregorian calendar).

The Zohar and 9/11

In a chapter called "End of Days" in *The Power of Kabbalah*, Yehuda Berg claims that the *Zohar* "speaks of the type of judgments that will strike the world's most powerful city" to launch an era related to the coming of the Messiah. Berg states that ancient Kabbalists "even calculated the exact Hebrew date from the *Zohar* and gives the date as September 11, 2001. He also claims that the *Zohar's* prologue "gives the actual name of a negative force that brings judgment into this world" and states it as "B laden." After expressing some reservations about prophecies, Berg writes: "still, we have the most important book of Kabbalistic wisdom giving us an exact date, a precise name, and a fairly accurate description of the events of 9/11" (*The Power of Kabbalah*, p. 208). Berg then states: "it's easy to be skeptical. And it's just as easy to be dazzled."

No, *total* skepticism is the only reasonable response. Berg's prophetic speculation is rooted in a completely superficial and selective reading. First, the relevant passage in the *Zohar* cites Rome as the city facing destructive forces: "And that day, WHICH IS MALCHUT, WILL CAUSE there to be ignited in the great city of Rome—WHICH IS THE SECRET OF BINAH OF KLIPOT—a flame of fire, WHICH IS THE JUDGMENTS OF THE LEFT." Second, the falling of "many towers and palaces" is part of a larger apocalyptic story that involves supernatural events not seen in 2001. Whatever the *Zohar* describes as the coming of the Messiah is still a future event. Third, the whole section on "the coming of the Messiah" is very, very confusing and bizarre, like much of the *Zohar*. Fourth, claiming that the prologue gives the name of the infamous terrorist Osama bin Laden will only work through confusion over some similarity in spelling.

In context, the actual spelling in the prologue is different from the one Berg gives. Further, and most important, the context makes it clear this has nothing to do with 9/11. Here is the relevant text:

> The sins caused him to go down to the lower levels and slay the lion. BECAUSE the lion refused to give up its prey as before! THIS IS AS THOUGH he killed it! THEREFORE, assuredly, "He slew the lion." "In the midst of a pit" (2 Shmuel 23:20) in front of the eyes of the Other Evil Side. And because the Other Side saw this, it gained courage and sent a dog to eat the offerings, ABOVE THE ALTAR, INSTEAD OF THE LION. And what is the name of that lion? Oriel, IS ITS NAME, as he had the face of a lion. And what is the name of that dog? Baladan is its name, BECAUSE BALADAN IS FORMED BY THE SAME LETTERS AS THE WORDS BAL (NOT) AND ADAM (MAN), WITH THE FINAL MEM EXCHANGED FOR A NUN. And He is not a human being, but a dog with the face of a dog.

Christian Response to Kabbalah

Incredibly, at one time some Christian scholars were completely taken up with the study of Kabbalah. During the late Renaissance, several Christian figures thought the Kabbalah could be used to prove Christian truth. The most famous Christian Kabbalists are Giovanni Pico della Mirandola (1463–94), Johann Reuchlin (1455–1522), Cornelius Agrippa (1486–1535), and Christian Knorr von Rosenroth (1631–89). Johann Kemper, a Jewish convert to Christianity who wrote a three-volume work on Kabbalah titled *The Staff of Moses*, was also influential.

With the emergence of Kabbalah into contemporary spirituality, how should Christians respond? Should believers see the Kabbalah as dangerous? Should it alarm us that Madonna and Karen Berg teach children Kabbalah? How does the gospel fit in with the world of *The Zohar* and the Kabbalah in general? Can Kabbalah advance Christian spirituality, as Philip Berg would suggest?

First, Christians should contrast the simplicity of the gospel with the utterly agonizing complexities of Kabbalah. These mind-numbing documents are virtually incomprehensible. I respect the right of Jewish scholars to view *The Zohar* as the epitome of brilliance and wisdom. One rabbi praised God that he was born after its publication so that he could be filled with its wisdom. But I have found the study of Kabbalah material as confusing and dreary as anything I have read in more than thirty years.

The Kabbalah Centre can achieve success only by offering "Kabbalah Lite." Madonna praised Yehuda Berg's book *The Power of Kabbalah* by noting that there is "no hocus pocus here, nothing to do with religious dogma." But the Kabbalah is *full* of magic and dogma. There one can find stories about how to create a spiritual robot, or how to put a curse on someone, or learn theology by adding up the value of specific letters in Genesis, Ezekiel, etc.

Second, Christians should be alarmed about a missing dimension in the Kabbalah. Yes, it includes specific non-biblical teachings—especially on astrology, reincarnation, and God's nature. Further, the method of interpretation Kabbalists have adopted wrecks the plain meaning of Scripture. This is important because a bad hermeneutic leads to bad theology. However, it is most significant that Jesus is absent from the Kabbalah. While this fits with an Orthodox Jewish perspective, it represents the greatest danger in the current fascination with Madonna's spiritual world.

KABBALISM

Typology	Judaism Esoteric
Early Author	Moses ben Shem Tov de Leon (d. A.D. 1305)
Website	www.kabbalah.com
Recommended Reading	Daniel C. Matt, *The Essential Kabbalah* (HarperSanFrancisco, 1996) Gershom Scholem, *Origins of the Kabbalah* (Princeton University Press, 1990)

■ Israel and Palestine

Understanding Islam, Judaism, and Christianity in the twenty-first century demands knowledge of the Palestinian issue and the way conflict over Palestine has shaped the self-identity of Muslims, Christians and Jews throughout the world. Public discourse since September 11 has often raised the Palestinian question as a factor in understanding and even defending Islamic extremism and the nature of terrorism. This has impacted Jewish-Muslim relations and has strengthened the resolve of many Christians, especially evangelicals, to support Israel.

Since the time of the prophet Muhammad, Islam has been in greater conflict with Christianity than with Judaism. Thus, we know of the Muslim attacks on Christian Europe and of the Christian Crusaders who sought to conquer the Muslim lands. Likewise, from A.D. 300 through 1950, Jews have had more to fear from the church than from the mosque.

However, with the decline of Christendom and the rise of the Jewish state, the last half of the twentieth century has seen a change in pattern. Now, Jewish people are more concerned with Islamic extremism than with the Christian threat. Muslim nations are more threatened by secular power than by Christian power. In the case of Israel, the turmoil is largely between Muslim and Jew.

Different Interpretations of the Palestinian Question

Studying the details of the history of the Palestinian question will leave anyone deeply discouraged for several reasons.

First, the conflict between Jew and Arab has been one filled with bloodshed. Jews and Arabs have fought five major wars in the half century since the founding of the State of Israel in 1948. That is one war per decade.

Second, the history of the Palestinian conflict is one of missed opportunities. Things could have been different. Jews started to return to Palestine in the late 1800s, and throughout the 120-year period that followed, both Jew and Arab chose certain roads that ensured further conflict. The wrong voices were heeded, the will for peace died, and the sword of revenge was taken up again.

Third, any student of Israeli or Palestinian history knows that ideological divisions run so deep that it is almost impossible to imagine a decisive turn toward peace. These divisions involve (a) radical differences in *religious* views, (b) competing *political* understandings, (c) divergent *historical* verdicts, and (d) opposing *moral* views about every aspect of the conflict.

KEY DATES IN ARAB/ISRAELI CONFLICT

1882—First wave of Jewish immigation to Palestine

1896—Theodore Herzl publishes *The Jewish State*

1897—First International Zionist Congress

1904—Second wave of Jewish immigration

1914—World War I begins

1916—Sykes-Picot agreement between Britain and France

1917—Balfour declaration in support of Jewish state

1919—Third wave of Jewish immigration

1920—Lebanon separated from Syria by French

1920—Arab revolt in Jerusalem (April)

1920—Formation of Haganah (Jewish underground army)

1924—Fourth wave of Jewish immigration

1929—Massacre of Jews in Hebron (August)

1931—Formation of the Irgun

1933—Hitler gains power in Germany

1933—Fifth wave of Jewish immigration

1936—Peel Commission on Palestine mandate

1939—World War II

1942—Jewish Holocaust dominates Nazi plans

1946—Irgun bombing of King David Hotel (July 22)

1947—Palestinians reject UN plan of partition

1948—Massacre of Palestinians at DeirYassin (April 9)

1948—Proclamation of Jewish state (May 14)

1948—War of Independence

1956—Sinai War

1964—Founding of the Palestinian Liberation Organization

1967—Six-Day War (June 5–10)

1972—Murder of Jewish Olympians in Munich (September 5)

1973—Yom Kippur War (October)

1974—Peace treaty between Jordan and Israel

1977—Anwar Sadat peace trip to Jerusalem (November 19)

1978—Camp David Accord (Sadat and Begin)

1979—Revolution in Iran under Ayatollah Khomeini

1981—Egyptian President Sadat assassinated (October 6)

1982—Israel invades Lebanon (June 6)

1982—Massacre of Palestinians at Sabra and Shatilla
(September 16–19)

1985—*Achille Lauro* hijacked by Palestinian terrorists
(October 7)

1987—First Uprising (Intifadah) by Palestinian youth

1991—Gulf War to liberate Kuwait

1991—Middle East peace talks in Madrid

1993—Oslo Peace Accords (Washington signing September 13)

1994—Jordan recognizes State of Israel

1995—Assassination of Yitzhak Rabin (November 4)

2000—Clinton's peace plans with Arafat and Barak fail

2000—Second Intifadah

2001—Dramatic increase in suicide bombing in Israel

2001—September 11 terrorist attacks in U.S.

2002—Sharon sends army into Jenin

2002—Proposal for peace by Saudi crown prince

2004—Death of Arafat (November 11)

2005—Mahmoud Abbas elected Palestinian leader

2005—Israeli forces leave Gaza and West Bank (August)

2006—Hamas defeats Fatah (January)

2006—Israeli-Lebanese war (July 12–August 14)

2007—Fighting between Hamas and Fatah

2008—Gaza under Israeli attack (December 27–January 19,
2009)

Four alternative interpretations capture the dominant perspectives among Israelis and Palestinians. Understanding the nature and power of these four paradigms is the necessary first step for any intelligible comprehension of the complex and tragic story of the Jewish-Arab conflict of the Middle East, which affects Jews and Muslims everywhere. For the sake of clarity, each of these positions is written in the voice of its advocate:

1. The Dominant Jewish Position

"The founding of the State of Israel is a moral and historical fact. Given the hatred of the Jews throughout history, and in the face of the Holocaust, the Jewish people had every right to recreate their homeland. This great victory for the world Jewish community occurred on May 15, 1948. For the first time in two thousand years we are home.

"Tragically, the Arab world chose not to accept the proposal of the United Nations to have two separate states in Palestine. Instead, Arabs chose to fight Israel in 1948, and have done so ever since. The Arab world wants Israel destroyed. Four of the wars since Independence in 1948 involved attacks on Israel by Arabs, including Palestinians. Our invasion of Lebanon was a necessary measure to wipe out terrorist bases in that country.

"Israel's aggression against the Palestinians is about legitimate self-defense. We cannot be at peace with a people who hate us, who want us destroyed. The world must not give nation status to a terrorist people. Decades of racist hatred toward the Jew and toward Israel, a hatred Islamic militants throughout the world fuel, has corrupted the Palestinian mind.

"The events of September 11 have sadly brought to America what Israel has faced for years: terrorists' wanton, hate-fueled killing of innocent people. We are grateful for the help of the United States in defending Israel's freedom. You have been our strongest ally in our fight for survival. Together we will stand strong against the forces that seek to destroy us.

"We hope, of course, that Palestinians will stop their hate of Israel, affirm our right to nationhood, and cease their terrorist activities against Jews in Israel and throughout the world. We are ready to negotiate at any time, providing that he and other Palestinians lay down their rocks and their bombs. Their continued war on Israel shows their obsession with our nation's destruction. We will not be moved."

2. The Moderate Jewish Position

"The birth of Israel is a joy to all Jews. It is a miracle from God, who brought us back to our land. But with this incredible gift comes enormous moral and spiritual responsibility. We cannot allow the forces of anti-Semitism to blind us to commitment to the ideals that have been our beacon of light through the centuries as a people with no land.

"There is much in the birth of Israel that stains our purity. From the start, and through the last century, we gave no serious moral thought to the rights and needs of the Arabs who were already here when we started to come home. Menachim Begin, who later became Prime Minister, even engaged in terrorist acts against the British in the mid-1940s. We secretly conspired against Arabs even as we publicly said we wanted Palestinians to have their own state.

"While there is no excuse for the Arab attacks on our nation, there is also no justification for what we have done to the Palestinians. Our invasion of Lebanon in 1982 was an unjust attack on another nation. The Palestinians have a right to their own country. We must overcome our own bigotry and hatred. We have often assaulted Palestinians the way Nazi Germany assaulted us. How can this be?

"We are becoming a terrorist nation against the Palestinians. Our secret defense forces have blown up Palestinian militia headquarters. We have destroyed Palestinian homes. We have razed entire villages. Our soldiers have engaged in torture of Palestinians. We have our hired assassins. We have our own zealots who match Islamic terrorists word for word, deed for deed. We must stop."

ISRAELI/PALESTINIAN CONFLICT MYTHS AND FACTS

1. Myth: When the Jews returned to Palestine in the late 1800s the land was empty.
   Fact: In 1881 there were about 400,000 Muslims living in the Holy Land, as well as more than 40,000 Christians and about 18,000 Jews.

2. Myth: The Palestinians just want peace.
   Fact: In both the West Bank and Gaza, Palestinian terrorist groups have no intention of ever having peace with Israel. On April 3, 2002, *The New York Times* reported on Hamas: "Bombers Gloating in Gaza as They See Goal Within Reach: No More Israel."

3. Myth: Only Palestinians are terrorists.

Fact: Jewish underground militia groups targeted both Arabs and the British during Britain's rule in Palestine. Menachim Begin, later Israel's prime minister, was a leader of the Irgun Z'vai Leumi (IZL), one of the Jewish terrorist groups.

4. Myth: Christians must back Israel because of Bible prophecy.
   Fact: Even if the Bible predicts the return of the Jews to the Holy Land, that in no way demands that Christians support Israel no matter what it does.

5. Myth: The Jews run the United States.
   Fact: Though the Jewish lobby is powerful in the United States, the American government has often been at odds with Israel's actions against Egypt, Jordan, Syria, Lebanon, and the Palestinians.

6. Myth: Israel deserves total blame for the Palestinian refugee crisis.
   Fact: Jewish complicity and action created the refugee problem, but hostility of the Arab nations toward the Palestinians compounded it. Further, Palestinian leaders for decades plotted to push the Jews into the sea.

3. The Extreme Palestinian Position

"Palestine has been a home of Arabs for hundreds of years. We lost our native land through Zionist aggression. We refused the United Nations partition of our land because it was our land. The British dominated us by force and they left us to the Zionist Jew to do the same. The Jewish pig stole our country from us.

"The Jews throughout the twentieth century attacked us. We engaged in *jihad* against them on four occasions because it is our duty to cleanse the earth of their filth. We will not stop until the Jews are forced into the ocean. The American fascists support Israel because Jews run America. The Jew runs the economies of the world, including those of Britain, Germany, and Japan.

"The Jews use the lie of the Holocaust to create sympathy for their cause. Hitler opposed the Jew for the same reason we do: The Jewish vermin will poison and destroy everything in its path. The Jews have even published their plans to run the world. Their leaders met and reported their attempted conquest in their *Protocols of the Elders of Zion*.

"The attack on the World Trade Center is probably a Zionist plot, cooked up by the American CIA in bed with the Israeli Mossad. If it is the work of Osama bin Laden, well, American Jewry is getting what it deserves. Either way, it is really the fault of the Jew. Jews were told to stay home from the World Trade Center on that day. They will never stop oppressing us because they have always stood against Allah and his true followers.

"The Jewish leaders of Israel are racist dogs. They assault our holy places. They humiliate us at all their checkpoints. They burn down our villages and raid our lands. They kill our leaders, rape our women, maim our children, and torture our soldiers. They cut off our water supplies, keep us from work, shut down our schools, and grind us into poverty. Allah will inflict upon them the fires of eternal hell."

4. The Moderate Palestinian Position

"It is a historical fact that we were here long before the Jews arrived in 1882. We have a moral right to nationhood. However, our path to freedom demands that we recognize the nation of Israel. Whether we like it or not, Israel is here to stay. We must stop our hatred of Jews and our talk of wiping Israel off the map. We made a terrible error when we refused the U.N. offer of statehood in 1947.

"We have engaged in brutal acts against innocent Israelis. Every terrorist act has dulled the growing spirit in Israel to grant us our own country. We have been our own worst enemies. We will not gain the international support we need until we stop our quest for blood. Osama bin Laden has hurt our cause and has brought great shame to Islam. We must not follow in his path.

"We have been racists against Israel. We have used the language of Hitler against the Jews. We have trusted anti-Semitic lies about Jews, including the bizarre theory that the Holocaust never happened. We stereotype Jews much like the rest of the world draws stereotypes of us. We will never learn to get along until we stop our bigotry and our hate. The throwing of stones must stop. Our bombing must stop.

"Following the way of Allah means we must be people of peace. Muhammad (Peace Be upon Him) taught us that war is to be used only as a last resort. Many Jews of good will (People of the Book) know that we deserve our own land. It is time for us to deal in good faith with Jewish leaders. The tragic events of September 11 show us that terror just breeds more terror. For the sake of our children, all children, let us return to the table of peace."

Responding to the Paradigms

Most people can understand that these paradigms represent different universes of discourse. However, we cannot let that fact leave us in despair that no progress can be made. So let me suggest some essentials in a proper response:

1. These four paradigms are not an exhaustive list of every view of the Palestinian question. For example, the reader might note the absence of a racist Jewish view that is parallel to the extreme Palestinian position. This is because racist perspectives are simply not popular among Jews in Israel or elsewhere. The extreme, radical, racist Jewish literature is hard to find, all things being equal. The exception here, of course, is the material and views propounded by the Jewish terrorist group founded by Rabbi Meir Kahane, the victim of an assassin's bullet in November 1990.

2. It will be hard for many readers to imagine that some Muslims really employ such racist language about Jews. Tragically, Muslims have duplicated "Christian" anti-Semitism in their attack on Jews. The extreme Palestinian paradigm is real and it is popular, just as Hitler's paradigm was real and popular in the 1930s and '40s. Some Muslims have the same view of the Jews as Hitler did.

   In Jeffrey Goldberg's article on Islamic extremism for *The New Yorker* magazine, he quotes a Muslim cleric from Egypt who had this to say: "Thanks to Hitler, of blessed memory, who on behalf of the Palestinians took revenge in advance, against the most vile criminals on the face of the earth. Although we do have a complaint against him, for his revenge was not enough." This is beyond vile.

3. Further, no amount of racism will undo the proof that the Holocaust is a real event in history. The case for a Palestinian state is morally bankrupt in direct proportion to any warrant given to Holocaust denial. The evidence of Hitler's extermination of the Jews is overwhelming, except to the morally blind. Christians and Muslims who deny the reality of Holocaust are either racist or ignorant beyond imagination.

   Michael Marrus notes in *The Holocaust and History* that Holocaust denial has the same credibility as the view that the earth is flat. Any reader can examine primary sources from Nazi Germany that document the vision and the plans to exterminate the Jewish people. Hitler's *Mein Kampf* made clear his racist agendas. He stated that behind every social problem was the Jew "like a maggot in a rotten corpse."

4. There is a virtually unbridgeable chasm between extreme Jewish and Muslim views on Palestine. The divide between a moderate Palestinian approach and even the dominant Jewish position is less significant. It is, of course, out of the middle ground of the moderate positions that peace has the most opportunity. But, for both Arab and Jew, it will not be peace at any price.

5. What stands in the way of peace is that the violence on both sides is rooted in a hardness of heart that refuses to acknowledge that the "other" (whether Jew or Arab) is to be treated differently than the paradigm of violence allows. On this, neither extreme wants to give ground by admitting fault, showing weakness, or granting that the situation is complex or that guilt is shared to any extent.

6. On this, the moderate Jewish paradigm will shock many readers because it raises very disturbing charges about Israel's treatment of the Palestinians. In the Western mind, Israel is often presumed innocent. Evangelical Christians, who believe that all Jews should trust Jesus as Messiah, often argue that criticism of Israel is against God's will. So, how can we even entertain these accusations?

   We examine them one by one, simply because we care about truth and justice. We should scrutinize them because there is no reason to imagine that Israel could be totally innocent. The case for Israel must not be based in the kind of zealous ideology that shows no regard for facts or openness to evidence. If Israel's policy toward Palestine is fundamentally right, it will not crumble with this or that admission of fault, unless, of course, the evidence of Israeli guilt builds to a breaking point.

In the last fifteen years the case for a Palestinian state has grown more popular among moderate Jews and many analysts who are very sympathetic to Israel. Hans Küng, the great German Christian theologian, wrote after the Gulf War in *Judaism: Between Yesterday and Tomorrow:* "The devastating consequences of the policy of occupation, including the moral consequences, are becoming increasingly clear to many Israelis. And as one who has so openly attacked the silence of Pius XII and the German bishops over the Jewish question, I may not keep silent over what Israelis are doing over the Palestinian question."

Jewish writers have echoed Küng's concerns. Amos Oz wrote in an editorial for *The New York Times:* "With or without Islamic fundamentalism, with or without Arab terrorism, there is no justification whatsoever for the lasting occupation and suppression of the Palestinian people by Israel. We have no right to deny Palestinians their natural right to self-determination."

He continues: "Two huge oceans could not shelter America from terrorism; the occupation of the West Bank and Gaza by Israel has not made Israel secure—on the contrary, it makes our self-defense much harder and more complicated. The sooner this occupation ends, the better it will be for Palestinians and Israelis alike."

Michael Lerner, the editor of *Tikkun* magazine and one of America's leading liberal Jewish activists, has made the same point most powerfully. Lerner, famous for his intellectual impact on Hillary Clinton, has received numerous death threats for his advocacy of a Palestinian state. However, his defense of the right of Palestinians to a homeland is in the context of strong denunciation of their terrorist attacks on Israel and the need for Palestinians to renounce their hatred of Jews.

▪ Holocaust Denial: The Case of Malcolm Ross

Malcolm Ross is one of the best-known Holocaust deniers in North America. The public school system in New Brunswick, on the east coast of Canada, removed Ross from the classroom as a result of his anti-Semitism. The Supreme Court of Canada ruled in favor of his dismissal, arguing that his racist views represented a break in the public trust that society must have in those who teach children. I was involved in the controversies surrounding Ross and spoke in interviews on local and national television about his case. His views parallel those of other Holocaust deniers. Here is a critique of his anti-Semitic views and his case in favor of denial of the Holocaust.

1. Initial Implausibility

Ross advocates many views so bizarre that his overall position is initially implausible. The following ideas illustrate the scope and nature of his conspiracy theories. These notions are gleaned from his four books: *Web of Deceit, The Real Holocaust, Christianity vs. Judeo-Christianity*, and *Spectre of Power.*

- Abortion is a Jewish plot to kill Gentiles
- Jewish faith is rooted in the "whore of Babylon"
- Jews control blacks and Civil Rights movement
- Christian publishers controlled by Jews
- Jews unduly influenced Churchill
- Communism is a Jewish plot
- Death camps are faked
- Evangelical support of Israel a Jewish plot
- Anne Frank's diary a fake
- Billy Graham fooled by Jews
- Heresy in Christian church a Jewish plot
- Higher Criticism of Scripture a Jewish plot
- Talmudic Jews believe intercourse with little girls is acceptable
- Talmudic Jews believe intercourse with the dead acceptable
- Jews still rule Russia

The faulty and paranoid nature of these ideas shows clearly why Ross's views must be resisted. These ideas are eccentric, mistaken, and harmful. It does not matter if other things he says are true. Theories like the above constitute proof that Ross is off target in his worldview and orientation. Is it surprising that his critics believe he is obsessed with the idea that the Jews are the embodiment of evil? Given the above theories, one can understand why the Jewish community in Canada and throughout the world is upset with him.

2. Lack of Scholarship and Research

Ross ignores the evidence of scholarship and reason against his views. Though his research might appear credible to the uninformed, he does not even make the most elementary academic move of reading the opposing point of view. He has not gone to Jewish people to ask them what their writings mean. On virtually any topic, he trusts anti-Semitic and racist literature and simply ignores other sources.

In his book *Christianity vs. Judeo-Christianity*, Ross argues that the Talmud condones Jewish men having sexual intercourse with little girls. The Talmudic passages Ross quotes are given the crudest interpretation possible. If Ross had talked to any Jewish rabbis, he would have discovered that the verses in question are given as a word of comfort for children who have been sexually assaulted. The virginity of the young child is not to be questioned since the blame lies solely with the man.

Ross also states that Jewish people cannot be trusted since they ask God every year to allow them to break their promises. Ross is referring to the *Kol Nidre* oath on this point, and he follows the standard anti-Semitic line that the oath proves that Jews are dishonest. When I visited Ross in his home, he showed me an article from a Jewish encyclopedia that confirmed his quotation of the thought. The same article stated, however, that absolution from a promise could only be gained in very unusual circumstances. When I pointed this out to Mr. Ross, he realized that he had misinterpreted the meaning of *Kol Nidre*. However, he has not retracted his false accusation.

In his book *The Real Holocaust*, Ross contends that "situation ethics" is a Jewish invention. I doubt if he could find a moral philosopher anywhere in the world who would agree with him. Contrary to Ross's assertion, Joseph Fletcher, the founder of situation ethics, is not a Communist.

Further, the scholars who have been properly critical of situation ethics never trace the roots of Fletcher's position back to the Talmud.

In the same vein, Ross tries to blame Jewish people for modern criticism of the Bible. He fails on two counts. First, he ignores the fact that Orthodox Jews have a high view of the inspiration of the Old Testament. Generally speaking, Jewish rabbis have been very conservative in their outlook and have not been open to enlightenment rationalism. Second, even minimal research would have shown Ross that Christians (and not Jews) started criticism of Scripture when debates on Protestant and Catholic authority led to doubt about the authority of Scripture itself. The complex story is told in detail in *The Cambridge History of the Bible* and in Richard Hopkin's classic studies on this chapter of intellectual history.

Ross adopts the standard view that the Jews hurt the church through the practice of usury—charging interest on borrowed money—during the Middle Ages. This should be suspected on grounds of common sense. Given the power of the Catholic Church in the medieval world, why would the pope allow the Jews to make all the money? Ross shows no sign that he knows about the research of Joseph Shatzmiller and others proving that Catholic leaders used Jews as a smokescreen to increase profits. Ross perpetuates the myth of the Jew as Shylock, the loan shark from *The Merchant of Venice.*

As the above shows, Malcolm Ross is caught in the web of the error because his research is sloppy. His first book, *Web of Deceit,* warns Canadians about the Illuminati, which he describes as "the most sinister secret organization ever conceived in the mind of Man." However, the group gets no mention at all in the next three books. Why the omission? Has Ross realized the fictitious nature of the Illuminati legends?

Ross follows standard racist ideology in his interpretation of the anti-Semitic forgery *The Protocols of the Elders of Zion.* Further, Ross uncritically accepts right-wing Catholic lies about Gregory Baum, the well-known Canadian Catholic theologian, just as he uncritically adopts the anti-Semitic arguments against Anne Frank's diary.

3. Denial of the Holocaust

Some Ross defenders have asserted that he does not deny the Holocaust. However, even a cursory reading of his books shows otherwise. Ross cites with approval Arthur Butz's notorious book *The Hoax of the Twentieth*

Century, which argues that the Holocaust is an invention of the Jews. Ross contends that only several thousand Jews died in the Second World War. He states that the Holocaust "never occurred," or at the least it is "grossly exaggerated." What kind of research does Ross do on this subject? His arguments are unconvincing and his evidence is pathetic.

For example, he states in *Web of Deceit* that the Holocaust could not have happened, since the majority of Jews left Germany before the war. Ross even refers to the Jewish publication *Community in Dispersion* for documentation of Jewish immigration from Germany after 1939. Only the uninformed would find this bit of information impressive. As any history of World War II and the Holocaust will state, the majority of the Jews the Nazis exterminated were from Poland and other countries surrounding Germany.

Ross also refers to a three-volume *International Red Cross Report* to back his skepticism. The Red Cross, he claims, found "no evidence of genocide." Ross adds: "because Christians are now learning to count, there's tremendous pressure to keep this information from getting out." Ross apparently has never consulted the Red Cross report directly; rather, he seems to have trusted the distorted picture of the report given in neo-Nazi literature.

Ross mistakenly believes the report is about concentration camps when, in fact, it is on the overall work of the Red Cross during World War II. More important, this report talks explicitly about the Nazi killing of the Jews. A special section on the Jewish people states: "Under national socialism, Jews had become in truth outcasts, condemned by rigid racial legislation to suffer tyranny, persecution and systematic extermination."

Ross refers to a *New York Times* article from 1948 as proof that the Holocaust never happened. The *Times'* military editor, Hanson Baldwin, made passing reference to the world population of Jews after the war, and the statistic he gives does not match with the losses the Jewish people suffered. Ross apparently does not know that the *Times* ran a correction of the statistic four days after the original article appeared.

When Malcolm Ross writes about the Holocaust, he shows only blindness about the obvious. The evidence for the reality of the Holocaust is overwhelming, except to those who hate the Jewish people. The University of Toronto historian Michael Marrus states in his book *The Holocaust in History* that the idea that the Holocaust never happened deserves as much respect as the opinion that the Earth is flat.

Of course, the uninformed can assess the evidence for the reality of the Holocaust. Anyone can read the primary documents from Nazi Germany that outline the goal of Hitler and his followers to free the world of the Jews. Ross gives no indication that he has ever systematically studied German documents on this issue. Has he read of Julius Streicher's hatred against Jews in the Nazi newspaper *Der Sturmer*? Has Ross read the minutes of the Wannsee Conference?

Has Ross read the brutal reports from the *Einsatzgruppen* as they told of their slaughter of Russian Jews? Has he read about the recommendation of SS Sturmbannfuhrer Hoppner to "sterilize all those Jewesses who are still fertile so that the Jewish population would be finally solved with the present generation"? Has he pondered Himmler's speech of October 1943, when the Nazi leader gave justification for the extermination of the Jews?

In 1942–44 the Allies knew of the Nazi campaigns against the Jews. For this reason, Winston Churchill argued for the bombing of the train tracks into Auschwitz. Anti-Semites like to believe that the Jews made up the Holocaust story in the 1960s. In the summer of 1944 Churchill referred to the Nazi Holocaust of the Jews as "probably the greatest and most horrible crime ever committed in the whole history of the world." The uninformed would be better off to learn their history lessons from Winston Churchill than from Malcolm Ross.

4. Blunders in Logic

Malcolm Ross is often inconsistent in his reasoning and commits blunders in logic. First, Ross contends that Jewish control of the media demands a mistrust of newspapers. But he trusts newspapers, even Jewish newspapers. He states, for example, that the Jews and Russians work together to stop peace in the Middle East. What is his source for this bizarre notion? He refers to a statement by the late King Faisal in *Newsweek* magazine. Likewise, *The New York Times* serves as his source for the absurd theory that the Jews control the Japanese economy. Ross even trusts the Soviet press on reports of a high percentage of Jews involved in the Russian Revolution. The methodology here is quite simple: Any person or newspaper is to be trusted when it tells us something bad about Jews.

Ross makes further blunders in logic when he deals with the Khazar theory. With a triumphant note, Ross tells of Arthur Koestler's explosive work *The Thirteenth Tribe*, which allegedly proved that modern-day Jews come from Turkey and not Palestine. According to this theory, the modern Jew's ethnic roots go as far back to the Khazar tribe that converted to Judaism in the eighth century. Once again, Ross fails to do adequate research. First, he tells us that Koestler's research has not been disputed but only suppressed. Ross is wrong. When *The Thirteenth Tribe* was released, the academic critique of its research was prompt, public, and generally negative.

But let's assume for the moment that Ross is right about the Khazar theory and that he is also correct in his suggestion that the Jews of Bible times became the white people of Europe and America. Ross is still in logical difficulty. Blaming modern Jews for the death of Jesus depends on tracing their ancestry back to biblical times. But, alas, it is the white race that goes back to the days of Jesus. So will Ross follow logic here and blame white people for their connection with the crucifixion? Will he start referring to modern Jews as Turks?

Ross believes that the Jews are behind Communism and that the Communists are in league with the Zionists who are running the United Nations. If so, why did the UN pass a resolution against Zionism in 1975? Ross believes the Jews have incredible influence in the Vatican. If so, why did it take so long for the Vatican to recognize the State of Israel? If the Jews run the television industry, why do they let Billy Graham preach the gospel to millions through television?

5. Threat to Freedom

Malcolm Ross advocates and tolerates ideas that constitute an incredible threat to freedom. Under the guise of free speech, he blesses ideas and actions that would undermine democracy. In fact, his book *The Spectre of Power* gives blessing to the regime of Adolf Hitler, a notion that should be particularly disturbing to Allied veterans who know the price paid to resist Nazism. Ross gives sanction to the following ideas: (a) the finances of Jewish people should be controlled by the state, (b) one should not talk to Jews, (c) it is doubtful that Jews should hold public office, (d) the government should carefully monitor the number of Jewish immigrants, (e) the Jews should wear distinguishing marks, and (f) Jewish books should be prohibited.

The lowest point in Ross's literature comes in the same book. After blessing Martin Luther's sickening statements about Jewish people, Ross asked rhetorically: "Why did this Reformer who loved his Lord and his country write such a vicious booklet about the Jews? And why, I wonder, did the German people, nearly 400 years later, elect a government that felt much the same way?" This quotation uses Luther to bless Hitler. We should resist Hitler even if Luther would not. And we must resist Luther at this point, however much we admire him for other things.

Luther believed that Catholics, Muslims, and Jews combined as an evil trinity against the gospel. Luther distrusted Jews so much because he believed they were as odious as the Muslims and the Catholics. Malcolm Ross trusts Catholic tradition in its hatred of Jews, and he trusts Luther for the same reason. It is ironic that Luther taught that Jews *and* Catholics were both of the devil and that Catholic leaders in the sixteenth century believed Luther was a plot of the Jews.

JEWISH EVANGELISM AND THE UNITED CHURCH OF CANADA

"To the Jew first," wrote the apostle Paul. "Not to the Jew," says the United Church of Canada, the country's largest Protestant group. In May 1998 Toronto's *Globe and Mail* gave front page coverage to a UCC report that suggests that Jewish people do not need to accept Jesus as Messiah.

What *The Globe* calls a "landmark document" was released under the title "Bearing Faithful Witness." Written by several UCC leaders (including then-moderator William Phipps), the report contains analysis of biblical teaching and the long tradition of anti-Semitism in the church.

It is, of course, the Holocaust that forms the background to the contemporary angst many Christians have about "our" right to witness to Jews. The slaughter of the Jews is no "hoax of the twentieth century," as one racist puts it. Church complicity (Protestant and Catholic) with Adolf Hitler is undeniable. Christian anti-Semitism combined with Nazi racist ideology to forge average German citizens into *Hitler's Willing Executioners* (to use the title of Daniel Goldhagen's controversial and chilling best seller).

This modern hatred of the Jews feeds on a wicked legacy left by many theologians of the past, including Martin Luther. The combination of Luther's biblical insights about the grace of God with his unbiblical contempt for Jews illustrates the truth in Luther's famous teaching that the believer is *simul justus et peccator* (simultaneously just and sinful).

Given this hatred of Jews, it is no wonder that many Jewish people find it hard to hear about Jesus. Has the UCC chosen the proper answer for our day? Given "Christian" participation in the murder *of* the Jews, would it not be better to give up the missionary mandate *to* the Jews?

The proper answer must be "No." But the consequent "Yes" to evangelism of all people (including Jews) must be said with certain humility, simply because there is so much blood in church history in relation to the mistreatment of Jews. Christians must think deeply about how Jewish people perceive the gospel, given the evil done in the name of Jesus toward the Jewish people.

"Bearing Faithful Witness" is on track when it comes to church transgressions toward the Jew. But it is a very unfaithful document when it comes to the biblical witness about the identity and place of Jesus Christ. The token mention of Scripture is utterly deceptive given the interpretive moves that deny the plain and repeated teaching of the New Testament. These hermeneutical twists are made with finesse under the guise of "modern" scholarship, "fresh" understandings, and "deeper" study.

The report notes that "Bible study is not a priority of most United Church adults." The authors should secretly hope that this continues to be the case. Otherwise, their report is doomed. As one reads the faithful witness of the early church about Jesus, a picture is evident of One who was "Lord of the Sabbath," God's "only Son," the "Messiah," the "King of the Jews," the "Lord."

This high Christology is everywhere in the New Testament. When one sees who Jesus is, what he has done, and what he offers, it is no wonder that Paul, the Jewish convert, would say to the Gentile Christians in Rome: "For I am not ashamed of the gospel of Christ: for it is the power of God unto salvation to every one that believeth" (Rom. 1:16). He adds: "To the Jew first." Ashamed of the church sometimes? Yes, of course. Ashamed of the gospel of Christ? May it never be!

Sephardic temple, Los Angeles, California

Photo: Gordon Melton

▨ Christian Response to Judaism

An adequate Christian response to Judaism must be developed along many lines. The following points can serve as a paradigm for continued reflection, especially in connection with the material provided in this chapter.

1. *Christians must recognize the divisions within Judaism and among Jewish people.* Evangelicals often have a one-dimensional vision of Jews as practitioners of Orthodox Judaism. A good percentage of Jews in America and Israel are secular, and the majority of Jews in both countries do not follow the Orthodox life.

DABRU EMET: SPEAK THE TRUTH

On September 10, 2000, *The New York Times* published a full-page ad, signed by leading rabbis from the United States and Great Britain, titled "*Dabru Emet*: A Jewish Statement on Christians and Christianity." The work was carried out under the auspices of the Institute for Christian and Jewish Studies in Baltimore (www.icjs.org). *Dabru Emet* is a Hebrew phrase from Zechariah 8:16.

The statement included eight key points:

1. Jews and Christians worship the same God.

2. Jews and Christians seek authority from the same book—the Bible (what Jews call "Tanakh" and Christians call the "Old Testament").

3. Christians can respect the claim of the Jewish people upon the land of Israel.

4. Jews and Christians accept the moral principles of Torah.

5. Nazism was not a Christian phenomenon.

6. The humanly irreconcilable difference between Jews and Christians will not be settled until God redeems the entire world as promised in Scripture.

7. A new relationship between Jews and Christians will not weaken Jewish practice.

8. Jews and Christians must work together for justice and peace.

Dabru Emet has received wide commendation from Christian and Jewish leaders. Only a handful of Orthodox rabbis signed the statement. Some Jewish leaders thought the document was too relativistic. Also, some have argued that the statement understates the connection between Christian tradition and Nazism.

2. *The Christian response to Judaism must recognize the disgusting realities of anti-Semitism that runs through church history.* It is very difficult for Jews to hear the gospel, given the ways Jews have been persecuted and killed in the name of Jesus. The scars of anti-Semitism run deep in the Jewish psyche, not only in terms of history, but also in terms of continuing hatred and persecution.

3. *Christians must also note the persistence of anti-Semitism in the church.* When I was engaged in public debate against Malcolm Ross, I received hate mail from fellow Christians who said I was going to hell for defending the Jews against a fine Bible believer like Malcolm Ross. As I have shown earlier, Ross is a racist who admires Hitler and defends the most obnoxious anti-Semitic actions and views.

4. *Christians must resist any notion that Jews are to be understood as "Christ killers."* It is quite obvious in Scripture that some Jewish leaders at the time of Christ wanted Jesus dead. These individuals deserve criticism for their blindness and hatred toward him and for their participation, in conjunction with key Roman leaders, in plotting his demise. However, this gives no credence to the long-standing diatribe against Jews in Christian tradition.

5. *Given both historic and contemporary persecution of Jews, Christians should support the existence of the State of Israel.* Affirmation of Israel does not demand uncritical acceptance of everything its government has done. Likewise, support of Israel does not have to be linked to a dispensationalist understanding of eschatology—that is the outlook that sees support of Israel as a part of Bible prophecy. From any theological angle, it is hard to imagine an effective Christian witness to Jews that parallels the belief that the Jewish people have no right to a homeland.

THE JEWISH RESPONSE TO JESUS

How do Jews today respond to Jesus? There are a variety of reactions, a fact that must be noted in Christian reflection on Judaism and Jews. First, the vast majority of Jews give very little consideration to the Person of Jesus. This should come as no surprise to Christians when we reflect on how little time we spend thinking about the leaders of other religions. How many Christians give much thought to Buddha or Muhammad or Krishna?

Second, there are Jews who react with outrage at the name of Jesus. This is most probably related to their sense of anger over Christian anti-Semitism and the way in which Christian faith means to them the end of Judaism. This response often involves outright dismissal of Jesus but could also include making nasty remarks about him, as is done in certain passages of the Talmud.

Third, there are an increasing number of Jewish scholars giving serious attention to the views of Jesus. Most significantly, Jacob Neusner, the most prolific Jewish author alive today, has devoted a whole book in response to Jesus. In *A Rabbi Talks with Jesus,* Neusner writes as if he is living in the time of Jesus and listening to him as he gives his Sermon on the Mount.

6. *Some protest must be made when both secular and Orthodox Jews mistreat Jews who have accepted Jesus as their Messiah.* Orthodox Jews have a right to create their own boundaries in assessing what constitutes Judaism. Likewise, the larger Jewish community has a right to complain about misappropriation of symbols that usually refer to Orthodox Jewish religion. However, the reaction to Messianic Jews sometimes goes far beyond legitimate debate and difference of opinion. It seems paradoxical that non-believing Jews or secular Jews are treated far better than Jews who trust in Jesus.

7. *Christian witness to Jews involves testimony about the Person and work of Jesus, a topic often repugnant to Jewish people.* However, in spite of anti-Semitism in the church, Christians can point to the grace represented in the death of Jesus, the power of his miracles, the courage in his actions, and the wisdom in his teaching. Christian confidence in

Jesus the Jew as Messiah for both Jews and Gentiles must not diminish. What more would one want in a Messiah?

JACOB NEUSNER ON THE MIRACLES OF JESUS

"The master's many miracles—healing leprosy, paralysis, and fever; calming the storm; driving out demons—stories about such wonders will have caught my attention. But I would have been used to wonders; the Torah made me expect them, and wonder-workers even then would not have disappointed me. Such things may have been necessary, but to me were trivial. For my concern would have lain not in finding supernatural proofs for the master's propositions, but in learning from him what he had to teach me about the Torah: analysis, argument, evidence. And to Jesus' own credit, he dismissed people who kept demanding a sign; what mattered was the message."

—from *A Rabbi Talks with Jesus*

JUDAISM TIMELINE: A.D. 70–1948

70—Destruction of Jerusalem and the second Temple
73—Last stand of Jews at Masada
120–135—Rabbi Akiva leads in Rabbinic Judaism
132–135—Bar Kokhba rebellion (Second Jewish Revolt)
200—Compilation of Mishnah
306—Council of Elvira forbids intermarriage with Jews
312–313—Emperor Constantine adopts Christianity
325—Council of Nicea forbids Jews from converting pagans to Judaism
400—Commentary on the Mishnah edited
410—Rome sacked by Visigoths
415—St. Cyril, the Bishop of Alexandria, orders persecution of Jews
500—Ostrogoth king Theodoric conquers Italy and protects Jews

587—Reccared of Spain adopts Catholicism and persecutes Jews

590—Pope Gregory the Great objects to forced baptism of Jews

626—Muhammad kills hundreds of members of Jewish tribe

638—Jews allowed to return to Jerusalem

691—Dome of the Rock built in Jerusalem

691—First reports of Jews in England

732—The French defeat Muslim invaders at Tours

740—Jewish kingdom of Khazar established

767—Karaite sect resists Talmudic traditions

807—Harun Al Rashid forces Jews to wear yellow badge

969—Fatamid Muslim rule in Palestine

1066—Jews settle in England after Norman Conquest

1071—Seljuk occupation of Jerusalem

1078—Pope Gregory VII prohibits Jews from holding offices

1095—Henry IV of Germany grants a charter to Jews

1187—Saladin recaptures Jerusalem, allows Jews to return

1135—Birth of Maimonides (d. 1204)

1144—First known charge of Jewish ritual murder (Norwich, England)

1195—Maimonides completes *The Guide to the Perplexed*

1204—First synagogue built in Vienna

1215—Fourth Lateran Council decrees Jews must wear yellow sign

1229—King Henry III of England forces high taxation on Jews

1243—Accusations about Jewish desecration of the Host in Germany

1254—French King Louis IX expels the Jews from France

1285—Blood libel in Munich, Germany, results in the death of 68 Jews

1290—English King Edward I expels the Jews from England

1322—Charles IV of France expels all French Jews

1389—Pope Boniface resists persecution of Jews

1415—Benedict XIII bans Talmudic study

1420—Pope Martin V bans forcible conversion of Jews

1453—Fall of Constantinople (Istanbul) to Ottoman Muslims

1479—Jews expelled from Spain

1505—Birth of Solomon ben Moses, famous Kabbalist

1516—Jews relegated to ghetto in Venice

1543—Luther writes *About the Jews and Their Lies*

1553—Talmud publicly burned in Rome

1626—Birth of Shabbatai Zvi (d. 1676)

1632—Birth of Spinoza

1636—Rhode Island grants religious liberty to Jews

1654—Arrival of Jews in New York

1655—Jews readmitted to England by Oliver Cromwell

1700—Birth of the Ba'al Shem Tov (d. 1760)

1729—Birth of Moses Mendelssohn (d. 1786)

1781—Austria rescinds law forcing Jews to wear badges

1791—French Jews granted full citizenship

1819—Birth of Isaac Wise, major American Reform leader (d. 1900)

1845—Birth of Baron Edmond James de Rothschild (d. 1934)

1858—Abduction of Edgar Mortara

1860—Birth of Theodore Herzl (d. 1904)

1873—Establishment of Union of American Hebrew Congregations

1881—Start of mass migrations of eastern European Jews

1886—Birth of David Ben-Gurion (d. 1973)

1894—The Alfred Dreyfus Affair

1896—Theodor Herzl publishes *The Jewish State*

1897—First Jewish Zionist Congress in Basle

1898—Birth of Golda Meir (d. 1978)

1913—Birth of Menachem Begin

1916—Sykes-Picot Agreement divides up Middle East

1917—Balfour Declaration favors Jewish Palestinian State

1920—Haganah (Jewish defense organization) founded

1923—Kemal Ataturk overthrows Ottoman rule in Turkey

1929—Hebron Jews massacred by Arab militants

1929—Birth of Anne Frank (d. 1945)

1931—Jewish underground group Irgun formed

1933—Hitler becomes German Chancellor

1937—Peel Commission recommends Holy Land partition

1938—Kristallnacht—destruction of German Jewish
   synagogues
1941—Lohamei Herut Yisrael (Lehi) or Stern Gang formed
1943—Warsaw Ghetto Uprising
1948—Creation of the State of Israel

JUDAISM

General Websites	World Jewish Congress: http://www.worldjewishcongress.org Institute for Jewish Christian Studies: www.icjs.org Judaism and Jewish Resources: http://shamash.org/trb/judaism.html Eliezer Segal (University of Calgary): www.acs.ucalgary.ca/~elsegal
Traditional Websites	Orthodox: www.ou.org Conservative: www.uscj.org Reform: http://urj.org and www.rj.org Kabbalah: www.kabbalah.com
Websites on Israel and Palestinian Issue	Academic Info Middle East: www.academicinfo.net/mestpeace.html Aljazeera: www.aljazeera.com The American Israel Public Affairs Committee: www.aipac.org Brookings Institution: www.brookings.edu Committee for Accuracy in Middle East Reporting in America: www.camera.org Council on Foreign Relations: www.cfr.org The Electronic Intifada: www.electronicintifada.net Ha'aretz: www.haaretzdaily.com/ Israel Government Gateway: www.info.gov.il/eng/ Israel Ministry of Foreign Affairs: www.mfa.gov.il/mfa Jerusalem Post: www.jpost.com The Jewish Virtual Library: www.jewishvirtuallibrary.org Jewish World Review: www.jewishworldreview.com Media Watch International: www.honestreporting.com Middle East Forum: www.meforum.org Middle East Media Research Institute: www.memri.org New York Review of Books: www.nybooks.com Tikkun: www.tikkun.org Washington Institute for Near East Policy: www.washingtoninstitute.org Washington Report on Middle East Affairs: www.wrmea.com

JUDAISM

Recommended Reading on Judaism	Hasia R. Diner, *The Jews of the United States* (Berkeley: University Of California Press, 2004)
	Hayim Halevy Donin, *To Be a Jew* (New York: Basic Books, 2001)
	Martin Gilbert, *The Jews in the Twentieth Century* (Toronto: Key Porter Books, 2001)
	D. D. Guttenplan, *The Holocaust on Trial* (New York: Norton, 2002)
	Samuel Heilman, *Defenders of the Faith* (New York: Schocken, 1992)
	Michael Marrus, *The Holocaust in History* (Toronto: Lester & Orpen Dennys, 1987)
	Daniel C. Matt, *The Essential Kabbalah* (HarperSanFrancisco, 1996)
	Jacob Neusner, *The Way of Torah* (Belmont: Wadsworth, 1997)
	Gershom Scholem, *Origins of the Kabbalah* (Princeton University Press, 1990)
Recommended Reading on Israel and the Palestinian Issue	Mitchell Bard, *Myths and Facts* (Chevy Chase, Maryland: AICE, 2002)
	Thomas Friedman, *From Beirut to Jerusalem* (Farrar Straus & Giroux, 1989)
	David Grossman, *The Yellow Wind* (Farrar Straus & Giroux, 1988)
	Efrahim Karsh, *Fabricating Israeli History* (London: Frank Cass, rev. ed. 2000)
	Walter Laquer & Barry Rubin, eds. *The Israel-Arab Reader* (Penguin, 2001)
	Benny Morris, *Righteous Victims* (Vintage, 2001)
	Michael Oren, *Six Days of War* (Oxford, 2002)
	Dennis Ross, *The Missing Peace* (New York: Farrar, Straus and Giroux, 2004)
	Tom Segev, *One Palestine, Complete* (Henry Holt, 2000)
	Avi Shlaim, *The Iron Wall* (W. W. Norton, 2001)
Christian Response to Judaism	Michael Brown, *Answering Jewish Objections to Jesus* (Grand Rapids: Baker, 2000, 2003) 3 volumes

10

MORMONISM

Mormon Tabernacle, Salt Lake City, Utah

Photo: Jim Beverley

In 1982 the Mormon Church reached the five million mark in membership. By 1994 the church's worldwide following exceeded eight million. At the beginning of the new millennium, the church claimed more than ten million members. Arguably, no religious group excels in public relations skills quite like the Church of Jesus Christ of Latter-day Saints. Why would any controversy persist over a church famous for its Tabernacle Choir, its wonderful pro-family ads, and a huge contingent of clean-cut missionaries deployed across the globe?

Joseph and Hyrum Smith, Carthage, Illinois

Photo: Gordon Melton

Early Mormon History

The history and authenticity of Mormonism hinges around a controversial nineteenth-century man named Joseph Smith, Jr. Smith was born December 23, 1805, in Sharon, Vermont, but moved with his family to Palmyra, New York, in 1816. Mormons believe that God the Father and Jesus appeared to Joseph Smith in the spring of 1820 and told him to restore the one true church. This episode is called the "First Vision" story and constitutes one of the most important historic claims of Mormonism.

Smith also claimed that on September 21, 1823, an angel named Moroni told him of gold plates containing the full gospel, buried in the hill Cumorah near Palmyra. Smith claimed to have discovered the gold plates in 1827 and translated their ancient writings into *The Book of Mormon,* which was published in 1830. The Mormon Church was founded that same year. Smith also claimed to receive direct revelations from God throughout his leadership as the first prophet of the church.

EARLY MORMON TEACHING

Early Mormons believed that Jesus was conceived as the result of the sexual union between God the Father (who has a body of flesh and bone) and Mary, who later married Joseph the carpenter. This view was based in part on early Mormon belief that the Holy Ghost is a separate God from the Father (who is called Elohim) and from the Son Jesus (who is called Jehovah). In contrast, Matthew 1:18 and Luke 1:34–35 assert that Jesus was conceived by the Holy Spirit, not by God-in-the-flesh.

Joseph Smith taught (and Mormons still believe) that the Garden of Eden was located in Jackson County, Missouri. He even claimed that rocks he found at Spring Hill, Missouri, were part of an altar once used by Adam. Smith also taught that Noah built his ark in North America.

Mormons settled in Ohio, Missouri, and Illinois after the early years in New York State. Members of the church were persecuted heavily during their time in Missouri, in part because of their radical claims about taking ownership in Jackson County. Smith proclaimed that Independence, Missouri, would be the site of the New Jerusalem predicted in the Book of Revelation. Smith himself was arrested in 1838 but escaped custody and returned to Illinois.

During the early 1840s Smith was the object of both internal dissent and external criticism, particularly regarding the practice of plural marriage, an accusation that Smith denied. Joseph Smith was jailed in Carthage, Illinois, on charges of ordering the destruction of a newspaper called the *Nauvoo Expositor*, a paper started by William Law, a leading ex-Mormon. Law had circulated the view that Smith believed in many gods and practiced polygamy. Smith and his brother Hyrum were killed by an angry anti-Mormon mob on June 27, 1844.

The Mormon movement split following Joseph Smith's death. Some church members followed James Jesse Strang (who was called King James I), while others formed the Reorganized Church (Joseph Smith III became president of this faction in 1860). Most Mormons, however, chose to follow Brigham Young's leadership. Young led Mormons west in 1946 and they arrived in the Salt Lake Valley of Utah in 1847.

Mormons practiced polygamy in Utah but were forced to abandon it under pressure from the U.S. government. Mormon president Wilford Woodruff issued a manifesto against polygamy in 1890, though some Mormon leaders continued the practice through the early years of the twentieth century. In 1896 Utah was admitted to the Union as a state, and by the turn of the century there were close to 300,000 Mormons living there.

THE MORMON MURDERS

In October 1985 Salt Lake City was rocked by a series of bomb explosions that killed two people. Mark Hofmann, a dealer in rare Mormon documents, was charged with their murder. The case is important for students of Mormonism because of Hofmann's dealings with top Mormon leaders. Evidence suggests that the Mormon leaders were not open about material in church archives nor about their full interaction with Hofmann.

For the whole story, consult Steven Naifeh and Gregory White Smith, *The Mormon Murders* (New York: Weidenfeld & Nicolson, 1988) and Linda Sillitoe and Allen Roberts, *Salamander: The Story of the Mormon Forgery Murders* (Salt Lake: Signature, 1989).

Mormon Beliefs

Capturing what Mormons believe involves some investigation because of the discrepancy between the ordinary reading of the LDS Statement of Faith and what is really meant by some of the Mormon doctrinal assertions. However, we must begin with the way that the Church of Jesus Christ of Latter-day Saints presents itself.

The Articles of Faith

1. We believe in God, the Eternal Father, and in His Son, Jesus Christ, and in the Holy Ghost.

2. We believe that men will be punished for their own sins, and not for Adam's transgression.

3. We believe that through the Atonement of Christ, all mankind may be saved, by obedience to the laws and ordinances of the Gospel.

4. We believe that the first principles and ordinances of the Gospel are: first, Faith in the Lord Jesus Christ; second, Repentance; third, Baptism by immersion for the remission of sins; fourth, Laying on of hands for the gift of the Holy Ghost.

5. We believe that a man must be called of God, by prophecy, and by the laying on of hands by those who are in authority, to preach the Gospel and administer in the ordinances thereof.

6. We believe in the same organization that existed in the Primitive Church, namely, apostles, prophets, pastors, teachers, evangelists, and so forth.

7. We believe in the gift of tongues, prophecy, revelation, visions, healing, interpretation of tongues, and so forth.

8. We believe the Bible to be the word of God as far as it is translated correctly; we also believe *The Book of Mormon* to be the word of God.

9. We believe all that God has revealed, all that He does now reveal, and we believe that He will yet reveal many great and important things pertaining to the Kingdom of God.

10. We believe in the literal gathering of Israel and in the restoration of the Ten Tribes; that Zion (the New Jerusalem) will be built upon the American continent; that Christ will reign personally upon the earth; and, that the earth will be renewed and receive its paradisiacal glory.

11. We claim the privilege of worshiping Almighty God according to the dictates of our own conscience, and allow all men the same privilege, let them worship how, where, or what they may.

12. We believe in being subject to kings, presidents, rulers, and magistrates, in obeying, honoring, and sustaining the law.

13. We believe in being honest, true, chaste, benevolent, virtuous, and in doing good to all men; indeed, we may say that we follow the admonition of Paul—We believe all things, we hope all things, we have endured many things, and hope to be able to endure all things. If

there is anything virtuous, lovely, or of good report or praiseworthy, we seek after these things.

Assessment of the Articles

It is helpful to imagine what would be said about these thirteen statements from a classical Christian perspective, if one knew nothing about Mormonism. The following reactions would be immediate:

On the positive side

- The view of God seems to reflect a Trinitarian outlook. (Article 1)

- There is a recognition of sin, and the need for atonement, faith, repentance, baptism, and the power of the Holy Ghost. (Articles 2, 3, and 4)

- Mormons recognize the need for care in the calling of leaders to ministry. (Article 5)

- Mormons want to have a faith rooted in the example of the early church. (Articles 6 and 7)

- Mormons claim to trust in the Bible as the Word of God. (Article 8)

- Mormons look forward to the return of Jesus Christ. (Article 10)

- Mormons affirm religious freedom, obedience to government, and moral purity. (Articles 11, 12, and 13)

On the negative side

Classical Christians would evidence concern over the following points, even without detailed knowledge of Mormon theology:

- Why is salvation linked to "obedience to the laws of the Gospel" in Article 3?

- Why is *The Book of Mormon* considered the word of God? (Article 8) And why is a restriction put on the Bible ("as far as it is translated correctly") when no such limitation is put on *The Book of Mormon*?

- Article 9 implies a belief in ongoing formal revelation from God, and this sounds typical of groups that are not in harmony with orthodox Christianity.

- Why is the restoration of Israel linked to the United States in Article 10?

DISTINCT MORMON CHURCHES 1844–2008

(Many of these groups are now defunct)

- Aaronic Order

- Apostolic United Brethren

- Center Branch of the Lord's Remnant

- Christ's Church

- Church of Christ (David Clark)

- Church of Christ at Halley's Bluff

- Church of Christ (Fetting/Bronson)

- Church of Christ (Restored)

- Church of Christ (Temple Lot)

- Church of Christ with the Elijah Message (Rogers)

- Church of Christ "With the Elijah Message," established anew in 1929

- Church of Jesus Christ (Bickertonite)

- Church of Jesus Christ (Bulla)

- Church of Jesus Christ (Cutlerite)

- Church of Jesus Christ (Drew)

- Church of Jesus Christ of Latter-day Saints (majority group)

- Church of Jesus Christ of Latter-day Saints (Strangite)

- Church of Jesus Christ of the Saints in Zion

- Church of Jesus Christ (Toney)

- Church of Jesus Christ (Zion's Branch)

- Church of the First Born of the Fullness of Times

- Church of the New Covenant in Christ

- Churches of Christ in Zion

- Confederate Nations of Israel

- Holy Church of Jesus Christ

- Independent Church of Jesus Christ of Latter-day Saints

- Millennial Church of Jesus Christ

- Community of Christ (formerly Reorganized Church of Jesus Christ of Latter Day Saints)

- Restoration Branches Movement

- Restored Church of Jesus Christ (Walton)

- Restoration Church of Jesus Christ of Latter-day Saints

- School of the Prophets

- School of the Prophets (Wood)

- True Church of Jesus Christ Restored

- United Order Effort

- Zion's Order, Inc.

Further Investigation

Enough serious issues arise from an initial glance at the Articles of Faith to indicate that more investigation into Mormonism is necessary. Is it possible that Mormonism teaches salvation by works? Assertion of belief in *The Book of Mormon* denies the Protestant principle of *sola scriptura*, as does the implicit endorsement of new revelation in Article 9. Likewise, eschatological beliefs about America suggest that Mormon leaders claim unique revelation that goes far beyond the Bible.

Expanded investigation prompts an even deeper reservation about the integrity of the Mormon Articles of Faith and the whole scheme of Mormon doctrine. This extends to those articles that seem orthodox at first glance. To be more specific:

1. Mormon affirmation of Father, Son, and Spirit does not mean commitment to a Trinitarian understanding of God.

2. The Mormon understanding of eternal life is not rooted in an emphasis on grace alone through faith alone. Rather, eternal life is linked to following the rules and procedures of the Mormon Church.

3. The Mormon desire to have a church rooted in the apostolic tradition simply means that they believe that the Church of Jesus Christ of Latter-day Saints is a duplication of the church created by Jesus eighteen centuries before Joseph Smith. Further, Mormons believe that their church is the only true church.

4. Mormon trust in the Bible is really subordinate to *The Book of Mormon* and the other Mormon scriptures (*Doctrine and Covenants* and *Pearl of Great Price*) that are not even mentioned in the Articles of Faith.

5. The Articles of Faith give virtually no indication of the central place given to Joseph Smith in Mormon life and thought. Though Mormons rightfully give Jesus supremacy in their Articles of Faith, the Mormon understanding of the gospel of Jesus Christ is radically altered by Mormon emphasis on the life and teachings of Joseph Smith.

MORMON TEMPLE RITUALS

In temples around the world Mormons continue to engage in special ceremonies created by Joseph Smith. Mormons get married for eternity in a "sealing" ceremony and also learn their secret names. Mormon males learn special handshakes and take secret vows related to the Aaronic and Melchizedekian priesthoods. Much of the temple ritual was adapted from Joseph Smith's experiences and training as a Mason.

Faithful Mormons also practice baptism for the dead in the belief that proxy baptism will save those who have never heard the Mormon message. While 1 Corinthians 15:29 mentions a group in Corinth who engaged in baptism for the dead, the practice is not mentioned anywhere else in the New Testament and has never been adopted by Christians.

Further Concerns

As one moves beyond the initial study of the Articles of Faith, the student of Mormonism discovers other issues in relation to Christian orthodoxy. Taking Mormonism at face value becomes very problematic when the extent of its divergence from orthodox Christianity becomes known. The following key charges are used to argue that Mormonism is either heretical or is a completely different religion from Christianity:

- Mormons believe that there are many gods and that these gods formed and organized the universe.

- Mormons believe that gods used to be men and grew up to become gods.

- Mormons believe that worthy Mormon males can become gods someday.

- Mormons believe that Elohim is the one God of planet Earth. Elohim, the Father of Jesus, has a god over him.

- Mormons believe that the eternal spirits who were less than valiant in a heavenly battle between Jesus and Lucifer were sent to Earth as humans but cursed with a dark skin.

- Mormons believe that Christian worship involves participation in sacred temple ceremonies including baptism for the dead, eternal sealing of marriage, and special washings and anointings.

- Mormons believe that they are to wear special endowment garments under their regular clothing.

- Mormons believe that Joseph Smith wrote an inspired version of the Bible.

- Mormons believe that natives in the Western hemisphere are descendants of Jews who came over to the West hundreds of years before the time of Jesus.

- Mormons believe that Jesus made a special trip after his resurrection to visit the native people of the Americas.

Critique of Mormonism

Though most Mormons are absolutely convinced that Mormonism is true, they do not examine the case against the basic authenticity of the unique features of Mormonism. While classical Christian churches can learn much from LDS wisdom in church growth and family emphasis, Mormons need to reexamine the case against their traditions.

1. Changing Revelation

The original revelations of Joseph Smith are not what Mormons read today. This is not a picky complaint about minor translation problems. Changes have been made to the early revelations and to historical documents because of changing doctrinal views or to cover up polygamy or intellectual blunders on the part of Joseph Smith.

Important and significant differences exist between the first and later editions of *The Book of Mormon*. Also, the first revelations that appear in *The Book of Commandments* (1833) are drastically altered when given under the title *Doctrine and Covenants* (1835). The original *History of the Church* has also changed to fit developing Mormon views and to hide unpleasant aspects of the life of Joseph Smith.

Those who are interested in the details of this point can examine for themselves alterations in texts by comparing original and later versions. Wilford C. Wood, a Mormon, has reproduced the first edition of *The Book of Mormon* and the original edition of *The Book of Commandments* in his two-volume work *Joseph Smith Begins His Work*. Mormons can use this work by a fellow Mormon to compare the wording of the first editions with later ones to see with their own eyes the radical extent of the changes made to alleged divine revelation.

These variations are unlike those that exist between Bible translations. The differences between the King James Version and the New International Version, for example, do not change the content or message of given passages. In contrast, the changes in Smith's alleged revelations can be drastic. Entire sections can disappear from an early version to a later one or whole paragraphs can be added.

Temple lot sign

Photo: Jim Beverley

PROPHETS OF THE MORMON CHURCH

1. Joseph Smith (1805–44)

2. Brigham Young (1801–77)
Sustained as Prophet: 1847

3. John Taylor (1808–87)
Sustained as Prophet: 1880

4. Wilford Woodruff (1807–98)
Sustained as Prophet: 1889

5. Lorenzo Snow 1814–1901
Sustained as Prophet: 1898

6. Joseph F. Smith (1838–1916)
Sustained as Prophet: 1901

7. Heber J. Grant (1856–1945)
Sustained as Prophet: 1918

8. George Albert Smith
(1870–1951)
Sustained as Prophet: 1945

9. David O. McKay (1873–1970)
Sustained as Prophet: 1951

10. Joseph Fielding Smith (1876–1972)
Sustained as Prophet: 1970

11. Harold B. Lee (1899–1973)
Sustained as Prophet: 1972

12. Spencer W. Kimball (1895–1985)
Sustained as Prophet: 1973

13. Ezra Taft Benson (1899–1994)
Sustained as Prophet: 1985

14. Howard W. Hunter (1907–95)
Sustained as Prophet: 1994

15. Gordon B. Hinckley (1910–2007)
Sustained as Prophet: March 12, 1995

16. Thomas Monson (1927–)
Sustained as Prophet: February 3, 2008

2. An Unstable Church

Some major doctrines of early Mormonism do not agree with the teachings of the current Latter-day Church. Examining the doctrinal changes one must keep in mind that Joseph Smith and Brigham Young, the first two Mormon prophets, believed that they were restoring the "one true church" to the world. It is quite ironic that what they introduced as true Christian faith has not always been preserved by the LDS leaders since their times.

This distinction is most crucial when it comes to *The Book of Mormon* itself. Modern-day Mormons do not really follow some of the book's key teachings. In fact, Joseph Smith himself turned his back on some of the clear doctrinal views expressed in *The Book of Mormon*. When Joseph Smith gave this volume to the public his orthodox Christian background was evident, even though the book's basic story (about the origins of American Natives and about Jesus' appearances in the New World) is incompatible with orthodox Christianity.

THE GODMAKER CONTROVERSY

In 1983 Jeremiah Films released *The Godmakers I*, a video that presented a powerful critique of Mormon history and doctrine. Though some liberal Christians attacked the video as bigoted and unfair, *The Godmakers I* presented Mormon beliefs with reasonable accuracy and exposed the false claims and immorality of Joseph Smith. While the video contains some careless arguments, and the cartoon presentation of Mormon beliefs lacks subtlety, the first *Godmakers* video is an excellent tool for Christian witness to Mormons.

The *Godmakers II* video, issued in 1992, contains some major faults that damaged its credibility. The depiction of the Mormon Temple Ceremony is outdated as it does not reflect the major changes made in the temple rituals in April 1990. The video also implies that Lillian Chynoweth, a former member of a split-off fundamentalist Mormon group, was a victim of murder by the Mormon Church. In fact, the evidence suggests that Chynoweth committed suicide.

Godmakers II also errs in suggesting a link between satanic rituals and Mormonism. This is grossly unfair to Mormons. The testimony of William Schnoebelen in the video should be treated with deep suspicion, given his careless regard for facts in his accounts as ex-Catholic, ex-Satanist, ex-Mormon. For these and other reasons, *Godmakers II* cannot be recommended as a witnessing tool.

Jerald and Sandra Tanner, the leading Christian scholars in the field of Mormon studies, have subjected the video to lengthy analysis in their work *Problems in The Godmakers II*.

One of the most serious issues involves the question of the plurality of gods. *The Book of Mormon* repeatedly asserts that there is only one God, that God is a Spirit, and that he is eternal. *The Book of Mormon* states: "God is unchangeable from all eternity to all eternity" (Moroni 8:18). However, Joseph Smith stated the opposite in April 1844 at the funeral of a Mormon elder named King Follett. He told the mourners: "We have imagined and supposed that God was God from all eternity. I will refute that idea and take away the veil" (*Teachings of the Prophet Joseph Smith*, p. 345).

Over time Smith came to believe that there are many gods, that God has a body, and that he is not eternal. When knowledgeable Mormons claim to believe in one God, what they are affirming is just acceptance of the one God who rules over our planet. Brigham Young, the second president of the Mormon Church, taught the heretical idea that Adam is the god for our planet. This is called the Adam-God doctrine, and it was believed by Mormons for generations, until Mormon prophet Spencer W. Kimball spoke formally against it.

Young also taught the doctrine called "Blood Atonement," which meant that one had to pay for some specific sins by having one's own blood shed. By this he was not speaking about earthly justice for crimes but rather spiritual justice and eternal forgiveness. He also denied priesthood to blacks and said that the Mormon Church would be apostate if it ever gave the priesthood to them before the resurrection. This teaching was overthrown by the famous announcement on June 9, 1978, from Prophet Kimball that all worthy Mormon males can become priests. What does this show about the prophetic status of Brigham Young? Likewise, the Mormon Church has never really faced the underlying racist theology behind the original ban on blacks, just as it has never seriously examined the racist statements of Brigham Young and other early Mormon leaders.

3. Character of the Founder

One should be suspicious about the Mormon gospel, given the dishonesty and arrogance of their first prophet, Joseph Smith. The lying and scheming behind his practice of plural marriage discredits him as a prophet of God. In the Mormon *History of the Church* (Vol. 6) Smith expresses his astonishment at being accused of having seven wives and claims that he only has one wife. In actual fact, as even Mormon historians admit, Smith was married to thirty-three women in addition to his first wife. Many of these wives were already married.

It must be remembered that average Mormons are raised to hold Joseph Smith in the highest esteem. Many Mormons believe that Joseph Smith will judge humanity at the end of time, along with Jesus Christ. Given this, it is virtually impossible for most Mormons to entertain notions that Joseph Smith was immoral, adulterous, deceptive, and arrogant, or a lawbreaker. However, anyone who reads Fawn Brodie's *No Man Knows My History*, probably the best biography of Smith, will recognize how his charismatic personality and tall tales captured the allegiance of the first generation of Mormons.

Smith was even arrogant enough to hint that in one sense he was better than Jesus himself. He stated: "I have more to boast of than ever any man had. I am the only man that has ever been able to keep a whole church together since the days of Adam. A large majority of the whole have stood by me. Neither Paul, John, Peter, nor Jesus ever did it. I boast that no man ever did such a work as I" (Joseph Smith, *Documentary History of the Church*, Vol. 6, pp. 408–9).

4. Discredited Sources

In 1835 Joseph Smith made one of his biggest blunders, one that gives some indication of his arrogance and the naïveté of his Mormon followers. In that year he came into possession of some Egyptian documents, which he purchased from a merchant who was traveling through Mormon territory. Smith looked at one of the Egyptian documents and announced that it was really written by Abraham, Israel's ancient patriarch.

"The Book of Abraham" was accepted by Smith's Mormon followers, and it became part of *The Pearl of Great Price,* one of the four scriptures of Mormonism. This whole episode illustrates both an ego ready to claim the ability to translate Egyptian and a group ready to accept anything that the Prophet states.

Since no Mormons at the time knew Egyptian, they could not correct the Prophet. However, in the twentieth century the documents that Joseph used were discovered and translated by competent Egyptologists. They have nothing to do with Abraham but contain directions for proper burial rites for an Egyptian mummy.

5. Incompetent Prophets

Joseph Smith and other Mormon prophets have failed to predict the future and, thus, come under the judgment of Jesus: "Beware of false prophets." Likewise, the Old Testament tells us not to fear those who are inaccurate in their prophecy (Deut. 18:21–22). Mormons often brag about Smith's prediction that a Civil War would start involving South Carolina (*Doctrine and Covenants,* 87:1–8), but this prophecy contains many problems. The basic fact of unrest in the South was already known in 1832 when Smith made his comments.

DID JOSEPH SMITH PREDICT THE AMERICAN CIVIL WAR?

Section 87 of *Doctrine and Covenants* is often used by Mormons as proof that Joseph Smith is a true prophet. However, major problems exist in the popular Mormon argument, as noted by Jerald and Sandra Tanner, authors of *The Changing World of Mormonism*. Here is a summary of their critique:

1. The prophecy states that "soon" there will be a division between the North and the South. Smith spoke in 1832, but Civil War did not break out until 1861.

2. Contrary to Smith's prophecy, war was not poured out "upon all nations."

3. The prophecy errs in stating that there will be a "full end of all nations."

4. Smith's revelation was not added to Mormon scripture until after the Civil War started.

5. Smith's 1832 alleged revelation actually follows a common understanding of the time that there were tensions between the North and the South. In fact, four days before Smith's prophecy the *Painsville [Ohio] Telegraph and Geauga Free Press* copied a New York article that also predicted Civil War.

Joseph Smith said that a temple would be built in his time in the state of Missouri, on a site he specified to be the New Jerusalem. The temple was never built (*Doctrine and Covenants*, 84:1–5). Smith also taught that Jesus Christ would return by about 1890 (*History of the Church*, Vol. 5, p. 336). Smith once declared that there were people on the moon who lived to be about one thousand years old and who dressed like Quakers. (Early Mormons even sang a hymn about these people.) Brigham Young further taught that there were people living on the sun (*Journal of Discourses*, Vol. 13, p. 271).

6. Problems with *The Book of Mormon*

The Book of Mormon forces the adoption of two opposing views. On the one side stands the Mormon claim that Joseph Smith was guided by an angel to gold plates buried 1,500 years earlier at the Hill Cumorah in upper New York State, now a sacred site for all Mormons. After discovery of these plates, Mormons believe that Smith was given supernatural power to translate them.

The second view is that this famous work is basically the product of Joseph Smith himself. This interpretation implies (or virtually demands) the understanding that Smith lied or was deluded about the book's alleged angelic origin. Though some liberal Mormons suggest a combination of divine-human elements for *The Book of Mormon,* the vast majority of Mormons and non-Mormons believe this is one case where a choice must be made between two radically opposing theories.

Mormons who defend the integrity of Smith's claim do so along the following lines.

First, they hold an implicit trust in Smith's integrity, in some sense similar to their trust in Jesus. What non-Mormons must remember here, again, is how difficult it is for most Mormons to entertain the possibility that Joseph Smith had major difficulty in telling the truth.

Second, Mormons believe that it would be impossible for a rather uneducated young man like Joseph Smith to have produced such a work by his mid-20s. They conclude from this that Smith's explanation of supernatural aid in bringing *The Book of Mormon* to light is the most satisfactory view of the origins of the sacred text. Apart from divine inspiration, how can one explain that the golden book associated with Joseph Smith has been accepted by millions?

Third, Mormons also claim that there are biblical passages that predict the emergence of *The Book of Mormon.* The most common biblical passage cited is from Ezekiel 37:15–17: "The word of the LORD came to me: 'Son of man, take a stick of wood and write on it, "Belonging to Judah and the Israelites associated with him." Then take another stick of wood, and write on it, "Ephraim's stick, belonging to Joseph and all the house of Israel associated with him." Join them together into one stick so that they will become one in your hand.'"

The passage continues: "When your countrymen ask you, 'Won't you tell us what you mean by this?' say to them, 'This is what the Sovereign

LORD says: I am going to take the stick of Joseph—which is in Ephraim's hand—and of the Israelite tribes associated with him, and join it to Judah's stick, making them a single stick of wood, and they will become one in my hand.' Hold before their eyes the sticks you have written on" (vv. 18–20).

There are several reasons to reject the traditional Mormon claims.

First, no good reason exists to trust Joseph Smith's integrity. He is no reliable witness on earthly matters and should not be trusted on divine ones, as noted earlier.

Second, the Ezekiel passage cited has nothing to do with *The Book of Mormon*. Even if one argued that the two sticks should be interpreted as two books, it is clear that the union of the sticks/books has to do with the unification of the twelve tribes of Israel, not *The Book of Mormon*.

Third, there is every indication that *The Book of Mormon* is a product of the nineteenth century. It deals with religious issues common to Smith's day, including debates over the proper name of the Christian church, the fate of the heathen, the proper mode of baptism, and so on.

Fourth, contrary to popular Mormon sentiment, no archaeological support exists for its version of events in the Americas from 2200 B.C. through A.D. 400 Archaeologists do not use *The Book of Mormon* as a field guide for the study of the geography and history of the Americas. In fact, the Smithsonian Institution in Washington sends out notices that *The Book of Mormon* is *not* used by its workers. Likewise, anthropologists repudiate the common Mormon view that American Natives are descendants of ancient Jews who migrated to the Western hemisphere.

Fifth, and very significantly, *The Book of Mormon* copies the King James Version of the Bible (1611), even down to the latter's use of italics. Why is the King James language being quoted in documents that were allegedly, according to Mormon teaching, written over one thousand years earlier? The easiest answer is that Joseph Smith neglected to think of all the ways in which his book might indicate that it was a product of his own time.

Finally, historians have tracked down other books that Smith used to produce *The Book of Mormon*. Of particular importance here is the work *View of the Hebrews* written by Ethan Smith and published in New York in 1823. Many of the concepts of *The Book of Mormon* duplicate Ethan Smith's earlier publication. In fact, one-time Mormon historian B. H. Roberts experienced an enormous crisis of faith in *The Book of Mormon* because of his close study of the parallels between the two works.

7. Imaginary Visions

Mormonism's integrity rests on the credibility of the First Vision story of Joseph Smith. In his personal history, Smith writes about his search for the true church when he was a teenager. "So, in accordance with this, my determination to ask of God, I retired to the woods to make the attempt. It was on the morning of a beautiful, clear day, early in the spring of eighteen hundred and twenty."

Smith writes: "I saw a pillar of light exactly over my head, above the brightness of the sun, which descended gradually until it fell upon me. When the light rested upon me I saw two Personages, whose brightness and glory defy all description, standing above me in the air. One of them spake unto me, calling me by name and said, pointing to the other— 'This is My Beloved Son. Hear Him!'"

The young teenager then asked which church to join. "I was answered that I must join none of them, for they were all wrong; and the Personage who addressed me said that all their creeds were an abomination in his sight; that those professors were all corrupt; that: 'they draw near to me with their lips, but their hearts are far from me, they teach for doctrines the commandments of men, having a form of godliness, but they deny the power thereof.'"

This First Vision story is a product of Smith's vivid imagination. First, the notion that every other church was wrong is impossible to reconcile with the promise of Jesus that the gates of hell would not prevail against the church. The claim of wholesale apostasy in all Christian churches is simply a fabrication of Joseph Smith. It speaks more of his pride and arrogance than it does about the state of churches in the United States or other parts of the world.

Second, it is particularly telling that Smith failed to remember the year of this alleged encounter. He states that he sought God's help when there was a revival going on in his area. That revival has been shown by Wesley P. Walters to have taken place in 1824, four years after Smith's date for the First Vision. How is it possible that Smith could forget the year of his face-to-face encounter with God the Father and Jesus Christ, his Son?

Adding to the uncertainty, Joseph Smith's famous First Vision account, which appears in *The Pearl of Great Price*, one of the Mormon scriptures, is contradicted by two other accounts from him. In other words, Smith cannot consistently recall and retell the most pivotal event of his life. The three accounts we have from Smith's own hand (written in 1832, 1835, and 1838) disagree on when the vision occurred, where it occurred, why it occurred, and who it was that appeared to Joseph.

Mormon apologists attempt to counter these contradictions by claiming here that critics of Smith's assertions are simply being picky. However, the discrepancies in his story do not represent matters of minute detail. Critics do not complain that Smith cannot remember how many leaves were on the trees during the divine visitation. Rather, they point out that his various accounts differ on significant items like date, place, rationale, and the identity of his divine guests.

8. Conflicts with the Bible

As classical Christians attempt to assess Mormonism, fundamental questions must be asked about whether key Mormon views are compatible with the teaching of Scripture. On this record, the contrast between Mormon views and biblical teaching is often stark and plain. For example, the Mormon view that there is more than one God is contradicted by clear biblical teaching in Deuteronomy 4:35, Isaiah 44:6–8, and John 17:3, among hundreds of other verses in the Bible that teach that only one God exists.

Further, the Mormon notion that God used to be a man is a stunning aberration from the mind of Joseph Smith. Smith's heretical view came to him late in his life and is contradicted by many verses both in *The Book of Mormon* and *Doctrine and Covenants*. That God is not a man is taught in Malachi 3:6 and Isaiah 44:6. Likewise, the Mormon view that God has a body of flesh and bones is contrary to Psalm 139:7–10, Jeremiah 23:24, and John 4:24.

No record of Mormon temple rituals can be found in Scripture and these rituals often contradict biblical teaching. Where in the New Testament or in early church history are Christians seen to wear special temple garments, engage in secret rites, and take bloody oaths? When it becomes obvious that the Mormon rites are largely borrowed from the Masonic Lodge, it is impossible to justify that Joseph Smith is reviving the lost Christian church.

9. Authoritarian and Narrow Leadership

The critical issues raised against Mormonism do not receive an objective hearing in Utah. Current Mormon leaders duplicate the pattern that has been set since the days of Joseph Smith, attributing critical questioning to Satan and using their ecclesiastical power to crush dissent and free inquiry. Smith employed his alleged prophetic status to excommunicate those who dared to challenge his authority. In fact, his wife faced such "divine" retribution when she dared to object to his lying and scheming over the practice of plural marriage.

Mormon leaders today use their enormous power to keep the hard questions from being faced. The Mormon Church has not defended itself on the most serious charges noted above. Even Mormon scholars complain about the secrecy and closed-door attitude of the church leadership concerning careful and sober examination of historical documents—documents that are not allowed into the public domain. A recent purge of alleged dissidents by the Mormon hierarchy shows how little the church cares for freedom and open scholarship.

10. Problems with "Inner Testimony"

Most Mormons do not know details about the case that can be made against the teachings and integrity of Joseph Smith. If pressed on the matter, many will simply refuse to face these hard issues that impact the essential fabric of their faith. Further, Mormons are trained to meet all doubts by referring to the "inner testimony" of the Holy Spirit that Joseph Smith is a prophet of God and that Mormonism is true.

This highly subjective defense of belief is rooted in a classic reference in *The Book of Mormon*: "And when ye shall receive these things, I would exhort you that ye would ask God, the Eternal Father, in the name of Christ, if these things are not true; and if ye shall ask with a sincere heart, with real intent, having faith in Christ, he will manifest the truth of it unto you, by the power of the Holy Ghost. And by the power of the Holy Ghost ye may know the truth of all things" (Moroni 10:4–5).

Given the strength of the objective evidence regarding the intellectual, moral, and spiritual failures of Mormon leader Joseph Smith, this subjective defense lacks credibility. Mormons urge others to ask God to show them by inner light that the Church of Jesus Christ of Latter-day Saints is the true church, that *The Book of Mormon* is the word of God, and so on. This "inner testimony" does not refute the evidence that proves that Joseph Smith is no reliable guide to truth.

While not every aspect of Mormonism is wrong, the basic and central message of Mormonism is false. Joseph Smith did not restore the gospel of Jesus. Rather, he distorted the Bible's plain teaching, denied clear Christian doctrines, and added to them his own untrue and harmful beliefs, thereby bringing discredit to those who follow his message. Mormons should reexamine their beliefs and fully embrace the gospel that is adequately described in the New Testament.

Mormon temple, Nauvoo, Illinois

Photo: Gordon Melton

RAVI ZACHARIAS AT THE MORMON TABERNACLE

Ravi Zacharias at Mormon Tabernacle

Photo: Jim Beverley

Evoking thoughts of the apostle Paul at the Greek Areopagus, Christian apologist Ravi Zacharias preached November 14, 2004, at the Mormon Tabernacle in Salt Lake City, Utah. Zacharias was the first major evangelical to preach there since D. L. Moody did so in 1899.

Thousands of Mormons and evangelicals packed the immense edifice in Temple Square to hear Zacharias preach on "Defending Jesus Christ as the Way, the Truth, and the Life." Zacharias argued that Jesus understood the depths of human depravity, that his atonement provides full redemption through grace, and that his resurrection is mankind's only hope. Zacharias also affirmed the doctrine of the Trinity.

Zacharias, a native of India, told *Christianity Today,* "I am absolutely grateful to the Lord for the opportunity and the courtesy extended to give me a hearing on such eternal matters. I still marvel that it came."

It almost didn't. The previous summer Zacharias called off his visit after fellow Christian apologetics expert Greg Johnson told the Mormon press that Zacharias had merely loaned his name as general editor to Walter Martin's *Kingdom of the Cults*, the classic work that includes a chapter on Mormonism. Johnson later apologized for mischaracterizing Zacharias's involvement. Richard Mouw, Fuller Seminary president, and other evangelical leaders convinced Zacharias to reconsider and preach at the Tabernacle.

Standing Together, a coalition of evangelical churches and ministries, and Robert Millet, a leading Mormon scholar, organized the event. The First Presidency of the Church of Jesus Christ of Latter-day Saints (LDS) approved Zacharias's appearance at the Tabernacle.

Greg Johnson, president of Standing Together, and Robert Millet, a professor at Brigham Young University, invited Zacharias to Utah for a three-part speaking engagement, with the Tabernacle as one of the venues. Zacharias also held a private meeting with Gordon B. Hinckley, the current leader of the LDS.

Greg Johnson and Robert Millet

Photo: Jim Beverley

Before Zacharias spoke, Mouw told the Tabernacle audience that evangelicals have sinned against Mormons by misrepresenting them, adding that he hoped evangelicals would "take part" in the 2005 events marking the 200th anniversary of Joseph Smith's birth.

Sandra Tanner, a former Mormon and president of Utah Lighthouse Ministry, said Mouw's apology was "overstated and hurts frontline evangelical witness to Mormons." Kurt Van Gorden, director of Utah Gospel Mission, echoed Tanner's concern and called Joseph Smith, the Mormon founder, "a false prophet." Bill McKeever, founder of Mormonism Research Ministry, told *Christianity Today* that the Fuller Seminary president's comments have already been used against evangelicals.

Mouw later said that he still believes Christian scholars should engage in "critical give and take" with their Mormon counterparts. He added, "I am deeply sorry for causing distress in the evangelical community." Mouw's apology has not been given enough attention by some of his critics. While Mouw can be very strong in raising objections to Mormon doctrine, at the same time he urges evangelicals to temper their concerns with love.

Tanner, the most influential critic of Mormonism, said she was "delighted by the clear gospel message that Ravi gave in the Tabernacle, but concerned about the use that the LDS church might make of the event."

Millet told *Christianity Today* that evangelicals shouldn't worry: "I can't foresee this being used in any typical public-relations sense. It is simply a sign that the LDS church is trying to build bridges with other faith communities." He also said "the LDS church is not changing its basic doctrine, though there is a greater emphasis now on the doctrine of grace."

Mormonism and Polygamy

Mormon founder Joseph Smith was married to Emma Hale in 1827. The first indication of Smith's interest in polygamy occured in 1831 when he privately advocated the practice to key Mormon leaders like W. W. Phelps. Evidence exists that Smith had an affair with Fanny Alger, a Smith maidservant, in 1835. Some Mormons have argued that Alger was secretly married to Joseph, but most Mormons contend that the Alger incident was simply a lie perpetrated against Smith.

Smith was sealed in marriage to Louisa Beaman in April 1841, and to many other women before his death in 1844. What makes Smith's polygamy utterly appalling is all the scheming and lying that are part of the tragic saga. Smith first lied to his wife about his liaisons with Mormon women, and then he used "divine" threats to force her acceptance of polygamy. Section 132:54 of *Doctrine and Covenants* states: "But if she will not abide this commandment she shall be destroyed."

Smith told Zina D. Huntington, one of his chosen girls, that an angel would strike him dead if she did not agree to plural marriage. Smith would even arrange mock marriages to hide his actions, the most notable of which was with a young girl named Sarah Ann Whitney. He would tell Mormon families to keep his wife in the dark; his letter to Sarah Ann's parents with that directive still survives. Smith would also arrange for a Mormon husband to be sent on a mission trip if that husband protested Smith's polygamous plans to marry that man's wife.

Early Mormon Polygamy

Most mainline Mormons are unaware of the details of early Mormon polygamy. They simply accept that Joseph only married older women (he married eleven women under the age of twenty), that the unions were never sexual (the diaries of early Mormons are reasonably clear that this was not the case), or that Smith was a reluctant participant in polygamy. In fact, Smith's zeal with regard to polygamy established the pattern for later Mormon leaders, including his successor, Brigham Young, who had twenty-seven wives.

Smith and other Mormon leaders violated American law in promoting polygamy and they attacked those few courageous Mormons who dared to question Smith's alleged revelations on the topic. Brigham Young argued that Mormon males who did not engage in polygamy would not enter heaven. Many Mormon leaders continued in polygamy even after the 1890 Manifesto was issued against the practice.

This breaking of both American and Mormon law became evident in 1904–07 at U.S. Senate Hearings involving Utah politician Reed Smoot. Even the sixth Prophet of the Mormon Church, Joseph F. Smith, admitted to disobedience to the Manifesto. The LDS Church has had to face the issue of polygamy since the Manifesto because of fundamentalist Mormons who refused to obey Salt Lake's prohibition.

Contemporary Polygamy

The largest contemporary polygamous group is the Fundamentalist Church of Jesus Christ of Latter Day Saints (FLDS). Warren Jeffs became the leader of this group in 2002 after the death of his father, Rulon T. Jeffs. The FLDS is based in the twin cities of Colorado City, Arizona, and Hilldale, Utah, in an area once known as Short Creek. The FLDS has also opened the YFZ (Yearning for Zion) Ranch in Eldorado, Texas.

The FLDS has followers in Bountiful, British Columbia, led by Bishop James Oler. Former Canadian leader Winston Blackmore was ousted by Warren Jeffs, but Blackmore retains a following in the secluded Canadian town and has been frequently interviewed by major Canadian media.

FLDS LEADERS

1. Lorin Woolley 1929–34	5. Charles F. Zitting 1954
2. J. Leslie Broadbent 1934–35	6. LeRoy Johnson 1954–87
3. John Y. Barlow 1935–49	7. Rulon T. Jeffs 1987–2002
4. Joseph W. Musser 1949–54	8. Warren Jeffs 2002–

In 1953 the FLDS group was raided by law enforcement as part of a crackdown on polygamy. This crisis in Mormon history is analyzed by Martha Sonntag Bradley in her book *Kidnapped from That Land* (University of Utah Press, 1996). The Yearning for Zion compound was raided by Texas authorities in March 2008, and children were later removed from their families under international media spotlight. The children were later returned after FLDS appeals to the Texas courts. Warren Jeffs was arrested in 2006 for crimes related to polygamy and was sentenced in 2007 to ten years to life.

Other polygamous groups include the True and Living Church, based in Manti, Utah, and led by James D. Harmston, and the Latterday Church of Christ (also known as the Kingston Clan). The second largest polygamist group is the Apostolic United Brethren, now under the leadership of Owen Allred. This group was led by Rulon Allred (b. 1906) until his murder in 1977. Allred's death was perpetrated by two female followers of Ervil LeBaron, the founder of the Church of the Lamb of God, another polygamous group. Ervil had his own brother Joel murdered on August 20, 1972. Joel had started the polygamous Church of the Firstborn of the Fullness of Times in 1955 and had excommunicated Ervil in 1971. Ervil died in prison in 1981. The details behind these cases take center stage in Jon Krakauer's *Under the Banner of Heaven* (New York: Doubleday, 2003).

Community of Christ temple, Independence, Missouri

Photo: Gordon Melton

THE KIDNAPPING OF ELIZABETH SMART

Public interest in Mormon polygamy increased dramatically after the kidnapping of Elizabeth Smart, a young woman who was abducted from her home on June 5, 2002. Smart was rescued from her captor, Brian David Mitchell, on March 12, 2003. Mitchell, who had worked as a handyman at the Smart home, views himself as Immanuel, God's messenger. He and his wife, Wanda Eileen Barzee, were charged in the Smart case with aggravated sexual assault, kidnapping, and burglary. Mitchell wanted Elizabeth Smart to become one of his seven divinely chosen wives.

Mitchell's views are documented in "The Book of Immanuel David Isaiah," a handwritten, twenty-seven-page collection of "revelations." At one point it is said of Wanda, "Therefore, Hephzibah Eladah Isaiah, thou art called and chosen to be a helpmeet unto my servant Immanuel David Isaiah, and to be his wise counselor and best friend, and to be submissive and obedient unto thy husband in all righteousness."

The document also attests to "seven diamonds" or testaments of Jesus Christ: (1) The Holy Bible (KJV), (2) *The Book of Mormon*, (3) The inspired words of the prophets of The Church of Jesus Christ of Latter-Day Saints, (4) "The Golden Seven Plus One" by Dr. C. Samuel West, (5) "Embraced By The Light" by Betty J. Eadie, (6) "The Literary Message of Isaiah" by Avraham Gileadi, and (7) "The Final Quest" by Rick Joyner.

Following the Smart kidnapping, Patricia Hearst appeared on *Larry King Live* and argued that Elizabeth Smart was a victim of brainwashing and that her situation paralleled Hearst's own kidnapping in 1974 by the militant Symbionese Liberation Front. Hearst had this message for Smart: "You have been so abused and so robbed of your free will and so frightened that you believe any lie that your abductor has told you. You think that either you will be killed if you reach out to get help or . . . your family will be killed."

While God tolerated or allowed polygamy in the Old Testament, monogamy remains the ideal and expressed teaching of the Bible (see Gen. 2:24; Deut. 17:17; Matt. 19:5; 1 Tim. 3:2, 12). The Mormon story of polygamy is a tale of tragedy birthed in lies and deception, one that has led to heartache as Mormon women in particular have experienced the pain associated with sharing their husband with others.

Sadly, there are no easy answers to the complexities connected with Mormon polygamy. First, there is the crucial issue of religious freedom involving adults who sincerely believe that it is their moral duty to practice polygamy. A group of polygamous Mormon wives from British Columbia intend to appeal to the Supreme Court of Canada that Canada's Charter gives them the right to practice polygamy. Second, in spite of the dark side of polygamy, any sane person should know that ripping Mormon polygamous communities apart is no path to freedom.

United States and Canadian courts must continue to address the real criminal issues related to the children victimized by polygamy's sexual ideology. Other moral issues must be faced as well, including the tragic reality that young Mormon men are forced out of their communes by older Mormon leaders who seek the young girls for themselves. The whole saga of Mormon polygamy proves the Puritan maxim that the chief result of sin is more sin. Brian Mackert reports on his own heartbreaking experience in *Illegitimate: How a Loving God Rescued a Son of Polygamy.*

TIMELINE OF MORMONISM

1805—Birth of Joseph Smith on December 23 in Sharon, Vermont

1812—Solomon Spalding writes manuscript about discovery of record of earlier civilization in a hill

1816—Smith family moves to Palmyra, New York

1820—Smith family engaged in "money-digging"—use of magic objects to find buried treasure

1820—Smith receives First Vision from God the Father and Jesus

1822—Smith family moves to Manchester, New York

1823—Ethan Smith publishes *Views of the Hebrews* in New York (second edition in 1825)

1823—On September 21–22 Angel Moroni tells Smith of gold plates containing Book of Mormon

1824—Major revival in upstate New York

1826—Smith tried—maybe arrested—for "glass-looking" on March 20

1827—Smith marries Emma Hale (age 22) on January 27

1827—Smith gets gold plates from Angel Moroni at Hill Cumorah

1828—Martin Harris takes copy of characters from gold plates to Prof. Charles Anthon at Columbia University in February

1828—Harris loses 116 pages of transcripts of gold plates in June

1829—John the Baptist confers Aaronic Priesthood on Joseph Smith and Oliver Cowdery in Harmony, Pennsylvania, on May 15

1829—Peter, James, and John confer Melchizedekian Priesthood on Smith and Cowdery

1829—Translation of *The Book of Mormon* completed

1830—*The Book of Mormon* printed on March 26

1830—The church organized on April 6

1831—Smith and wife move to Kirtland, Ohio, in January–February

1831—Some Mormons move to Independence, Missouri

1831—Smith receives revelation on July 20 that Zion site is to be in Independence, Missouri

1832—Brigham Young joins church on April 14

1832—Smith arrives in Missouri on April 24

1833—Smith completes translation of New Testament on February 2

1833—Word of Wisdom revelation given to Smith on February 27

1833—Mormons subject to mob attacks in Jackson County, Missouri

1833—*Book of Commandments* published

1834—Eber D. Howe's *Mormonism Unveiled* published

1835—*Doctrine and Covenants* accepted as scripture

1835—Smith acquires Egyptian texts and translates them

1836—Jesus appears to Smith and Cowdery in Kirtland Temple, along with Moses, Elias, and Elijah on April 3 (*D&C*, 110)

1836—Smith reportedly has affair with Fanny Alger

1837—Smith and Sidney Rigdon start Kirtland Safety Society Anti-Banking Company and later are fined for unauthorized banking

1838—Smith starts writing *History of the Church*

1838—Military group known as Danites formed in June

1838—Mormons attacked by mobs in Missouri

1838—Smith arrested and later escapes from custody and returns to Illinois

1839—Smith and other Mormon leaders travel to Washington, DC

1840—Smith publically announces baptism for the dead

1841—Smith marries Louisa Beaman, aged 26

1842—Smith starts teaching on plurality of gods

1842—Smith joins Masonic Lodge and in May introduces temple ceremonies similar to Masonic ones

1843—Smith starts to translate Kinderhook plates

1843—Smith dictates revelation on plural marriage on July 12

1844—Smith announces candidacy for LDS president

1844—*Nauvoo Expositor* first—and only—issue charges Smith with polygamy

1844—Smith killed on June 27 in gun battle while prisoner in Carthage

1844—Sidney Rigdon excommunicated on September 8

1846—On February 4 Mormons begin trek to Utah

1847—Brigham Young and first group of pioneers enter Salt Lake Valley

1848—Crops saved by flock of seagulls eating crickets

1850—*Deseret News* begins publication in Salt Lake City

1852—First public announcement of doctrine of polygamy

1856—Brigham Young gives Blood Atonement speech

1857—Mountain Meadows Massacre (120 Arkansas travelers killed in Utah)

1877—John D. Lee executed for leadership in massacre

1880—John Taylor becomes president of church on October 10

1880—*The Pearl of Great Price* accepted as scripture

1889—Wilford Woodruff becomes LDS president

1890—Manifesto about suspension of polygamy

1893—Salt Lake City Temple dedicated

1898—Lorenzo Snow becomes LDS president

1901—Joseph F. Smith becomes LDS president

1918—President Smith receives vision of redemption of the dead (*D&C*, 138)

1918—Heber J. Grant becomes LDS president

1945—George Albert Smith becomes LDS president

1951—David O. McKay becomes LDS president

1961—Metropolitan Museum in New York presents LDS church with fragments of papyri once owned by Joseph Smith

1964—Jerald and Sandra Tanner publish *Mormonism: Shadow and Reality*

1970—Joseph Fielding Smith becomes LDS president

1972—Harold B. Lee becomes LDS president

1973—Spencer W. Kimball becomes LDS president on December 30

1976—Two revelations added to Mormon canon (become *D&C*, 137–138 in 1981)

1978—Revelation that lifts ban on priesthood of blacks accepted on September 30

1981—New editions of Mormon scriptures published in September

1985—Mark Hofmann sells forged documents to church leaders and plants bombs in two locations in Salt Lake City to kill suspected critics

1985—Ezra Taft Benson becomes LDS president on November 10

1994—Howard Hunter becomes LDS president on June 5

1995—Gordon B. Hinckley becomes LDS president on March 12

1995—"The Family: A Proclamation to the World" published on September 23

1997—Membership reaches 10 million in November

2002—Winter Olympics in Salt Lake City

2003—Elizabeth Smart rescued from polygamist Brian David Mitchell

2004—DNA evidence contradicts Mormon claim of link between Natives and Jews

2004—Ravi Zacharias preaches in Mormon Tabernacle

2004—Grant Palmer, LDS scholar, excommunicated

2005—LDS Church celebrates bicentennial of birth of Joseph Smith

2006—Arrest of FLDS prophet Warren Jeffs on crimes related to polygamy

2007—Jeffs found guilty at trial and sentenced ten years to life

2008—Thomas Monson becomes LDS president

2008—Texas authorities raid FLDS commune in Eldorado

MORMONISM
(CHURCH OF JESUS CHRIST OF LATTER-DAY SAINTS)

Typology	Christian Protestant Restorationist Sectarian
Founder	Joseph Smith (1805–44)
Headquarters	Salt Lake City
Home Website	www.lds.org
Critic Sites	Utah Lighthouse Ministry: www.utlm.org Mormonism Research Ministry (Bill McKeever): www.mrm.org Mormon Central (Michael Marquardt): www.xmission.com/~research/central Recovery from Mormonism: www.exmormon.org Watchman Fellowship: www.watchman.org Institute for Religious Research: www.irr.org
Recommended Reading	Richard Abanes, *One Nation Under Gods* (New York: Four Walls Eight Windows, 2002) Will Bagley, *Blood of the Prophets: Brigham Young and the Massacre at Mountain Meadows* (University of Oklahoma Press, 2002) S. I. Banister, *For Any Latter-day Saint* (Star Bible Publications, Fort Worth, Texas 76118) Francis J. Beckwith, Carl Mosser, and Paul Owen, eds. *The New Mormon Challenge* (Grand Rapids: Zondervan, 2002) Fawn M. Brodie, *No Man Knows My History* (New York: Alfred A. Knopf, 1977) Todd Compton, *In Sacred Loneliness* (Salt Lake: Signature, 1997) Michael Marquardt, *The Rise of Mormonism: 1816–1844* (Longwood: Xulon, 2005) Michael Marquardt and Wesley Walters, *Inventing Mormonism* (Salt Lake: Signature, 1994) Bill McKeever and Eric Johnson, *Mormonism 101* (Grand Rapids: Baker, 2000) Richard and Joan Ostling, *Mormon America* (San Francisco: HarperSanFrancisco, 1999) Grant Palmer, *An Insider's View of Mormon Origins* (Salt Lake: Signature, 2002) David Persuitte, *Joseph Smith and the Origins of The Book of Mormon* (Jefferson: McFarland & Company, 2000) Simon Southerton, *Losing a Lost Tribe* (Salt Lake: Signature, 2004) Jerald and Sandra Tanner, *The Changing World of Mormonism* (Chicago: Moody Press, 1980) Richard Van Wagner, *Mormon Polygamy: A History* (Salt Lake City, UT: Signature Books, 1986) Dan Vogel, *Joseph Smith: The Making of a Prophet* (Salt Lake: Signature, 2004)

11

THE NEW AGE

James Van Praagh, famous medium

Photo: Warwick's Books, La Jolla, California

The New Age represents one of the few new religious movements that has had a major impact on modern life and culture and traditional patterns of religion. While Mormonism has spread in powerful and dynamic ways around the globe, especially in the last thirty years, and the Jehovah's Witnesses have enjoyed some numerical growth, most of the famous sectarian movements of the last three centuries remain insignificant in size and influence.

Over the last century the New Age movement has become increasingly diverse and disorganized. It is a highly fragmented movement, full of competing groups and rival leaders and limited by its often flighty grasp on spiritual and organizational reality.

Still, the New Age has had a major impact on Western culture, particularly since Shirley MacLaine went public with her conversion to New Age teachings. The New Age is *everywhere*. Many of its underlying themes have become part of pop culture. Many New Age ideas appear in ordinary discourse. Given its spread and impact, evangelicals must be concerned about the New Age—but this demands paying extra attention to its real nature, spirit, intent, and goals. If evangelicals misunderstand its true nature, Christian witness to the New Age will be seriously hampered.

Definition of the New Age

The New Age should be viewed as a diverse spiritual movement that rose to prominence in the 1970s and 1980s, rooted in the esoteric traditions of Eastern and Western religion. It focused on the belief that the planet had reached a fresh stage of religious transformation involving humanity's divine potential to achieve healing, higher consciousness, and planetary peace in the dawning of the true Age of Aquarius.

Key Ideas of the New Age

Common themes and ideas permeate the New Age movement, this despite major differences between given groups, the ever-present splits that occur after the death of a group leader, and the ongoing rivalries between competing or jealous leaders in various groups and branches of the New Age. While the following list of themes differs somewhat from those leading researchers (Wouter J. Hanegraaff, Hans Sebald, Christof Schorsch, and J. Gordon Melton) give on the New Age, certain basic ideas emerge in their studies:

1. *All the world's great religions teach essentially the same truths.* New Age writers regularly affirm the unity of religions. This widespread New Age view received its first major exposure at the World's Parliament of Religions in Chicago in 1893. It was repeated at the second

parliament held in the same city in 1993 and at the third parliament in Cape Town, South Africa, in 1999.

2. *Human beings are divine.* It is no secret that New Age writers have little patience for the Christian doctrine of original sin. Rather, New Agers emphasize the "God within," or one's "God consciousness," or the inherent divinity of all humanity. The film *Out on a Limb* captured this idea when Shirley MacLaine spread her arms wide as she looked out to the Pacific Ocean and exclaimed, "I Am God."

3. *Human beings have potential to achieve higher consciousness and divine perfection.* This theme, which flows out of the affirmation of human divinity, lies at the very heart of New Age ideology. In fact, this affirmation is probably one of the most deeply held and widely spread ideas of the New Age—and helps to explain the allure of the New Age to millions of people.

4. *Reincarnation and karma provide the true and best explanation about the past and future of human beings.* This popular New Age idea shows the pervasive influence of Eastern religion, particularly Hindu teaching. The New Age, however, puts a significant spin on reincarnation and karma. New Age groups and leaders have downplayed the dark side of karma (that your sins will find you out) and reincarnation (you can return in another life as a worm or bug or virus). Rather, the New Age focuses on one's potential in future lives and in collecting merit for the next life.

5. *Psychic claims are often true and the occult world provides important paths and tools to achieve higher consciousness.* Though the New Age is not to be identified with the occult *per se*, and not all New Agers accept the manifold psychic claims that permeate our world, New Age religion is largely sympathetic to paranormal/psychic views and is usually open to occult traditions. This explains why New Age groups and teachers show up at psychic fairs and why so many New Agers follow and adopt the latest fads in the world of the occult.

6. *Science in its truest vision and best exponents conforms to New Age teaching.* Contrary to popular perception, the New Age claims to have a deep love for science. The New Age interest in science is best expressed in the writings of Fritjof Capra, author of *The Tao of Physics,* and Robert

Pirsig, who wrote *Zen and the Art of Motorcycle Maintenance.* Ken Wilber, a leading New Age theoretician, constantly explores scientific theories in his writings. Marilyn Ferguson, author of the famous book *The Aquarian Conspiracy,* is well known for her work on brain research.

7. *Alternative and holistic medicine is a helpful corrective to the West's obsession with traditional Western medicine.* The New Age has a preoccupation with health issues. New Agers claim that modern medicine depends on a truncated view of science and medicine and so fails to capture the holistic nature of humans (as body *and* spirit) and thereby reduces medicine to mere technology. The New Age movement accepts almost anything in alternative medicine—from practices readily accepted in Western hospitals (like acupuncture) to more unusual therapies like reading one's body aura or getting emotional help from talking to dolphins.

8. *The task of the New Age is to bring peace to planet Earth and achieve harmony between all humans and tribes and nations.* Though the New Age tends to be very individualistic, the major New Age voices have always argued for peace. The "Aquarian Conspiracy" that Marilyn Ferguson describes is not a secret conspiracy of evil New Age manipulators taking control of the world. It is, rather, an open conspiracy of all good people working together to transform the political, educational, and social orders so that we move a step back from the brink of nuclear disaster and create a rich, wonderful planet full of beauty, truth, and goodness.

9. *Morality is relative and Christian and religious absolutes are often harmful.* The New Age takes particular offense at moral and religious absolutism. The power of moral relativism is illustrated by Shirley MacLaine's defense of her affair with a married British politician by saying that they used to be lovers in a previous life. New Age literature constantly criticizes the moral absolutes of Christianity, especially concerning sexuality. Many New Age leaders have defended their sexual practices with followers in terms of a higher wisdom unencumbered by absolutes.

10. *This is a New Age for humanity and incredible transformation immediately awaits our world.* New Agers tend to be incredibly optimistic about the present and future possibilities of the planet, in large part because

so many New Age leaders and groups believe that the spirit world has pointed in various ways to our time as the moment for planetary change for the good. This idea is expressed in widely different terms, depending on which group or leader is speaking, but there is a common theme of transformation that is coming now or very soon.

11. *Eternal Spirit Masters and Teachers have been presenting the New Age message to humanity for thousands of years.* This key idea captures two realities. First, the New Age affirms human need for divine guidance. While there is no unanimity as to who these Masters are, there is agreement that divine instruction is available. Second, the New Age message is actually *not* new, according to New Age thinkers. The Masters and Teachers have given their revelations to previous ages, through various spirit guides and teachers, including Jesus of Nazareth.

12. *An Energy pervades the universe that is beyond the physical that unites all things and provides the source for inner healing, human potential, and planetary change.* Various New Age health practices and most New Age philosophies affirm the reality of a cosmic energy that can be tapped into to achieve divine potential. This energy will be expressed in different terms and will be absorbed through various techniques, depending on the cultural tradition and the specific New Age group.

■ The New Age "Secret"

Have you heard "the secret"? Thanks to Rhonda Byrne, a former Australian television producer, you should have. She is the mastermind behind the runaway best seller *The Secret*.

The title was released in DVD format in March 2006 and then released in a book version in November of the same year. Demand was so great for the book that Simon & Schuster ordered the largest second-printing run in company history. Byrne and other Secret teachers have appeared on *Larry King Live*, *The Oprah Winfrey Show*, *Nightline*, *ABC News*, *Ellen DeGeneres*, and *The Today Show*.

What is the Secret? According to Byrne, it is what is called the Law of Attraction (referred to in Secret circles as LOA)—the idea that all humans attract everything into their lives through the power of thought. The film pictures the universe as one giant cosmic genie who says to each person: "Your wish is my command."

London, UK, bookstore announces The Secret

Photo: Jim Beverley

Byrne states in her book: "There isn't a single thing that you cannot do with this knowledge. It doesn't matter who you are or where you are, The Secret can give you whatever you want."

Jack Canfield, creator of the Chicken Soup for the Soul series, says the Secret is the basis for all his wealth and success. Joe Vitale, a famous marketing expert, pictures the LOA this way: "This is really fun. It's like having the Universe as your catalog. It is you placing your order with the Universe. It's really that easy."

The DVD shows a woman wishing for a necklace, and she suddenly receives it. A boy wishes for a new bike, and it shows up like magic. A man gets the car of his dreams by visualizing it. The book states that getting a million dollars and getting one dollar amount to the same thing.

THE MISSING TEACHER

The first edition of *The Secret* in DVD format contained extensive teachings from Esther Hicks, one of the most famous proponents of the Law of Attraction (LOA). What distinguishes Hicks from other LOA teachers is an explicit link to the spiritual realm, in her case through a collective spirit entity known as "Abraham."

In 2006 Esther and her husband, Jerry, with the guidance of Abraham, parted ways with Rhonda Byrne over contractual disagreements involving property rights. This breakup created significant buzz in the Secret community. The original edition has become somewhat of a collector's item.

The Hickses refuse to give their ages and talk reluctantly about their past. Both come from abusive home environments.

Esther is a native of Utah and is Jerry's fifth wife. They were married in 1980 and took part in New Age channeling in the mid-1980s in Phoenix. Esther claims that Abraham contacted her in 1985, and she began doing Abraham sessions at Christmas the same year. There is little change in Esther's voice when Abraham speaks through her, though he uses the continuous present tense: "We are appreciating your presence."

Some Abraham devotees were upset that Esther and Abraham were cut out of the DVD. The Hickses put a very positive spin on events, including notice of the fact that they made $500,000 in royalties.

However, in one teaching session "Abraham" stated that Esther "suffered a great deal" because of the cancelled agreement and that what Byrne did "was not nice." Hicks told one British journalist that "probably the most victimized I have felt was over the Secret." She is not listed as a Featured Teacher on *The Secret* website, but she is thanked in the preface to the book.

Oprah Winfrey did a radio interview with Hicks and also had an exchange with Abraham on her radio show. Winfrey described the experience of talking to Abraham as "weird," but Hicks's talks with Winfrey and her connection with the Secret has created exponential interest in Abraham's revelations.

> Abraham offers standard New Age views but presents a stunning portrait of Hicks: "That which Jesus Christ was, Esther is now. Not Esther alone. That which Buddha was, Esther is now. That which Muhammad was, Esther is now." The Hickses travel in a luxury bus valued at $1.4 million to provide seminars with Abraham throughout North America. Seminars usually cost $195.

But this is not magic, according to Secret teachers. The Secret is a law, like the law of gravity, created at the beginning of time. Bob Proctor, one of the most famous proponents of the Secret, writes: "Wherever you are—India, Australia, New Zealand, Stockholm, London, Toronto, Montréal, or New York—we're all working with one power. One Law. It's attraction!"

Byrne says she discovered the Secret in late 2004 in the midst of a dark time in her life. "I began tracing The Secret back through history. I couldn't believe all the people who knew this. They were the greatest people in history: Plato, Shakespeare, Newton, Hugo, Beethoven, Lincoln, Emerson, Edison, Einstein."

Critics Speak Out

Who could complain about positive thinking backed by such pedigrees? Actually, *The Secret* has received enormous criticism from both secular and Christian circles.

There are already four anti-Secret books on the marketplace. In one of them, *The Secret Revealed,* James L. Garlow and Rick Marschall suggest that adoption of the philosophy of *The Secret* will lead to the death of American culture. Byrne has also been lampooned on several shows, including *Saturday Night Live* and *Boston Legal.*

On the website Salon.com, Peter Birkenhead wrote a savage attack about Oprah's endorsement: "By continuing to hawk *The Secret,* a mishmash of offensive self-help clichés, Oprah Winfrey is squandering her goodwill and influence, and preaching to the world that mammon is queen."

Maureen Dowd satirized *The Secret* in her column for *The New York Times,* as did Lynn Yaeger in *The Village Voice.* Yaeger wrote: "I am standing half naked in the fitting room at Barneys with a $3,300 Lanvin gold lamé evening dress and a $5,650 pleated Prada frock puddled at my feet and I am smiling for one full minute—harder than it sounds—in an attempt to feel my feelings, which will in turn send out a powerful signal to the universe."

She continues: "I am a human transmission tower, according to Rhonda Byrne, the author of the Oprah-endorsed runaway best seller *The Secret,* and in that capacity I can miraculously transform myself from a woman who buys everything on triple markdown to a happy, high roller whose shopping addiction is funded by the universe itself."

In spite of these criticisms, *The Secret* remains a best seller, and there is no end to testimonials about its transforming powers. More than 1,500 reviewers gave it five of five stars on the amazon.com website.

One delighted reviewer wrote: "I simply cannot say enough about how much this film has affected my life for the better. I bought 100 copies of it and have been sending it to all of my favorite people on the planet. When I watched it, I was jumping up and down and laughing and clapping with joy. It's so simple to understand, and it's presented in such a fun way—it will be the best money you've ever spent."

On *The Secret* forum a significant number of Christians have argued that there is no contradiction between the gospel and *The Secret. Is it possible that critics are overstating their case?* they wonder. *After all, would Rhonda Byrne really be advocating the kind of materialism mocked by Yaeger?*

She seems like a wonderful, sincere, and caring person. And doesn't The Secret *have a tremendous section on gratitude? The Bible promises material rewards to the faithful, doesn't it? Do we not reap what we sow? Did Jesus not tell us to ask and receive? Further, isn't the phenomenal success of* The Secret *proof that it is true?*

The last question is the easiest to answer. *The Secret* is no more proven true for its best-seller status than cigarettes are proven healthy through wide sales.

There is actually no big secret behind Byrne's success. Combine adequate capital with a savvy producer (Byrne once did a show titled *The World's Best Commercials*), top marketers (Vitale and Proctor), famous author (Canfield), and influential spiritual leaders (Esther Hicks and Michael Beckwith); produce a great-looking product (the book is beautiful and the DVD has some amazing cinematography), and the result is sales, sales, and more sales.

Ultimately, how should *The Secret* be viewed? A proper response, Christian and otherwise, must involve legitimate appreciation for everything that is true and beautiful. *The Secret* recognizes the importance of gratitude, something that Oprah noted on one of her shows.

Further, *The Secret* can be praised for its emphasis on being positive and optimistic. This surely matches to some degree the wisdom in Proverbs and the principles in Paul's epistle to the Philippians. Likewise, *The Secret* does capture in part the ways in which we shape our own destinies and program our futures through our thoughts and desires.

The Secret's Dangerous Teachings

I wish that one could stop with these good points. However, the weaknesses in *The Secret* virtually annihilate its merits.

There is no need here to question the intentions of Byrne. She comes across in her publications and interviews as a sincere, warm, and caring person. But her product is largely bogus unless all you want in life is what Steve Salerno, a critic of the self-help movement, calls "a quick jolt of formless inspiration that fades as fast as the winter sun."

Why such a harsh verdict? Beyond the glossy veneer of *The Secret* there are very serious spiritual, physical, and moral dangers, especially from the perspective of the Christian message.

First, various teachings in *The Secret* defy reason and common sense. For example, *The Secret* states that asking the universe for something *not* to happen actually causes it to happen.

"The law of attraction doesn't compute *don't* or *not* or *no*, or any other words of negation," Byrne states. The book argues that not wanting a bad haircut is translated as "I want bad haircuts," and not wanting to catch the flu is the same as saying, "I want the flu, and I want to catch more things."

If this were true, there would be plane crashes every day because of all the passengers who are hoping and praying that the flight they're on doesn't crash. And what about people who pray not to get cancer? Is God (another name for the universe, according to *The Secret*) obligated by the Law of Attraction to give them cancer? If we pray, "Lead us not into temptation," are we really asking for temptation to come our way?

The Secret also has outlandish views on health issues. Here's one: "Food cannot cause you to put on weight unless you *think* it can." How many medical doctors would agree with that statement? And how many would tell their overweight patients to simply "think 'thin thoughts'" to get their weight down?

Regarding age, the book advises: "Aging is limited thinking, so release those thoughts from your consciousness and know that your body is only months old." *The Secret* even states that one can *think* one's way to "the perfect state of health, the perfect body, the perfect weight, and eternal youth."

Even more dangerous, it argues that you cannot catch a disease "unless you think you can." Several doctors have warned that *The Secret* can be fatal if you follow its medical advice.

Second, no amount of rationalization can hide the overt hedonism and materialism, especially in the DVD version of *The Secret*. It is too much about cars, houses, and money, even with the occasional comment about giving to others. Critics have had a field day with the money angles.

Blair Warren notes that *The Secret* DVD supposedly provides *all* the resources needed to understand the Law of Attraction. But wait—there are additional courses you should take with at least one Secret teacher for $3,500. And Canfield and Proctor offer The Science of Getting Rich seminars for $1,995. And Vitale (known as "Mr. Fire" in the marketing world) has a DVD out for $79.97 that supposedly helps a person "truly transcend *The Secret*."

Virtually all twenty-four official Secret teachers offer new products to buy. One Secret teacher will even do private consultations for $700 per hour. It looks as if *The Secret* is not really giving students *all* the resources they need.

Third, *The Secret* moves out of the realm of Christian truth in its adoption of a New Age view of humanity. As one might expect, there is no mention of sin in either the book or the DVD. The word *evil* appears only once in the book.

And humans are granted divinity in the most hyped verbiage. "You are eternal life. You are God manifested in human form, made to perfection. You are God in a physical body. You are all power. You are all wisdom. You are all intelligence. You are perfection. You are magnificence. You are the creator. You are the Supreme Mind." The nature and uniqueness of God is obliterated in *The Secret*, at great cost to the truth about both God and His fallen creatures.

Fourth, what *The Secret* says about life's tragedies is profoundly disturbing. It states that our thoughts, either conscious or unconscious, are the cause for *all* pain and negativity in our lives. Byrne writes: "You cannot be harmed unless you call harm into existence by emitting those negative thoughts and feelings."

Though some Secret teachers such as John Assaraf and Lee Brower are retreating from this fatalistic view, Byrne has reaffirmed her earlier position. Here is what she said in response to a question about the Holocaust: "First, there is no one to blame. Secondly, the law of attraction is absolute; it is impersonal and it is precise and exact."

Bob Beverley, a Christian pastor and psychotherapist, has written about the unrealistic view of *The Secret*: "You can hear the cries of people in the Bible. There is no crying in *The Secret*."

He continues: "If anything like *The Secret* were true, Shakespeare need not have taken the immense trouble to teach us about family strife as in *Hamlet* or jealousy as in *Othello*; he could merely have felt the need for peace in his soul and emitted it to seventeenth-century England. Likewise there would be no need for Churchill's speeches and British sons dying on the shores of Normandy—they all could have magnetically begun to attract peace."

Fifth, Byrne does not picture Jesus as the true Secret, as the real source for joyful and abundant living. Jesus is not even listed as one of the past teachers of the Secret.

The book mentions Jesus just once by name, and what it states about him is mistaken. We are told he was a millionaire who lived a more affluent lifestyle than many present-day millionaires.

Certainly, no one expects a book on car mechanics to focus on Jesus. However, any work or philosophy that deals with human joy and fulfillment, true wealth and life's tragedies that does not have Jesus at its center has missed the boat.

The apostle Paul makes this clear in the second chapter of his letter to the Colossians. He tells us: "I want you woven into a tapestry of love, in touch with everything there is to know of God. Then you will have minds confident and at rest, focused on Christ, God's great mystery.

"All the richest treasures of wisdom and knowledge are embedded in that mystery *and nowhere else*. And we've been shown the mystery! I'm telling you this because I don't want anyone leading you off on some wild-goose chase, after other so-called mysteries, or 'the Secret'" (vv. 2–4, *The Message*, emphasis added).

Resources on *The Secret*

Response Books

- Bob Beverley, Kevin Hogan, Dave Lakhani, and Blair Warren, *The Secret Behind The Secret Law of Attraction* (Network 3000 Publishing, 2007): This multi-authored work offers a tough and wide-ranging response to *The Secret*. It deals with marketing issues, theology, psychotherapy, and the world of self-help. Three of the four authors are experts in persuasion and marketing while Beverley (my twin brother) is a psychotherapist and Christian pastor.

- James L. Garlow and Rick Marschall, *The Secret Revealed* (FaithWords, 2007): This wide-ranging work would be far better if it adopted less sarcasm and ridicule in response to New Age ideas. The authors are properly alarmed at the errors of *The Secret,* but they hurt their case by overkill and by reading Rhonda Byrne and her fellow Secret teachers in their worst light.

- Ed Gungor, *There Is More to The Secret* (Thomas Nelson, 2007): Gungor has written a winsome and optimistic critique, but this work suffers somewhat by its argument that the Law of Attraction is true. Further, by putting a Christian spin on the Law of Attraction, Gungor tends to understate the vast gulf between the Secret and the gospel.

- James K. Walker and Bob Waldrep, *The Truth Behind The Secret* (Harvest House, 2007): This is the best of the explicitly Christian replies now available. The authors provide both comprehensive background and critique to *The Secret*. They have good material on whether quantum physics proves the Secret (it does not). They also have helpful data on various Secret teachers and traditions, though they overstate the link to Christian Science.

Other Book Resources

Steve Salerno, *Sham: How the Self-Help Movement Made America Helpless* (Crown, 2005)

Internet Sources

thesecretlie.com

thetruthisthesecret.com

Steve Salerno blog: shambook.blogspot.com/

■ New Age Groups

Arcane School

The Arcane School is one of the many New Age groups that emerged in the twentieth century. It was founded by Alice Bailey (1880–1949) and her husband Foster and is one of the most important schools to emerge out of the larger Theosophical tradition. Within fifty years of its founding by Helena Petrova Blavatsky (1831–91) in 1875, Theosophy became one of the most dominant aspects of Western esotericism.

Alice was born in Manchester, England on June 16, 1880. She moved to India in 1899 where she worked at the YWCA and was married in 1907 to Walter Evans, her first husband. They moved to Cincinnati where Walter studied for the Episcopal priesthood at Lane Theological Seminary. The couple separated in 1915 after moving to California. Alice first heard about Theosophy from friends in Pacific Grove, California. She became editor of *The Messenger*, the journal of the Theosophy society, in 1917. Two years later she met Foster Bailey, the society's national secretary.

In November 1919 Alice claimed to have received channeled messages from a spiritual being known as Djwhal Khul or "The Tibetan." This claim created enormous controversy among Theosophists who believed that Blavatsky was the final channel. Foster sided with Alice, and they were forced to leave the movement. They moved to New York and married in 1921. They formed the Lucis Trust to publish Alice's revelations and also started the Arcane School. Alice died in 1949; Foster led the School till his own death in 1977.

In addition to her alleged contacts with Djwhal Khul, Alice Bailey claimed that she had a supernatural encounter as a teenager with another

Spirit Master. She thought it was Jesus Christ but later learned that it was Koot Hoomi, one of the members of the Great White Brotherhood who had first appeared to Madame Blavatsky. Bailey's writings were often rooted in her continuing contact with "The Tibetan" from 1919 until her death.

The Arcane School flourished at a time when Theosophists had been hurt by the failure of the famous mystic Krishnamurti (1895–1986) to accept his role as the Maitreya or modern Messiah. Alice Bailey spent considerable time on the message that Christ would reappear, not as Jesus Christ or as Krishnamurti, but as a Cosmic Spirit who has always dwelt with any in all religions who pursue love. Bailey wrote: "If people look for the Christ Who left His disciples centuries ago, they will fail to recognize the Christ Who is in process of returning. His advance guard is already here and the Plan which they must follow is already made and clear. Let recognition be the aim."

Bailey is most famous for her transmission of "The Great Invocation," probably the most influential prayer in New Age circles. The prayer went through three versions, and the most popular dates from 1945. It reads:

> From the point of Light within the mind of God
> Let light stream forth into the minds of men.
> Let Light descend on Earth.

> From the point of Love within the Heart of God
> Let love stream forth into the hearts of men.
> May Christ return to Earth.

> From the Centre where the Will of God is known
> Let purpose guide the little wills of men—
> The purpose which the Masters know and serve.

> From the Centre which we call the race of men
> Let the Plan of Love and Light work out
> And may it seal the door where evil dwells.

> Let Light and Love and Power restore the Plan on Earth.

ARCANE SCHOOL

Typology	Western Esoteric
Major Figure	Alice Bailey (1880–1949)
Main Website	www.lucistrust.org

Church Universal and Triumphant

The Church Universal and Triumphant, or CUT, is one of the best-known New Age groups. Originally named Summit Lighthouse, CUT was founded by Mark Prophet in 1958. The church has its roots in the Theosophical tradition (Madame Blavatsky) and its offshoot I AM, founded by Guy and Edna Ballard. Prophet was born in 1918 in Wisconsin and claimed to have been contacted in his teens by the Ascended Master El Morya. He stated that he rejected the supernatural visitor's message until the early 1950s.

In 1961 Mark met Elizabeth Clare Wulf, a former Christian Scientist, and they were married in 1963, after Mark's divorce from his first wife. The new couple moved their headquarters to Colorado. Mark died in 1973. Elizabeth, a native of New Jersey, took over leadership of Summit Lighthouse.

Both Mark and Elizabeth Prophet taught that they were restoring the lost teachings of Jesus, and they argued that Jesus traveled in India and Tibet before beginning his public ministry. Elizabeth taught that she was Catherine of Siena in a previous life, while her husband taught that he had previously existed as the third-century Christian theologian Origen and as Mark the Evangelist, companion to the apostle Peter.

Summit Lighthouse was renamed the Church Universal and Triumphant in 1974 on the basis of an alleged revelation from Pope John XXIII through Mrs. Prophet. At the time, headquarters was near Santa Barbara, California, though later the church moved to Malibu (at a site known as Camelot) and then to Montana in 1986. The church had previously purchased the former ranch of Malcolm Forbes near Yellowstone Park.

After the move to Montana, Mrs. Prophet's messages became increasingly apocalyptic and stressed a survivalist mentality. The church was mocked for its building of bomb shelters, and critics complained that the movement was stockpiling weapons. Members were encouraged to have supplies that could last for seven years and were given the opportunity to purchase in bulk from the church.

Through the 1980s, Mrs. Prophet taught members that a major catastrophe could possibly occur at some point prior to March 15, 1990. She even observed that the national March obsession with college basketball finals gave America's enemies an opportunity to strike. Cheri Walsh, a former member, writes: "I was on the night shift in the bomb shelter. I was glad because if anything happened it would probably be in the middle of the night and I would already be there." The group spent enormous sums preparing shelters that would survive a nuclear apocalypse. Church membership declined through the 1990s following several major organizational changes and the decline of Mrs. Prophet's health.

In 1999 Mrs. Prophet stepped down from church leadership after being diagnosed with Alzheimer's disease. After her first husband's death, she remarried three times. She has five children—Sean, Erin, Moira, Tatiana (all adults), and Seth, who was born in 1994. All of the adult children left the movement, experienced periods of hostility to the church and their mother, and later achieved some reconciliation with her. Sean Prophet has adopted an atheistic worldview but defends his mother against charges that she was insincere in her beliefs.

CHURCH UNIVERSAL AND TRIUMPHANT	
Typology	Western Esoteric
Founders	Mark and Elizabeth Prophet
Home Website	www.tsl.org
Critic Sites	www.lifeincut.com www.blacksunjournal.com (Sean Prophet)
Recommended Reading	Erin Prophet, *Prophet's Daughter* (Guilford: Lyons Press, 2009) Bradley C. Whitsel, *The Church Universal and Triumphant* (Syracuse: Syracuse University Press, 2003)

A Course in Miracles

A Course in Miracles (ACIM), one of the most popular texts in the New Age movement, has found its way into a few mainline Christian denominations. The story of its origin has been complicated by stormy litigation surrounding copyright battles over the three-volume work. The standard story is that ACIM is a product of channeling from Jesus to a woman named Helen Schucman. The Jesus of ACIM conforms to standard New Thought teaching, with no emphasis upon Jesus as the unique Son of God.

Schucman, a secular atheist, became associate professor of medical psychology at the Columbia-Presbyterian Medical Center in New York City in 1958. In the summer of 1965 she reported dramatic dreams in which she heard from a Voice. In October of that year the Voice told her: "This is a course in miracles; please take notes." With the help of William Thetford, her boss, she began channeling almost fifteen hundred pages of material. The process lasted until September 1972 and resulted in *A Course in Miracles.* Schucman died in 1981, followed by Thetford seven years later.

In 1973 the ACIM was edited by Ken Wapnick, who had become friends with Helen and Bill. In 1975 the text was shown to Judy Skutch, president of the Foundation for Parasensory Investigation. Skutch changed her organization to the Foundation for Inner Peace (FIP) that same year and registered the copyright of ACIM under "Anonymous (Helen Schucman)." In these formative years it was regularly claimed that Jesus was the ultimate source of ACIM. In fact, Wapnick stated at one point, "It was very clear to me that Helen could not have written it and I just could not imagine it having any other source than Jesus himself."

In 1995 the Foundation for Inner Peace reached an agreement with Penguin Books to allow the publisher to hold copyright for ACIM. The next year the New Christian Church of Full Endeavor was sued for distributing ACIM on its own. That began a lengthy legal battle and period of turmoil among the groups (including Robert Perry's Circle of Atonement) that use the text as a source of truth. Litigation continued until April 2004, when the court ruled that *A Course in Miracles* could not be copyrighted. That decision rose largely because the earliest versions of ACIM were not distributed with copyright notice.

The fame of *A Course in Miracles* has been extended through the writings and teaching of famous New Thought teacher Marianne Williamson. She rose to fame with her 1992 book *A Return to Love* and her appearances on *The Oprah Winfrey Show.* She was for several years the spiritual leader of Renaissance Unity Spiritual Fellowship, based in Warren, Michigan. Born in Houston in 1952 and raised Jewish, Williamson turned toward Unity's esoteric Christian vision in 1977.

Williamson has been a professional speaker since 1983 and the founder of Project Angel Food. She is also president of the Global Renaissance Alliance, a worldwide network of peace activists. She works with figures such as Deepak Chopra, Barbara Marx Hubbard, and Neale Donald Walsch. She has a political and civic emphasis in her teaching, as in her book *A Healing for America*.

ACIM is also a central element in the teaching of Jon Mundy, a former Methodist pastor and co-founder of Interfaith Fellowship in New York City.

A COURSE IN MIRACLES	
Typology	Western Esoteric
Websites	Foundation for Inner Peace (Judith Skutch Whitson): www.acim.org Foundation for *A Course in Miracles* (Ken Wapnick): www.facim.org Marianne Williamson: www.marianne.com, www.renaissancealliance.org Course in Miracles Society: www.jcim.net Northwest Foundation for "A Course in Miracles" (Paul Tuttle): www.nwffacim.org New Christian Church of Full Endeavor: www.newchristianchurch.com Circle of Atonement (Robert Perry): www.circleofa.com Jon Mundy: www.miraclesmagazine.org
Recommended Reading	D. Patrick Miller, *The Complete Story of the Course* (Fearless Books, 1997)

Freemasonry

Freemasonry is included in this book for four reasons. First, there are elements of a religious nature in the ethos and rites of the Masonic Lodge. Second, there are Masons, historically and in the present, who view Masonry as a religious movement. Third, Freemasonry has exercised an enormous influence on Western esoteric religious life. Lastly, nasty charges against Masonry are so pervasive that they impact study and proper understanding of the Lodge and other esoteric movements.

Freemasonry is a fraternal order known for its secret rituals and the use of secret signs. The origins of Freemasonry are usually traced by scholars to the founding of the Grand Lodge in London on June 24, 1717. There is historic evidence of Masonic ritual in Scotland in the preceding century. Most Masons follow the York Rite though the Scottish Rite, with its 33 degrees, is the subject of more speculation.

Should Christians join the Masonic Lodge? Is Christian faith compatible with Masonry? These questions have generated enormous controversy since the earliest days of freemasonry. Roman Catholic popes have condemned Masonry and many Protestant denominations forbid membership in the Lodge. The Southern Baptist Convention had a major debate over Masonry in the mid-1990s, with political and verbal assaults on all sides.

The war over Masonry stems in part from the extreme charges laid against the Lodge. Both Christian and secular writers argue that Masons exercise enormous international power for evil purposes. In his book *The New World Order*, Pat Robertson, the host of *The 700 Club*, targeted the Lodge as a part of the emerging global conspiracy against the gospel. Stephen Knight, a British journalist, created a storm on the secular front with *The Brotherhood*, his political exposé of Masonry. His untimely death after the book's publication led to charges that he was murdered under orders from the Lodge.

According to various critics, Masonry is racist, pagan, occultic, and demonic. It is argued that top Masons (like Albert Pike) admit that Lucifer is the god of the Lodge. Further, Masons are said to kill to protect their secret and bloody rituals, and their ideology is said to denigrate the Bible, Jesus, and God. Critics argue that Masons worship the figure Hiram, said to be a stone mason from the days of Solomon. It is also charged that Masons turn a blind eye to criminal acts done by fellow members and that average Masons are the victims of cultic mind control.

Jim Shaw and Tom McKenney contend in *The Deadly Deception* that key Masonic symbols are sexual in nature and represent a revival of pagan mystery religion. Texe Marrs includes the Masons in the schemes of the Antichrist to establish One World Order. William Schnoebelen, who claims to be an ex-Satanist, ex-Mormon, and ex-Mason, argues that Masons are involved in many of the fifty thousand ritual murders that take place every year in North America. Ed Decker, a famous cult expert, states in *What You Need to Know About Masons* that Lodge members infiltrate libraries across the United States to steal anti-Masonic books and "sensitive" Masonic documents.

What is one to make of such incredible accusations? First, they must be examined carefully, especially since they represent popular sentiment against Masonry. Second, they must be assessed individually since some might be true while others are half-true or totally false. If these charges are largely true, the Masonic order represents an evil empire that defies comprehension. If largely untrue, many Masons will properly resent much of the "Christian" witness about the Lodge.

Masonic temple, London, England

Photo: Jim Beverley

In addition to the extremely negative view of Masonry, there are two other general assessments. There are those who argue that Masonry, while not the evil force suggested above, is essentially religious in nature and is not compatible with Christianity since it teaches a deistic version of God, gives only lip service to biblical truth and the Lordship of Christ, and advocates secrecy involving bloody oaths. The false accusations about Satanism and overt evil hurt effective witness to Masons about the gospel. This view is defended by Steven Tsoukalas, one of the most informed researchers in primary Masonic writings.

There is also the view that Masonry is not a religion. For most Masons, the Lodge is simply a fraternal order of males. Masons must believe in God but no specific designation or description of God is allowed simply because the Lodge is a place where all religions can be represented. Nothing in Masonry forces a Christian to deny any essential gospel claims, whether the supremacy of Christ or salvation by grace alone. The wild and extreme claims about the Lodge are a result of bigotry and lies. This perspective is defended by Wallace McLeod, a former classics professor, and one of the world's leading Masonic historians.

What does the evidence suggest as the best reaction to Masonry? First, the wildest accusations against the Lodge are largely a result of fabrication and poor research on the part of careless and extreme critics. For example, the charge that Albert Pike, a leading nineteenth-century Masonic scholar, advocated the worship of Lucifer is untrue. The hoax against Pike was started by Leo Taxil, a pen name for Gabriel Antoine Jogand-Pages, an anti-Masonic writer who invented a quote from Pike to incite a vendetta against the Lodge.

While Masons are to care for fellow members, their oaths forbid them to break the law or harbor any criminal. Accusations about Masonic murders are strong in only one case, a famous one involving ex-Mason William Morgan. This New York resident was killed in 1826, probably at the hands of a few zealous Masons who were enraged by his exposé of the secret rituals of Masonry. Kenneth Lanning, the FBI's expert on Satanic ritual theories, has argued persuasively that there is no hard evidence to support the wild but popular theory that an alleged evil group (like Satanists or Masons) are on a killing spree involving fifty thousand ritual murders per year in North America alone. That is more than twice the total of all other kinds of homicide for the entire continent.

Do Masons steal anti-Masonic books from libraries? Ed Decker says so but provides no objective evidence. Ron Carlson, another cult watcher, charges that Masons take Albert Pike's pro-Masonic work *Morals and Dogma* out of libraries because of Pike's alleged occultic and demonic views. Masonic scholars Arturo de Hoyos and Brent Morris replied to this accusation with a long list of libraries where Pike's work is available, including libraries in Carlson's home state. De Hoyos and Morris also provide extensive refutation of many of the other extreme charges against Masonry.

The charge that Masonry has some occult connections and is a revival of ancient mystery religion has some truth to it. As Tsoukalas shows in *Masonic Rites and Wrongs*, Albert Pike recast many Masonic rituals by drawing parallels with what he knew of ancient Egyptian religion. Today, most Masons have little regard for Pike's mystical and mythical musings. Likewise, while key occult figures like Helena Blavatsky and Aleister Crowley have used Masonic ritual, the vast majority of Masons have no interest in esoteric occult paths.

Are all concerns about Masonry unjustified? No, there remain some substantial issues to address in the remaining divide represented by Tsoukalas and McLeod. Of paramount concern is the fact that some Masonic rituals can be easily interpreted as offering a religious path to light, truth, and heaven. This seems evident, for example, in the readings given in Lodge funeral services. It is also important to note that some Masons have argued that Masonry is a religion, though this is an older view and has never been the self-understanding of Masons as a whole.

Masonic writings about explicit Christian themes often leave a lot to be desired. This valid concern is not about the popular false accusation that Masons worship Baal or that Masons intend to discredit the gospel. While there is some very careless teaching about God in Scottish Rite ritual (in the 25th through 27th degrees, for example), most Masons belong to the Blue Lodge. The crucial issue here is that some leading Masonic writers, including Pike, have often undermined a Christian understanding of God and Jesus Christ by overt sympathies to all religions and by misapplication of biblical texts. While a generic view of God opens the Lodge to all faiths, it can easily create the impression that Masons believe that all roads lead to heaven.

Finally, there is the famous issue of secret and bloody oaths. In fairness, as McLeod points out, there are no secrets in Masonry anymore. In fact, the rituals were made public as early as 1730 in Samuel Prichard's *Masonry Dissected*. While Masons do not take the oaths literally, even a symbolic reading of them has little merit. Thankfully, Masons have taken steps in recent years to downplay the significance of the oaths and to remove them from Masonic ceremonies.

The history of Masonry reflects something of the deeper currents in changing religious ideology. The earliest Masonic writings manifest a more explicit Christian focus. Then, through the last century an unhealthy preoccupation with pluralism led some Masons to downplay Christian interpretation of Masonic rites. With the rise of secularism in this century, and with a greater sensibility to specific religious claims, most Masons are now very insistent that the Lodge is not a church of any sort. However, the burden of a divided history, one that contains both overt Christian claims alongside a relativistic picture of God, continues to make the question of Masonry a complicated one.

After considerable debate the Southern Baptist Convention decided to make Masonic Lodge involvement a matter of personal Christian conviction. That view deserves respect only when and where it is clear that Masons believe that their practices are not religious in nature. This can be accepted more readily of the three degrees of the Blue Lodge than of the thirty-three degrees in Scottish Rite Masonry. Tsoukalas argues persuasively that Scottish Rite teachings are often in obvious conflict with the Bible's teaching. Masons have to avoid the plain meaning of words to harmonize the two.

In the end, legitimate Christian response to the Masonic Lodge must involve three clear indictments. First, every Christian should be alarmed and ashamed at the false and outrageous charges against Masonry that are spread widely in Christian circles as a result of paranoid and careless research. Second, Christians have every right to complain about explicit teachings in Scottish Rite Masonry that are incompatible with the gospel. In this regard, leading Masonic scholars would do well to interact with the case laid out by Tsoukalas on these matters. Third, Masons of any sort who look to Masonry as a religion and consequently ignore the gospel cannot receive the endorsement of the Christian church.

FREEMASONRY	
Official Sites	Grand Lodge of London: www.grandlodge-england.org Masonic Quarterly magazine: www.mqmagazine.co.uk Library and Museum: http://freemasonry.london.museum
Other Important Websites	Quatuor Coronati Lodge No. 2076: www.quatuorcoronati. com Canonbury Masonic Research Cent: www.canonbury.ac.uk Centre for Research into Freemasonry: www.shef.ac.uk/~crf Masonic Info: www.masonicinfo.com
Recommended Reading	Arturo de Hoyos and S. Brent Morris, *Is It True What They Say About Freemasonry?* (Silver Spring: Masonic Information Center, 1997) Gary Leazer, *Fundamentalism & Freemasonry* (New York: M. Evans and Company, 1995) David Stevenson, *The Origins of Freemasonry: Scotland's Century, 1590-1710* (Cambridge University Press: 1990) Steve Tsoukalas, *Masonic Rites and Wrongs* (Presbyterian & Reformed Publishing, 1995)

Heaven's Gate

Heaven's Gate represents one of the more tragic episodes in modern religion: the faith-motivated suicide of twenty-one women and eighteen men whose bodies were discovered on March 26, 1997, in a house in San Diego, California. Members of the California-based UFO group, led by Marshall Herff Applewhite, believed that suicide was simply about leaving behind the body ("container"), after which the soul would go to sleep until "replanted" in another "container." Eventually the soul would be "grafted" onto a being at the "level above human" on board a UFO spaceship. The timing of these suicides was triggered in part by the appearance of the Hale-Bopp comet.

Applewhite was among the thirty-nine Heaven's Gate followers who took their own lives. They ingested applesauce or pudding mixed with drugs and then suffocated themselves with plastic bags. The victims ranged in age from mid-20s to 72. When their bodies were discovered, they were all dressed in unisex clothing and wearing Nike shoes. Some of the men were castrated—an indicator of the anti-body ideology of the group. The website of the group still announces, "Red Alert: Hale-Bopp Brings Closure to Heaven's Gate." Rio DiAngelo, a lone survivor who later killed himself, told the Associated Press in 2002: "What I've gained from this group is phenomenal. If he [Applewhite] is just a gay music teacher from Texas, how he could teach all these advanced ways of being that really work?"

Heaven's Gate was the creation of Applewhite and Bonnie Lu Nettles. The two started their apocalyptic group in 1975 in Houston, Texas, under the name Total Overcomers Anonymous. They had some public exposure in the early years but remained a small sect on the fringe of society. Nettles died in 1985 from cancer, and Applewhite continued to lead the few who had adopted his message. Applewhite originally went by the nickname Bo and later was called Do (pronounced "Doe"). She was known first as Peep, then as Ti.

Applewhite was born into a traditional Christian family, studied at Union Theological Seminary, and then pursued a career in music and the performing arts. Nettles studied in the metaphysical tradition, had connections with Theosophy, and participated in channeling. When with Nettles, Applewhite experienced visions and paranormal events that the two claimed included contact with space beings. Members viewed the two of them as "the Two"—a reference to the two prophets mentioned in Revelation 11. The group also viewed some biblical events as accounts of visits from UFOs.

The group believed that Jesus was a "Representative" sent by the beings of the kingdom level above human to teach about entrance into the kingdom of God. Humans who were inspired by demons killed "the Captain" (another term for Jesus), and his teachings were changed into "watered-down Country Club Religion." Applewhite and Nettles claimed to represent a new chance for humanity to hear what Jesus had taught two thousand years ago. Applewhite stated, "The same grace that was available at the end of the Representative's mission 2,000 years ago is available now with our presence. If you quickly choose to take these steps toward separating from the world, and look to us for help, you will see our Father's Kingdom."

HEAVEN'S GATE

Typology	Western Esoteric UFO Religion
Founders	Marshall Applewhite and Bonnie Lu Nettles
Homepage	www.heavensgate.com
Recommended Reading	Wendy Gale Robinson, "Heaven's Gate: The End?" *Journal of Computer Mediated Communication*: http://jcmc.indiana.edu/vol3/issue3/robinson.html

MSIA: Movement of Spiritual Inner Awareness

John-Roger Hinkins, a former Mormon, founded the Church of the Movement of Spiritual Inner Awareness (MSIA) in 1968, legally in 1971. He was born Roger Hinkins on September 24, 1934, in Utah. He claims to have been visited by two trance-channelers when he had a near-death experience in 1963. Newly aware of his "spiritual personality" named John, he created the name John-Roger "in recognition of his transformed self." John-Roger (often referred to as J-R) devoted himself to writing and teaching full time, first devising a series of six seminars and eventually developing the *Soul Awareness Discourses*, a series of 144 monthly lessons designed to be completed in a twelve-year study. John-Roger has written some fifty books, including *Spiritual Warrior* and *When Are You Coming Home?*

MSIA teaches that John-Roger was the "Mystical Traveler" from 1963 through 1988. The Mystical Traveler holds, or "anchors," the Traveler Consciousness on the planet at a particular time. In 1988 the mantle passed to John Morton, the spiritual director of MSIA who has studied with John-Roger since 1975. They describe the Mystical Traveler Consciousness as a "way show-er into the higher, spiritual levels." MSIA teaches that Jesus was human and a Mystical Traveler, according him an elevated status they describe as "similar to being President of Earth." According to the group, "the Christ Consciousness is the spiritual line of energy undergirding MSIA."

Controversy has surrounded MSIA. At one time it was accused of basically being a duplication of Eckankar. MSIA leaders dismissed parallels with that movement as arising from shared truth rather than as being intentional and unacknowledged borrowing. MSIA was the focus of intense media scrutiny in 1994 when Michael Huffington was running for the U.S. Senate. *Time* magazine referenced the involvement of his wife, well-known journalist Arianna Huffington, with MSIA and noted that the American Family Foundation, a cult-watching group, had labeled the group as "destructive." John-Roger co-authored the *New York Times* best seller *Life 101*, published in 1991, with his follower Peter McWilliams. After McWilliams left the group, he wrote a bitter memoir called *Life 102: What to Do When Your Guru Sues You* (Los Angeles: Prelude Press, 1994). McWilliams died of cancer in 2000 but reached reconciliation with the movement before his death.

MSIA leaders John-Roger (foreground) and John Morton

Photo: David Sand

MSIA AFFIRMATION ON JESUS

Jesus Christ is the head of the Church of the Movement of Spiritual Inner Awareness, and the Traveler's work through MSIA (Soul Transcendence) is based on Jesus' work. Jesus was a Mystical Traveler, and he made it possible for all people to enter the Soul realm; before that time, this was available to only a few people. John-Roger's and John Morton's work of Soul Transcendence builds upon Jesus' work and makes it possible for people to go above (transcend) the Soul realm, into the heart of God.

MSIA describes its purpose as "to teach Soul Transcendence, which is becoming aware of yourself as a Soul and as one with God, not as a theory but as a living reality. Your Soul is the highest aspect of yourself, where you and God are one. MSIA provides a variety of tools and techniques that allow you to experience your Soul and, therefore, your own Divinity." MSIA incorporates elements of Sant Mat, Christianity, Buddhism, and Taoism.

Followers are encouraged to release themselves from earthly attachments. The soul has been trapped in "the material world" that is suffering, and everyone is doomed "to continue a cycle of death, rebirth and reincarnation." They refer to their practices as "spiritual exercises." These involve meditation, controlled breathing, and sacred chants for gaining greater health, achieving mental clarity, and increasing energy.

MSIA	
Typology	Western Esoteric
Founder	John-Roger (born Roger Hinkins)
Current Leader	John Morton
Homepages	www.msia.org www.john-roger.org www.ndh.org
Recommended Reading	James R. Lewis, *Seeking the Light* (Los Angeles: Mandeville Press, 1998) Diana G. Tumminia, "Heart and Soul," in James R. Lewis & Jesper Aagaard Petersen, eds. *Controversial New Religions* (New York: Oxford, 2005)

New Thought

New Thought refers to the metaphysical tradition associated with Phineas Parkhurst Quimby (1802–66) and his ideological heirs. Quimby is one of the original figures in the theory of "mind over matter." He was influenced by mesmerism and hypnotism. He opened an office in Portland, Maine, in 1859. Though he started no church, Franz Anton Mesmer had an impact, either directly or indirectly, on famous religious leaders such as Warren Felt Evans (1817–89); Julius Dresser (1838–93); Horatio Dresser (1866–1954); Mary Baker Eddy, the founder of Christian Science (1821–1910); Emma Curtis Hopkins (1853–1925); Charles and Myrtle

Fillmore, the founders of the Unity School of Christianity; and Ernest Holmes, the founder of Religious Science (1877–1960).

There has been considerable debate over Mary Baker Eddy's debt to Quimby in her works, including *Science and Health with Key to the Scriptures*, published in 1875. In the 1890s Julius Dresser and his wife accused Eddy of stealing Quimby's basic ideas. It is fair to say that Mrs. Eddy downplayed her debt to Quimby and that she also departed from his theology and healing in a number of significant ways.

Emma Curtis Hopkins is often called the founder of New Thought. She was born in Connecticut in 1849 (and not in 1853, as usually stated). She was one of the early students of Mary Baker Eddy and became editor of the *Christian Science Journal* in 1884. After a falling out with Mrs. Eddy, Hopkins moved to Chicago and started her own work. Her last years were spent in New York City. She is often praised for the prominent role that women played in her ministry and teaching.

NEW THOUGHT AFFIRMATIONS

- We affirm the inseparable oneness of God and humankind, the realization of which comes through spiritual intuition, the implications of which are that we can reproduce the Divine perfection in our bodies, emotions and all our external affairs.

- We affirm the freedom of each person in matters of belief.

- We affirm the Good to be supreme, universal and eternal.

- We affirm that the kingdom of God is within us, that we are one with the Father, that we should love one another and return good for evil.

- We affirm that we should heal the sick through prayer and that we should endeavor to manifest perfection "even as our Father in heaven is perfect."

- We affirm our belief in God as the Universal Wisdom, Love, Life, Truth, Power, Peace, Beauty and Joy, "In whom we live and move and have our being."

- We affirm that our mental states are carried forward into manifestation and become our experience through the Creative Law of Cause and Effect.

- We affirm that the Divine Nature expressing Itself through us manifests Itself as health, supply, wisdom, love, life, truth, power, peace, beauty and joy.

- We affirm that we are invisible spiritual dwellers within human bodies continuing and unfolding as spiritual beings beyond the change called physical death.

- We affirm that the universe is the body of God, spiritual in essence, governed by God through laws which are spiritual in reality even when material in appearance.

The best-known contemporary groups associated with New Thought are the International Divine Science Association, the Unity School of Christianity, Religious Science International, the United Church of Religious Science, and Seicho-No-Ie, a Japanese movement started in 1930 by Masaharu Taniguchi. Of these groups, the Unity School is the largest, founded by Charles and Myrtle Fillmore.

Charles Fillmore was born in Minnesota on August 22, 1854. In 1876 he moved to Texas and met his future wife Mary Myrtle Page, a teacher, who was born in 1845 in Ohio. Charles and Myrtle were married in 1881 and moved to Kansas City, Missouri, in 1884. In 1886 Myrtle was influenced by the teaching of E. B. Weeks, a follower of Emma Curtis Hopkins. Myrtle came away from the meetings with Weeks with an affirmation: "I am a child of God and therefore I do not inherit sickness." Over the next two years Myrtle achieved a new level of healing from a constant threat of tuberculosis.

Charles became convinced of the New Thought healing paradigm after he heard Hopkins in Chicago. He and Myrtle started the magazine *Modern Thought* in 1889 (later renamed *Unity Magazine*), and the Unity Society of Practical Christianity was incorporated in 1903. Charles wrote *Christian Healing* in 1909 and started radio broadcasts in 1922. Myrtle, called the "Mother of Unity," died in 1931. Two years later Charles married Cora Dedrick and also wrote *The Metaphysical Bible Dictionary*. Charles retired that same year but continued to travel and teach until shortly before his death in 1948.

NEW THOUGHT

Typology	Western Esoteric
Founder	Emma Curtis Hopkins
Websites	New Thought Alliance: http://newthoughtalliance.org New Thought Movement Homepage: http://websyte.com/alan/#7 Unity School of Christianity (Charles and Myrtle Fillmore): www.unityworldhq.org United Church of Religious Science (Ernest Holmes): www.religiousscience.org Seicho-No-Ie (Masaharu Taniguchi): www.snitruth.org Quimby website: www.ppquimby.com
Recommended Reading	Gail Harley, *Emma Curtis Hopkins* (Syracuse University Press, 2002) Neal Vahle, *The Unity Movement* (Philadelphia: Temple Foundation Press, 2002)

Nuwaubian Nation

This esoteric group, based most recently in Eatonton, Georgia, is the creation of Dwight York, who goes by several other names including Malachi Z. York. The movement has been subject to intense scrutiny since the arrest of York in 2002 on child-sex charges. He pleaded guilty to over seventy sex charges on January 24, 2003. However, he petitioned the court on June 30, 2003, for abandonment of this plea. In late 2004 the courts refused a new trial and York was sentenced to 135 years in prison. He is imprisoned in a super-maximum security facility in Florence, Colorado, the same site that holds Terry Nichols, Zacarias Moussaoui and Theodore (Ted) Kaczynski.

Two hundred FBI agents and eighty sheriff's deputies raided Nuwaubian headquarters on May 8, 2002, and took York and his "main wife," Kathy Johnson, into custody. Their arrests culminated a four-year investigation into allegations of sexual abuse against children. Johnson pleaded guilty in April 2000 to knowing a felony was taking place and doing nothing.

York started a mission known as Ansaar Pure Sufi in 1967 in Brooklyn, New York, and he referred to himself as Imaam Isa. The group later identified themselves as Nubians and then took the title of Nubian Islamic Hebrews. Orthodox Muslims viewed the group and its leader as heretical, but York accused Muslims of mistranslation of the Qur'an.

In 1993 the group purchased over four hundred acres near Eaton-ton, Georgia. York referred to the state as the "Mecca of Nubians"; and they developed an Egyptian theme on the property, including the building of small pyramids. Ex-members state that York lived in splendor while they endured cramped and squalid housing.

While in Georgia, York continued to claim that they were a Sufi group but also said that they were the Ancient Mystic Order of Melchizedek. York is also known as Nayya Malachizodok El and Chief Black Eagle. He speaks confidently of the power of his writings to his followers: "You can't be fooled by any religious doctrines of any kind. No, not now a days! You have your first tool, this Holy Tablet, not someone else's interpretation. Your own scripture that will dispel all the lies causing all falsehood to perish. Making the truth come to light."

Nuwaubians believe that they are descended from Egyptians who walked to America before the continents divided and that they are the true Native Americans. The group also teaches that blacks are the superior race. York's followers also claim that he is from another planet and that he is the incarnation of God.

One unofficial Nuwaubian website gives elaborate details about extra-terrestrials that now live on planet Earth. One species is said to be the Deros, a group of obese cave dwellers with low intelligence, led by Yaba-haan. The Deros have elephant-like noses and are hatched from eggs that are four to six feet in diameter. The site claims that some obese humans are descended from the Deros.

Before York's arrest in 2002, Nuwaubians came into frequent conflict with local officials for building permit and zoning violations. The sect accused county officials of racism, and both Jesse Jackson and Al Sharpton visited the group to support their concerns. Some had speculated that York's daughter Hagar York-El might lead the group.

In spite of York's incarceration he retains a devoted cadre of believers who proclaim his innocence.

NUWAUBIAN NATION	
Typology	Western Esoteric
Founder	Malachi Z. York
Main Websites	www.nuwaubiaholylandofthenuwaubians.com www.geocities.com/Area51/Corridor/4978
Recommended Reading	Bill Osinski, *Ungodly* (Indigo, 2007)

Raelians

The Raelian movment is a modern-day esoteric UFO religion, led by a Frenchman named Rael. Raelians received enormous worldwide attention when they announced that the first cloned baby was born on December 26, 2002. The subsequent media hunt for "Clone Baby Eve" (with DNA proof to be provided) waned in January 2003 after a whirlwind of political protest and legal threats.

The Raelian movement traces its origin to December 13, 1973, when Rael (Claude Vorilhon) claims that he was contacted by an extraterrestrial named Yahweh Elohim. Vorilhon, then a French journalist, describes Elohim as about four feet tall, with long dark hair, almond-shaped eyes, and olive skin. He is said to have told Rael: "We were the ones who made all life on earth, you mistook us for gods, we were at the origin of your main religions. Now that you are mature enough to understand this, we would like to enter official contact through an embassy." The alien creature is said to have emerged from a UFO near Clermont-Ferrand in central France.

Raelians believe that humans are not created by God or random evolution but by a team of super-scientists who used DNA to create humans in their image. Humanity's fall is related to forbidden scientific knowledge being passed on to some early humans. Rael's mission is to provide the true message to the world and create an embassy in Jerusalem that can serve as a landing base for the extraterrestrials. Rael first advanced his message through an organization known as MADECH, founded in 1974.

Rael claims that the extraterrestrials took him to their planet on October 7, 1975. He states that he had sexual encounters with six female robots while he was there and that he was also introduced to cloning. The movement developed a Clonaid Program, directed by Brigitte Boisselier, and believes that human cloning represents the path to gaining eternal life.

Raelians promote UFO message

Photo: Jonathan Tobin

According to Rael, who believes he is the Messiah, the space creatures also taught the same message to Moses, Buddha, Muhammad, and Jesus. However, that revelation got scrambled and distorted through history. For example, Jews and Christians believe that Elohim is one of the names of God in Genesis when actually it should be translated "those who came from the sky"—a clear reference to the UFO aliens.

The group's scientific pursuits on cloning have been taken very seriously. Cloneaid CEO Brigitte Boisselier has a double doctorate in chemistry and worked for twelve years in a respected French chemical firm before moving to Quebec to work with Rael. Boisselier announced the birth of "Eve" at a Florida news conference on December 27, 2002. The group got 30 million hits on their website as a result.

The scientist said that the baby weighed seven pounds and was created through the use of DNA from the skin cells of the mother, an American citizen. U.S. journalist Michael Guillen was supposed to be given proof of the cloning, but Rael stopped the verification procedures in early January 2003.

Raelians Q&A

1. What does Rael think of himself?

Rael believes that he is the Messiah awaited by Old Testament Jews. He even claims that high-level rabbis in Israel have privately recognized his messianic status but the government refused to cooperate and accept Jerusalem as the embassy base. As a result, Rael states that Israel lost its chance for peace.

2. Why do Raelians want to establish an embassy for the space creatures?

Rael claims that the extraterrestrials, or Elohim, do not want to scare humans by an unexpected visit. When planet Earth prepares an embassy for them, then they know they will have "free air space and an official welcome."

3. Why does the Raelian movement claim to be atheistic?

They use the term *atheist* with reference to their objection to traditional views of God. Their religious devotion is directed toward Rael, his mythological claims, and his deference to modern science.

4. Why have Raelians called for a boycott of products from France?

They object to the French government's bigotry against new religious movements, a claim that has real validity. They also make the bizarre claim that the French secret service was behind the deaths of members of the Solar Temple. Members of the group actually took part in a well-orchestrated mass suicide in Switzerland, France, and Quebec in 1994 and 1995.

5. Has Rael written any books?

He wrote *The Book That Tells the Truth* in French in 1974, followed by his best seller *Extra-Terrestrials Took Me to their Planet* in 1976. He has also authored *Let's Welcome Our Fathers from Space* (1979), *Sensual Meditation* (1980), and the more recent *Yes to Human Cloning* (2001).

6. What is the prevailing scientific attitude to human cloning?

Most scientists, including Ian Wilmot who cloned Dolly (the famous sheep), are opposed to human cloning because of health risks and belief that it is morally wrong. However, Italian embryologist Dr. Severino Antinori has announced plans to clone humans. Several U.S. states currently have legislation banning human cloning.

7. Where does one find great Christian reflection on cloning and bioethics?

The Center for Bioethics and Human Dignity, based in Bannock-burn, Illinois, offers impressive resources from a Christian perspective. John Kilner (Ph.D., Harvard), the Center's president, addresses major issues in bioethics in a series of edited volumes. The Center also provides great material on its website. James C. Peterson's work *Genetic Turning Points* (Eerdmans) is a comprehensive study of the ethics related to human genetic intervention.

8. How should Christians respond to Raelians and their message?

First, Christians should be concerned about defending the civil rights of Raelians, given the group's controversial and eccentric views. They deserve the full protection of international law, like all humans. Second, Rael's 60,000 followers are obviously looking for meaning and transcendence. Though his spacecraft theories are irrational, there is nothing strange about the group's longing for eternal life, a hope that can be anchored in Jesus.

RAELIANS

Typology	Western Esoteric UFO Religion
Founder	Claude Vorilhon (b. 1946) now known as Rael
Home Websites	www.rael.org www.clonaid.com
Academic Sites on Cloning	The Roslin Institute: www.roslin.ac.uk Dolan DNA Learning Center: www.dnalc.org U.S. President's Council on Bioethics: www.bioethics.gov The Center for Bioethics and Human Dignity: www.cbhd.org
UFO Critic Site	UFO Skeptic—Philip Klass: www.csicop.org/klassfiles
Recommended Reading	Susan Palmer, *Aliens Adored* (Rutgers University Press, 2004)

Ramtha School of Enlightenment

The Ramtha School of Enlightenment features the work of JZ Knight, one of the most influential and well-known New Agers. A native of New Mexico, Knight was born Judith Darlene Hampton on March 16, 1946. Knight claims that her roots in poverty gave her inner strength to resist conformity. "I wasn't the pretty little girl that was born into the *Leave It to Beaver* family that had to do everything right and belong to all the right clubs and do all the right things and read all the right books and wear all the right clothes. I was just one of a lot of kids that a poor woman had, and she was trying to keep her family together. That freedom allowed me to learn, and it allowed me to develop an interior strength."

Knight states that in February 1977 she was contacted by a 35,000-year-old warrior from the eternal realm. "Beloved woman, I am Ramtha the Enlightened One, and I have come to help you over the ditch. It is called the ditch of limitation. I am here, and we are going to do grand work together." Knight claims that Ramtha once lived in the northern part of the lost continent of Atlantis. Knight channeled Ramtha for the first time in November 1978. Knight achieved fame and wealth in the 1980s, particularly after being endorsed by actresses Shirley MacLaine and Linda Evans.

A MESSAGE FROM RAMTHA

I am Ramtha, a sovereign entity, who lived a long time ago upon this plane called Earth, or Terra. In that life I did not die; I ascended, for I learned to harness the power of my mind and to take my body with me into an unseen dimension of life.

In doing so, I realized an existence of unlimited freedom, unlimited joy, unlimited life. I have come to tell you that you are very important and precious to us, because the life that flows through you and the thought that is coming to every one of you—however you entertain it—is the intelligence and life-force that you have termed God.

To prevent your worshiping me, I have not come to you in my own embodiment. Instead, I have chosen to speak to you through an entity who was my beloved daughter when I lived upon this plane. My daughter, who graciously allows me to use her embodiment, is what is termed a pure "channel" for the essence that I am. When I speak to you, she is no longer within her body, for her soul and spirit have left it completely.

—selected from *Ramtha: The White Book* (Yelm: JKZ Publishing, 2005), pp. 21-22

Knight has been criticized over the years for the high cost of her public teaching and private channeling sessions. As well, there was some controversy over JZ advising followers to put money into Arabian horses. JZ later reimbursed some disgruntled investors. She has also been attacked by the anti-cult movement for breaking up families who were divided about moving to Knight's new headquarters in Yelm, Washington.

She married Jeff Knight, her third husband, in 1984, claiming that Ramtha told Jeff that he was married to JZ in a previous life and that they were soul mates. Their marriage ended in a bitter court battle. Jeff claimed that he was under undue influence from Ramtha when he and JZ initially reached agreement on the divorce settlement. The courts dismissed allegations of brainwashing in relation to Ramtha School of Englightenment. Jeff, who was bisexual, died in 1994.

Knight claims that various scientists have performed tests that prove that she is not deliberately faking her experiences with Ramtha. In 1997 an Austrian court ruled that JZ has sole rights to channel Ramtha, contradicting claims by Julie Ravel, a Berlin woman, to be the proper agent of Ramtha. Ramtha is alleged to have said through JZ that "the world does not need another guru. The world does not need another priest. The world does not need another preacher. The world does not need another spiritual interpretation of the stars. What the world needs is truth."

RAMTHA SCHOOL OF ENGLIGHTENMENT	
Typology	Western Esoteric
Founder	JZ Knight
Homepage	www.ramtha.com
Recommended Reading	JZ Knight, *A State of Mind* (New York: Warner, 1987) J. Gordon Melton, *Finding Enlightenment* (Hillsboro: Beyond Words, 1998)

Share International

Share International is one of the many esoteric groups that became popular during the rise of the New Age movement in the 1970s and 80s. This group became especially noteworthy because of the strident claims made by its founder Benjamin Creme about the emergence of the Christ figure known as Maitreya. Creme is one of the most important and fascinating figures in New Age circles. Creme was was born in Scotland in 1922. He developed an interest in occult and esoteric writings after World War II. He was particularly shaped by the ideas of Alice Bailey, founder of the Lucis Trust and one-time Theosophist. Creme also had contact with the Aetherius Society, a UFO group.

Creme has concentrated his spiritual energy on the appearance of Maitreya, a special world teacher and Christ figure expected by many New Agers. His followers formed the Tara Center and Share International to focus on the message of Maitreya's appearance. In 1974 Creme claimed that Maitreya was providing messages through him about his emergence on the planet. Creme often gave public lectures about "The Reappearance of the Christ."

On April 25, 1982, he even placed full-page ads in seventeen newspapers to announce that "The Christ Is Now Here." Later, on May 14, he told reporters in London that it was their duty to look for Maitreya who had taken the form of a Pakistani and was in the Brick Lane area of London. When Maitreya did not appear Creme cast the blame on the media's apathy. Share International and its leader continue to focus on the soon return of Maitreya.

The movement has this to say about Maitreya: "He has been expected for generations by all of the major religions. Christians know Him as the Christ, and expect His imminent return. Jews await Him as the Messiah; Hindus look for the coming of Krishna; Buddhists expect Him as Maitreya Buddha; and Muslims anticipate the Imam Mahdi or Messiah. The names may be different, but many believe they all refer to the same individual: the World Teacher, whose name is Maitreya." As is common in the esoteric tradition, Share International makes a distinction between Jesus and the Christ, but uniquely teaches that Jesus, who has lived in Rome since 1984, is a disciple of the Christ force.

Creme teaches that Maitreya is responsible for the fall of Communism, the end of apartheid, the emergence of environmental consciousness, etc. Share International expects that Maitreya will be revealed to the whole world in a Day of Declaration. Maitreya will appear on worldwide television, and all humans will be able to hear him telepathically in their own language. This apocalyptic event will also include a worldwide experience of miraculous healings.

The Maitreya announcements caused much concern among evangelicals and became a central item in their critique of the New Age during the 1980s. Constance Cumbey's famous work *Hidden Dangers of the Rainbow* (1983) gave particular attention to Creme's pronouncements. It was even popular to suggest that Maitreya fit the description of what the Antichrist would be like. Focus on the New Age as a central element in evangelical eschatology has waned since the resurgence of militant Islam in our post-9/11 world.

SHARE INTERNATIONAL (BENJAMIN CREME)

Typology	Western Esoteric
Homepage	www.shareintl.org

Solar Temple

The Order of the Solar Temple represents the darker side of new religious movements. This esoteric movement was started by Joseph Di Mambro (1924–94), a French citizen, who had a background in the Rosicrucian Order AMORC (Ancient and Mystical Order Rosae Crucis) from

1956 through the late 1960s. Di Mambro started several esoteric groups in the 1970s and moved to Geneva with his followers in 1978. The Solar Temple group started in 1984, rooted ideologically in modern-day revivals of the Knights Templar (the medieval order) under Jacques Breyer and Raymond Bernard.

Belgian doctor Luc Jouret (1947–94) joined Di Mambro in the early 1980s, and he became the visible presence in the various groups associated with Di Mambro. Di Mambro taught that his daughter Emmanuelle would become the chief spiritual guide for humanity. He deceived followers by using hidden technology in rituals to convince them that they alone could see the Masters who guided Di Mambro. The Masters were actually holographic images.

In October 1994, fifty-three members perished in Switzerland and in the Canadian province of Quebec. Fifteen committed suicide and thirty-eight were murdered, including (in Quebec) a young couple named Tony and Nicki Dutoit and their three-month-old baby. Tony was the chief technologist of the group and had begun to speak about the use of holographs to deceive members.

The couple also disobeyed Di Mambro's command that they not have a child. Beyond this provocation, they named him Christopher Emmanuel, a not so subtle reference to the founder's daughter. Di Mambro referred to the child as the Antichrist and ordered his execution, along with his parents. Sixteen more followers died in France in December 1995, and five more perished in Quebec in March 1997. These three separate tragedies have led to much speculation about the group, including the claim that Princess Grace of Monaco was connected with the movement.

Surviving writings from Di Mambro and Jouret show two leaders consumed with their self-importance and their belief that the death of the group would awaken the world to its sacrificial mission. "We are the Star Seeds that guarantee the perennial existence of the universe, we are the hand of God that shapes creation. We are the Torch that Christ must bring to the Father to feed the Primordial Fire and to reanimate the forces of Life, which, without our contribution, would slowly but surely go out. We hold the key to the universe and must secure its Eternity."

The apocalyptic ending of the group came in part from its radical beliefs. Solar Temple leaders were also influenced by ongoing financial difficulties, defections of key members, police investigations, and internal dissent over the nature and direction of the group. In the end, however,

Solar Temple members lived out through death their group's philosophy. An internal document gave this as a hope: "Like the Phoenix We might be reborn from our ashes. Through the Sword of Light . . . Raised toward the Levels Above, what is refined should depart from the world of density . . . And ascend toward its Point of Origin."

In June 2001 Michel Tabachnik, a music conductor, was acquitted of murder charges related to the sixteen deaths of Solar Temple members that took place in the Vecors region of France in December 1995. Tabachnik claimed that he had left the Solar Temple in 1992, two years before the first suicides in Switzerland in October 1994.

SOLAR TEMPLE	
Typology	Western Esoteric
Founder	Joseph Di Mambro
Recommended Reading	James R. Lewis, "The Solar Temple Transits," in James R. Lewis & Jesper Aagaard Petersen, eds. *Controversial New Religions* (New York: Oxford, 2005) Jean-François Mayer, "Our Terrestrial Journey Is Coming to an End," *Nova Religio* (April 1999) Catherine Wessinger, *How the Millennium Comes Violently* (New York: Seven Bridges, 2000)

Spiritualism

Spiritualism is traced to the alleged supernatural psychic powers of the Fox sisters (Margaret, Kate, and Leah) of Hydesville, New York, thirty-five miles east of Rochester. In 1848, Margaret, then 14, and her younger sister Kate (age 12) claimed that disturbing noises in their house were made by a spirit who would answer questions from the girls by tapping on the walls. The Fox family claimed that the spirit was that of Charles B. Rosna, a peddler who had been murdered in the house about five years earlier. Margaret and Kate became national celebrities and were joined by their older sister, Leah.

Both Margaret and Kate struggled with alcoholism in later years. Leah died in 1890, Kate in 1892, and Margaret a year later. The Fox home is now owned by the National Spiritualist Association of Churches. The NSAC is the oldest spiritualist organization, founded in 1893 in Chicago. In 1899 the organization adopted a Declaration of Principles. The fifth principle states: "We affirm that communication with the so-called dead is a fact, scientifically proven by the phenomena of Spiritualism."

Since 1848 Spiritualism has been mainly identified by its individual practitioners. The most famous is probably Edgar Cayce. Born in Kentucky in 1877, Cayce gave his first "reading" in 1901 after recovery from laryngitis. He worked as a photographer until his popularity as a medium demanded his total time and energy. Cayce gave over 14,000 "readings" or medium sessions during his life. He started the Association for Research and Enlightenment in Virginia Beach, Virginia, in 1931. Cayce died in 1945.

DECLARATION OF PRINCIPLES (SPIRITUALISM)

1. We believe in Infinite Intelligence.

2. We believe that the phenomena of Nature, both physical and spiritual, are the expression of Infinite Intelligence.

3. We affirm that a correct understanding of such expression and living in accordance therewith, constitute true religion.

4. We affirm that the existence and personal identity of the individual continue after the change called death.

5. We affirm that communication with the so-called dead is a fact, scientifically proven by the phenomena of Spiritualism.

6. We believe that the highest morality is contained in the Golden Rule: "Whatsoever ye would that others should do unto you, do ye also unto them."

7. We affirm the moral responsibility of individuals, and that we make our own happiness or unhappiness as we obey or disobey Nature's physical and spiritual laws.

8. We affirm that the doorway to reformation is never closed against any human soul here or hereafter.

9. We affirm that the precepts of Prophecy and Healing are Divine attributes proven through Mediumship.

Principles 1–6 adopted in Chicago, Illinois, 1899
Principles 7–8 adopted in Rochester, New York, 1909
Principle 9 adopted in St. Louis, Missouri, 1944
Principle 9 revised in Oklahoma City, 1983
Principle 9 revised in Westfield, New Jersey, 1998

One of the most famous modern psychics is James Van Praagh. He claims that he is able to "bridge the gap between two planes of existence, that of the living and that of the dead, by providing evidential proof of life after death via detailed messages." He calls himself a "telephone to the spirit world." After its publication in 2001, his book *Talking to Heaven* topped the best-seller list of *The New York Times*, boosted by repeated appearances on the major television talk shows.

Van Praagh is a native of Queens, New York. He was raised in a staunch Roman Catholic home but by his teen years had dismissed Catholicism as an "archaic belief system." He moved to Los Angeles after high school, worked on the fringes of show business, all the while developing the psychic abilities he says every human possesses. Van Praagh claims that his paranormal gifts were evident from his earliest years.

Van Praagh also promotes Hindu teaching on karma and reincarnation. Believing each human is "perfect if we would only seek our divinity," he invites his admirers to explore the spirit world through attending séances and use of the Ouija board. He also promotes a range of practices such as having one's aura read and developing one's *chakras* (alleged spiritual power points within the body). In *Reaching to Heaven* Van Praagh adopts the New Age message of the power of the mind. He illustrates this by writing: "If our thoughts dwell on poverty and illness, we will draw these conditions to us. If we elevate our thoughts to a higher frequency level, we will reap harmony and abundance. This is a fixed universal law that cannot be changed."

SPIRITUALISM	
Typology	Western Esoteric
Homepages	National Spiritualist Association of Churches: www.nsac.org Spiritualist National Union (UK): www.snu.org.uk Association for Research and Enlightenment: www.edgarcayce.org James Van Praagh: www.vanpraagh.com
Critical Sites	CSICOP: www.csicop.org Society for Psychical Research: www.spr.ac.uk American Society of Psychical Research: www.aspr.com
Recommended Reading	Ruth Brandon, *The Spiritualists* (New York: Knopf, 1983) Martin Gardner, *Science: Good, Bad, and Bogus* (New York: Avon, 1981) James Randi, *Flim Flam* (Buffalo: Prometheus, 1982)

Swedenborgianism

Swendenborgians trace their faith to the famous scientist and religious leader, Emanuel Swedenborg, who was born in Stockholm in 1688 and died in London on March 29, 1772. He had a reputation as a man of letters and was also involved in the political life of his country. His early work for his country earned him a pension from the king when he made the transition to the study of spiritual issues.

Swedenborg's life was changed in 1743 and 1744 when he is said to have received contact from the spiritual realm. Within two years he claimed regular communication with angelic beings. Out of this alleged divine revelation Swedenborg wrote prolifically. By 1756 he finished the twelve volumes of *Arcana Coelestia* (Heavenly Secret), which provided an esoteric commentary on Genesis and Exodus. He also wrote *Heaven and Hell* (1758), *Treatise on the Four Doctrines* (1760–1), *Conjugal Love* (1768), and many other books. The American editions of his works run to thirty volumes.

Swedenborg remained discreet about his spiritual writings for many years. It was only after he became known as a clairvoyant that attention was drawn to him as the author. His followers claim that he saw, through psychic powers, a fire that destroyed parts of Stockholm in 1759. Swedenborg did not start a church in his own country and tried to protect those who were charged with heresy for adopting some of his views. Though Swedenborgians often claim complete originality about him, there is evidence that he was influenced by Kabbalism, the esoteric Jewish tradition.

Swedenborg's influence went far beyond the boundaries of the several churches devoted to his teaching. His emphasis on an esoteric interpretation of Christianity, use of inner revelation, and appeal to the angelic realm attracted considerable interest across Europe and particularly in London. His belief that esoteric religion can be rational was a comfort to many religious leaders in a time when Enlightenment rationalism was undermining faith. He had an influence on Goethe, Immanuel Kant, Ralph Waldo Emerson, and William Blake.

Blake's rather open sexual theories may be traced in part to the influence of Swedenborg. Blake and his wife attended the First General Conference of the Swedenborgian New Jerusalem Church in London on April 14, 1789. They did not become members, and while Blake (1757–1827) could be very critical of Swedenborg's overall philosophy, some of his libertarian views made an impact on Blake. Both Swedenborg and Blake were influenced by the radical views of Count Zinzendorf (1700–60), the leader of the Moravians, though Swedenborg distanced himself from Zinzendorf in his later years.

The British roots of Swedenborgianism can be traced to Robert Hindmarsh, a one-time Methodist, who formed a group for the study of Swedenborg in 1787. The American church was formed in 1817 but experienced schism in 1890. There are now at least four Swedenborgian bodies, each with a worldwide mission. The sociological study of Swedenborgian movements owes most to Jane Williams-Hogan, a professor at Bryn Athyn College in Pennsylvania.

Swedenborg's views influenced the early leaders in American Spiritualism, and he played a part in the development of New Thought and the broader esoteric traditions of the late nineteenth century. D. T. Suzuki, the famous Zen teacher, referred to Swedenborg as "the Buddha of the north." The most famous Swedenborgians are Helen Keller and John Chapman (1774–1845). Chapman spread Swedenborg's teaching as he planted apple trees in the Midwest. We know him as "Johnny Appleseed."

Swedenborg's theology contrasts with Christian orthodoxy at several crucial points. His understanding of the Trinity denies the affirmations of the Nicene Creed. He also taught that the last judgment took place in 1757 and that a new church began in 1770, representing the second coming of Christ. He adopted an allegorical interpretation of the Bible, avoiding the literal or plain sense interpretation of the text. Further, his understanding of Christian faith was based on private revelation, a fact that makes Christian truth hinge on the subjective experiences of one person. This is a dangerous theological method and foundation for Christian theology and philosophy.

SWEDENBORGIANISM

Typology	Western Esoteric
Church Websites	Swedenborgian Church of North America (Newtonville, MA): www.swedenborg.org [formerly General Convention] New Church/General Church of the New Jerusalem (Bryn Athyn, PA): www.newchurch.org The Lord's New Church which is Nova Hierosolyma: www.thelordsnewchurch.com General Conference of the New Church: www.generalconference.org.uk/
Resource Websites	The Swedenborg Foundation: www.swedenborg.com The Swedenborg Society: www.swedenborg.org.uk/ Swedenborg Online: www.heavenlydoctrines.org
Recommended Reading	Ernst Benz, *Emanuel Swedenborg* Trans. Nicholas Goodrick-Clarke (West Chester, Pennsylvania: Swedenborg Foundation, 2002) Interview with Jane Williams-Hogan in *Relioscope* (Jean-Francois Mayer): http://religion.info/index.shtml

Thelema (Aleister Crowley)

Thelema, a Greek word that means "will" or "volition," is the term given to the religious philosophy of Aleister Crowley and the movement connected to him. Crowley had only a small following during his lifetime, but his occult views are now espoused by many groups and he had a significant impact on Gerald Gardner, the founder of modern witchcraft.

Aleister Crowley was born on October 12, 1875, in England. He came from a wealthy and religious home. His parents were members of the Plymouth Brethren, one of the most conservative Christian groups. Crowley attended Cambridge but did not graduate. In 1898 he joined the Hermetic Order of the Golden Dawn, an occult group, but was forced out two years later by W. B. Yeats. In 1903 Crowley married Rose Kelly. The next year he traveled to Egypt with his wife.

Crowley and his disciples believe that he received supernatural dictation over a three-day period beginning on April 8, 1904. The material received became known as the *Liber Al vel Legis*, or *Book of the Law*. This work contains Crowley's most famous phrase: "Do what thou wilt shall be the whole of the Law." Crowley believed that the revelation in Egypt marked a new age for humanity, with Crowley as its chief prophet. He viewed his Thelemic philosophy as Magick (spelled with a *k* to differentiate it from mundane stage magic).

In 1910 Crowley developed connections to the Ordo Templi Orientis (OTO), an occult group founded a few years before by Theodor Reuss, and eventually became its OHO (Outer Head of the Order). Crowley's first marriage ended in 1909. After his divorce, he continued to travel and spent time in the United States. He then settled for several years in Sicily. While there he wrote *Diary of a Drug Fiend,* one of his most controversial works. Mussolini kicked Crowley out of Italy in 1923 after the death of Raoul Loveday, one of his students. He remarried in 1929, but his remaining years were fraught with poor health and financial woes. He died in England on December 1, 1947.

ALEISTER CROWLEY TIMELINE

1875—Born in England. Parents from Plymouth Brethren movement
1887—Death of father
1895—Leaves Trinity College, Cambridge
1896—Claims mystical experience in Stockholm
1898—Joins Hermetic Order of the Golden Dawn
1899—Begins long association with Allan Bennet
1900—Golden Dawn Order has schism over Crowley
1901—Becomes 33rd degree Mason in Mexico
1902—Learns yoga in Ceylon with Bennet
1903—Marriage to Rose Kelly in Scotland
1904—Claims revelation for *The Book of the Law*
1907—Founding of A.A. (Argenteum Astrum)
1909—Divorced from Rose Kelly
1912—Crowley initiated by Reuss into OTO
1914—Leaves for the U.S.
1915—Helps Charles Stansfield Jones in Vancouver
1917—Editor of *The International*
1920—Abbey of Thelema founded in Cefalu, Sicily
1923—*Diary of a Drug Fiend* published
1923—Mussolini kicks Crowley out of Sicily
1923—*The Confessions* completed
1928—Israel Regardie becomes Crowley's assistant

1929—Maria de Miramar and Crowley marry
1932—Regardie and Crowley end their working relationship
1934—Crowley suffers loss in libel action against Nina Hamnett
1935—Crowley declares bankruptcy
1937—*The Equinox of the Gods* published
1940—Grady Louis McMurtry visits Crowley
1944—*The Book of Thoth* published
1947—Death on December 1 and cremation in Brighton

Crowley deliberately challenged the traditional mores of his time. He wrote pornography, referred to himself as a Satanist, and stated that he was the Great Beast 666. He composed the Gnostic Mass as an alternative to the Catholic Mass. Crowley taught that the greatest spiritual transformations occur through Sex Magick and radicalized the sex rites found in the Ordo Templi Orientis. Three of the OTO degrees created by Crowley celebrate specific sexual practices. Crowley even seemed to believe that his Sex Magick could create a divine child.

THELEMA TIMELINE

1838—Birth of Franz Hartmann
1851—Birth of Carl Kellner (aka Renatus)
1855—Birth of Thedor Reuss (aka Merlin or Peregrinus)
1858—Birth of Leopold Engel
1875—Aleister Crowley born on October 12
1875—Birth of Jane Wolfe
1885—Kellner meets Dr. Franz Hartmann (1838–1912)
1888—Order of the Golden Dawn founded
1890—l'Eglise Gnostique founded by Jules Doinel (1842–1903)
1895—Kellner and Theodor Reuss discuss Academia Masonica
1897—S. L. MacGregor Mathers takes control of Order
1898—Aleister Crowley joins Order of the Golden Dawn
1900—Monte Verità commune started by Henri Oedenkoven and
      Ida Hofmann
1902—Reuss parts company with Leopold Engel
1902—Kellner and Reuss agree to start Oriental Templar Order

1902—Reuss starts publication of masonic journal *The Oriflamme*

1904—Crowley claims revelation in Cairo from astral realm

1904—Eglise Gnostique Catholique Apostolique founded by Julius Houssaye

1905—Death of Carl Kellner on June 7

1907—Crowley starts Argenteum Astrum

1907—Birth of Israel Regardie

1909—Crowley begins to publish *Equinox*

1910—Crowley admitted to the three degrees of OTO by Reuss

1912—Rudolph Steiner starts Anthroposophical Society

1912—Crowley appointed head of British and Irish OTO by Reuss

1913—John Yarker dies

1913—Crowley composes the Gnostic Mass

1914—Steiner ends his relationship with Reuss

1914—Crowley travels to New York in October

1914—Charles Stansfield Jones appointed head of OTO in Vancouver

1914—Birth of John W. "Jack" Parsons (Belarion)

1915—Crowley and Jane Foster have son

1915—Winifred T. Smith (Frater 132) starts Agapé Lodge in Vancouver

1917—Police raid Crowley's Lodge in England/Crowley resigns as Grand Master

1917—Birth of Phyllis Seckler (nee Pratt) aka Soror Meral

1917—Reuss arranges conference in Monte Verità

1918—The Gnostic Mass published in *The International* by Crowley

1919—Crowley returned to England

1921—C. S. Jones appointed OTO head in North America

1921—Crowley and Reuss have dispute over OTO leadership

1923—Reuss dies on October 28

1925—Steiner dies

1926—Pansophical Lodge closed/restarted as Fraternitas Saturni

1931—Birth of Marcelo Motta

1933—Gnostic Mass celebrated in Hollywood by W. T. Smith, Jane Wolfe, and R. Kahl

1935—Agapé Lodge No. 2 (USA) holds first meeting

1939—Phyllis Seckler joins OTO

1943—Crowley confers 9th degree on McMurtry (Hymenaeus Alpha 777)

1945—L. Ron Hubbard and Jack Parsons meet

1946—Hubbard splits from Parsons

1946—McMurtry designated as Crowley's representative in U.S.

1947—Crowley dies

1947—Karl Johannes Germer heads OTO

1949—Jack Parsons takes oath of Antichrist

1950—Charles Stansfield Jones dies

1952—Parsons dies in home explosion

1955—Germer expels Kenneth Grant from OTO

1955—Birth of William Breeze (aka Hymenaeus Beta)

1958—Jane Wolfe dies

1961—Grady McMurtry moves to Washington

1962—Karl Germer dies on October 25

1962—Hemann Metzger leads OTO in Europe/Kenneth Grant leads British OTO

1963—Mellinger blocks Metzger's bid for leadership of OTO

1969—OTO restarted by Grady McMurtry (Hymenaeus Alpha 777)

1969—McMurtry asserts leadership of OTO

1969—McMurtry, Meral, Burlingame, and Grimaud resume initiations

1970—Frederick Mellinger dies on August 29

1971—Ordo Templi Orientis registered in California by McMurtry

1973—Temple of Thelema founded (Phyllis Seckler aka Soror Meral)

1975—Sascha Germer dies in April

1975—Seckler and McMurtry divorce

1976—OTO documents transferred to McMurtry from Germer's estate

1983—Gerald Yorke dies

1985—Israel Regardie dies

1985—McMurtry wins lawsuit against Marcelo Ramos Motta in San Francisco

1985—Grady Louis McMurtry dies on July 12

1985—Frater Hymenaeus Beta appointed head of OTO

1987—Motta dies on August 26
1996—Sabazius X appointed Grand Master of OTO Grand Lodge
    in U.S.
2003—Death of Helen Parsons Smith
2004—Death of Phyllis Seckler (aka Soror Meral)
2008—Paris exhibition of Crowley's paintings

Since Crowley's death, there have been extended ideological and legal battles over which group is the proper heir to the OTO name. This story is convoluted because of ambiguity in Crowley's directives to his leading disciples and the complexities of intellectual debate about the major claimants to Crowley's title. The top claimants are usually said to be Gerald McMurtry (1918–85), Kenneth Grant (1924–), and Marcelo Ramos Motta (1931–87).

Several U.S. court decisions have recognized McMurtry as the legal heir to Crowley's OTO, and this branch is certainly the largest. McMurtry was succeeded at his death by Frater Hymenaeus Beta, now considered head of the OTO. The U.S. branch of the OTO is led by Sabazius X. The OTO carries on its public worship through the Ecclesia Gnostica Catholica, which is the liturgical branch of Crowley's movement.

THELEMA LEADERS IN RITUAL MAGICK

Aleister Crowley (1875–1947) [Baphomet]
Karl Germer (1885–1962) [Saturnus], OTO head from
    1947 to 1962
Kenneth Grant (1924–), British OTO member; claimed
    OTO headship in 60s
Eugen Grosche (1888–1964), Founder of Fraternitus
    Saturni
Charles Stansfield Jones (1886–1950) [Parzival], OTO head
    in Canada
Carl Kellner (1851–1905)
Arnold Krumm-Heller (1879–1949), OTO leader in Mexico
Grady McMurtry (1918–85) [Hymenaeus Alpha 777]

Hermann Metzger (1919–90) [Paragranus], Swiss OTO
  leader
Marcelo Motta (1931–87), claimant to OTO leadership
Jack Parsons (1914–52) [Belarion]
Israel Regardie (1907–85), student of Crowley
Theodor Reuss (1855–1928) [Merlin or Peregrinus]
Winifred Talbot Smith (1885–1937) [Frater 132]
Heinrich Tränker (1880–1956), OTO head in Germany
Jane Wolfe (1875–1958)

THELEMA (ALEISTER CROWLEY)

Founder	Aleister Crowley (1875–1947)
Homepage	U.S. Grand Lodge (OTO): http://oto-usa.org
Resource Websites	Aleister Crowley Society: www.lashtal.com Association for the Study of Esotericism (ASE): http://www.aseweb.org/ Esoterica (online journal related to ASE): www.esoteric.msu.edu/ European Society for the Study of Western Esotericism: www.esswe.org/ www.thelemapedia.org http://user.cyberlink.ch/~koenig (Peter Koenig)
Recommended Reading	Martin Booth, *A Magick Life: The Biography of Aleister Crowley* (London: Hodder & Stoughton, 2000) Richard Kaczynski, *Perdurabo: The Life of Aleister Crowley* (Tempe: New Falcon, 2002) Lawrence Sutin, *Do What Thou Wilt* (New York: St. Martin's, 2002) John Symonds, *The Beast 666: The Life of Aleister Crowley,* (London: Pindar Press 1997, orig. 1951)
Special Note	Marco Pasi provides superb analysis of Crowley in "The Neverendingly Told Story: Recent Biographies of Aleister Crowley," in *Aries: Journal for the Study of Western Esotericism,* III, 2 (2003). Hugh Urban has an important essay on "Unleashing the Beast: Aleister Crowley, Tantra and Sex Magic in Late Victorian England," in *Esoterica V* (2003), 138–192.

Theosophy

Theosophy is one of the most significant religious movements of the nineteenth century. It is always associated with Helena Petrova Blavatsky, who had a singular impact on the ideology behind New Age spirituality, even though she died almost a century before New Age became a recognized term.

HPB (as she is often known) was born in 1831 in Ukraine and was raised in an upper-class family in Russia. Her mother died when Helena was entering her teen years, and she married a General Blavatsky when she was 16. After three months, she left him and then traveled the world for two decades.

Blavatsky had early interests in the occult and was associated in 1858 with Daniel D. Home, a prominent medium in France. She dabbled in other forms of Spiritualism for more than a decade. After moving to New York in 1873, she had some contact with William and Horatio Eddy, two of America's leading Spiritualists. The impact of Spiritualism on Blavatsky was considerable. She would spend the rest of her life telling her own version of contact with the spiritual realm.

Madame Blavatsky claimed to transmit messages from the Great White Brotherhood, the Ascended Masters who guide humanity. Blavatsky taught that her messages usually came from two beings: Master El Morya and Master Koot Hoomi. Theosophists do not view the Masters as angelic beings but rather as individuals who have completed the cycles of reincarnation. (Nothing racist is implied in the use of the word *White* in reference to the brotherhood.)

Blavatsky claimed that she learned about the Ascended Masters through her travels in Egypt and Tibet. Her theories show knowledge of Buddhist thought and Egyptian mythology, though critics have doubted her credibility both on whether she actually traveled in Tibet and on her ideology as a whole. Her thought gives place to both Buddha and Jesus, though not in typical Buddhist or Christian fashion. The historical Jesus is identified with the eternal spirit Bodhisattva Maitreya, who is head of the love/wisdom department of the brotherhood.

Blavatsky founded the Theosophical Society in 1875 in cooperation with Henry Steel Olcott and William Q. Judge. Blavatsky's *Isis Unveiled* was released in 1877. The next year she and Olcott moved to India and settled in Adyar, near Madras, in 1882. They had a working relationship with a Hindu group until Blavatsky was suspected of trickery.

In 1884 Emma Cutting Coulomb, a longtime confidante, charged Blavatsky with making fraudulent claims about having psychic power. Richard Hodgson investigated Coulomb's charges on behalf of the Society for Psychical Research. In December 1885 Hodgson wrote a damning report against Blavatsky that plagued her for the rest of her life and continues to affect the image of the Theosophical Society to the present day.

In 1887 Blavatsky settled in London and began writing her book *The Secret Doctrine*, which was published two years later. She died on May 8, 1891. Theosophy underwent schism after Blavatsky's death. One group, following Olcott, has its headquarters in India, while the other, following Judge, established headquarters in Pasadena, California. Theosophy has formed the ideological basis for many esoteric movements not formally connected with the two major Theosophical groups.

THEOSOPHY	
Typology	Western Esoteric
Major Figure	Helena Petrova Blavatsky (1831–91)
Main Websites	http://ts-adyar.org (India-based group) www.theosociety.org (Pasadena-based group)
Other Sites	www.blavatskyarchives.com www.blavatsky.net www.theohistory.org (James A. Santucci)
Recommended Reading	Peter Washington, *Madame Blavatsky's Baboon* (New York: Schocken, 1995) K. Paul Johnson, *The Masters Revealed* (State University of New York Press, 1994)

UFO Cults

UFO Cults is the term for a broad range of small, diverse, and independent groups who variously believe that "alien beings" are "out there" and that their existence is of vital importance to human life on earth. Speculation about life beyond Earth's boundaries has existed for centuries but contemporary interest dates to June 24, 1947, when Kenneth Arnold, a pilot, claimed to see nine Unidentified Flying Objects or UFOs near Mount Rainier, Washington.

The major UFO-style New Age groups are the Aetherius Society, the Unarius Academy of Science, the Urantia Brotherhood, and the Raelian movement. The suicide debacle of the Heaven's Gate group in 1997 cast a gloom over New Age UFO groups and UFO interests in general but the passing of time has dulled the impact of Heaven's Gate on believers in the New Age UFO groups. The religious-based UFO groups have a dogmatic commitment to the claims of their leaders and the alleged spiritual revelations from aliens.

Of course, even secular-minded UFO advocates believe passionately in the truth of their claims about extraterrestrial life and in the widespread belief that the United States government is engaged in a cover-up about space ships. In addition to the Kenneth Arnold case, there is unanimity among advocates that a spaceship crashed in Roswell, New Mexico, in the first week of July 1947. This is known as the Roswell Incident. The U.S. military claims the incident is simply a case of a crashed weather balloon. There is an International UFO Museum and Research Center in Roswell.

Another significant case involves the allegation that that the U.S. government operates Area 51, a military compound ninety miles north of Las Vegas, as a site where alien craft can be examined. Bob Lazar, a leading UFO advocate, made this notion famous with his assertion in 1989 on Art Bell's *Coast to Coast* radio program that he had worked with alien spacecrafts in the area. Area 51 is a military site used by the Air Force to test new fighter planes, but the Air Force denies Lazar's claims.

J. Allen Hynak, who died in 1986, was one of the world's leading UFO advocates. He was a professor of astronomy and a consultant to the U.S. Air Force's Project Blue Book, which investigated UFO claims until the project was shut down in 1969. In 1973 Hynak published the classic work *The UFO Experience: A Scientific Study*. Also, along with Philip Imbrogno and Bob Pratt, he co-authored *Night Siege*, a whole book on the Westchester Country "Boomerang" sightings, involving hundreds of reports in the 1980s about a V-shaped craft hovering both north of New York, in the Hudson River Valley, and over Connecticut.

Critics of UFO sightings and UFO religions reject all claims that there is proof of real alien visits to planet Earth. The skeptics do not argue that that every claim can be disproved or that the believers are all liars. Their approach is to argue that most of the cases can be explained better by alternative explanations. One of the major groups attacking the credibility of UFO reports is the Committee for the Scientific Investigation of the Claims of the Paranormal, popularly known as CSICOP. Their UFO specialist is Philip J. Klass, author of *UFOs: The Public Deceived*, a number of other books, and *The Klass Files*.

UFO CULTS	
Typology	Western Esoteric
General Websites	Mirrored site with focus on Area 51: www.ufomind.com The International UFO Museum and Research Center: www.iufomrc.org The National UFO Reporting Center: www.nuforc.org Center for UFO Studies (J. Allen Hynek): www.cufos.org Committee for the Scientific Investigation of Claims of the Paranormal: www.csicop.org Center for the Study of Extraterrestrial Intelligence: www.cseti.com

Unarius

Unarius is a UFO-oriented movement founded in Los Angeles in 1954 by Ernest L. Norman (1904–71), aka Archangel, and his wife Ruth E. Norman (1900–93), aka Archangel Uriel. Unarius is an acronym for Universal Articulate Interdimensional Understanding of Science. Unarius teaches that a "Pleiadean star ship" will bring missionary-like "Space Brothers" to the Earth, and we will become "the final world to join an alignment of thirty-three planets forming an interplanetary confederation for the spiritual renaissance of humankind on Earth."

The Unarian "Science of Life" curriculum is based on mastering the "mind-body system." To progress spiritually, followers undergo "past life therapy" for unresolved problems from previous lives. Ruth Norman claimed fifty-five past lives, including those of Mary of Bethany (that is, Mary Magdalene). Mrs. Norman announced that as Mary Magdalene she had been engaged to Jesus of Nazareth, who was a previous incarnation of Ernest L. Norman. She claims that in her current incarnation she was once again "by the side of the man who had taught from the hillsides of Galilee, before the plots against him resulted in his crucifixion and the subsequent distortion of his true teachings by his disciples, under the negative leadership of the one who changed his name from Saul of Tarsus to Paul."

Antare kissing hand of Uriel

Photo: Diana Tumminia

After Ruth died in 1993, the leadership of the movement passed to Charles Spiegel, who used the spiritual name of Antares. Spiegel joined the movement in 1960 and wrote many volumes about Unarius themes. Spiegel believed that he had previously lived as Napoleon Bonaparte and wrote an autobiography about this past life called *The Confessions of I, Bonaparte*. He also claimed to have channeled messages from Ruth Norman after her departure. Spiegel died on December 22, 1999.

On October 12, 1984, Ruth Norman said that she had received contact from Alta, from the planet Vixall, who told her that a spacecraft from Myton would land in the Bermuda Triangle in the year 2001. By 2010, thirty-one other spaceships will have arrived, each holding one thousand "Space Brothers" who will work out of the seventy-three-acre plot reserved for them near El Cajon, California.

When the 2001 prediction failed, members were told that the Earth's leaders were not mentally receptive to the Space Brothers' visit. In the mid-1970s an earlier failed prophecy was similarly explained. When the Space Brothers were about to come to Earth, Ruth Norman and other Unarians were recalling their past lives in Egypt. It was revealed that some Unarian students had killed the great Masters Isis and Osiris just as their Space Brothers were about to take them back to their planet. Ruth taught that she was the incarnation of Isis and her husband Ernest had been

Osiris in a previous life. In the words of the Unarius website: "These two beings had returned to the earth plane, overshadowed by the Archangels Raphiel and Uriel, to help the very same souls who had murdered them in the past!"

The movement does not claim to be a religion but a truly scientific spirituality. The most important academic work on Unarius has been done by Diana G. Tumminia.

UNARIUS	
Typology	Western Esoteric and UFO-Oriented
Founders	Ernest L. Norman (1904–71), Ruth E. Norman (1900–93)
Homepage	www.unarius.org
Recommended Reading	Diana G. Tumminia, *When Prophecy Never Fails* (Oxford University Press, 2005)

Urantia

Urantia is a small modern esoteric movement connected to followers of *The Urantia Book*, a work of 2,097 pages said to be a revelation from celestial beings for Urantia (planet Earth). The book was first published in 1955 and is promoted by the Urantia Foundation. Its earthly story owes most to two people: psychiatrist William S. Sadler (1875–1969) and one of his patients, who claimed to receive the divine revelations that became *The Urantia Book*.

In 1923 Sadler, who had a Seventh-day Adventist background, organized a forum to discuss material from the patient. They met at 533 Diversey Parkway in Chicago. *The Urantia Book* presents a complex cosmology, with hundreds of constellations, each with hundreds of inhabited worlds. Urantia describes five "epochal" events in the history of humankind, the fourth being the life of Christ and the fifth being the writing of *The Urantia Book* itself.

The Urantia Book teaches that God used beings called "Creator Sons" to create various universes in time and space. Earth's Creator Son is Michael, who created Nebadon, our local universe. Michael incarnated on Earth as Jesus of Nazareth. *The Urantia Book* claims to provide a huge amount of new information about the life of Jesus, in addition to offering unusual interpretations of classical Christian teaching about Jesus.

Page 2090 of *The Urantia Book* proclaims: "The time is ripe to witness the figurative resurrection of the human Jesus from his burial tomb amidst the theological traditions and the religious dogmas of nineteen centuries. What a transcendent service if, through this revelation, the Son of Man should be recovered from the tomb of traditional theology and be presented as the living Jesus to the church that bears his name, and to all other religions!"

The Urantia Foundation does not usually identify Sadler or any Forum members in order to "preclude future generations from venerating the participants." However, the Foundation had to go over the details about Sadler's life and the emergence of the text in ongoing litigation over the ownership of *The Urantia Book*. The legal case centered on a dispute with the Michael Foundation and Harry McMullan III. The Urantia Foundation was upset with the Michael Foundation and McMullan for publication of *Jesus: A New Revelation*. This volume contains material from section 4 of *The Urantia Book*. In March 2003 a U.S. appeals court ruled that the Urantia Foundation could not renew its copyright on *The Urantia Book*. In October of the same year the U.S. Supreme Court refused to review the decision.

URANTIA ON GOD AND JESUS

About two thousand years ago, one of these divine sons of God incarnated himself on Urantia, in part, in order to help us mortals realize that we, too, are sons of God, indwelt by a divine light. "The kingdom of God is within you." This inner guidance can lead us in timeless evolution, life after life, toward perfection. Jesus literally meant it when he commanded, "Be ye perfect." But there is an added reason for Jesus' incarnation. By his life in the flesh he was earning his own sovereignty. *The Urantia Book* teaches that this same Son, who became the carpenter of Nazareth, was the actual and literal creator of the earth, the solar system, and our entire "local" universe, with its potential of ten million inhabited worlds. And out of all those possible planets where he might have lived his life of the flesh, he chose to come to ours—probably because of our great need.

Six times before, on other spheres, this divine Son of God had bestowed himself and lived the life of one of his own creatures; thereby, with this seventh and final one, in the likeness of the lowest order, earning complete and absolute sovereignty over the universe he created. Jesus did not come to Urantia to placate a God of wrath, nor to offer himself as a ransom by dying on the cross. The cross was wholly man's doing, not God's requirement. He came to say that God is a loving Father, that man is a son of the eternal God, and that all men are brothers. By these seven bestowals, he enriched his divine and perfect personality, making it not only complete, but replete. He thus became the Son of Man, in addition to being the Son of God.

As the case suggests, there has been considerable controversy over the nature of *The Urantia Book* and the manner of revelation with Sadler's patient. Martin Gardner, probably the greatest living writer on fringe science, suggests in his work *Urantia: The Great Cult Mystery* that the individual in question was Wilfred Custer Kellogg, Sadler's brother-in-law. Gardner also argues that *The Urantia Book* makes major errors on scientific issues and that it plagiarizes from other sources.

Martin Gardner, famous critic of New Age, Norman, Oklahoma

Photo: Jim Beverley

The plagiarism charge relates to the exhaustive research done by Matthew Block. Block was a believer in Urantia and viewed the connections between the sacred text and human sources as a signal of the brilliant creativity of the revelators who spoke to and through Sadler's patient. However, recently Block has become more skeptical and has expressed greater appreciation for the work of Gardner. Block now believes that *The Urantia Book* was put together by Sadler with his son's help in the later stages of compilation.

The divide between Urantia and classical Christian faith is fundamentally about whether one accepts *The Urantia Book* as divine revelation and as an accurate commentary on God and Christ and cosmology. Urantia apologists repeatedly rest their case on the trust that Dr. Sadler and his patient were recipients of modern revelation. Given the human sources at work in *The Urantia Book*, its key errors on testable items about the universe, and its denial of major biblical teaching, Christians should resist claims that it is new revelation from God.

URANTIA	
Typology	Western Esoteric
Founder	William S. Sadler (1875–1969)
Websites	The Urantia Foundation: www.urantia.org The Official Urantia Foundation Truth Page: www.freeurantia.org The Urantia Book Fellowship: www.urantiabook.org Square Circles Publishing: www.squarecircles.com A New Picture of Jesus: www.truthbook.com
Recommended Reading	Martin Gardner, *Urantia: The Great Cult Mystery* (Buffalo: Prometheus, 1995)

New Age Leaders

Franz Alper (1930–)

A native of Brooklyn, New York, Franz Alper is best known in New Age circles for his focus on crystals and the lost city of Atlantis. Alper released a three-volume channeled work in 1982 under the title *Exploring Atlantis*. He claimed that his views were from extraterrestrial beings who settled in the lost city before it was destroyed. He was also associated with the Church of Tzaddi, part of the spiritualist movement.

Jose Arguelles (1939–)

Jose Arguelles is the New Age leader behind the famous Harmonic Convergence, the theory that a massive shift in human consciousness was to take place on August 16–17, 1987, in preparation for the final transformation of humanity in 2012. On those two days thousands of New Agers who accepted his prediction gathered at special sacred sites (also known as "power spots") to share in the collective moment. Mount Shasta in California was the most popular destination, but others journeyed to locations in Egypt and Peru.

Mount Shasta, sacred site for New Agers in Northern California

Photo: Vicki & Chuck Rogers

Arguelles based his prediction on various factors from ancient Mayan teaching, astrology, and data from those who claimed to have had contact with UFOs. He even used Revelation 14:3 to argue that 144,000 enlightened teachers needed to celebrate the Convergence. New Age celebrities like John Denver and Shirley MacLaine participated in the two-day event.

Along with his wife Lloydine, Arguelles continues to teach on Mayan cosmology. He also claimed that on his fifty-eighth birthday he came to recognize that his essential being is an entity known as ValumVotan, the "Closer of the Cycle."

Alice Bailey (1880–1949)

Alice Bailey and her husband Foster were co-founders of the Arcane School, an influential break-off movement from Theosophy. Alice, a native of England, had Anglican roots but became attracted to esotericism after separating from her first husband in 1915. She claimed that Koot Hoomi, one of the Ascended Masters in Madame Blavatsky's teaching, had actually contacted her when she was a teenager.

Alice and Foster were married in 1921. By this time Alice was receiving messages from Djwhal Khul ("The Tibetan"), another Master, but this created enormous controversy among Theosophists who believed that Blavatsky was the final channel. The Baileys left Theosophy and started the Lucis Trust to publish Alice's revelations. In 1923 they also started the Arcane School. Alice died in 1949. Foster led the School until his own death in 1977.

ALICE BAILEY ON THE SECOND COMING

"A truth hard for the orthodox thinker of any faith to accept is the fact that Christ cannot return because He has always been here upon our Earth, watching over the spiritual destiny of humanity; He has never left us but, in physical body and securely concealed (though not hidden), He has guided the affairs of the Spiritual Hierarchy, of His disciples and workers Who are unitedly pledged with Him to Earth service. He can only re-appear. If people look for the Christ Who left His disciples centuries ago, they will fail to recognise the Christ Who is in process of returning. The Christ has no religious barriers in His consciousness. It matters not to Him of what faith a person follows. The Son of God is on His way and He cometh not alone. His advance guard is already here and the Plan which they must follow is already made and clear. Let recognition be the aim."

Internet Source

www.lucistrust.org

Guy Ballard (1878–1939)

Guy Ballard, a native of Kansas, made a significant contribution to American esotericism through his founding of the I AM movement in the 1930s in cooperation with his wife Edna. Ballard claimed that while he was visiting Mount Shasta, California, in 1930 the Ascended Master Saint Germain appeared to him. Saint Germain appointed him, his wife and their son Donald as the Accredited Messengers of the Seventh Golden Age.

The Ballards started the Saint Germain Foundation in 1932. Guy Ballard wrote *Unveiled Mysteries* in 1934 and *The Magic Presence* the next year. He and his wife toured America in the latter half of the decade, starting informal groups and lecturing on the teachings from Saint Germain. Ballard and his wife were targets of much criticism, especially from Gerald Bryan, a former student, who published a number of pamphlets that became the basis for his 1940 book *Psychic Dictatorship in America*.

Gerald died on December 29, 1939. His wife led the movement through the next three decades until her death in 1971. The movement survived serious criminal charges in the 1940s, ones that were eventually settled by rulings of the United States Supreme Court in favor of the group's religious liberty.

Elbert Benjamine (1882–1951)

Elbert Benjamine is known for his writings on various occult topics (under the pen name C. C. Zain) and his specialized works on astrology. He was associated for decades with the Brotherhood of Light, an occult group based in Denver; and in 1932 he incorporated The Church of Light to spread Brotherhood teachings. Benjamine claims that early contact with the Great White Brotherhood in 1907 set the direction for his life. He began research on what he called the twenty-one branches of occult science in 1914 and over the next two decades wrote twenty-four books on the various themes. He then wrote six books on astrology, including *The Influence of the Planet Pluto* (1939).

The Brotherhood and The Church of Light trace their origin back to a secret group that emerged in Egypt in 2440 B.C. The church teaches that Thales, Pythagoras, and Plato were taught by the Brotherhood. Benjamine was chosen by the Brotherhood to teach "The Religion of the Stars" in our emerging Age of Aquarius. The Church of Light is now based in Brea, California.

Internet Source

Church of Light: www.light.org

Annie Besant (1847–1933)

Annie Besant, a native of London, is one of the most important leaders in the Theosophical movement founded by H. P. Blavatsky and Colonel Henry Steel Olcott. She was born as Annie Woods and was influenced by her mother's Anglican faith, particularly in moral formation. Besant married Anglican clergyman Frank Besant in 1867, but they separated in 1873, in part because of Annie's growing disenchantment with orthodox Christianity.

Besant was associated with the Freethought tradition of Charles Bradlaugh from 1874 to 1887. By 1888 she developed a deep interest in Theosophy, particularly through reading Blavatsky's work *The Secret Doctrine*. She joined Theosophy in 1889 and quickly became one of Blavatsky's most trusted aides. Besant worked with Olcott and William Q. Judge in leadership after Blavatsky's death in 1891; however, personal rivalries led Judge and the American Theosophists to break away from Besant and Olcott in the mid-1890s.

Besant moved to India, the movement's international headquarters, after she became the president of the society in 1907, following the death of Olcott. She worked for two decades on India's political and social problems and had some significant contact with Gandhi, the famous reformer, though she did not accept his principle of non-cooperation. Besant also devoted most of her later life as a Theosophist to introducing the world to Jiddu Krishnamurti as the "World Teacher," a term she borrowed from Blavatsky. Charles Leadbeater, a longtime associate of Besant, introduced her to Krishnamurti in 1909, when the boy was 15. He was tutored for his role as a Messiah figure and was practically worshiped by Besant and other Theosophists for two decades. Krishnamurti renounced his role in 1929. Besant died in 1933.

Eileen Caddy (1917–2006)

Eileen Caddy is famous for her work in the Findhorn Community, the Scottish New Age retreat, which she co-founded with her husband Peter and Dorothy Maclean. Both Peter and Eileen left previous marriages to be with one another. They developed the spiritual community in the early 1960s and remained together until the late 70s.

Eileen Caddy is the author of several works, including *God Spoke to Me*, published in 1971. Her autobiography, *Flight into Freedom*, was released in 1988. The Findhorn website posts a devotional every day from her bestselling book *Opening Doors Within*. The quotation for October 27 reads in part: "Many new ideas and concepts are being born, and each one has to be tried out, understood, loved and cherished. When you are at the spearhead of the New Age, you must be willing to go ahead fearlessly and try out the newest of the new." She died in 2006.

Peter Caddy (1917–94)

Peter Caddy is one of the principal founders of the Findhorn Community in Scotland. A native of England, Caddy had interests in the occult while in his twenties. Caddy traveled in India during his time with the RAF in World War II. After the war he married Sheena Govan, who shared his occult interests; but their relationship ended when Caddy fell in love with Eileen Combe in the early 1950s.

Peter and Eileen started Findhorn in the mid-1960s, along with Dorothy Maclean. Peter divorced in 1982 and remarried. He and his new wife Paula then started The Gathering of the Ways center in Mount Shasta, California. Peter was killed in a car accident in Switzerland in 1994. Findhorn Press carries his memoir, *In Perfect Timing*.

Edgar Cayce (1877–1945)

Edgar Cayce is one of the most prominent psychics of modern times. A native of Kentucky, Cayce gave his first "reading" in 1901 after recovery from laryngitis. He worked as a photographer until his popularity as a medium demanded his total time and energy. Cayce gave over 14,000 "readings" or medium sessions during his life. He started the Association for Research and Enlightenment in Virginia Beach, Virginia, in 1931.

Cayce would normally do a reading while lying on a couch with his hands folded across his stomach. He would enter a self-induced sleep state and then respond to questions about any individuals. Cayce believed that this psychic activity and belief in reincarnation was compatible with his Christian faith.

Andrew Cohen (1955–)

Andrew Cohen is one of the more successful esoteric teachers in the United States. He was born in 1955 in a secular Jewish home. His spiritual journey began with an experience of enlightenment in Rome when he was 16. In the '80s he traveled to India and eventually became a disciple of Harivansh Lal Poonja. Poonja taught Hindu advaitism, the theory that all is one and that humans are divine.

Cohen separated from Poonja in the early '90s and has since taught as a distinct guru. He has authored several books including *My Master Is My Self, Autobiography of an Awakening* and *Living Enlightenment.* His work is carried out under the organizational name EnlightenNext (also the name of the group's magazine) and is based in Lenox, Massachusetts.

Some ex-members have critiqued Cohen for alleged manipulation and narcissism, most notably his own mother, Luna Tarlo, in *The Mother of God* (1997). André van der Braak wrote of his journey with Cohen in *Enlightenment Blues: My Years with an American Guru* (2003).

Internet Source

www.andrewcohen.org

Terry Cole-Whittaker

Terry Cole-Whittaker is the founder of Adventures in Enlightenment and is one of the major teachers of prosperity consciousness. She became a pastor of the United Church of Religious Science congregation in La Jolla, California, in 1977 but broke away from the New Thought group in 1982. Cole-Whittaker had incredible early success in her independent ministry but experienced spiritual and organizational crisis in 1985. She then started Adventures in Enlightenment.

She is the author of *What You Think of Me Is None of My Business* and *Every Saint Has a Past, Every Sinner a Future.* This latter book reflects her sense of her own struggles in life, including several failed marriages. She is building The International Institute of Sacred Knowledge near New Delhi, India. Cole-Whittaker claimed in a 2001 interview with *In Light*

Times that her message of prosperity has changed in one very important respect: "Instead of accumulating everything for ourselves, let's serve God and humanity selflessly, and our heart's desire naturally will come to us as a result of our faith and surrendered attitude."

Internet Source

Cole-Whittaker website: www.terrycolewhittaker.com

Ignatius Donnelly (1831–1901)

Modern-day interest in the lost continent of Atlantis owes most to Philadelphia native Ignatius Donnelly. He spent many years in politics and journalism in Minnesota and then devoted two years to research for his famous book *Atlantis: The Antediluvian World*. The work went through many printings in both England and the United States. A revised edition by Egerton Sykes came out in 1949.

Betty Eadie

Betty J. Eadie became famous in 1992 through the publication of *Embraced by the Light*, a record of her own near-death experience (NDE). The book describes Jesus' appearance to Eadie when she "died" during surgery in 1973. Her writings are "dedicated to sharing what I learned during my brief stay in heaven."

Her experience led her to explore aspects of psychology, including the study of hypnosis and the human response to death. *Embraced by the Light* sold six million copies and was on *The New York Times* best-seller list for two years. Eadie has since written three other books and travels widely to talk about what awaits humanity after death. Born in rural Nebraska, Eadie, a mother and grandmother, lives in Seattle, Washington.

In *Embraced by the Light* Eadie wrote about the love she felt when she met Jesus in her near-death experience. "All my life I had feared him, and I now saw—I knew—that he was my choicest friend. Gently, he opened his arms and let me stand back far enough to look into his eyes, and he said, 'Your death was premature; it is not yet your time.' No words ever spoken have penetrated me more than these. Until then, I had felt no purpose in life; I had simply ambled along looking for love and goodness but never really knowing if my actions were right. Now, within his words,

I felt a mission, a purpose; I didn't know what it was, but I knew that my life on earth had not been meaningless."

Internet Source

www.embracedbythelight.com

Ralph Waldo Emerson (1803–82)

Ralph Waldo Emerson, a major American poet, philosopher and literary figure, has had a significant impact on the esoteric tradition in America. He left the Unitarian ministry to pursue a career as a writer and lecturer. Emerson was a leading advocate for Transcendentalism, with Henry Thoreau, Nathaniel Hawthorne and William Wordsworth. His 1836 essay "Nature" expounded Transcendentalism's central idea, the principle of the "mystical unity of nature."

An excerpt from his 1938 address at Harvard Divinity School captures the essence of Emerson's philosophy. "It is the office of a true teacher to show us that God is, not was; that He speaketh, not spake. The true Christianity—a faith like Christ's in the infinitude of man—is lost. None believeth in the soul of man, but only in some man or person old and departed. Ah me! no man goeth alone. All men go in flocks to this saint or that poet, avoiding the God who seeth in secret. They cannot see in secret; they love to be blind in public. They think society wiser than their soul, and know not that one soul, and their soul, is wiser than the whole world."

Internet Source

http://www.transcendentalists.com/1emerson.html

Virginia Essene (1928–)

Virginia Essene is one of the leading New Age channelers. Messages from "The Master known as the Christ" were published in 1986 under the title *New Teachings for an Awakening Humanity*. She says that they were rooted in energy she received from Jesus when she was visiting Israel in 1984. Essene has also released channeled revelations with Ann Valentin under the titles *Cosmic Revelation* and *Descent of the Dove*. She now leads The Share Foundation, a non-profit organization in Santa Clara, California, and is a minister in the Church of Antioch.

Marilyn Ferguson (1938–2008)

Marilyn Ferguson, a Colorado native, is the author of *The Aquarian Conspiracy*, published in 1980 and one of the most important books in the New Age movement. In the 1970s Ferguson worked on research about the brain and human consciousness. She also paid significant attention to the major social changes having an impact on the global community. Out of this she wrote her famous book about what she believed were the necessary paradigm changes for the health of the human race.

Her work aimed to provide an overall view about the possibility of improving planet Earth, whether in terms of education, ecology, politics, or spirituality. In a 1995 essay Ferguson talked about the possibilities emerging in the growing New Age spirit: "Spaceship Earth, Gaia, a New Atlantis, planetary tribe, partnership, community, holism . . . these are not just ideas whose time has come. These are visions that transcend time. The concepts emerging now have the potential to shape a planetary civilization. Quite suddenly, too, we are not afraid to talk about the soul. Wildly popular films and books address spiritual issues. The whispers of the soul grow louder."

In the early 1980s Ferguson became the popular target of some evangelical Christian writers who accused her of being part of a satanic conspiracy to bring in the One World Church of the Antichrist. Constance Cumbey, author of *Hidden Dangers of the Rainbow*, suggested that the numbers 666 were hidden in the design on the cover of *The Aquarian Conspiracy*. Ferguson died of an apparent heart attack in October 2008.

Charles Fillmore (1854–1948)

Charles Fillmore was born in Minnesota on August 22, 1854. In 1876 he moved to Texas and met his future wife Mary Myrtle Page, a teacher, who was born in 1845 in Ohio. Charles and Myrtle were married in 1881 and moved to Kansas City, Missouri, in 1884.

In 1886 Myrtle was influenced by the teaching of E. B. Weeks, a follower of Emma Curtis Hopkins, an advocate of Christian Science and founder of New Thought. Myrtle came away from the meetings with Weeks with an affirmation: "I am a child of God and therefore I do not inherit sickness." Over the next two years Myrtle achieved a new level of healing from a constant threat of tuberculosis.

Charles became convinced of the Christian Science/New Thought healing paradigm after he heard Hopkins in Chicago. He and Myrtle started the magazine *Modern Thought* in 1889 (later renamed *Unity Magazine*), and the Unity Society of Practical Christianity was incorporated in 1903. Charles wrote *Christian Healing* in 1909 and started radio broadcasts in 1922.

Myrtle, called the "Mother of Unity," died in 1931. Two years later Charles married Cora Dedrick and also wrote *The Metaphysical Bible Dictionary*. Charles retired that same year but continued to travel and teach until shortly before his death in 1948.

Internet Source

http://charlesfillmore.wwwhubs.com

The Fox Sisters

The Fox sisters (Margaret, Kate, and Leah) are considered the founders of the modern Spiritualist movement. In 1848, Margaret, then a teenager, and her younger sister Kate claimed that disturbing noises in their house in Hydesville, New York, were made by spirits who would answer questions from the girls by tapping on the walls. Their older sister, Leah, joined in the drama and soon the Fox sisters were national celebrities.

Margaret and Kate suffered from alcoholism, and this affected both their personal lives and their medium work. In 1888 Margaret announced that she and Kate were frauds and that Leah had forced them to continue their hoax. Margaret said that she and Kate created the tapping sounds by putting their toes out of joint. The next year Margaret retracted these accusations and launched an unsuccessful national tour to bolster her status as a medium.

Leah died in 1890, Kate in 1892, and Margaret a year later.

Matthew Fox (1940–)

Matthew Fox is the founder of Creation Spirituality. He was silenced by the Vatican in 1989 and then expelled from the Dominican order in 1993. He became an Episcopal priest the next year. Fox is now president of the University of Creation Spirituality and a major inspiration for New Agers.

Fox was born in Wisconsin in 1940 and was ordained a priest in 1967. His book *On Becoming a Musical, Mystical Bear* (1972) laid the foundation for his continuing work in a theology that emphasized the positive side of the created order. The Vatican reacted to what they perceived as his downplaying of original sin and also his openness to non-orthodox understandings of Christian faith and other religions. Many traditional Catholics objected in particular to Fox's work with Starhawk, the famous witch.

Fox expressed his deep interplay between faith and creation in his work *Original Blessing*. In his description of Creation Spirituality he states that "we experience that the Divine is in all things and all things are in the Divine (Panentheism) and that this mystical intuition supplants theism (and its child, atheism) as an appropriate way to name our relation to the Divine and experience the Sacred."

Fox has attempted to revive church worship for young people through his creation of "Techno-Cosmic Masses," which combine the wisdoms of ancient liturgy and spirituality with modern dance, music, drama, and poetry, all presented via modern technology. Fox says this of the power of the Techno-Cosmic Mass: "Transformation happens. Transformation is possible. Hope happens. Beauty flows. Fun occurs. Memory is unleashed and tapped into. The ancestors return. Boundaries melt. Boredom ceases. Creativity breaks out. Depression disappears. Empowerment takes place. Community comes to pass."

Fox situates himself between what he regards as classical mystical Christianity and the New Age. He writes: "Certain ecclesial guardians of the ancestral powers feel the forms we have are just fine even if no one shows up; at the other extreme we have new agers who want to throw the past out entirely. In the middle there is the Techno Cosmic Mass movement wherein we are deconstructing and reconstructing the worship of our ancestors with the able leadership of the first postmodern generation."

Fox has masters degrees and a doctorate in spirituality, and has written over twenty books, including *Confessions: The Making of a Postdenominational Priest* (1996) and the recent *Creativity: Where the Divine and Human Meet.*

Internet Sources

www.creationspirituality.com

http://www.matthewfox.org/sys-tmpl/door

Joseph Gelberman (1912–)

A native of Hungary, Joseph Gelberman is a New Age rabbi with roots in Jewish orthodoxy. After his family perished in the Holocaust, Gelberman moved to America and trained as a rabbi in New York City. He departed from orthodoxy in the early 1960s while serving as a rabbi in Princeton. He then founded the Little Synagogue in lower Manhattan and became a popular New Age speaker in the '70s and '80s. He was connected with the start of The New Light Temple in 1977. He is the author of several books, including *To Be . . . Fully Alive*, *Zen Judaism*, and *Kabbalah As I See It*. He is currently the rabbi of The New Synagogue in New York City.

Internet Source

http://www.interfaith.org

George Ivanovitch Gurdjieff (c. 1866–1949)

George Ivanovitch Gurdjieff is one of the most enigmatic modern esoteric teachers. His date of birth is a matter of some speculation (1866, 1872, and 1877 are the usual dates given). A native of Armenia, he traveled through Asia and the Middle East for a couple of decades, moved to Russia in 1912, but had to flee during the Marxist revolution in 1917. Gurdjieff settled in Paris and started The Institute for the Harmonious Development of Man in 1922. Russian philosopher P. D. Ouspensky (1878–1947) met Gurdjieff in 1914 and became one of his most famous interpreters.

Gurdjieff sought to awaken humanity from spiritual, psychological and intellectual slumber. He often used shocking language or directives to his students to break down what he thought were their false pretensions and ideologies. He sought to unite Western science with Eastern wisdom, but his fragmented and obscure writings remain very difficult to understand. Constance Jones offers a guide to his thought in her work *The Legacy of G. I. Gurdjieff* (2005).

Internet Source

Website: www.gurdjieff.org

Steven Halpern (1947–)

Steven Halpern is one of the leaders in the field of New Age music. In the late '60s and early '70s he began to compose music that he believed would lead to health and healing. *Keyboard Magazine* says that Halpern is one of the twelve contemporary musicians who altered the way we play and listen to music. Halpern has produced many recordings, and he wrote a book in 1985 called *Sound Health* that deals with his philosophy of music.

Halpern suggests in one of his newsletters that great musicians like Mozart received their messages from the Spirit. He also refers to the inspiration that country singer Alan Jackson said was behind his famous response to 9/11: *Where Were You (When the World Stopped Turning)*. Halpern writes: "I salute Alan Jackson for being a messenger, and for acknowledging he didn't do it alone."

Internet Source

www.stevehalpern.com

"John-Roger" Hinkins (1934–)

John-Roger Hinkins is the founder of the Church of the Movement of Spiritual Inner Awareness or MSIA. Born Roger Hinkins into a Mormon family in Utah in 1934, Hinkins got a degree in psychology from the University of Utah in 1958 and began teaching high school. He traces his emergence to the day in 1963 when a Mystical Traveler named "John" entered his body after Hinkins came out of a nine-day coma following surgery to remove a kidney stone. Hinkins then took on the name John-Roger.

Hinkins's own spiritual teaching began in May 1968 and more formally in 1971 with the incorporation of MSIA. Hinkins has been charged with stealing ideas from Eckankar, another spiritual movement. Hinkins denies formal membership in ECK but acknowledges attending meetings in this and other metaphysical movements in the early 1960s. David Christopher Lane, a scholar of esotericism, has been very critical of Hinkins in terms of his connections to Eckankar and also to alleged sexual misconduct.

Hinkins claimed that in 1988 the Mystical Traveler moved on to John Morton, though Hinkins continues to be a major presence in MSIA. Hinkins's message is one of self-affirmation rooted in Divine acceptance.

He said in 1997: "The most obvious mistake we make in our lives is not loving ourselves no matter what. At the moment when we've made an emotional feeling-level mistake, there's one thing we need more than anything else in the world, and that is to be loved past all that, to be loved into the Divinity, the divineness, the holiness of God's breath upon us. Yet we often won't do this because, as I said, we make a mistake and then we punish ourselves more, even though that isn't what we need."

Internet Source

www.john-roger.org

www.msia.org

Jean Houston (1941–)

Jean Houston is one of the leaders in the study of the transformation of the human consciousness. Houston rejected her Roman Catholic schooling early in life, turned to drugs in the '60s and early '70s (along with her husband Robert Masters) as a potential means for enlightenment, and then shifted her attention to meditation and the potential of the human mind. Her interest in human potential may have some roots in her mother's background in Christian Science.

Houston worked closely with Margaret Mead, the famous anthropologist, and the well-known mythologist Joseph Campbell. For thirty years she and her husband have co-directed the Foundation for Mind Research, now situated in Pamona, New York. She is also the founder of The Mystery School, which offers cross-cultural studies for "Inspired Living in the Radical Now: Inventing Solutions for the Wildest of Times." On the school's website Houston states: "Beneath the surface crust of consciousness there is a new nature waiting to bud when the old nature has withered. This nature lies within us all and is open to the path that leads from chaos to creation."

Houston has written eighteen books, including *Mystical Dogs, Public Like a Frog*, and *The Hero and the Goddess*. She has drawn media attention for careless claims about her educational background, and there was controversy over her connection with Hillary Clinton at the White House.

Internet Source

www.jeanhouston.org

Geraldine Innocente (?–1961)

Geraldine Innocente is the co-founder (along with Mary Innocente, her mother) of The Bridge to Freedom Activity, one of the groups that emerged from the I AM movement founded by Guy and Edna Ballard. The Innocentes broke away from I AM in 1951 and Edna Ballard attacked the new group.

Geraldine channeled messages from the Ascended Master El Morya, which were published under the pseudonym Thomas Printz. Geraldine taught that her father, Gus, was previously incarnated in the time of Jesus and helped him carry the cross. Geraldine died in 1961, and Lucy Little-john led the movement through 1989.

The Bridge is now headquartered in Kings Park, New York.

Ken Keyes, Jr. (1921–95)

Ken Keyes, Jr. is most well known as the author of *The Hundredth Monkey*, published in 1982. The work introduced New Agers to the idea that when a "critical mass" of humanity adopts an idea an almost miraculous paradigm shift can occur in the larger population. Keyes's idea was based on a report from Lyall Watson in 1979 about research that allegedly proved psychic transmission between monkeys when a group of them attained a new habit. Masao Kawai, a key scientist involved in the scientific study, has repudiated Watson's version of events.

A native of Atlanta, Keyes turned to New Age ideas in 1970 when he was looking for fulfillment following two divorces in ten years. He released *Handbook to Higher Consciousness* in 1975 and started the Ken Keyes College in Coos Bay, Oregon, in 1982.

Keyes was admired most for his positive attitude in spite of being confined to a wheelchair since a polio attack in 1946. Keyes wrote: "To be upset over what you don't have is to waste what you do have."

Near the end of his life Keyes developed Caring Rapid Healing workshops that merged his work in positive thinking with EMDR, the rapid eye movement therapy developed by Francine Shapiro. From this interest he wrote his last book *Your Road Map to Lifelong Happiness* that was published just six months before his death in December 1995.

Krishnamurti (1895–1986)

Jiddu Krishnamurti is one of the most enigmatic and important figures in both Eastern and Western religious traditions. A native of Andhra Pradesh, India, Krishnamurti was chosen by Theosophy leaders Charles Leadbeater and Annie Besant in 1909 to be the World Teacher or Maitreya, a Christ figure who was to usher in a new human order. Krishnamurti was given Alcyone as a spiritual name, and the Order of the Star of the East was founded to focus on Krishnamurti's role.

By the mid-1920s Krishnamurti was teaching in the United States and other countries. On August 2, 1929, at a Star meeting in Holland, he openly rejected claims that he was the World Teacher, though he announced his intent to continue as a spiritual advisor to any who would listen. His speech was a blow to Leadbeater, Besant, and other Theosophists who had spent two decades grooming him as the Messiah.

Krishnamurti continued his world travels till his death in California in 1986. His image as a great Spirit Master suffered greatly in 1991 with the release of Radha Rajagopal Sloss's memoir *Lives in the Shadow with J. Krishnamurti.* Sloss, the daughter of Krishnamurti's longtime assistant D. Rajagopal and his wife Rosalind, documented a twenty-five-year affair between Krishnamurti and Rosalind. The book is written without malice, though it has been attacked by modern devotees of the famous Indian teacher.

Internet Source

Krishnamurti Foundation of America: www.kfa.org

Elisabeth Kübler-Ross (1926–2004)

Elisabeth Kübler-Ross is the famous author of *On Death and Dying.* A native of Zürich, Switzerland, she graduated from medical school in 1957 and moved to United States the following year. Kübler-Ross was appalled at the treatment of dying patients at the hospital where she worked in New York City. Over the next decade she reached out to the terminally ill and listened to them. *On Death and Dying,* her first work, told the story of what she learned from her dying patients. The book, published in 1969, made her a world authority on the topic.

Kübler-Ross has been the object of some scorn for her belief in fairies and spirit guides. In one interview she speaks about taking pictures in hopes of capturing an image of her spirit guide. "I took my husband's expensive camera, went up a small hill, looked into the woods and said aloud, 'If I have a guide, I'd like to see him or her materialize in a photograph.' I pointed the camera at the trees, took two pictures, went home and forgot about the whole thing. Weeks later when the pictures were developed, there, on one of them, was the figure of a tall American Indian with a hand stretched out towards me. Needless to say I was thrilled! That was my first encounter with one of my guides."

Kübler-Ross suffered a series of strokes in 1995 and withdrew from public life. She died in 2004.

Internet Source

www.elisabethkublerross.com

Charles Leadbeater (1854–1934)

Charles Leadbeater was one of the early leaders in Theosophy and had a significant impact on Annie Besant, the second president of the Theosophical Society. Born in England, he was an Anglican priest before turning to Buddhism, esoteric movements, and the occult world. He met Besant in 1890, and they worked on several books together espousing Theosophical views.

In 1906 accusations of sexual misconduct with young boys led to his expulsion from the movement. He was reinstated in 1908, in large part because of Besant's trust in his integrity. In 1909 Leadbeater introduced Krishnamurti as the coming World Teacher. She and Leadbeater groomed Krishnamurti in his messianic role, one that he rejected in 1929, just five years before Leadbeater's death in 1934.

John Lilly (1915–2001)

The New Age fascination with dolphins owes much to John Lilly, a neurologist and specialist on dolphin research. Lilly, a native of Minnesota, wrote several scientific studies about dolphins and opened the Human/Dolphin Foundation in 1981 in Malibu.

Lilly was trained as an M.D. and in psychoanalysis and was also widely known for his openness to LSD.

Internet Source

www.johnclilly.com

Shirley MacLaine (1934–)

Shirley MacLaine has probably done more than any one person to introduce New Age concepts simply because of the huge publicity surrounding her spiritual journey. Born in Richmond, Virginia, MacLaine had some connection with Southern Baptist Church life in her early years.

Her interest in New Age ideas coincided with the breakdown of her marriage to Steve Parker, from whom she was divorced in 1977. MacLaine wrote about her conversion to New Age philosophy in her 1983 best seller *Out on a Limb*. However, it was the movie release of the book in the fall of 1987 that made her views and experiences even more widely known. She made the cover of *Time* in its report on the New Age. Her extravagant claims have made her the object of jokes in the comedy circuit. In one famous incident, MacLaine lost her temper on *The David Letterman Show* when she was grilled about her past lives.

She is also the author of *Dancing in the Light* and *It's All in the Playing*. Her latest book *The Camino* documents her 500-mile trek along a pilgrim's path in northern Spain. She claims that her journey led her spiritually back through thousands of lives to the start of the universe.

Internet Source

www.shirleymaclaine.com

HAS REINCARNATION BEEN CUT OUT OF THE BIBLE?

Shirley MacLaine and other New Age teachers argue that Christians used to believe in reincarnation until the church abandoned this teaching in the sixth century. MacLaine even suggests that Catholic leaders ordered verses supporting reincarnation to be cut out of the Bible.

Fact: With the possible exception of Origen, early church fathers did not believe in reincarnation.

Fact: Origen's views on the preexistence of the soul are not the same as New Age ideas on reincarnation.

Fact: No verses have been cut out of the Bible; the idea is pure fantasy. We have thousands of copies of the New Testament written before the sixth century with no sign of cutting and pasting.

Franz Anton Mesmer (1734–1815)

Franz Anton Mesmer, a native of Germany, is a significant figure in the history of esotericism and New Age religion because of his emphasis on the role of the mind in healing. The term *mesmerism* is coined from his name and he was a practitioner of what we now call hypnosis. Mesmer, a native of Germany, also used magnets to promote healing and taught that he could magnetize water, paper, and even dogs. He would magnetize a tree and have sick people dangle by rope from its branches.

Ruth Montgomery (1913–2001)

Ruth Montgomery is both a famous chronicler and an exponent of the New Age. Born in Illinois, she spent decades in journalism before turning her attention to the psychic realms. She became Washington correspondent for *The New York Daily News* in 1944 and was president of the National Press Club in 1950.

Montgomery developed an interest in the occult in the late '50s and wrote a major book on the famous psychic Jeane Dixon in 1965. She also believed she was in touch with Spirit Guides and attended séances with the famous medium Arthur Ford. Even after Ford's death in 1971, Montgomery claimed that Ford was speaking through her.

Montgomery helped to make famous the notion of Walk-ins—a reference to enlightened Spirit beings from the eternal realm who are allowed to take over the bodies of souls who are ready to leave the earth. Montgomery claimed in one interview that Charles Colson is a "Walk-in" as were George Washington and Abraham Lincoln.

Montgomery died January 10, 2001.

Henry Steel Olcott (1832–1907)

Henry Steel Olcott, born in New Jersey, was an agriculturalist, military investigator, lawyer, and journalist. He fought with Union forces in America's Civil War and had a long-term interest in Spiritualism. While he was studying the psychic work of the Eddy brothers in Vermont in 1874, Olcott met the famous Madame H. P. Blavatsky. The next year the two of them founded the Theosophical Society, along with William Q. Judge.

Olcott became president of the Society and traveled with Blavatsky to India to develop the movement there. While remaining active in

Theosophy, Olcott also became a Buddhist in 1880. He was later instrumental in arranging for Anagarika Dharmapala, a prominent Buddhist monk, to speak at the World's Parliament of Religions in Chicago in 1893. His organizational skill and travels are credited with much of Theosophy's growth. He died in Adyar, Madras, India, in 1907.

Phineas Parkhurst Quimby (1802–66)

Phineas Parkhurst Quimby, a native of Maine, was one of the first people in America to introduce the concept of mental energy as a major factor in medical and spiritual health. He was influenced by mesmerism and hypnotism. He opened an office in Portland, Maine, in 1859 and taught his version of healing to several students who became famous as religious leaders: Warren Felt Evans (1817–89), Annetta and Julius Dresser (early leaders in New Thought), Mary Baker Eddy (the founder of Christian Science), and Emma Curtis Hopkins (one-time Eddy follower who founded a New Thought school).

There has been considerable debate over Eddy's debt to Quimby in her works, including *Science and Health with Key to the Scriptures*, published in 1875. In the 1890s the Dressers accused Eddy of stealing Quimby's basic ideas. It is fair to say that Eddy owed some of her thought to Quimby, but she departed from his theology and healing in a number of significant ways.

Internet Source

Website: www.ppquimby.com

Baba Ram Dass (1933–)

Baba Ram Dass is one of the most famous New Age and esoteric teachers in the world. He was born Richard Alpert in 1933 and was raised in a Jewish home. He was dismissed from Harvard University in 1963, following his controversial research on LSD with his colleague Timothy Leary. In 1967, while traveling in India, he became a devotee of the Hindu teacher Neem Karoli Baba. In 1970 Baba Ram Dass accompanied the famous Swami Muktananda (1908–82) on the latter's first tour of America.

*Famous New Age teacher Baba Ram
Dass teaching in Hawaii*

Photo: Jessica Rigney

Ram Dass started the Hanuman Foundation in 1974. His book *Be Here Now*, published in 1971, has sold over one million copies and has gone through over thirty printings. The book is one of the most important works in modern esotericism. Ram Dass works currently with the Seva Foundation, the Social Venture Network, and the Institute for Dying, among other service institutions. He has talked openly about his homosexual past in several interviews.

On February 19, 1997, Ram Dass suffered a severe stroke, but he has recovered enough to maintain some public speaking. He said in an interview with *USA Today* that "I had been superficial and arrogant and the stroke helped me to be humble. I had gotten power from helping people and now I need help for everything. That was the grace. The stroke happened to the ego, and when I could witness the pain, my life got better."

One of his latest works is *One Liners: A Mini-Manual for a Spiritual Life,* which includes the statement: "The shadow is our greatest teacher for how to come to the Light."

Internet Source

www.ramdasstapes.org/

James Redfield (1950–)

James Redfield is one of the most widely read of current New Age leaders. He is the author of the famous work *The Celestine Prophecy,* which he self-published in 1993. The book had remarkable sales across the United States, and the rights to it were bought by Warner Books in 1994. The work remained on *The New York Times* best-seller list for three years.

The Celestine Prophecy uses a fictional journey to Peru as the context for imparting Nine Insights for spiritual maturity. He followed that work with *The Tenth Insight* in 1996. Redfield has also written *The Secret of Shambhala: In Search of the Eleventh Insight,* and co-authored *God and the Evolving Universe.*

A native of Alabama, Redfield found his Methodist roots did not provide enough answers about true spirituality. He studied Eastern religion while pursuing a degree in sociology. Redfield counseled abused teens for over fifteen years and during that time became fascinated with the human potential movement. He stopped his therapy practice in 1989 and devoted over two years to write *The Celestine Prophecy.* He is now involved with the Global Renaissance Alliance and also works at preserving America's forests.

Redfield and his wife, Salle, live in Florida. Salle teaches courses in meditation and produces the online *Celestine Journal* with her husband.

REDFIELD'S ELEVEN INSIGHTS

1. A Critical Mass

There is a new enlightenment sweeping human culture that is based on a critical mass of humans who have entered life as a spiritual journey.

2. The Longer Now

A more comprehensive worldview, one that is concerned with purpose and fundamental reality, is replacing the secular and technological preoccupations of the last five centuries.

3. A Matter of Energy

Humans now recognize that we live in a world of energy and not a material universe. Energy can be projected so that the flow of helpful coincidences increases.

4. The Struggle for Power

Human history has been marred by the urge to dominate and use power to hurt others.

5. The Message of the Mystics

The mystics of the ages have taught us to connect with our inner divine energy so that we are not consumed by power.

6. Clearing the Past

As humans connect to the divine energy there is a greater awareness of our past failures in taking energy from others.

7. Engaging the Flow

Working on personal mission leads to a questioning that brings us along the mystical path with the wisdom from other humans.

8. The Interpersonal Ethic

Our help to others increases the chances of synchronistic development in our own lives.

9. The Emerging Culture

As humanity progresses on the path of spirituality we will be transformed so that we unite with the eternal realm in a breaking of the cycle of life and death.

10. Holding the Vision

Humans must join together in maintaining the spiritual vision that has been the unconscious quest of humans throughout history.

11. Extending Prayer Fields

The future for humanity involves a growing dependence on prayer, on positive thinking, on faith, particularly as humanity joins together in common spiritual vision.

Internet Source

www.celestinevision.com

David Spangler (1945–)

David Spangler is one of the intellectual leaders of the New Age, especially in terms of its theoretical basis and political aspirations. Spangler was born in Columbus, Ohio, but moved with his family to Morocco in 1951, returning to America in 1957. After he moved to Los Angeles when he was 20, he worked with psychic Myrtle Glines for a five-year period. Spangler had connections with some theosophical groups in the late '50s and had a major mystical experience when he was 7 and riding in the car with his parents.

Spangler worked in the Findhorn Community in Scotland from 1970 through 1973. Along with Dorothy Maclean, he founded the Lorian Association in 1974 in California and became a major speaker and guide to the emerging New Age community in the United States. In his book *Blessing* Spangler says this of himself: "I don't call myself a spiritual teacher, although that name is often applied to me. I feel that each of us has an indwelling spirit—a unique and personal connection with the sacred—which is our true spiritual teacher."

Though he is not skeptical of mystical experiences, Spangler has been critical of the apocalyptic emphasis in some New Age circles and has distanced himself in a polite way from some of its more popular practices and theories. In *A Pilgrim in Aquarius* he reports on being dismissed by a *Time* magazine reporter because he did not want to equate the New Age with the use of crystals.

He writes: "I think if we must have a symbol for the New Age, a much better image would be the cell. The cell is a fluid organization, a highly complex and structured system that is still flexible and dynamic; it is an organic crystal. On the other hand, unlike crystals, there's no profit in cells. It's hard to wear one on a pendant around your neck (although you could just display the neck: it has plenty of cells and all free)."

After 9/11 Spangler claimed that he received a message from a being in the Spirit world who spoke of the tragedy in redemptive terms. "I have spoken of this as a sacrificial act made by the Soul of America. Did those who were killed have any choice in the matter? What we see is that many of those who perished had indeed made an agreement at a soul level to participate in this sacrificial act, to make it their portal for entry into our world; others did not but were drawn into the event for a great many reasons personal to them and their destinies. They could not have avoided it."

Internet Source

www.davidspangler.com

Brad Steiger (1936–)

Brad Steiger, formerly Eugene Olson, is a native of Iowa and one of the most widely read writers on New Age phenomena. He claims that when he was 5 years old he had contact with an alien and a near-death experience when he was 11. In 1973 Steiger authored a book called *Revelation,* which documented accounts of people claiming direct contact with supernatural beings. In *Gods of Aquarius,* published in 1976, he focused on UFO contactees and gave significant attention to what he called Star People, humans who come from a special gene pool linked to visits by extraterrestrials.

Steiger continued this theme in works written with his second wife, Francie Pascal, including *The Star People.* Following the breakup of their marriage in the mid-1980s, Steiger wrote *The Fellowship* where he contin-ued the subject without much reference to the actual term *Star People*. In 1987 Steiger married Sherry Hanson, and together they have written more than twenty volumes on paranormal themes and other topics.

Internet Source

www.bradandsherry.com

Rudolf Steiner (1861–1925)

Rudolf Steiner is the founder of Anthroposophy. He was a specialist in the works of Johann Wolfgang von Goethe. At the start of the twen-tieth century, Steiner had contact with the Theosophical Society and with occult movements. He then developed his own spiritual movement, based in part on ideas gleaned from Goethe and from the metaphysical groups of his day. Steiner wrote forty books, and his six thousand lectures are collected in three hundred volumes. The Anthroposophical Society was founded in 1912.

Though Steiner had some sense of the importance of the historical Jesus, he separated the Christ from Jesus. In a 1913 lecture he stated: "That Being Who lived in Jesus from his thirtieth to thirty-third years gave the impulse humanity needed for its development at a time when its youthful forces were beginning to decline. In recapitulation, I can say that a new understanding of Christ is a necessity today. Spiritual science not only tries to lead us to Christ; it *must* do so. All the truths it advances must lead from a spiritual contemplation of man's development to a com-prehension of Christ. Men will experience Christ in ever greater measure, and through Christ they will discover Jesus."

Internet Source

www.anthroposophy.org

Whitley Strieber (1945–)

Whitley Strieber is the author of the 1987 best seller *Communion*, which tells the story of Strieber's abduction by aliens at his family's cabin in Upstate New York. What has made the book significant is that Strieber had prior credibility as an author and researcher, with no apparent need for money or evidence of psychological imbalance. However, critics have insisted that Strieber knew this work would make a lot of money. They also draw attention to significant lapses of memory in his reporting on other alleged events in his life.

Other skeptics have suggested that any initial plausibility that might be granted to Strieber's *Communion* work disappears in light of his ongoing regular contact with the alien realm. It is just too much, too often, and too good to be true. Strieber is now selling a book called *The Key*, which tells the story of his encounter at 3 A.M. in a hotel room in Toronto on June 6, 1998, with a highly intelligent human that he calls "Master of the Key." He stated that the Master admitted having no Canadian identification papers, so Strieber argues that perhaps he survives outside traditional Canadian boundaries through his possible link with the descendants of the Knights Templar who came to Newfoundland centuries earlier.

Likewise, Strieber's website shows almost no limits to his acceptance of the wildest range of paranormal claims, including crop circles, out-of-body experiences, and lost worlds.

Internet Sources

www.unknowncountry.com

www.beyondcommunion.com

James Van Praagh (1958–)

James Van Praagh, one of North America's best-known mediums, says that he is able to "bridge the gap between two planes of existence, that of the living and that of the dead, by providing evidential proof of life after death via detailed messages." He calls himself a "telephone to the spirit world." After its publication in 2001, his book *Talking to Heaven* topped the best-seller list of *The New York Times*, boosted by repeated appearances on the major television talk shows.

Van Praagh is a native of Queens, New York. He was raised in a staunch Roman Catholic home, but by his teen years had dismissed Catholicism as an "archaic belief system." He moved to Los Angeles after high school and worked on the fringes of show business, all the while developing the psychic abilities he says every human possesses. Van Praagh claims that his paranormal gifts were evident from his earliest years. A frequently told story goes that in first grade he told his teacher about injuries her son sustained in a car crash moments before she received first news of the accident.

Van Praagh promotes Hindu teaching on karma and reincarnation. Believing each human is "perfect if we would only seek our divinity," he invites his admirers to explore the spirit world through attending séances and use of the Ouija board. He also promotes a range of practices such as having one's aura read and developing one's *chakras* (spiritual power points within the body, used in yoga).

In *Talking to Heaven* Van Praagh adopts the New Age message of the power of the mind. He illustrates this by writing: "If our thoughts dwell on poverty and illness, we will draw these conditions to us. If we elevate our thoughts to a higher frequency level, we will reap harmony and abundance. This is a fixed universal law that cannot be changed."

Internet Source

www.vanpraagh.com

Neale Donald Walsch (1943–)

Neale Donald Walsch is the famous author of the *Conversations with God* series. Raised in a Roman Catholic home in Milwaukee, he claims that his mother encouraged him in an open quest for spiritual truth. When he asked her once why she did not attend church regularly, she replied: "I don't have to go to church—God comes to me. He's with me and around me wherever I am."

By his teenage years Walsch was reading famous scriptures of the Eastern traditions. After spending two years in college, he wandered from job to job, finally settling in public relations on the West Coast. By this time he had already gone through several failed marriages. After relocation in Oregon, Walsch was involved in a serious car accident in which his neck was broken. After a year of rehab, another failed marriage, and a period of homelessness, he regained a steady job.

Walsch was filled with despair and life seemed to have no meaning. In February 1992 he awoke in the middle of the night and wrote a letter to God in which he asked: "What does it take to make life work?" He claims that he received a divine answer and began recording his now-famous conversations with God. His first book of dictation became an instant best seller.

In response to the recent sex scandals in the Catholic Church, Walsch has suggested that organized religion makes a serious mistake in advocating restrictive sexuality and the worship of God. He writes: *"Conversations with God* tells us that religion in its highest form has nothing to do with serving or worshipping God, for the simple reason that God does not need servicing or worshipping. Religion in its highest form has to do with serving and worshipping ourselves, and all humankind."

Walsch resides in Oregon with his wife, Nancy. Together they run the Conversations with God Foundation.

Internet Source

www.cwg.org

Ken Wilber (1949–)

Ken Wilber, a native of Oklahoma, is one of the most prolific and seriously studied New Age leaders. His early interests in medicine gave way to an ongoing study of psychology, mysticism, and religion. He wrote *The Spectrum of Consciousness,* one of the most influential works in the field of Transpersonal Psychology, though he has since distanced himself from the movement.

Wilber is one of the few New Age academics who read widely in mainstream philosophy and science. He has attempted to develop a comprehensive worldview that takes into account all aspects of human research. His recent books include *A Brief History of Everything* and *Boomeritis,* an attempt to introduce his views in the form of a postmodern novel. In 1998 Wilber founded the Integral Institute to foster cross-discipline research.

Wilber is viewed by some intellectuals as one of the most important thinkers of all time, while others accuse him of being incomprehensible. These critics might cite the following from his *A Brief History of Everything*: "Abide as Emptiness, embrace all Form. The liberation is in the Emptiness, never in the Form, but Emptiness embraces all forms as a mirror of all its objects. So the Forms continue to arise, and, as the sound of one hand clapping, you are all those Forms. You are the display. You and the universe are One Taste. Your Original Face is the purest Emptiness, and therefore every time you look in the mirror, you see only the entire Kosmos."

His work provides an argument that rationalism and science alone cannot reach truth and that a secular philosophy will ultimately lead nowhere. He stated in *The Marriage of Sense and Soul* that "neither sensory empiricism, nor pure reason, nor practical reason, nor any combination thereof can see into the realm of Spirit. In the smoking ruins left by Kant, the only possible conclusion is that all future metaphysics and authentic spirituality must offer direct experiential evidence."

Ken Wilber

Photo: Genpo Merzel Roshi

Wilber's most moving work is *Grace and Grit* (1991), a series of reflections on his life with his wife, Treya, who was diagnosed with cancer one week after their marriage in 1983. She died in early 1989. Wilber's accounts of his last days with her are heartbreaking. Ten years after her death he wrote: "I am immeasurably more, and immeasurably less, because of her presence. Immeasurably more, for having known her; immeasurably less, for having lost her. But then, perhaps every event in life is like that: filling you up and emptying you out, all at the same time."

In the introduction to the 1999 edition of *Grace and Grit* he offered this understanding of the self and survival after death: "You triumph over death, not by living forever, but by living timelessly, by being present to the Present. You are not going to defeat death by identifying with the ego in the stream of time and then trying to make that ego go on forever in that temporal stream. You defeat death by finding that part of your own present awareness that never enters the stream of time in the first place and thus is truly Unborn and Undying."

Wilber is often critical of New Age fads and the shallowness in some New Age spirituality. He wrote in *One Taste*: "Real compassion kicks butt and takes names. If you are not ready for this fire, then find a New Age, sweetness-and-light, perpetually smiling teacher. But stay away from those who practice real compassion because they will fry your ass, my friend."

Wilber has been criticized for his contradictory advice about the controversial teacher Adi Da, formerly known as Da Free John and Bubba Free John, head of the Adidam community. Wilber has said that Adi Da is the most brilliant spiritual teacher of our time and yet has also warned about his wild side. In response to criticism about his ambivalence he stated that he could no longer recommend Adi Da as a guide.

Internet Sources

http://wilber.shambhala.com

www.worldofkenwilber.com

www.integralinstitute.org

Marianne Williamson (1952–)

Marianne Williamson is one of the leading speakers and inspirational writers in New Age circles, rising to fame with her 1992 book, *A Return to Love*. She is a minister in the Unity Church founded by Charles and Myrtle Fillmore and was for several years the spiritual leader of Renaissance Unity Spiritual Fellowship based in Warren, Michigan. Williamson was born in Houston, Texas, in 1952 and was raised in a Jewish home. She turned toward Unity's esoteric Christian vision through reading the famous work *A Course in Miracles* in 1977 when she was going through a major crisis in her life.

Williamson has been a professional speaker since 1983 and is the founder of Project Angel Food. She also is president of the Global Renaissance Alliance, a worldwide network of peace activists. She works with figures like Deepak Chopra, Barbara Marx Hubbard, and Neale Donald Walsch. She has a political and civic emphasis in her teaching, as in her book *A Healing for America*, and resists the individualism of much New Age religion.

Internet Sources

www.marianne.com

▨ A Christian Response to the New Age

Classical Christianity is clearly much different from New Age religion. First, the religions of the world do *not* agree on essentials; in fact, the differences are as significant as the similarities. The popular view that "all religions are the same" is both unbiblical and untrue to reality. Do New Agers really believe that their religion is the same as Southern Baptist or Mormonism?

Second, the New Age teaching of humanity's divinity has dangerous implications. The Christian can affirm that humans are made in the image of God, but humans are not divine *per se* and have no right to say, "I am God." New Age teachers ignore or downplay the Bible's teaching about the Fall and original sin. Failure to see humans as sinful involves denial of the obvious.

Third, humanity finds its hope not in realizing some mystical higher consciousness but in knowing and living out the grace and love of God as expressed in Jesus. There is nothing wrong, of course, in having ideals about achieving greater things for God. On one level, the positive focus of the New Age can serve as a corrective to negatively oriented and gloomy versions of Christian faith.

Fourth, reincarnation and karma are rooted in Hinduism and Buddhism, not in Jewish and Christian teaching. The New Testament has no teaching of karmic destiny or of souls involved in eternal rounds of death and life. The biblical teaching on salvation by grace alone and by faith alone directly contradicts the works-righteousness at the heart of New Age theories on karma and reincarnation.

It bears emphasis that New Agers often refer to reincarnation in a glamorous way, speaking about past lives in Rome or Atlantis, or past existences as a wolf or lion. In the process, they neglect the more traditional Buddhist and Hindu teachings that reincarnation can also involve becoming a bug in the intestine of a pig or a virus in the stomach of a cow. These possibilities take the glamour out of New Age theories of karma.

Fifth, the New Age is on very dangerous ground in its affirmation of psychic reality and the occult. On the one hand, many psychic and occult practices are simply untrue. New Agers often buy into the latest fads in the world of psychic or occult teachers and practitioners. And even if certain occult activities are real, that does not mean it is wise to participate in them. Scripture commands us to forbid trying to contact the dead, whether or not it can be done.

Sixth, the New Age has a distorted view of science, especially when it comes to claims that various aspects of physics somehow prove New Age ideology. New Age writers often promote a pseudo-scientific understanding of reality. On these issues New Agers should pay attention to the work of Martin Gardner, the famous mathematician and scholar who wrote regular exposés of the irrational schemes and ideas that falsely pass for science.

Seventh, the New Age interest in alternative medicine has some merit (that topic is covered in more detail later in this chapter). Still, New Agers must exercise great care in the realm of alternative medicine. Many alternative medical paths are rooted in bad science, bad medicine, and bad motives. While typical Western medical practices are not infallible, New Age medicine has far more potential for harm than New Agers usually imagine.

Eighth, Christians cannot disagree with the New Age wish for peace on planet Earth. The failure to see how much this is truly part of the New Age movement—that it represents the real and honest wishes of New Agers—is a significant error among evangelicals. Christians must recognize, however, that the New Age solution for the planet is largely about an ideology foreign to the gospel of Jesus Christ.

Ninth, New Age relativism undermines the credibility of its leaders and belief system. New Age arguments against clear moral absolutes will not regain the loss of moral authority in our postmodern world. Further, New Age leaders lose their credibility as the weak moral foundations of New Age lead to emotional, financial, and sexual abuse of followers.

Tenth, New Age claims that the world is about to enter a new dawn or an Age of Aquarius deserve little respect. Not only have New Age leaders been wrong in past predictions about this phenomenon, but the New Age also lacks the proper foundation for confidence about the future. Further, speculation about an emerging Golden Age for humanity is rooted largely in the New Age's overly optimistic understanding of human perfection.

Eleventh, the New Age affirmation that Eternal Spirit Masters have been teaching the New Age message cannot be reconciled with the Christian faith. First, there is virtually no historical support for the existence of many New Age Masters, like the leading members of Theosophy's Great

White Brotherhood. Second, the New Age emphasis on spirit beings is ultimately a distraction from God's revelation that Jesus is the Way, the Truth, and the Life, that he is the culmination of all of God's prophets, and that he is the unique Son of God.

Twelfth, the New Age emphasis on an eternal energy realm is a poor substitute for reliance on God's Holy Spirit. Christians can celebrate, of course, that New Agers realize we are spiritual beings and that this is not merely a material world. The New Age focus on impersonal forces, however, often leads followers to adopt dangerous and misleading paths to the so-called divine energy. Humans are to anchor their lives in the love of God and not in the uncertain power fields of the New Age.

WHAT DO YOU SEE WHEN YOU LOOK IN THE MIRROR?

To find out whether you are in tune with New Age ideas, do a little exercise. Stand in front of a mirror and ask, "What do I see?" New Age ideology would teach you to say this: "I see God, since I am God, since all humans are God." Christian faith teaches you to give another answer: "I see a creature of God, made in the image of God, but a fallen creature hurt by sin and unrighteousness. I see a human for whom Christ died."

Jesus Christ and the New Age

Almost all religious movements seek to place Jesus in a place of honor, and the New Age movement is no exception. New Age groups treat the name of Jesus with respect. In the vast majority of New Age movements, Jesus is believed to be a teacher of New Age doctrine. His name is invoked to prove spiritual support for this or that New Age group, tradition, leader, idea, or practice. A high view of Jesus so pervades New Age traditions that it is difficult to reference a single famous New Age leader or group that scorns or ridicules the name of Jesus.

This does not mean, of course, that the New Age understanding of Jesus is correct. The high place New Agers give to Jesus does, however, present an opportunity for witness, since New Agers would agree with Christians that Jesus was a great teacher and spiritual leader. Given this common ground, it is important for both Christians and New Agers to have an accurate understanding of Jesus of Nazareth.

KEY NEW AGE IDEAS ABOUT JESUS

1. Jesus is one of the greatest Spiritual Masters, if not the greatest.

2. Jesus was open to New Age spirit beings in his mission on earth.

3. Jesus of Nazareth was open to "The Christ" and was a vessel for "The Christ."

4. Jesus was not always the Christ and is not the only Christ figure.

5. The Christ now works apart from Jesus of Nazareth.

6. Jesus represents the highest ideal that humanity can reach.

7. Jesus did not die to atone for the sins of the world.

8. The second coming of Jesus is not to be understood literally.

9. Jesus went to India when he was young in order to learn from Eastern religion.

10. Jesus believed in reincarnation.

11. Jesus is now an Enlightened Master on a level with other Spiritual Masters.

12. Jesus speaks to our day through mediums and channeling.

13. Jesus is not the only way to heaven. Jesus is not the only mediator and Savior.

14. The life and teaching of Jesus is not presented accurately in the Gospels.

15. An accurate picture of Jesus can be found in New Age books such as *The Unknown Life of Jesus, The Aquarian Gospel of Jesus the Christ, A Course in Miracles,* and *The Urantia Book.*

A Christian who believes that the Gospels and the rest of the New Testament provide the foundation for a proper understanding of Jesus cannot but feel saddened by the New Age picture of Jesus. Even its positive comments about Jesus are not fully Christian in their direction and underlying premises. All its remaining points about Jesus show a radical departure from the plain meaning of biblical material and the traditions of all Christian churches. The New Age understanding of the term *Christ*, and its view of his death, second coming, and nature all illustrate that a religious movement can say nice things about Jesus and yet completely misunderstand the truth about him.

What does this discrepancy suggest about the New Age and its leaders? On the positive side, the New Agers' desire to have Jesus on their side is a testimony to the power of Jesus as an icon and a symbol of truth and goodness. When witnessing to New Agers, it is also encouraging to realize that a typical New Ager respects Jesus as a Teacher and Spiritual Master. This can provide the foundation for further discussion about his true identity, teaching, and mission.

How can a group be so positive about Jesus and yet be so far removed from an accurate assessment of him? Ultimately, the New Age failure to envision and follow the authentic Jesus amounts to its most serious error.

While New Age advocates claim to honor Jesus, their teaching about him shows a plain disregard for New Testament teachings. At its heart, Christian witness to the New Age involves the argument that New Agers should pay attention to what Jesus said about himself. Jesus claimed to be the only eternal Son of God, the One who dwelt with the Father from all eternity, and the one who gave himself in his death so that human beings might be forgiven. Only in Jesus' life, teaching, death, resurrection, and ascension can the New Ager find the only solid rock on which to build genuine concern about making planet Earth a better place to live and gaining assurance of eternal life.

■ Channeling and the New Age

One of the most interesting and controversial aspects of the New Age is channeling. This involves the alleged communication of spirit beings through humans as mediums. The guidance from a disembodied spirit can occur in various forms. Often the New Age channeler goes into a trance and claims to communicate directly from the eternal realm. This is what JZ Knight, one of the most famous spirit guides, says happens to her when she gives revelations from Ramtha, a 35,000-year-old warrior. In some cases the voice of the channeler changes, either in accent or tone or pitch. The channeling can also occur in the form of automatic writing, as Urantia followers claim happened when *The Urantia Book* was given to William Sadler's patient.

The practice of channeling reached its highest point just after Shirley MacLaine published her life story in book form and then in film, both under the title *Out on a Limb*. In fact, channeling became a very lucrative business choice in the mid-'80s through the mid-'90s, with famous channelers making as much as $300 per hour for private sessions. In the 1800s the term *channeling* was unknown, but the same practice occurred with reference to the work of a medium or psychic. What today would be called a trance session or channeling would have been called a séance in the early 1900s.

Some significant changes in the focus of psychic activity have occurred from the 1850s to our day. In general, psychics or spirit mediums in the nineteenth century dealt with offering "proof" of life after death by giving messages from someone's deceased relative or friend. While popular psychics like James Van Praagh are still doing this today, New Age channeling has generally been preoccupied with providing extensive spiritual guidance from specific spirit teachers. In the 1880s one would likely hear words from a deceased mother, whereas today one is probably going to receive a message from a divine Master.

One of the more famous modern cases of channeling involves Sun Myung Moon, the controversial founder of the Unification Church. When Moon first visited America he had a session with the well-known medium Arthur Ford, who channeled an entity known as Fletcher. Moon wanted to know about the eternal realm's view of his work and mission in the United States. Though Moon is not New Age, he had several sessions in 1965 with Ford, whose views often echoed New Age thought. Fletcher resisted Moon's dogmatic assertions of his own movement's supremacy and tried to lead the Korean leader to a more pluralistic understanding of Christianity and other religions.

Options in Understanding Channeling

There are several ways to understand and explain the phenomenon of channeling. It is helpful to list the major options in interpretation adopted by New Agers and by critics of the New Age, including Christian writers. Consider a range of five perspectives:

Option One: All of the famous channelers provide the truth and link humanity to real spirit beings who provide the liberating New Age message for the planet.

Option Two: The spirit beings are real but demonic in nature and purpose. On this perspective, either channelers know they are in the hands of demonic forces or they are deceived about the true nature of the spirits behind their guidance. Many conservative Christians adopt this view.

Option Three: The channelers are sincere, but the spirit guides do not exist and there is nothing supernatural about channeling. The channelers are honest but deluded about their authenticity. Their mistaken view comes from gullibility, hallucination, hypnotic states, drug use, peer group pressure, wish fulfillment, or some combination of these factors.

Option Four: The channelers are frauds and con artists who know that the spirit guides are not real. There is no overt satanic activity, but Satan uses the false claims of channeling and the erroneous devotion to channeled messages to keep New Agers blind to the true revelation in Jesus Christ.

Option Five: Some channeling or psychic activity that does not advance anti-Christian teaching can be interpreted as simply an extra-special ability that some humans have to know things from the eternal realm. For example, some humans have incredible musical abilities, others have an extraordinary compassion, while others happen to receive accurate information from the "other side."

Since the New Age message is not compatible with the gospel, New Age channeling is fundamentally wrong and untrue. This would apply even if the channeling brought a real message from a spirit being. Given this, how should Christians react to the other options?

The correct answer involves deciding which option fits which particular case. In other words, channeling can be explained best by using all the options to help explain the different types of channelers and messages. Some channelers are under demonic influence, but at other times there is no real channeling at all. In the latter situation, the channeler would be either sincere (but wrong) or a con artist.

Most New Age channelers seem to sincerely believe that they truly receive messages from spirit beings. Therefore, channeling is seldom about outright fraud. Nor do demons deliver most messages. New Age channeling is usually best explained with reference to gullibility and wish fulfillment on the part of the channeler and the New Age believers.

New Age channeling is a diverse and complex topic. Therefore, it is much better to allow for a number of explanations that can increase the chances of presenting an accurate assessment of cases. Any message purportedly from the spirit world that presents a revelation that does not revere the triune God and does not exalt Jesus, the only Savior, however, is fundamentally from the Evil One, either directly or indirectly.

New Agers believe crystals have special power

Photo: fearlessvk

New Age Medicine

The issue of New Age medicine represents a very complex issue. The evangelical community has been uncertain about what to think of holistic health and alternative medicine in general and has expressed particular concern about "New Age" medicine. The complexity of the topic arises out of several factors.

First, it is impossible for any one person to keep track of all the current alternative health practices, let alone keep up with new alternative medical procedures that arise every year. It takes hours simply to type a list of all available New Age therapies and theories.

Second, it is very difficult to find careful research on alternative medicines. This is partly because the medical establishment tends to ignore alternative medicine. Also, many who advocate alternative medical theories have little interest in proving their case to the scientific establishment.

Third, some serious spiritual and theological issues are at stake in responding to some holistic health practices and theories. This means that one must move beyond the necessary questions about the actual medical and scientific credibility of a given practice to deal with issues related to spiritual authenticity and faithfulness to the gospel.

The topic has grown more complicated in the last three decades because some practitioners of alternative medicine have tried to increase their appeal by labeling their methods "New Age." This has led to extra confusion in the public debate about holistic medicine and to debate among Christians about the proper response to medical procedures commonly associated with the New Age. Is all New Age medicine bogus and/or demonic? Is all alternative medicine quackery? Consider ten crucial guidelines:

1. Most Christians do not have the necessary medical and scientific training to judge alternative medical therapies. They must rely on people they trust who know enough to provide proper medical/scientific analysis of this or that therapy.

2. The many types of alternative/holistic medical therapies and ideas should not be lumped together for either wholesale blessing or condemnation. Thousands of procedures and drugs are part of the world of alternative medicine. Such diversity cannot be dealt with in sweeping generalities, either positive or negative.

3. Any alternative or holistic medical practice that involves belief in false religious teaching or engaging in ungodly or anti-Christian ritual must be avoided. For example, if the alleged cure for cancer involves taking a pill while chanting to an Egyptian god, the biblical command against idolatry and worship of false gods binds the Christian, and he or she should avoid the procedure.

4. Traditional medicine deserves respect for its emphasis on scientific testing and careful investigation. Alternative medicines have not always shown similar openness to extended scrutiny. Holistic health advocates would have a far better reception if they allowed for the kind of analysis associated with standard medical research.

5. The fact that a suspect individual or group started a specific medical treatment or belief does not necessarily disqualify it. Thus, while acupuncture has is roots in ancient Chinese folk religion, this does not mean that all acupuncture is fraudulent or demonic. Also, chiropractic medicine should not be ruled out simply because one of its founders was interested in non-Christian views.

6. In relation to the emotional and psychological dynamic in health, Christians should find the right balance between the foolish notion that the mind has unlimited power and the mechanistic and reductionist view that health has nothing to do with human emotion. "Positive thinking" has power, but that power has a limit. Further, it is better to trust in the power of God than in the power of the human mind.

7. The fact that a particular "New Age" or holistic practice cannot be explained scientifically does not mean that Christians should automatically conclude that the practice must be demonic. It is entirely possible that a specific practice or drug works, and one day a perfectly natural and scientific explanation will be found for its effectiveness.

8. Christians must distinguish medical practices that are wrong by their very nature from techniques and therapies that are wrong only if abused. Evangelicals too easily adopt the "slippery-slope" argument that a given alternative medicine is wrong because it might lead to a practice that is clearly wrong. One must examine how slippery is the slope leading from something good in itself to the abuse of that good.

9. Christians need to be aware that traditional medicine can be blind to legitimate alternative medical procedures. Western-based science has an almost automatic dismissal of anything outside the boundaries of traditional medicine. This bias can lead to blindness about truly healthy therapies and a rejection of new theories that actually work, even if they are non-traditional.

10. Medicine attracts a lot of quackery. Christians need an adequate level of suspicion about how medical con artists manipulate the sick into following costly therapies that may actually harm or kill the patient. The biblical command to "test the spirits" is a good principle to keep in mind when dealing with the latest fads in fringe medicine, whether called New Age or not.

CAN YOU TRUST YOUR DOCTOR?

John Ankerberg and John Weldon's popular work *Can You Trust Your Doctor?* is one of the most significant evangelical works on New Age medicine. Ankerberg and Weldon are two highly influential evangelical cult watchers. Their book too readily condemns some alternative medical procedures simply because of bad roots (the genetic fallacy) or the possibility of future occult involvement (the slippery slope argument). On balance, *Can You Trust Your Doctor?* contains a wealth of helpful material. If it errs on the side of caution, in terms of medicine, that is the right way to go.

■ Constance Cumbey and the New Age

Constance Cumbey's book *Hidden Dangers of the Rainbow* sold very well and demonstrated that she had widely read New Age literature. She was the first source for many Christians when the New Age movement became popular. However, her paranoid reading of New Age authors seriously mars her work. She overstates the organizational nature of the New Age, misreads Marilyn Ferguson's book *The Aquarian Conspiracy*, and gives far too much prominence to Benjamin Creme's wild theories about the return of Maitreya, a Messiah figure in Buddhism. Cumbey also hurt her credibility by being closed to criticism of her work by fellow evangelicals.

■ The New Age and Biblical Prophecy

Most evangelical responses to the New Age have leaned heavily on prophecy theories to describe the nature and future of the New Age. In particular, Constance Cumbey, Texe Marrs, and Dave Hunt have all argued that the New Age fits into the work of the Antichrist and the beginning of the Great Tribulation. Their theories, however, should be treated with great reservation. First, evangelicals have a pathetic record when it comes to guessing the identity of the Antichrist. Evangelical books on prophecy are usually riddled with guesswork and after-the-fact interpretations. Second, these writers overstate the power and organizational realities of the New Age movement. They also consistently treat New Age leaders as if they were in willing cooperation with Satan. There is little reason to believe this.

NEW AGE (WESTERN ESOTERICISM)

Scholarly Sites	Esoterica (Online Journal): www.esoteric.msu.edu Association for the Study of Esotericism: www.aseweb.org European Society for the Study of Western Esotericism: www.esswe.org/ Alternative Spiritualities and New Age Studies: www.asanas.org.uk Centre for Research into Freemasonry: www.shef.ac.uk/ The Alchemy Web Site (Adam McLean): www.levity.com/alchemy
Recommended Reading	Catherine Albanese, *A Republic of Mind and Spirit* (New Haven: Yale, 2006) Russell Chandler, *Understanding the New Age* (Dallas: Word, 1988) Antoine Faivre, *Access to Western Esotericism* (Albany: State University of New York Press, 1994) Douglas Groothuis, *Unmasking the New Age* (1986). Wouter J. Hanegraaff, Senior Editor, *Dictionary of Gnosis & Western Esotericism* (Leiden: Brill, 2005) Wouter J. Hanegraaff, *New Age Religion and Western Culture* (Albany: State University of New York Press, 1998) James Lewis and J. Gordon Melton, eds. *Perspectives on the New Age* (Albany: State University of New York Press, 1992) J. Gordon Melton, *New Age Encyclopedia* (Detroit: Gale, 1990) Elliot Miller, *A Crash Course on the New Age* (Grand Rapids: Baker, 1989) Ted Peters, *The Cosmic Self* (New York: HarperCollins, 1991) John A. Saliba, *Christian Responses to the New Age Movement* (London: Cassell, 1999)

12

ORTHODOXY

Christ the Savior Church, Moscow, Russia

Photo: Eileen Barker

In 1990, Franky Schaeffer left the evangelical fold and joined the Greek
Orthodox Church. Franky, son of the famous apologist/writer and L'Abri
founder Francis Schaeffer, has not kept his conversion to Orthodox Christianity a secret. In a string of articles, books, and videos he has become
an apostle for Eastern Orthodoxy. In one book, *Dancing Alone,* Schaeffer accuses evangelicals of being alone with the Bible, alone in personal
conversion, with no regard for tradition, proper liturgy, and legitimate
ecclesiastical authority.

For the first time evangelical Christians are giving Orthodoxy its
due. Schaeffer may be the loudest convert, but he is not alone. Frederica
Mathewes-Green, a regular contributor to *Christianity Today* magazine,

penned *Facing East: A Pilgrim's Journey into the Mysteries of Orthodoxy.*" In *Becoming Orthodox,* Peter Gillquist, a former Campus Crusade for Christ leader, tells the story of 2,000 American evangelicals who have joined this ancient church.

Orthodox church with view of Mt. Ararat, Turkey

Photo: Steffen Schuelein, Georgia Tourism Association

ORTHODOX CHRISTIANITY 101

- The Orthodox Church affirms the doctrine of the Trinity.

- The Orthodox Church is the visible expression of the body of Christ.

- Orthodox Christians unite under the Patriarch of Constantinople.

- Orthodoxy affirms the truth of the Seven Ecumenical Councils.

- Orthodoxy values both Scripture and tradition.

- Justification involves faith in and obedience to God.

- Church life is exercised through seven sacraments.

- Infants are to be baptized into the church.

- Baptism and the Eucharist provide spiritual life to believers.

- The Bible is to be understood through Orthodox tradition.

- The Orthodox Church honors and prays to the saints, including Mary.

- Saint Peter was the first among equals in church leadership.

- Praying for the dead is part of Christian life.

- Mary was a perpetual virgin.

- Mary was kept free from sin.

- Mary was assumed into heaven.

- Icons are to be venerated as part of divine liturgy.

- The Holy Spirit proceeds from the Father alone.

- Christians outside of Orthodoxy should return to the mother church.

- The goal of the Christian life is deification, becoming one with God.

There are about 300 million Orthodox believers worldwide. The Orthodox believe that they are the "one, holy, catholic, and apostolic church" spoken of in the Apostles' Creed. There are about fifteen different churches that unite under the banner of Orthodoxy, the most well known being the Russian and Greek Orthodox Churches, though pride of place goes to the Churches of Constantinople, Alexandria, Antioch, and Jerusalem, because of their ancient roots.

The Orthodox are committed to various early creeds, to the teachings of the Seven Ecumenical Councils, and to an affirmation of Apostolic succession from Saint Peter to His All-Holiness Bartholomew, the head of the Church of Constantinople and Ecumenical Patriarch to all Orthodox

Communions. The Orthodox believe that Roman Catholics left the one church in 1054, with the famous schism over papal supremacy and other doctrines. This split was sealed in blood when Roman Catholic armies on the Fourth Crusade ransacked Constantinople in 1204 in a three-day siege of murder, rape, and theft that defies comprehension.

Rila Monastery, Bulgaria

Photo: Eileen Barker

Certain distinctives in Orthodox liturgy will be jarring to evangelicals. Like Roman Catholics, the Orthodox place a great deal of emphasis on Mary and pray to the saints and for the dead, practices that seem foreign to the traditions of the New Testament, though Protestant disregard of Mary is also unbiblical. The Orthodox use of icons can be celebrated by anyone who has appreciation for art and beauty in worship. The judgment that iconography is idolatry goes too far, given the clear Christ-centered nature of the Orthodox liturgy. However, evangelicals have every right to object to the historic Orthodox insistence on the use of icons in worship. Daniel Clendenin, editor of *Eastern Orthodox Theology*, asks that Orthodox consider their undue emphasis on the use of icons. "Does it really serve any useful purpose, given this murky theological history of the icon, to continue to insist with the Council of 787 that Christians who reject icons are evil, pernicious, and subversive heretics?"

Serbian Orthodox church, Libertyville, Illinois

Photo: Gordon Melton

Of more concern is the Orthodox understanding of salvation, at least at some points. Thankfully, Christ is the only source of salvation in Orthodoxy, even though the Orthodox venerate Mary and the saints. Likewise, evangelicals can applaud Orthodox recognition that redemption is rooted in grace alone. That is, Orthodox doctrine explicitly condemns salvation by works.

Vardzia Cave Monastery, Georgia

Photo: Steffen Schuelein, Georgia Tourism Association

Artwork, Rila Monastery, Bulgaria

Photo: Eileen Barker

However, the Orthodox focus on the deification of humanity (*theosis*), emphasis on the sacraments, and reservations about justification by faith alone can give pause. Orthodox Christians neither have a magical view of baptism, nor do they believe in salvation by works. But their emphases here can dull the sense of need for personal trust in the work of Christ and assurance of salvation in Christ. These concerns led a task force at Biola University to conclude that at crucial points evangelical doctrine and Orthodox theology are incompatible.

While Clendenin has a more positive assessment of evangelical and Orthodox unity, he also objects to the view that the Orthodox Church is the one, holy, catholic, and apostolic church. "I believe that it is reasonable, even compelling, to affirm that we see the Spirit working all across the world to inaugurate God's kingdom, far outside the narrow confines of Orthodoxy."

MOVING "TOWARDS FULL COMMUNION"

This fraternal encounter which brings us together, Pope Benedict XVI of Rome and Ecumenical Patriarch Bartholomew I, is God's work, and in a certain sense his gift. We give thanks to the Author of all that is good, who allows us once again, in prayer and in dialogue, to express the joy we feel as brothers and to renew our commitment to move towards full communion. This commitment comes from the Lord's will and from our responsibility as Pastors in the Church of Christ. May our meeting be a sign and an encouragement to us to share the same sentiments and the same attitudes of fraternity, cooperation and communion in charity and truth. The Holy Spirit will help us to prepare the great day of the re-establishment of full unity, whenever and however God wills it.

Common Declaration by Pope Benedict XVI and Patriarch Bartholomew I
November 30, 2006

Alexander Nevsky Cathedral, Sofia, Bulgaria

Photo: Eileen Barker

ORTHODOX TIMELINE

325 —First Ecumenical Council

330 —Constantine names Constantinople as eastern capital

381 —Second Ecumenical Council

431 —Third Ecumenical Council

451 —Fourth Ecumenical Council

532 —Hagia Sophia under construction

553 —Fifth Ecumenical Council

638 —Jerusalem conquered by Muslims

680 —Sixth Ecumenical Council

730 —Emperor Leo III bans veneration of icons

787 —Seventh Ecumenical Council

800 —Pope Leo III crowns Charlemagne emperor

815 —Emperor Leo V bans images

843 —Empress Theodora restores veneration of images

858 —Photius becomes patriarch

862 —Cyril and Methodius sent to Slavic people as missionaries

867 —Photius deposes Pope Nicholas III

988 —Prince Vladimir of Russia becomes Orthodox

1054—Schism between East and West

1204—Fourth Crusaders sack Constantinople

1261—Emperor Michael Palaeologus returns Constantinople to Byzantine rule

1389—Ottoman army defeats Serbs at Battle of Kosovo

1439—Council of Florence attempts reunion of East and West

1448—Russian church breaks from Constantinople

1453—Muslim armies conquer Constantinople

1652—Liturgical reforms by Patriarch Nikon of Moscow lead to dissent

1794—Saint Herman guides mission to Alaska.

1848—Saint Innocent of Alaska is consecrated as North America's first Orthodox bishop.

1917—Russian Revolution deposes patriarch

1965—Pope Paul VI and Patriarch Athenagoras I nullify excommunications of 1054

2003—Russian Orthodox Church breaks with Episcopal Church

2006—Meeting of Pope Benedict XVI and Patriarch Bartholomew I

Uspensky Cathedral in Helsinki, Finland

Photo: Hans Raabe

ON THE EUCHARIST

The most awesome ceremony in the Orthodox Church is the *Mysterion* (sacrament) of the Holy Eucharist. This ceremony was instituted by Jesus Christ the day before His Crucifixion, as He enriched His Church forever with the Divine Gifts, His own Body and Blood. This ceremony of the Holy Eucharist is both His sacrifice for the salvation of man and a sacred *mysterion*. The Holy Eucharist is the seal of the proclamation of the communion with God. It is the only Sacrament offered by the Church in which the elements of bread and wine not only carry the Grace of God, as a *mysterion*, but are "changed" into and "is" the very Body and the very Blood of Christ, being a propitiatory sacrifice.

Source: Greek Orthodox Archdiocese of America

SEVEN ECUMENICAL COUNCILS

Council	Date	Location	Decision
First	A.D. 325	Nicea, Asia Minor,	Defined divinity of Jesus
Second	A.D. 381	Constantinople	Clarified deity of Holy Spirit
Third	A.D. 431	Ephesus	Mary defined as theotokos (Mother of God)
Fourth	A.D. 451	Chalcedon	Fuller definition of deity of Christ
Fifth	A.D. 553	Constantinople	Reconfirmed Trinity
Sixth	A.D. 680	Constantinople	Affirmation of true humanity of Jesus
Seventh	A.D. 787	Nicea, Asia Minor	Approval of icons in worship

*Easter procession 2008, Svetitskhoveli
to Jvari, Mtskheta, Georgia*

Photo: Christian Schnurer, Georgia Tourism Association

TOP COUNTRIES WITH ORTHODOX MEMBERS

Country	Number of Orthodox
Russia (Orthodox Church)	106,000,000
Ethiopia	31,520,000
Ukraine (Moscow patriarch)	26,000,000
Romania	19,400,000
Greece	9,312,300
Egypt	9,000,000
Bulgaria	5,750,000
Serbia	5,239,000
Belarus	5,100,000
Ukraine (Kiev patriarch)	4,000,000
Georgia	3,087,500
India (Orthodox Syrian Church)	2,500,000
USA (Orthodox Church in America)	2,500,000
Moldova	2,250,000
Armenia	2,220,000
Eritrea	1,920,000
USA (Greek Orthodox Archdiocese)	1,500,000
Russia (Armenian Apostolic Church)	1,420,000
Kazakhstan	1,390,000
Russia (Ukrainian Orthodox in Russia)	1,300,000
Macedonia	1,200,000
Bosnia-Herzegovina	1,070,000
India (Mar Thoma Syrian Church)	1,050,000

Source: World Christian Database 2008

ORTHODOX CHRISTIANITY

Typology	Christian
Leader of Orthodoxy	Ecumenical Patriarch of Constantinople
Patriarchate and Church Websites	Ecumenical Patriarchate: www.patriarchate.org Patriarchate of Alexandria: www.greekorthodox-alexandria. org Patriarchate of Antioch: www.antiochpat.org Patriarchate of Jerusalem: www.jerusalem-patriarchate.org Patriarchate of Moscow: www.mospat.ru Patriarchate of Serbia: spc.org.yu Patriarchate of Romania: www.patriarhia.ro Patriarchate of Bulgaria: bulch.tripod.com/boc/ Patriarchate of Georgia: www.patriarchate.ge/ Church of Greece: www.ecclesia.gr Church of Albania: www.orthodoxalbania.org Church of Poland: www.orthodox.pl Church of Czech—Slovakia: www.pravoslav.gts.cz Church of Finland: www.ort.fi Church of Estonia: www.orthodoxa.org Orthodox Church of America: www.oca.org Orthodox Church of Canada: www. orthodoxchurchofcanada.org
Other Sites	Orthodox World Links: www.theologic.com/links Orthodox Faith: www.orthodoxfaith.com Orthodox Net: www.orthodoxnet.com Orthodoxy in America: http://orthodoxyinamerica.org Pokrov: Dealing with Victims of Abuse: www.pokrov.org
Recommended Reading	Victoria Clark, *Why Angels Fall* (New York: St. Martin's, 2000) Daniel B. Clendenin, editor, *Eastern Orthodox Theology* (Grand Rapids: Baker, 2003) Clendenin, *Eastern Orthodox Christianity* (Grand Rapids: Baker, 2003) Donald Fairbairn, *Eastern Orthodoxy through Western Eyes* (Louisville: Westminster John Knox Press, 2002) Frederica Mathewes-Green, *At the Corner of East and Now* (New York: Jeremy P. Tarcher/Putnam, 2000) Robert L. Saucy, John Coe, and Alan Gomes, Task Report on "Eastern Orthodox Teachings in Comparison with the Doctrinal Position of Biola University" (May 1998) James Stamoolis, ed. *Three Views on Eastern Orthodoxy and Evangelicalism* (Grand Rapids: Zondervan, 2004) Timothy Ware, *The Orthodox Church* (Baltimore: Penguin, 1964)

13

PROTESTANTISM

Moody Church, Chicago, Illinios

Photo: Gordon Melton

Protestant is the designation given to those groups that trace their identity back to the sixteenth century and the work of Martin Luther, John Calvin, and the leaders of the Anabaptist movement. The term *Protestant* rose out of the fact that Luther protested what he regarded as errors and abuses in the Roman Catholic Church of his time. The essentials of Protestant Christianity are often identified as belief in Scripture alone, grace alone, faith alone, and Christ alone.

Protestants now make up the second largest body of Christians in the world, next to the Roman Catholic communion. While Roman Catholic leaders warned in the sixteenth century about the dangerous precedent set by Luther in splitting the church, they had no idea how fragmented

Protestantism itself would become. The number of Protestant groups both in North America and worldwide is easily overwhelming.

The many groups within the Protestant world may be interpreted in terms of larger "families" within the Protestant tradition. Most of the specific groups fall under fourteen major denominational or family traditions. Further, these traditions are best approached in terms of chronology, since earlier Protestant traditions form the matrix for ongoing developments.

John Knox home, Edinburgh, Scotland

Photo: Jim Beverley

Four family traditions of Protestantism emerged in the sixteenth century: Lutheran, Reformed, Free Church/Anabaptist, and Anglican. Baptists started in the seventeenth century, and the Pietistic/Methodist grouping began in the eighteenth century. The nineteenth century witnessed the emergence of the Churches of Christ (Stone-Campbell Restoration), the Adventist family, and the Holiness churches. Five more Protestant families started in the twentieth century: Pentecostalism, fundamentalism, evangelicalism, the charismatic church, and the Emergent Church.

These family traditions are not exhaustive of all Protestant groups. However, these traditions or denominations provide the framework to understand various sectarian or cultic movements that seem, at first sight, to be unique and distinct from the larger Protestant world. For example, the Jehovah's Witnesses are clearly rooted in the Adventist family, even though the movement claims to be the only true Christian church. Likewise, the Mormon Church is a product of the larger restorationist movement that swept the United States in the nineteenth century. The Family International (formerly the Children of God) gained some of its dynamic from the broad currents of charismatic, fundamentalist, and evangelical church life of the 1960s.

Many charismatic and emergent church leaders would not want to be listed in a group of denominations. Yet, while it is not popular to be viewed as a denomination, every significant renewal movement or independent group of churches takes on the realities of denominational life by virtue of the necessities of organization, bureaucracy, promotion, and shared identity.

All the Protestant families noted have been influenced by the broad philosophical and theological currents that have dominated Western Christianity in the last five centuries. Each denomination or family has its own particular reading in relation to the Enlightenment, liberal theology, evangelicalism, postmodernism, and so on. Trends in philosophy and theology create divisions within and across the various Protestant families. This means, for example, that a moderate Southern Baptist might find more in common with a liberal Presbyterian than with a conservative in the Southern Baptist Convention.

PROTESTANTS	
Typology	Christian
Recommended Reading	J. Gordon Melton, *Encyclopedia of American Religions* (Detroit: Gale: 2002) Hans J. Hillerbrand, ed. *The Protestant Reformation* (New York: Harper & Row, 1969)

◼ Adventism

Adventist Christian groups trace their roots to the ministry and views of William Miller. Miller was born in 1782 and fought in the War of 1812. A convert from deism, he became preoccupied with eschatology and determining when the second advent of Jesus Christ would take place. He initially argued for a date in October 1843 and then added one year to his calculations. When the second coming did not take place as he predicted, Miller and most of his followers admitted error in what became known as "the Great Disappointment." Miller died in 1849.

TOP TEN ADVENTIST SUBGROUPS IN U.S.

Name	Web Address	Founded	Followers
Jehovah's Witnesses	www.watchtower.org	1872	2,382,000
Seventh-day Adventist Church	www.adventist.org	1844	1,138,000
Advent Christian Church	www.areachurches.com/ adventinfo.html	1854	24,800
Church of God (Seventh-day) (Denver)	www.bible.ca/cr-church-God-7thday.htm	1858	11,200
General Conference of Church of God (Seventh-day)	http://cog7.org	1860	6,600
Church of God General Conference (Abrahamic Faith)	www.abc-coggc.org/coggc/ index.htm	1816	5.248
New Beginnings Fellowship	http://newbeginnings fellowship.com	1965	4,600
Association for Christian Development	www.godward.org	1974	1,000
Primitive Advent Christian Church	www.adherents.com/Na/ Na_539.html#3249	1930	610

The Advent Christian General Conference formed in 1860 and has about 35,000 members in North America. The largest Adventist group is the Seventh-day Adventist Church, known for its emphasis on health care, Sabbath-keeping, and the controversies surrounding Ellen G. White, the prophetess of the movement. The Worldwide Church of God (WCG), founded by Herbert W. Armstrong, has also been controversial. While Armstrong was alive the WCG had a clearly sectarian ethos. After his death in 1986 the church gradually adopted an overtly evangelical Christian identity. This transformation occurred through the leadership of Joseph Tkach, Sr. (Pastor General 1986–1995) and his son Joseph Tkach, Jr. (1995–present).

The Adventist tradition also influenced Charles Russell, the founder of the Jehovah's Witnesses. Though Russell held an unorthodox view on the Trinity, his interests in biblical eschatology were rooted in Adventism. Various Bible Student groups are part of the Adventist legacy as well, given their allegiance to the views of Russell. These groups opposed the teachings of Judge Rutherford, who took over the Watchtower Society in 1917. The most well-known Bible Student groups are the Laymen's Home Missionary Movement, the Pastoral Bible Institute, and the Dawn Bible Students Association.

Internet Sources

Advent Christian General Conference: www.adventchristian.org

The Journal: www.thejournal.org

Seventh-Day Adventist Church: www.adventist.org

Worldwide Church of God: www.wcg.org

Dawn Bible Students Association: www.dawnbible.com

Pastoral Bible Institute: www.heraldmag.org

▨ Anabaptists

The term *Anabaptist* refers to radical or Free Church Protestants who departed from the Lutheran and Reformed traditions on infant baptism, church-state relations, use of violence, church government, and separation from the world. Vigorous debate has occurred about the origins of the Anabaptist tradition in the sixteenth century, questioning to what extent Anabaptist ideas can be traced to reform movements before Martin Luther and to violent reactionary elements after Luther's posting of the 95 Theses in 1517.

*Anabaptist Brethren Bruxy Cavey, teaching
pastor, The Meeting House, Oakville, Ontario*

Photo: The Meeting House

Most scholars are content to trace Anabaptism to the community of Christians who were rebaptized in 1525 in Zürich. On January 18 of that year Conrad Grebel debated his longtime friend Ulrich Zwingli, the famous Swiss Reformer, on the issue of infant baptism. Those who sided with Grebel chose to renounce their baptism as infants. Zwingli won the city council to his defense of the Lutheran-Reformed perspective and the Anabaptists were declared heretical. Immediately Conrad Grebel and his followers became victims of persecution. On January 5, 1527, Felix Manz was drowned in the lake near Zürich for his profession of believer's baptism.

EARLY ANABAPTIST CHRONOLOGY

1525—Debate between Conrad Grebel and Ulrich Zwingli on
    infant baptism (January 18)
1525—Baptism of Georg Blaurock by Conrad Grebel in Zurich
1525—Execution of Thomas Müntzer, supporter of the German
    Peasants War
1526—Death of Conrad Grebel
1526—Hans Hut baptized by Hans Denck in Augsburg
1527—Execution by drowning of Felix Manz in Zürich (January 5)

1527—Schleitheim Confession

1527—Martyrdom of Michael Sattler (chief author of Schleitheim Confession)

1528—Martyrdom of Balthasar Hubmaier and his wife Elizabeth

1529—Georg Blaurock burned at the stake in Tyrol

1529—Suppression of Hutterites

1533—Rothmann becomes Anabaptist through Melchior Hoffman's followers

1534—Death of Hoffman in Strassburg prison

1534—Rise of apocapytic movement in Munster ("the New Jerusalem")

1534—Jan Matthys killed in Munster

1534—John of Leiden (aka Jon Bockelson) declared King in Munster

1535—Violent suppression of Münster group

1536—Execution of Jacob Hutter in Innsbruck

1544—Calvin writes critique of Schleitheim Confession

1561—Death of Menno Simons

The earliest critics of Anabaptism attempted to discredit the movement through associating it with the practices of Thomas Müntzer, a supporter of the German Peasants War who was executed in 1525. Anabaptists were also criticized by reference to the apocalyptic rebellion in Münster, Germany, in 1534–35. While the leaders in Münster had connections with some Anabaptist thinkers of the day, it is quite unfair to associate Anabaptism in any simplistic way with this isolated and bizarre revolution. Most Anabaptists of the sixteenth century and since have repudiated violence and have been staunch defenders of pacifism.

As early as 1527 a group of Anabaptists expressed some of their beliefs in what has become known as the Schleitheim Confession. Seven articles outlined commitment to believer's baptism, church discipline (the ban), pacifism, participation in the Lord's Supper, separation of church and state, denial of oath taking, and the work of the Christian pastor. One part of the Schleitheim Confession reads: "The government magistracy is according to the flesh, but the Christian's is according to the Spirit; their houses and dwelling remain in this world, but the Christian's are in heaven; the weapons of their conflict and war are carnal and against the flesh only, but the Christian's weapons are spiritual, against the fortification of the devil."

We now know Anabaptists through the famous groups that rose from that tradition: the Mennonites, Hutterites, Amish, and the Brethren. (The Anabaptist Brethren groups are distinct from the Plymouth Brethren, the famous dispensational movement started by John Nelson Darby in the nineteenth century.) The Bruderhof, a communal group now based in the United States, are a recent new addition to the Anabaptist world.

The Mennonites are the largest Anabaptist group in the world, followed by the Brethren. The Old Order Mennonites shun many aspects of modern society, as do the Hutterites and Amish. The latter groups are famous for their old-style communal living. The 1985 film *Witness* by Peter Weir brought an awareness of Amish culture to Hollywood and to the general public. The film contrasted the darker sides of mainstream society with the peaceful Amish community.

ANABAPTISTS	
Typology	Christian Protestant
Homepages	Mennonite World Conference: www.mwc-cmm.org Church of the Brethren (Elgin, Illinois): www.brethren.org Brethren Church (Ashland, Ohio): www.brethrenchurch.org Fellowship of Grace Brethren Churches: www.fgbc.org Bruderhof Homepage: http://www.churchcommunities.org/
Recommended Reading	Franklin H. Littell, *The Origins of Sectarian Protestantism* (New York: Macmillan, 1964)

Amish

The Amish trace their roots to Jacob Ammann, the Anabaptist leader who instigated separation from the larger Mennonite community in 1693. Ammann, in conflict with Mennonite leader Hans Reist, believed that Mennonites were becoming undisciplined in their spiritual life, particularly related to the implementation of the ban. Early Amish identity was also shaped by the writings of Uli Ammann (unknown relationship to Jacob Ammann).

Most people know of the Amish because of their communal lifestyle and their old-fashioned ways, including the use of horse and buggy as a primary means of transportation. The Amish migrated to America in the eighteenth century. Most Amish communities are found in Lancaster County, Pennsylvania, and in Holmes County, Ohio, though Amish dwell in twenty other states as well as in Canada. In 2004 a reality TV series *Amish in the City* featured five Amish teenagers facing modern life in Hollywood.

Brethren

Given that male disciples of Jesus are called brothers in the New Testament, it is not surprising that a number of churches go by the name *Brethren*. The origin of one of the most significant of these groups can be traced to Germany with the rise of an Anabaptist Brethren movement in 1708. Alexander Mack (1679–1735) and seven others were founders of what was known as the Schwarzenau Brethren, named after the town where they formed. Like earlier Anabaptists, Mack's group adopted believer's baptism and contended that Christians should be separate from the state. They also promoted pacifism and had strict standards of holiness.

The Anabaptist Brethren are distinct from the Plymouth Brethren, which formed much later in England.

Soon after their start the Brethren were persecuted by Lutherans and Reformed leaders. They took refuge in Holland and in 1719 Peter Becker led some of the Brethren to Pennsylvania. The Brethren retained a strong ethnic identity in the nineteenth century and chose the title German Baptist Brethren in 1871. They experienced major schism in 1883 and further splits in the early twentieth century, the latter involving dissent over the fundamentalist-modernist controversy.

The earliest break in unity among the Brethren revolved around the controversial leadership of Brethren minister and publisher Henry R. Holsinger. Holsinger was an advocate for Sunday schools, better education and salaries for pastors, foreign missions, and a more liberal view of dress codes. Following his discipline for his dissent against more traditional Brethren values, he was ousted from the fellowship and started his own group in 1883. This new group, based in Ashland, Ohio, is now known as the Brethren Church. It has about 15,000 members. The larger Church of the Brethren has about 150,000 members and is based in Elgin, Illinois. There are other Anabaptist Brethren groups, including the Dunkard Brethren and the Fellowship of Grace Brethren Churches

(Winona Lake, Indiana), the latter forming as a split from the Ashland group.

Recent decades have seen a deeper unity between the various groups with joint participation in social projects and a major encyclopedia on the Brethren.

AN APPEAL FOR UNITY

"I do not believe that God is happy with the Brethren and our continuing efforts to justify our stubborn positions. I do not believe God will bless the Brethren until we admit our wrongdoing and humbly ask God to forgive us our trespasses as we forgive those we feel have trespassed against us.

"On a personal basis, I have admitted to God the stubbornness of the Ashland Brethren and the sin of our separation and failure to work with all segments of the Brethren family. I have asked God to forgive us for not making the needed effort to heal the break in the family and once again to work together in harmony and love. I feel like our failure to heal this break in the family has damaged each of our denominations in numerous and major ways.

"I ask the Church of the Brethren branch of our family to forgive us and join with us as a renewed family to serve God together. There is much we can do together!"

—Emanuel "Buzz" Sandberg, former executive director of The Brethren Church Offices, Ashland, Ohio. He first voiced this appeal for unity in the Brethren family at the Ecumenical Luncheon at the 2000 Annual Conference in Kansas City.

Bruderhof

The Bruderhof is a Christian Anabaptist communal group founded in 1920 in Germany by Eberhard Arnold. Arnold died in 1935. Before and during the Second World War, Bruderhof communities were victims of Nazi persecution. Many Bruderhof members relocated to Britain from 1939 to 1941, but they were forced to leave, so most then settled in Paraguay. Heinrich (Heini) Arnold led the movement from 1935 until his death in 1982.

The Bruderhof started a new community called the Woodcrest Hof in Rifton, New York, in 1954. In 1959 the membership experienced a crisis when Arnold shut down the European community and the one in Paraguay. Many followers were expelled from the group at the time. Details of this trauma in the group's history became public when Ramon Sender, one ex-member, began a network for Bruderhof apostates in 1989 using the *Keep in Touch* (KIT) newsletter. Sender started the Peregrine Foundation to expand the reach of Bruderhof critics. The foundation's press has published Elizabeth Bohlken-Tumpe's *Torches Extinguished*. She is the granddaughter of the Bruderhof founder. Her book is an alternative to the group's work *Torches Rekindled* (Plough Publishing).

The Bruderhof were connected for several decades with two major Hutterite groups, but this tie was severed in 1990. The Hutterite elders were upset that the Bruderhof had an open policy about public education of their children. They also objected to Bruderhof participation in a public rally against the death penalty. "Have we ever heard of Hutterites marching with other denominations, or taking part in such activities? No! Never in Hutterite history or in biblical history." They concluded that the use of candles in Bruderhof worship could lead to idolatry, and the use of courts to settle disputes between Christians was against Hutterite tradition.

The Bruderhof group is now led by Johann Christoph Arnold. Under his leadership, the spiritual community has taken aggressive steps, including litigation, against KIT members, media groups critical of the movement, and several scholars. The community also protested a documentary aired on March 27, 1997, by the CBS newsmagazine *48 Hours*.

Bruderhof leaders tried to pressure Oxford University Press to stop publication of Julius Rubin's work *The Other Side of Joy*, a study of tensions in the Bruderhof community; however, Rubin's work was released by Oxford University Press in 2000 after considerable delay. SPCK Publishing (The Society for Promoting Christian Knowledge) in Britain sold the entire first run of their book *Harmful Religion* (1997) to the English Bruderhof community. The first edition of the book included a chapter on the group by Rubin. The legal and media controversies of the Bruderhof have subsided since 2000.

Typical of other Anabaptists, the Bruderhof are opposed to military service, and the group campaigns actively for peace initiatives. Johann Christoph Arnold maintains a presence outside Bruderhof circles, meeting several times with Cardinal Joseph Ratzinger, now Pope Benedict XVI, and also with Pope John Paul II in 2004. In these settings Arnold has pursued Vatican recognition of its persecution of Anabaptists in the sixteenth century. Arnold also speaks publicly with former NYPD officer Steven McDonald for the Bruderhof antiviolence program called Breaking the Cycle. McDonald was shot in 1986 in the line of duty and left paralyzed from the neck down.

BRUDERHOF	
Typology	Christian Protestant Anabaptist
Critic Site	The Peregrine Foundation: www.perefound.org
Recommended Reading	Elizabeth Bohlken-Tumpe, *Torches Extinguished* (San Francisco: Carrier Pigeon Press, 1993) Julius H. Rubin, *The Other Side of Joy: Religious Melancholy among the Bruderhof* (New York: Oxford University Press, 2000) Merrill Mow, *Torches Rekindled: The Bruderhof's Struggle for Renewal* (Rifton, NY: Plough, 1990)

Hutterites

The Hutterites are a communal Anabaptist group who trace their identity back to the work of Jacob Hutter, who was part of an Anabaptist group in Tyrol in the late 1520s during a time of intense persecution. Hutter moved to Moravia and became a church elder in 1533. In November 1535 he was arrested and tortured, then put to death on February 2, 1536.

During the Thirty Years War (1618–48), Hutterites received protection in Transylvania. In 1755 the community revived its identity, seizing an opportunity to renew its communal and spiritual roots. Many Hutterites moved to the United States in 1874, with others migrating to Canada in 1918.

North American Hutterites divide into three groups: (1) Schmiedeleut, (2) Dariusleut, and (3) the Lehrerleut. Both Dariusleut and Lehrerleut Hutterites are found in Washington, Montana, Saskatchewan, Alberta, and British Colombia. The Schmiedeleut are principally located in Minnesota, North and South Dakota, and Manitoba. There are about 40,000 Hutterites in North America. These three major Hutterite groups differ in geographical location and minor differences in dress codes. The

Dariusleut are led by Elder Martin Walter (Spring Point Colony, Alberta) and the Lehrerleut are led by Elder John Wipf of the Rose Town Colony in Saskatchewan.

The Schmiedeleut Hutterites experienced a schism in 1992 and are now divided into the Hutterian Brethren and the Committee Brethren. The Hutterian Brethren are led by Elder Jacob Kleinsasser and based in Crystal Spring, Manitoba. A large group of Schmiedeleut Hutterites separated from Kleinsasser (who became the leading elder in 1979) over disputes about his leadership.

Internet Source

www.hutterites.org

Mennonites

The Mennonites are the largest Anabaptist grouping. They trace their heritage to Menno Simons, the sixteenth-century Anabaptist leader. Simons was born in 1496 and became a Catholic priest in 1524. His first doubts about Catholic doctrine were soon raised over the issue of transubstantiation; then in 1531 he questioned the practice of infant baptism. While he objected to political radicalism in Anabaptism (his brother was killed in 1535 in the Munsterite rebellion), he was increasingly drawn to the Anabaptist position on Scripture and church life. Simons left the Catholic Church in 1536 and was ordained by Obbe Philips, a disciple of Melchior Hoffman. He died in 1561.

There are more than two hundred Mennonite groups (including Brethren in Christ) in the world, located in sixty-five countries with approximately thirty-five of these in North America. The total membership of the Mennonite Church in 2003 stood at close to 1,300,000. Currently, more Mennonites live in Africa than in North America, though membership in both continents is near 450,000. The largest Mennonite bodies in North America are the Brethren in Christ, Mennonite Brethren, Mennonite Church Canada, and Mennonite Church USA. Mennonite groups range from small, Old Order communes to large denominations. Many Mennonite churches collaborate with the Mennonite World Conference.

Many Mennonites have looked to the 1632 Dordrecht Confession of Faith for expression of classical Anabaptist teaching. In terms of pacifism

Article XIV states: "As regards revenge, that is, to oppose an enemy with the sword, we believe and confess that the Lord Christ has forbidden and set aside to His disciples and followers all revenge and retaliation, and commanded them to render to no one evil for evil, or cursing for cursing, but to put the sword into the sheath, or, as the prophets have predicted, to beat the swords into ploughshares."

Internet Source

Mennonite World Conference: www.mwc-cmm.org

Anglicans

The word *Anglican* refers principally to the Church of England and other churches that are part of the worldwide Anglican Communion. This body of churches submits to the leadership of the archbishop of Canterbury, the primate of the Church of England, who is first among equals of the leaders (primates—also termed archbishops or presiding bishops) of the various Anglican bodies.

Anglican church, Tunis, Tunisia

Photo: Eileen Barker

Westminster Abbey, London, England

Photo: Derek Beverley

The Anglican Communion includes the Episcopal Church, the official name for the Anglican Church in the United States. There are about 80 million Anglicans worldwide and more than two million in America. Outside England the largest numbers of Anglicans are located in Nigeria, Uganda, and Australia. Anglicans trace their roots to the work of Saint Augustine in Britain in the sixth century; he is viewed as the first archbishop of Canterbury. Anglicans often consider themselves both Catholic and Protestant, signifying a desire to be in apostolic succession from Peter and yet separate from Roman Catholicism.

Generally, Anglicans unite in adherence to the historic creeds, *The Book of Common Prayer*, the decisions of the Lambeth Conferences (held every ten years), and the leadership of the archbishop of Canterbury. Anglican tradition has also been deeply influenced by the Thirty-Nine Articles of the Church of England. (King Henry VIII led the Church of

England away from papal allegiance in 1534.) These articles contain several classic objections to specific Catholic doctrines, such as purgatory. The famous document also states, "For Holy Scripture doth set out unto us only the Name of Jesus Christ, whereby men must be saved."

Rowan Williams became the 104th archbishop of Canterbury on February 27, 2003. The archbishop is appointed by the British Parliament in consultation with Anglican leaders; the British monarch is the official head of the Church of England. The archbishop of Canterbury has no legal authority over Anglican churches outside the Church of England. Archbishop Williams succeeded George Carey, who was highly regarded for his evangelical Anglican perspective.

TOP TEN ANGLICAN SUBGROUPS IN U.S.

Name	Web Address	Founded	Followers
Episcopal Church	www.episcopalchurch.org	1578	2,247,819
Charismatic Episcopal Church	http://netministries.org/see/churches/ch03356	1992	200,000
Communion of Evangelical Episcopal	www.theceec.org	1993	38,000
Anglican Mission in America	www.theamia.org/	2000	14,100
Anglican Church in America	www.acahome.org	1981	9,500
Reformed Episcopal Church	http://rechurch.org	1873	9,300
Anglican Catholic Church in North America	www.anglicancatholic.org	1978	8,200
Anglican Orthodox Church of North America	www.anglicanorthodoxchurch.org	1963	7,100
Episcopal Missionary Church	www.emchome.org	1992	4,800
United Episcopal Church	http://united-episcopal.org	1981	1,200

Source: World Christian Database 2008

Some Anglican churches are not in unity with the See of Canterbury, the Church of England, and the worldwide Anglican Communion. Melton's *Encyclopedia of American Religions* lists sixty-five distinct Anglican churches in the United States alone. The major breakaway churches are the Anglican Catholic Church, the Anglican Province of Christ the King, and the United Episcopal Church of North America. These churches have usually broken away because of disagreements over alterations in *The Book of Common Prayer*, biblical authority, the ordination of women, and homosexuality.

The appointment of the openly gay Gene Robinson as the bishop of New Hampshire in 2003 has increased the likelihood of further schisms in the Anglican Communion. Peter Jasper Akinola, archbishop of the Church of Nigeria, has stated that the Nigerian churches are in "impaired Communion" with the Episcopal Church USA. In October 2004 the Lambeth Commission on Communion released the Windsor Report, a document that attempts to address how Anglicans should respond to the crisis created by Robinson's election and by a move to bless gay unions by an Anglican diocese in British Columbia.

St. Paul's Cathedral, London, England

Photo: Jim Beverley

ANGLICANS

Typology	Christian Protestant
Leader	Archbishop of Canterbury
Homepages	Anglican Communion: www.anglicancommunion.org Anglicans Online: www.anglicansonline.org Episcopal Church (USA): www.ecusa.anglican.org Anglican Church in Canada: www.anglican.ca The United Episcopal Church of North America: http://united-episcopal.org
Recommended Reading	John Moorman, *A History of the Church of England* (Harrisburg, PA: Morehouse, 1980)

▧ Baptists

Most church historians trace Baptist roots back to the work of Englishmen John Smyth (1570–1612) and Thomas Helwys (d. 1616). Smyth was an Anglican priest who dissented from his heritage on church-state relations, ecclesiastical hierarchy, and infant baptism. As part of a persecuted Separatist movement in seventeenth-century England, Smyth fled to Holland. He founded a church there in 1609, and his associate Thomas Helwys founded a Baptist church in England in 1611.

Both Smyth and Helwys adopted an Arminian theology and believed that Christ died for all human beings. This stance represents the General Baptist tradition, in contrast to the Particular Baptists, who advance a Calvinist view on predestination, the extent of the atonement, and eternal security. The Particular Baptist movement began in England in the 1630s when a group of Separatists adopted believer's baptism and a Baptist understanding of the church, yet within a dominant Calvinist theology. The Particular Baptists formulated their theology in the London Confession of Faith of 1644.

Some historians have argued that Baptists can be traced back to the Anabaptist tradition of the sixteenth century. However, this view ignores not only early Baptist objections to being identified as Anabaptists but also the significant differences between the two Protestant paradigms, particularly in relation to pacifism and church discipline.

The view that Baptists have survived in an unbroken lineage since Christ has little scholarly support. This position is often called Landmarkism and created a schism in the Southern Baptist Convention in the mid-1800s. The main proponents of this view were James Graves, James

Pendleton, and Amos Dayton. The perspective is defended most famously in *The Trail of Blood* by J. M. Carroll (1858–1931).

TOP TEN BAPTIST SUBGROUPS IN U.S.

Name	Web Address	Founded	Followers
Southern Baptist Convention	www.sbc.net	1845	20,536,000
National Baptist Convention of America	www.nbca-inc.com	1880	4,100,000
Progressive National Baptist Convention	www.pnbc.org	1961	2,000,000
American Baptist Churches	www.abc-usa.org	1639	1,762,000
Baptist Bible Fellowship International	www.bbfi.org	1950	1,600,000
Christian Churches and Churches of Christ	www.mun.ca/rels/ restmov	1935	1,213,000
Christian Church (Disciples of Christ)	www.disciples.org	1809	710,000
American Baptist Association	www.abaptist.org	1905	350,000
National Primitive Baptist Convention	http:// natlprimbaptconv. org/	1865	254,000
National Association of Free Will Baptists	www.nafwb.org	1701	292,000

Source: World Christian Database 2008

Melton's *Encyclopedia of Religions in America* identifies sixty-five distinct Baptist bodies. Of these, thirteen have memberships of more than 100,000. The largest Baptist body in the United States is the Southern Baptist Convention, comprising more than 20 million members, making it the largest Protestant grouping in the United States. In 2004 the Southern Baptists, who have generally avoided ecumenical endeavors, voted to leave the Baptist World Alliance (BWA). At the beginning of 2005 the BWA had 210 member bodies, representing more than 31 million Baptists.

Baptist identity centers on the autonomy of the local congregation and the affirmation of believer's baptism. Baptists historically have resisted acceptance of infant baptism as practiced in Catholic and mainline Protestant churches. Baptists are often perceived as fundamentalists, in part because of the conservative trends in the Southern Baptist Convention and the influence of conservative Baptists such as Jerry Falwell. Falwell, former pastor of Thomas Road Baptist Church in Lynchburg, Virginia, became famous through his leadership of the Moral Majority.

Airport Baptist Church in Vishakhapatnam,
Andra Pradesh, India

Photo: Courtesy of Blair Clark

Baptist leaders have often placed great stress on religious freedom, in part because Baptists were persecuted by state-sponsored churches in Europe in the seventeenth century. Roger Williams, one of the most famous American Baptists, argued for religious freedom in the early republic. This image of Baptists defending religious liberty is something of an antidote to the popular image of Baptists as narrow-minded and judgmental.

BAPTISTS	
Typology	Christian Protestant
Founders	John Smyth (1570–1612) and Thomas Helwys (d. 1616)
Home Websites	Baptist World Alliance: www.bwanet.org American Baptist Churches: www.abc-usa.org National Baptist Convention of America: www.nbca-inc.com National Baptist Convention, USA: www.nationalbaptist.com Progressive National Baptist Convention: www.pnbc.org Southern Baptist Convention: www.sbc.net
Recommended Reading	William H. Brackney, *A Genetic History of Baptist Thought* (Macon: Mercer, 2004)

■ Charismatics

Charismatic Christianity is a stream of the church that puts emphasis on the "sign-gifts" of the Holy Spirit: prophecy, healings, and speaking in tongues, as mentioned in 1 Corinthians 12. Historians often date the origin of the modern charismatic movement to April 3, 1960. On that day Dennis Bennett announced to his congregation at St. Mark's Episcopal Church in Van Nuys, California, that he had spoken in tongues. Reports in *Newsweek* and *Time* about the ensuing controversy led to national awareness of charismatic gifts in mainline Protestantism. In 1967 charismatic gifts became a significant reality in Roman Catholic worship. One manner in which many Charismatics differ from Pentecostals is that the latter usually believe speaking in tongues is the exclusive sign of the baptism of the Holy Spirit.

Both the Pentecostal and charismatic worlds have been influenced significantly by John Wimber (1934–97), leader of the Vineyard movement. Wimber's music ministry, views on healing and prophecy, and style of leadership influenced Christian pastors and congregations worldwide. Wimber had a significant impact on both the Kansas City Prophets (a movement connected with Mike Bickle) and the Toronto Blessing (a revival movement started in 1994 and led by John Arnott).

Mike Bickle's Kansas City Fellowship (KCF) became a major charismatic center in the late 1980s, following Wimber's embrace of Bickle and the prophets (John Paul Jackson, Bob Jones, and Paul Cain) connected with KCF. Paul Cain was a healing revivalist in the 1950s and began a second ministry with Bickle and Wimber. In the fall of 2004 Cain was disciplined over allegations of sexual sin and alcoholism. Jones is now connected with Rick Joyner, who leads MorningStar Ministries in North Carolina. (Bob Jones has no connection with the Jones dynasty connected to the famous Bob Jones University.) John Paul Jackson heads Streams Ministries International, based in New Hampshire.

The Toronto Blessing is one of the most famous and controversial renewal movements in the charismatic world. The revival's start is dated to January 20, 1994, when Randy Clark, a visiting Vineyard pastor, spoke about his spiritual renewal under the ministry of Rodney Howard-Browne, a South African evangelist based in Florida. Clark's preaching led to strange manifestations that night and in the ongoing revival—people falling over, laughing, screaming, and shaking violently. In the first two years of the Blessing some enthusiasts even imitated animal behavior, but this practice stopped after considerable controversy.

Aspects of the Toronto Blessing were duplicated in Pensacola, Florida, in the ongoing revival that began on Father's Day 1995 at the Brownsville Assembly of God congregation. Steve Hill, a visiting evangelist, was reporting at the time on his personal spiritual renewal at Holy Trinity Church, Brompton, England—another congregation touched by the renewal in Toronto. The Brownsville congregation was led by John Kilpatrick from 1981 to 2003.

Hank Hanegraaff critiqued the more sensational components in the Vineyard movement, the Kansas City Prophets saga, the Toronto Blessing, and the Brownsville renewal in his best-selling book *Counterfeit Revival*. On the other hand, Jack Deere, a former Old Testament professor at Dallas Theological Seminary, defended these renewals in his work *Surprised by the Power of the Holy Spirit*. Mainstream charismatic life is chronicled today in the monthly issues of *Charisma* magazine, published by Stephen Strang.

A charismatic Christian style is still dominant in parts of the Roman Catholic and mainline Protestant world. More importantly, much of the incredible growth of Christian faith in the Third World involves a charismatic dimension. Many missiologists argue that the charismatic or Pentecostal worldview ties in with the supernatural worldviews of South American and African cultures.

CHARISMATICS	
Typology	Christian Protestant
Websites	Toronto Airport Christian Fellowship: www.tacf.org Brownsville Revival: www.brownsville-revival.org
Recommended Reading	Stanley M. Burgess, ed., *The New International Dictionary of Pentecostal Charismatic Movements* (Grand Rapids: Zondervan, 2002) Harvey Cox, *Fire from Heaven* (Reading, MA: Addison-Wesley, 1994) Vinson Synan, *The Century of the Holy Spirit* (Nashville: Thomas Nelson, 2001)

▪ Church of Christ (aka Stone-Campbell Restoration Movement)

In the early nineteenth century, in the midst of a proliferation of Protestant denominations, several Christian leaders in the southern United States campaigned for the restoration of a single Church of Christ. The most well-known advocates of this return to "primitive" Christianity are Barton Stone (1772–1844), Thomas Campbell (1763–1854), and his son Alexander Campbell (1788–1866). Restorationists deplored the concept of denominations and argued that the New Testament only knows one body of Christ.

The Campbells were Presbyterian in their roots, as was Barton Stone. Other Restorationists came from Methodist backgrounds (James O'Kelly, 1757–1826) and from the Baptist church (Abner Jones, 1772–1841; Elias Smith, 1769–1846). Stone and other Presbyterians advanced their new Restorationist outlook in the famous document known as "The Last Will and Testament of the Springfield Presbytery" issued in 1804 in Kentucky. Stone is usually granted authorship of this document. Alexander Campbell and Stone met for the first time in 1824.

The focus on one Church of Christ rooted in the Bible alone was an ideal never to be realized. Melton's *Encyclopedia of Religions in America* lists sixteen distinct bodies that have emerged from the original movement. Divisions occurred over different understandings of baptism, women in leadership, use of instrumental music in worship, whether or not to use one Cup during communion, and whether Sunday school is biblical. The movement also experienced schism over the issue of charismatic gifts. Pat Boone was excommunicated by the Church of Christ in Inglewood,

California, in 1971. As is often the case, a movement designed to restore unity in the church actually led to greater splintering.

The major Restoration groups today are the Christian Church (Disciples of Christ), the independent Christian Churches and Churches of Christ, and Churches of Christ (Non-instrumental). The Christian Church (Disciples of Christ) is the most mainstream of the three Restoration groupings, and the one most easily seen as a denomination. The independent Christian Churches/Churches of Christ are more conservative than the Disciples but less conservative than the Churches of Christ (Non-instrumental). The Non-instrumental group split from the Disciples in 1906. Independents made a final break with the Disciples in 1968.

Cabin of David Lipscomb, noted Church of Christ minister and educator, whose estate became Nashville Bible School; later named Lipscomb University, Nashville, Tennessee

Photo: Gordon Melton

Since the Stone-Campbell movement emphasizes local church autonomy, the various streams in the movement are identified through common doctrine and practice. Theological stress is put on the Bible alone as guide, believer's baptism (by immersion), evangelism, and a strong Christian character. The different groups find unity in their various educational institutions, publications, and conferences.

The controversial International Churches of Christ (ICOC), founded by Kip McKean, are also rooted in the Church of Christ tradition from Stone-Campbell. The ICOC is also referred to as the Boston Church of

Christ, the Boston Movement, and the Crossroads Movement. The ICOC is frequently targeted as cultic. Mainline Church of Christ groups have distanced themselves from McKean, and his resignation from the top leadership position in 2002 has created a crisis in the movement.

Ultra-conservative Church of Christ members deny salvation to those outside their "one church." This verdict would be based either on arguments against the validity of baptism in mainline churches or about practices (like instrumental music in worship) that allegedly illustrate the spiritual death in non-Church of Christ circles. Some critics of instrumental music in worship argue that this practice is satanic and rooted in the darkest pagan rituals. Further, the strictest Church of Christ members believe that it is absolutely necessary to be baptized as a believer (no infant baptism) in order to be saved. Moderates in the Church of Christ tradition do not deny salvation to those outside of their religious group, nor do they have a legalistic view on the necessity of baptism.

CHURCHES OF CHRIST	
Founders	Barton Stone, Thomas Campbell, Alexander Campbell
Church Websites	Christian Church (Disciples of Christ): www.disciples.org Churches of Christ: http://church-of-christ.org, http://cconline.faithsite.com/
Other Websites	Restoration Movement (Hans Rollmann): www.mun.ca/rels/restmov World Convention: http://worldconvention.org
Recommended Reading	William Baker, ed., *Evangelicalism & the Stone-Campbell Movement* (Downers Grove: InterVarsity, 2002) Douglas A. Foster, Paul M. Blowers, Anthony L. Dunnavant and D. Newell Williams, editors, *The Encyclopedia of the Stone-Campbell Movement* (Grand Rapids: Eerdmans, 2004)

Emergent Church

The Emergent Church refers to a new movement among evangelical Christians that builds on a deep engagement with postmodern culture through appreciation of key components in a postmodern outlook. The Emergent Church is usually identified with Brian McLaren, author of *A Generous Orthodoxy* and voted one of the twenty-five leading evangelicals by *Time* magazine. Other Emergent Church leaders include Leonard Sweet, Dan Kimball, Sally Morgenthaler, Erwin McManus, Andrew Jones (Internet name: Tall Skinny Kiwi), Doug Pagitt, Tony Jones, and Karen

Ward. The movement receives its best intellectual support from Dallas Willard, Andrew Perriman, Scot McKnight, and two recently deceased leaders, Robert Webber and theologian Stan Grenz.

THE EMERGENT CHURCH'S IDENTITY

Brian McLaren

Photo: Fuzz Kitto

"I am an evangelical Christian. I love God, I seek to follow Jesus and confess him as Lord, I love the Bible and seek to understand it and live by it in my daily life. I love to help people become disciples of Jesus and grow in Christ through their whole lives. I seek to love my neighbors, whatever their religious background, and I seek to love my enemies as well. I'm not perfect, and I have a lot of flaws and blind spots, but I am pouring out my life to bring the Gospel to the postmodern world. The Gospel is the only hope we have."

—Brian McLaren, 2008

Robert Webber has pictured the Emergent movement as a third alternative to traditional evangelicals and pragmatic evangelicals. The former refers to an older evangelical paradigm that places emphasis on apologetics and sound doctrine. By pragmatic Webber means the seeker-sensitive paradigm, connected most famously with Bill Hybels and Rick Warren. Emergent leaders believe that the older models of evangelical Christianity fail, either because of an outdated epistemology or because of a capitulation to a consumer view of religion.

The Emergent Church movement embraces paradox and balances competing realities. Leonard Sweet states that "our faith is ancient. Our faith is future. We're old-fashioned. We're new-fangled. We're orthodox. We're innovators. We're postmodern Christians." McLaren writes that he can be viewed as "Missional, evangelical, Post/Protestant, Liberal/Conservative, Mystical/Poetic, Biblical, Charismatic/Contemplative, Fundamentalist/Calvinist, Anabaptist/Anglican, Methodist, catholic, Green, Incarnational, Depressed-Yet-Hopeful, Emergent, Unfinished."

Both Charles Colson and D. A. Carson have criticized the Emergent Church for being too sympathetic to postmodernism and too open to relativism. These two concerns bear serious note but must not be overstated. The Emergent Church is far more concerned to address postmodernism and relativism than to embrace either or both uncritically. Robert Webber has noted: "A postmodern setting demands relationship, participation, community, symbol, servanthood and the like. The radical re-norming of biblical priorities coupled with an absolute rejection of slick marketing, showy worship and phony verbal games precede the birth of an honest, genuine, authentic community passionately engaged with being the truth."

FUNDAMENTALIST ATTACKS ON THE EMERGENT CHURCH

Warren Smith, Roger Oakland, and David and Deborah Dombrowski view Emergent as non-Christian and as a powerful New Age conspiracy to seduce the church. Sadly, these four writers engage in sloppy scholarship, careless logic, and extreme overstatement. Their legitimate concerns about Emergent get lost in their use of invective, misrepresentation, and guilt by association. They employ the same tactics in their attempts to discredit Rick Warren as a false teacher and in targeting Leighton Ford—Billy Graham's brother-in-law—as part of the Emergent conspiracy.

Evangelicals and fundamentalists who adopt an extreme overreaction to Emergent are missing out on some significantly beneficial characteristics offered by Emergent. Yes, Emergent leaders are sometimes snobbish and occasionally blunder in theology, but they are brothers and sisters in Christ doing creative mission to our postmodern world.

Emergent Church places a great deal of emphasis on worship in community. This arises out of emphasis on the relational and the subjective element in Christian faith. McLaren and other Emergent leaders are very critical of the seeker-sensitive movement because of its alleged preoccupation with entertainment. Sally Morgenthaler argues: "The new worship paradigm contends that unbelievers can respond positively to a worship that has been made culturally accessible to them; it also proposes that unbelievers come to church, not primarily to investigate the 'claims of Christ,' but to investigate the 'Christ in us.'"

R. Albert Mohler, Jr., president of Southern Baptist Theological Seminary, stated this indictment of McLaren: "Embracing the worldview of the postmodern age, he embraces relativism at the cost of clarity in matters of truth and intends to redefine Christianity for this new age, largely in terms of an eccentric mixture of elements he would take from virtually every theological position and variant." This is far too harsh and distorts McLaren. However, McLaren should be more aware of the epistemological complexities involved in his critique of traditional evangelicalism. He and other Emergent leaders should also correct an implicit elitism in the movement and be more careful in argument, rhetoric, and treatment of major Christian doctrines.

EMERGENT CHURCH

Typology	Christian Protestant Evangelical
Websites	Brian McLaren: www.brianmclaren.net/ Leonard Sweet: www.leonardsweet.com Dallas Willard: www.dallaswillard.org Chad Hall: www.coolchurches.com John C. O'Keefe: www.ginkworld.net Mark and Jeanette Priddy: www.allelon.org Emergent Village: www.emergentvillage.com Next Wave: www.the-next-wave.org The Ooze (Spencer Burke): www.theooze.com
Recommended Reading	Brian McLaren, *A Generous Orthodoxy* (Grand Rapids: Zondervan, 2004) D. A. Carson, *Becoming Conversant with the Emerging Church* (Grand Rapids: Zondervan, 2005) Eddie Gibbs and Ryan Bolger, *Emerging Churches: Creating Christian Community in Postmodern Cultures* (Grand Rapids: Baker, 2005) Doug Pagitt and Tony Jones, eds. *An Emergent Manifesto of Hope* (Grand Rapids: Baker, 2008)

Florida Outpouring

A revival in Lakeland, Florida, broke all records in 2008 for the speed with which a revival becomes worldwide news. On April 2 of that year Canadian preacher Todd Bentley began what was meant to be a five-day conference at the 700-seat Ignited Church, pastored by Stephen Strader. The meetings continued through mid-April when *God TV* began worldwide coverage. By July, NBC, *Nightline,* and Fox had covered the revival as well. However, reports in mid-August that Bentley was leaving his wife led to evaporation of interest in the revival.

The Florida Outpouring received attention because of extravagant claims that it was "the most contagious, transferable and tangible anointing" in history. Astounding reports surfaced of angelic visitations, prophecies, visions, conversions, miraculous healings, and even raisings from the dead. Similar to the Kansas City Prophets/Vineyard phenomenon (1990 Mike Bickle/John Wimber), the Holy Laughter movement (1993 Rodney Howard-Browne), the Toronto Blessing (1994 John Arnott) and the Brownsville revival (1995 John Kilpatrick) in some ways, the Florida Outpouring developed faster and became more controversial than all of these.

Todd Bentley was born in 1976 in British Columbia and was raised by a single mother. A troubled child and teen, Bentley experienced a dramatic conversion in 1994 and began in ministry in 1998. Until his recent marriage troubles, he led Fresh Fire Ministries (FFM) in Abbotsford, British Columbia. He and his wife Shonnah are the parents of three children. FFM operates Uganda Jesus Village for children. The FFM statement of faith adopts a standard evangelical and charismatic paradigm.

Why did such controversy surround the Lakeland event and the Florida Outpouring?

First, Bentley's appearance and tastes alarmed some Christians. His love for tattoos, ultimate fighting, Christian rock music, and even motorcycles has been used as proof that he is a false prophet. These things have been seized upon in many Internet sites whose creators contend that Bentley has risen to prominence to deceive Christians in the latter days.

Second, Bentley's reports on angels, heavenly visitations, and numerous encounters with angels, including one named Emma and another named Winds of Change, caused concern among some Christians. Bentley claims to have been caught up in a pillar of fire to heaven where angels operated on him. He also says he has met Abraham and Paul in the heavenly realm. Lee Grady, editor of *Charisma* magazine, waved a yellow flag of caution, asking the leaders of the Lakeland revival to balance their spiritual experiences with biblical integrity. Grady wrote: "We have no business teaching God's people to commune with angels or to seek revelations from them. And if any revival movement—no matter how exciting or passionate—mixes the gospel of Jesus with this strange fire, the results could be devastating."

Third, others have challenged the accuracy of Bentley's various healing reports. Critics complained that few of the miracles received objective medical verification. Bentley responded in an interview that he had hired four staff members to work on proof for the healings and the claimed resurrections from the dead. Lynne Breidenbach, a one-time media advisor, reports that the staff had difficulty getting medical verification of miracles because of legal concerns.

In spite of these concerns, the Lakeland revival was endorsed by major charismatic and Pentecostal leaders, including John Kilpatrick, Bob Jones, Patricia King, Randy Clark, Paul Cain, and John Arnott, the pastor of the Toronto Airport Christian Fellowship. Arnott and his wife Carol attended Lakeland in May, and he told the crowd: "It's just amazing what God is doing here. Carol and I are here tonight to absolutely bless this, with everything in us."

On June 23, 2008, Arnott, Che Ahn, Bill Johnson, Rick Joyner, Peter Wagner and others gave their apostolic blessing to Bentley. Wagner, head of the International Coalition of Apostles, decreed that Bentley's authority, favor, influence, and revelation would increase. In mid-August, however, the board of Bentley's Fresh Fire Ministries announced that Bentley was separating from his wife and that he had "entered into an unhealthy relationship on an emotional level with a female member of his staff." Bentley quickly stepped away from ministry and canceled all speaking engagements. A few hundred people continued to gather every evening at the Ignited Church through August and September.

Two extreme views of the Florida Outpouring remain. Critics say the revival is influenced by Satan and that Bentley is a con artist who is in ministry for money. On the other side, fans of the revival have claimed it is clearly of God, that Bentley was one of the most anointed Christian leaders on Earth, and that those who have doubts and raise questions about the Outpouring are being influenced themselves by demonic spirits.

Regardless of which view is held, those who anointed Bentley in June 2008 owe their constituencies an apology for their rush to bless him without seriously engaging his personal struggles and the deeper flaws in the revival. While God may have used the revival to bless people and to bring the lost to salvation, this does not negate the need to address the major problems in Bentley's life and ministry and in the Florida Outpouring.

Peter Wagner issued an explanation for his involvement and admitted that he did not know Bentley when he participated in the apostolic blessing. Arnott, Joyner, and Bill Johnson acknowledged knowing that Todd Bentley and his wife had experienced marital struggles in the past but they were unaware of his relationship with the staff member.

Fundamentalism

The term *fundamentalist* is often used to describe right-wing elements in any religion. This entry will use it in its classical sense as a reference to the reactionary movement within Protestantism that arose to protest liberalism in Christian thought. The twentieth-century conflict between liberals and fundamentalists is part of a larger story about the breakdown in confidence in classical Christian faith that spanned the previous three centuries.

The Reformation of the sixteenth century led, ironically, to a crisis in epistemology as initial doubts about Catholicism gave way to doubts about the Christian faith itself. Skepticism about central Christian beliefs was muted in the seventeenth century but became explicit among Enlightenment figures in the next century. David Hume doubted miracles; Voltaire questioned biblical authority; and Immanuel Kant doubted the proofs for God's existence. Questions were even raised about the divinity of Jesus.

Doubts about classical Christian faith increased in the nineteenth century with Darwin's theory of evolution and with new arguments about the unity of religions. Further, the Bible was being subjected to rigorous analysis, not only in relation to Old Testament source criticism, but also in connection with evidence for the historical Jesus. All of the above formed the matrix for both the rise of liberal theology and conservative reaction by Catholics and Protestants.

FUNDAMENTALISM TIMELINE 1889–1959

1889—Moody Bible Institute founded

1892—Heresy trial of Charles Briggs

1909—J. Frank Norris begins ministry in Fort Worth, Texas

1910—Start of *The Fundamentals* pamphlet series (completed in 1915)

1919—W. B. Riley starts World's Christian Fundamental Association

1922—Harry Emerson Fosdick's sermon "Shall the Fundamentalists Win?"

1923—J. Gresham Machen's *Christianity and Liberalism* published

1924—Dallas Theological Seminary founded

1925—Scopes Trial on evolution

1926—T. T. Shields opposes liberalism among Canadian Baptists

1927—Bob Jones University founded

1929—Westminster Theological Seminary founded

1934—*Sword of the Lord* founded by John R. Rice

1936—Founding of the Orthodox Presbyterian Church

1941—American Council of Christian Churches founded

1948—International Council of Christian Churches founded

1949—Billy Graham revival meetings in Los Angeles

1949—Evangelical Theological Society founded

1956—Jerry Falwell founds Thomas Road Baptist Church

1959—Jack Hyles begins ministry in Hammond, Indiana

Fundamentalists were strongly opposed to the various strands of skepticism and in particular were appalled that liberal theologians would deny the miraculous and abandon a literal understanding of major Christian doctrines. Early fundamentalist leaders affirmed the inerrancy of the Bible, the deity of Christ, his virgin birth, the substitutionary atonement, and Christ's second coming. They defended these doctrines in a twelve-volume series known as *The Fundamentals*, released between 1910 and 1915.

The fight between liberals (or modernists) and fundamentalists split denominations and led to conflicts at institutions such as Princeton Theological Seminary. J. Gresham Machen left Princeton and founded Westminster Theological Seminary as a fundamentalist alternative. Harry Emerson

Fosdick, one of the leading modernists, argued against fundamentalist intolerance in his 1922 sermon "Shall the Fundamentalists Win?"

After the Scopes trial in 1925, fundamentalists became increasingly withdrawn from mainstream denominational life and from the wider culture. This insularity led to adoption of an even more narrow perspective and a louder polemic about classical Christian doctrines and what seem to outsiders like secondary issues. Thus, fundamentalist preachers became preoccupied with issues such as dancing, card playing, movie attendance, and social drinking. Modern fundamentalists often endorse only the King James Version and denounce contemporary Christian music.

*J. Frank Norris statue, Arlington, Texas
(Norris, 1877–1952, was a longtime pastor,
First Baptist Church, Fort Worth, Texas.)*

Photo: Gordon Melton

During World War II, a more irenic version of fundamentalism appeared and became known as evangelicalism. It has been principally identified with evangelist Billy Graham. Other early evangelical leaders included Harold Ockenga, Carl F. H. Henry (the first editor of *Christianity Today* magazine), and Charles Fuller (the founder of Fuller Theological Seminary). These evangelicals retained a conservative doctrinal framework but placed more emphasis upon academic learning, cultural engagement, and tolerance on issues of secondary importance.

FUNDAMENTALISM	
Typology	Christian Protestant
Fundamentalist school and publishing sites	David Cloud site: www.wayoflife.org The Sword of the Lord: www.swordofthelord.com Bob Jones University: www.bju.edu
Recommended Reading	Joel Carpenter, *Revive Us Again* (New York: Oxford University Press, 1997) James Davison Hunter, *Evangelicalism: The Coming Generation* (Chicago: University of Chicago, 1987) George M. Marsden, *Fundamentalism and American Culture* (Oxford: Oxford University, 1980) Martin E. Marty, *Modern American Religion, Vol 1. The Irony of It All, 1893–1919* (Chicago: University of Chicago Press, 1986)

■ Kansas City Prophets

In 1988 John Wimber, leader of the famous Vineyard movement, developed a close association with Mike Bickle, then senior pastor of the Kansas City Fellowship (KCF). Bickle's ministry had become popular through its promotion of Bob Jones, John Paul Jackson, and Paul Cain, who became known as the Kansas City Prophets. Wimber's fame launched Bickle and the KCF prophets into greater international prominence and controversy.

In 1990 the Kansas City Prophets, Wimber and Jack Deere (a leading charismatic apologist) were accused by some Australian Christians of denying the sufficiency of Scripture and neglecting the cross of Christ. The Vineyard church strongly denied the accusations. In May of the same year Ernie Gruen, a leading Pentecostal pastor in Kansas, issued a 200-page critique of KCF. He accused Bob Jones of engaging in wild speculation, false predictions, and bizarre visions. Gruen's report also argued that Bickle's fellowship had an elitist element, arising out of its focus on a new breed of super Christians.

The story of John Wimber's involvement with Bickle and the Kansas City Prophets was chronicled in David Pytches's 1991 naïve work *Some Said It Thundered.* In late 1991 Bob Jones was disciplined for sexual misconduct and withdrew from ministry for several years. In 1992 Wimber became less focused on the prophetic, though he continued to travel with Bickle and Paul Cain. Bickle broke away from the Vineyard in 1996, in large part because of Wimber's negative reaction to John Arnott and the Toronto Blessing renewal.

Paul Cain, a native of Texas, is by far the most famous of the Kansas City Prophets. Born in 1929, Cain was raised a Baptist and was a figure in healing revivals through the 1950s. He had some association with William Branham, one of the most famous healers. After 1959 Cain basically withdrew from public ministry until he connected with Mike Bickle in the mid-1980s. Cain maintained a worldwide itinerary from 1988 to 2004, often in association with Bickle, Jack Deere and Rick Joyner. In late 2004 these three exercised church discipline against Cain because of his alcoholism and homosexual behavior. In 2005 Cain admitted his wrongdoings and asked for forgiveness from the Christian community.

Bickle now leads the International House of Prayer and the Friends of the Bridegroom ministry in Kansas City. John Paul Jackson founded Streams Ministries International in 1993, after working in Kansas City and then the Anaheim Vineyard. He is now based in New Hampshire. Bob Jones, a native of Arkansas, has regained his status as a major player in prophetic circles. He claims that a supernatural spirit being appeared to him on August 12, 2004, identified himself as the "Watcher," and prophesied a "new day" for the church.

Focus on the Kansas City Prophets as a group lessened dramatically after the start of the Toronto Blessing in 1994 and the Brownsville revival in 1995. By then, however, each of the prophets had his own independent status. More important, prophetic focus had become a major staple among charismatics worldwide, due in large part to the endorsement of Mike Bickle and John Wimber. While the Kansas City Prophets do not deserve the nastiest indictments against them, their prophecies are often mistaken if specific and are otherwise either vague or reckless.

KANSAS CITY PROPHETS

Typology	Christian Protestant Charismatic
Websites	Mike Bickle: www.fotb.com Paul Cain: www.paulcain.org Bob Jones: www.bobjones.org John Paul Jackson: www.streamsministries.com
Recommended Reading	James A. Beverley, *Holy Laughter & The Toronto Blessing* (Grand Rapids: Zondervan, 1995) Mike Bickle, *Growing in the Prophetic* (Lake Mary, Florida: Creation House, 1996) Jack Deere, *Surprised by the Power of the Holy Spirit* (Grand Rapids: Zondervan, 1996) Hank Hanegraaff, *Counterfeit Revival* (Dallas: Word, 1997) John MacArthur, *Charismatic Chaos* (Grand Rapids: Zondervan, 1992) David Pytches, *Some Said It Thundered* (Nashville: Thomas Nelson, 1991) Carol Wimber, *John Wimber: The Way It Was* (London: Hodder and Stoughton, 1999)
Cautionary Note	Hank Hanegraaff's work *Counterfeit Revival* contains important critique of charismatic Christianity, but the book is marred by its negative tone and overstated concerns. Pytches's book *Some Said It Thundered* errs in the opposite direction since it offers a naïve and flawed reporting.

■ Local Church (Witness Lee)

The Local Church is a controversial Christian movement rooted in the ministries of Watchman Nee (1903–72) and Witness Lee (1905–99). Nee was converted to Christ in 1920 and influenced by both Methodism and the Plymouth Brethren tradition. Lee was born in northern China, raised in a Christian home, and became a close associate of Watchman Nee in the 1930s. Lee moved to Taiwan in 1949. Watchman Nee and his Local Church movement experienced persecution by Communist authorities in the early 1950s. Nee was sentenced to prison in 1956 and remained there till the end of his life.

The Local Church grew quickly under Witness Lee in Taiwan and other parts of Southeast Asia. Lee moved to the United States in 1962 and settled in southern California, where he carried on a regular teaching and preaching ministry until 1997, two years before his death. Living Stream Ministries continues to publish his material, now available in more than fourteen languages and four hundred separate volumes. LSM also publishes *The Recovery Bible,* a title that reflects Local Church teaching that it is part of God's recovery of the original New Testament Church.

Controversy about Witness Lee began in the mid-1970s when the Local Church in Berkeley was attacked by Jack Sparks, a leader in the Christian World Liberation Front (CWLF). The CWLF developed the Spiritual Counterfeits Project (SCP), the famous evangelical cult-monitoring group. Sparks wrote a chapter against the Local Church in his work *The Mindbenders* (1977), and Neil Duddy and the SCP attacked Lee's movement in *The God-Men* (1977, revised edition 1981). The publisher withdrew *The Mindbenders* from circulation in 1983 and published an apology in eighteen major U.S. newspapers. After a lengthy court case the Local Church won a $12 million judgment in 1985 against SCP. SCP was forced into bankruptcy and reemerged under Chapter Eleven protection.

Protestant church, Kunming, China

Photo: Gordon Melton

In 1999 John Ankerberg and John Weldon included the Local Church in their *Encyclopedia of Cults and New Religions*. In 2001 leaders in the Local Church wrote the two authors and publisher to protest their inclusion in the book, asking for a meeting to process the issue. Harvest House and the authors refused to meet with Local Church representatives and started legal proceedings against the Local Church in late 2002. In response, the Local Church started its own legal action against the publisher. A Texas court ruled against the Local Church in 2006, and the next year the United States Supreme Court refused to hear the case.

In August 2004, I spent considerable time with Local Church leaders at their headquarters in Southern California. This gave me the opportunity to expand on previous study of the controversies about Witness Lee and the Local Church. I came away from my intense dialogue convinced that the Local Church is basically an evangelical Christian group. However, there remain four areas where the Local Church needs to improve in terms of its theological stance and communication.

First, the movement is inclined to elitism because of the way Witness Lee pictured the movement in terms of recovery of the Lord's church. Like so many other restorationists, Lee failed to see that the unity of the church is not really solved by starting another group. Second, the rhetoric in Local Church literature about other Christian groups is occasionally far too negative and inconsistent with their otherwise open stance. Third, the Local Church adoption of Eastern Orthodox teaching on *theosis* or Christians becoming Godlike is unfortunate, given the scanty biblical witness to that idea. Finally, Local Church leaders are far too reluctant to detect or admit errors in the teaching of Witness Lee.

Fuller Seminary leaders announced in 2006 that their two-year dialogue with Local Church leaders led them to affirm the evangelical stance of the Local Church. Their report stated that "the teachings and practices of the local churches and its members represent the genuine, historical, biblical Christian faith in every essential aspect." The same verdict was reached by Answers in Action and the Christian Research Institute. Withdrawing some of Witness Lee's more controversial and careless remarks from circulation should broaden evangelical consensus of the Local Church. A 2007 Open Letter to the Local Church from major evangelical scholars makes this same request.

The Open Letter also called on Local Church leaders to "publicly renounce the use of lawsuits and the threat of lawsuits against evangelical

Christians to answer criticisms or resolve conflicts." The Local Church replied by defending their litigation against Harvest House and invited evangelicals to do a more serious study of the context and background of the quotes cited in the Open Letter. Even if the context helps in ongoing dialogue, some of Lee's statements are too extreme and should be withdrawn from widespread distribution.

LOCAL CHURCH	
Founders	Watchman Nee and Witness Lee
Websites	Living Stream Ministries: www.lsm.org Contending for the Faith: www.contendingforthefaith.com Affirmation and Critique: www.affcrit.com

Lutherans

Lutheran churches trace their existence back to the German reformer Martin Luther, the famous monk who protested doctrinal errors and moral lapses in the popular Catholicism of his day. Luther is most famous for his 95 Theses, a document that targeted the sale of Indulgences—buying souls out of purgatory through payments to the Catholic Church. Luther's critique led to a trial before Catholic authorities and to his eventual excommunication in 1521. Luther stated at a hearing at the Diet of Worms: "Unless I am convinced by Scripture and plain reason—I do not accept the authority of the popes and councils, for they have contradicted each other—my conscience is captive to the Word of God. I cannot and I will not recant anything for to go against conscience is neither right nor safe. God help me. Amen. "

The Augsburg Confession of 1530 cemented the differences between Luther and his Catholic opponents. This confession is part of *The Book of Concord*, published in 1580, which also includes Luther's Small Catechism, Large Catechism, and his Smalcald Articles (from 1537). In his writings Luther objected to celibacy, the worship of saints, and the doctrine of purgatory. Luther also became increasingly critical of the office of the pope. In his Smalcald Articles he states: "The Pope is the very Antichrist, who has exalted himself above, and opposed himself against Christ because he will not permit Christians to be saved without his power, which, nevertheless, is nothing, and is neither ordained nor commanded by God." His chief objection to the papacy rose out of his argument for salvation by grace alone, through faith alone.

TOP TEN LUTHERAN SUBGROUPS IN U.S.

Name	Website	Founded	Followers
Evangelical Lutheran Church in America	www.elca.org	1623	4,850,776
Lutheran Church Missouri Synod	www.lcms.org	1847	2,440,864
Wisconsin Evangelical Lutheran Synod	www.wels.net	1850	389,252
Association of Free Lutheran Congregations	www.aflc.org	1897	39,409
Synod of Evangelical Lutheran Churches	www.nesynod.org	1902	24,500
Evangelical Lutheran Synod	www. evangelicallutheransynod. org	1917	20,429
American Association of Lutheran Churches	www.taalc.com	1987	17,900
Latvian Evangelical Lutheran Church in America	www.dcdraudze.org/church	1946	15,900
Estonian Evangelical Lutheran Church	www.eelk.ee/eng_ EELCabroad.html	1941	15,600
Church of the Lutheran Confession	www.clclutheran.org	1959	8,500

Source: World Christian Database 2008

A large majority of Lutheran churches belong to the Lutheran World Federation, founded in 1947. In 2004 the LWF comprised 138 member churches, representing 65 million Lutherans from seventy-seven countries. The Evangelical Lutheran Church in America (ECLA) is part of this Federation. Membership in the ECLA is almost 5 million, making it the largest Lutheran church in the United States. The more conservative Lutheran Church-Missouri Synod has almost 2.5 million members while the Wisconsin Evangelical Lutheran Synod, another conservative Lutheran group, has more than 400,000.

Lutherans have always held Luther in high esteem, and his writings play a significant part in the training of Lutheran ministers. However, in recent years Lutherans have also distanced themselves from darker sides of Luther's ideology, particularly his rantings against the Jews. Luther grew increasingly intemperate about Jews, culminating in his 1543 work *Concerning the Jews and their Lies.* His writings were cited by Hitler to justify Nazi policy. The Lutheran World Federation condemned Luther's anti-Semitism in 1984.

Luther statue, Worms, Germany

Photo: Gordon Melton

On October 31, 1999, the Lutheran World Federation and the Roman Catholic Church ratified a Joint Agreement on Justification at an official ceremony in Augsburg, Germany. This ecumenical achievement was a result of three decades of scholarly engagement between Lutherans and Catholics. More conservative Lutherans, like the Lutheran Church-

Missouri Synod, refused to endorse the agreement, arguing that it represented a compromise of historic Lutheranism.

LUTHERAN	
Typology	Christian Protestant
Founder	Martin Luther (1484–1546)
Websites	Confessional Evangelical Lutheran Conference: www.celc.info International Lutheran Council: www.ilc-online.org Lutheran World Federation: www.lutheranworld.org Evangelical Lutheran Church in America: www.elca.org Lutheran Church Missouri Synod: www.lcms.org Wisconsin Evangelical Lutheran Synod: www.wels.net
Recommended Reading	Richard Cimino, ed. *Lutherans Today* (Grand Rapids: Eerdmanns, 2003) Victor Shepherd, *Interpreting Martin Luther: An Introduction to His Life and Thought* (Vancouver: Regent Press, 2008)

Methodists

The Methodist tradition in Protestantism is always traced to the lives of John Wesley (1703–91) and his brother Charles (1707–88), the famous hymn writer. The Wesleys were raised in the Church of England and attended Oxford University. After a failed ministry in America, John Wesley found himself spiritually depressed; this melancholy disappeared when he experienced conversion at a Moravian meeting in London on May 24, 1738. Here are his famous words about his transformation: "I felt my heart strangely warmed. I felt I did trust in Christ, Christ alone, for salvation; and an assurance was given me that he had taken away my sins."

John Wesley spent the rest of his life preaching the message of Christian grace. He severed relations with the Moravians, but he never left the Church of England, though his practices created strains within Anglican circles. Wesley's itinerant preaching grew because of the encouragement of George Whitefield, the famous revival preacher. Wesley sent Francis Asbury (1745–1816) to the Americas in 1771. Asbury, Thomas Coke, and others formed the Methodist Episcopal Church.

Methodists divided early on along racial lines, with the formation of the African Methodist Episcopal Church in 1816. Later, in 1845, the larger Methodist movement split over the issue of slavery and the Methodist Episcopal Church, South was formed. This split was formally healed with a reunion of the two groups in 1939. The United Methodist Church, the largest American Methodist body, stands in this lineage, and was officially founded in 1968.

John Wesley can also be considered the spiritual founder of churches in the Holiness tradition. Wesley's theology and ministry laid the roots for the Salvation Army, the Church of the Nazarene, the Christian and Missionary Alliance, the Church of God (Anderson, Indiana), the Wesleyan Church, and the Glenn Griffith churches, among others. More than 120 distinct groups exist in the Methodist and Holiness traditions in North America. The vast majority of Methodist churches, both American and otherwise, belong to the World Methodist Council.

Methodist Hall, London, England

Phtoo: Jim Beverley

Tablet commemorates UN meeting at Methodist Hall, London, England

Photo: Derek Beverley

Methodist churches divide along liberal and conservative theological agendas. Like many denominations, mainline Methodist groups face a crisis over how to handle homosexuality and the ordination of homosexuals. In March 2004 the Reverend Karen Dammann of Seattle was found not guilty of engaging in "practices incompatible with Christian teachings," even though she admitted to being a practicing homosexual. Conversely, in December 2004 a United Methodist court in Pennsylvania removed Reverend Irene Elizabeth Stroud from ministry, citing her open lesbian relationship. The United Methodist Church has a policy against ordination of "self-avowed, practicing homosexuals."

METHODISTS	
Typology	Christian Protestant
Founder	John Wesley
Homepages	World Methodist Council: www.worldmethodistcouncil.org United Methodist Church: www.umc.org African Methodist Episcopal Church: www.ame-church.com African Methodist Episcopal Zion Church: www.amez.org Christian and Missionary Alliance: www.cmalliance.org Christian Methodist Episcopal Church: www.c-m-e.org Church of the Nazarene: www.nazarene.org Evangelical Free Church of America: www.efca.org Evangelical Covenant Church: www.covchurch.org Evangelical Congregational Church: www.eccenter.com Evangelical Methodist Church of America: www.emchurch.org Southern Methodist Church: www.southernmethodistchurch.org Moravian Church in America: www.moravian.org
Recommended Reading	Thomas Oden, *John Wesley's Scriptural Christianity* (Grand Rapids: Zondervan, 1994)
Special Note	Victor Shepherd's web material on Methodism is particularly important in relation to theological developments in the United Church of Canada. Shepherd, a professor at Tyndale Seminary in Toronto, was the expert witness in the 1996 Bermuda case in which the Supreme Court of Bermuda accepted his testimony that a local Methodist church had the right to remove itself from the United Church of Canada jurisdiction because of the latter's deviation from historic Methodism. Most important, the judge also ruled that the local church had the right to keep its property. See www.victorshepherd.on.ca

TOP TEN HOLINESS SUBGROUPS IN U.S.

Name	Web Address	Founded	Followers
Church of the Nazarene	www.nazarene.org	1907	803,000
Salvation Army	salvationarmyusa.org	1880	422,543
Christian & Missionary Alliance	www.cmalliance.org	1881	390,000
Church of God (Anderson)	www.chog.org	1880	211,000
Wesleyan Church	www.wesleyan.org	1843	197,000
Free Methodist Church of North America	www.freemethodistchurch.org	1860	57,700
Missionary Church	www.mcusa.org	1889	45,100
Volunteers of America	http://www.voa.org/	1896	43,600
Church of God (Holiness)	www.cogh.net	1890	28,300
Churches of Christ in Christian Union	www.cccuhq.org	1909	19,100

Source: World Christian Database 2008

New Apostolic Reformation

Cindy Jacobs, a prominent prophet in the charismatic world, declared several years ago that God would use C. Peter Wagner to "change the face of Christianity" and that this change "will be like unto what Martin Luther did." Wagner, now based in Colorado Springs and president of Global Harvest Ministries and chancellor of the Wagner Leadership Institute, claims to be the apostle of the New Apostolic Reformation (NAR). NAR leaders argue that its churches are "the fastest growing in all areas of the world."

Wagner also leads the International Coalition of Apostles (ICA) and the New Apostolic Roundtable. He is in partnership with prominent pastors, including Mel Mullen (Red Deer, Alberta), Naomi Dowdy (Singapore) and Harold Caballeros (Guatemala). Beyond Jacobs's endorsement, Wagner's apostolic authority is also blessed by prophets Paul Cain, Rick Joyner, and Bill Hamon.

Peter and Doris Wagner

Photo: Global Harvest Ministries

For more than two decades C. Peter Wagner has been at the center of controversy in Christian circles. In 1982 he and John Wimber, the leader of the Vineyard movement, began teaching a course on "Signs, Wonders and Church Growth" at Fuller Seminary in Pasadena, California. The hands-on course created a fury of protest because of its charismatic orientation. Wagner was later connected to the controversial Kansas City Prophets led by Mike Bickle.

The New Apostolic Reformation has gained fierce critics. Wagner and his fellow apostles are on the list of some cult-watch groups. One site even suggests that NAR leaders engage in mind-control and are motivated by financial greed. Others contend that Wagner is setting the scene for the Antichrist and that he is a dupe of the "Latter Rain," a Pentecostal movement that originated in North Battleford, Saskatchewan, in 1948. Milder critics express caution about Wagner's spiritual mapping theories and accuse him of naïveté about healings and prophecy.

The most negative interpretations of Wagner merit attention only because of their popularity. Painting him as a pawn or player in the hands of Satan and the end-times is profoundly misleading. Wagner and his colleagues are deeply committed to intercessory prayer and missions; both he and his wife, Doris, served for fifteen years as missionaries in Bolivia. Financially, both Global Harvest Ministries and the Wagner Leadership Institute belong to the Evangelical Council for Financial Accountability (ECFA).

Wagner's proposals include virtually nothing unique, other than the statement that he is the lead apostle in a new apostolic movement. The major characteristics of Wagner's movement represent a variation on old-fashioned Pentecostalism or new-fashioned charismatic Christianity. For the sake of argument, assume that God wants to restore apostles. Wagner and his Roundtable members deserve the title of apostle only if the term is used across the entire church of those in positions of crucial leadership. This honors the breadth of the universal church and deflates the self-referential elitism in Wagner's group.

NEW APOSTOLIC REFORMATION

Typology	Christian Protestant Charismatic
Leader	C. Peter Wagner
Homepage	Global Harvest: www.globalharvest.org
Recommended Reading	C. Peter Wagner, *The New Apostolic Churches* (Regal, 1998)

Pentecostalism

Pentecostalism is the largest Protestant family worldwide. The combined charismatic-Pentecostal movements represent the fastest-growing spiritual tradition in many countries. The largest Trinitarian Pentecostal groups in the United States are the Assemblies of God and the Church of

Rodney Howard-Browne, a Pentecostal evangelist from South Africa

Photo: Jim Beverley

God (Cleveland). The tradition has been prone to splits; Melton's *Encyclopedia of American Religions* identifies almost 400 different Pentecostal and charismatic groups. The earliest Pentecostals divided along racial lines. The most significant doctrinal division in Pentecostal history occurred in 1913–14 over teaching that Jesus is the Father, Son, and Holy Spirit. This is known as Jesus-Only or Oneness Pentecostalism. The largest Oneness body is the United Pentecostal Church, formed in 1945.

As David Barrett and Todd Johnson show in their ongoing research on global religious trends, the sweep of Pentecostalism and charismatic Christianity is one of the most astounding developments in the Christian story since 1900. The continuing popularity and growth in this tradition makes it imperative that leaders within the tradition address some of its obvious weaknesses, including correction of anti-intellectual tendencies in Pentecostal rhetoric, abandonment of simplistic understandings of the Spirit, and curtailing of exaggerated claims related to healing, visions, and prophecies.

True Jesus Church, Malaysia

Photo: Gordon Melton

TOP TEN PENTECOSTAL APOSTOLIC BLACK CHURCHES

Name	Web Address	Founded	Followers
Church of God in Christ	www.cogic.org	1895	7,500,000
Full Gospel Baptist Church Fellowship	www.fullgospelbaptist.org	1993	1,400,000
Pentecostal Assemblies of the World	www.pawinc.org/	1906	1,400,000
United Pentecostal Church International	www.upci.org	1914	816,000
Assemblies of the Lord Jesus Christ	aljc.org	1952	161,000
Deliverance Evangelistic Church	www.decministry.org	1960	136,000
United Church of Jesus Christ (Apostolic)	www.unitedchurchofjesuschrist.org	1945	123,000
Pentecostal Church of God	www.pcg.org	1919	96,000
Pentecostal Churches of the Apostolic Faith	www.pcaf.net	1957	79,500
Mount Sinai Holy Church of America	mtsinaiholychurch.org	1924	73,100

Source: World Christian Database 2008

TOP TEN PENTECOSTAL SUBGROUPS IN U.S.

Name	Web Address	Founded	Followers
Assemblies of God	www.ag.org	1906	2,830,861
Church of God (Cleveland)	www.churchofgod.org	1886	1,013,488
Rhema Bible Churches	www.rhema.org/church	1960	610,000
International Church of the Foursquare Gospel	www.foursquare.org	1918	412,000
International Convention of Faith Ministries	www.icfm.org	1978	230,000
Association of Vineyard Churches	http://www.vineyardusa.org/	1978	165,000
Church of God of Prophecy	www.cogop.org	1923	158,000
Deliverance Evangelistic Church	www.decministry.org/ fellowshipchurches.asp	1960	136,000
Pentecostal Church of God	www.pcg.org	1919	96,000
Fellowship of Christian Assemblies	www.fcaoc.org	1922	61,700

Source: World Christian Database 2008

The New Testament emphasis on the Holy Spirit lies at the heart of the worldwide Pentecostal movement. Pentecostals usually trace their modern roots to the ministry of Charles Parham (1873–1929), founder of the Bethel Bible School in Topeka, Kansas. On January 1, 1901, Agnes Ozman, one of Parham's students, spoke in tongues. Parham himself and about half the student body also spoke in tongues during the next several days. Parham spread the Pentecostal message through his Apostolic Faith movement.

RESOURCES ON PENTECOSTALISM AND CHARISMATIC CHRISTIANITY

The best one-volume work is Stanley M. Burgess, editor, *The New International Dictionary of Pentecostal Charismatic Movements* (Grand Rapids: Zondervan, 2002). On the debates about the Health and Wealth gospel, the two most important works are Robert Bowman Jr., *The Word-Faith Controversy* (Grand Rapids: Baker, 2001) and Andrew Perriman, *Faith, Health and Prosperity* (Carlisle: Paternoster, 2003). For data on the Kansas City Prophets, Rodney Howard-Browne, and the Vineyard movement, see my book *Holy Laughter & The Toronto Blessing* (Grand Rapids: Zondervan, 1995).

For general data on healing revivalism see David Edwin Harrell Jr., *All Things Are Possible* (Bloomington: Indiana University Press, 1975) and his *Oral Roberts: An American Life* (Bloomington: Indiana University Press, 1985). The most important study on William Branham is Douglas Weaver, *The Healer-Prophet* (Macon: Mercer University Press, 1987). David Reed has studied Oneness Pentecostalism in his new work *In Jesus' Name* (U.K.: Deo, 2008). Harvard professor Harvey Cox chronicles charismatic Christianity in *Fire from Heaven* (Reading: Addison-Wesley, 1994). Vinson Synan's, *The Century of the Holy Spirit* (Nashville: Thomas Nelson, 2001) is also important.

In 1905 William J. Seymour (1870–1922), a black Holiness preacher, met Charles Parham in Texas and adopted his theology. In 1906 Seymour began work at the Azusa Street Mission in Los Angeles. The church (based at 312 Azusa St.) experienced a three-year revival from 1906 through 1909 that launched Pentecostal doctrine and practice to the entire world. Seymour's congregation rebuffed a takeover by Parham in late 1906. After the revival subsided Seymour gradually lost influence in wider Pentecostal circles. He died on September 28, 1922.

Pentecostals emphasize the sign-gifts of the Holy Spirit, which include the gifts of speaking in tongues, discernment, prophecy, and divine healing. Speaking in tongues is viewed by Pentecostals as the initial sign of the baptism of the Holy Spirit. The early Pentecostals often believed that those who spoke in tongues were actually speaking in foreign languages, like the early Christians in the second chapter of Acts. Pentecostals now hold that most tongues-speaking involves divinely inspired utterances that lie outside ordinary human language.

Pentecostalism is often associated with its famous healers, including Kathryn Kuhlman (1907–76), William Branham (1909–65), A. A. Allen (1911–70), Oral Roberts (1918–), Benny Hinn (1952–), and Rodney Howard-Browne (1961–). Other significant Pentecostal leaders include Thomas Ball Barratt (1862–1940), Aimee Semple McPherson (1890–1944), David du Plessis (1905–87), Demos Shakarian (1913–93), Pat Robertson (1930–), and David Yong-gi Cho (1936–).

PENTECOSTALISM

Typology	Christian Protestant
Scripture	Bible
Websites	Assemblies of God: http://ag.org Church of God in Christ, Inc. (Memphis, Tennessee): www.cogic.org Church of God (Cleveland, Tennessee): http://www.churchofgod.org Rodney Howard-Browne: www.revival.com Brownsville Revival: www.brownsville-revival.org
Recommended Reading	Stanley M. Burgess, editor, *The New International Dictionary of Pentecostal and Charismatic Movements* (Grand Rapids: Zondervan, 2002) David Reed, *In Jesus' Name* (U.K.: Deo, 2008)

▓ Plymouth Brethren

Plymouth Brethren is the designation for those who follow in the heritage of John Nelson Darby (1800–82), a Bible teacher who separated from the Church of Ireland in 1827. While Darby did not start this fellowship of independent Christians, he was their most famous leader. The Plymouth Brethren are known for their detailed study of Scripture. Sadly, their biblical acumen has often been overshadowed by their frequent schisms, particularly among the Exclusive Brethren, who followed Darby's isolationism. The less sectarian heirs of Darby are known as Open Brethren. F. F. Bruce, well-known evangelical scholar, was part of this tradition.

The darkest hours in Exclusive Brethren history came in the later years of the ministry of James Taylor, Jr., who became head of the group in 1959. His leadership was marked by legalism and ruthless sectarianism.

His career ended in scandal because of alleged sexual misconduct at a meeting in Aberdeen, Scotland, in July 1970, as reported in newspapers in the United Kingdom and North America. His control over his group was such, however, that he was able to oust or silence most critics and command total trust as the "Elect Vessel" of the Lord for his worldwide following. The "Jims" (the nickname for those who followed the Taylorites) excused his vulgar language in worship, excessive drinking, overt sexual behavior, and ruthless treatment of any who dared question him.

Granville Chapel, Vancouver, BC, Canada

Photo: Derek Beverley

The Plymouth Brethren movement influenced wider conservative Christian circles in its focus on eschatology. Darby laid the groundwork for the widespread adoption of pre-millennialism that has become the dominant paradigm in evangelical prophetic writing. He stressed the view that Christ will return before the Tribulation to take believers to heaven. This Rapture theory is part of the prophetic outlook adopted in the popular *Left Behind* novels, authored by Tim LaHaye and Jerry Jenkins.

Darby also held a high view of the authority of Scripture, including the belief that the Bible is without error. Generally, the Plymouth Brethren accept the literal interpretation of Scripture. The inerrancy position and literal interpretation of Scripture became major elements in the fundamentalist movement of the early twentieth century.

One interesting difference between fundamentalists and some Plymouth Brethren groups involves the use of alcohol. Fundamentalists have often advocated total abstinence, while Plymouth Brethren leaders have often supported wine drinking on the basis of Jesus' changing water into wine at the wedding in Cana mentioned in the Gospel of John, chapter 2.

It is difficult to track contemporary Plymouth Brethren life, since the various groups often maintain a low public profile. The more exclusive groups have no major internet presence and are not interested in academic study of their history and ideology. Ex-members of the exclusive tradition often describe their past religious life as "cultic" and "destructive."

PLYMOUTH BRETHREN

Typology	Christian Protestant Fundamentalist
Early Leader	J. N. Darby
Websites	www.peebs.net brethrenonline.org www.mybrethren.org

■ Presbyterian-Reformed

Reformed and Presbyterian churches trace their roots back to John Calvin (1509–64), the famous Protestant leader. He was born in France and studied at the University of Paris. Raised Catholic, Calvin was influenced by Renaissance humanism and the ideology of Erasmus (d. 1536), the influential Dutch thinker. Calvin's conversion to Protestantism resulted from his ongoing study of the Bible and his experience of Catholic suppression of Protestant movements in France. Calvin left France in 1533 and settled in Basel, Switzerland. He released the first edition of his *Institutes of the Christian Religion* in 1536, the same year that he moved to Geneva. After a brief exile in Strasburg (1538–41), Calvin spent the rest of his life in Geneva.

REFORMER ABRAHAM KUYPER

Abraham Kuyper is one of the most influential reformed thinkers of modern times. Born in the Netherlands in 1837, Kuyper studied arts and theology in Leiden. He was influenced by the writings of the Polish reformer John à Lasco. After he became a pastor, Kuyper grew increasingly alarmed by the liberal theology of the state-controlled church. In 1870 he became one of the pastors in the church in Amsterdam, and in 1874 he was elected as a member of parliament. Six years later, in 1880, Kuyper helped found the Free University of Amsterdam, and in 1886 he helped found the Netherlands Gereformeerde Kerken (NGK). This secession from the larger state church (the Netherlands Hervormde Kerk—NHK) is known as the Doleantie, which means "mourning." Kuyper delivered the Stone Lectures at Princeton in 1898 and became president of the Netherlands in 1901. He died in 1920.

Calvin's theology and understanding of church government became a dominant force in the spreading Protestant movement. His heritage is found largely in the Reformed and Presbyterian Church traditions, but Calvinistic theology has also had a significant impact on Anglican and Baptist history. Calvin is most famous for his teaching on predestination. He was criticized by other reformers for his complicity in the execution of Servetus (d. 1553), the Spanish radical who advanced an unorthodox interpretation of the Trinity. Though Calvin had an affinity with the main contours of Luther's thought, the two most famous Protestants never met.

Calvin's thought formed the doctrinal framework for the Scots Confession (1560), written by John Knox and others; Belgic Confession (1561); Heidelberg Catechism (1563); Canons of Dordt (1619); and the famous Westminster Confession (1646). It also had a significant impact on the London Baptist Confession of Faith (1689). Though these statements reflect Calvin's theology to a great degree, his *Institutes* and biblical commentaries provide a far broader and richer interpretation of Christian doctrine and life. For example, the first section of the *Institutes* places great emphasis on the leading of the Holy Spirit in the discovery of Christian truth.

The Reformed tradition took particular hold in Switzerland, France, Scotland, the Netherlands, and Hungary in the sixteenth and seventeenth centuries, though the Huguenots in France suffered heavy persecution. Many Huguenots fled to the British colonies in America, including the father of Paul Revere. Reformed and Presbyterian churches in Britain and the Netherlands have had the most impact in spreading Calvinistic Christianity to the United States and other parts of the world, particularly South Africa and Korea.

THE FAMOUS FIRST QUESTION

Q. 1. What is the chief end of man?
A. Man's chief end is to glorify God and to enjoy him forever.

—Westminster Shorter Catechism (1647)

The Reformed Ecumenical Council unites 10 million members from 39 Presbyterian and Reformed denominations from 25 countries. The International Conference of Reformed Churches is a smaller conservative union, which includes the Orthodox Presbyterian Church. The OPC, led by J. Grecham Machen, formed in 1934 in reaction to liberalism at Princeton Theological Seminary. The World Alliance of Reformed Churches represents the largest ecumenical grouping, with more than two hundred churches representing 75 million believers from more than 100 countries. The World Alliance includes The Presbyterian Church (USA), the United Church of Christ, and the United Church of Canada.

PRESBYTERIAN-REFORMED

Typology	Protestant
Founder	John Calvin
Scripture	Bible
Homepages	International Conference of Reformed Churches: www. icrconline.com World Alliance of Reformed Churches: www.warc.ch
Recommended Reading	Calvin's *Institutes of the Christian Religion* Victor Shepherd, *The Nature and Function of Faith in the Theology of John Calvin* (Vancouver: Regent Publishing, 1983)

Purpose-Driven Worship at Willow Creek

Photo: Courtesy of Willow Creek Community Church

Purpose-Driven/Seeker-Sensitive Churches

Purpose-Driven and Seeker-Sensitive churches include two of the largest churches in America. The Seeker-Sensitive movement can be traced to the Willow Creek Church (aka Willow Creek Community Church) near Chicago, Illinois, founded by Bill Hybels. The Purpose-Driven movement has its roots in the ministry of Rick Warren, founding pastor of the Saddleback Community Church in Southern California. Warren is known most famously for his two best-selling works *The Purpose Driven Church* and *The Purpose Driven Life*. The latter has sold more than 25 million copies.

Willow Creek Church started in October 1975 in a rented movie theater. After considerable growth over two years, the church purchased ninety acres of land in South Barrington, Illinois, in 1977, now the site of the main church sanctuary and headquarters.

The local Willow Creek Church operates at three other sites in Illinois, with more than 20,000 members, while the Willow Creek Association reaches more than 10,000 different churches in thirty-five countries.

The Saddleback Valley Community Church held its first service at Easter in 1980. Rick Warren and his wife, Kay, moved to Orange Country the previous December with plans to launch a church that reached the non-churched. Their first Bible study had seven in attendance. Now more than 20,000 people attend Saddleback church services each weekend, and more than 350,000 pastors and church leaders have been trained in Purpose-Driven seminars. Warren has been called America's most influential pastor.

REVISITING THE SEEKER-SENSITIVE CHURCH

In the summer of 2007 Willow Creek founder Bill Hybels admitted he blew it. He told participants at his Leadership Summit that he was facing the "wake-up call" of his entire ministry. With the assistance of Greg Hawkins, Willow's executive pastor, Hybels discovered that key practices of the seeker-sensitive paradigm had not worked.

Hybels states: "Some of the stuff that we have put millions of dollars into, thinking it would really help our people grow and develop spiritually—when the data actually came back it wasn't helping people that much. Other things that we didn't put that much money into and didn't put much staff against is (sic) stuff our people are crying out for."

Hawkins says that Willow Creek recognizes the need to make big changes. "Our dream is that we fundamentally change the way we do church—take out a clean sheet of paper and rethink all of our old assumptions. Replace it with new insights. Insights that are informed by research and rooted in Scripture. Our dream is really to discover what God is doing and how He's asking us to transform this planet."

This news represents a very, very sobering reality. Willow Creek's impact does not stop at the mother church in South Barrington, Illinois. Hybels's influence stretches across more than thirty-five countries and to thousands of other churches. The fault lines discovered in the summer of 2007 run deep and long. It is no wonder that Hybels said that the new research from Hawkins "rocked" his world.

Hawkins and Willow Creek staffer Cally Parkinson document these findings in their new book, *Reveal*. Parkinson states: "We've just finished doing research with over 500 churches and almost half of them are not seeker-targeted or seeker-sensitive. Based on these churches, the flaws discovered by REVEAL are not unique to Willow Creek, or the seeker movement. Our findings suggest that all churches could do a better job of helping people grow spiritually."

Hybels admits the mistakes made in the planning and implementation of the Willow Creek dream. He has said that he lost nights of sleep in the realization that he had been wrong on some "church growth stuff" for thirty years, but he has faced these things honestly, and with humility. Thankfully, both Willow Creek and Saddleback Church have thoroughly orthodox statements of faith on all essential Christian doctrines. Their errors have been due to improper strategy, not to improper truth. The research shows that Willow Creek, for example, has done a superb job in reaching non-Christians and young Christians, but has not done as well in helping mature Christians grow deeper in the Lord. Evangelical churches of all styles would do well to engage in self-examination and critique as Willow Creek has done.

Both Warren and Hybels receive significant criticism from Emergent Church leaders who suggest that the two have been seduced by a commercial mind-set that views church as a form of entertainment. Fundamentalist Christians are even harsher in their criticism, including the outrageous allegation that an occult spirit is behind *The Purpose Driven Life*. More commonly, both Warren and Hybels are charged with pragmatism, spiritual shallowness, and offering a man-centered, New-Age style religion. They are also frequently criticized for their connection with Robert Schuller, the founder of California's Crystal Cathedral.

These negative allegations are largely based on superficial and unfair analysis of both leaders and their respective movements. The statements of faith of both Saddleback and Willow Creek are thoroughly orthodox. Both Warren and Hybels have based their entire ministry model on reaching the unsaved, a fact that seems lost to most critics. They both openly acknowledge Jesus Christ as the only Savior, a fact that thoroughly discredits any suggestion that they are New Age. Warren was completely candid about his Christ-centered faith in a May 2005 forum in Key West, Florida, with some of America's leading journalists.

Both Warren and Hybels acknowledge learning some practical techniques from Robert Schuller in relation to church growth. However, Hybels and Warren do not duplicate Schuller's emphasis on positive thinking and they are far more orthodox in their writings. It deserves note that the Crystal Cathedral has a thoroughly orthodox Statement of Faith as well. It includes these affirmations: "Man is by nature sinful and cannot make himself good. He can only be made righteous by accepting God's forgiveness for sin through Jesus' sacrifice on the cross." Of course, conservative Christians have every right to complain when Robert Schuller strays from his own church's orthodoxy to emphasize positive thinking instead.

Rick Warren receives his most severe criticism from conservative Christians, including Ken Silver, Warren Smith, Paul Proctor, Ingrid Schlueter and the Lighthouse Trails Research Project (Dave and Deborah Dombrowski). Richard Abanes has provided detailed and careful response to such critics on his website and through his book *Rick Warren and the Purpose that Drives Him.* Abanes's work is also a corrective to the flawed biography on Warren written by George Muir.

PURPOSE-DRIVEN AND SEEKER-SENSITIVE CHURCHES	
Founders	Rick Warren (Saddleback) and Bill Hybels (Willow Creek)
Websites	Rick Warren and Saddleback: www.saddleback.com, www. purposedrivenlife.com Willow Creek Church: www.willowcreek.org Willow Creek Association: www.willowcreek.com Richard Abanes site: www.abanes.com
Recommended Reading	Richard Abanes, *Rick Warren and the Purpose that Drives Him* (Eugene: Harvest House, 2005)

▓ Quakers

Quakers is the popular term for The Society of Friends, the spiritual movement that traces its roots back to George Fox, a dissenting Christian leader of seventeenth-century England. Fox was born at Drayton-in-the-Clay, England, in 1624 and raised in the Church of England, but he developed an independent spirit about certain traditions in both society and church life.

Known for his focus on inward spirituality and enlightenment by the Holy Spirit, Fox refused to use the word *church* about buildings. He found little theological or spiritual help from either orthodox Christian pastors or various sectarian groups. This deprivation led him to write: "And when all my hopes in them and in all men were gone, so that I had nothing outwardly to help me, nor could tell what to do, then, oh, then, I heard a voice which said, 'There is one, even Christ Jesus, that can speak to thy condition'; and when I heard it my heart did leap for joy."

Fox's public ministry began in 1648, and he was imprisoned in Derby just two years later, in 1650. A judge referred to Fox and his followers as "Quakers" because of their emphasis on trembling before God's Word. In 1653 Fox was arrested again, taken to London, and met with Oliver Cromwell. Cromwell was impressed by Fox's spirituality and met with him twice more. Fox was jailed at least six times between 1654 and 1674, usually for refusing to take oaths or for disturbing religious order. He married Margaret Fell in 1669 and traveled to America in 1671. Fox died in 1691.

Quakers prefer to call themselves "Friends." They number about 350,000, spread throughout seventy countries of the world. The three major Quaker groupings are the Friends General Conference (FGC), Friends United Meeting (FUM), and the Evangelical Friends International (EFI). The Friends World Committee for Consultation (FWCC) serves as a larger unifying body, based in London, England. The EFI, with strong influence from the Holiness movement, claims an explicit Christ-centered emphasis, based in affirmation of Scripture. The broader Quaker tradition is more liberal and sympathetic toward other religions. This perspective is defended in Chuck Fager's *Without Apology* (Kimo Press, 1996).

Quakers are famous for their silence in worship, though they also hold meetings where sermons are given. Friends put great emphasis on the equality of believers, a perspective that accounts for the absence of clergy in worship and also explains why anyone may speak a word based on the leading of the Spirit. Quakers stress the Inner Light and do not participate in the Lord's Supper or practice any form of baptism. Friends are famous for their social protest of war and were notably one of the first groups to speak out against the slave trade in America.

The most famous Quaker in American history is William Penn (1644–1718), the founder of the state of Pennsylvania. Susan B. Anthony (1820–1906), one of the pioneers of the women's suffrage movement, was a Quaker too. Contemporary author Richard J. Foster (*Celebration of Discipline*) is also a Quaker, though he writes mainly for broad evangelical Christian audiences.

QUAKERS

Typology	Christian Protestant
Websites	Friends General Conference: www.fgcquaker.org Friends United Meeting: www.fum.org Evangelical Friends International: www.evangelicalfriends.org/ Friends World Committee for Consultation: http://fwccworld.org General site: www.quaker.org
Recommended Reading	Hugh Barbour and J. William Frost, *The Quakers* (New York: Greenwood, 1988)

Seventh-day Adventism

Seventh-day Adventist identity lies in three key notions: (a) the view that 1844 is predicted in the Bible as the time when Jesus would begin an Investigative Judgment in the heavenly realm, (b) Christians should worship on the Sabbath, and (c) Ellen G. White (1827–1915) is a prophet for the end-time church. Adventists are also known for their emphasis on vegetarianism and obedience to relevant Old Testament laws.

Historically, considerable tension has existed between Seventh-day Adventism and the evangelical Christian community. Relations between evangelicals and Seventh-day Adventists improved considerably through the dialogue that took place between Adventists and Donald Barnhouse and Walter Martin in the 1950s. In the last twenty-five years, however, there has been an increase of suspicion about Seventh-day Adventism by evangelicals. This has come in part because of the handling of research from Desmond Ford and Walter Rea, two prominent scholars within the Adventist tradition.

All things being equal, Seventh-day Adventists should be regarded as a community of faith in essential agreement with evangelical Christianity. Adventists should be admired for their emphasis on healthy living. In fact, Adventists have made major advancements in medicine. The movement also fosters obedience to the ethical principles of Scripture. Further, for the most part, the Adventist statement of Fundamental Beliefs is orthodox.

Evangelical Christians, however, should also note the following concerns about key issues in Adventist doctrine and ethos:

1. The continued emphasis on 1844 as a significant date in biblical prophecy marks the weakest component in Adventist doctrine. William Miller, a Baptist, predicted that the end of the world would occur in 1844 and was wise enough to admit his enormous error. Unfortunately, Seventh-day Adventists tried to rescue the prophecy by saying that it was really about the beginning of an Investigative Judgment in heaven by Jesus. This is the biggest biblical and intellectual blunder in Seventh-day Adventism.

   Scriptural evidence against the Investigative Judgment theory has been provided by various Adventist scholars themselves, including Desmond Ford and Raymond Cottrell. Cottrell, a distinguished leader, wrote against the Investigative Judgment in late 2001, shortly before his death.

2. The Adventist emphasis on Ellen G. White as a prophet is not warranted, given her false teaching on various doctrinal issues (like the "shut door"), certain medical views, and her mistaken prophecies. Further, there are troubling issues related to alleged plagiarism in her writings, raised most significantly by Walter Rea in his work *The White Lie*. While copyright issues were somewhat different in Mrs. White's day, her borrowing from others seems extreme, especially when she claimed divine inspiration for sections of her books that were copied without credit.

3. Adventist focus on the law often leads to works-righteousness in the movement, a fact readily evident in the testimonies of ex-members. Obedience to the commands of God is a necessary part of Christian life, but the Adventist emphasis on Sabbath-keeping and Old Testament food laws can easily overshadow the doctrine of salvation by grace alone.

4. The Seventh-day Adventist love for the second coming of Jesus is to be admired. However, this great reality is marred by an unhealthy focus on eschatology, particularly given the ways in which Adventists write themselves into the center of God's end-time work. Various Christian groups argue that Scripture foretells the rise of their particular movement; this has been a regular theme in the polemic of both Jehovah's Witnesses and the Seventh-day Adventists.

5. The leadership of the Seventh-day Adventist Church has failed at crucial times to address the core weaknesses in their ideology. Ellen G. White is defended at all costs. There are few if any Protestant groups that honor their founder in the way that Adventists heap praise on Mrs. White. This leads to a fortress mentality in the movement. Sadly, Adventist scholars who dare to question key items are far too often dismissed, ignored, or sidelined. This was particularly true in the church's dealings with Desmond Ford and his case against the theory of Investigative Judgment. Church leaders broke their promises about granting Ford a safe and fair hearing in 1980 when they processed his research.

SEVENTH-DAY ADVENTISM

Typology	Christian Protestant
Key Leader	Ellen G. White
Scripture	Bible
Homepages	www.adventist.org www.whiteestate.org
Critic Websites	Dale Ratzlaf: http://www.ratzlaf.com Gary Gent site: www.ex-sda.com Seventh-day Adventist Outreach (Mark Martin): www.exadventist.com Truth or Fables (Robert Sanders): www.truthorfables.com John Cusaac site: www.xsda.net
Recommend Reading	*Questions on Doctrine* (Original edition, 1957; Berrien Springs: Andrews University Press, 2003, annotated edition) Desmond Ford, *Daniel 8:14, The Day of Atonement and the Investigative Judgment* (Casselberry, Florida: Euangelion Press, 1980) Jerry Gladson, *A Theologian's Journey* (Glendale: Life Assurance Ministries, 2000) Gary Land (ed.), *Adventism in America* (Grand Rapids: Eerdmans, 1986) Ronald Numbers, *Prophetess of Health* (Knoxville: University of Tennessee, 1992) Ronald Numbers and Jonathan Butler, eds., *The Disappointed* (Knoxville: University of Tennessee, 1993) Geoffrey Paxton, *The Shaking of Adventism* (Grand Rapids: Baker, 1977) Walter Rea, *The White Lie* (Turlock: M&R Publications, 1982)

■ Toronto Blessing

The Toronto Blessing refers to the famous charismatic renewal that began at the former Toronto Airport Vineyard Church on January 20, 1994. In late 1995 and early 1996 the church left the larger Association of Vineyard Churches and became known as the Toronto Airport Christian Fellowship (hereafter TACF). Pastors John and Carol Arnott, a husband-wife team, are founders of the congregation.

Anointed Pentecostal minister Joshua Mills, New Wine International, at Toronto Airport Christian Fellowship

Photo: Jim Beverley

The Blessing renewal began under the ministry of Randy Clark, a Vineyard pastor from St. Louis, who was holding a revival campaign in early 1994. Clark outlined his own experience of spiritual awakening through the work of Rodney Howard-Browne, a Pentecostal evangelist from South Africa, who now heads Revival Ministries International in Tampa, Florida. Howard-Browne gained fame through manifestations of "holy laughter" that characterized his revival meetings.

The initial campaign in Toronto continued after Clark returned to St. Louis. The Blessing gained international attention as news spread throughout the charismatic Christian world about a supernatural "Holy Ghost" revival in Toronto. By the summer and fall of 1994 thousands were flocking to Toronto for the meetings held six nights every week. *Toronto Life* magazine billed the "Blessing" the top tourist attraction of

1994. Visitors continued to come to Toronto by the thousands from every part of the globe throughout 1995 and early 1996. Since then TACF has given more focus to special conferences and to travel to various countries to export the renewal around the world.

From the outset of the renewal, critics like Hank Hanegraaff, author of *Counterfeit Revival*, accused TACF leaders of using hypnotism and psychological control to manipulate the crowds into frenzied bouts of laughter, shaking, rolling on the floor, moaning, groaning, crying, and falling down (known as being "slain in the Spirit"). What drew particular concern from Vineyard leader John Wimber were episodes of people acting or sounding like animals during the worship services.

In early 1996 TACF formed Partners in Harvest, a non-denominational organization that seeks to unite charismatic groupings of ministries and churches. There are now about one hundred participating member organizations from the United States, Canada, and more than a dozen other countries in Europe, the United Kingdom, Africa, and South America.

TACF became the target of fresh criticism in 1999 following reports from the church leaders that God was filling people's cavities with real gold. TACF released a video about the alleged miracles called "Go for the Gold," and their website featured pictures from people who claimed that God had performed dental work on them. Attendance increased as reports circulated about the supernatural claims. The focus on dental miracles subsided when further research on the claims undermined their veracity.

Though local membership involves about one thousand people, TACF has enormous worldwide outreach through its weekly television program, resource materials, and International Leaders School of Ministry. As well, the church has been visited by several million people since 1994 and maintains links with the most prominent leaders in the charismatic and Pentecostal world, including Benny Hinn.

Toronto Blessing leaders are sincere Christians, not deserving of the wild polemics against their character and motives. The Blessing has led to many conversions to Christ and to authentic spiritual renewal, gains that cannot be denied. However, the movement has also hurt charismatic Christian life through its wild excesses and through overemphasis on the strange manifestations connected to the Blessing.

TORONTO BLESSING	
Typology	Christian Protestant Charismatic
Websites	Toronto Airport Christian Fellowship: www.tacf.org
Recommended Reading	John Arnott, *The Father's Blessing* (Lake Mary, FL.: Creation House, 1995) James A. Beverley, *Holy Laughter & The Toronto Blessing* (Grand Rapids: Zondervan, 1995) Guy Chevreau, *Catch the Fire* (London: Marshall Pickering, 1994) Margaret Poloma, *Main Street Mystics* (Alta Mira Press, 2003)

■ The Vineyard

The Association of Vineyard Churches is most commonly associated with John Wimber, one of the leading charismatic Christians of the twentieth century. Wimber was born in 1934 in the American Midwest. His alcoholic father left the family when John, an only child, was very young. He had no introduction to Christian faith in his youth. In 1955 Wimber married his wife, Carol, a nominal Roman Catholic. Gifted in music, he began his career as a writer for The Righteous Brothers. John and Carol separated in 1962, but their marriage was saved when John turned to God for help.

In the early 1970s Wimber served as co-pastor of an evangelical Quaker church in Southern California. From 1974 to 1978 he worked with the Fuller Institute of Evangelism and Church Growth. In 1977 Wimber became identified with Chuck Smith and the Calvary Chapel movement. On Mother's Day in 1980, Wimber's Calvary church in Yorba Linda experienced a major revival, one that included radical charismatic behavior. In 1982 Wimber left Calvary Chapel and became leader of a small group of churches known as the Vineyard, founded in 1974 by Kenn Gulliksen.

Wimber started teaching course MC 510 on "Signs, Wonders and Church Growth" at Fuller Seminary in Pasadena in 1982. This class, co-taught with Peter Wagner, acquired worldwide interest after *Christian Life* published a special report on the course. In 1985 Fuller Seminary put Wimber's popular and controversial course on hold. It was later brought back into the curriculum, and Wimber remained an adjunct faculty member until 1992.

The Vineyard movement experienced an internal reorientation in 1988 when Wimber embraced the prophetic movement connected with

Mike Bickle's Kansas City Fellowship (KCF). For the next three years Wimber traveled internationally with Bickle and with Paul Cain, Bob Jones, and John Paul Jackson, the three leading prophets connected with the Kansas City movement. Wimber distanced himself from the prophetic focus in 1991.

In 1994 and 1995 Wimber and other Vineyard leaders were drawn into the controversy surrounding "the Toronto Blessing," the renewal movement that originated at the Toronto Airport Vineyard. Wimber had grown increasingly concerned about some of the religious ecstasy involved, particularly related to duplication of animal behavior. In December 1995 Wimber pressured the Toronto congregation, led by John Arnott, to leave the Association of Vineyard Churches.

The Vineyard has often been targeted as heretical and occultist by right-wing Christians. These charges are far too extreme. Vineyard leaders follow standard evangelical doctrine and have no demonstrated interest in the darker side of religion. However, the Vineyard movement has been prone to subjectivity and excessive focus on sensationalist elements in charismatic Christian life. These weaknesses were corrected by Wimber in his reaction to the Kansas City Prophets and the Toronto Blessing.

Wimber died in 1997. Today The Vineyard has about six hundred churches in the United States, led by Bert Waggoner.

VINEYARD	
Typology	Christian Protestant
Websites	Association of Vineyard Churches, USA: www.vineyardusa. org Vineyard International Consortium: www.vineyard.org
Recommended Reading	James Beverley, *Holy Laughter & The Toronto Blessing* (Grand Rapids: Zondervan, 1995) Carol Wimber, *John Wimber: The Way It Was* (London: Hodder & Stoughton, 1999)

Worldwide Church of God

The Worldwide Church of God (WCG) was started as the Radio Church of God in 1933 by Herbert W. Armstrong. Armstrong was born in 1892 and joined the General Conference of the Church of God, part of the Adventist tradition, in 1927. He was ordained in 1931. In 1933 Armstrong linked with the newly formed Church of God, Seventh Day, led by Andrew N. Dugger. Armstrong lost his credentials with that group in 1937 but continued an independent ministry. He moved his base of operations to Pasadena, California, in 1947 and ordained his son Garner Ted (1930–2003) in 1955. The Radio Church of God was renamed the Worldwide Church of God in 1968.

The WCG became well known in the late '60s and early '70s through its television program, *The World Tomorrow,* and its free magazine *The Plain Truth.* In his teaching Herbert W. Armstrong focused on themes common to Adventists: eschatology, emphasis on Old Testament law, and keeping of the Sabbath. However, he also taught that the WCG was "the" church of Christ and that he was the only "Apostle" of God's end-time work. Armstrong and his son advocated a form of British-Israelism as well, arguing that the Jews of the Old Testament became the people of the British Empire and the United States.

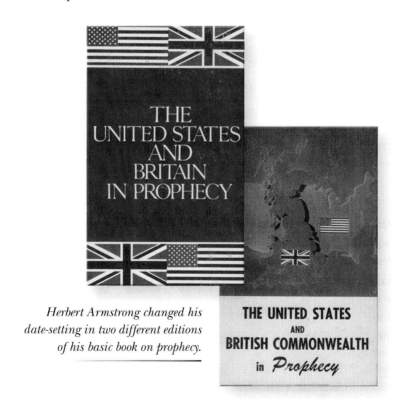

Herbert Armstrong changed his date-setting in two different editions of his basic book on prophecy.

WORLDWIDE CHURCH OF GOD TIMELINE

1831—William Miller begins preaching Adventist message

1842—Gilbert Cranmer adopts Adventist outlook

1843—October date for Advent changed to 1844

1844—Failure of October 22 prophecy

1845—Cranmer observes Saturday as Sabbath

1846—Ellen G. Harmon and James White wed

1849—William Miller dies

1858—Cranmer organizes several congregations in Michigan

1863—First issue of *The Hope of Israel* published by Cranmer

1863—Seventh-day Adventist Church organized

1881—Death of James White

1884—The General Conference of the Church of God organized

1892—Birth of Herbert W. Armstrong (HWA)

1903—Death of Gilbert Cranmer

1914—Andrew N. Dugger edits *The Bible Advocate*

1915—Death of Ellen G. White

1927—Baptism of HWA

1930—Birth of Garner Ted Armstrong

1931—HWA ordained by The Church of God

1933—Dugger starts Church of God, Seventh Day (Salem, West Virginia)

1933—HWA starts preaching on KORE radio and joins Dugger's church

1937—HWA removed as minister from Dugger's church

1947—HWA moves Radio Church of God to Pasadena

1955—Garner Ted Armstrong ordained

1958—Herbert's oldest son, Richard David, dies from injuries from car accident

1967—Death of Herbert's wife, Loma

1968—Radio Church of God renamed to Worldwide Church of God (WCG)

1974—East Coast Rebellion against WCG

1975—Raymond C. Cole forms Church of God, The Eternal

1975—Death of Dugger

1976—Start of *Ambassador Report* (John Trechak)

1977—HWA marries Ramona Martin

1978—Garner Ted kicked out of WCG and forms Church of God, International

1979—State of California launches then drops suit against WCG

1986—HWA dies and Jospeh Tkach, Sr. becomes Pastor General

1989—Philadelphia Church of God formed (Gerald Flurry)

1992—Global Church of God founded by Roderick Meredith

1994—Tkach announces WCG membership not under Sabbath and food laws

1995—United Church of God founded by David Hulme

1995—Garner Ted Armstrong resigns from CGI

1995—Joseph Tkach, Jr. becomes head of WCG after death of father

1997—*Transformed by Truth* released by Joseph Tkach, Jr.

1998—Garner Ted starts Intercontinental Church of God

1998—David Hulme leaves UCG and starts Church of God, an International Community

1998—Roderick Meredith starts Living Church of God

2003—Death of Garner Ted; son Mark becomes president of ICG

2004—WCG sells significant parts of its Pasadena property

Prior to Armstrong's death in 1986, the Worldwide Church of God became embroiled in controversy. Several ex-members wrote critically about Armstrong's wealth and dictatorial style. The most prominent critic was John Trechak, who began publishing *The Ambassador Report* in 1976. In 1978 Herbert excommunicated his son Garner Ted, who then started the Church of God, International, based in Tyler, Texas. In 1979 the State of California initiated legal action against the Worldwide Church of God in relation to alleged financial improprieties, but the suit was quickly dropped.

After Herbert's death the WCG went through major doctrinal changes under Joseph Tkach, Sr., its new Pastor General. In his boldest move, Tkach preached a sermon on Christmas Eve 1994 that clearly spelled out that church members were not obligated to obey Old Testament law related to diet and Sabbath. Tkach was succeeded in 1995 by his son Joseph Tkach, Jr. The WCG continued to become more evangelical in its ideology, adopting a Trinitarian understanding of God and a grace-based understanding of salvation. The church became part of the National Association of Evangelicals in 1997.

WORLDWIDE CHURCH OF GOD

Typology	Christian Protestant Adventist
Founder	Herbert W. Armstrong (1892–1986)
Current Leader	Joseph Tkach, Jr
Website	www.wcg.org
Major WCG Splits	Church of God, International (1978–) Founder: Garner Ted Armstrong: www.cgi.org Philadelphia Church of God (1989–) Founder: Gerald Flurry www.pcog.org Global Church of God (1992–99) Founder: Roderick Meredith Christian Educational Ministries (1995–) Founder: Ron Dart www.borntowin.net/newsite/ United Church of God (1995–) Founder: David Hulme www.ucg.org Church of God, an International Community (1998–) Founder: David Hulme www.church-of-god.org Intercontinental Church of God (1998–) Founder: Garner Ted Armstrong www.intercontinentalcog.org Living Church of God (1998–) Founder: Roderick Meredith www.livingcog.org
Websites About the WCG and Other Church of God Groups	Servant News: www.servantsnews.com The Journal: News of the Churches of God: www. thejournal.org The Painful Truth: www.herbertwarmstrong.com
Recommended Reading	Joseph Tkach, Jr. *Transformed By Truth* (Multnomah, 1997) J. Michael Feazell, *The Liberation of the Worldwide Church of God* (Zondervan, 2001)

The departure of the WCG from many of Armstrong's views created an enormous crisis among its membership. Many WCG pastors broke away and started their own groups. The most well-known new groups that follow the teachings of Herbert Armstrong are the Philadelphia Church of God; the United Church of God; Church of God, an International Community; and the Living Church of God. After six years of litigation the Philadelphia Church of God, founded by Gerald Flurry, reached an agreement with the WCG to hold copyright on the writings of Herbert W. Armstrong.

In 1998 Garner Ted Armstrong was ousted from the Church of God International and formed the Intercontinental Church of God. He died in 2003 and leadership passed to his son Mark. Joseph Tkach, Jr. believes that he and his father helped move the WCG toward biblical orthodoxy. He wrote about this in his 1997 work *Transformed by Truth*. "We searched the Scriptures diligently to discover the right twist to this doctrine or the correct slant to that one. We got lost in minutiae and largely missed the real treasure, Jesus Christ Himself."

ROMAN CATHOLICISM

The Vatican, Vatican City

Every attempt to understand the story of Jesus Christ and his impact on world history must engage the Roman Catholic Church. This is true for three reasons. First, the claims of the Roman tradition that the pope is the Vicar of Jesus and that the Roman Church is the church of Jesus demands careful analysis. Second, the size and antiquity of Catholicism commands the need for attention, even if one does not accept it as identical with the earliest Christian community. Third, every other form or paradigm of Christianity has been influenced by the Catholic story, even those groups that are virulent in their opposition to Roman doctrines. It is simply a fact that Catholic leaders, saints, and institutions have shaped the way that Orthodox, Protestant and other Christian movements form their own identity.

Pope Benedict XVI

Photo: Mike Fairbanks

According to the World Christian Database, Catholics are found in 239 countries of the world. As of 2005 there were more than one billion Catholics on Earth, making it by far the largest body of Christians. There are more than one million Catholics in seventy-eight separate countries of the world. Further, twenty-two of these countries have more than ten million Catholics each. And of these twenty-two, five countries (Brazil, Mexico, USA, Philippines, and Italy) have more than 50 million Catholics, while eight other countries, including France, Columbia, Spain, Poland, and Argentina, have more than 25 million Catholics.

It is ironic that Christian groups that view Roman Catholicism as heretical derive much of their basic theological identity from Catholic history. Therefore, the Protestant urge to ignore history from postbiblical times to Martin Luther is clearly wrongheaded, even if one retains many Protestant objections to Catholic doctrine and practice. Protestant critique of Rome must go hand-in-hand with appreciation for Augustine, Saint Francis, Aquinas, and other luminaries of the Catholic story.

■ The Role of the Pope

Roman Catholicism cannot be understood without knowledge of the position and role of the pope in Catholic history and thought. What Catholics believe about the papal office is the subject of much confusion and enormous debate, now and through the centuries.

What is the official Catholic teaching about the pope? In brief, Catholic orthodoxy teaches that (a) the pope is the head of the church of Jesus Christ, (b) that he is infallible when he teaches on matters of faith and morals, (c) that Saint Peter was the first pope, (d) that the Holy Spirit has provided and will continue providing the church with a succession of popes from Saint Peter to the end of time, and (e) that popes, like all humans, are sinful and in need of the mercy of Jesus.

ROMAN CATHOLICISM 101

- There is one God in the Trinity of Father, Son, and Spirit.

- The Bible is the infallible Word of God.

- Laity is to read and obey the Bible.

- Jesus Christ is the only Savior and one mediator.

- Sacred tradition and Scripture should receive equal reverence.

- Sacred Scripture contains the Deuterocanon.

- Catholic doctrine is supported by Scripture and/or Sacred Tradition.

- The church of Jesus Christ "subsists in the Catholic Church."

- The pope is infallible when he teaches on faith and morals.

- The pope has "full, supreme and universal power over the whole Church."

- The pope teaches in unity with church councils.

- The church includes the "separated brethren" who should return to the Mother Church.

- Salvation is not by works.

- Baptism (in fact or intent) is necessary for salvation.

- Infant baptism brings one into the body of Christ.

- Transubstantiation is the true view of the Eucharist.

- Penance (confession/conversion from sin) is necessary for salvation.

- The priesthood is for males only.

- Celibacy is the normal requirement for priests.

- It is right to pray for the dead.

- It is right to pray to the saints, especially Mary.

- Mary is subordinate to Jesus Christ.

- Mary is the "Mother of God."

- Mary can be called mediatrix.

- The Immaculate Conception of Mary is truth.

- Mary was a perpetual virgin.

- Mary was assumed into heaven.

- Mary is "pre-eminent, wholly unique" among Christians.

- Catholic orthodoxy is biblical Christianity.

- The whole body of Christ "cannot err in belief."

- Penance is to be offered in the Confessional at least once a year.

- It is the sacred duty of Christians to evangelize the world.

- The devil is real.

- Purgatory is a true doctrine.

- Heaven and hell are eternal.

Swiss Guard at the Vatican, Vatican City

Photo: Jim Beverley

This last point needs special focus because many Protestants believe that Catholic affirmation of papal infallibility means that the pope is sinless. The doctrine has never been understood this way in Catholic thought. The Catholic Church has always taught that popes can and do sin, that they must confess their sins like all humans, and that infallibility is restricted to their role as teacher and defender of the faith. Pope Benedict XVI, like other popes, has a confessor.

The actual wording of Catholic documents about infallibility deserves notice. In *The Dogmatic Constitution on the Church*, from Vatican II, the bishops of Rome affirmed the primacy of the pope in relation to Christ's establishment of the church. Section 18 of the document, known in Latin as *Lumen Gentium*, states that Jesus "placed Blessed Peter over the other apostles, and instituted in him a permanent and visible source and foundation of unity of faith and communion."

ELECTING A NEW POPE

The College of Cardinals, the highest ranking clergy in the Roman Catholic Church, chooses a new pope. According to rules John Paul II established, the cardinals are to meet no sooner than fifteen days and no later than twenty days following a pope's death in order to elect a new pontiff.

Only cardinals who are under eighty are eligible to vote, and they do so by secret written ballot. They take an oath to maintain rigorous secrecy about the election of a new pope. The voting takes place in the Sistine Chapel, which must be "swept" electronically to prevent spying. During the election, the cardinals are to have no contact with the outside world.

Cardinals receive ballots on which is written the Latin words for "I elect as Supreme Pontiff." The cardinals are to write a name on the ballot and file to the altar, one by one, where the Cardinal Chamberlain who supervises the election announces the votes. A two-thirds majority is necessary, up until a possible thirty rounds of voting.

After that, the cardinals can choose a simple majority to elect the head of the Catholic Church.

The person the cardinals choose is asked if he accepts the election and, if so, what name he chooses as pope. Tradition suggests that the first evidence of a new pope is when white smoke rises from the chapel. A Vatican official announces, *"Habemus Papam!"* (We have a Pope!), and the new pontiff delivers a blessing from the main balcony of the Vatican.

Section 22 defends the authority of all Catholic bishops but immediately notes that "the college or body of bishops has no authority unless it is understood together with the Roman Pontiff, the successor of Peter as its head. The pope's power of primacy over all, both pastors and faithful, remains whole and intact. In virtue of his office, that is, as Vicar of Christ and pastor of the whole Church, the Roman Pontiff has full, supreme, and universal power over the Church."

Lumen Gentium states that the infallibility of the pope is set in the broader context of the infallibility that is granted to the Catholic Church as a whole and to the bishops when they act in unity with the Supreme

Pontiff. However, it also notes the supremacy of the pope on infallibility. Section 25 states that the pope is granted infallibility "when, as the supreme shepherd and teacher of all the faithful, who confirms his brethren in their faith, by a definitive act he proclaims a doctrine of faith or morals."

*Saint Charbel Maklouf (1828–98)
of Lebanese Maronite community*

Photo: Massimo Introvigne

CARDINAL RATZINGER (NOW BENEDICT XVI) ON CATHOLIC ORTHODOXY

In 1984 Joseph Ratzinger, then Head of the Sacred Congregation for the Doctrine of the Faith (formerly called the Holy Office), granted journalist Vittoria Messori an extensive interview. The English version of the interview was published the next year under the title *The Ratzinger Report*. The following summary expresses the major points of Cardinal Ratzinger on a range of very important matters:

- The Office of the Sacred Congregation is a legitimate and caring institution.

- Heresy still exists and Catholic orthodoxy must be defended.

- The teachings of Vatican II agree with both Vatican I and the Council of Trent.

- An understanding of the church is central in theology.

- In both the church and the world the priesthood has become undervalued.

- The individualism of the modern era radically harms theology and the church.

- There is a loss of belief and attention to the role of the Catechism in church life.

- It is wrong that the church and the Bible have been divorced in liberal Catholic thought.

- It is tragic that the Son of God has been reduced in modern theology.

- It is also tragic that God the Father has been forgotten in modern theology.

- Original Sin has been neglected.

- Permissive morality has harmed society.

- Women must not be ordained.

- Feminism is a very dangerous ideology.

- Distinction between genders is very important.

- Mary is the key for a proper understanding of womanhood.

- Fatima is a precious part of Catholic faith.

- Pluralism in Catholic liturgy is a fine reality.

- The traditional view of the Eucharist is an absolute.

- The devil is real.

- Purgatory is a true doctrine.

- The angelic world is a reality.

- The charismatic movement has been helpful in the church.

- The Bible is a Catholic Book.

- Liberation theology is dangerous.

- Missionary work is necessary.

- Jesus is the only Savior.

- The infallibility of the pope is a crucial doctrine.

Catholic church, Beijing, China

Photo: Gordon Melton

Notre Dame cathedral, Paris, France

The text then makes this important point. "And therefore his definitions, of themselves, and not from the consent of the Church, are justly styled irreformable, since they are pronounced with the assistance of the Holy Spirit, promised to him in blessed Peter, and therefore they need no approval of others, nor do they allow an appeal to any other judgment."

Lumen Gentium also teaches that the faithful are to accept the decisions of bishops when they speak together on core issues. It then expands this in relation to the pope: "This religious submission of mind and will must be shown in a special way to the authentic magisterium of the Roman Pontiff, even when he is not speaking ex cathedra; that is, it must be shown in such a way that his supreme magisterium is acknowledged with reverence."

The teaching of Vatican II reflects, of course, the declaration of papal infallibility that was made most famously at Vatican I in 1870. There has been enormous intellectual debate over the internal politics of Vatican I. Likewise, the announcement of infallibility led to internal dissent within the church, protest from outside the church, and academic debate over the origins of papal infallibility in Catholic history.

FROM THE PARISH TO THE VATICAN

It can seem a long way to the Vatican from the local Catholic parish. To illustrate how a Catholic might envision that mental and spiritual journey, think of a Catholic who attends the Star of the Sea parish, south of Boston, Massachusetts. The parish is composed of about four hundred Catholic families. There are almost 3,000 priests in the 292 parishes that make up the Archdiocese of Boston.

The archdiocese is led by Sean Cardinal O'Malley, who is the spiritual head of the fourth largest diocese in the United States, with just over two million members. Cardinal O'Malley reports directly to the Vatican, but he also relates to over four hundred other bishops who work through the National Conference of Catholic Bishops, located in Washington, D.C.

The Boston archdiocese is one of 195 dioceses in the United States, which together serve the 62 million Catholics who comprise about 23 percent of the country's entire population. Only three other countries of the world have a larger Catholic population—that of the Philippines (67 million), Mexico (124 million), and Brazil (180 million).

Cardinal O'Malley has regular contact with the Vatican because of his membership in the College of Cardinals. All bishops in the diocese are also bound by Canon Law to visit Rome regularly to report on their local work. The bishops of the Archdiocese of Boston are confirmed in their office by the pope and are subject to the Code of Canon Law, which binds all priests and bishops.

Members of the Star of the Sea parish relate to the wider Catholic world through the educational services provided by the archdiocese and by the various orders of the Catholic Church. In the Boston archdiocese alone there are 176 schools. More than 5,500 Catholic sisters serve the Catholic faithful. The four hundred Catholic families of the Star of the Sea parish are also united with Catholics all over the world through the common liturgy of the church, including Mass, celebration of Feast Days, and the use of the rosary.

Church of Nuestra Senora de Los
Dolores in Valparaiso, Chile

Photo: Hans Raabe

The declaration itself, however, is quite clear. On July 18, 1870, the bishops in Rome stated: "We teach and define as a divinely revealed dogma that when the Roman Pontiff speaks *ex cathedra*, that is, when, in the exercise of his office as shepherd and teacher of all Christians, in virtue of his supreme apostolic authority, he defines a doctrine concerning faith or morals to be held by the whole Church, he possesses, by the divine assistance promised to him in blessed Peter, that infallibility which the divine Redeemer willed his Church to enjoy in defining doctrine concerning faith or morals."

The bishops then concluded: "Therefore, such definitions of the Roman Pontiff are of themselves, and not by the consent of the Church, irreformable." The parallels between this statement and those at Vatican II are obvious. In 1870 the bishops added a warning about dissent: "So then, should anyone, which God forbid, have the temerity to reject this definition of ours: let him be anathema."

TIMELINE OF JOHN PAUL II—
KAROL JOSEF WOJTYLA

1920— Born on May 18 in Wadowice, Poland

1929— Death of his mother Emilia, who was born in 1884

1932— Death of his brother Edmund

1938— Receives confirmation as a Roman Catholic

1941— Death of father

1942— Begins study for priesthood

1946— Ordained as priest; moves to Rome for further study

1948— Earns doctorate in philosophy; returns to Poland for priesthood duties

1954— Begins teaching at Catholic University of Lublin

1958— Ordained bishop

1962— Participates in Second Vatican Council

1964— Becomes archbishop of Krakow

1967— Appointed cardinal by Pope Paul VI

1974— Attends celebrations in Rome for Paul VI

1978— Elected pope after death of John Paul I

1979— First papal visit to Poland

1979— Küng removed as Catholic theologian in Germany

1980— Addresses UNESCO in Paris

1981— Assassination attempt on May 13 by Mehmet Ali Agca, a Turk

1982— Joint statement with Robert Runcie, archbishop of Canterbury

1983— Writes letter for the 500th anniversary of Martin Luther's birth

1984— Releases document on Liberation theology

1985— Message to Ronald Reagan and Mikhail Gorbachev (November 17)

1986— Visit to Rome's main synagogue (April 13)

1987— Visit by His Holiness Dimitrios, the Ecumenical Patriarch of Constantinople

1988— Apostolic Letter on the Dignity and Vocation of Women

1989— Gorbachev visits Vatican in December

1990— Diplomatic relations with Soviet government

1991— Letters to President Bush and Saddam Hussein to try to avert war

1992— Approval of new *Catechism of the Catholic Church*

1993— Agreement reached on relations between Rome and the State of Israel

1994— Release of *Crossing the Threshold of Hope*

1995— Addresses UN General Assembly on October 5

1996— Yasser Arafat has audience with Pope in Vatican

1997— Pastoral visits to Sarajevo and Lebanon

1998— Encyclical Letter *Fides et ratio* (on faith and reason)

1999— Joint Declaration on Justification with Lutheran World Federation

2000— Release of *Memory and Reconciliation* and *Dominus Iesus*

2001— Travel to Greece, Syria, and Malta

2002— Prayer for Peace at Assisi with world religion leaders

2005— Death on April 2

■ Scripture and Tradition

At Vatican II the bishops of Rome finalized a statement on Scripture and tradition. Dated November 18, 1965, it bears the Latin title *Dei Verbum*, and is known in English as *The Dogmatic Constitution on Divine Revelation*. As with all doctrinal matters, Vatican II documents claim to be consistent with the teachings of both the Council of Trent (1545–63) and Vatican I (1869–70). Likewise, Roman teachings on Scripture and tradition since Vatican II claim to be in continuity with preceding doctrinal views from the popes and bishops of the Catholic Church.

Like evangelicals, the Catholic Church affirms God's revelation in both deeds and words. God has given both a general revelation to all of humanity and a final revelation in Jesus Christ, such that "no new public revelation is to be expected." For Rome, as for Protestants, the gospel in Jesus is the ultimate and finished revelation, though, obviously, Catholics do not find this belief inconsistent with affirmation of Marian visions. Catholics would say that nothing in any authentic Marian statement could possibly contradict what God has fully given in her Son.

Statue of Mary, Palermo, Sicily

Photo: Gordon Melton

The Catholic Church affirms the clarity of God's gift in Scripture and tradition. According to *Dei Verbum*, his revelation can be known "with ease, with firm certainty, and without the contamination of error."

There was no postmodern angst at Vatican II. Similarly, there is a confidence of knowing God's truth in *The Code of Canon Law*, in the Catholic *Catechism*, and in the writings of John Paul II, both in his official publications and in his more private work.

John Paul's 1998 encyclical *Fides et Ratio* (Faith and Reason) laments the erosion of confidence in truth. He states that modern philosophy has "given rise to different forms of agnosticism and relativism which have led philosophical research to lose its way in the shifting sands of widespread skepticism. Recent times have seen the rise to prominence of various doctrines which tend to devalue even the truths which had been judged certain." He adds later: "To bear witness to the truth is therefore a task entrusted to us Bishops; we cannot renounce this task without failing in the ministry which we have received."

Catholic confidence in truth extends beyond philosophical knowledge to the revelation God has given in both Scripture and tradition. The apostolic authority of the church is preserved through a "continuous line of succession until the end of time" (*Dei Verbum*, 754), and, by God's providence, there will be a "growth in insight" about God's revelation, and the church will be "always advancing." This notion of development owes much to Cardinal John Henry Newman (1801–90), the famous Anglican leader who converted to Rome in 1845.

Catholics do not claim that tradition takes precedence over Scripture, or vice versa. Rather, sacred tradition and Scripture form a unified whole and there are to be "equal feelings of devotion and reverence" toward both. According to *Dei Verbum*, they make up "a single sacred deposit of the Word of God, which is entrusted to the Church." This deposit of revelation is "entrusted to the living teaching office of the Church alone" in its servant role to the Word of God. Scripture, tradition, and the church magisterium (the pope and his bishops) "are so connected and associated that one of them cannot stand without the others."

Catholic orthodoxy affirms the inspiration, inerrancy, and sufficiency of Scripture, though, of course, these claims extend beyond the Protestant canon to include the deuterocanonical books (several pre-New Testament-era books Protestants deem non-canonical, or apocryphal). Interpretation of Scripture demands discovering of its original meaning, though the church teaches that the student of the Bible needs tradition and the "analogy of faith" (central orthodox beliefs) in order to know the original intent of authors. The Old Testament has "imperfect" elements in it because it awaits the fuller truth of the new covenant in Jesus. The revelation about Jesus in the Gospels is historically true and the writers give "the honest truth about Jesus."

Dei Verbum asserts that the church has always had a high regard for Scripture. Christians are to be "nourished and ruled by Scripture." Access to Scripture is to be "wide open." The Catholic Church must provide contemporary translations of Scripture. Further, all Christians can read translations done in cooperation with "separated brethren." The study of the sacred page is "the very soul of sacred theology." *Dei Verbum* cites the famous words of Saint Jerome (c. 347–420?): "Ignorance of the Scriptures is ignorance of Christ" and then states: "May the Word of God speed on and the treasures of Revelation fill the hearts of men."

Catholic church, Malta

Photo: Eileen Barker

Doctrine of the Church

The Catholic understanding of the church can be derived from Vatican II's declaration on the church. The text, known in Latin as *Lumen Gentium*, runs to seventy-three pages in Austin Flannery's edition of *Documents of Vatican II*. Sixty-nine paragraphs under eight chapters deal with the Mystery of the church, the people of God, the hierarchy of the church, the laity, the call to holiness, the clergy and members of orders, the pilgrim church, and a section on Mary under the title "Our Lady."

Of most importance are the statements about the identity of the church. Paragraph 8 argues that the "holy Church" sustained by Christ is "an entity with visible delineation." This church is both hierarchical and mystical, both visible and spiritual, both earthly and heavenly. These facets of the church "form one complex reality" and are not to be viewed as separate realities. The document then states: "This Church constituted and organized in the world as a society, subsists in the Catholic Church, which is governed by the successor of Peter and by the Bishops in communion with him, although many elements of sanctification and of truth are found outside of its visible structure."

CATHOLICISM AND CHILD SEX ABUSE

The decade from 1992 to 2002 saw an explosion of allegations of sexual abuse of children by Roman Catholic priests. Father Andrew Greeley, the famous Catholic novelist and sociologist, calls the crisis "the greatest scandal in the history of religion in America." Every diocese in America has received at least one charge of pedophilia. In 1997 the church paid out $120 million to eleven victims of sexual abuse by Father Rudy Kos.

Abuse cases abound in other countries as well. One of the most notorious involved evidence of a culture of pedophilia in Mount Cashel, a Christian Brothers orphanage in Newfoundland, Canada. This involved complaints of abuse from the 1950s through the 1970s. Most of the priests charged were found guilty.

Victims of Clergy Abuse Linkup organized in 1992, the same year Barbara Blaine founded SNAP, the Survivors Network of those Abused by Priests (www.snapnetwork.org). Blaine has been critical of the American Catholic Bishops and the Vatican in relation to a new round of abuse cases that surfaced in 2002, particularly in the Archdiocese of Boston. *The Boston Globe* conducted a major investigation of the Boston scandals, and Cardinal Law was forced to resign as archbishop of Boston because of his inept handling of the crisis.

Many Catholic thinkers are enraged by what they perceive as the dishonesty of the Catholic hierarchy in its muddled response to the sexual abuse scandal. Garry Wills stated in *The New York Review of Books:* "The problem is not with the Church, with the people of God, but with those who claim to be the Church, in a structure honeycombed with pretense, hypocrisy, and evasion. The core of solid belief, the common sense of the faithful, the deep belief in the saving truths of the creed, will stand more solid after this clumsy scaffolding of lies thrown up around it has collapsed."

Of significance is both that the church of Christ is identified with the Roman Church and that the bishops at Vatican II also recognized that the church of Christ cannot be equated solely with Rome. This is expressed clearly in Paragraph 15: "The Church recognizes that in many ways she is linked with those who, being baptized, are honored with the name of

Christian, though they do not profess the faith in its entirety or do not preserve unity of communion with the successor of Peter."

Lumen Gentium makes it clear that modern Catholic orthodoxy does not teach that one must be a Roman Catholic to be saved. The document makes it plain, however, that the bishops of Rome believe that faithful Christians should return home: "In all of Christ's disciples the Spirit arouses the desire to be peacefully united, in the manner determined by Christ, as one flock under one shepherd, and He prompts them to pursue this end. Mother Church never ceases to pray, hope and work that this may come about."

Black Madonna, Barcelona, Spain

Photo: Kaarina Hsieh

The Vatican's openness to non-Catholic Christians also extends to members of other religions. In paragraph 16 of *Lumen Gentium,* the bishops declared: "Those also can attain to salvation who through no fault of their own do not know the Gospel of Christ or His Church, yet sincerely seek God and moved by grace strive by their deeds to do His will as it is known to them through the dictates of conscience." The document even demonstrates a positive attitude about atheists of good will, though it does not explicitly state if they will be saved apart from conversion to Christ.

Statue of John Paul II, Salt Mine Church, Wieliczka, Poland

Photo: Hans Raabe

The Doctrine of Salvation

An understanding of the Roman Catholic view of salvation involves a grasp of a range of issues, some of them representing very complicated issues in the history of Christian doctrine. This is demonstrated in Alister McGrath's *Iustitia Dei: A History of the Christian Doctrine of Justification* or Hans Küng's famous work *Justification.* In spite of technicalities, however, the basic Catholic understanding of salvation can be grasped by focusing on official Catholic documents and by examination of the extensive Roman Catholic-Lutheran dialogue on justification over the past forty years.

Contrary to popular Protestant opinion, Roman Catholic doctrine does *not* teach that works save a person. The Council of Trent, which was convened in response to the Protestant Reformation, states in Canon One: "If anyone says that man can be justified before God by his own works, whether done by his own natural powers or through the teaching of the law, without divine grace through Jesus Christ, let him be anathema."

The 1983 U.S. Catholic-Lutheran report on "Justification by Faith" states: "Our entire hope of justification and salvation rests on Christ Jesus and on the gospel whereby the good news of God's merciful action in Christ is made known; we do not place our ultimate trust in anything other than God's promise and saving work in Christ."

On October 31, 1999, the Catholic Church and the Lutheran World Federation signed a Common Statement in Augsburg, Germany, that gave consent to the following statement: "Justification takes place by grace alone, by faith alone, the person is justified apart from works." This astounding agreement was rooted in the 1997 "Declaration on the Doctrine of Justification" and from earlier theological reports, including a 24,000-word U.S. Lutheran-Catholic statement issued in 1983.

The 1999 Agreement also clarified the Catholic understanding of merit. If a believer has merit before God, it is only and always rooted in the grace of God that enables the justified sinner to obey God's will. Merit can never be understood in the sense that the Christian deserves reward for any work on his or her own. Likewise, the Christian's works are a response to the prior grace of God. According to Catholicism, the full biblical teaching on justification includes the reality that the justifying grace of God actually changes the sinner. The sinner is both *declared* righteous and *made* righteous.

In relation to a broader understanding of salvation, the Catholic Church also teaches that baptism is necessary for salvation, in fact or intent. Infants who are baptized are received into the body of Christ. Unbelievers who accept Christ are to be baptized. Those who truly accept Christ but are not baptized will only be saved because of the grace of God that forgives their ignorance, based on the recognition that it would be their intent to be baptized if they knew the true teaching of the gospel.

The Vatican continues to teach the following related to salvation: (a) A Christian can lose his or her salvation through denial of the faith; (b) a distinction is to be made between mortal and venial sins, the former referring to grave offenses and venial to lesser sins; (c) the Catholic priest can forgive sins in the sense of proclaiming to the repentant person that his or her sins are washed away because of their trust in the gospel; (d) the Christian can have assurance of salvation rooted in confidence of the grace of Christ; (e) the priest can suggest indulgences as a proper expression of true repentance; and (f) purgatory awaits Christians who upon death need further cleansing of their sin.

Shrine of the Immaculate Conception, Washington, D.C.

Photo: Gordon Melton

■ The Sacraments

The seven sacraments form an essential component in Catholicism and give us a picture of the Catholic understanding of salvation, church order, and some of the main elements of the Christian life. Official Catholic teaching on the sacraments is presented below from *The Code of Canon Law.* Pope John XXIII called for a new Code on January 25, 1959, and the church began the long process of revising the old Code of 1917. The new Code was promulgated on January 25, 1983.

The Code contains 1,752 Canons, dealing with everything from the office of the pope to procedures for discipline of priests to the arrangement of worship during the church year. Canons 840 through 1,165—a total of 326 codes—cover the material on the sacraments. Canon 841 states that the sacraments receive their validity by the authority of the Catholic Church in Rome. Canon 844 stipulates that the sacraments are generally for Catholics and are to be administered only by proper Catholic authorities.

CHRIST'S SACRIFICE DURING MASS

"[Christ], our Lord and God, was once and for all to offer himself to God the Father by his death on the altar of the cross, to accomplish there an everlasting redemption. But because his priesthood was not to end with his death, at the Last Supper 'on the night when he was betrayed,' [he wanted] to leave to his beloved spouse the Church a visible sacrifice (as the nature of man demands) by which the bloody sacrifice which he was to accomplish once for all on the cross would be represented, its memory perpetuated until the end of the world, and its salutary power be applied to the forgiveness of the sins we daily commit.

"The victim is one and the same: the same now offers through the ministry of priests, who then offered himself on the cross; only the manner of offering is different.

"In this divine sacrifice, which is celebrated in the Mass, the same Christ who offered himself once in a bloody manner on the altar of the cross is contained and is offered in an unbloody manner."

—The Council of Trent

The following summary presents some of the most important canons on each sacrament:

1. Baptism

- Baptism is necessary for the other sacraments to take place (C842).

- Baptism, Confirmation, and Orders cannot be repeated (C845).

- Baptism (in fact or intent) is necessary for salvation (C849).

- Infants are to be brought to baptism by their Catholic parents (C851).

- The water for baptism is to be blessed (C853).

- Adults are to be confirmed soon after baptism (C866).

- Infants in danger of death are to be baptized if possible, even if the parents are non-Catholic (C868).

- If possible, aborted fetuses are to be baptized (C871).

2. Confirmation

- Confirmation involves the decision of the individual to continue in the path of faith begun at baptism (C879).

- Confirmation involves anointing, laying on of hands, and the proper wording to invoke the reception of the Holy Spirit (C880).

- Confirmation is to take place at the age of discretion (C891).

3. The Eucharist

- The doctrine of transubstantiation is the true understanding of the Lord's Supper (C899).

- Mass can be offered for the living and the dead (C901).

- The Eucharist is to be celebrated only with churches in full communion with Rome (C913).

- Children must be aware of the meaning of Eucharist before participating (C913).

- Eucharist is to be observed by every Catholic at least once a year (C920).

- The bread is to be unleavened (C926).

- The bread is to be reserved in a special place for the faithful to observe (C934).

- There is to be a special lamp near the place where the host is placed for observation and safe-keeping (C940).

- The faithful can hold a procession to give honor to the host (C944).

- Offerings related to Mass are to be done in accordance with Canon Law (C945–948).

TRANSUBSTANTIATION

"Because Christ our Redeemer said that it was truly his body that he was offering under the species of bread, it has always been the conviction of the church of God, and this holy council now declares again, that by the concentration of the bread and wine there takes place a change of the whole substance of the bread into the substance of the body of Christ our Lord and of the whole substance of the wine into the substance of his blood. This change the holy Catholic Church has fittingly and properly called transubstantiation."

—The Council of Trent, 1551

4. Penance

- The sacrament of penance involves confession of sin, sorrow, reformation, absolution, and reconciliation (C959).

- Individual confession and absolution is the "only ordinary way" to be reconciled to God and the church (C960).

- Penance is to be expressed in the confessional (C964).

- Only the priest is to hear confession (C965).

- In extreme conditions the ordinary rules can be relaxed (C976–977).

- The priest is not to reveal what he hears in confession (C983).

- For penance to be valid there must be conversion from sin (C987).

- Catholics must offer penance at least once a year (C989).

- Indulgences can be suggested by the priest (C992–997).

5. Anointing the Sick

- This is the sacrament of healing, involving the use of blessed oil with appropriate spiritual counsel (C998).

- The priest can carry oil with him in order to administer the sacrament (C1003).

- This anointing is not for any who "obstinately persist in manifest serious sin" (C1007).

6. Orders

- Those to be ordained to the priesthood must take a vow of celibacy (C1037).

- Ordination is not for those who have committed homicide, nor for those who have helped procure abortions (C1084).

7. Marriage

- A valid marriage must be ratified by consummation (C1061).

- The marriage of a Catholic and non-Catholic must receive the permission of the Catholic authorities (C1141).

- The Catholic in a mixed marriage must agree to raise children in the Catholic faith, and the partner must be told of this agreement (C1125).

- Marriages are dissolved by death (C1141).

- Divorce can take place if an unbelieving partner separates from the marriage (C1143).

- Separation can take place in the case of adultery or in the case of serious danger to the spirit and body of a marriage partner (C1152–1153).

VATICAN STRUCTURE

I. Secretariat of State
   1. Section for General Affairs
   2. Section for Relations with States
II. Congregations
   1. Doctrine of the Faith
   2. Oriental Churches
   3. Divine Worship and the Discipline of the Sacraments
   4. Causes of Saints
   5. Evangelization of Peoples
   6. Clergy
   7. Institutes of Consecrated Life and Societies of Apostolic Life
   8. Catholic Education
   9. Bishops
III. Tribunals
   1. Apostolic Penitentiary
     Vatican body responsible for granting and use of indulgences
   2. Supreme Tribunal of the Apostolic Signature
     Top judicial body for Church and Vatican City State
   3. Tribunal of the Roman Rota
     Vatican judicial branch that handles appeals and nullification of marriages
IV. Pontifical Councils
   1. Laity
   2. Promoting Christian Unity
   3. Family
   4. Justice and Peace
   5. "Cor Unum" (Latin: "One Heart"—Council deals with Aid and Human Development Worldwide)
   6. Pastoral Care of Migrants and Itinerant People
   7. Health Pastoral Care
   8. Legislative Texts
   9. Inter-religious Dialogue
   10. Culture
   11. Social Communications

Catholic church, west shore of Nova Scotia, Canada

Photo: Jim Beverley

Mary and Roman Catholicism

The Roman Catholic understanding of Mary is pivotal in the long-standing tensions between orthodox Protestants and Catholics. Both traditions affirm the virgin birth of Jesus, the claim that Mary conceived by the supernatural operation of the Holy Spirit and that she had never had sexual relations with anyone before the birth of Jesus Christ. The Protestant-Catholic agreement on this point is rooted in the plain biblical teaching in Matthew and Luke about the birth of Jesus.

These are the additional teachings about Mary that form the basic fabric of Catholic teaching and practice:

1. *Catholics believe that Mary was a perpetual virgin, that she never had sexual relations with Joseph, her husband.* This teaching appears in the current *Catechism of the Catholic Church*: "The deepening of faith in the virginal motherhood led the Church to confess Mary's real and perpetual virginity even in the act of giving birth to the Son of God made man." In Catholic tradition, Mary is honored as Aeiparthenos, the "Ever-Virgin."

   In Catholic tradition, there has been some emphasis on the view that Mary's hymen was not broken during the birth of Jesus. As well, a popular tradition holds that she experienced no pain during the birth of Jesus. Both of these views remain in the realm of popular Catholic piety and have not been officially taught by the Magisterium of the church.

SELECTION FROM THE MARIAN PRAYER OF SAINT THOMAS AQUINAS

O most blessed and sweet Virgin Mary,
  Mother of God, filled with all tenderness,
  Daughter of the most high King,
  Lady of the Angels,
  Mother of all the faithful,
On this day and all the days of my life,
  I entrust to your merciful heart my body and my soul,
  all my acts, thoughts, choices,
  desires, words, deeds,
  my entire life and death,
So that, with your assistance,
  all may be ordered to the good
  according to the will of your beloved Son, our Lord Jesus
  Christ.

2. *Mary can also be called* Theotokos, *or Mother of God.* This was affirmed at the Council of Chalcedon in 451. The *Cathechism* proclaims the teaching in this manner: "Called in the Gospels 'the mother of Jesus,' Mary is acclaimed by Elizabeth, at the prompting of the Spirit and even before the birth of her Son, as 'the mother of my Lord.' In fact, the One whom she conceived as man by the Holy Spirit, who truly became her Son according to the flesh, was none other than the Father's eternal Son, the second person of the Holy Trinity. Hence the Church confesses that Mary is truly 'Mother of God' (*Theotokos*)."

3. *Catholics also believe that prayers are to be offered to the Virgin Mary.* Out of this Catholic tradition comes the most famous of prayers: the *Ave Maria,* which is Latin for "Hail Mary." In English, the prayer reads: "Hail Mary, full of grace, the Lord is with thee. Blessed art thou amongst women and blessed is the fruit of thy womb Jesus. Holy Mary, Mother of God, pray for us sinners, now and at the hour of our death. Amen." Prayers to Mary are a central element in the rosary, and prayers to her form a key part in Mass and in Feast Days in her honor.

4. *Roman Catholic tradition also affirms the Immaculate Conception of Mary, the view that Mary was born without original sin.* Pope Pius IX proclaimed this on December 8, 1854. The declaration is contained in the text known as *Ineffabilis Deus.* Before the proclamation, Pius IX stated that his declaration is "by the inspiration of the Holy Spirit, for the honor of the Holy and undivided Trinity, for the glory and adornment of the Virgin Mother of God, for the exaltation of the Catholic Faith, and for the furtherance of the Catholic religion, by the authority of Jesus Christ our Lord, of the Blessed Apostles Peter and Paul, and by our own."

He then decreed: "We declare, pronounce, and define that the doctrine which holds that the most Blessed Virgin Mary, in the first instance of her conception, by a singular grace and privilege granted by Almighty God, in view of the merits of Jesus Christ, the Savior of the human race, was preserved free from all stain of original sin, is a doctrine revealed by God and therefore to be believed firmly and constantly by all the faithful."

5. *Catholic orthodoxy also teaches the Assumption of Mary, the idea that Mary was preserved from bodily death and received directly into heaven.* Pope Pius XII formalized this teaching on November 1, 1950, in the document known as *Munificentissimus Deus.* Pius XII invoked the name of Pius IX in the latter's declaration of Mary's Immaculate Conception and said that he also wrote a letter to all Catholic bishops asking them: "Do you, venerable brethren, in your outstanding wisdom and prudence, judge that the bodily Assumption of the Blessed Virgin can be proposed and defined as a dogma of faith? Do you, with your clergy and people, desire it?"

Based on papal tradition and the positive consensus of his colleagues, Pius XII proclaimed that "for the honor of her Son, the immortal King of the Ages and the Victor over sin and death, for the increase of the glory of that same august Mother, and for the joy and exultation of the entire Church; by the authority of our Lord Jesus Christ, of the Blessed Apostles Peter and Paul, and by our own authority, we pronounce, declare, and define it to be a divinely revealed dogma: that the Immaculate Mother of God, the ever Virgin Mary, having completed the course of her earthly life, was assumed body and soul into heavenly glory."

St. Charles Church, Vienna, Austria

Photo: Hans Raabe

6. *Catholicism also claims that Mary serves as a co-mediatrix in the work of salvation. The Catechism of the Catholic Church* states this idea in the context of a glowing description of Mary's role and status. It first states that "by her complete adherence to the Father's will, to his Son's redemptive work, and to every prompting of the Holy Spirit, the Virgin Mary is the Church's model of faith and charity. In a wholly singular way she cooperated by her obedience, faith, hope, and burning charity in the Savior's work of restoring supernatural life to souls. For this reason she is a mother to us in the order of grace."

The section concludes: "Taken up to heaven she did not lay aside this saving office but by her manifold intercession continues to bring us the gifts of eternal salvation. Therefore the Blessed Virgin is invoked in the Church under the titles of Advocate, Helper, Benefactress, and Mediatrix."

Given this view, it is no wonder that *Lumen Gentium,* a document from Vatican II, says that Mary is a "preeminent and wholly unique member of the Church."

Main altar, St. Michael's Cathedral, Toronto, Canada

Photo: Derek Beverley

7. *The Catholic Church affirms various visions and apparitions of Mary.* The most celebrated cases involve claims of Marian visions at Guadalupe, Mexico (1531); La Salette, France (1846); Lourdes, France (1858); and Fatima, Portugal (1917). In recent years Catholics have been drawn to alleged Marian apparitions at Bayside, New York (1970); Medjugorje, Bosnia-Herzegovina (1981); and Clearwater, Florida (1996). There are hundreds of other reports of Marian visions through the centuries, with varying degrees of followers and Vatican support. Miracles are often reported in conjunction with given apparitions, or there is often adoration of relics associated with Mary.

THE FATIMA APPARITION

In 1917 three Portugese children (Lucia dos Santos, now a Carmelite nun, and her cousins Francisco and Jacinta Marto, both since deceased) claimed that the Virgin Mary appeared to them on six different occasions between May 13 and October 17 at Fatima, seventy miles north of Lisbon.

On May 13, 2000, Pope John Paul II presided over a beatification ceremony at Fatima for the Marto children. Cardinal Angelo Sodano, his Secretary of State, announced that the famous Third Secret of Fatima had to do with the attempted assassination of John Paul on May 13, 1981. On June 26 the Vatican released the text of the Third Secret, along with a commentary by the Congregation for the Doctrine of the Faith, headed by Joseph Cardinal Ratzinger.

Hans Küng, the famous German theologian, has stated that he sees the Fatima revelations "as pious projections of the children, especially of the eldest sister, Lucia." He also believes that the pope's interpretation amounts to prophecy after the fact. Father Richard McBrien, professor of theology at the University of Notre Dame, shares Küng's skepticism. He does not believe in Marian apparitions in general, nor does he accept the pope's recent interpretation. "The third secret speaks of a bishop in white dying. The pope was only wounded. None of the other details of the secret correspond with the shooting incident in Saint Peter's Square."

Cardinal Sodano said the Third Secret pictured a pope who made his way in a ruined city "with great effort towards the Cross amid the corpses of those who were martyred." The pope then "falls to the ground, apparently dead, under a burst of gunfire." The relevant part of the primary text says that while the pope was "on his knees at the foot of the big Cross he was killed by a group of soldiers who fired bullets and arrows at him."

Father Richard John Neuhaus (1936–2009) saw no dichotomy between the pope's "devotional expression and the Vatican's theological explanation." He stated that Catholics should have no problem in believing in the message of Fatima. "God works in all kinds of mysterious ways, but Catholics should not confuse such apparitions with the doctrinal structure of the Christian faith."

Ralph MacKenzie, who co-authored *Roman Catholics and Evangelicals* with Norman Geisler, believes that "the apparitions of Fatima are not heretical in the classical sense but are outside the realm that most evangelicals embrace." He also believes that "there seems to be a discrepancy between the text and the pope's interpretation. Some creativity will be necessary to reconcile the differences."

Paul Carden, Executive Director of the Centers for Apologetics Research in San Juan Capistrano, has argued that the recent debate about Fatima "opens a window on Catholic policy and shows the Vatican's very delicate dance with extreme elements in the Catholic Church."

Carden, a leading cult-watcher, believes that most evangelicals do not realize the significance of the Marian focus in Catholic piety: "It is virtually inevitable that a focus on Mary distorts the Gospel." Carden spent six years in Brazil and said that he has seen firsthand how obsession with Marian visions "generates movements that descend into cultism."

Lucia turned over her handwritten account to the Vatican in 1957. Both Pope John XXIII and Pope Paul VI examined the text of the Third Secret but chose to keep it secret. The current pope stated that as John Paul II thought of the assassination attempt against him, he was drawn to the suffering images of Fatima. Ratzinger asked: "Was it not inevitable that he should see in it his own fate?"

▓ Roman Catholicism Q&A

1. What are the common major documents about Catholics and evangelicals?

On March 29, 1994, Charles Colson and other evangelical leaders released a statement with Catholic leaders called "Evangelicals and Catholics Together." On October 7, 1997, "The Gift of Salvation" presented the common ground between evangelicals and Catholics on issues related to the gospel, justification, and mission. The Alliance of Confessing Evangelicals has expressed serious reservations about both major documents, accusing both camps of neglecting critical issues related to key Reformation themes.

Sistene Chapel, Vatican City

Photo: Jim Beverley

2. How can one really know what is going on in Rome?

Contrary to many conspiracy theories, there are few secrets in Rome. The Vatican is like any large and famous organization in that it is very difficult to keep people from talking, especially when there is profound disagreement over a particular decision by Roman authorities. As well, hundreds of journalists, many of whom work for secular newspapers with no vested interest in protecting the Vatican, cover the Vatican. *Inside the Vatican*, by Thomas Reese, offers a detailed picture of what goes on there day to day.

3. Do the Jesuits run the Vatican?

No. Though the Jesuit order, started in 1540 under Ignatius of Loyola (1491–1550), has been and is one of the most powerful of the Catholic orders, the Jesuits have always been under the control of the pope—or have paid a price for rebellion. Because of internal jealousy and external political pressure, the Vatican suppressed the order from 1773 to 1814.

There are more than twenty thousand Jesuits serving in the world today.

4. Why did the church condemn Galileo?

Contrary to popular perception, Galileo's censoring was not rooted in Roman Catholic rejection of science. Galileo (1564–1642) adopted the Copernican view that the sun was at the center of the universe in his 1613 *Letter on Sunspots*. The dominant scientists of Galileo's day opposed his views, as did Catholic leaders who believed that Copernican views were contrary to the plain teaching of Scripture. A year after Galileo published *A Dialogue on the Two Great World Systems* (1632) the Roman Inquisition of 1633 placed him under house arrest. John Paul II admitted in 1979 that the church had erred in its treatment of Galileo.

5. Who is Alberto Rivera?

Chick Publications circulate the works of Alberto Rivera, who claimed to be a Jesuit priest and bishop in the Catholic Church. Rivera, who died in 1997, also claimed that he was hired to destroy Protestant churches by getting them to abandon the King James Version of the Bible and adopt ecumenism and the charismatic movement. Rivera's life story was the subject of devastating criticism by Gary Metz in a 1981 *Cornerstone* magazine report. Rivera's former colleagues provided Metz with clear evidence of Rivera's lies and delusions about his claims of espionage for the pope.

6. What is Opus Dei?

In 1928 Josemaria Escriva founded Opus Dei, a controversial lay movement in Catholicism. Escriva was born in Spain in 1902. He was ordained to the priesthood in 1925 and began his ministry in Madrid. He moved to Rome in 1946 and led Opus Dei until his death in 1975. John Paul II canonized him on October 6, 2002.

Critics of the movement charge that it is sectarian and cultic and allege that its founder was a man of bad temper and poor taste who had far too much sympathy for authoritarian political movements, right-wing Vatican ideologues, and a masochistic spirituality that obsesses on self-inflicting of pain.

The current leader or prelate of Opus Dei is Javier Echevarría. The Opus Dei website is www.opusdei.org. The Opus Dei Awareness Network (Executive Director: Dianne DiNicola) provides critical perspective on the movement. Its web address is www.odan.org.

Confession booth, St. Michael's Cathedral, Toronto, Canada

Photo: Derek Beverley

7. Was John Paul I murdered?

John Paul I assumed the papacy on Saturday, August 26, 1978, and died on Thursday, September 28, just thirty-three days into his rule. Sister Vincenza, his housekeeper, discovered his body on Friday morning. His is the eleventh shortest pontificate in Catholic history.

David Yallop argues in his book *In God's Name* that Vatican insiders who wanted the new pope silenced over his plans to expose corrupt financial practices in the Vatican may have murdered him. There was no autopsy, so Yallop's case cannot be proved, but his book documents the sordid details of key Vatican leaders' illegal banking practices.

8. What are indulgences?

Indulgences refer to the practice in Catholicism whereby the temporal punishment of a Christian's sin is remitted through the authority of the church. Orthodox Catholics believe that the church can draw on the spiritual treasury of Christ and the saints to transfer their merit and holiness to cover the sins of the penitent, both on earth and in purgatory.

The abuse of indulgences in the sixteenth century was a major factor in the protests of both Martin Luther and John Calvin, key leaders of the Protestant Reformation. In their day, the church tied the granting of indulgences directly to monetary giving to the Vatican and even calculated how much time a purgatorial sentence was reduced in proportion to cash flow. The Reformers mocked the abuses but also disagreed with indulgences in principle, believing that they contradicted both salvation by grace and the full atonement of Christ.

9. Who are the new Catholic apologists?

In the last two decades, a new generation of Catholic intellectuals has sought to defend traditional Catholic teaching from typical Protestant attacks. Much of this work is done through Catholic Answers, which features the work of Karl Keating, its president and founder, James Akin and Mark Shea, among others, and publishes the magazine *This Rock*. Mitchell Pacwa, Scott Hahn, and Dave Armstrong are other well-known apologists for Catholic orthodoxy. The Catholic Answers web address is www.catholic.com.

These new apologists have found sloppy Protestant critique of Rome an easy target, but their answers are less persuasive when they deal with well-informed Protestant thinkers or when they seek to address the more serious objections to Catholic views on papal infallibility, the role of Mary, the nature of salvation, and the proper interpretation of scriptural authority.

10. How does one discover official Catholic teaching?

The Vatican's website (www.vatican.va) provides extensive links to official Catholic teaching. Also, the entire range of Catholic doctrine is presented in the *Cathechism of the Catholic Church* and in the revised *Code of Canon Law*.

Catholic church, Ho Chi Minh City, Vietnam

Photo: TD

11. Was Pope Pius XII sympathetic to Hitler?

John Cornwell created considerable controversy with his very unsympathetic portrayal of Pius XII in his work *Hitler's Pope*. Cornwell claims that he started the book in order to defend the wartime pope against popular charges that he failed to protect Jews, a view made famous by Rolf Hochhuth's 1963 play *The Deputy*. In the process of research, Cornwell came to believe that Pius XII had deep anti-Semitic tendencies and failed to exercise all of his papal power to stop Hitler.

Cornwell's views have come under sharp criticism from various historians, Catholic and otherwise. However, even many defenders of Pius XII recognize the limitations of his probably well-intended diplomacy. William Arthur Purdy writes in the *Encyclopedia Britannica* that "the oblique allusions of traditional diplomacy, which came naturally to him and which often seemed to him much clearer than they seemed to others, were no longer appropriate to the savagery and cynicism of a death struggle for world domination and of deliberate genocide."

12. What is Medjugorje?

Medjugorje is a small town in Bosnia-Herzegovina made famous since June 24, 1981, by claims that five children have seen visions and heard messages from the Virgin Mary. Millions of Catholics have visited the town in the past two decades. Defenders of the Medjugorje apparitions claim that Mary gives revelation every day. The bishops of the former Yugoslavia stated in a 1991 report that "on the basis of the investigations so far, it cannot be affirmed that one is dealing with supernatural apparitions and revelations."

The Vatican quoted the bishops positively in a 1998 letter about Medjugorje but also said that the skeptical opinions of the local Bishop Ratko Peric are to be considered his personal views, not necessarily reflecting the views of the Vatican, which has yet to deliver a final verdict. A pro-Medjugorje website can be found at www.medjugorje.org.

■ Catholic-Evangelical Agreements and Disagreements

The Roman tradition has done much to preserve many central teachings of the gospel. Evangelicals must celebrate their agreement with Catholics on every essential doctrine and in all areas where we can unite on moral and social issues. Evangelicals share with orthodox Catholics a confession of the triune nature of God, the supremacy of Jesus Christ as the only Savior and Lord, the authority of the Bible, the necessity of evangelism, and the hope of eternal life with God.

Alongside gratitude for all aspects of true unity with Catholics must also come evangelical openness to learn from Rome where the Catholic tradition has something to teach Protestants in general and evangelicals in particular. Roman Catholics have had a higher appreciation for church unity, which is in stark contrast to the fragmentation that has dominated Protestant history. Likewise, however deep our differences are over doctrines related to Mary, the Catholic appreciation for her is a rebuke to

Protestant neglect. Also, evangelicals need to recapture the sense of awe and majesty found in Catholic worship.

However, evangelicals have rightly challenged Roman Catholic tradition at these most important points: (a) the church as Roman, (b) the doctrine of papal infallibility, (c) aspects of the doctrine of salvation, (d) certain teachings about Mary, (e) aspects of the emphasis on a celibate priesthood, and (f) Catholic traditions in harmony with biblical revelation.

Here are some important questions relating to differences between Catholics and evangelicals:

1. **Where is the church of Jesus Christ?**

Vatican II teaches that Protestants and Orthodox Christians should return to Rome as the home of the church of Jesus. While Vatican II resisted the temptation to say that the church of Jesus is the Catholic Church, the bishops in Rome made it clear that Rome is the Mother Church.

The identification of the church of Jesus with the Roman Church is marred at every point where the history of Catholicism shows flagrant disregard for both truth and goodness. Evangelicals often forget that orthodox Catholicism teaches not only the infallibility of the pope but also the infallibility of the church. On the latter, it is very difficult to reconcile this notion with any attention to the dark stains that have blotted Roman history.

When Pope John Paul II startled the world with his Lenten apology in the spring of 2000, he spoke with humility about the sins of Catholics past and present. "The children of the Church know the experience of sin, whose shadows are cast over her, obscuring her beauty. For this reason the Church does not cease to implore God's forgiveness for the sins of her members."

How can Catholics affirm church infallibility given the sin of its members?

This becomes especially problematic when the sins involve popes, archbishops, and, more important, structural and ideological defects that were or are part of the institutional life of the Vatican itself. In this regard, the sordid aspect of the Crusades or the innocent lives lost at the hands of Roman inquisitors should make any Catholic realize that the church of Jesus cannot be equated so easily with Rome.

Maronite Cathedral of Saint George, Beirut, Lebanon

Photo: Massimo Introvigne

2. Is the pope infallible?

Evangelical objection to papal infallibility should not be about arguments over whether Peter was in Rome. The issue of infallibility is also not about the debate over whether God could have made all popes infallible. On this, I would think that evangelicals should grant the obvious: that all things are possible with God.

The crux of the debate is simply whether in fact the popes have been infallible. On this, I think the record of papal history is clear: Popes have made flagrant and serious errors in their teachings in regard to both faith and morals. For example, (a) a church council condemned Pope Honorius I for teaching heresy about the will of Christ, (b) popes erred in their condemnation of the views of Galileo, (c) many popes throughout history have advocated views that furthered anti-Semitism, and (d) many popes have taught views that have created false views of women and sexuality.

Though Catholic orthodoxy does not teach that the popes themselves are sinless, it is hard to respect the doctrine of papal infallibility in the case of popes who have shown themselves capable of any evil. Must Catholics extend this notion of infallibility to popes who bribed their way into office, who killed and raped? Should infallibility be imagined of Pope Alexander VI, a monster of iniquity who had the Florence preacher Savonarola tortured? What shall we say of the infallibility of popes who called for crusades, inquisitions, and persecutions—whether of Muslims, Jews, witches, gypsies, Protestants, atheists, or fellow Catholics?

PROTESTANT MYTHS ABOUT ROMAN CATHOLICISM

Myth: Catholicism teaches that the pope is sinless.

Fact: Like all Catholics, the popes are sinful and are to go to confession. The current pope has a priest who hears his confession regularly.

Myth: Catholicism officially teaches that salvation comes by human effort.

Fact: The Council of Trent condemned any who teach salvation by works. Salvation by grace alone has been affirmed at the Second Vatican Council, in the recent *Catechism of the Catholic Church,* and in the official declarations with Lutherans on the doctrine of justification.

Myth: Catholics leave Christ on the cross.

Fact: Catholic use of the crucifix is not meant to suggest that Jesus remained on the cross. Roman Catholics have always affirmed the resurrection of Jesus after his death at Calvary.

Myth: Priests can forgive sins even if Catholics do not repent.

Fact: Through the gospel of Jesus, the priest can proclaim the good news of forgiveness but only to those who have Christ's grace and repent of their sin.

Myth: Catholicism is the revival of ancient Babylonian paganism.

Fact: Catholic faith and doctrine is a result of gradual development, based on the thought of Cyprian, Athanasius, Augustine, Pope Leo the Great, Pope Saint Gregory I (Gregory the Great), Thomas Aquinas, and Saint Francis, among many others. Catholicism is not linked to Babylon, contrary to the flawed theories of Alexander Hislop's popular book *The Two Babylons,* published in 1858.

3. How are we saved?

Thankfully, the Catholic-Lutheran dialogue has led to remarkable unity on many issues connected with justification. However, evangelicals have every right to continue to question whether the Roman sacramental scheme has made salvation something different in many degrees from the picture Scripture gives. For example, does the emphasis on infant baptism lull Catholics into a false sense of security about their status as members of the body of Christ? Has emphasis away from forensic justification, the legal declaration of salvation, led many Catholics to believe in works righteousness? Has the focus on Mary and on the priesthood led some Catholics to forget the centrality of Christ?

Further, Catholic leaders should pay close attention to the fact that evangelical Christians find so many of their Catholic friends out of touch with biblical themes of faith and grace. Why do so many Catholics believe that salvation is by works? Questions like this one should be asked in hopes of giving many Catholics a more profound awareness of the simplicity of salvation offered in Christ.

4. Who is Mary?

The unique Catholic views about Mary depend almost solely on acceptance of papal infallibility and the veracity of Roman tradition. Many Catholic dogmas about her are long removed from what could possibly be derived from the beautiful teachings about Mary in the Gospel infancy stories of Jesus. The view that Mary is sinless or that she was assumed into heaven is a giant leap from the important fact that she was faithful to Jesus in his hour of death.

Beyond this, a plain reading of biblical material about her would not lead one to imagine that she was born sinless or that she was a perpetual virgin. Likewise, the growing adulation of Mary throughout Catholic history is out of proportion even with her significant calling as Jesus' mother. This focus on Mary has led to incredible gullibility among the Catholic faithful in regard to Marian visions and ritual.

5. Are traditions biblical?

Evangelicals often understate the importance of tradition and overemphasize an individual approach to Scripture. The Catholic focus on tradition is not wrong in and of itself. However, the emphasis on tradition, when combined with the doctrine of infallibility, creates a setting where doctrines, ideas, and practices can develop that are not in full harmony with Scripture.

This can be asked of Catholic traditions about purgatory and indulgences. Further, the long tradition of priestly celibacy has led to some very dark moments in both the past and present, not only in terms of the abuse of children, but also in regard to the way in which many women feel like second-class citizens in their church. Also, Catholic traditions have often been mixed with pagan customs in ways that detract from the main teachings of the gospel.

ROMAN CATHOLICISM	
Typology	Christian
Catholic Websites	The Holy See: www.vatican.va Catholic Answers: www.catholic.com New Advent: www.newadvent.org Zenit News: www.zenit.org Dave Armstrong site: http://socrates58.blogspot.com/
Critic Websites	Alpha & Omega Ministries (James White): www.aomin.org Christian Witness to Roman Catholicism (Robert Zins): www.cwrc-rz.org
Recommended Reading	Boston Globe Investigative Staff, *Betrayal* (Boston: Little, Brown, & Co., 2002) Norman Geisler & Ralph MacKenzie, *Roman Catholics and Evangelicals* (Grand Rapids: Baker, 1995) David I. Kertzer, *The Popes against the Jews* (New York: Vintage, 2001) Hans Küng, *Infallible? An Inquiry* (Garden City: Doubleday, 1971) Hans Küng, *The Church* (New York: Sheed and Ward, 1968) Richard McBrien, ed., *HarperCollins Encyclopedia of Catholicism* (New York: HarperCollins, 1995) Thomas P. Rausch, ed. *Catholics and Evangelicals* (Downers Grove: InterVarsity, 2000) Garry Wills, *Papal Sin* (New York: Doubleday, 2000)

SATANISM

*Magus Peter H. Gilmore, High Priest, celebrating
40th anniversary of the Church of Satan in 2006*

Photo: Courtesy of the Church of Satan

The term *Satanism* conjures up images of black robes, dark rooms, naked bodies, slain animals, tortured humans, and dead babies. After all, it is commonly assumed that Satanists worship the Prince of Darkness and as a result love darkness and all the nefarious deeds associated with it. Many people assume as well that the ritual satanic abuse of humans and animals reaches its height on Halloween night. This image of Satanism is based on historic perceptions going back nearly one thousand years that have been augmented by recent Hollywood stereotypes of Satanism and by the work of Anton LaVey. LaVey is the author of *The Satanic Bible* and the founder of The Church of Satan.

This chapter will explore Satanism in its historic and contemporary context and attempt to distinguish between fact and fiction about the many issues and personalities involved in the study of Satanism.

■ Debate about Satanic Ritual Abuse

In the past three decades there has been fierce debate about the nature and extent of Satanism in contemporary society. This bitter controversy has involved many Protestant denominations, the Roman Catholic Church, and the Mormon Church—each with differing verdicts about alleged satanic ritual abuse (SRA). Arguments about SRA also involve opposing views about trauma memory, multiple personality disorder (now usually termed "dissociative disorder"), and the extent of child sexual abuse.

Several evangelical Christian writers have popularized the view that Satanism is widespread. Some psychiatrists, judges, and police officers have adopted this position, but others in mental health fields and law enforcement have strongly resisted it. The controversy over Satanism has led to criminal charges involving pastors and day-care workers and many legal battles over child custody. Families have been bitterly divided over claims of ritual abuse by both fathers and mothers.

Though the controversy has subsided somewhat in the past few years, two basic positions have been paramount in the literature about Satanism.

First, it has been argued that Satanism is reaching an epidemic level in our society, that it is expressed through ritual slaughter of animals, the birthing of babies specifically for ritual killing, and the raping of women in satanic covens. According to this theory, participants in satanic ceremonies are forced to drink blood and urine, eat feces and body parts, and engage in sexual orgies. Some hold that Satanists often produce child pornography. Some claim that there are fifty thousand ritual killings per year in the United States. Some psychologists claim to have verified this perspective through the recovery of repressed memories of victims of SRA.

A second position argues that the recent scare over Satanism is largely paranoia. According to this view, there is no solid evidence of satanic ritual abuse involving organized groups of devil worshipers. No babies are being killed in sacrifice to Satan. Overly zealous evangelicals and gullible health professionals have been duped by rumors, the wild stories of children, and the hysteria generated by sloppy "cult cops." According to this perspective, psychologists obsessed with proving satanic ritual abuse have created false memories in alleged victims.

Four Types of Satanists

It is now common in literature on Satanism to distinguish four categories or types of Satanism. These categories are often discussed in the debates about contemporary Satanism.

- First, there are those who dabble in Satanism and occult activity. This includes teenagers who focus on music with satanic lyrics.

- Second, there are self-styled Satanists, individuals, for example, who explain their criminal behavior by referring to the devil's leading. The serial killer Richard Ramirez is a case in point.

- Third, there are formal religious groups who claim to worship Satan and revel in their departure from mainstream religion. The most famous group is the Church of Satan. The Temple of Set is also a well-known organization devoted to Satanism. Neither Anton LaVey nor Michael Aquino, the founders of the Church of Satan and the Temple of Set, respectively, advocate criminal behavior.

- Fourth, it is alleged that there are thousands of Satanists who form an international network involved in satanic ritual abuse, as noted above.

There is no debate about the existence of the first three types of Satanism. No one denies the reality of satanic motifs in pop culture, or the self-styled Satanist loner who engages in criminal behavior. Likewise, the Church of Satan is one of the best-known religions (or anti-religions), thanks both to the media savvy of its founder and the controversy surrounding its origin and continued existence. In spite of common recognition of these forms of Satanism, evangelical Christians remain divided about the realities of satanic ritual abuse.

Assessing Claims about Satanism

In reacting to the debates about modern Satanism, Christians bring two important truths to the topic.

First, and most important, the Christian worldview asserts the primacy and sovereignty of God over Satan and evil. This fundamental doctrine provides a rationale for not giving undue attention to Satan or overstating the powers of the demonic. As boundless as evil seems, its scope is not infinite. Emphasis on the omnipotence of God serves as a necessary corrective to overemphasis on Satan.

Second, Christian recognition of the reality of evil provides the intellectual framework for taking claims about Satanism seriously. Accounts of both natural and supernatural evil can be assessed as possible given the biblical recognition of the depth and extent of spiritual and moral darkness in the human race and in the demonic realm. Ironically, Christian recognition of evil also presents the proper ideological ground for realizing that false claims about evil and Satanism can be taken as another example of intellectual and moral depravity.

With these two fundamental propositions in mind, the following principles can be brought to bear in contemporary debates about Satanism:

- As noted in the chapter on witchcraft, Christians must make distinctions between the various forms of witchcraft and Satanism. Therefore, any serious discussion of Satanism must pay serious attention to the differences between typical Western witchcraft and Satan worship.

- Claims about SRA should be handled case-by-case so that real instances of evil are distinguished from false allegations.

- The theory that SRA is an epidemic has not been proven, and the burden of proof is on those who advocate this perspective.

- It is not helpful to question the spiritual integrity of those who, in good conscience, hold differing theories about the pervasiveness of SRA.

- All things being equal, those who report a case of SRA should be treated with tenderness and compassion.

- Since false allegations of SRA can ruin those accused, the testimony of alleged victims needs to be weighed very seriously.

- Children can lie or be misled, so their testimony about sexual and satanic abuse needs to be examined critically.

- False testimony about SRA involving children has damaged the prosecution of authentic cases of child abuse.

- Human memory is not infallible. Therefore, "repressed memories" of SRA may turn out to be false.

- Given the reality of evil such as the Holocaust and child pornography, claims about SRA are possible and should be investigated.

Main Altar at Black House

Photo: Courtesy of the Church of Satan

TIMELINE RELATED TO SATANISM AND RITUAL ABUSE

1966—Anton LaVey founds Church of Satan

1969— *The Satanic Bible* (author: LaVey)

1969—Sharon Tate and others killed by followers of Charles Manson

1972— *The Satan Seller* (author: Mike Warnke)

1973—*Sybil*, an account of MPD, multiple personality disorder (author: Flora Rheta Schreiber)

1975—Temple of Set founded by Michael Aquino

1980— *Michelle Remembers* (Michelle Smith and Laurence Pazder)

1983—First major SRA case in Bakersfield, California

1983—Ritual allegations in McMartin Case in California

1984—Fells Acre Daycare case, Malden, MA (Amirault family)

1985—Kelly Michaels charged in Wee Care case in New Jersey
    Sean Sellers (Oklahoma) claims killings caused by Satan

1986—Rebecca Brown, *He Came to Set the Captives Free*

1987—Maury Terry, *The Ultimate Evil* (about the Son of Sam case)

1988—Lauren Stratford, *Satan's Underground* (alleged ex-Satanist)
    Ellen Bass and Laura Davis, *The Courage to Heal*
    Paul Ingram (Olympia, WA.) charged with SRA against his two daughters
    October 25, Geraldo Rivera show on Satanism

1989—Little Rascals Day Care case (Edenton, North Carolina)
    April 11, Mark Kilroy and others murdered in ritual (Matamoras, Mexico)

1990—McMartin trial ends after seven years

1991—Reports of SRA in Mormon Church (Salt Lake City)

1992— *Cornerstone* magazine exposes Mike Warnke
    False Memory Syndrome Foundation (FMSF) formed in Philadelphia
    SRA Case in Wenatchee, Washington
    SRA Case in Martensville, Saskatchewan

1993—Kelly Michaels wins appeal in Wee Care case

1995—Geraldo Rivera apologizes for gullibility about extent of SRA
    Frontline documentary "Divided Memories"

1997—Death of Anton LaVey

1998—Trial in Houston against therapists

1999—Karla LaVey founded First Satanic Church, San Francisco

2001—Peter H. Gilmore heads Church of Satan

2002—Criminal charges against Order of Perdition founder
    Russell J. Smith

2003—Ingram released from prison and passed polygraph test

2003—SRA case in Lewis Island, Scotland

2006—Martensville SRA case settled (Saskatchewan)

2007— *The Satanic Scriptures* (Gilmore)

The Mike Warnke Story

Mike Warnke is most famous as a Christian comedian and as the author of *The Satan Seller*, published in 1972. Warnke claimed that in 1965–66 he was the head of a 1,500-member satanic coven in California. For two decades, no one questioned Warnke's testimony. Then, in 1992, *Cornerstone* magazine (from Jesus People USA in Chicago) published

"Selling Satan: The Tragic History of Mike Warnke." Mike Hertenstein and Jon Trott authored this 24,000-word exposé, which showed beyond reasonable doubt that Warnke had fabricated reports of his satanic activity. The article also documented Warnke's failed marriages and lavish lifestyle. The article was later expanded into a book under the same title, *Selling Satan* (Cornerstone Press).

The *Cornerstone* article led to other inquiries about Warnke. Word Records dropped its contract with him and his ministry virtually collapsed. Warnke said that some of his critics were actually Satanists. He maintained the basic integrity of his account but admitted exaggerating the number of people in his coven. He also acknowledged his failings as a father and husband. In 1993 he submitted to spiritual discipline under several Christian leaders, a process that continued for several years. Warnke and his current wife, Susan, now conduct a speaking ministry through their organization, Celebrations of Hope. Warnke dealt with some of the controversy surrounding his ministry in *Friendly Fire*, published in 2002.

Internet Sources

Celebrations of Hope: www.mikewarnke.org

Cornerstone article: www.cornerstonemag.com

Rebecca Brown, M.D.

Rebecca Brown is the author of *He Came to Set the Captives Free* (Chick Publications), which offers one of the most amazing stories ever written about modern Satanism. Brown claims that God used her to perform exorcisms on hundreds of demon-possessed patients while she was a doctor in Indiana. Her most significant case involves a woman named Elaine, who was allegedly the bride of Satan, having married him in a secret ceremony in a Presbyterian church. Brown also maintains that Elaine flew with Satan on his private jet to the Vatican, where she took part in planning meetings with the pope and other conspirators, including some famous rock stars.

Although millions of Christians believed the contents of Brown's book, in late 1989, Personal Freedom Outreach's major investigation on "Drugs, Demons and Delusions" exposed her life story. Among other things, PFO reported that:

- Rebecca Brown was originally known as Ruth Irene Bailey. She changed her name in 1986 through petition to the Superior Court of California, County of San Bernardino.

- Bailey was born on May 21, 1948, in Shelbyville, Indiana. After working as a nurse, she earned her M.D. in 1979 and did her residency at Ball Memorial Hospital in Muncie, Indiana.

- In 1980 Bailey developed a close relationship with Edna Elaine Knost, a patient at the hospital and a native of New Castle, Indiana. Elaine was married in 1966, but her husband filed for divorce after a few months.

- Bailey was asked to leave Ball Memorial because of complaints about her attempts at exorcisms on patients. Bailey started a general practice in Lapel, Indiana, in 1982. However, the Indiana Medical Licensing Board revoked Bailey's right to practice medicine in September 1984. Bailey was charged with misdiagnosis of patients and misuse of prescriptions.

- Bailey was able to convince Jack Chick, the controversial publisher, that she had rescued Elaine from Satanism, even though the Medical Board found her guilty of mistreating the woman when she was her patient.

On December 10, 1989, Rebecca Brown (nee Bailey) married Daniel Yoder. Brown claims that Yoder was raised in a wealthy Jewish family and educated in Switzerland. His family arranged a marriage with a woman named Kai. After Kai became a Christian, Yoder's family had her and Daniel kidnapped and sent to Israel. According to *Unbroken Curses* (authored by Brown and Yoder), "Daniel was chained to a wall and forced to watch as Kai, his first and only love, was tortured to death!" Brown states that Daniel escaped to the United States and became a Christian. Yoder and Brown met in November 1989, and they were married a month later.

Personal Freedom Outreach has provided evidence of fraud Yoder committed in 1991. He pled guilty in a court in Iowa in the spring of 1992. Daniel and Rebecca now live in Clinton, Arkansas. They operate a speaking and writing ministry under the name Harvest Warriors.

Internet Sources

Personal Freedom Outreach: www.pfo.org

Rebecca Brown/Daniel Yoder: www.harvestwarriors.com

The Paul Ingram Case

In 1988 two daughters of Paul Ingram, a deputy sheriff in Olympia, Washington, charged him with sexual abuse involving satanic rituals. Fellow police officers and his Christian pastor pressured him to plead guilty. He did so and was sentenced to twenty years in prison. However, after pleading guilty, he argued that his confession was obtained under duress. The court denied him a new trial. He was released from prison in 2003 and passed a polygraph test about his innocence. One of his daughters continues to maintain that her father was guilty.

Social psychologist Richard Ofshe (University of California, Berkeley) was involved in the case and argued that Ingram was the victim of both police and church leaders. Ofshe was even able to persuade Ingram to admit to sexual abuse that Ofshe simply invented. Medical reports showed no physical marks on the two daughters consistent with their claims of sexual and satanic abuse. The case is analyzed in Lawrence Wright's *Remembering Satan* (New York: Random, 1994). Karen Olio and William Cornell criticized Ofshe's work in the case in "The Façade of Scientific Documentation" in the journal *Psychology, Public Policy, and Law* (Vol. 4, #4).

The McMartin Pre-school Trial

One might expect that the longest trial in U.S. history would involve litigation between huge corporations or a protracted criminal trial involving the Mafia. In actual fact, the longest trial was about allegations of child sex abuse and satanic ritual abuse against day-care workers in Southern California. In September 1983 police arrested a man named Ray Buckey. He was the son of Peggy Buckey who ran the McMartin Pre-School program in Manhattan Beach. The school was founded by Peggy's mother, Virginia McMartin. In 1984 Ray, Peggy, Virginia, and several of the day-care workers were indicted on 208 different charges of child abuse.

There were several different trials related to the McMartin School; but in the end, after six years, no one was convicted. The trial cost the state of California $15 million.

Conflicting views remain about the whole tragic saga. Some view the case as a prime example of a crazed witch-hunt. On this view, the accused were innocent victims of a mass hysteria that led to forced confessions from scared children. The opposite view is that Buckey, McMartin, and others got away with ritual murder because of their ability to hide any evidence of crimes against the children.

The McMartin incident was part of a larger panic about ritual abuse that gripped North America during the 1980s. Initially the McMartin case led to greater funding for groups devoted to the protection of children. Over time, however, the legal system became far more skeptical about claims of ritual and satanic abuse. Former FBI Special Agent Ken Lanning, their longtime specialist on satanic ritual abuse, has argued that false allegations involving Satanism led to increased doubts about true allegations of sex abuse.

MCMARTIN PRE-SCHOOL TRIAL: CHRONOLOGY

August 1983—Judy Johnson claims her son Billy was sexually molested by Ray Buckey.

September 7, 1983—Ray Buckey is arrested.

September 8, 1983—Police Chief Harry Kuhlmeyer issues letter to 200 McMartin parents about suspected abuse.

November 1983—Kee MacFarlane of Children's Institute International starts interviews with children in case.

January 1984—McMartin Pre-school closed.

March 1984—Indictment against Ray Buckey, Peggy Buckey, Virginia McMartin, Peggy Ann Buckey (Ray's sister), Mary Ann Jackson, Bette Raidor, and Babette Spitler.

December 1984—ABC's *20/20* reports on McMartin case.

March 1985—A group of parents and an archaeological firm hired by district attorney search for secret tunnels; none is discovered.

September 1985—Doubts about case raised by some of the prosecutors.

January 1986—Preliminary hearing ends and charges are dropped against five of the seven defendants. Ray Buckey and Peggy Buckey remained charged.

December 1986—Judy Johnson dies.

July 1987—Start of first trial.

February 1989—Ray Buckey released on bail.

January 1990—Peggy Buckey acquitted and jury is hung on charges against Ray Buckey. District attorney announces a second trial against him.

July 1990—Second trial ends with hung jury. District attorney decides against third trial.

1995—Virginia McMartin dies of natural causes.

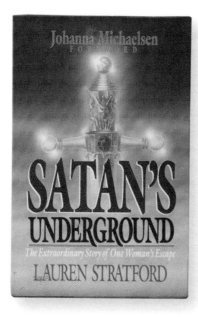

Photo: From Satan's Underground: The Extraordinary Story of One Woman's Escape *by Lauren Stratford,* © 1988 *by Lauren Stratford; used by permission of the publisher,* Pelican Publishing Company, Inc.

Lauren Stratford

Lauren Stratford is the alleged ex-Satanist who authored *Satan's Underground,* her own testimony. Stratford claimed she was the victim of satanic ritual abuse at the hands of a sex ring headed by a man she identified as Victor. Harvest House released Stratford's work in 1988, but the publisher withdrew it from circulation after considerable controversy. Pelican then chose to publish the book. Later, Bob and Gretchen Passantino of Answers in Action and Jon Trott, a researcher with Jesus People USA, gathered evidence calling Stratford's integrity into question. Their investigation was published in *Cornerstone* magazine in 1990. Johanna Michaelson, a Christian writer, and Stratford's brother-in-law, Hal Lindsey, author of *The Late Great Planet Earth,* defended her testimony.

Incredibly, after years of telling about her life in Satanism, Stratford developed another identity. In the 1990s she postured herself as Laura or Lauren Grabowski, a child survivor of a Nazi concentration camp. In actual fact, Lauren Stratford (aka Grabowski) was born Laurel Willson on August 18, 1941, in Tacoma, Washington. She was adopted at birth, and her real life story is one of true emotional trauma; but overwhelming evidence shows that she fabricated her testimony as a Satanist and then as a Holocaust survivor. Her original critics published a devastating second critique in *Cornerstone* magazine in 1999.

Stratford died in April 2002. Kathleen and Bill Sullivan, who run a ministry for victims of ritual abuse, have a memorial to Stratford and completely dismiss the *Cornerstone* critique. The Sullivans's organization is called PARC-VRAMC, which stands for "positive activism, remembrance and commemoration" to honor "victims of ritual abuse and mind control."

The Sullivans, and others who defend Stratford, do not respond to specific evidence provided in *Cornerstone* magazine. Rather, they either question the integrity of the researchers involved or point out the positive impact of Stratford's message. It is undeniable that many people were helped through every truth Stratford shared. However, this fact does not absolve her or her apologists from her false testimony about Satanism and Holocaust survival.

Underwager and Wakefield: Accusations of Pedophilia

The vicious controversy over memories of SRA and sexual abuse is illustrated by allegations against Ralph Underwager and Hollida Wakefield, two of the leading psychologists who have testified about the possibility of false memories in both children and adults. In 1990 they gave an interview to the editor of *Paidika*, a journal published in Holland that deals with pedophilia and contains material in favor of adult-child sexual relationships.

The journal published the interview in 1993, and immediately Underwager and Wakefield were charged with approving of pedophilia. What makes the interview problematic is that some statements do sound, even in their immediate context, sympathetic to pedophilia. However, the psychologists responded at length in their publication *Issues in Child Abuse Accusations* (1994) stating that their statements were misunderstood because critics did not understand the wider context of the interview. Underwager and Wakefield also wrote of their categorical disapproval of pedophilia. "We do not believe sexual contact between an adult and a child is ever acceptable nor can it ever be positive. We have never accepted or condoned sexual acts between adults and children as positive or acceptable."

In spite of these clear statements, accusations continued. It was alleged that Underwager and Wakefield were "known pedophiles" and regular speakers at the conferences of NAMBLA (North American Man/Boy Love Association), charges that are totally untrue. Critics continue to cite the *Paidika* interview in discussions about memory and satanic and sexual abuse. The False Memory Syndrome Foundation is often attacked on the basis of its connection with Underwager.

Underwager and Wakefield worked together at the Institute for Psychological Therapies in Minnesota. They were married in 1978. Ralph Underwager died in December 2003.

Anton Szandor LaVey

Photo: Courtesy of the Church of Satan

■ Anton LaVey and the Church of Satan

Anton LaVey was born in 1930 in Cook County, Illinois. His birth name was Howard Stanton Levey, and he was the son of Michael and Gertrude Levey. He founded the Church of Satan in 1966 and wrote *The Satanic Bible* in 1969. The church was headquartered at LaVey's home at 6114 California Street, San Francisco. His parents gave him the house in 1971. Contrary to popular perception, the property was never used as a brothel.

There are several items about LaVey and his history that are debated. He may have had an affair with Marilyn Monroe, but there is no conclusive proof. The evidence seems clear that he influenced the making of Roman Polanski's 1968 film *Rosemary's Baby*. LaVey was never wealthy, and the Church of Satan has never had a huge membership. LaVey did not die on October 31, 1997 (Halloween), but on October 29 of that year.

After LaVey's death, his longtime partner, Blanche Barton, led the church. In 2001 Peter H. Gilmore became High Priest and his wife Peggy Nadramia replaced Barton as High Priestess in 2002. The church now uses a mailing address in New York City.

In 1989 one of LaVey's daughters, Zeena, disowned him and went public with criticisms about her father. Karla, another of LaVey's daughters, founded the San Francisco-based First Satanic Church on October 31, 1999. Karla announced that membership was subject to careful screening and allegiance to her father's legacy. She wrote: "My father's death is a tragedy and a loss. He was the closest person in my life and I, along with many others, miss him profoundly. Through his works he will remain a part of our lives, giving us guidance and inspiration. I am determined to continue, in every way I can, to uphold and expand on his ideals, his teachings, his traditions, and his visions. I call on others to do the same."

Some early members of the Church of Satan parted company with LaVey in 1975, claiming that he was using the church for his personal and financial needs. Michael Aquino, one ex-member, formed the Temple of Set (Set is the Egyptian god of darkness) as an alternative satanic movement. The Temple of Set website probably has LaVey in mind when it states: "A person who claims to be a Satanist but who denies Satan is simply using the title for ulterior motives such as personal glamorization or commercial exploitation."

THE NINE SATANIC STATEMENTS (ANTON LAVEY)

1. Satan represents indulgence, instead of abstinence!

2. Satan represents vital existence, instead of spiritual pipe dreams!

3. Satan represents undefiled wisdom, instead of hypocritical self-deceit!

4. Satan represents kindness to those who deserve it, instead of love wasted on ingrates!

5. Satan represents vengeance, instead of turning the other cheek!

6. Satan represents responsibility to be responsible, instead of concern for psychic vampires!

7. Satan represents man as just another animal, sometimes better, more often worse than those that walk on all-fours, who, because of his "divine spiritual and intellectual development," has become the most vicious animal of all!

8. Satan represents all of the so-called sins, as they all lead to physical, mental, or emotional gratification!

9. Satan has been the best friend the church has ever had, as he has kept it in business all these years!

▨ Satanism: Q&A

1. Does *The Satanic Bible* outsell the Christian Bible?

No, this is a myth spread both in some Christian and some occult circles. The Bible is still by far the world's best seller.

2. Is *The Satanic Bible* dangerous?

Yes. It offers an immoral, anti-Christian, degrading, selfish, and destructive worldview. Some Christians might need to read it to be informed observers about Satanism.

3. Should Christians take part in games like the Ouija board?

No, and for two reasons. First, most of the time the game does not work unless you ask it questions to which you already know the answers. Second, if spirits work through the game, then one is in territory Scripture has forbidden.

4. Do witches and Satanists have some rituals in common?

Yes, witches and some Satanists might have the same holy days, or say the same chants on occasion, or follow similar rituals. However, the pagan/witch and Satanist adopt radically different philosophies, especially since Satanism is atheistic.

5. Why do members of LaVey's Church of Satan say "Hail Satan!" if they do not believe that he is a real being?

Matt G. Paradise, a member of the Church of Satan and the webmaster at Superhighway to Hell, answered this question when he wrote: "'Hail Satan!' is often another way of saying 'Hail Me!' Since we Satanists embody the qualities of the archetype of Satan, it stands to reason that the phrase is both apropos and analogous. You very well could say 'Hail Me!' instead, but keep in mind this . . . 'Hail Satan!' is also a salute to our achievements (both collective and, more importantly, individual), ethics, and heritage. It is a statement of pride in defiance of a polyglot, egalitarian, and ignorant way of life represented by the nauseating Christ ethos and its followers. If we have signed any pact with Satan, it is this."

6. Is there a danger in focus on Satanism?

Yes, there is some danger since (a) Christians have been too gullible in acceptance of claims that cannot be proved or have been disproved, (b) the devil gets more credit than he deserves, with insufficient attention to the ways in which God limits the hand of Satan, and (c) Christians do not pay sufficient attention to other evils that dominate our world. For example, when we focus on the alleged massive ritual killing of children, we lose focus on the fact that thousands of children die every day of starvation.

7. Are there really 50,000 ritual murders every year in North America?

No. The investigative work of Kenneth Lanning, formerly the FBI specialist in the study of ritual abuse allegations, has discredited this figure, which is twice the number of other types of murder. Those who advance this number offer no clear evidence to support their case. Al Carlisle, one alleged authority on this topic, has contended that there are at least six hundred ritual murders every year in Las Vegas alone (see Jerry Johnston, *The Edge of Evil*, p. 4). After I read this I phoned the Las Vegas Police Department and was told that the total homicide rate for the city was roughly eighteen per year. The officer interviewed had heard of no satanic ritual killings at all.

STATEMENT FROM FORMER FBI AGENT ON SATANISM

Many people do not understand how difficult it is to commit a conspiracy crime involving numerous co-conspirators. One clever and cunning individual has a good chance of getting away with a well-planned interpersonal crime. Bring one partner into the crime and the odds of getting away with it drop considerably. The more people involved in the crime, the harder it is to get away with it. Why? Human nature is the answer. People get angry and jealous. They come to resent the fact that another conspirator is getting "more" than they. They get in trouble and want to make a deal for themselves by informing on others.

Until hard evidence is obtained and corroborated, the public should not be frightened into believing that babies are being bred and eaten, that 50,000 missing children are being murdered in human sacrifices, or that Satanists are taking over America's day-care centers or institutions. No one can prove with absolute certainty that such activity has not occurred. The burden of proof, however, as it would be in a criminal prosecution, is on those who claim that it has occurred.

—Kenneth V. Lanning, Special Agent, FBI Academy, Quantico, Virginia (1992)

8. Is satanic ritual abuse a myth?

Not at all. The point above is about the *extent* of SRA. Every year there are ritual killings done in the name of Satan. Though these killings are limited in number, they are real.

Item: Daniel Ruda, 26, and his wife Manuela, 23, argued before a German court that their killing of Frank Haagen in July 2001 was not their responsibility since they were obeying Satan's command. Haagen was struck on the head with a hammer and stabbed sixty-six times. The couple also drank their victim's blood.

Item: Donnie James Clayburn, 19, was charged with desecration of graves and arson in Carter County, Oklahoma, in 2001. He claimed to be the head of a satanic group, and three others have been implicated with him in the criminal-religious acts.

Item: Portugese rock musician Antonio Jore of the band Agonizing Terror was sentenced recently to twenty-five years in prison after admitting to killing his parents in a satanic ritual.

9. Where did Anton LaVey get his ideas?

La Vey was influenced by the ideologies of Friedrich Nietzsche (1844–1900) and the philosopher Ayn Rand. He was also shaped by the writings of Herbert Spencer and Max Stirner.

10. Is a Christian harmed by owning *The Satanic Bible*?

Spiritual harm comes through following *The Satanic Bible*, not owning it. Of course, thankfully, the vast majority of Christians have no need to purchase or read it.

11. Does Freemasonry advocate the worship of Satan?

No. This is a rumor spread largely by gullible and misleading evangelicals. Accurate details about the teachings of the various degrees in Freemasonry are available in Steven Tsoukalas, *Masonic Rites and Wrongs* (Presbyterian and Reformed), probably the best critique of the Masonic Lodge.

12. Should Christians trust Chick Publications on witchcraft and Satanism?

Jack Chick has published many fine tracts and comics that present the basics of the gospel. However, his wild and unproven conspiracy theories about Freemasons, the Catholic Church, the charismatic movement, Nazis, and Christians who use versions of the Bible other than the King James Version ruin his material on witchcraft and Satanism.

13. What led to the demise of claims about rampant sexual and satanic ritual abuse by the mid-1990s?

Criminal prosecutors started to realize that many cases had fallen apart in the previous decade. As well, Frederick Crews makes this important observation in *The New York Review of Books* (March 11, 2004): "Like the Salem witch hunt three centuries earlier, the sex panic had no internal brake that could prevent its accusations from racing beyond all bounds of credibility. The stirring motto 'Believe the children' began to sound hollow when preschoolers who finally agreed that they must have been inappropriately touched went on to describe having been dropped into a pool of sharks or turned into a mouse. The medical records of some alleged rape victims showed that they had still been virgins at a later period. And many patients, when urged to dig deeper after producing a vague scene or two, reduced the process to self-travesty by conjuring surreal orgies with Daddy's bridge partners, visiting uncles, and the family pets."

14. How should debates among psychologists about memory and trauma be interpreted?

Unless one is an expert in psychological testing, it is difficult to know who to trust in the nasty controversies about recovered memory. The opposing views have credible psychologists on each side. The stakes are high in the controversy simply because no one wants psychologists who are too skeptical about memories of abuse to betray truly victimized children. Likewise, no one wants false allegations spread by psychologists who are too ready to believe false claims of abuse to ruin innocent human beings. Readers should consult the leading theorists noted in the bibliography and read critical reviews from all sides. Most important, if one wants to speak with authority on this subject, it is imperative to explore specific cases in great depth.

15. Why should Christians distinguish between white witches and Satanists?

First, both witches and Satanists want the distinction to be made. Second, there are simply no scholars who argue that witches = Satanists. Third, those few witches who claim to be Satanists also deny belief in a literal Satan, as Christians would define the term. Fourth, many evangelical Christian testimonies about Satanism have been thoroughly discredited. Fifth, false understandings and gross exaggerations ruin the Christian witness to witches and Satanists.

TEACHINGS OF *THE SATANIC BIBLE*

- **New Light:** "The twilight is done. A glow of new light is borne out of the night and Lucifer is risen, once more to proclaim: 'This is the age of Satan! Satan Rules the Earth!'" (pp. 23–24).

- **Hatred for God:** "I gaze into the glassy eye of your fearsome Jehovah, and pluck him by the beard; I uplift a broad-axe, and split open his worm-eaten skull" (p. 30).

- **Contempt for Christ:** "Behold the crucifix; what does it symbolize? Pallid incompetence hanging on a tree" (p. 31).

- **Hatred for Enemies:** "Hate your enemies with a whole heart, and if a man smite you on the cheek, SMASH him on the other! He who turns the other cheek is a cowardly dog!" (p. 33).

- **Self-Salvation:** "Say unto thine own heart, 'I am mine own redeemer'" (p. 33).

- **Seven Deadly Sins:** "The seven deadly sins of the Christian Church are: greed, pride, envy, anger, gluttony, lust, and sloth. Satanism advocates indulging in each of these 'sins' as they all lead to physical, mental, or emotional gratification" (p. 46).

- **True Satanists Are Selfish:** "Anyone who pretends to be interested in magic or the occult for reasons other than gaining personal power is the worst kind of hypocrite" (p. 51).

- **The Origin of Satan:** "Satan as a god, demi-god, personal saviour, or whatever you wish to call him, was invented by the formulators of every religion on the face of the earth for only one purpose— to preside over man's so-called wicked activities and situations here on earth. Consequently, anything resulting in physical or mental gratification was defined as 'evil'—thus assuring a lifetime of unwarranted guilt for everyone!" (pp. 62–63).

- **Against Child-Sacrifice:** "Under no circumstances would a Satanist sacrifice any animal or baby!" (p. 89).

- **Invocation to Satan:** "In the name of Satan, the Ruler of the earth, the King of the world, I command the forces of Darkness to bestow their Infernal power upon me!" (p. 144).

■ Satanism Internet Sources

Christian Ministry to Satanists

Refuge Ministries (Jeff Harshbarger, ex-Satanist): www.refugeministries.cc

Data on SRA Cases, Memory and Psychological Issues

David Baldwin's Trauma site: www.trauma-pages.com

False Memory Syndrome Facts: www.fmsf.com

False Memory Syndrome Foundation: www.fmsfonline.org

Jennifer Freyd (psychologist, University of Oregon): http://dynamic.uoregon.edu/~jjf

Institute for Psychological Therapies (Ralph Underwager and Hollida Wakefield): www.ipt-forensics.com

International Society for the Study of Disassociation: www.issd.org

Elizabeth Loftus (psychologist on memory issues): www.seweb.uci.edu/faculty/loftus

Ontario Consultants on Religious Tolerance: www.religioustolerance.org

Ken Pope (psychologist on memory issues): www.kspope.com

Recovered Memories of Sexual Abuse: www.jimhopper.com

Recovered Memory Project (Ross Cheit): www.recoveredmemory.org

Anna Salter (psychologist on sexual abuse): www.annasalter.com

SMART (Stop Ritual Abuse and Mind Control Today): http://ritualabuse.us/

Witchhunt Information Page (Jonathan Harris): http://www.geocities.com/jgharris7

Satanic Groups

Church of Satan (Anton LaVey): www.churchofsatan.com

First Satanic Church (Karla LaVey): www.satanicchurch.com

Temple of Set (Michael Aquino): www.xeper.org

■ Bibliography

Evangelical Christian

Rebecca Brown, *He Came to Set the Captives Free* (Chino: Chick Publications, 1986).

G. Richard Fisher, Paul Blizard, and Kurt Goedelman, "Drugs, Demons and Delusions," *Journal of Personal Freedom Outreach* 9 (October–December, 1989)—a critique of the claims of Rebecca Brown.

Jerry Johnston, *The Edge of Evil* (Dallas: Word, 1989).

Bob Larson, *Satanism* (Nashville: Nelson, 1989).

Moody Monthly, "Evil in the Land" Special Report on Satanism (March 1989).

Bob & Gretchen Passantino, *Satanism* (Grand Rapids: Zondervan, 1995).

Lauren Stratford, *Satan's Underground* (Eugene: Harvest House, 1988)—the now-discredited testimony of an ex-Satanist.

Jon Trott and Mike Hertenstein, *Selling Satan: The Tragic History of Mike Warnke*, (Chicago: Cornerstone Press, 1993).

Reinder Van Til, *Lost Daughters* (Grand Rapids: Eerdmans, 1997)—an account of family breakups over false allegations of ritual abuse and incest, including Van Til's own family.

Mike Warnke, *The Satan Seller* (Plainfield: Logos, 1972).

Other Material

Ellen Bass and Laura Davis, *The Courage to Heal* (New York: Harper & Row, 1988).

Daniel Brown, Alan W. Scheflin, and D. Corydon Hammond, *Memory, Trauma Treatment, and the Law* (New York: Norton, 2003).

Mary DeYoung, *The Ritual Abuse Controversy: An Annotated Bibliography* (McFarland & Company, 2002).

Paul & Shirley Eberle, *The Abuse of Innocence* (Buffalo: Prometheus, 1993). Deals with the McMartin case.

Jennifer Freyd, *Betrayal Trauma* (Cambridge: Harvard University Press, 1996).

Robert Hare, *Without Conscience: The Disturbing World of the Psychopaths Among Us* (Guilford Press, 1999).

Robert Hicks, *In Pursuit of Satan* (Buffalo: Prometheus, 1991).

Michael Langone and Linda Blood, *Satanism and Occult-Related Violence* (American Family Foundation, Box 2265, Bonita Springs, FL 33959).

Kenneth V. Lanning, *Investigator's Guide to Allegations of Ritual Child Abuse* (Quantico: FBI Academy, 1992).

Elizabeth Loftus & Katherine Ketcham, *The Myth of Repressed Memory* (New York: St. Martin's, 1994).

Kathryn Lyon, *Witch Hunt* (New York: Avon Books, 1998).

Richard McNally, *Remembering Trauma* (Cambridge: Harvard University Press, 2003).

Gareth Medway, *Lure of the Sinister* (New York: New York University Press, 2001).

Debbie Nathan and Michael Snedeker, *Satan's Silence* (New York: Basic Books, 1995).

Richard Ofshe & Ethan Watters, *Making Monsters* (New York: Scribner's, 1994).

Mark Pendergrast, *Victims of Memory* (Hinesburg, Vermont: Upper Access, 1995).

Kenneth Pope and Laura Brown, *Recovered Memories of Abuse: Assessment, Therapy, Forensics* (American Psychological Association, 1996).

Dorothy Rabinowitz, *No Crueler Tyrannies* (New York: Wall Street Journal Books, 2003).

Carl Raschke, *Painted Black* (New York: Harper & Row, 1990).

James T. Richardson, Joel Best and David G. Bromley, eds, *The Satanism Scare* (New York: De Gruyter, 1991).

Martha Rogers, Guest Editor, "Special Issue: Satanic Ritual Abuse," *Journal of Psychology and Theology* (Fall 1992, Vol. 20, #3).

Daniel Ryder, *Breaking the Circle of Satanic Ritual Abuse* (Minneapolis: CompCare Publishers, 1992).

David K. Sakheim and Susie E. Devine, *Out of Darkness* (New York: Lexington Books, 1992).

Michelle Smith & Lawrence Pazder, *Michelle Remembers* (New York: Congdon & Lattes, 1980).

Tim Tate, *Children for the Devil* (London: Michelin House, 1991).

Lenore Terr, *Unchained Memories* (New York: Basic, 1994).

Maury Terry, *The Ultimate Evil* (New York: Doubleday, 1987). Son of Sam case.

Hollida Wakefield & Ralph Underwager, *Return of the Furies* (Chicago: Open Court, 1994).

Lawrence Wright, *Remembering Satan* (New York: Random, 1994). On the Paul Ingram case.

Church headquarters, Toronto, Canada

Photo: Derek Beverley

The Church of Scientology is one of the most controversial new religious movements. The church has been involved in many major legal cases involving its tax-exempt status, its status as a religion, and its perceived threats to psychiatric medicine. The claims of Scientologists and the counterclaims of critics are so diametrically opposed to one another that it is difficult to sort through the competing views and get beyond extreme rhetoric about the church.

L. Ron Hubbard, a well-known writer, started the church in 1954. Born in 1911 in Tilden, Nebraska, he traveled widely in his youth and during his two years as a student at George Washington University. He saw Navy service in World War II. After the war, he came into contact with Jack Parsons, a disciple of the famous occult leader Aleister Crowley. Hubbard had already developed an interest in the human unconscious and explored this topic in his most famous work, *Dianetics*, which was published in 1950.

SCIENTOLOGY TIMELINE

1911— LRH born on March 13 in Tilden, Nebraska

1924— Lives in state of Washington

1927— Visits China—1927–28 (father in Guam)

1929— Studies at Swavely Prep School in Virginia

1930— Attends Woodward School for Boys

     Joins Marine Reserve in May (discharged October 22, 1931)

     Studies at George Washington University

1933— Marries Margaret Louise Grubb on April 13

1934— Career begins in pulp fiction writing

     Birth of LRH, Jr. (May 7)

1938— Writes non-fiction work called *Excaliber*

1941— War duty through April 1945

1945— Meets Jack Parsons in California

1946— Marries Sara Northrup on August 10

1947— Divorced from first wife on December 24

1950— Birth of Alexis Valerie Hubbard on March 8

     Dianetics published

1951— Divorce from Sara

1952— Marries Mary Sue Whipp

1954— Church of Scientology founded on February 18

1959— LRH, Jr. leaves Scientology

1960— Birth of David Miscavige (April 30)

1962— LRH writes JFK

1963— FDA raids Washington Church on January 4

1965— Australia bans Scientology

1966— British Inquiry

     John McMaster becomes the first Clear

     Guardian's Office founded

     Narconon (anti-drug) Program launched

1967— Sea Organization created

1968— Release of OT IV-VII (OT VII was not released until 1970)

1969— Citizens Commission on Human Rights founded

1970— Celebrity Center opened

1971— Death of Susan Meister
     John Foster report
     Paulette Cooper, *The Scandal of Scientology*
1972— Applied Scholatics founded
1973— Rehabilitation Project Force established
     FDA returns seized material to church
1975— Flag Offices formerly at sea relocated to Clearwater
1976— Suicide of Quentin Hubbard
1977— FBI raid on Scientology offices on July 7
1978— Gilman Hot Springs property purchased
     Hubbard writes training films
1980— *St. Petersburg Times* does series on Scientology
     Hubbard releases *The Way to Happiness*
     Reader's Digest article against Scientology
1981— Gerry Armstrong leaves church
1982— Management crisis and reorganization
     Religious Technology Center incorporated
     Battlefield Earth published
1983— Raid on Toronto church in March
     Australia recognizes Scientology as religion
     LRH, Jr. interview in *Penthouse* magazine
1984— IRS rules against church on tax exemption
     Say No to Drugs program started
1986— LRH dies at 8 P.M. Friday, January 24
     Release of Hubbard's *The Road to Freedom* music album
     Lawrence Wollersheim wins court case
1988— OT VIII released
     Cruise ship *Freewinds* used for OT VIII training
     Association for Better Living and Education (ABLE)
     founded
1990— *Los Angeles Times* does six-part series
     Narconon New Life Center opens in Chilocco, Oklahoma
     Jon Atak's *A Piece of Blue Sky* published
1991— *Time* cover story on Scientology by Richard Behar (May 6)
     David Miscavige meets with IRS Commissioner
1992— Ted Koppel interviews Miscavige on *Nightline*
     Celebrity Center reopened in Hollywood

1993— IRS grants tax-exempt status to all church corporations
Fishman court exhibit includes sacred documents
John Travolta launches Drug-Free Marshal program
1994— Vicki Aznaran settles lawsuit with church
1995— Death of Lisa McPherson
1996— Karin Spaink wins Internet case
1997— *Wall St. Journal* reports on IRS tax settlement
Supreme Court of Italy recognizes Scientology as religion
Miscavige interview in *St. Petersburg Times* (October 25)
1999— British government denies charity status to Scientology
Sweden grants Scientology recognition as a religion
2000— Keith Henson charged with bomb threat
Lisa McPherson's death ruled accidental
2002— New Zealand and Austria recognize Scientology
Former leader Steve Marlow leaves church
2004— McPherson civil case settled
Marty Rathbun defects
2005— Media storm over Tom Cruise's attack on psychiatry
Marc Headley and Jeff Hawkins leave church
"Trapped in the Closet" *South Park* episode (November 6)
2006— Janet Reitman writes "Inside Scientology" for *Rolling Stone*
"The Return of Chef" on *South Park* (March 22)
2007— Keith Henson arrested and serves brief time in jail
Scientology recognized as religion in Spain and Portugal
Mike Rinder leaves church
2008— Church issues statement against Andrew Morton's
biography of Tom Cruise
Jenna Miscavige goes public against church
Project Chanology holds public protests against church
(February 10)
Actor Jason Beghe leaves church
Church attacks Anonymous rallies

During Hubbard's tenure as Church of Scientology leader, government agencies in the United States, England, and Australia investigated the church. Hubbard founded the Guardian's Office (GO) in 1966 to protect the church. The GO engaged in illegal activities in the 1970s that resulted in a massive FBI raid on the church on July 7, 1977. Several top Scientologists went to jail, including Hubbard's wife, Mary Sue. Following the trial, the Guardian's Office (GO) was replaced with the Office of Special Affairs (OSA). Hubbard died in 1986.

Chapel at London, UK, headquarters

Photo: John A. Raineri; courtesy of the Church of Scientology

New Leadership

Under its current leader, David Miscavige, the Church of Scientology has enjoyed major gains and suffered significant setbacks. Scientology was featured in a major exposé by *Time* magazine in 1991 but won tax exemption from the IRS in 1993. Two years later, the death of church member Lisa McPherson at the Scientology headquarters in Clearwater, Florida, created enormous controversy. Her death was ruled accidental in 2000.

Hollywood stars have brought prestige to Scientology, though Tom Cruise created enormous negative publicity in the summer of 2005 because of his attack on psychiatry.

Scientology claims that humans are spiritual beings. This is expressed in the belief that we are more than mind and body. Scientology teaches that human beings are really *thetans*, a term expressing the belief that humans are immortal. A complex set of causes has blocked our knowledge of our true identity as thetans. Scientology calls the path of freeing the spirit/thetan of its encumbrances and reaching its true potential the "bridge to total freedom."

One of the goals along the bridge to total freedom is to become "clear." This state is reached through a dual process of taking Scientology classes and engaging in a process of counseling called "auditing." In these auditing sessions Scientologists use a device known as an *e-meter*, which they believe keeps track of the workings of the inner spirit (or thetan). After a person has reached "clear," instruction and counseling continue to assist him or her to attain the ultimate goal: becoming an *Operating Thetan* (OT).

Currently, Scientology offers eight levels of OT. Scientologists view all of the documents of instructional material related to OT as confidential and sacred. The church has sought to keep this material off the Internet.

L. Ron Hubbard

Photo: Courtesy of the Church of Scientology

HUBBARD'S OCCULT CONNECTION

One of the most famous and controversial incidents in the life of L. Ron Hubbard relates to his contact with the famous rocket scientist and occultist Jack Parsons (1914–52), who was born in Pasadena, California, and spent most of his life there, working for Cal Tech. Parsons was fascinated with rockets at an early age and became one of the most important figures in the history of jet propulsion.

Hubbard was introduced to Parsons in August 1945. Their relationship was complicated almost immediately because Parsons's girlfriend, Sarah Northrup, fell in love with Hubbard. Parsons was torn between his very liberal policies about sex and his intense jealousy. In spite of his emotions, Parsons allowed Hubbard into his occult ideology and practice. Parsons was a devoted follower of Aleister Crowley, the famous British occult master.

Hubbard served as scribe in January 1946 during Magick rituals performed by Parsons. Hubbard also took an active part in some rituals during March of the same year. In April Hubbard and Sarah left for Florida and took $10,000 from Allied Enterprises, a company that Hubbard, Sarah, and Parsons had started. In June Parsons tracked down the pair and sued Hubbard in Dade County, Florida Circuit Court. The court ordered Hubbard to pay the rocket scientist's legal fees. Hubbard and Sarah married in August 1946, even though Hubbard did not divorce his first wife until the following year.

The church explains the Parsons saga by maintaining that Hubbard was sent by Navy intelligence to investigate Parsons. Parsons died on June 17, 1952, as a result of an explosion at his home.

For further reading see John Carter, *Sex and Rockets: The Occult World of Jack Parsons* (Los Angeles: Feral House, 2004).

Analyzing Scientology

The battle over Scientology is so nasty that careful analysis is necessary to sort through false claims, wild rhetoric, and biased views. However, despite the controversy, five things are clear in terms of overall reaction to Scientology. First, in spite of what some critics argue, it is obvious that Scientology is a religion, a fact seen clearly in the zeal and commitment of its members. Second, the fact that Scientology is a religion should not stop critique of its failings, particularly in abuses connected with the Rehabilitaton Project Force. Third, the sacred texts of the Church of Scientology should be granted standard copyright protection. Fourth, Scientologists deserve to be granted the same freedom to exercise their religion as members of other faiths. Fifth, critics of Scientology should have the liberty to exercise free speech against Scientology.

SCIENTOLOGY 101

- Man is a spirit (thetan) with body and mind.

- Human survival includes eight dynamics or drives:

  1. Self: the drive to survive as an individual

  2. Creativity: the urge for family, sex, and children

  3. Group: the urge to form group identity

  4. Species: the drive to continue as a species

  5. Life Forms: the urge to survive as living realities

  6. Physical Universe: the drive for the physical to continue

  7. Spiritual Dynamic: the urge to survive as spiritual being

  8. Infinity: the urge to know the Supreme Being (God, the infinite)

- The thetan is eternal and beyond both body and mind.

- Scientology procedures bring humans to the state of Clear.

- The highest goal for a human is to become an Operating Thetan.

- Auditing sessions form the key tool in spiritual analysis and growth.

- Humans often experience their past lives through auditing.

- Humanity needs a drug-free and psychiatry-free world.

- The Sea Org is the fraternal body of full-time Scientologists.

- The Religious Technology Center is the fundamental church authority.

- L. Ron Hubbard is the founder of the Scientology religious philosophy.

Ultimately, Scientology is a modern form of Gnosticism. Though Scientologists claim no incompatibility with Christian faith, this new religion essentially offers an alternative understanding of reality. This can be seen along several important lines.

First, Scientologists base their philosophy on the writings of L. Ron Hubbard rather than on the documents of the Bible.

Second, Scientology material clearly shows that Hubbard, not Jesus, is viewed as the ultimate bearer of truth.

Third, Scientology offers a different understanding of humanity in terms of origin, history, and salvation. Scientologists believe in past lives, for example, contrary to historic Christianity. Likewise, the Scientology bridge to freedom is not anchored in the death of Christ as atonement.

Fourth, the esoteric/secret documents of Scientology illustrate a non-Christian metaphysic. The reader can see this in Hubbard's own handwriting when he gave instruction about a being called Xenu in the Operating Thetan III material. While Scientologists have the right to view the hidden material as sacred, critics have equal right to raise questions about the validity of such.

Finally, the absence of Jesus in Scientology discourse is further proof of the distinction that must be made between Scientology and Christian faith. Ultimately, one has to choose between the paradigm of L. Ron Hubbard and Jesus in relation to life's meaning, human identity, and the path of liberation.

Anonymous rally, London, UK

Photo: Paul Williams

SCIENTOLOGY

Typology	Western Esoteric
Websites	Scientology: www.scientology.org Religious Technology Center: www.rtc.org L. Ron Hubbard: www.lronhubbard.org Dianetics: www.dianetics.org Narconon: www.narconon.org Freedom Magazine: www.freedommag.org
Critical Websites	*Special Note:* I have listed below the most famous sites critical of Scientology. While I share many of the concerns of critics, I urge readers to be cautious in accepting the claims of critics and the counterclaims of Scientology without further study. The battle over Scientology is so nasty that careful analysis is necessary to sort through false claims, wild rhetoric, and utterly biased views. Operation Clambake (Andreas Heldal-Lund): www.xenu.net Secrets of Scientology (Dave Touretzky): www-2.cs.cmu.edu/~dst/Secrets/ Exposing the Con (Arnie Lerma): www.lermanet.com Tilman Hausherr: http://home.snafu.de/tilman/ Stop Narconon: http://stop-narconon.org/ About Lisa McPherson: www.lisamcpherson.org/ Gerry Armstrong: www.gerryarmstrong.org Fact Net: www.factnet.org Steve Fishman: www.xs4all.nl/~fishman Xenu TV (Mark Bunker): http://xenutv.bogie.nl Narconon Exposed (Chris Owen): www-2.cs.cmu.edu/~dst/Narconon Ask the Scientologist: http://askthescientologist.blogspot.com/ A.R.S. Webpage Summary: www.altreligionscientology.org Ex-Scientology Kids: www.exscientologykids.com Counterfeit Dreams (Jeff Hawkins): http://counterfeitdreams.blogspot.com/ Wikipedia on Scientology: http://en.wikipedia.org/wiki/Scientology Ex-member John Peeler: http://bts2free.blogspot.com/
Recommended Reading from Scientology	L. Ron Hubbard, *Scientology: A New Slant on Life* (Los Angeles, CA: Bridge Publications, 2007) *The Scientology Handbook* (Los Angeles, CA: Bridge Publications, 1994) *What Is Scientology?* (Los Angeles, CA: Bridge Publications, 1998)
Other Reading	Jon Atack, *A Piece of Blue Sky* (New York: Lyle Stuart, 1990) Stewart Lamont, *Religions Inc.* (London: Harrap, 1986) James Lewis, ed., *Scientology* (New York: Oxford, 2009) J. Gordon Melton, *The Church of Scientology* (Salt Lake: Signature, 2000) Russell Miller, *Bare-faced Messiah* (New York: Henry Holt, 1987)

17

SIKHISM

Gurdwara, Abbotsford, British Columbia, Canada

Photo: Derek Beverley

The Sikh faith is traced to the work of Guru Nanak (1469–1539), an Indian spiritual reformer, who paved the way for the emergence of a new world religion in what is now northern India. Nanak, who lived about the same time as Martin Luther, offered an alternative to Hinduism and Islam. Sikhs believe that God has given Nanak and his nine successors the ultimate revelation of truth. This truth is embodied in the Sikh Bible, which is called the *Adi Granth.* All faithful Sikhs venerate and adore this volume, which is 1,430 pages long, and view it as the ultimate Guru.

Sikhs hold that there is one Creator God, who is not to be represented in images or idols. The Sikh's highest spiritual duty is to praise God, particularly in song and recitation of scripture, and to obey his commands.

Today faithful Sikhs are identified by appearance in terms of following what are known as the five k's: (1) *kes*: uncut hair, (2) *kirpan*: wearing of dagger, (3) *kara*: wearing of steel bracelet, (4) *kangha*: wearing of comb, and (5) *kachh*: wearing of knee-length shorts.

THE TEN SIKH GURUS

1. Guru Nanak (1469–1539)

2. Guru Angad (1504–52)

3. Guru Amar Das (1479–1574)

4. Guru Ram Das (1534–81)

5. Guru Arjan (1563–1606)

6. Guru Hargobind (1595–1644)

7. Guru Hari Rai (1630–61)

8. Guru Hari Krishan (1656–64)

9. Guru Tegh Bahadur (1621–75)

10. Guru Gobind Singh (1666–1708)

Major media accounts of conflict in the Canadian Sikh community have influenced popular impressions of the Sikh faith in recent years. There has been litigation in Canada over whether Sikh police officers can wear their turbans to work and whether Sikh children should be allowed to wear their ceremonial daggers (*kirpan*) to school. A debate in British Columbia over whether chairs and tables should be used in the Sikh temple created an international controversy. Most important, the crash of an Air India flight on June 22, 1985, raised questions about the militancy of the international Sikh community.

Some of the tensions related to Sikh identity were readily resolved. The RCMP, Canada's national police force, suffered no great loss when Sikh officers were granted the right to wear the turban. The debate over using tables was settled when Giani Rattan Singh of Surrey, British Columbia, repented of this radical departure from the traditional Sikh custom of everyone sitting on the floor of the temple.

Sikh flag

Photo: Derek Beverley

The question of violence and Sikhism is more complicated. First, the Air India crash was just one dreadful part of a broader conflict between militant Sikhs and Hindus that reached its apex twenty-five years ago. On June 5, 1884, the Indian government ordered a raid on the Sikh Golden Temple, a military action that left many dead. That led to the assassination of Prime Minister Indira Gandhi by two of her Sikh bodyguards. This in turn led to widespread attacks on Sikhs all across India.

Second, these recent episodes of violence in the Sikh world must be seen in the larger context of Sikh history. Some of Nanak's religious claims put him at odds with some Hindus and Muslims. These religious differences led eventually to political hostility and military campaigns against Sikhs. This trail of oppression and bloodshed led Sikhs to adopt a militant stance against enemies, first Hindu authorities, then Muslim, then British. Of course, it needs to be remembered that military conflicts were episodic. There was often peace between Sikhs and the various ruling parties in northern India.

Sikhs believe that the violence in their tradition does not represent the essence of Sikhism. Essentially, Sikhism involves the adoption of the spiritual teachings of the ten gurus. They place great emphasis on the miracle stories connected with Nanak and several of the other gurus. Scholars who question the historicity of these miracles are viewed as subversive. W. H. McLeod, one of the greatest modern scholars of Sikhism, has been subject to intense verbal attack for his critical questioning of various Sikh traditions. According to orthodox Sikhs, questions should not even be raised about either the original text of the Sikh Bible or the reports of supernatural events in the life of Nanak and other Sikh gurus.

Guru Nanak opposed the Hindu caste system to a great degree and he also objected to the Muslim emphasis on pilgrimage to Mecca. He did retain the Hindu doctrine of karma and reincarnation. Sikhs believe that the human's earthly life represents an opportunity to escape the cycle of death and rebirth. Though Sikhism places great significance on the work of the ten gurus, there is generally no clergy class in the religion. An organizational body known as the SGPC or Shrimani Gurudwara Prabandhah Committee, based in Amritsar, India, settles issues in belief and practice, at least for the majority of Sikhs who acknowledge its authority.

Golden Temple, Amritsar, India

Photo: Jim Beverley

RULES FOR SIKH LIVING

- A Sikh should pray to God before launching off on any task.

- Learning Gurmukhi (Punjabi in Gurmukhi script) is essential for a Sikh.

- A Sikh should, in no way, harbor any antipathy to the hair of the head with which his child is born.

- A Sikh must not take hemp (cannabis), opium, liquor, tobacco, in short any intoxicant.

- Piercing of the nose or ears for wearing ornaments is forbidden for Sikh men and women.

- A Sikh should not kill his daughter, nor should he maintain any relationship with a killer of a daughter.

- The true Sikh of the Guru shall make an honest living by lawful work.

- A Sikh shall regard a poor person's mouth as the Guru's cash offerings box.

- A Sikh should not steal, form dubious associations, or engage in gambling.

- He who regards another man's daughter as his own daughter, regards another man's wife as his mother, has coition with his own wife alone, he alone is a truly disciplined Sikh of the Guru.

- A Sikh, when he meets another Sikh, should greet him with *Waheguru ji ka Khalsa, Waheguru ji ki Fateh* [The Khalsa is Waheguru's; victory too is His!]. This is ordained for Sikh men and women both.

- It is not proper for a Sikh woman to wear a veil or keep her face hidden by veil or cover.

- For a Sikh, there is no restriction or requirement as to dress except that he must wear Kachhehra and turban.

—From the *Rehat Maryada* (Code of Conduct), 1945

In the last century Sikhs have maintained significant unity. However, this came as a result of the weakening of Sikh traditions and groups opposed to the powerful Tat Khalsa movement that came to dominate Sikh life at the end of the nineteenth century. The Tat Khalsa leaders won control of the Golden Temple and the other major centers of Sikh life in India. Other Sikh traditions continued in spite of Tat Khalsa power, and the twentieth century witnessed the emergence of a few new Sikh groups. The most controversial is probably the 3HO (the Healthy, Happy, Holy Organization), founded by Yogi Bhajan, who died in October 2004.

Sikh life centers on the *gurdwaras* (the term for places of worship), which are open to anyone willing to obey simple rules. Shoes are to be removed and feet are to be washed before entering the gurdwara. Respect is to be given to the *Adi Granth* that is placed in the gurdwara every morning.

The spiritual center of Sikh life is the beautiful Golden Temple in Amritsar, India. I visited the Temple one evening and also the next afternoon in the summer of 2000 while I was doing research in India. I saw firsthand the famous provision of free food for all visitors and also witnessed the procession of the Sikh Bible being stored away for the night.

▓ Sikhism Q&A

1. Is the Sikh Bible like the Christian Bible?

The *Adi Granth* reads largely like the Old Testament psalms. There is little historical narrative or doctrinal exposition.

2. Was Guru Nanak a real historical figure?

Yes. There is no reason to doubt that he existed. However, the miracle traditions about him are very unreliable.

3. Who is the best scholar to read on Sikhism?

W. H. McLeod is considered by many academics to be the greatest and most influential modern scholar of Sikhism. However, many traditional Sikhs view McLeod with deep suspicion because he questions the historical reliability of various Sikh traditions, particularly concerning Guru Nanak.

4. Why did Sikhs get so upset about chairs and tables being used in the Sikh gurdwaras in British Columbia?

This went against the centuries-old tradition of having everyone sit on the floor as a sign of equality.

5. Why do Sikhs follow the five k's?

Sikhs believe God has commanded these customs.

6. What do Sikhs think of Jesus?

Most Sikhs respect Jesus. However, they give ultimate loyalty to the ten gurus and to the *Adi Granth*.

7. Is it fair to be suspicious of Sikhism as a violent religion?

While there is a deep militancy in Sikh history and ideology, Sikhs have often been attacked unjustly, especially in the eighteenth and nineteenth centuries. Sikh teaching allows for military response, and the gurus adopted a "just war" tradition. Just war theory involves the view that under special conditions it is morally right to use military force.

8. Do Sikhs really object to the caste system?

Sikh doctrine affirms all humans as equal before God without regard to a person's social status. Sikhs claim that this denial of caste is shown most clearly in the custom of shared meals (*langar*) at the gurdwara. However, this affirmation of essential human equality must be balanced with the recognition that Sikhs in India and elsewhere follow various social customs that involve caste distinctions. The same holds true for some Indian Christians who retain caste distinctions in spite of professed belief in equality.

9. How should Christians witness to Sikhs?

Witness should be respectful of the beautiful things in Sikh culture. This creates the proper setting for loving witness to what is the most important part of Christian faith: the Person and work of Jesus Christ. Christians have to remember that Sikh doctrine forbids the worship of Jesus as divine, so this represents one of the major stumbling blocks for preaching the gospel to Sikhs.

SIKHISM	
Sikh Websites	www.sikhs.org http://thesikhencyclopedia.com http://allaboutsikhs.com www.sikhnet.com
Recommended Reading	Hew McLeod, *Discovering the Sikhs: Autobiography of a Historian*. Delhi: Permanent Black (2004) _____, *Sikhism* (London: Penguin, 1997) Pashaura Singh and N. Gerald Barrier, eds., *Sikhism and History* (New Delhi: Oxford, 2004) Patwant Singh, *The Sikhs* (New York: Knopf, 2000)

18

UNIFICATION CHURCH

Sun Myung Moon speaks at Washington Times*'s 25th Anniversary, 2007.*

Photo: FFWPU International

On February 6, 2003, more than eight thousand Unificationists gathered in Korea to witness the second marriage of Sun Myung Moon and his wife, Hak Ja Han. Unificationists believe this event to be the fulfillment of the Marriage Supper of the Lamb described in the Apocalypse of John. At the same time Unificationists also witnessed the coronation of Moon as King of all Humanity. The followers of Sun Myung Moon believe that these events are crowning examples of the constant interplay between the drama of Moon's life and the unfolding events in the Spirit realm.[1]

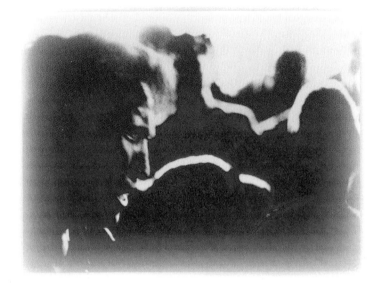

Moon in early years of church

Photo: FFWPU International

The Reverend Sun Myung Moon was born in January 6, 1920, in what is now North Korea. Moon's parents converted to the Presbyterian faith when he was ten years old. Unificationists believe that Jesus appeared to Moon on April 17, 1935, and that he was asked to fulfill the mission of Jesus. This began a nine-year period of spiritual searching for Moon, in the midst of study in Seoul (1938–41) and Japan (1941–43).

Moon was married for the first time in November 1943. His wife gave birth to a son in April 1946, and two months later Moon traveled to North Korea. He did not see his family for six years. He was arrested in 1946, later released, and then taken prisoner by Communist authorities in 1948. United Nations' forces freed Moon on October 14, 1950. He then began an arduous trek to the South and was eventually reunited with his wife and son in November of 1952.[2]

Moon's marriage ended in 1953, a result of the years of separation, his wife's lack of appreciation for Moon's spiritual calling, and the pastor's neglect of his wife. Moon officially launched the Holy Spirit Association for the Unification of World Christianity in 1954, though he had been preaching since 1946 and had gathered a small group of loyal followers.[3]

In 1959 Young Oon Kim, one of the most important Unification theologians, was sent to America.[4] The next year Reverend Moon married again, this time to Hak Ja Han, the young daughter of a devoted follower. Mrs. Moon was born on January 6, 1943, and has given birth to thirteen children. She is known as True Mother and has exercised increasing influence in the Unification Church.

Moon visited the United States in 1965 and toured various states, paying particular attention to his encounter with the famous medium, Arthur Ford. Ford claimed to receive messages from his spirit guide, "Fletcher," about Moon's significance, though the medium did not endorse explicit claims about the alleged uniqueness of Moon. The sessions show a conflict between Moon's exclusivism and Ford's more inclusive esotericism.[5]

Reverend Moon moved permanently to the United States in December 1971. The church received notoriety for its giant rallies at Madison Square Garden (September 18, 1974), Yankee Stadium (June 1, 1976), and the Washington Monument (September 18, 1976), while Moon became one of the most visible targets of the anti-cult movement. His followers were often subject to kidnapping and deprogramming.[6]

The United States government charged Moon with income tax evasion on October 15, 1981. Though powerful religious groups protested Moon's indictment, the Korean leader was found guilty and sentenced to eighteen months in prison. He began serving his sentence in Danbury, Connecticut, in the summer of 1984 and was released from a Brooklyn halfway house on August 20, 1985. Moon viewed his trial and imprisonment with serenity and received significant sympathy during his time in custody.[7]

Young Oon Kim, first missionary to America

Photo: FFWPU International

Moon's followers were elated with Moon's meetings with Mikhail Gorbachev on April 11, 1990, and with North Korean leader Kim Il Sung in November 1991. These strategic meetings were viewed as evidence of Moon's complete supremacy over Communism. Moon took credit both for the fall of the Berlin Wall in 1989 and for the victory of the Allied Forces in the Persian Gulf War in 1991.

Since the mid-1990s Reverend Moon has invested heavily in the purchase of land and development of Unification projects in South America. New Hope East Garden, located in western Brazil, provides a vast site for educational and ecological work. The church has also purchased thousands of acres of land in Uruguay. Unificationists regularly visit both countries for spiritual exercises, though the South American projects have received less attention in recent years.[8]

In 1998 Nansook Hong, Moon's former daughter-in-law, published a devastating memoir about life inside the church titled *In the Shadow of the Moons*. In it, Hong accused her ex-husband Hyo Jin Moon of adultery, drug addiction, and physical and emotional abuse. Further, she claimed that Sun Myung Moon had an illegitimate child who was raised by another Unification family.[9]

Unificationists were shocked by the death of Moon's son, Young Jin, on October 27, 1999. Though police ruled his death a suicide, Reverend Moon proclaimed that the death was providential and that his son died as a "sacrifice" so that Satan could not make a direct attack on the True Parents.[10] Two years later a minor tempest swelled when Roman Catholic African Archbishop Emmanuel Milingo wed Unification member Maria Sung. Milingo later renounced the marriage after a private meeting with the pope and accused the Unification Church of brainwashing him.[11]

The Unification movement has survived these recent crises though Hong's book created considerable internal turmoil. However, criticism against Sun Myung Moon is met by most followers with complete confidence in what they believe God has revealed through his life. Moon's directions are obeyed as God's commands, even if these instructions reverse longstanding Unification traditions.[12] The key is trust in God's ongoing revelations to Moon and the theology given to him from the eternal realm.

Moon at early worship, Korea, 2007

■ Unification Theology

The Unification movement retains the outline, though not always the substance, of classical Christian doctrine. *Divine Principle,* the famous Unification "Bible," has been the centerpiece in Unification evangelism and in-house teaching. Academics have often overstated the importance of *Divine Principle.* Moon has always made it clear that his ongoing teachings and sermons themselves constitute the most important source of modern revelation.[13]

The Unification Church is committed to monotheism but does not adopt a Trinitarian understanding of God. Though Moon adopts the use of *Father, Son,* and *Holy Spirit* in his language about God, his sermons exhibit no interest in a Nicean understanding of God. Further, *Divine Principle* explicitly distances Unification doctrine from a classical understanding of the Son and the Spirit, though Moon constantly emphasizes his relationship with Jesus and his dependence on God's Spirit.[14]

Moon teaches that Satan sexually seduced Eve and then she engaged in sex with Adam before the providential time allowed by God. A ransom motif dominates Moon's interpretation of God's relationship with Satan. Satan has humans in captivity and God has to work within the boundaries of the protocol that exists between God, Satan, and humanity. The sins of the first couple extend to their blood lineage. God has been looking for a Messiah who would be the new Adam who finds a new Eve.[15]

Moon's understanding of salvation involves the redemption of humanity through the restoration of the family. This explains why he puts such great emphasis on the marriage ceremony ("the Blessing") as a central component in Unification ritual. Before Unificationists are married (usually in the famous mass weddings) they engage in the Holy Wine ceremony where they partake of wine derived from Moon's own wedding ceremony in 1960.[16]

Moon's more esoteric teachings about Jesus build upon explicit views given in *Divine Principle* that (a) Jesus was not sent to die on the cross, (b) Calvary was a secondary option that resulted largely from the disobedience of John the Baptist, and (c) the ideal plan for Jesus was to have found a true Eve to restore humanity. Part of the alleged success of Moon is that he has been able to provide a bride for Jesus in the spirit realm.[17]

Unificationists frequently complain that their teaching on Jesus is misrepresented. At an early scholarly conference on Unification theology, Lynn Kim contended: "We never ever say Jesus failed. That's put on us from outside. We don't ever talk of Jesus as a failure."[18] British scholar George Chryssides has defended Unificationists in his important work, *The Advent of Sun Myung Moon.* "Unification Church members often find themselves foisted with the belief that Jesus' mission was a failure. *Divine Principle* does not say this at any point, and UC members feel justifiably indignant when their critics persistently ignore their attempts to explain what they really believe about Jesus."[19]

The chief obstacle to this apologetic is the explicit teaching of the Unification leader himself. Moon stated in 1974 that he "must go beyond the failure of Adam, the failure of Abraham, the failure of Moses, the failure of Jacob, Moses and John the Baptist, and Jesus."[20] Moon has also objected to the prayer of Jesus in Gethsemane and his lament at Calvary that he felt forsaken by God. "Father does not accept Jesus' Gethsemane prayer, and the prayer of Jesus Christ on the Cross . . . he does not buy that kind of terrible statement."[21] Moon even contends that Jesus had a streak of selfishness in his walk with God, unlike the Korean leader.[22]

The traditional Christian view of the cross is being challenged in the recent call from Moon for churches to take down the cross. This campaign is being carried out through the American Clergy Leadership Conference and focus on Black church leaders.[23] This action is defended both on the basis of God's original ideal and the desire to remove a major stumbling block to Jews and Muslims. Andrew Wilson, a leading Unification scholar and a Jew, has argued "by emphasizing the act of rejecting and crucifying Jesus Christ, the cross sets up a high wall between those who accept Jesus and those who do not."[24]

Both the general contours and the specifics of the Unification system are defended by reference to the claim that God has given new revelation through and about Sun Myung Moon. This apologetic is adopted in the very first section of *Divine Principle* and is emphasized repeatedly in Moon's sermons. It also emerges in the alleged spirit revelations that have dominated Unification life in the last quarter century.

Unification palace in South Korea

Photo: FFWPU International

■ The Heavenly Ministry of an Ascended Son

Reverend Moon's second son, Heung Jin, sustained severe head injuries as a result of a car accident near Hyde Park, New York, in December 1983. He died in early January 1984. Moon claimed immediately that his son's loss was a providential act allowed by God in order to protect Moon's calling. "If the sacrifice of Heung Jin Nim had not been made, either of two great calamities could have happened. Either the Korean nation could have suffered a catastrophic setback, such as an invasion from North; or I myself could've been assassinated."[25]

Heung Jin was buried in Korea on January 8. Reverend Moon proclaimed a week later that his son had a new mission that freed him to travel between his spirit world and our physical world. Moon also proclaimed that Heung Jin became a leader to Jesus in the spirit realm and that he had assumed the role of "the commander-in-chief" to those who are unmarried in the spirit realm.[26]

On February 28, 1984, Heung Jin was married posthumously to Hoon Sook Pak, the daughter of Colonel Bo Hi Pak, one of Moon's top aides. Colonel Pak stated that his son-in-law's sacrifice "carries far greater importance than the crucifixion of Jesus Christ."[27] According to Moon, his son needed to be married in order to move from prince to king in the spirit realm. Hoon Sook was positive about her unusual marriage. "I will never forget in my whole life and for eternity this greatest honor of being Heung Jin Nim's bride, which I do not deserve."[28]

Shortly after the death of Heung Jin, Unificationists in different parts of the world claimed to be receiving messages from him. Most of the alleged revelations took place in 1984 and 1987 and were published in book form under the title *The Victory of Love*. In one message dated March 29, 1987, Heung Jin said: "If you are afraid of me or if you fear that I will give you a heavy burden you're like a baby crying at the feet of Santa. I have more precious gifts in my bag than Santa could ever have and today I wish to give to each one of you the tools that you need to build the Kingdom of Heaven."[29]

Revelations are also claimed from Saint Francis, Paul, Kierkegaard, and Jesus. The latter speaks both of his submission to Heung Jin and the True Parents. "I will show them that the Lord of lords and the King of kings and the king of glory is our precious Lord Sun Myung Moon and his beloved bride Hak Ja Han. They reign as king and queen of the entire universe. I, Jesus of Nazareth, known as the Christ, bow in humility before them. Any who will follow me must do the same."[30]

If the death of Heung Jin can be seen as a Calvary for Sun Myung Moon, Heung Jin's postmortem ministry amounts to a second Easter. To this day Heung Jin remains the central child in the ongoing life of the Korean Messiah. Heung Jin's messages from the spirit realm have been foundational to the Unification movement since his death in 1984, even as these revelations have been transmitted in rather unusual ways.

▓ Another Heung Jin?

In the summer of 1987 Unificationist leaders heard that Heung Jin had returned to Earth in the body of a church member from Zimbabwe. The Japanese missionary to Zimbabwe informed Chung Hwan Kwak, one of Moon's top aides, about the ministry of Heung Jin through the physical form of Cleopus Kundiona. In August 1987 Kwak traveled to Africa and met with the black Unificationist. In November "Black" Heung Jin came to America and met the Moon family at East Garden.

Takeru Kimiyama, a leading Japanese Unificationist, described the meeting: "Father and Mother were waiting in the reception area. Heung Jin Nim ran over to father and practically jumped into his arms, saying, 'Father! Father!' Then he embraced Mother tightly, crying, 'Mother! Mother!' He sounded like he was weeping."[31] Black Heung Jin led the church in revival meetings in New York, Washington, San Francisco, and other cities. Many Unificationists greeted him openly and wrote glowing testimonies about his positive impact on them. Other members, including some of the True Children, were skeptical of his claim to be the embodiment of Moon's deceased son. In fact, his greeting of his alleged parents was done in a manner oblivious to Korean custom and Unification protocol.

Reverend Kwak suggested a positive attitude about Black Heung Jin: "If you had a relationship with Heung Jin before, don't try to question him about your former experience together. Many small details of our experience on Earth are unneeded and forgotten when we go to the spirit world. We should have an open, humble, and penitent mind and accept him 100 percent."[32]

In his public meetings Black Heung Jin urged serious confrontation about sin in the movement, and members were given severe conditions for repentance. In this connection, there were complaints from some members about excessive physical discipline at the hands of the black Unificationist. There were reports about broken bones and of members being detained against their will. There were also complaints that Black Heung Jin had a legalistic understanding of sexual issues.

The biggest controversy surrounding Black Heung Jin arose from the beating of Bo Hi Pak, the father of Heung Jin's bride. Black Heung Jin disciplined Pak in a private session at the church's training center in Tarrytown, New York. Unificationists told me that Bo Pak was beaten so badly that he was unrecognizable. He required surgery to relieve pressure on his brain. Michael Isikoff of *The Washington Post* reported that Col. Pak was admitted to Georgetown hospital for tests for almost a week.[33]

Reverend Moon allowed Black Heung Jin to continue his ministry at conferences through the early part of 1988 and then told him to return to Zimbabwe. Later that same year it was clear that Black Heung Jin had distanced himself from the ideology and practice of the Unification movement. He reportedly impregnated the wife of the Japanese missionary to his country and taught that he was the Lord of the Second Advent and that Reverend Moon was a precursor to his ministry.

The Unification Church did not publish much material from Black Heung Jin. His counsel to the apostle Paul was included along with messages from the ascended Heung Jin in *A Victory of Love*. "Paul had resentment because some people said he failed. He did not fail; it was Peter who failed his mission. I told him, 'Paul, you did not fail.' He grabbed me and exclaimed, 'Is it really true?' And I assured him it was." Black Heung Jin also claimed that he had some direct words for John the Baptist: "You failed, but now you should just go ahead; help the dispensation of restoration. Don't sleep and don't cry about your head being cut off."[34]

■ Revelation for Ancestral Liberation

Though the Unification movement has never abandoned belief in the spirit realm, the debacle with Black Heung Jin created some unease about spirit mediums. However, since 1995 church members have been directed by Sun Myung Moon to pay particular attention to two different mediums that are in contact with Heung Jin and others in the spirit world. The first is Mrs. Hyo Nam Kim who receives messages from both Heung Jin and from Dae Mo Nim, the deceased mother of Hak Ja Han (Mrs. Sun Myung Moon).

Dae Mo Nim is actually the honorific title given both to Soon-Ae Hong (Hak Ja Han's mother) and to Mrs. Kim. Reverend Moon's mother-in-law was born on February 22, 1914. She was involved with several of the native Korean churches that had an influence on Sun Myung Moon's theology. She met Moon in 1955, joined his church, and saw her daughter married to him in 1960. She lived with the Moon family in the United States for many years. She returned to Korea in 1979 and died in early November 1989.

Workshop in London, UK. Spirit medium Dae Mo Nim on far left

Photo: John A. Raineri

After her death she was assigned a mission in the spirit realm by the True Parents. She was told to work with Heung Jin to help liberate the ancestral realm and subjugate Lucifer to God's plans. Mrs. Hyo Nam Kim was given the responsibility to be the earthly partner to Dae Mo Nim. Mrs. Kim was born on March 13, 1952, and was a relatively unknown figure in the church until her public ministry for Dae Mo Nim began in 1995.[35]

Mrs. Kim claims that she was chosen to work with Dae Mo Nim in 1979. After Dae Mo Nim's death, Mrs. Kim passed a series of tests over a period of two years. She was able to find five sacred trees and a sacred body of water that were chosen by Reverend Moon as holy sites. She endured a forty-day prayer vigil without sleep where she made 10,300 full bows to Dae Mo Nim. She also had to plunge into icy cold water in the dead of winter in order to resist Satan. Mrs. Kim adopted a hairstyle to match that of Dae Mo Nim. Angels are said to have changed the color of her eyes to match those of her heavenly mentor.

Mrs. Kim leads renewal and liberation workshops at the Unification retreat center at Chung Pyung Lake in Korea. Reverend Moon has ordered all Unificationists to participate in her ongoing ministry. Moon believes that Mrs. Kim is helping Heung Jin and the heavenly Dae Mo

Nim work with his own mother (Choong Mo Nim) to redeem the souls of ancestors and to renew the lives of Unificationists on Earth. Church members are urged to liberate their ancestral lineage from demonic influence and from the toll of human iniquity that plagues generations. Details about one workshop said it costs $1,400 to liberate both sides of a family, though this figure only involves the first generation.

Mrs. Kim can be blunt as she engages in spiritual warfare. At one conference in England in 1998 she stated: "The children must be kept quiet! There are many spirits here out of your bodies yelling and screaming at me. When I get spirits out with the help of angels they try and come to plead their case; there are so many now out in front of me yelling and screaming, talking to me. I am talking to you but also to the spirits at the same time. The children are making so much noise; I am having a difficult time talking to you. Those of you with children who make noise: please calm them down or take them out."

She also offers very specific guidance about purity. "I see people wearing shirts so short that they are showing their belly buttons and trousers so long that they drag on the floor—our second generation should not do such things—we should look neat and clean. God is clean and pure and God is a beautiful God so we must keep ourselves clean and neat. So boys, young men should not have long hair; Satan likes that a lot. Also no earrings on the ears. You should make yourself look neat and clean so that God can love you."[36]

In a speech to husbands at Chung Pyung Lake Mrs. Kim warned of the danger of smoking and drinking. "For those who smoke, you must understand that the smell lingers, even years after you quit. It's in your skin, in your body, down to the bone. And you may not believe me, but both drinking and smoking lead to the sexual fall. Smoking creates such a low spiritual atmosphere and invites many low spirits. Smoking and drinking open up many holes in your spirit for satanic spirits to invade."[37]

Mrs. Kim's work gained particular fruition at the mass Unification Blessing held at RFK Stadium in Washington, D.C., on November 29, 1997. On that day she was able to work with Dae Mo Nim to liberate many ancestors from the spirit realm. The founders of the world's great religions were able to attend the ceremony, including Buddha, Jesus, Muhammad, and Confucius. In early 1999 Mrs. Kim sent 106 missionaries to America from the spirit world, including Aquinas, John Calvin, Martin Luther, Saint Matthew, and even doubting Thomas. Also, the Unification movement just announced that Mrs. Kim has dispatched angels to leading hospitals in the world to do research that can be used at the retreat center.[38]

Hyun Jin Moon, president, Unification Church International

Photo: Andrea Mozer

Heung Jin and a Scholar's Revelations

The second aspect of Unification spirit mediumship involves Dr. Sang Hun Lee, a famous Unification scholar who died on March 22, 1997. Immediately after his death Young Soon Kim claimed to be receiving messages from Heung Jin and from Dr. Lee. The first revelations from 1997 and 1998 were published in the book *Life in the Spirit World and on Earth* and include details about his death and his wishes for his immediate family.

The book also contains passing comments about details of life in the spirit realm, explanations of Unification doctrine, and records of Dr. Lee's meeting with leading religious and political figures. Lee tells Young Soon Kim that the cars used in heaven can move very fast based on thought projection. Unificationists have special privileges, and a prison holds those who have committed grave sins. Spirit beings cannot improve without help from their family members on Earth, a notion that fits with the ancestral liberation done by Dae Mo Nim.

According to Lee, Jesus is lonely in the spirit realm and will not advance to heaven until the True Parents arrive. Mary and Joseph are strangers to one another. Buddha regrets that he did not know about God, Lee states, while Confucius spends a lot of time in meditation in the snow. Muhammad was difficult to visit, Socrates was egotistical and argumentative, and Judas was resistant to talking. Eve admitted to Lee that she found Lucifer irresistible, confirming Unification teaching that Eve had sex with the fallen angel.

Lee also met with the former North Korean leader Kim Il Sung who told him that "North Korea will perish" unless his son learns to follow Reverend Moon. Lee found Karl Marx shouting Communist slogans while surrounded by shabby buildings and people "who looked like remnants of a defeated army." Lenin was plotting a revolution in the spirit realm, while Hitler was hanging naked on a tree, being attacked by angry mobs of former victims. *Life in the Spirit World and on Earth* also contains a letter from Jesus that states that he is not worthy of the love of Sun Myung Moon.[39]

The revelations from Dr. Lee have continued. In 1999 Young Soon Kim received a lot of material about and by Lucifer, including letters of repentance that were written to God. In 2000 Lee sent an elaborate set of new confessions from Saint Augustine. This was followed the next winter and spring by statements from four major religious leaders (Buddha, Confucius, Muhammad, and Jesus). In the summer and fall of 2001 Lee passed on messages from 120 Christian leaders that were released under the title "God Is the Parent of Humankind." (This ran as an advertising supplement in *The Washington Times*.)

Young Soon Kim also received a major report from Lee about a meeting he conducted on Christmas Day 2001 with the leaders of the five major religions. The fathers of Buddhism, Hinduism, Confucianism, and Islam met with Jesus to proclaim their total alignment with the True Parents. This document was translated from Korean into English and then published in July 2002 in some of the major newspapers of the world as "A Cloud of Witnesses." In 2002 Lee also sent messages from 120 Communist leaders and then from twelve journalists to record their endorsement of Moon. In 2003 the Unification movement released Lee's channeled messages from thirty-six deceased presidents of the United States, all testifying to their recognition of the truth and importance of Reverend Moon's life and message.[40]

The general theme of the entire corpus from Lee involves a multifaceted endorsement of Moon, expressed in unequivocal manner, making it abundantly clear that the Korean prophet is the true Messiah, the Lord of Lords, and the ultimate eternal answer to all problems, both on earth and in the spirit world. Though some Unification scholars have tried to argue for an ecumenical reading of these documents, their pleadings seem hollow in light of the dogmatic and exclusivist language of all the messages.

▧ Spirit Revelations and the Mind of a Messiah

How should Christians respond to these alleged revelations? Stanley Johannesen, a Canadian scholar, has made a point about Moon's *Divine Principle* that is relevant as a way of interpreting Sun Myung Moon. Johannesen suggested that the text of the movement is ideologically unstable and that it contains "a vast, and swiftly accumulating, burden of anxious responsibility." He worried that the book's "extraordinary demands on personality" could lead either to "the narcotizing of temperament in self-defense or the radical internalizing of cosmic mission in the form of compulsive, megalomaniacal work obsession with fantasies of superhuman personal significance and authority."[41]

While Johannesen hoped for maturation in Unification faith, his concerns bear scrutiny in relation to the issue of divine revelation through Moon's son and other mediums. The Korean Messiah reveals in his sermons and in the recent focus on spirit revelations an anxiety that illustrates an extraordinary demand on self, one that has manifested in terms of a "cosmic mission" that is compulsive and narcissistic, with constant assertions of "superhuman personal significance and authority."

The revelations from Heung Jin and the other Unification mediums have a compulsive tone to them and share an obsessive emphasis on defending Sun Myung Moon. In his sermons Moon is also too concerned about self-apologetic. He brags about his grasp of literature[42] and even boasts about his head size.[43] Moon claims that he could have won "dozens of different doctorates in different fields."[44] Moon asked this question in one sermon: "What if I did not exist? It would be as if all the world were here but were empty."[45]

In 1976 Moon told his followers: "I really keep the FBI busy trying to keep track of me. After the Washington Monument Rally their biggest question was what in the world I would do next. Even Satan is saying, 'What is Reverend Moon's next move? Where should I take my big guns?' But most important is that even God is asking, 'Where are you going next?' My plan is simple and clear, I am inexorably moving toward the absolute center of the universe."[46]

Scholars of Unificationism have in Moon's sermons a wealth of primary material about his understanding of self, particularly in relation to his belief in God's calling in his life. This self-understanding is mirrored in the spirit revelations from his son and other mediums. The picture of grandiosity that emerges in his sermons synchronizes with the unrelenting focus and apologetic given to Moon in the alleged communications from beyond. This is a pattern that contrasts both Moon's explicit commands to humility and the sacrificial and humble path chosen by most of his followers.[47]

■ Appeal of the Unification Church

At the height of what has been called "the great American cult scare" of the 1970s, the appeal of Sun Myung Moon and his church was often explained on the basis of brainwashing theories.[48] It is still commonly believed that certain religious groups known as "cults" recruit members through brainwashing techniques.[49] Eileen Barker showed in her work *The Making of a Moonie* that there is little to support brainwashing as a plausible theory for why people joined the Unification Church, or remained in the movement.[50]

Better explanations lie in the more mundane realities of religious and social life. First, many of Moon's unique ideas are rooted to some extent in the religious milieu of Korea during his early years. There were several groups contending that the Messiah prophesied in the New Testament would come from Korea. Second, Moon's first followers would have been drawn to his dynamic and passionate faith and to a visionary who endured torture and jail for his beliefs. Whatever one may say critically about Moon, he is an incredible survivor.

Converts to the Unification Church have often been introduced to Sun Myung Moon through an extensive series of lectures about the *Divine Principle*. This apologetic material would leave the impression, especially among the uninformed, that the Unification ideology was rooted in careful biblical study and the unfolding of progressive revelation. Moreover, Unificationists have always believed that Moon's life and mission clearly duplicated that of Jesus.

Beyond this, the Unification Church has always excelled at public relations and image. Church publications have constantly documented the fact that many of the world's leading academics have taken part in Unification-sponsored events. Moon has continually attracted famous politicians, clergy, media figures, and even Hollywood stars. *The Unification News* and *Today's World* picture Moon in poses with figures like Jerry Falwell and President George H. W. Bush. Ex-Polish leader Lech Walesa attended the Unification-sponsored World Summit on Leadership and Governance in Seoul in February 2003.[51]

George H. W. Bush speaks at Washington Times's *Anniversary. The newspaper was started by Moon.*

Photo: FFWPU International

Moon has obviously gained credibility through his many educational, media, political, and religious organizations. He achieved significant attention when he founded *The Washington Times* in 1982, as he was facing income tax charges by the United States government. He also owns the *Segye Times* (Korea) and *The Middle East Times* (Cairo) and took over

United Press International (UPI). He is the founder of the International Conference on the Unity of the Sciences, the Professors World Peace Academy, the Summit Council for World Peace, and the World Media Conference, among other educational and political enterprises.

He also started the Sun Moon University in Korea and the movement runs Bridgeport University in Connecticut. Moon is also credited with initiating the International Highway Project attempting to unite China and Korea and Japan. Moon has founded ballet and dance schools (most notably "The Little Angels" program) and is also involved in support of the World Culture and Sports Festival. He created the Women's Federation for Peace in Asia.

Critics of Moon often refer to the Unification "front groups."[52] Though Unification organizers sometimes hide Moon's connection, the diverse portfolio of the movement is best understood as a genuine attempt at addressing all aspects of life in terms of a Unification worldview. Unificationists receive strong justification for their faith in light of Moon's wide-ranging vision and also in relation to the incredible endorsements given by the leaders who participate in his multifaceted projects and conferences.

The 176-page volume *The Hope of All Ages* illustrates the apologetic power of Moon's projects. Released on the occasion of Moon's eighty-second birthday, the book contains elaborate commendations of Moon by political, academic, and religious leaders, including E. V. Hill (former pastor of Mt. Zion Baptist Church), Kessai Note (president of the Marshall Islands), Dan Quayle (former U.S. vice-president) and Dae Wood (Korean Buddhist priest and poet), among many others. There are several writers who argue that Sun Myung Moon should be nominated for the Nobel Prize for peace. The praise of the many authors is often directed toward Moon's vision as expressed in the conferences, organizations, newspapers, and educational institutions that he finances.[53]

Of course, the direct appeal of the Unification Church lies in the power of a utopian vision fostered by a dedicated and committed following. The movement's esoteric message is one of radical love for God, professed allegiance to Jesus Christ, openness to all religions, and deep commitment to solving the world's problems. In spite of his egocentrism and his anti-Christian teachings, Moon has inspired a generation of highly moral and loving disciples. Moon's followers are his best advertisement as they work tirelessly to obey their messiah's call to love and to serve.

UNIFICATION CHURCH	
Typology	Christian Sectarian
Founder	Sun Myung Moon (1920–)
Websites	Family Federation for World Peace and Unification: www. ffwpui.org True Parents Organization: www.tparents.org Unification Home Page (Damian Anderson): www. unification.net
Critic Websites	Craig Maxim: www.geocities.com/craigmaxim Allen Tate Wood: www.allentwood.com
Recommended Reading	Eileen Barker, *The Making of a Moonie* (Oxford: Basil Blackwell, 1984) James A. Beverley, "Spirit Revelation and the Unification Church," in James R. Lewis and Jesper Aagaard Petersen, eds. *Controversial New Religions* (New York: Oxford, 2005) George Chryssides, *The Advent of Sun Myung Moon* (New York: St. Martin's, 1991) Michael Inglis, ed. *40 Years in America* (New York: HSA, 2000) Massimo Introvigne, *The Unification Church* (Salt Lake: Signature, 2000) Nansook Hong, *In the Shadow of the Moons* (Boston: Beacon,1998)

Endnotes

1 This material on the Unification Church is reprinted by permission of Oxford University Press, Inc from James Lewis and Jesper Aagaard Petersen, eds., *Controversial New Religions* (New York: Oxford University Press, 2005). See my chapter in Ronald Enroth, ed., *A Guide to New Religious Movements* (InterVarsity Press, 2005).

2 For biographical data on Moon's early years see Michael Breen, *Sun Myung Moon* (West Sussex: Refuge, 1997

3 On the Church see Massimo Introvigne, *The Unification Church* (Salt Lake: Signature, 2000).

4 The most significant work on the American Unification movement is Michael Inglis, ed. *40 Years in America* (New York: HSA, 2000). The historical material is written by Michael Mickler, a leading Unification scholar.

5 For details on the Ford meetings, see my doctoral dissertation on *The Religious Teaching of Sun Myung Moon* (Toronto: University of Saint Michael's College, 1994).

6 See David Bromley and Anson Shupe, Jr., *"Moonies" in America* (Beverly Hills: Sage, 1979).

7 For a sympathetic portrayal of Moon's tax case see Carlton Sherwood, *Inquisition* (Washington: Regnery Gateway, 1991).

8 See Moon, "New Hope Farm Declaration," (April 3, 1995), available at www. unification.org. For critical perspectives on Moon's South American ventures see Tom Gibb, "Brazil Probes Moonie Land Purchases," *BBC News* (February 28, 2002), available at http://bbc.co.uk.

9 Nansook Hong, *In the Shadow of the Moons* (Boston: Beacon, 1998). See also James A. Beverley, "Moon Struck," *Christianity Today* (November 16, 1998). In a conversation I had with Nansook Hong in Toronto she reversed her opinion expressed in an interview with Mike Wallace that Reverend Moon was a con artist. Upon further reflection she stated that she thought he was totally convinced of his messianic status.

10 James A. Beverley, "Son's Death Shakes Up Unification Church," *Christianity Today* (December 13, 1999).

11 For details on the Milingo affair see the reports at www.cesnur.org and www. archbishopmalingo.org.

12 One of the most significant changes involved Moon's announcement at the church's 40th anniversary in 1994 that focus was to turned from the church to the newly founded Family Federation for World Peace and Unification.

13 In 1997 Moon announced the new tradition of Hoon Dok Hae in which disciples spend 6 A.M. to 7 A.M. every day in the study of the most important of Moon's sermons.

14 Moon's sermons are replete with references to his unparalleled obedience to God, but there are also frequent hints that God is fortunate to have Moon on his side. "I know I am the only person on earth who truly knows God and can comfort him. God has now said I have done enough and He told me to relax because He has been comforted by me, but that is the one command from God that I am defying." See Moon, "The Stony Path of Death" (April 27, 1980), p. 5.

15 See Moon, "CAUSA Seminar Speech" (August 29, 1985), p. 4.

16 Couples also participate in what is known as the Indemnity Stick ceremony. With roots in Korean shamanism, Moon mandates the couple to beat each other on the posterior. This physical discipline is to teach both the need for human involvement in the salvific process and the pain and humiliation connected with physical abuse. After the Blessing and a period of waiting, married couples follow a special Three-Day ceremony during which specific sexual positions are followed in order to reverse the impact of the distorted sexuality that brought humanity's fall. For analysis see Ed Mignot, "Married Rituals in Tongil," *Areopagus* (Trinity, 1989), pp. 36–37.

17 According to Moon, Jesus is the product of a sexual relationship between Mary and Zechariah, the father of John the Baptist. Joseph never discovered who was the real father of Jesus. Moon even claims that Mary and Joseph purposefully left Jesus behind in Jerusalem when he was visiting at Passover at age 12. Moon states in one sermon that Jesus was actually at the temple "because he was forsaken by his mother and father!" Moon adds: "The fact that Jesus could not get married was directly due to the failure of responsibility on Mary's part. How can Mary be a great woman?"

18 Lynn Kim, quoted in Darrol Bryant and Susan Hodges, eds., *Exploring Unification Theology* (New York: Rose of Sharon, 1978), p. 31.

19 George Chryssides, *The Advent of Sun Myung Moon* (New York: St. Martin's, 1991), p. 32. Chryssides's work is usually accurate but contains strained apologetics. His inadequate attention to esoteric literature is documented in my Ph.D. thesis. See James A. Beverley, *The Religious Teachings of Sun Myung Moon* (University of Saint Michael's College, 1994), 321 pp.

20 Moon, "Human Life" (December 1, 1974), p. 11.

21 Moon, "Address to the Prayer and Fast Participants" (July 29, 1974), p. 6.

22 Moon, "The Way Our Blessed Family Should Go" (August 28, 1971), p. 12.

23 See www.aclc.info for website data. Some Christian clergy have reported supernatural events in the removal of the cross from their churches.

24 Wilson, "Removing the Curse of the Cross" (Lecture at Unification-sponsored conference in Jerusalem in May 2003). Available at www.tparents. org.

25 Moon, "Let Us Go over the Hill" (February 7, 1984), p. 9.

26 Moon, "The Necessity for the Day of Victory of Love" (January 15, 1984), p. 12.

27 *Today's World* (January–February 1984), p. 7.

28 *Blessing Quarterly* (Winter 1984–85), p. 11.

29 *The Victory of Love* (New York: HAS-UWC, 1992), p. 42.

30 Ibid., p. 65.

31 See *Today's World* (January 1988), p. 28.

32 "Guidance from Rev. Kwak," *Today's World* (January 1988), pp. 26–27.

33 See *The Washington Post* (March 30, 1988).

34 *The Victory of Love*, p. 259.

35 The most detailed study on Mrs. Kim is found in Chang Skik Yang, "Understanding Dae Mo Nim's Earthly Activity" (4 Part Series at www. tparent.org).

36 Mrs. Kim, "The Chung Pyung Providence," Lecture at Cleeve House (December 1998).

37 Mrs. Kim, "Living a Life with No Shadows," Lecture at Chung Pyung (January 2002).

38 For full documentation on data about Mrs. Kim see the material under "Dae Mo Nim" at www.tparents.org.

39 See Sang Hun Lee, *Life in the Spirit World and on Earth* (New York: FFWPU, 1998).

40 The various documents from Lee can be seen at www.tparents.org.

41 See Johannesen, in Frank Flinn, ed., *Hermeneutics and Horizons* (New York: Rose of Sharon, 1982), pp. 310–311.

42 Moon, "Today in the Light of Dispensational History" (February 23, 1977), p. 13.

43 Moon, "Good Day" (July 3, 1977), p. 7 and "Day of All Things" (June 13, 1980), p. 7.

44 Moon, "The Blessing" (February 20, 1977), p. 13.

45 Moon, "Our Family in Light of the Dispensation" (March 1, 1977), p. 15.

46 Moon, "The Final Warning Concerning Good and Evil," (December 26, 1976), p. 9. Moon has even argued that God had finally learned the true meaning of love because of him. "God has to be educated. People will say that I am a heretic, but it is true. God doesn't know about love—He hasn't experienced it before. God has no sexual organs, so until a man becomes one with God, He cannot experience making love to a woman. Through me, God has done this." See Moon, "God's Day Morning Address" (January 1, 1990), p. 2.

47 For concerns about spiritual grandiosity, see comments in Dick Anthony, Bruce Ecker and Ken Wilber, eds., *Spiritual Choices* (New York: Paragon, 1987), pp. 69, 167–168, 190, 341.

48 See David Bromley and Anson Shupe, *Strange Gods* (Boston: Beacon, 1981).

49 For an example of recent scholarly exchange about brainwashing, see Benjamin Zablocki and Thomas Robbins, eds., *Misunderstanding Cults* (Toronto: University of Toronto Press, 2002). Also note Jack Hitt, "The Return of the Brainwashing Defense," *The New York Times* (December 15, 2002).

50 Eileen Barker, *The Making of a Moonie* (Oxford: Basil Blackwell, 1984).

51 For information on the program see the website of the Family Federation for World Peace and Unification at http://www.familyfed.org.

52 For a very helpful and extensive listing of such "front" groups see the data on the Unification Church at www.freedomofmind.com. The site features the work of Steve Hassan, an ex-Unificationist and one of the most influential exit counselors dealing with new religions. Other significant ex-member sites are at www.xmoonies.com (Craig Maxim) and www.allentwood.com (Allen Tate Wood).

53 Thomas G. Walsh, Gordon L. Anderson, and Theodore Shimmyo, eds., *Hope of All Ages* (Tarrytown: Interreligious and International Federation for World Peace, 2002).

19

WITCHCRAFT

(WICCA)

Stonehenge, United Kingdom

Photo: TD

Brooks Alexander states in his book *Witchcraft Goes Mainstream* that "the Halloween witch is dead" and has been replaced by an image of "a young, beautiful, sexually magnetic maiden who reveres Nature, honors a goddess, practices magic, and wields mysterious psychic powers." This transformation to a more positive image of witchcraft has taken place in the last two decades. Part of the reason for this change has to do with the powerful appeal of various Hollywood ventures (*Buffy the Vampire Slayer*) and the enormous appeal of the *Harry Potter* books.

The modern fascination with witchcraft creates the need for careful analysis, especially since stereotypes about the occult have had enormous impact for about eight centuries.

The subject of witchcraft covers an array of topics, many of them extremely controversial. What should one think of the inquisition against witches that dominated European society for four centuries? Do witches have special powers? Are modern pagans practitioners of evil? Are witches the same as Satanists? These are the issues explored in this chapter.

SELECTION FROM THE WITCHES' CREED
(DOREEN VALIENTE)

Hear now the words of the witches,
The secrets we hid in the night,
When dark was our destiny's pathway,
That now we bring forth into light.

The birth and rebirth of all nature,
The passing of winter and spring,
We share with the life universal,
Rejoice in the magickal ring.

Four times in the year the Great Sabbat Returns,
And the witches are seen,
At Lammas and Candlemas dancing,
On May Eve and old Hallowe'en.

The power was passed down the ages,
Each time between woman and man,
Each century unto the other,
Ere time and the ages began.

This world has no right then to know it,
And world of beyond will tell naught,
The oldest of Gods are invoked there,
The Great Work of magick is wrought.

For two are the mystical pillars,
That stand at the gate of the shrine,
And two are the powers of nature,
The forms and the forces divine.

The dark and the light in succession,
The opposites each unto each,
Shown forth as a God and a Goddess:
Of this did our ancestors teach.

And Do What You Will be the challenge,
So be it in love that harms none,
For this is the only commandment.
By magick of old be it done.

Types of Witchcraft

Nothing is more important in the correct understanding of witchcraft than to make careful distinctions about its various types. Since the Middle Ages it has been commonplace to believe that all witches are Satan worshipers who engage in ritual killing, sexual orgies, and various diabolical acts. This stereotype of the witch, which many evangelical Christians spread, continues today, both in secular and religious circles.

For the sake of accuracy, witchcraft should be understood in four different ways in relation to actual beliefs and practices in our world:

1. *Witchcraft* can refer to the practice of sorcery by witch doctors in pre-industrial, non-technological societies. This involves tribes in Africa and South America and also applies to practitioners of voodoo in Haiti and other countries. This type of witchcraft can involve actions ranging from the effective use of potions as medicine to gruesome rites like grave robbing and ritual killing of babies. In most cases, the witches who practice sorcery do not believe in Satan. Rather, they engage in rituals as part of their animistic worldview that is part of their tribal history and identity.

Starhawk, one of the famous contemporary pagan leaders

Photo: sofree roots

2. *Witchcraft* is also the term given to those who follow the pagan path idolized in *The Da Vinci Code.* Such witches worship gods and goddesses, honor Mother Earth, participate in covens, celebrate sexuality in their rituals, and follow the cycles of nature for their holy days. Such practitioners are often known as "white witches" because they do not believe in Satan and explicitly deny intent to harm anyone. These witches follow various traditions, both ancient and recent.

3. Some witches also call themselves Satanists. These witches follow "the dark side" and believe that true living involves self-centeredness and engaging in all the lusts of the flesh. This type of witchcraft is exemplified by Anton LaVey, the founder of the Church of Satan and author of *The Satanic Bible.* Though most people find it shocking, LaVey (1930–97) and his followers clearly deny that they believe in a literal Satan, as most Christians understand him. Rather, LaVey invokes Satan as a metaphor for a life in direct opposition to Christian principles of peace, gentleness, and love. Further, the Church of Satan denies involvement in satanic ritual abuse (SRA) or any other criminal acts.

4. Finally, some witches follow Satan, call themselves Satanists, and engage in satanic ritual abuse. These witches form a criminal element in various countries of the world. Usually such Satanists operate as loners or in wicked concert with a handful of others. Some serial

killers represent themselves as Satanists. In the 1980s it was popular to believe that Satanists killed 50,000 people every year in the United States. This satanic panic died down as law enforcement, including the FBI, and court officials failed to find evidence to back up such astounding claims. (I have examined this issue further in the chapter on Satanism.)

SELECTIONS FROM "PRINCIPLES OF THE WICCAN BELIEF"

- We practice Rites to attune ourselves with the natural rhythm of life forces marked by the Phases of the Moon and Seasonal Quarters and Cross Quarters.

- We seek to live in harmony with Nature, in ecological balance offering fulfillment to life and consciousness within an evolutionary concept.

- We conceive of the Creative Power in the Universe as manifesting through polarity—as masculine and feminine—and that this same Creative Power lives in all people and functions through the interaction of the masculine and feminine.

- We recognize both outer worlds and inner, or psychological, worlds—sometimes known as the Spiritual World, the Collective Unconscious, the Inner Planes, etc.

- We do not recognize any authoritarian hierarchy, but do honor those who teach, respect those who share their greater knowledge and wisdom, and acknowledge those who have courageously given of themselves in leadership.

- Calling oneself "Witch" does not make a witch—but neither does heredity itself, or the collecting of titles, degrees and initiations. A Witch seeks to control the forces within him/herself that make life possible in order to live wisely and well, without harm to others and in harmony with Nature.

- Our animosity toward Christianity, or toward any other religion or philosophy-of-life, is to the extent that its institutions have claimed to be "the only way" and have sought to deny freedom to others and to suppress other ways of religious practice and belief.

- We do not accept the concept of "absolute evil," nor do we worship any entity known as "Satan" or "The Devil" as defined by the Christian tradition. We do not seek power through the suffering of others, nor do we accept the concept that personal benefit can only be derived by denial to another.

—Council of American Witches, Minneapolis, April 11–14, 1974

The Da Vinci Code and Witchcraft

As amazing as it may seem, Dan Brown's best-selling novel *The Da Vinci Code* will be for some time the most significant book in shaping popular understanding about witchcraft. Occult themes surface frequently in Brown's writings. *The Da Vinci Code* is preoccupied with general pagan themes but also makes some very strident claims about witchcraft and Freemasonry. Brown's earlier novel *Angels & Demons* deals explicitly with the Masons and the Illuminati. How accurate are Brown's views on witchcraft?

Witches and the Vatican in *The Da Vinci Code*

The Da Vinci Code actually defends a theory about witchcraft both witches and Christians would find hard to believe. Brown argues that early, authentic Christianity was a version of pagan religion. This "true" Christian and pagan gospel has also been spread by witches, both ancient and modern. According to the novel, witches experienced the full wrath of the Vatican. This was "a brutal crusade to 'reeducate' the pagan and feminine-worshipping religions."

Frontispiece to
Heinrich Institoris'
Malleus Maleficarum

The Da Vinci Code then states:

The Catholic Inquisition published the book that arguably could be called the most blood-soaked publication in human history. *Malleus Maleficarum*—or *The Witches' Hammer*—indoctrinated the world to "the dangers of freethinking women" and instructed the clergy how to locate, torture, and destroy them.

Those deemed "witches" by the Church included all female scholars, priestesses, gypsies, mystics, nature lovers, herb gatherers, and any women "suspiciously attuned to the natural world." Midwives also were killed for their heretical practice of using medical knowledge to ease the pain of childbirth—a suffering, the Church claimed, that was God's rightful punishment for Eve's partaking of the Apple of Knowledge, thus giving birth to the idea of Original Sin.

During three hundred years of witch hunts, the Church burned at the stake an astounding five *million* women. The propaganda and bloodshed had worked. Today's world was living proof. Women, once celebrated as an essential half of spiritual enlightenment, had been banished from the temples of the world. There were no female Orthodox rabbis, Catholic priests, nor Islamic clerics.

The days of the goddess were over. The pendulum had swung. Mother Earth had become a *man's* world, and the gods of destruction and war were taking their toll. The male ego had spent two millennia running unchecked by its female counterpart.

COVENANT OF THE GODDESS CODE OF ETHICS

An ye harm none, do as ye will.

- Since our religion and the arts and practices peculiar to it are the gift of the Goddess, membership and training in a local coven or tradition are bestowed free, as gifts, and only on those persons who are deemed worthy to receive them. However, a coven may expect each of its members to bear a fair share of its ordinary operating expenses.

- All persons have the right to charge reasonable fees for the services by which they earn a living, so long as our religion is not thereby exploited.

- Every person associated with this Covenant shall respect the autonomy and sovereignty of each coven, as well as the right of each coven to oversee the spiritual, mental, emotional and physical development of its members and students in its own way, and shall exercise reasonable caution against infringing upon that right in any way.

- All persons associated with this Covenant shall respect the traditional secrecy of our religion.

- Members of this Covenant should ever keep in mind the underlying unity of our religion as well as the diversity of its manifestations.

- These ethics shall be understood and interpreted in light of one another and especially in light of the traditional laws of our religion.

PENANCE FOR WITCHCRAFT

"Have you shared the belief of many women in Satan's retinue? That during the silence of the night, after lying down on your bed and while your husband rests on your breast, you have the power to leave through the closed door, though you are a bodily being, and to traverse through space with other women who are like you? That you have the power to kill with invisible weapons baptized Christians redeemed by the blood of Christ; to eat their flesh after cooking it and to replace their heart with straw, or a piece of wood, or some other thing? That after eating your victims you have the power to revive them, or to give them a respite for living? If yes, 40 days fasting and a penance for seven years."

—Burchard of Worms, *Decretum*, Book XIX (A.D. 1008)

There are two major blunders in the novel's polemic about the Vatican attack on witchcraft. First, Brown makes a huge mistake about the scope of the Inquisition. Brown puts the number of deaths at five million, but historians who specialize in the study of witchcraft now consistently state that the number is actually no more than 100,000. Of course, this is a staggering figure but nowhere near five million. Modern witches have often placed the number at nine million.

Some pagan scholars are speaking out against the popular but flawed belief that millions were killed in "The Burning Times." Jenny Gibbons writes in "Recent Developments in the Study of The Great European Witch Hunt":

> We Neopagans now face a crisis. As new data appeared, historians altered their theories to account for it. We have not. Therefore an enormous gap has opened between the academic and the 'average' Pagan view of witchcraft. We continue to use outdated and poor writers, like Margaret Murray, Montague Summers, Gerald Gardner, and Jules Michelet. We avoid the somewhat dull academic texts that present solid research, preferring sensational writers who play to our emotions. For example, I have never seen a copy of Brian Levack's *The Witch Hunt in Early Modern Europe* in a Pagan bookstore. Yet half the stores I visit carry Anne Llewellyn Barstow's *Witchcraze*, a deeply flawed book which has been ignored or reviled by most scholarly historians.

Witchcraft vendor in La Paz, Bolivia

Photo: Neil Liddle

Brown's novel also significantly distorts the nature of the church polemic against the alleged witches. The attack was not about "the dangers of freethinking women" or really about female scholars, gypsies, priestesses, mystics, nature lovers, herb gatherers, midwives or "women suspiciously attuned to the natural world."

Richard Abanes points out in his reply to Dan Brown that the phrase "the dangers of freethinking women" is not, as the novel implies, a direct quotation from the notorious *Malleus Maleficarum*.

The Da Vinci Code spins a verbal web to make it look like persecution of witches was essentially an attack on female pagan scholars and female nature lovers. Dan Brown neglects to mention that the church also targeted males as witches. Further, nowhere in the novel do we read the fact that accusations against alleged female witches were often made by females. Of course, this correction against Brown's bias is not meant to deny the deeply misogynist impulses at work in the targeting of many females as witches.

Dan Brown has also adopted the faulty notion that midwives were special targets. Recent scholarly work has shown that being a midwife actually increased the chance of protection from accusation and trial.

The novel also misleads readers when it gives the impression that the assault on witches was basically an operation of the Vatican. Protestants were just as involved in the persecution of alleged witches. In fact, in some areas of Europe, Protestant leaders engaged in more killing of witches than Catholic inquisitors. This is not meant to deny the involvement of the Vatican.

Some Catholic critics of *The Da Vinci Code* have tried to whitewash the issue by arguing that witches were put to death by the state and not by the church. This is simply disingenuous, even though it is true that secular courts were often harder on witches than the Inquisition courts. However, no amount of denial can overcome the obvious fact that the Catholic Church engaged in the persecution, torture, and killing of witches. In 1484 Pope Innocent IV issued *Summis Desiderantes,* a formal document approving the work of Jakob Sprenger and Heinrich Kramer, the two authors of the *Malleus Maleficarum.*

The most significant fact to remember about the witchcraft craze is that church officials, both Catholic and Protestant, and lay Christians believed that witchcraft was real and that it was essentially about Satanism, radical evil power, and unimaginably wicked deeds. The *Malleus Maleficarum* and other similar treatises speak against witches who slaughter babies, have sex with demons, poison their neighbors, and bring plagues to countries.

To give an idea of the specifics involved, here is the record (obtained under torture) of Pierre Vallin, a Frenchman accused of witchcraft in 1438, taken from Jeffrey B. Russell's *A History of Witchcraft*:

> Pierre confessed to invoking Beelzebub. He had served the Devil for sixty-three years, during which time he had denied God, trampled and spat on the cross, and sacrificed his own baby daughter. He went regularly to the synagogue, where he copulated with Beelzebub, who had taken the form of a girl and where he and the other witches ate the flesh of innocent children.

TIMELINE FOR WITCHCRAFT TRIALS (1000–1800)

1008— Burchard of Worm's *Decretum*

1022— Heretics burned at Orleans

1144— Blood libel accusations against Jews (Norwich)

1140— Gratian's *Decretum*

1163— Persecution of Cathars in Cologne

1184— Waldensians condemned as heretics

1215— Fourth Lateran Council

1232— Pope Gregory IX (1227–1241), *Vox in Rama*

1324— Trial of Alice Kyteler in Kilkenny, Ireland

1368— Nicolas Eymeric, *Directorium Inquisitorum*

1384— "Luciferans" tried in Brandenburg

1400— Witch trials in Lausanne (Peter von Greyerz)

1428— Trials in Valais (Switzerland)

1430— Trial of Joan of Arc

1484— Pope Innocent IV issues *Summis desiderantis*

1486— Jakob Sprenger and Heinrich Kramer publish *Malleus Maleficarum*

1490— King Charles VIII issues edict against witchcraft

1532— *Constitutio Criminalis Carolina* allows torture and death for witchcraft

1542— King Henry VIII condemns witchcraft in statute

1547— King Edward VI repeals statute of 1542

1563— Queen Elizabeth I delivers statute against witchcraft

1563— Johann Weyer publishes *De praestigiis daemonum*

1566— Agnes Waterhouse executed

1580— Jean Bodin, *Daemonomanie des sorciers*

1581— Trials in the Archbishopric of Trier

1584— Reginald Scot, *The Discoverie of Witchcraft*

1590— Bavarian trials under Duke Wilhelm V the Pious

1590— North Berwick trials (Scotland)

1597— *Daemonologie* by King James VI of Scotland (later King James I of England)

1604— Witch Statute of King James I

1609— Case involving convent possession in Aix-en-Provence

1628— Johannes Junius, mayor of Bamberg, tried for witchcraft

1631— *Cautio criminalis* (Friedrich von Spee)
1632— Case of convent possession (Loudun)
1643— Convent possession (Louviers)
1647— Matthew Hopkins publishes *Discovery of Witches*
1652— Anne Bodenham trial
1674— Anne Foster trial in Northampton
1679— Beginning of *Chambre d'ardente* affair
1692— Witchcraft craze in Salem
1736— Statute of James I (1604) repealed
1787— Austrian witchcraft laws repealed

Another case Russell mentions involves a woman named Walpurga Hausmannin, who was burned to death in 1587:

> Arrested and tortured, she admitted to having intercourse with the Devil and making pact with him, riding out at night on a pitchfork, trampling on the consecrated host, keeping a familiar [evil spirit] named Federlin as a lover, manufacturing hail storms, and committing a long list of *maleficia* relating to her duties as midwife. She crushed the brain of Dorothea Wachter's baby while delivering it. She sucked the blood out of one of the twin children of the publican Kuntz.

What about the underlying premise of *The Da Vinci Code*: that those accused of witchcraft were actually practitioners of ancient paganism who were simply celebrating sexuality and the sacred feminine? Were the witches legitimate heirs of Isis, Artemis, Aphrodite, and Jesus and his wife, Mary Magdalene? Is this true? Most contemporary witches and pagans would not include Jesus and Mary Magdalene in the lineage of practitioners of the craft. Of course, this may change as pagans come under the spell of Dan Brown's novel. The interest in Mary Magdalene as the goddess of the early church has increased noticeably since the release of *The Da Vinci Code*.

In any case, many modern witches are beginning to realize the flimsy evidence for the belief that the rituals and traditions of current witchcraft extend back in history like an unbroken chain. In other words, one must make clear distinctions between the actual beliefs and practices of ancient pagans, the so-called witches of Europe and colonial America, and today's witchcraft community.

▓ Vampire Religion

Since the release of Bram Stoker's *Dracula* in 1897, vampires have increasingly captured the human imagination. This is illustrated in the last several decades by the success of various novels (Anne Rice, *Interview with a Vampire*), television shows (*Buffy the Vampire Slayer*), comic books (*Vampirella*), and even scholarly studies (J. Gordon Melton's *The Vampire Book*).

What makes the vampire theme most significant is that a growing number of humans claim to be vampires. Further, vampire life and ideology is being considered as a religious path. Internet sites provide details on how to get blood from donors, where to get the best fangs, and what are the best ways to handle "the Beast" (the inner urge to drink blood). Some vampire elders stress the "psychic-vamp path," that is, the alternative lifestyle of avoiding blood sports and simply feeding off of human energy. Individuals who are solely into role plays are known vampyres.

Self-professed vampires usually describe themselves as light-sensitive, prone to nocturnal living, susceptible to migraines, and capable of sensing the presence of other vampires. They also claim above-average strength and intelligence. Most vampires say that the essence of being a vampire is the need for blood: "We require blood to survive. Why this is I do not know, but it does not change the fact it is necessary. To feed charges a vampire—renews them, strengthens them, simply invigorates them and sets every nerve on fire." Vampires who use blood are known as *sanguinarians* (from the Latin root word for bloodthirsty) or as sang vampires. Blood is usually obtained through a donor and seldom involves biting on the neck.

Most vampires recognize they have an image problem. Michelle Belanger and Father Sebastian, two famous vampires, co-authored a thirteen-point code of ethics known as *The Black Veil*. It was even mentioned in an episode of *CSI: Vegas* that dealt with vampires. One of the codes reads: "Do not allow your darkness to consume you. You are more than just your hunger, and you can exercise conscious control. Do not be reckless. Always act with a mind toward safety."

Vampire elders actually warn that the vampiric life is very difficult. One famous vampire states: "There are far more depressed (and manic-depressive) vampires out there than healthy, happy ones. We're a horribly unstable lot prone to deep and even suicidal bleakness and tend to mostly suffer through various bi-polar-esque see-saws of stability. It's not easy fighting a primal, horridly powerful need to feed your Hunger." Night Angel, another vampire, writes: "This isn't something I want nor would I want it if I did not have it already."

Though some vampires claim to be Christians, the ethos of the vampire culture is basically antagonistic to the gospel. Generally, vampires who are spiritually inclined are more attuned to witchcraft and the New Age than to any form of Christian faith. Some vampires are openly hostile about Jesus. Many show a distinct preference for sadomasochism and the bondage scene. Often the blood rituals in vampire life take place as part of sexual encounters. The Temple of the Vampire is one of the more well-known groups for vampires inclined to religion.

VAMPIRES	
Typology	Western Esoteric
Websites	www.sanguinarius.org www.drinkdeeplyanddream.com http://sphynxcatvp.nocturna.org www.vampiretemple.com
Recommended Reading	J. Gordon Melton, *The Vampire Book* (New York: Visible Ink, 1998)

Witches Q&A

1. What is the popular stereotype of witches?

According to Jeffrey B. Russell, one of the great experts on witchcraft, by the end of the Middle Ages there were eight common beliefs about witches:

1. Witches flew in the night.
2. Witches had made a pact with the devil.
3. Christianity was repudiated.
4. Witches met in secret at night.
5. Witches desecrated the crucifix and the Eucharist.
6. Witches engaged in orgies.
7. Witches sacrificed children.
8. Witches took part in cannibalism.

2. Are witches Satanists?

Most witches are not Satanists, do not believe in Satan, and do not practice satanic rituals. Most witches perform rituals inherited from Gerald Gardner, the founder of modern witchcraft. Most witches do not believe that it is right to hurt other human beings. A few witches believe in using magic for selfish purposes or to seek revenge on an enemy.

3. What do witches want Christians to know about their beliefs?

According to Margot Adler, a leading author on witchcraft, witches want Christians to realize that modern paganism or witchcraft is not rooted in Satanism. Witches believe that their religion is rooted in ancient religions that offered unity with nature and union with the gods and goddesses behind creation.

Tomb of famous Voodoo priestess Marie Laveau, New Orleans, Louisiana

Photo: Gordon Melton

WICCAN RITUAL

Nineteen women, including a visiting Italian feminist and a well-known writer, sat nude in a circle in a darkened room. Molded candles of yellow hung by thongs from a loft bed. The small, bright flames cast a pattern of light and shadow. . . .

A bathtub was filled with cool water, scented with musk and flower petals. A flutist played soft music while the women, one by one, entered the water, bathed and were towel-dried by the others. There was laughter and a sense of ease.

After a short ritual a goblet was filled to the brim with wine and passed sunwise around the circle. The most powerful moment was yet to come; the pouring of libations to the goddesses and heroines of old. Each woman took a sip, then dipped her fingers into the wine and sprinkled a few drops into the air and onto the floor. As she did so, she invoked a particular goddess, gave thanks, or expressed a personal or collective desire. . . . The ritual ended with the music of drums and flutes.

Fruit was brought out and shared—a large bowl carved from a watermelon, filled with blueberries and pieces of honeydew and cantaloupe. There were plates filled with olives and dates. There was a foamy strawberry drink and a huge block of ice cream covered with berries and one large spoon. It was to feel transported to another age, some great festival perhaps, an ancient college of priestesses on a remote island somewhere in the Aegean. . . .

—Margot Adler, from *Drawing Down the Moon*

4. Do any witches want to be called Satanists?

Yes. Anton LaVey started the Church of Satan and proudly describes himself as a Satanist. He stated that the "white" witches are really hypocritical wimps. As well, Michael Aquino, the founder of the Temple of Set, is willing to be called a Satanist. Both LaVey and Aquino use the terms *witch* and *Satanist* to gain notoriety and attention. Both say that they do not believe in the literal Christian devil.

5. Do witches kill animals and humans?

Most witches or neo-pagans find the ritual killing of animals and humans completely abhorrent and would disassociate themselves from any witch who engaged in any such evil. Witches realize that some self-styled or psychotic witch might practice such destruction, but this in no way means that most or all witches endorse the mutilation and killing.

6. Why do witches perform their rituals in secret?

Actually, only some witches engage in secret ritual. Many covens meet in public and invite participants and observers. Other groups meet in secret because they believe that their knowledge is special and should be given only to those who are willing to be trained in the process of learning.

7. What is the appeal of witchcraft?

In an age of technology and science, witchcraft has an appeal like any other religion. It offers an explanation for life and it claims to offer communion with the deities behind creation. Witchcraft also offers a process to gain power and control in one's life, with the allure of becoming part of an elite and secret society.

8. Is witchcraft part of the New Age Movement?

While witches and New Agers agree in some of their basic beliefs, witchcraft offers a very specific part of the occult tradition. It is less public than the New Age Movement and offers much more specific rituals and practices.

9. Do witches have special powers?

While it may be true that some witches can perform miraculous events, most witches would probably suggest that they are simply in touch with the powers of nature. There is no need to resort to an overt demonic influence behind witchcraft unless there was proof that there was evil, supernatural power in operation.

10. Do witches cast spells?

Yes. Most engage in casting spells for good fortune and good health. A witch can cast a spell against someone who is being abusive or trying to bring harm. Generally, the pagan community states that negative spells should only be used as a last resort.

Ritual bowls used to mix potions for spells,
Occult Store, Toronto, Canada

Photo: Derek Beverley

11. How do we know that the average witch or neo-pagan is not part of a worldwide satanic conspiracy that engages in ritual murder, child abuse, pornography, drug smuggling, etc.?

The burden of proof here is on those who would argue for the existence of this conspiracy. Kenneth Lanning, who was for years the FBI specialist on Satanism, believes there is no hard evidence to support such an astounding claim. He also argues that sloppy rhetoric or exaggeration actually hurts the legal case against real cases of occult crime.

12. What can the average Christian do about local rumors about witches engaging in satanic activities?

Read some basic literature on witchcraft to be informed. Try to document specific allegations and concerns. Be willing to talk with the relevant members of the Wiccan community to allow them to answer concerns and accusations.

13. What do witches think of Jesus?

Most witches would speak of Jesus with respect, though it is obvious that their message is not in unity with the New Testament. Further, Christians need to remember that witches often have a deep antagonism toward Christianity as a religion, even as they speak highly of Jesus. Witches are usually pluralistic on the truth of different religions, and they do not follow Jesus as the only Savior and as the only Son of the eternal God.

14. Should Christians attend a witchcraft meeting?

No. The only exception would involve Christians who are trained to study the occult and are not tempted by witchcraft. Obviously, any Christian who attends a Wiccan coven, for example, should observe and not participate in the worship. This would follow the example of the apostle Paul when he witnessed pagan worship in Athens (see Acts 17:22–23).

KEY FACTS ABOUT WITCHCRAFT

- The Goddess is the central concept among witches.

- Some witches view the Goddess as a personal guide. Z. Budapest, a witch, states: "I relate to the Goddess, every day, in one way or another. I have a little chitchat with Mommy." (Budapest, in Adler, *Drawing Down the Moon*, p. 105)

- Witches often meet at *esbats*, the term for meetings on the full moon.

- Seasonal ritual meetings (Halloween, for example) are called *sabbats*.

- Typical covens have about a dozen members.

- There are three stages of involvement in a coven, from initiate to second degree, and then third degree initiation in either a symbolic or physical sexual ritual.

- The knife used in magic ritual is called the *athame*.

- During ritual, witches usually gather in a circle; maintain an altar; place candles at north, east, south, and west; and offer praise and petition to the goddesses and gods, which are often represented in the form of statues.

- Most witches come from a middle-class background.

- A decade ago significant debate arose among witches about dropping the "w" word: *witch*. Though the word is associated with evil and Satanism, witches have generally opted for retaining the word (with its sense of mystery and power) and fight to overcome what they perceive as gross misunderstanding.

- Witches often take the following initiation oath: "I . . . in the Presence of the Mighty Ones, do of my own free will and accord most solemnly swear that I will ever keep secret and never reveal the secrets of the Art. . . . And may my weapons turn against me if I break this my solemn oath."

- Witches debate whether the Goddess is objectively real or a symbolic way of relating to the modern world. Witches also debate the nature and extent of the power of their magic.

■ Aidan Kelly and Witchcraft Historicity

For nearly forty years Aidan Kelly, one of the leading witches in the United States, has studied the origins of the rituals modern Wiccans and neo-pagans practice. In his important and very controversial work *Crafting the Art of Magic*, Kelly argues that (a) Gerald Gardner, a British civil servant, invented modern witchcraft in 1939 and (b) witches are incorrect to believe that modern rites of pagans can be traced back to earlier times.

Though personally painful for Kelly to discover, his textual and historical research on the famous Wiccan text *Book of Shadows* shows that Gardner is its main author. It is not a magic ritual guide handed down through the generations, as many witches believe. While Gardner used material from Charles Leland, Margaret Murray, Aleister Crowley, and others, the evidence seems strong that the text of *Shadows* is largely a creation of the 1940s and '50s.

While some witches dispute Kelly's views, most witches now argue that their faith does not depend on the historical continuity of ritual traditions. While Kelly retains his commitment to Wicca (and liberal Catholicism), his research shows the mythic nature of Wiccan historical claims. While it is plausible that Gardner joined a group of witches who thought they had inherited pagan rituals, there is no strong reason to believe that their rituals were any older than half a century.

Kelly has also argued that Gardner included masochistic sexual practice in his coven rituals. While this is debatable, early Gardnerian covens engaged in sexual intercourse as part of the final initiation into the highest degree. Most covens have abandoned Gardner's interest in sex magic, though specific groups still adopt the practice of going "sky-clad" (nude) during ritual.

CHRONOLOGY OF MODERN WITCHCRAFT

1884—Gerald Brosseau Gardner born in England (June 13)

1889—*The Key of Solomon the King* published

1899—Charles Leland publishes *Aradia: Gospel of the Witches*

1890—Sir James Frazier publishes *The Golden Bough*

1908—Gardner moves to Borneo

1909—Aleister Crowley publishes *The Equinox*

1921—Margaret Murray publishes *The Witch Cult in Western Europe*

1929—Birth of Alexander Sanders

1929—Aleister Crowley publishes *Magick in Theory and Practice*

1936—Gardner settles in England

1939—Gardner allegedly initiated into a witch coven

1947—Gardner meets Aleister Crowley on May 1

1947—Death of Aleister Crowley (December 1)

1948—Robert Graves publishes *The White Goddess*

1949—Gardner publishes *High Magic's Aid* under pseudonym of Scire

1951—Death of Dorothy Clutterbuck (January 12)

1951—Britain repeals witchcraft laws (June)

1953—Doreen Valiente joins Gardner's group and becomes High Priestess

1954—Gardner publishes *Witchcraft Today*

1955—The *Sunday Pictorial* equates witchcraft and Satanism

1956—Violet Firth (aka Dion Fortune) publishes *Moon Magic*

1957—Fred Lamond joins Gardner's coven

1957—Valiente and Ned Grove leave Gardner's coven in summer

1962—Tim Zell and Robert Christie found The Church of All Worlds

1963—Raymond Buckland starts Gardnerian coven in U.S.

1964—Gardner dies

1964—Doreen Valiente initiated, by Robert Cochrane, into new coven

1968—Zell begins publication of *The Green Egg*

1969—*King of the Witches* published about Sanders

1971—Stewart Farrar initiated into Alexandrian coven

1972—Susan B. Anthony coven formed by Z. Budapest

1973—Tim Zell marries Morning Glory

1973—Raymond Buckland leaves Gardnerian movement

1974—Selena Fox forms Circle Sanctuary

1975—Covenant of the Goddess formed

1979—Margot Adler publishes *Drawing Down the Moon*

1979—Starhawk publishes *The Spiral Dance*

1983—Isaac Bonewits starts Druid group *Ár nDraíocht Féin* (ADF)

1984—*The Witches' Bible* published

1986—Five members protest ADF policies at Pagan Spirit Gathering

1988—Alexander Sanders dies

1991—Publication of Aidan Kelly, *Crafting the Art of Magic*

1997—*The Witches' Voice* Internet site started

1999—Death of Doreen Valiente

2000—Death of Stewart Farrar

Crystal ball and ritual products, Occult Shop, Toronto, Canada

Photo: Derek Beverley

▓ Christian Witness to Witches

1. Christian witness to the Wiccan community will be ruined at the outset if we follow the popular, and false, view that all witches are Satanists. We need to imagine what it is like for peaceful, loving witches to be accused of worshiping Lucifer and engaging in ritual murder. It would be very difficult for them to be open to the gospel from people making such wild and false claims.

2. Christian testimony must by rooted in gentleness and love. Most Wiccans believe in living in harmony with nature, with the earth, with all creation. Given this, and in light of the ruthless persecution during "The Burning Times," can the Christian church share the truth in kindness and love? Such gentle witness is also necessary given the dominant nasty interpretation of witchcraft among many Christians.

A POSITIVE CHRISTIAN APPROACH

"The pagans I have met differ in no wise from the rest of humanity. They also possess that God-shaped hole that leaves them empty and restless until filled by the one true God. Having seen the worst side of Christian polemics, they have little use of a merely verbal faith. But they are influenced by Christians whose lives have been changed by Jesus Christ and who manifest that change through the fruit of the Spirit. Having heard our words, they need to see our Christian love in practice."

—J. Gordon Melton, "A Christian Response to Witchcraft," *Christianity Today*, October 21, 1983, p. 25

3. Witchcraft ultimately fails in the mythic and legendary nature of its gods and goddesses. The Roman, Celtic, Nordic, and Greek deities dwell only in the followers' imaginations. The lack of historical trustworthiness concerning Artemis or Zeus or Diana or Isis is in direct contrast to the historical nature of the Gospel accounts of Jesus Christ.

4. Christians can remember the point that C. S. Lewis often made about the myths and legends from other times. While they are not historically true, they can prepare individuals with a sense of anticipation and longing for God's real intervention in history. One can remember Paul's reference to the faint realities of Greek religion (Acts 17) as a pointer to that story of Jesus that "was not done in a corner" (Acts 26).

THE WITCHES' VOICE

The Witches' Voice (www.witchvox.com) is the most significant Internet site concerning modern witchcraft and paganism. Fritz Jung and Wren Walker, who live together in Clearwater, Florida, started this award-winning site on February 1, 1997. It is commercial-free and provides an astounding amount of information as well as thousands of links to various pagan leaders and groups.

Analysis of this website provides primary documentation about the core realities of contemporary witchcraft. It becomes obvious that the ancient stereotypes about witches do not describe the beliefs and practices of modern-day witches and pagans. Most significant, The Witches' Voice proves how misleading it is to argue that witches are really Satanists or that most pagan groups engage in overt evil and ritual abuse.

5. Just as we expect witches to be open to self-criticism, so Christians must show willingness to face up to those blunders and sins that run through our own history, particularly in earlier times when the church had nearly ultimate power. Christians should also engage in protecting the rights of law-abiding witches to practice their religion.

6. Christian leaders should process accusations of satanic ritual abuse against specific witches (or others) with extreme caution. This is necessary for two reasons. First, if the charges are true, this involves the most serious of crimes, and anyone dealing with the criminals involved is in serious danger. Second, if the claims are not true, the accused can face total ruin simply on the basis of wicked gossip and rumor.

WITCHCRAFT	
Typology	Western Esoteric
Witchcraft Groups, Leaders, and Sites	*Ár nDraíocht Féin* (ADF): www.adf.org Isaac Bonewits: www.neopagan.net Raymond Buckland: http://geocities.com/SoHo/Workshop/6650/ Circle Sanctuary: www.circlesanctuary.org Church of All Worlds: www.caw.org Covenant of the Goddess: www.cog.org Stewart and Janet Farrar (and Gavin Bone): http://www.callaighe.com Selena Fox: www.mhtc.net/~selena/ Gerald Gardner: www.geraldgardner.com Henge of Keltria (Druid): www.keltria.org Order of Bards, Ovates, and Druids (OBOD): http://druidry.org Reformed Druids of North America: www.geocities.com/mikerdna Doreen Valiente: www.doreenvaliente.com The Wiccan-Pagan Times: www.twpt.com The Witches' Voice: www.witchvox.com Z. Budapest: www.zbudapest.com
Academic Websites About the Witchcraft Inquisition	Gender Studies and witchcraft: www.gendercide.org Doug Linder on Salem trials: http://www.law.umkc.edu/faculty/projects/ftrials/salem/salem.htm Seventeenth-century New England: www.17thc.us/index.php?id=12
Christian Ministry to Witches	Ex-witch Ministries: www.exwitch.org Spiritual Counterfeits Project: www.scp-inc.org/
Scholarly Works on Modern Witchcraft	Graham Harvey, *Contemporary Paganism* (New York: NYU Press, 1997) Ronald Hutton, *The Triumph of the Moon* (London: Oxford University Press, 1999) Aidan A. Kelly, *Crafting the Art of Magic* (St. Paul: Llewellyn, 1991) T. M. Luhrmann, *Persuasions of the Witch's Craft* (Cambridge: Harvard University Press, 1989) Sarah Pike, *Earthly Bodies, Magical Selves* (Berkeley: University of California, 2001) *The Pomegranate: The International Journal of Pagan Studies* (Chas Clifton, editor) Shelley Rabinovich and Jim Lewis, eds., *The Encyclopedia of Modern Witchcraft and Neo-Paganism* (Citadel, 2002)

WITCHCRAFT

Recommended Reading on the Witchcraft Inquisition	Bengt Ankarloo and Stuart Clark, editors, *The Athlone History of Witchcraft and Magic in Europe* (London: Athlone, 1999), 5 volumes Robin Briggs, *Witches & Neighbors: The Social and Cultural Context of European Witchcraft* (Penguin Books, 1998) Carlo Ginzburg, *Ecstasies: Deciphering the Witches' Sabbat* (Chicago: University of Chicago, 2004) Brian P. Levack, *The Witch-Hunt in Early Modern Europe* (New York: Addison-Wesley, 1995) Darren Oldridge, *The Witchcraft Reader* (London: Routledge, 2002) Jeffrey B. Russell, *A History of Witchcraft* (New York: Thames and Hudson, 1980) Geoffrey Scarre and John Callow, *Witchcraft and Magic in Sixteenth and Seventeenth-Century Europe* (Palgrave, 2001)
Books by Modern Witches	Margot Adler, *Drawing Down the Moon* (Boston: Beacon 1986) second edition Stewart Farrar, *The Witches' Way* (London: Robert Hale, 1985) Gerald B. Gardner, *Witchcraft Today* (Rider, 1954) Ellen Hopman and Lawrence Bond, *Being a Pagan* (Destiny Books, 2001) Starhawk, *The Spiral Dance* (Harper and Row; 1979) Doreen Valiente, *The Rebirth of Witchcraft* (London: Robert Hale, 1989)
Christian Response	Brooks Alexander, *Witchcraft Goes Mainstream* (Harvest House, 2004) David Burnett, *Dawning of the Pagan Moon* (Nashville: Nelson, 1991) Craig Hawkins, *Goddess Worship, Witchcraft and Neo-Paganism* (Grand Rapids: Zondervan, 1998) Philip Johnson and Gus diZerega, *Beyond the Burning Times: A Pagan and Christian in Dialogue*, edited by John W. Morehead (Oxford: Lion Hudson, 2008)

APPENDICES

APPENDIX A:
RELIGIONS AS FAMILY TRADITIONS

Here is an outline of the family model of religions Gordon Melton and I use in our work at the Institute for the Study of American Religion. A similar model is used by David Barrett and Todd Johnson for their World Christian Database.

Level 1	Level 2	Level 3	Level 4
Baha'i			
	Babis		
Buddhism			
	Theravada		
		Burmese	
		Cambodian	
		Lao	
		Sri Lankan	
		Thai	
		Vietnamese	
	Mahayana		
		Chinese	
		Japanese	
			Nichiren
			Shin
			Shingon
			Tendai
			Zen
		Korean	
	Vrajayana		
		Bhutan	
		Tibetan	
		Mongolian	

Level 1	Level 2	Level 3	Level 4
Christianity			
	Western Catholic		
		Roman Catholic	
		Old Catholic	
		Post-Vatican Traditionalists	
	Eastern Orthodoxy		
	Eastern Non-Chalcedonian		
	Protestant		
		Lutheran	
		Anglican	
		Reformed/ Presbyterian/ Congregationalist	
		European Free Church	
		Baptist	
		Methodist/Pietist	
		Adventist	
		Latter-day Saints	
		Holiness	
		Pentecostal/ Charismatic	
		Fundamentalist/ Evangelical	
		Emergent	
Confucianism			
Hinduism			
	Vashnava		
	Saivite		
	Shaktiite		
	Smarti		
	Yogi		

Level 1	Level 2	Level 3	Level 4
Islam			
	Sunni		
	Shi'a		
		Ismailis	
		Bohoras	
	Sufi		
	Sectarian		
Jainism			
Judaism			
	Orthodox		
	Hasidism		
	Reform/Liberal		
	Conservative/ Reconstruction		
	Kairites		
Modern New Religious Traditions			
	African Initiated Churches (nontraditional)		
	Cargo cults		
	Pagan revivalism (northern Europe)		
	Unificationism (Sun Myung Moon)		
	Unitarianism (Universalism)		
Satanism			
	Church of Satan (Anton LaVey)		
	First Satanic Church (Karla LaVey)		
	First Church of Satan (John D. Allee)		
	Temple of Set (Michael Aquino)		

Level 1	Level 2	Level 3	Level 4
Shintoism			
	Shrine Shinto		
	Sectarian Shinto		
Sikhism/ Sant Mat			
Taoism			
	Yigandao		
Traditional Ethnic-linguistic Religions			
	African		
	Afro-American (Voodoo, Santeria, Macumba)		
	Native American		
	Chinese		
	East Asian (not Chinese)		
	Oceania		
	South Asian		
Unbelief			
	Humanism		
	Atheism		
	Rationalism		
	Deism		

Level 1	Level 2	Level 3	Level 4
Western Esotericism			
	Gnostic		
	Mandean		
	Rosicrucianism		
	Swedenborgianism		
	Spiritualism		
	Theosophy		
	Liberal Catholic		
	Ceremonial Magic		
	Metaphysical/New Thought		
	Neo-Paganism		
	New Age		
Zoroastrianism			

APPENDIX B: TAOISM

Taoism is one of the most complex of the world religions because of controversial issues related to its history and nature. Even the very term *Taoism* raises problems simply because many scholars now believe that it should be spelled *Daoism*. Taoism is still retained by many academics simply because of its popularity.

Taoism is always traced to Laozi (Lao-tzu in the older Wade-Giles terminology), said to have lived in the sixth century before Christ. Scholars of Taoism either doubt his existence or believe that the popular legends about him have little historical value. Some even debate that Laozi is a person's name since it can be translated as "Old Master." Tradition states, however, that Laozi is the author of the *Tao-te Ching* (or *Daodejing*), one of the most widely translated texts in history. Again, according to Taoist tradition, Laozi was a court archivist and lived at the same time as Confucius. In the more religious strand of Taoism, Laozi is viewed as a deity.

The second most well-known Taoist text is the *Zhuangzi*, which is also the name of the alleged author. Zhuangzi is said to have lived about 300 B.C. The current text associated with him dates from the fourth century A.D. and so it is impossible to know for sure what can be traced back to Zhuangzi. Most scholars view the *Zhuangzi* as a composite text. One scholar, W. C. Graham, believes that five separate voices framed the work as we know it today.

Taoism first appears as an overt religious movement with the emergence of the "Way of the Celestial Master" in the second century A.D. From then until the rise of Communism, Taoism retained an ideological hold in Chinese life and culture and was often the preferred religion of Chinese rulers. During the Cultural Revolution many Taoist temples were destroyed.

In both the *Tao-te Ching* and *Zhuangzi* there is frequent discussion of the Way. *Tao* or *Dao* is usually translated as "Way." The famous opening line of the *Tao-te Ching* (which means "Classic of the Way") reads: "The Way that can be spoken of is not the constant Way." There is no unanimity on the meaning of the "Way" in either Taoist tradition or among scholars of the religion. Is Taoism essentially religious, philosophical, ethical, or political? Alan Chan argues in his entry on Laozi in *The Stanford Encyclopedia of Philosophy* that "such categories form a unified whole in Daoist thinking and are deemed separate and distinct only in Western thought."

Many argue that "the Way" ultimately refers both to a path of ethics and the ultimate source of reality. Chinese tradition would often refer to the Dao as the source for *qi,* or energy, and the cosmic forces of *yin* and *yang.* Dao is more concretely understood as a moral path for humanity, and this emphasis is dominant in Confucian usage of the term. If Dao is understood as something akin to a Creator, this is not to be understood in the sense of a personal God but rather as a supernatural Force. The transcendence of the Dao is best captured by the fact that the term *Dao* is often associated with the classical Chinese notion of *Wu,* or nothingness.

TAOISM	
Founder	
Websites	Daoist Studies (James Miller) www.daoiststudies.org Fabrizio Pregadio http://www.venus.unive.it/dsao/pregadio/ Russell Kirkland www.arches.uga.edu/~kirkland Taoism Information Page (Gene Thursby) http://www.religiousworlds.com/taoism/index.html Chad Hensen Chinese Philosophy Page http://www.hku.hk/philodep/ch Taoist Culture and Information Centre http://eng.taoism.org.hk/ Center for Daoist Studies (Louis Komjathy and Kate Townsend) www.daoistcenter.org
Recommended Reading	Livia Kohn, ed., *Daoist Handbook* (Leiden: Brill, 2000) Livia Kohn, *Daoism and Chinese Culture* (Cambridge: Three Pines Press, 2001) Stephen Little, ed., *Taoism and the Arts of China* (Chicago: Art Institute of Chicago, 2000) James Miller, *Daoism: A Short Introduction* (Oxford: Oneworld Publications 2003) Fabrizio Pregadio, ed., *The Encyclopedia of Taoism* (London: Curzon Press, forthcoming) Isabelle Robinet, *Taoism: Growth of a Religion* (Stanford: Stanford University Press, 1997) Liu Xiaogan, "Taoism," in Arvind Sharma, ed., *Our Religions* (San Francisco: HarperCollins, 1993)

APPENDIX C:
INTRODUCTION TO BRAINWASHING
AND DEPROGRAMMING

▨ Introduction

For over three decades religious groups have often been interpreted by reference to the theory of brainwashing. It is frequently claimed that cults are those groups that engage in mental coercion and psychological pressure to convert followers and retain members. Under the brainwashing model the coercion involved is not said to be physical in nature. People are not held captive by physical chains but by the emotional trickery of the alleged cult leader.

The brainwashing model has spread widely in our society and is often present in journalistic accounts of cult groups. Brainwashing theories are popular in movies about religion, and it is almost a truism to say that odd religions engage in the mental coercion of followers. David Snow and Robert Machalek argued in a 1984 article that brainwashing was the most popular explanation for conversion to new religions. In spite of popularity, however, the theory of brainwashing has been the object of long, intense, and bitter dispute among scholars and religious leaders.

▨ Advocates

Current brainwashing theories about religious conversion are usually traced back to the seminal research of Edgar Schein and Robert J. Lifton. Lifton is the author of the famous study *Chinese Thought Reform and the Psychology of Totalism*, published in 1961. Chapter 22 is the most oft-cited part of the book for its elaboration of eight psychological realities that are part of an ideologically totalistic environment. The eight are: milieu control, mystical manipulation, demand for purity, cult of confession, "sacred science," loading the language, doctrine over person, and dispensing of existence. These are Lifton's phrases and are often expressed in more popular terms by other cult-critics.

In the 1970s Lifton's study of Chinese political brainwashing was used as a basis for arguing that new religious movements engaged in the same thought reform techniques or brainwashing as the Chinese communists. Lifton's eight signs of totalism are still used today in attempts by the anti-cult movement to defend the brainwashing thesis. Anti-cult websites frequently list his eight characteristics of totalism in critiques of the alleged cult groups that endanger the family and society.

The view that "cults" engage in brainwashing led to the obvious conclusion that cult members are not really free and that society has a right to rescue them from their captors. This led to the practice of deprogramming, often with the use of physical force, to free the enslaved cult member from his or her group and to reverse the impact of brainwashing. Many members of the Unification Church, for example, were kidnapped from the group and taken to an isolated place in order to be deprogrammed.

Ted Patrick was the most infamous deprogrammer in America's cult wars. Patrick was involved initially in trying to free members of the Children of God, a radical communal group founded by David Berg (aka Moses David) in California in 1968. Patrick, known as "Black Lightning," is the author of *Let Our Children Go!* (Dutton, 1976). He also defended his views on brainwashing and deprogramming in a famous interview with *Playboy* magazine.

The brainwashing model is defended by Steve Hassan (an ex-Unificationist), Flo Conway and Jim Siegelman, Willa Appel, James and Marcia Rudin (famous Jewish exit counselors), and is a dominant viewpoint in the International Cultic Studies Association, originally the American Family Foundation. Brainwashing was also a major paradigm in the ideology of the old Cult Awareness Network (originally Citizens Freedom Foundation) before CAN went bankrupt in 1996.

Among academics, Louis J. West (deceased), Harvard's John Clark (deceased), Richard Ofshe, and Margaret Singer (deceased) have been the most famous defenders of the view that some religious groups engage in mental coercion. Singer presented her case in a famous article in *Psychology Today* called "Coming Out of the Cults." Singer had been at the center of legal battles both over individuals involved in new religions and about the legitimacy of the very concept of brainwashing.

Singer realized the term *brainwashing* conveys a simplistic understanding of thought reform. She preferred language like the "systematic manipulation of social influences" in her descriptions of how new religions recruit members. She argued that "cults" engage in the following tactics to ensnare unsuspecting individuals: isolation, hypnosis, group pressure, love bombing, lack of privacy, change of diet, sleep deprivation, control of individual's time, hyperventilation, guilt, and fear.

Critics

Singer's views came under particular attack from many in the academic community. Thomas Robbins and Dick Anthony wrote a major critique of her views in 1980. In 1983 Singer was asked by the American Psychological Association (APA) to chair a Task Force on Deceptive and Indirect Methods of Persuasion and Control (DIMPAC). A report was submitted to the APA. However, on May 11, 1987, the APA's Board of Social and Ethical Responsibility for Psychology (BSERP) told Singer and colleagues on the Task Force that their report was unsatisfactory because it lacked scientific rigor.

Singer lost the legal grounding for appearing in court as an expert witness in *U.S. v. Fishman* (a case involving a former member of Scientology). In later legal action she also lost her bid to sue the group of academics who did the most to undermine the credibility of her theories. In spite of this, Singer remains a hero in the anti-cult community and her views are still defended by psychiatrists and psychologists convinced of the reality of brainwashing.

Along with Anthony and Robbins, James Lewis, J. Gordon Melton, James Richardson, Stuart Wright, Eileen Barker, David Bromley, and a number of other academics have led the attack on brainwashing as an explanatory tool in religious life. These scholars are often dismissed as "cult apologists" by the anti-cult network. However, their main concern is not about defending the spiritual or moral integrity of new religions but about critique of brainwashing theories that they believe are false and dangerous.

Though the rulings against Singer gave brainwashing theorists a setback in the United States, legal battles over new religions in Europe in the last decade have led to renewal of debate over thought reform. Stephen Kent, a Canadian scholar, has tried to help various European governments adopt brainwashing as an explanatory tool in formal reaction to new religions like the Unification Church and Scientology. Further, Benjamin Zablocki is trying to revive Lifton's model of thought reform in a renewed defense of the reality of brainwashing. Zablocki has also written very critically of famous new religion scholars, including Melton and Lewis.

Conclusion

Consistent rulings against forcible deprogramming led to a change of vocabulary and tactics in the anti-cult world. First, the use of the term *deprogrammer* was generally dropped in favor of the designation *exit-counselor*. Second, apart from a few cases, the use of violence against cult members was stopped and kidnapping came to a halt. The threat of hefty fines and imprisonment led to an abandonment of physical coercion.

Though there has been a more open dialogue between advocates and critics of brainwashing in recent years, the topic continues to divide scholars and even those critical of new religions. Religious liberty advocates remain wary of European governments that use brainwashing theories to attack religious groups. The religious groups under threat are often the well-known new religions but can also be Protestant groups like Baptists and Pentecostals.

In my view, the brainwashing theory has been overused in response to new religions. It is too convenient that the "cults" are always found guilty of thought reform, as if the methods of these hundreds of "cults" are so radically different from older, larger religions. In my study of many of the "cults," I have found there to be little charisma or power at work, not to mention brainwashing. Even the most famous cult groups are often particularly adept at both poor recruitment and poor retention of members.

However, critics of brainwashing have often failed to be sufficiently enraged by the manipulation and ruination of people in certain religious groups that repress human beings in the name of religion. Scholars must not miss the evidence of the systemic and powerful social engineering of members that wipes away individual freedom and power. Even if that is not equivalent to brainwashing, it is a reality that deserves serious attention and moral indignation.

APPENDIX D:
RESOURCES ON WORLD AND
NEW RELIGIONS

General Scholarly Resources

Allan H. Anderson, *African Reformation* (African World Press, 2001)

Eileen Barker, *New Religious Movements: A Practical Introduction* (HMSO, 1995)

David Barrett, George Kurian, Todd Johnson, *World Christian Encyclopedia* (Oxford University Press, 2002)

Stanley M. Burgess, ed., *The New International Dictionary of Pentecostal and Charismatic Movements* (Zondervan, 2002)

Paul Marshall, ed., *Religious Freedom in the World* (Freedom House, 2000)

Richard P. McBrien, ed., *The HarperCollins Encyclopedia of Catholicism* (1995)

J. Gordon Melton, *Melton's Encyclopedia of American Religions*, 8th ed. (Gale, 2009)

J. Gordon Melton and Martin Baumann, eds. *Religions of the World* (ABC-Clio, 2002)

Timothy Miller, ed. *America's Alternative Religions* (State University of New York Press, 1995)

Christopher Partridge, ed. *New Religions* (Oxford University Press, 2004)

James T. Richardson, *Regulating Religion* (Kluwer, 2004)

Scott W. Sunquist, ed., *A Dictionary of Asian Christianity* (Eerdmans, 2001)

Evangelical Scholarship

James A. Beverley, *Religions A to Z* (Thomas Nelson, 2005)

Winfried Corduan, *Neighboring Faiths* (InterVarsity, 1998)

Gavin D'Costa, ed., *Christian Uniqueness Reconsidered* (Orbis, 1990)

Ronald Enroth, ed. *A Guide to New Religious Movements* (InterVarsity, 2005)

Irving Hexham, Stephen Rost, and John Morehead II, eds. *Encountering New Religious Movements: A Holistic Evangelical Approach* (Kregel, 2004)

Hendrik Kraemer, *The Christian Message in a Non-Christian World* (Harper, 1938)

Richard Kyle, *The Religious Fringe* (InterVarsity, 1993)

Walter Martin, *The Kingdom of the Cults* (Bethany, 2003)

Walter Martin, Jill Martin, and Kurt Van Gorden, *The Kingdom of the Occult* (Thomas Nelson, 2007)

Gerald McDermott, *God's Rivals: Why God Allows Different Religions* (InterVarsity, 2007)

Terry Muck and Frances S. Adeney, *Christianity Encountering World Religions* (Baker Academic, 2009)

Stephen Neill, *Christian Faith and Other Faiths* (InterVarsity, 1984)

Harold A. Netland, *Dissonant Voices* (Eerdmans, 1991)

Larry A. Nichols, George A. Mather, and Alvin J. Schmidt, *Encyclopedic Dictionary of Cults, Sects, and World Religions* (Zondervan, 2006)

Tim S. Perry, *Radical Difference: A Defence of Hendrik Kraemer's Theology of Religions* (Wilfred Laurier, 2001)

Clark Pinnock, *A Wideness in God's Mercy* (Zondervan, 1992)

Terrance L. Tiessen, *Who Can Be Saved?* (InterVarsity, 2006)

Ruth Tucker, *Another Gospel* (Zondervan, 1989)

Ravi Zacharias, *Jesus Among Other Gods* (Word, 2000)

INDEX

▪ C

▓ E

▓ F

▪ G

■ H

▓ I

▪ J

■ L

Q

Q & A:
    Christian Science, 107-109
    Cults, 20-22
    Waco, 40-46
Quakers, 570-572, 577
Quayle, Dan, 692
Queen Elizabeth I, 708
Quimby, Phineas Parkhurst, 97, 99, 107, 419-420, 473
Qur'an, 218-220, 222-223, 225-227, 231-232, 234, 237-252, 256, 258-260, 269-
    270, 272, 423
Qutb, Sayyid, 263, 277

R

Rabbinical Council of America, 318
Rabin, Yitzhak, 330
Radhakrishnan, Sarvepalli, 215
    Selected Writings, 215
Rabinowitz, Dorothy, 655
    No Crueler Tyrannies, 655
Radio Church of God, 478-580
Rael (aka Claude Vorilhon), 424-428
    Book That Tells the Truth, The, 427
    Extra-Terrestrials Took Me to their Planet, 427
    Let's Welcome Our Fathers from Space, 427
    Sensual Meditation, 427
    Yes to Human Cloning, 427
Raelians/Raelian movement, 424-428, 447
Raidor, Betta, 642
Ram Dass, 189 (*see also* Alpert; Baba Ram Dass)
Ram Tzu (*see* Liquorman)
    No Way for the Spiritually Advanced, 177
Rama, 172
Ramadan, 222, 224, 230, 233, 239,
Ramadan, Tariq, 233, 239
    In the Footsteps of the Prophet, 233, 239
Ramaiah, S. A. A., 181-182

■ S

▪ T

U

▓ V

von Greyerz, Peter, 708
von Spee, Friedrich, 708
    Cautio criminalis, 708
voodoo, 699, 712 [caption]
Vreeland, Nicholas, 64
    Tibet Center in Manhattan, 64

W

Wach, Joachim, 1
Wachter, Dorothea, 709
Waco, Texas, 19, 20, 35-38, 40-46, 131, 132
Wade-Giles, 733
Waggoner, Bert, 578
Wagner, C. Peter, 540, 541, 555-556, 577
    Doris (wife) [caption], 556
Wagner Leadership Institute, 555, 556
Wakefield, Hollida (with Ralph Underwager), 644-645, 655
    Issues in Child Abuse Accusations, 644
    Return of the Furies, 655
Waldrep, Bob (with James K. Walker), 403
    Truth Behind The Secret, The, 403
Walesa, Lech, 691
Walsh, Cheri, 407
Walker, James K. (with Bob Waldrep), 403
    Truth Behind The Secret, The, 403
Walker, Mary, 254
    Living Islam (BBC2 series), 254
Wall Street Journal, 660
Wallace, Mike, 694
Walsch, Neale Donald, 409, 481-482, 484
    Nancy (wife), 482
    publication:
        Conversations with God series, 481
Walsh, Thomas G. (with Gordon L. Anderson and Theodore Shimmyo), 696
    Hope of All Ages (editors), 696
Walter, Elder Martin, 523
Walters, J. Donald (Swami Kriyananda), 178-179, 199
Walters, Wesley P., 374

▪ X

▪ Y